Thos W. A[...]
Jan 1982

The Fiscal Impact Handbook

The Fiscal

Impact Handbook

estimating local costs and revenues of land development

Robert W. Burchell
David Listokin

In collaboration with:
Robert W. Lake; Franklin J. James, Jr.;
W. Patrick Beaton; Nathan Edelstein

With the assistance of:
Rodney E. Engelen; Darwin G. Stuart;
Robert B. Teska; Michael Levin

THE CENTER FOR URBAN POLICY RESEARCH
P.O. BOX 38
NEW BRUNSWICK, NEW JERSEY 08903

Copyright, 1978, Rutgers— The State University of New Jersey
All rights reserved. Published in the United States by the Center for Urban Policy Research, New Brunswick, New Jersey 08903

Third Printing—February, 1980

Copyright of this document is limited to form and composition and is retained by Rutgers University. The United States Government reserves the right of a royalty free, non exclusive and irrevocable license to reproduce or publish the work in this form, if it should be determined at any time that the report is not readily available to the public.

The research and studies forming the basis for this report were conducted pursuant to a contract with the U.S. Department of Housing and Urban Development (HUD). The statements and conclusions contained herein are those of the contractor and do not necessarily reflect the views of the U.S. Government in general or HUD in particular. Neither the United States nor HUD makes any warranty, expressed or implied, or assumes responsibility for the accuracy or completeness of the information herein.

Library of Congress Cataloging in Publication Data

Burchell, Robert W.
 The fiscal impact handbook.

 Bibliography: p.
 Includes index.
 1. Municipal services—Finance. 2. Tax revenue estimating. 3. Cities and towns—Growth. I. Listokin, David, joint author. II. Title.
HD4431.B85   352'.12   78—6216
ISBN 0-88285-045-8

Contents

INTRODUCTION AND ORGANIZATION 1
    Why Fiscal Impact Analysis?
    Definition and Concepts
    Fiscal Impact Analysis and Other Evaluative Strategies
    Calculating Costs
    Calculating Revenues
    General Applicability
    Why the Handbook?
    Organization of the Handbook
    Analyst's Guide

PART 1. CALCULATING COSTS: METHODS OF FISCAL IMPACT COST PROJECTION. 11
    CHAPTER 1. RELATING METHODS TO TASKS AND CONTEXTS OF FISCAL IMPACT ANALYSIS. 15
    INTRODUCTION
    What Methods are Used, Where, When?
        Per Capita Multiplier Method
        Case Study Method
        Service Standard Method
        Comparable City Method
        Proportional Valuation Method
        Employment Anticipation Method
    Method Choice/Employment and the Interpretation of Results
    The Use of Multiple Methods in Pursuit of a Single Fiscal Impact Solution
    The Settings for the Demonstrated Cost Calculations
    CHAPTER 2. PER CAPITA MULTIPLIER FISCAL IMPACT METHOD 25
    Background
    Application

Basic Assumptions
Procedures
  Step 1 Obtain Information on Budgets, Current Population and Assessments
  Step 2 Categorize Local Expenditures into Five Municipal Service Categories Plus the School District Function.
  Step 3 Obtain Total Annual Municipal (by service category) and School District Expenses (including operating and debt service costs)
  Step 4 Assign a Share of Annual Per Capita and Per Pupil Expenditures
  Step 5 Calculate Net Annual Per Capita and Per Pupil Expenditures
  Step 6 Calculate Anticipated Total Resident and School Population by Housing Type
  Step 7 Calculate Residentially-Induced Total Annual Municipal and School District Total Expenses
  Step 8 Calculate Municipal Costs for Inclusive Nonresidential Uses
  Step 9 Determine Total Annual Public Costs and Distribute Costs Both by Municipal Service and by Municipal and School District Operating Versus Debt Service Expenditures
  Step 10 Project Total Annual Revenues
  Step 11 Calculate the Cost-Revenue Surplus or Deficit
Data Requirements
Sophistication of User
Advantages and Disadvantages
    Advantages
      Simplicity/Low Cost
      Operational Utility
      Acceptability
    Disadvantages
      Richness of Detail
Interpreting Results

CHAPTER 3. CASE STUDY FISCAL IMPACT METHOD 45

Background
Application
Basic Assumptions
Procedures
  Step 1 Contact Local Officials
  Step 2 Categorize Public Service Functions and Delineate Responsibilities
  Step 3 Determine Excess and Deficient Service Capacity
  Step 4 Project Population Increases and Population Induced Demand
  Step 5 Determine Anticipated Local Service Response
  Step 6 Project Total Annual Public Costs
  Step 7 Project Total Annual Public Revenue
  Step 8 Calculate the Cost-Revenue Impact
Data Requirements
Sophistication of User
Advantages and Disadvantages
    Advantages
      Richness of Detail
      Operational Utility
      Acceptability
    Disadvantages
      The Accuracy of Public Projections
Interpreting Results

Contents   vii

CHAPTER 4. SERVICE STANDARD FISCAL IMPACT METHOD. . 67
Background
Application
Basic Assumptions
Procedures
   Step 1 Determine Population and Student Increase Resulting from Growth
   Step 2 Project Number of Public Employees Resulting from Growth
   Step 3 Calculate Average Operating Costs
   Step 4 Project Total Annual Operating Costs
   Step 5 Project Total Annual Capital Costs
   Step 6 Project Total Annual Public Costs
   Step 7 Project Total Annual Public Revenues
   Step 8 Calculate the Cost-Revenue Surplus or Deficit
Data Requirements
Sophistication of User
Advantages and Disadvantages
      Advantages
         Richness of Detail
         Operational Utility
         Acceptance
         Simplicity/Low Cost
      Disadvantages
Interpreting Results

CHAPTER 5. COMPARABLE CITY FISCAL IMPACT METHOD. . . 97
Background
Application
Basic Assumptions
Procedures
   Step 1 Determine Population/Student Growth
   Step 2 Obtain Appropriate Expenditure Multipliers and Calculate the Rate of Change in the Multipliers
   Step 3 Calculate Current Average Operating and Capital Expenditures Per Capita
   Step 4 Calculate Future Average Operating and Capital Expenditures Per Capita
   Step 5 Determine Net Costs Attributable to Growth
   Step 6 Project Total Annual Public Revenues
   Step 7 Calculate the Cost-Revenue Impact
Data Requirements
Sophistication of User
Advantages and Disadvantages
      Advantages
         Time and Cost
         Availability of Required Data
      Disadvantages
         Validity of the Expenditure Multipliers
         Detail
         Acceptance
Interpreting Results

CHAPTER 6. PROPORTIONAL VALUATION FISCAL IMPACT METHOD 119
Background
Application

Basic Assumptions
Procedures
  Step 1 Assemble and Prepare Base Data
  Step 2 Assign a Share of Existing Municipal Expenditures to Total Local Non-residential Uses
  Step 3 Project the Future Total Municipal Operating Costs Induced by the Future Non-residential Use
  Step 4 Assign Total Annual Non-residential Facility Costs to Component Service Categories
  Step 5 Project Total Annual Public Revenue
  Step 6 Calculate the Cost Revenue Impact
Data Requirements
Sophistication of User
Advantages and Disadvantages
    Advantages
      Time and Cost
      Availability of Required Data
      Acceptance
    Disadvantages
      Validity of the Refinement Coefficients
Interpreting Results

CHAPTER 7. EMPLOYMENT ANTICIPATION FISCAL IMPACT METHOD 135

Background
Application
Basic Assumptions
Procedures
  Step 1 Determine Per Capita Municipal Expenditures by Service Category
  Step 2 Obtain Anticipated Employment for the New Commercial or Industrial Facility From Developer Estimates or by Multiplying the Average Number of Employees Per Square Foot for a Comparable Facility
  Step 3 Using Known Direction of Growth Over the Previous Decade and Current Population Size, Choose the Applicable Percentage Increase Per Employee, by Service Category, in Per Capita Municipal Costs
  Step 4 Multiply the New Employment Increment by the Percentage Increase in Per Capita Costs Per Employee to Obtain Total Percentage Increase for Each Service
  Step 5 Multiply the Percent Increase in Per Capita Expenditures Per Service Category by the Existing Per Capita Dollar Expenditure in that Service Category to Obtain the Per Capita Dollar Increase for Each Service
  Step 6 Multiply Dollar Per Capita Expenditure Increase in Each Service Category by the Existing Population to Obtain the Municipal Cost Increase for Each Municipal Service Assignable to the Nonresidential Facility
  Step 7 Project Total Annual Public Revenues
  Step 8 Calculate the Cost-Revenue Impact
Data Requirements
Sophistication of User
Advantages and Disadvantages

Contents

  Advantages
    Operational Utility
    Detail
    Simplicity/Cost
  Disadvantages
  Interpreting Results

PART 2. CALCULATING REVENUES: METHODS OF FISCAL IMPACT REVENUE PROJECTION 149

CHAPTER 8. REVENUE TRENDS 153
 Municipal and School District Revenue Resources
 Intergovernmental Transfers
  Overview
  Regional Patterns
 Own Source Revenues
  Taxes
   Property Tax
   Overview
   Regional Patterns
  Sales Tax, Income Tax, and Other Taxes
   Overview
   Sales Tax
   Income Tax
   Other Taxes
   Regional Patterns
  Charges and Miscellaneous Revenue
   Overview
   Regional Patterns
 Summary — The Revenue Systems of Municipalities and School Districts

CHAPTER 9. PROJECTING MUNICIPAL AND SCHOOL DISTRICT OWN SOURCE REVENUES 179
 Own Source Revenues: Property, Income, Sales and Other Taxes..........
  Real Property Tax ....
  Personal Property Tax
  Earned Income Tax
  Sales Tax
   Residential Development
   Non-residential Development
  Real Property Transfer Tax
  Occupation and Business Privilege Tax
  Per Capita Tax
  Transient Occupancy Tax
 Own Source Revenues: Miscellaneous Revenues and User Charges
  Interest Earnings
  Fees and Permits
  Fines, Forfeitures and Penalties
  User Charges for Special Services
  User Charges for Water, Sewerage and Sanitation Services

CHAPTER 10............................ 195
SECTION I. PROJECTING MUNICIPAL AND SCHOOL DISTRICT INTERGOVERNMENTAL REVENUES
 Intergovernmental Transfers: State
  Redistribution of State-Levied Sales Taxes

    Redistribution of State Levied Income Tax
    Redistribution of State Levied Motor Fuels Tax
    Redistribution of State Levied Cigarette and Alcohol Taxes
    Redistribution of Incorporated/Unincorporated Business Tax
    State Road/Street Lighting Aid
    Redistribution of Public Utilities Franchise/Gross Receipts Tax
    State Aid to Urban or Rural Areas
    State Homestead and Property Tax Relief Reimbursement
    Educational Support
    Educational Basic Support via Flat Grants
    Educational Basic Support via Foundation Aid
    Educational Basic Support via Variable Guarantees
    Educational Assistance via Categorical Aid
    Educational Assistance via State Apportioned Federal Programs
   Intergovernmental Revenue: Federal
    State-Local Fiscal Assistance Act of 1973 (Federal Revenue Sharing) Public Law 92–512; 86 STAT 919
    Comprehensive Employment and Training Act (CETA) of 1972-Public Law 93–203; 87 STAT 839.
    Public Works Employment Act of 1976 (Anti-recession or Countercyclical Aid) Public Law 94-369; 90 STAT 999
    Community Development Block Grants (CDBGs) (Title I of the Housing and Urban Development Act of 1974) Public Law 93–382; 88 STAT 633
    Educational Assistance in Federal Impact Areas Public Law 81–874; 64 STAT 1100
  SECTION II. EXAMPLE REVENUE CALCULATIONS FOR ALTERNATIVE FISCAL IMPACT METHODS 222

PART 3. GENERAL APPLICABILITY — ARE FISCAL IMPACT CONSIDERATIONS ACCEPTABLE MUNICIPAL ACTIVITIES OR REQUIREMENTS? 236
  CHAPTER 11. CURRENT LEGAL STANDING 239
  Fiscal Impact Considerations: Are They Permissible Municipal Concerns?
    Scope of Survey
    Enabling Legislation and Its Specification of the Ability to Undertake Fiscal Impact Analysis.
      Comprehensive Planning
      Zoning
      Subdivision Controls
      Planned Unit Developments
      Annexation
      State-wide Land Use Plans
    Interpretating Enabling Legislation
    Summary
  Fiscal Impact Considerations: Are They An Authorized Use of the Police Power?
    Methodology
    Preliminary Results
    The Setting
    Fiscal Impact: A Valid Consideration
    Fiscal Impact: Not a Valid Consideration
    The New Jersey Story
    Summary

Contents

CHAPTER 12. FIELD EXPERIENCE: FISCAL IMPACT ANALYSIS IN THE UNITED STATES.................................... 257
    Fiscal Impact Analysis: Use and Method Application
        For What is Fiscal Impact Analysis Used?
        What Fiscal Impact Analysis Methods are Used?
    Fiscal Impact Analysis: Geographic, Fiscal and Legal Context
        Regional Incidence of Cost-Revenue Analysis
        Fiscal Impact Analysis and the Legal Environment
    Fiscal Impact Analysis: Scope of Study and Data Resources
        Fiscal Impact Analysis Costs: Scope Considered, Data Bases Drawn Upon
        Fiscal Impact Analysis Revenues: Scope Considered, Data Bases Drawn Upon
        Other Fiscal Impact Characteristics
    Fiscal Impact Analysis: Author, Audience and Significance of Study
        Author and Time Commitments
        Practitioner Reaction to Current Practice
    Summary

PART 4. ADDITIONAL DATA: MULTIPLIERS AND MODELS USED IN FISCAL IMPACT ANALYSIS..................................... 272

CHAPTER 13. DEMOGRAPHIC MULTIPLIERS FOR STANDARD AND SPECIALIZED HOUSING TYPES: ORIGINS, USES DERIVATIONS.. 275
    Background
    Calculating Demographic Multipliers
    Public Use Samples and Demographic Multipliers: Standard Housing Types
        Samples
        Definitions
        Household Size and School-Age Children Multipliers: Standard Housing Types
    Field Surveys and Demographic Multipliers: Specialized Housing Types
        Samples
        Definitions
            Vacation Homes
            Condominums
            Housing for the Elderly
            Singles Residences
        Housing Size and School-Age Children-Multipliers: Specialized Housing Types
    Regional and Temporal Variation of Demographic Multipliers
        Regional Variations
        Temporal Variations
    Conclusion: Which Multipliers are Used; Where?

CHAPTER 14. USING CENSUS DATA TO CALCULATE DEMOGRAPHIC MULTIPLIERS............................ 291
    Public Use Samples
    Geography in Public Use Data
        State Public Use Samples
        County Group Public Use Samples
        Neighborhood Public Use Samples
    Household Descriptions in the Public Use Samples
    Sample Size in the Public Use Samples

Housing Type Specifications Using Public Use Samples
    Defining Housing Structure Types
    Housing Unit Space: Rooms and Bedrooms
Calculation of Demographic Multipliers/Profiles
    Multipliers
    Socio-economic Profiles
Data Processing and the Public Use Samples
    Where to Get the Data
Programming and Using the Public Use Samples

CHAPTER 15. USING FIELD SURVEYS TO CALCULATE DEMOGRAPHIC MULTIPLIERS 303
Deciding to Undertake a Survey
    Potential Benefits of Surveys
    Potential Costs of Surveys
Sample Design and Survey Methods
    Choosing the Target Population
    Sample Design
Questionnaire Design
    Estimating Demographic Multipliers
    Other Potential Questions
    Questionnaire Layout and Survey Efficiency
        Interview Notes and Pre Interview Data
        Preamble for Interviews
    Computer Coding and Question Design
The Determination of Sample Size
The Mechanics of Sample Surveys: After the Field Work
Conclusion

CHAPTER 16...
SECTION I. GROSS INCOME MULTIPLIERS FOR RESIDENTIAL AND COMMERCIAL PROPERTIES. 323
The Organization of the Information and How It Was Obtained
Gross Income Multiplier Procedural Guide: Need and Basic Strategy
Calculating Residential Real Property Value: Garden and High Rise Apartments
    Determine Net Operating Income
        Step 1 Determine Annual Gross Income
        Step 2 Calculate Effective Annual Gross Income
        Step 3 Calculate Total Annual Expenses
        Step 4 Determine Annual Net Operating Income
    Determine the Capitalization Rate
        Step 5 Calculate the Capitalization Rate
        Step 6 Determine Real Property Value
        Step 7 Derive Income Multiplier
    Summary
Calculating Nonresidential Real Property Value: Shopping Centers
    Determine the Operating Balance
        Step 1 Determine Actual Annual Operating Receipts
        Step 2 Calculate Effective Annual Operating Receipts (not computed)
        Step 3 Calculate Total Annual Operating Expenses
        Step 4 Determine Operating Expenses
    Determine the Capitalization Rate
        Step 5 Calculate the Capitalization Rate
        Step 6 Determine Real Property Value
        Step 7 Derive Operating Receipts Multiplier
    Summary

Calculating Nonresidential Real Property Value: Office Space
    Determine Net Income
        Step 1 Determine Total Annual Operating Income
        Step 2 Calculate Total Annual Effective Income
        Step 3 Calculate Total Annual Operating Expenses
        Step 4 Determine Annual Net Income
    Determine the Capitalization Rate
        Step 5 Calculate the Capitalization Rate
        Step 6 Determine the Real Property Value
        Step 7 Derive Operating Income Multiplier
    Summary

SECTION II. INPUT DATA USED TO DETERMINE REAL PROPERTY VALUE OF RESIDENTIAL AND COMMERCIAL PROPERTIES 341

CHAPTER 17. COMPUTER MODELS FOR FISCAL IMPACT ANALYSIS 345

Model Description
    Alachua County Economic Model (ACEM)
    Community Development Model (CDM)
    Community Impact Model (CIM)
    The Community Development Impact Model (CODIM)
    Cost Revenue Analysis Model (CRAM)
    Fiscal Impact Model for Rural Industrialization (FIMRI)
    Fiscal Impact Research Project (FIRP)
    Municipal Impact Evaluation System (MUNIES)
    New Haven Model (NHM)
    Public Finance Model (PFM)
    Provincial Municipal Simulator (PROMUS)
    Selle Model (SELLE)
Methods and Techniques
    Use of Technique by Models
Data Base and Data Base Sources
Revenues Considered
Troublesome Issues
    Impact Over Time
    Inflation
    User Sophistication
    Cost of Implementation
Conclusion

APPENDIX 1. NATIONAL SUMMARY OF CASE LAW RELATING TO COST-REVENUE 361

    ALABAMA
    ARKANSAS
    CALIFORNIA
    COLORADO
    CONNECTICUT
    FLORIDA
    GEORGIA
    ILLINOIS
    KANSAS
    LOUISIANA
    MARYLAND
    MASSACHUSETTS
    MICHIGAN

MINNESOTA
MISSISSIPPI
MISSOURI
NEBRASKA
NEVADA
NEW HAMPSHIRE
NEW JERSEY
NEW YORK
NORTH CAROLINA
OHIO
PENNSYLVANIA
RHODE ISLAND
TENNESSEE
VIRGINIA
WASHINGTON
DISTRICT OF COLUMBIA

APPENDIX 2. EXPERIENCE OF THE FIELD: ANNOTATED LITERATURE SEARCH 378
Annotation Organization
Using the Matrix
Definitions
Summarized Information for Each Study
    1. Subject, Jurisdictional Focus, Method and Land Use Analyzed . 383
    2. Geographical, Fiscal and Legal Context 393
    3. Scope of Study, Data Resources 403
    4. Author, Audience and Significance of Study 413
    5. Sources and Prices of Annotated Fiscal Impact Studies 423

Glossary 431
Source of Definitions 441
Bibliography 467
Index 467

Exhibits

PART 1. CALCULATING COSTS: METHODS OF FISCAL IMPACT COST PROJECTION

CHAPTER 1.
Exhibit 1-1.   Relating Methods to Contexts and Tasks of Fiscal Impact Analysis 17
Exhibit 1-2.   Geographical and Problematical Contexts of Fiscal Impact Cost Calculation Demonstrations 23

CHAPTER 2.
Exhibit 2-1.   Per Capita Multiplier Fiscal Impact Method: Summary of Procedures 28
Exhibit 2-2.   General Parameters of a New Jersey, Township, 1976 29
Exhibit 2-3.   Municipal and School District Expenditures by Service Category, Township, New Jersey, 1976 30
Exhibit 2-4A. Regional and National Demographic Multipliers for Common Configurations of Standard Housing Types, Total Household Size by Housing Type and Size 34
Exhibit 2-4B. Regional and National Demographic Multipliers for Common Configurations of Standard Housing Types, School-Age Children by Housing Type and Size 35
Exhibit 2-4C. Regional Demographic Multipliers for Common Configurations of Specialized Housing Types, Total Household Size by Housing Type and Size 36
Exhibit 2-4D. Regional Demographic Multipliers for Common Configurations of Specialized Housing Types, School-Age Children by Housing Type and Size. 36
Exhibit 2-5.   Using the Per Capita Multiplier Method to Evaluate the Fiscal Impact of a Development Proposal 38
Exhibit 2-6.   Municipal and School District Expenditures by Service Category Assignable to the 3,000 Unit PUD 39
Exhibit 2-7.   Computation Sheet for Revenue Projection 40
Exhibit 2-8.   Per Capita Multiplier Method: Data Requirements and Sources 41
Exhibit 2-9.   Time Estimates to Use the Per Capita Multiplier Method 42

CHAPTER 3.

Exhibit 3-1.	Case Study Fiscal Impact Method: Summary of Procedures	48
Exhibit 3-2.	Relationship of Census of Governments Service Categories and Line-Item Budget Classifications	51
Exhibit 3-3.	Using the Case Study Method to Evaluate the Operating Fiscal Impact of a Development Proposal	53
Exhibit 3-4.	Using the Case Study Method to Evaluate the Capital Fiscal Impact of a Development Proposal	54
Exhibit 3-5.	Projection of Resident and School-Age Children Populations	55
Exhibit 3-6.	Computation Sheet for Revenue Projection	59
Exhibit 3-7.	Case Study Method: Data Requirements and Sources	61
Exhibit 3-8.	Time Estimates to Use the Case Study Method	64

CHAPTER 4.

Exhibit 4-1.	Service Standard Fiscal Impact Method: Summary of Procedures	71
Exhibit 4-2.	Full Time Public Employment Per 1,000 Population and Pupils for Municipal and School District Services, by Municipal/School District Size and Region of the United States (Northeast Region)	73
Exhibit 4-3.	Full Time Public Employment Per 1,000 Population and Pupils for Municipal and School District Services, by Municipal/School District Size and Region of the United States (North Central Region)	74
Exhibit 4-4.	Full Time Public Employment Per 1,000 Population and Pupils for Municipal and School District Services, by Municipal/School District Size and Region of the United States (Southern Region)	75
Exhibit 4-5.	Full Time Public Employment Per 1,000 Population and Pupils for Municipal and School District Services by Municipal/School District Size and Region of the United States (Western Region)	76
Exhibit 4-6.	Using the Service Standard Method to Evaluate the Fiscal Impact of Land Use Alternatives	78
Exhibit 4-7.	Relationship of Census of Governments Service Categories and Line-Item Budget Classifications	81
Exhibit 4-8.	Salary, Statutory and Material, and Total Operating Costs per Employee by Service Function	83
Exhibit 4-9.	Annual Capital-to-Operating Expenditure Ratios for Municipal and School District Services by Municipal/School District Size and Region of the United States (Northeast Region)	85
Exhibit 4-10.	Annual Capital-to-Operating Expenditure Ratios for Municipal and School District Services by Municipal/School District Size and Region of the United States (North Central Region)	86
Exhibit 4-11.	Annual Capital-to-Operating Expenditure Ratios for Municipal and School District Services by Municipal/School District Size and Region of the United States (South)	87
Exhibit 4-12.	Annual Capital-to-Operating Expenditure Ratios for Municipal and School District Services by Municipal/School District Size and Region of the United States (West)	88
Exhibit 4-13.	Computation Sheet for Revenue Projection	91
Exhibit 4-14.	Service Standard Method: Data Requirements and Sources	93
Exhibit 4-15.	Time Estimates to Use the Service Standard Method	94

CHAPTER 5.

Exhibit 5-1.	Comparable City Fiscal Impact Analysis Method: Summary of Procedures	101
Exhibit 5-2.	Municipal and School District Median Operating Expenditure Multipliers by Population Size and Growth Rate	103

Exhibits xvii

Exhibit 5-3.	Municipal and School District Median Capital Expenditure Multipliers by Population Size and Growth Rate	106
Exhibit 5-4.	Using the Comparable City Method to Evaluate the Fiscal Impact of Land Use Alternatives	109
Exhibit 5-5.	Per Capita/Per Student Cost Calculations by Service Function	111
Exhibit 5-6.	Computation Sheet for Revenue Tabulation	113
Exhibit 5-7.	Comparable City Method: Data Requirements and Sources	115
Exhibit 5-8.	Time Estimates to Use the Comparable City Method	116

CHAPTER 6.

Exhibit 6-1.	Proportional Valuation Fiscal Impact Method: Summary of Procedures	122
Exhibit 6-2.	Basic Data Required to Implement the Proportional Valuation Method in a Texas Community	123
Exhibit 6-3.	Refinement Coefficients for the Proportional Valuation Fiscal Impact Method	124
Exhibit 6-4.	Typical Impact of Nonresidential Uses on Various Local Public Service Categories	127
Exhibit 6-5.	Using the Proportional Valuation Method to Evaluate the Fiscal Impact of a Proposed Nonresidential Development	128
Exhibit 6-6.	Computation Sheet for Revenue Tabulation	129
Exhibit 6-7.	Proportional Valuation Method: Data Requirements and Sources	131
Exhibit 6-8.	Time Estimates to Employ the Proportional Valuation Method	132

CHAPTER 7.

Exhibit 7-1.	Employment Anticipation Fiscal Impact Method: Summary of Procedures	137
Exhibit 7-2.	Expenditure Multipliers Measuring the Demand Generated Impact of Commercial Activity upon Six Categories of Per Capita Municipal Expenditures	140
Exhibit 7-3.	Expenditure Multipliers Measuring the Demand Generated Impact of Industrial Activity upon Six Categories of Per Capita Municipal Expenditures	141
Exhibit 7-4.	Using the Employment Anticipation Method to Estimate the Fiscal Impact of a Development Proposal	142
Exhibit 7-5.	Computation Sheet for Revenue Tabulation	144
Exhibit 7-6.	Employment Anticipation Method: Data Requirements and Sources	145
Exhibit 7-7.	Time and Cost Estimates to Employ the Employment Anticipation Method	146

PART 2. CALCULATING REVENUES: METHODS OF FISCAL IMPACT REVENUE PROJECTION

CHAPTER 8.

Exhibit 8-1.	Reliance on Revenue Sources by Municipalities and School Districts, United States (1972)	155
Exhibit 8-2.	Change in Revenue Sources within Municipalities and School Districts (1942-1972)	155
Exhibit 8-3.	Change in Revenue Source Dependency in Municipalities and School Districts (1957-1972)	156
Exhibit 8-4.	Intergovernmental Transfers in Municipalities and School Districts by Region (1972)	158
Exhibit 8-5.	Rank Order of States for Intergovernmental Support of Municipal and School District Operations (1972)	159
Exhibit 8-6.	Contribution of Taxes to Local Revenue (1972)	159

xviii THE FISCAL IMPACT HANDBOOK

Exhibit 8-7.	Contribution of Property Tax to Local Revenue (1972)	160
Exhibit 8-8.	Reliance on Property Tax (1942-72)	161
Exhibit 8-9.	Regional Reliance on Property Tax by Type of Government (1972)	161
Exhibit 8-10.	Rank Order of States for Property Tax Support of Municipal and School District Operations (1972)	162
Exhibit 8-11.	Sales Taxes Imposed by Local Jurisdictions, by State (1976)	163
Exhibit 8-12.	Income Taxes Imposed by Local Jurisdictions, by State (1976)	166
Exhibit 8-13.	Reliance on Taxes by Municipalities and School Districts (1942-1972)	171
Exhibit 8-14.	Regional Patterns of Use of Sales, Income and Other Taxes in Municipalities and School Districts (1972)	172
Exhibit 8-15.	Changes in Use of Charges and Miscellaneous Revenues for Municipalities and School Districts (1942-1972)	173
Exhibit 8-16.	Rank Order of States in User Charges and Miscellaneous Revenues to Support Municipal Operations (1972)	174
Exhibit 8-17.	Rank Order of States in User Charges and Miscellaneous Revenues to Support School District Operations (1972)	174
Exhibit 8-18.	Revenue Sources of Municipalities and School Districts (1972)	175
Exhibit 8-19.	Municipalities' Reliance on Various Sources of Revenues, by Region (1972)	176
Exhibit 8-20.	School Districts' Reliance on Various Sources of Revenues, by Region (1972)	177

CHAPTER 9.
Exhibit 9-1.	Local Revenues for which Calculation Procedures are Illustrated	180
Exhibit 9-2.	Computation Sheet for Revenue Projection	183

CHAPTER 10.
Exhibit 10-1.	Municipal Revenues by Source	224
Exhibit 10-2.	School District Revenues by Source	229
Exhibit 10-3.	Market Value of Real Property for 3,000 Unit PUD (New Jersey and Illinois)	232
Exhibit 10-4.	Market Value of Real Property for 3,000 Unit PUD (California and Georgia)	233
Exhibit 10-5.	Pre- and Post-Growth Property Valuation and Student Population	234

PART 3. GENERAL APPLICABILITY—ARE FISCAL IMPACT CONSIDERATIONS ACCEPTABLE MUNICIPAL ACTIVITIES OR REQUIREMENTS?

CHAPTER 12.
Exhibit 12-1.	Subject, Jurisdictional Focus, Method, Land Use Type, and Land Use Form Analyzed	259
Exhibit 12-2.	Geographical and Fiscal Context	262
Exhibit 12-3.	Scope of Study and Data Resources	265
Exhibit 12-4.	Author Audience and Significance of Study	268

PART 4. ADDITIONAL DATA: MULTIPLIERS AND MODELS USED IN FISCAL IMPACT ANALYSIS

CHAPTER 13.
Exhibit 13-1.	Regional and National Demographic Multipliers for Common Configurations of Standard Housing Types for Total Household Size by Housing Type and Number of Bedrooms	279

Exhibits

Exhibit 13-2. Regional and National Demographic Multipliers for Common Configurations of Standard Housing Types for School-Age Children by Housing Type and Number of Bedrooms 280
Exhibit 13-3. Region and Subregion into Which Various States Fall for the Purpose of Demographic Multipliers 282
Exhibit 13-4. Regional Demographic Multipliers for Common Configurations of Specialized Housing Types for Total Household Size by Housing Type and Number of Bedrooms (Field Surveys 1970-75) 284
Exhibit 13-5. Regional Demographic Multipliers for Common Configurations of Specialized Housing Types for School-Age Children by Housing Type and Number of Bedrooms (Field Surveys 1970-75) 284

CHAPTER 14.
Exhibit 14-1. Household and Person Data From the Public Use Sample Required to Calculate Demographic Multipliers 299
Exhibit 14-2. Sample Fortran Program for Editing the Output of the PUSH Program .. 300

CHAPTER 15.
Exhibit 15-1. Sample Size and the Reliability of Survey Estimates of Demographic Multipliers 311

CHAPTER 16.
Exhibit 16-1. Gross Income Multipliers for Newly Constructed Residential and Commercial Properties by Region of the United States 325
Exhibit 16-2. Input Data to Derive Real Property Value for New Residential Uses..... 327
Exhibit 16-3. Input Data to Derive Real Property Value for New Commercial Uses (Shopping Centers) 333
Exhibit 16-4. Input Data to Derive Real Property Value for New Commerical Uses (Office Space) 337
Exhibit 16-5. Input Data Used to Derive Gross Income Multipliers for Garden Apartments 341
Exhibit 16-6. Input Data Used to Derive Gross Income Multipliers for Mid to High-Rise Elevator Apartments 342
Exhibit 16-7. Input Data Used to Derive Gross Income Multipliers for Regional Shopping Centers 342
Exhibit 16-8. Input Data Used to Derive Gross Income Multipliers for Community Shopping Centers 343
Exhibit 16-9. Input Data Used to Derive Gross Income Multipliers for Neighborhood Shopping Centers 343
Exhibit 16-10. Input Data Used to Derive Gross Income Multipliers for Office Space ... 344

CHAPTER 17.
Exhibit 17-1. Basic Techniques Used to Project Costs in the Fiscal Impact Section of the Cost-Revenue Model 349
Exhibit 17-2. Data Resources Drawn Upon: Cost-Revenue Models/Costs and Revenues Considered 354
Exhibit 17-3. Troublesome Issues in Fiscal Impact Analysis and Their Handling by Cost Revenue Models 356

Preface

The three key elements of planning — the physical, the social, and the fiscal — are mutually interdependent. The success of the planning process is dependent upon an appropriate balance and analytical competence with which to integrate them. Despite this significance, they have received great variance not only in attention but also in the provision of appropriate analytical tools with which to evaluate them. The physical sector dominated the field through the early part of the 1960s when, at overly long last, it was complemented by some measure of focus on social impacts. Lagging both of these, however, has been the provision of appropriate firm building blocks of fact with which to structure fiscal impact appropriately. Increasingly it is this last element of the triad which has moved into the center of public attention.

The work presented here is intended to provide the key elements of input in this vital sphere. Its intended audience are concerned citizenry, governmental officials, both on the local and broader spheres, and the professionals in the field; the consultants and the academics who service the need for knowledge. The **goal** of this study is not to advocate one form or another of developmental pattern, not to define what is a "good" ratable versus a "bad" one, but rather to provide the numbers surrounding fiscal impact. What are the realities of municipal service costs and pressures for various forms of improvement? How are these matched by the offset of revenues?

In our experience at CUPR we have seen all too frequently fallacious fiscal impact statements being misused either to preclude or endorse development. The zoning struggle in many cases is similar to the Dance of the Seven Veils, with fiscal impact being used as the first of these, serving as a cloak for a variety of other goal structures. The target of the research effort presented here is rather to provide a common meeting ground of fact, the quantification necessary to do adequate fiscal planning, of mixing and matching various forms of physical improvement in a fashion which will permit both heterogeneity and fiscal competence.

The quantification of the parameters in this field is a most complex one. On the cost side of the ledger we have been faced with the enormous variety of both residential and nonresidential configurations. When, in turn, these are considered within the diversity of the United States, with cost elements varying both regionally and also substantially by the size of the governmental units involved—the very scale of cities altering some of the cost elements — the scope of the research becomes evident.

Nor is the other side of the scale—the income sector—one which the researcher can face with equanimity. The rapid changes in revenue sharing of various kinds, both on the state and federal level, have left earlier cost revenue analyses (practically exclusively focused on local impact, community costs versus immediately derived community revenues) hopelessly behind the realities of municipal finance.

The sheer growth in both data resource and complexity of analysis which was required in order to cope with these problems has involved an intensive work effort of more than two years. We are indeed fortunate in the competence, energy and profound grasp of the two principal investigators of the study, Drs. Burchell and Listokin, for the success that has been achieved.

This is a working document. It provides the key data inputs and a flexible format intended for utility in the field. We at the Center are extremely proud of the opportunity to have worked on this study, and we invite the criticisms and suggestions of all the elements of our audience in pursuing it through the future.

GEORGE STERNLIEB
Director
Center for Urban Policy Research

ACKNOWLEDGEMENTS

The preparation of this study would have been impossible without the assistance and cooperation of many individuals. Dr. George Sternlieb must be singled out for invaluable assistance and guidance. The work is also a tribute to the nature of the Center for Urban Policy Research as a research organization. The Center has sufficient flexibility to pursue a topic, should the situation warrant, far beyond the limits of the topic's initial financial support.

Our joint authors made significant contributions. Dr. W. Patrick Beaton was responsible for initial drafts of the Comparable City Method and the tabular material of the Employment Anticipation Method. Dr. Franklin J. James, Jr. provided initial drafts of the sections on using the Public Use Samples and survey methods to derive demographic multipliers. Mr. Robert W. Lake provided the tabular material on demographic multipliers and performed the statistical tests to determine their geographic and temporal variation. Nathan Edelstein, Esq., did both original work on and subsequently polished the legal chapter.

Personnel from Barton-Aschman Associates, Mssrs. Robert B. Teska, Rodney E. Engelen, Darwin G. Stuart and Michael Levin, commented upon drafts and oversaw field work relating to specialized demographic multipliers and the field testing of fiscal impact methods.

The Department of Housing and Urban Development gave the initial financial support that made this study possible. We especially commend HUD's Government Technical Representatives, Dr. Louis Rose and Mr. Stevenson Weitz, for their detailed review of and comments on, submitted documents.

The handbook was overseen throughout its development by User and Technical Committees. The User Committee included Dr. E.E. Brickell, Director, Division of the Superintendent, Virginia Beach City Public Schools; Mr. Fred Bryant, Assistant Planning Director, Charlotte-Mecklenberg Planning Board; Ms. Beatrice Cohen, Planning Director, Easton, Pa.; Mr. Walter Doyle, Chairman, East Windsor, N.J. Planning Board; Mr. William D. Kirk, Jr., Vice President, Richard P. Browne Associates, Wayne, N.J.; Mr. Naphtali H. Knox, Director, Palo Alto Department of Planning and Community Development; Dr. Lee E. Koppelman, Executive Director, Nassau-Suffolk

Regional Planning Board; Mr. James R. Leva, Vice President, Jersey Central Power and Light Company; Mr. Stuart Meck, Planner, Miami Valley Regional Planning Commission; Mr. Harvey S. Moskowitz, President, Harvey S. Moskowitz Planning Associates, Livingston, N.J.; Mr. Eugene Oross, President, E. Eugene Oross Associates, New Brunswick, N.J.; Mr. Douglass Powell, Director, Middlesex County, N.J. Planning Board; Mr. Arthur K. Rothschild, Vice President, W.R. Grace Properties, Inc., Philadelphia, Pa.; and Mr. Warren W. Wilson, Senior Research Analyst, The Rouse Company.

The Technical Committee consisted of Mr. Richard R. Almy, Director of Research and Technical Service Department, International Association of Assessing Officers; Mr. J. Thomas Black, Assistant Research Director, The Urban Land Institute; Ms. Carol Berenson, Research Associate, National Association of Counties Research Foundation; Dr. Bernard Frieden, Professor, Department of Urban Studies and Planning, Massachusetts Institute of Technology; Ms. Judith Getzels, Senior Research Associate, American Society of Planning Officials; Mr. Allan A. Hodges, Assistant Executive Director, American Institute of Planners; Dr. Frank Kristof, Vice President, Planning and Program Development, Urban Development Corporation, New York; Dr. Thomas Muller, Senior Research Associate, Urban Institute, Washington, D.C.; Mr. John E. Lynch, Director, Program Operations, Office of Economic Adjustment, Department of Defense; Ms. Mary Nenno, Associate Director for Program Operations, National Association of Housing and Redevelopment Officials; Mr. Donald Priest, Research Director, Urban Land Institute, Washington, D.C.; Mr. Randall Scott, Institute Fellow, Environmental Law Institute; and Professor Jerome G. Rose, Chairman, Department of Urban Planning, Rutgers University. All of these individuals provided extremely useful and structural emphases that improved the organization and substantive content of the handbook immeasurably.

Staff members at the Center for Urban Policy Research were of great assistance. These include: Dr. Kristina Ford, Ms. Natalie Borisovets, Thomas R. Fitzgerald, Ms. Debra Ann Berger, Mr. William Rainwater, Ms. Deborah Ramsey, Mr. Stephen R. Seidel, Mr. Shrikant Sinha and Mr. James Marchetti.

Mrs. Mary Picarella, Mrs. Joan Frantz, Mrs. Lydia Lombardi, and Mrs. Anne Hummel, the mainstays of the Center for Urban Policy Research's administrative and typing staff, all performed valuable duties in preparing the manuscript. Ms. Barbara Fishel, edited the very complex manuscript and Mssrs. Daniel Sohmer and J. Carl Cook, current and interim directors of publication, deserve special credit for shaping the book and guiding it through the publication process.

The principal authors, of course, assume responsibility for any errors or misinterpretations that remain.

Robert W. Burchell
David Listokin

The Fiscal Impact Handbook

INTRODUCTION AND ORGANIZATION

Why Fiscal Impact Analysis?

In times of continued inflation and consequent strain on municipal budgets, elected officials and municipal department heads must be aware of the public costs associated with private development, major rezonings, annexations, or alternative land use plans. They need to project resident and school-age children populations attributable to development, the numbers of public employees—policemen, firemen, teachers, etc.—who must be hired, and the kinds of municipal facilities needed to serve the changing population.

This handbook provides municipal officials, local staff planners, city managers/business administrators, and private planning consultants access to the information they need to make these decisions. It includes simple, straightforward procedural guides to estimate the costs and revenues associated with development. Persons who are involved in the public service costs and revenues of local growth can use the methods and data in this basic field manual to calculate fiscal impact of planned development.

Several benefits are associated with fiscal impact analysis. The community can project service requirements of anticipated development. It can monitor the cost of land use decisions—the decision to zone for single-family houses or garden apartments, the decision to rezone for commercial rather than residential development. And it can maintain a reasonable long-term balance by comparing fiscally beneficial decisions with those that are not.

Definition and Concepts

Fiscal impact analysis, as used in this handbook, is:

> A projection of the direct, current, public costs and revenues associated with residential or nonresidential growth to the local jurisdiction(s) in which this growth is taking place.

Certain terms in this definition must be clearly understood. The following paragraphs define them.

Fiscal impact analysis, as used in this handbook, considers only *direct* impact. It projects only the primary costs that will be incurred and the immediate revenues that will be generated. Direct or primary costs include, for example, salaries for instructors to teach new students generated by a large subdivision, or for policemen to control traffic at a new shopping center. Direct or primary revenues include property and sales taxes and intergovernmental monies generated as a direct consequence of the particular growth increment. Indirect impacts are not specifically treated due to (1) the near impossibility to predict accurately the secondary consequences of growth and (2) the recurring potential for double counting when primary and secondary impacts are viewed simultaneously. In the first case, will a shopping center increase real property values of adjacent parcels or does the presence of an immediate market enhance the value of the shopping center? In the second, should property tax revenues from an off-site nonresidential development which in part is supported by a residential development be considered the primary impact of the nonresidential development or the secondary impact of the residential development? This handbook considers no differential property value loss or gain relative to proximate development nor does it attribute secondary revenues to a residential development due to property or sales tax increases of a nonresidential facility benefitting from the nearby population. In the first case, it is assumed that the "contagion effects" of land uses in the long run will net to zero. In the second, the revenue contributions of any land use are considered only when that land use's primary impact is under scrutiny.

Fiscal impact analysis examines *current* costs and revenues. It tallies the financial effect of a planned unit development, urban renewal complex, new town, shopping center, etc., by considering the current costs and revenues such facilities would generate if they were completed and operating today. This approach recognizes that development or redevelopment often requires several years and that inflation will increase costs and revenues over time. It also assumes, however, that the rising costs of providing public services will be matched by an essentially comparable increase in revenues—that the relative relationship of costs and revenues will change little over time.

Fiscal impact analysis is concerned with *public* (governmental) costs and revenues. It does not consider *private* costs of public actions, i.e. the costs passed on to developers or consumers through local land use regulations or building, health, and fire codes. Thus, special assessments on real property or the value of land dedications required of developers are considered private revenues. Private services provided by homes associations and community trusts are also considered private expenditures.

Tallying and comparing *costs and revenues* is a significant part of fiscal impact analysis. Costs include operating expenses (salaries, and statutory and material expenses) and capital outlays, either directly incurred by a public jurisdiction or paid to others as a result of a specific development. Revenues comprise all monies a government receives from external sources as a result of the development or redevelopment. Revenues counted in this handbook include municipal and school district own source (local) contributions (taxes, charges, and miscellaneous revenue) and state and federal intergovernmental transfers.

Fiscal impact analysis is further concerned with the cost and revenue implications derived from *population and/or employment change*. These changes are broadly defined as residential and/or nonresidential entrance into or departure from a community. The fiscal impact analysis may be a prediction or a *post hoc* evaluation and may evaluate population and/or employment change in either the private or public sectors (i.e., a builder attempting to develop a mixed use planned unit development or a local authority seeking municipal approval for a public housing project or a civic center).

Finally, costs are projected to only the *local jurisdictions* in which the population or employment change is taking place. In most instances, the local jurisdiction is the town, township, borough, or parish for municipal costs and the school district(s) for primary and secondary school district expenditures. This handbook does not consider services administered by and revenues flowing to utilities, special districts, county governments, regional authorities, and states.

Emphasizing projections of exclusively local costs reflects user demand. Local governments—either municipal or school district—provide most services to residential and nonresidential properties. Police and fire protection, road maintenance and repair, education, etc., represent types of local government services. Local property owners most often share the cost of these services. Impacts on the cost are of vital interest to the local population; fiscal impact analyses volunteered by developers or required by local ordinances are the result. Services provided by special districts are usually paid for with user charges. They typically do not affect the local population directly. County government services in areas where local governments also provide services to property frequently involve major road construction or repair and institution or agency maintenance. Their impact on local residents is small and not of vital concern.

Fiscal Impact Analysis and Other Evaluative Strategies

In this handbook, *fiscal impact analysis* is used interchangeably with *cost-revenue analysis*. It is not synonymous, however, with the terms cost benefit or cost effectiveness. The basic difference in the three terms is the scope of the analysis. Cost benefit analysis is the broadest of the three techniques. It compares both the tangible and intangible costs and revenues of a particular project or program. Costs and benefits may include public expenditures as well as individual, community, or environmental gains or losses. Cost effectiveness analysis considers only the economic costs of the cost benefit analysis but emphasizes the least cost approach to realizing a given objective's success. It usually considers the range of alternative actions, given a fixed level of resources. Cost-revenue analysis, on the other hand, focuses exclusively on the costs and revenues associated with a specific form of growth. The result of such an analysis is a statement of net governmental surplus or deficit expressed in purely financial terms—dollars, manpower, service units, etc.

These three approaches may be distinguished by their analyses of the impact of a publicly assisted housing development in a middle income community. A *cost benefit analysis* would assess not only dollar impact of the development but also the project's potentially negative and positive impacts on the neighborhood. It would weigh the value of a heterogeneous community and an improved housing environment for residents against negative effects such as increased congestion. A *cost effectiveness analysis* would establish the maximum level of acceptable costs to the community by ascertaining which types of publicly assisted developments result in minimal local expenditures—housing for families, the elderly, or the disabled, for example. A *cost-revenue analysis* would determine only the difference between the cost of providing the municipal services the project requires and the expected municipal income it generates.

In this handbook, fiscal impact analysis is used in its narrowest form, i.e., as a financial auditing tool that considers only net local public costs and revenues. This approach ignores all other nonfiscal costs or benefits and costs or benefits which may be conferred differentially, i.e., on one group in a community at the expense of another. The handbook's aim is to provide a fiscal foundation for development planning but not to serve as a surrogate for the latter. Fiscal impact analysis is an essential beginning step in the overall evaluative process.

Calculating Costs

There are two basic approaches to municipal cost allocation: *average costing* and *marginal costing*. Average costing is by far the more common field application. Costs are attributed to a new development according to average cost per unit of service (municipal and school district services) times the number of units the development is estimated to require. This method does not consider existing excess or deficient capacity that might exist for particular services or the possibility that a new development might fall at the threshold level, calling for major new capital construction to accommodate increased growth. Both of these deficiencies could invalidate an average cost assumption. Marginal costing, however, takes both of these potential deficiencies into account. Marginal costing relies heavily on careful analysis of existing demand/supply relationships for local governmental and school services.

The average cost and marginal cost approaches are two different ways to assess the cost of governmental services growth imposes. Average costing views the relationship as linear while marginal costing views growth as having a more cyclical impact on local expenditures. In the extremely long run, however, the two techniques will yield similar estimates of growth impact. The difference is that at times the marginal cost estimate will lag behind the average cost projection while in other instances the marginal cost estimate will lead or exceed the average cost figures. For example, marginal costs may be low in communities where unused facilities are available for an increased population; they are high when new facilities are to be built and new services provided that are greater than those immediately needed by the incoming population. Choosing either the average costing or marginal costing approaches will depend on what the fiscal impact analyst seeks — a best average estimate of the fiscal effects of growth, in which case he will select the average costing approach, or a more intimate projection, in which case he will opt for the marginal costing technique.

This handbook presents six different methods to analyze cost-revenue impact. They are relatively simple and straightforward in nature, based on the derivation of either average or marginal cost-revenue characteristics from recent municipal and school district budgetary data. It is assumed that the recent cost-revenue characteristics of individual land uses will be maintained in the future. Because of their simplicity, these fiscal impact analysis techniques do not represent forecasting "models" of the more rigorous type (typically based upon sophisticated statistical analysis or mathematical modeling), rather, they represent ad hoc analysis techniques for estimating the likely cost-revenue impact of different land-use development patterns, based upon recent historical experience in a given locality.

Three of the six fiscal impact analysis techniques — *Per Capita Multiplier, Service Standard,* and *Proportional Valuation* — represent average costing approaches, while the three remaining techniques — *Case Study, Comparable City* and *Employment Anticipation* — represent marginal costing strategies.*

All but two of the six methods — Proportional Valuation and Employment Anticipation — are used for estimating the impacts of residential activity. The remaining two are applicable for

---

*This categorization into average costing and marginal costing reflects the *application* of the method. The Per Capita Multiplier, Service Standard and Proportional Valuation methods assume future costs are extensions of current averages. This assumption is most applicable when the city's service capacity closely reflects the population's service demands. The Case Study, Comparable City, and Employment Anticipation methods assume a substantial service change. The city, as a result of growth, must provide new services. Relying on either excess or deficient service capacity related to economies or diseconomies of scale results in new service costs which are significantly different from past averages.

Introduction 5

nonresidential land uses, while the Case Study is used for both residential and nonresidential projections. Since the same methods for revenue estimation may be utilized under any technique, emphasis is given to differences in the estimation of public service costs. To facilitate their use each cost estimation method is presented in a standard format:

- Background (history and development of method, with a brief example).
- Application (review of population size, growth rate, development context, and planning activity which each technique is most suitable).
- Basic Assumptions (how costs are assumed to vary; the method is sensitive to this variation).
- Procedures (detailed listing of each analysis procedure).
- Data Requirements (tabular listing, by analysis step, of data requirements and sources).
- Sophistication of User (mathematical and technical requirements of method).
- Advantages and Disadvantages (including estimate of effort required to apply method, level of detail of results, short-term versus long-term impact estimates, reliance on local data, etc.).
- Interpreting Results (cost-revenue surplus or deficit and what this means according to the method chosen).

The six fiscal impact analysis methods are briefly summarized in the following paragraphs.

Per Capita Multiplier Method

This is the most versatile fiscal impact analysis method. A sample of local fiscal impact analyses undertaken from 1970–1973 showed that 70 percent of the evaluations employed either this method or a slight variation of it. The Per Capita Multiplier technique relies on average municipal costs per person, average school costs per pupil, and the number of persons or pupils generated by various housing types to project future municipal and school district costs. It is most appropriately applied to moderately sized municipalities, between 10,000 and 50,000 residents, with moderate projected population growth. In such communities, it is assumed that the best estimate of future costs is current per capita cost multiplied by the future population increment.

The demographic multipliers employed in this method have been developed from U.S. Census data for eleven regions throughout the country. For each region the number of residents and the number of school-age children associated with eight standard and five specialized housing types are presented.

Case Study Method

The Case Study Method is the second most frequently used method, having been used in approximately 15 percent of the fiscal impact analyses to date. It is employed for both residential and nonresidential analyses in very large or very small cities which typically exhibit significant excess or deficient service capacity so great that average costs, extended into the future, appear inappropriate.

The method projects future local costs based on specific future service demand determined by interviewing municipal department heads and school district administrators. The Case Study Method assumes that each department head knows best the functional capacity of his agency and can respond most accurately to specific questions of future service extensions or retrenchments. Each determination of local service excess or deficiency is based on first-hand knowledge of existing local conditions. The results are either subtracted from or added to the best estimate of operating and capital demands imposed by growth.

Service Standard Method

The Service Standard Method is used in approximately 10 percent of the fiscal impact analyses nationally. Its application is similar to that of the Per Capita Multiplier Method—midsize, moderate growth communities.

The Service Standard Method provides more detail than the Per Capita Multiplier Method. Future manpower estimates by specific service function are available from the former while only gross expenditures by service category are derived from the latter. This method uses U.S. Census of Governments data to obtain averages of manpower per 1,000 population and capital-to-operating expenditure ratios for eight common municipal functions. Multiplying the expected municipal and school district populations by service manpower requirements and by local salaries, statutory obligations, and expenses per employee provides an estimate of future fiscal impact.

Manpower ratios are tabulated for municipalities and school districts by population size and geographic area. Tables have been prepared for four regions of the country, with eleven population categories per region.

Comparable City Method

The Comparable City Method has been used only slightly to date, but its future use should increase. It is ideal for projecting long-term views of the future or large scale development, both situations which significantly change population size or growth rate. This method relies on these two variables to develop new service ratios based on economies or diseconomies of scale. The method assumes that cities of comparable population size and growth rate expend money for municipal services and education at relatively similar levels across five basic municipal service categories and education. If the fiscal impact analyst can predict a new population size obtained at a specific growth rate, he can adjust current expenditures based on communities of comparable size and growth rate. He thus applies ratios of future to current expenditures to existing per capita costs and multiplies by the total projected future municipal and school population of the community as a whole to obtain an estimate of the future local servicing obligation. Tables of expenditure multipliers are found within this method for municipal/school district size categories ranging from less than 1,000 to over 1,000,000, for positive and negative growth rates from 0 percent to over 2 percent, and for each of the five categories of municipal services and for school district services.

Proportional Valuation Method

The Proportional Valuation Method is a quick and easy procedure to determine the fiscal impact of *nonresidential* facilities. It has been used for more than a decade. The method is ideally suited to employment-generating facilities which exhibit neither relatively excessive nor slight number of employees per square foot. The analyst assigns a share of solely *municipal* costs to an incoming nonresidential facility (a shopping center, industrial complex, etc.) based on the facility's proportion of total local real property valuation. The method tends to overstate municipal servicing obligation for very large nonresidential facilities and understate them for very small ones. Refinement coefficients have been developed to scale down projected impact when new nonresidential facilities are significantly *larger* than the average local nonresidential facility and to *scale up* projected impact when they are significantly *smaller* than the average.

Employment Anticipation Method

The Employment Anticipation Method is also used for determining the municipal servicing costs for incoming *nonresidential* facilities. The method, because it is new, has not been widely used. It is most appropriate for nonresidential facilities having either significantly more or significantly fewer employees per square foot than normal, thus imposing larger or smaller municipal costs based on the public service needs of these employees. The method assumes that municipal service costs are related to the number of employees a nonresidential facility introduces locally. For both industrial and commercial uses, coefficients are developed which state that for every new employee, service cost in the general government, public safety, public works sectors, etc. will increase by given percentages. The practitioner multiplies the number of future employees by these coefficients and obtains the percent increase in each service function expenditure. The percent increase times the existing dollar expenditure is the servicing cost assignable to the new nonresidential facility.

Calculating Revenues

Each of the six cost estimation methods uses the same techniques to estimate local government tax revenues associated with different land uses, development projects, and plan alternatives. In general, relatively simple multiplier or ratio techniques are used to project the many different sources of service-supporting income which might be relevant for a particular community. Estimating revenues is complicated by the fact that local revenue sources are steadily becoming more diversified.

The primary sources of income are local (own source) revenues (property, sales, and income taxes, charges and fees for services) and intergovernmental transfers (payments from federal and state governments). Intergovernmental transfers are becoming more important, property taxes are becoming somewhat less important, and other taxes, notably sales and income taxes and charges are being used more widely. Despite these trends, however, the local property tax remains the prime source of locally produced tax revenue.

This handbook presents methods to project some thirty different sources of revenue. About half consist of own source or locally generated tax revenues; the remainder are for intergovernmental transfers from both the state and federal governments. Only a portion of these potential revenue sources will be applicable in any given locality. The handbook stresses the user's employing his judgment to identify those revenue sources on which to concentrate. When any one of the thirty different revenue sources constitutes a potentially important local revenue source, procedural guides and examples for projecting source-specific revenues are included. These recommended methods have been derived from the various cost-revenue studies which were reviewed as a part of the project as well as from prototypical state transfer formulas and federal program-allocation guides. As such, they represent the most frequent types of revenue source estimation procedures observed in field practice. The user should still check the specifics of revenue generation in his locale to determine whether there are unique aspects in a particular revenue generation system which would call for adaptations or alterations of the methods provided here (for example, changes in the population or land use class against which some local tax revenues are collected).

General Applicability

Fiscal impact considerations are legally authorized or fertile grounds for authorization can exist within the confines of numerous planning or planning-related tasks. Because economy and efficiency have long been basic objectives of planning and land development, fiscal projections can be used to achieve these goals. Fiscal impact considerations could easily be required as part of a comprehensive plan. They are similarly pertinent in cases of special exception or permitted use (for instance, as part of the PUD approval process) to ensure local fiscal stability throughout the multiple stages of a large development; or in variances or rezonings to provide documentation that undue hardship to an individual property owner is mitigated by the community's general economic benefit or that the fiscal situation has so changed in a community that the existing zoning bears no relationship to reality and is in fact counterproductive to orderly growth. These are key parameters in granting these forms of relief.

Fiscal impact considerations are further authorized for use in annexations; they assess the likely financial outcome of the merger to both jurisdictions and prevent annexations which would benefit one jurisdiction at the expense of the other. Fiscal impact considerations are within the purview of state land use laws which attempt to coordinate the often conflicting economic objectives of smaller units of government.

Fiscal impact analyses can be inappropriate, however, and it is important to be aware of the potential for their misuse. The practitioner should realize that every land use does not benefit the community and while it is possible to assess relative fiscal merit, it does not follow that those land uses that either are not as beneficial as others or impose a local liability can necessarily be excluded.

Where fiscal impact analysis has a history, the courts have in part specified its role. *Fiscal considerations, while the concern of local land use policy, are neither the sole concern, nor may they be the basis on which to exclude totally a category of land use.* Fiscal impact analysis is a local accounting mechanism which provides insight into the fiscal effect of land use decisions. Analyses will inform local authorities, for instance, that certain forms of residential development will not be "profitable" while others will, and that generally most forms of nonresidential uses will be more "profitable" than residential. The courts have said then that localities may indeed use this type of information to plan for the future; however, the fiscal implications of particular development or zone change are only one element within the planning process. In several instances the courts have recognized that municipalities also have to provide housing for those who work nearby, answer regional as well as local needs, and provide residential opportunities for those who are economically disadvantaged.

Why the Handbook?

The purpose of this handbook is to assemble and disseminate practitioner-oriented fiscal impact methods. Initially it was assumed that operable methods existed in the field and were capable of being packaged for field use without extensive refinement. This proved to be definitely not the case. At the time of the initiation of this study, only one operable method for analyzing residential fiscal impact (Per Capita Multiplier Method) and one for nonresidential fiscal impact (Proportional Valuation Method) existed. While these methods had obvious inherent operational shortcomings, alternatives were even more poorly developed. The Case Study Method was used sparingly because it relied on subjective impact projections. The Service Standard Method was used infrequently because it relied on numerous professional group, union, and trade standards to convert future service population demands to annual operational service cost estimates. The resulting projection proved extremely uneven between service categories as there were often numerous "standards" (many times conflicting) for some departments and few, if any, standards for others. The Comparable City Method lacked a national data base and had been used only in a few instances in the Northeast. The Employment Anticipation Method was essentially nonexistent. *All* the methods, even the ones in use, lacked both a capital facilities component and the ability to

Introduction

partition total municipal costs among specific service categories. Finally, few of the methods considered the range of costs (operating, statutory, and capital) that were integral parts of both municipal and school district daily operations, and even fewer were concerned with the wide array of local revenue sources. Intergovernmental transfers, for instance, the fastest growing municipal revenue component, were almost always ignored.

Field practice reflected the unsure state of fiscal impact analysis. Of nearly 140 fiscal impact analyses surveyed in the course of this study:

- Twenty percent were either incomplete, incomprehensible, or incorrect (with arithmetic or conceptual mistakes).
- In over half of the locations where the study was undertaken, the presiding local official could not gauge the study's accuracy.
- Sixty percent of the cases contained no replicative capacity without the specific local consultants and staff planners who prepared the initial report.
- Even though demand existed for further fiscal impact analyses at over one-third of the locations, they were not repeated.

The foregoing suggests the need for a manual that would assemble fiscal impact methods, standardize the methods to include the full range of costs and revenues, collect and augment necessary data, and finally, provide the analyst with guidance about how, when, and where to use this planning tool most effectively as an element of local land use policy. This handbook is directed to those ends.

Organization of the Handbook

This handbook consists of four parts, encompassing several chapters each. Parts 1 and 2 present the actual procedures to project costs and revenues resulting from local population change.

Part 1 begins with an overview of the dynamics of local public expenditures in the United States (Chapter 1). It then summarizes the specific steps necessary to implement each of the six fiscal impact analysis methods (Chapters 2 through 7). Each strategy is described in terms of where it is applicable, what its assumptions are, how it is to be applied, what the method's demands are in terms of data and user sophistication, what its advantages or disadvantages are, and, finally, how its results should be interpreted. Each fiscal impact method is illustrated with a full example at one site.

Part 2 complements the previous cost discussion by demonstrating procedures for estimating local revenues generated by new growth. It provides an overview of the range of municipal and school district revenues and their changing relationships over the past decade (Chapter 8). It continues by presenting detailed steps to estimate both local revenues and intergovernmental transfers (Chapters 9 and 10). The revenue calculations are further illustrated by showing actual revenue projections at the specific sites where costs were calculated.

Part 3 discusses the kinds of land use activities that typically require fiscal impact considerations and the situations where fiscal impact analysis may be inappropriate or may not be the correct criterion upon which to base land use policy (Chapter 11). This review is important to the user because it clearly specifies the potential benefits and pitfalls of being fiscal impact "conscious." This Part also considers current field practice, that is, the state of the art of fiscal impact analysis (Chapter 12). It examines which methods are used in particular situations, which data resources are relied upon, which range of costs and revenues are considered, and finally, what is the current level of user satisfaction with fiscal impact analysis.

Part 4 provides supplementary data essential to those who are undertaking fiscal impact analyses. Chapter 13 summarizes demographic multipliers (household size and school-age children) for housing units of different configurations, sizes, and locations. These multipliers are used in most fiscal impact methods to project the incremental population and school load resulting from growth. Chapters 14 and 15 show how to calculate demographic multipliers from either local surveys or from the U.S. Census data if the general multipliers in this handbook do not accurately reflect local conditions. Chapter 16 demonstrates how to project the value of multifamily and nonresidential properties if only gross income is known. Chapter 17 presents background information on computer models for fiscal impact analyses.

A glossary of terms, an index, and a bibliography close the work. The glossary defines over 200 technical and legal terms used in the handbook, covering such subjects as real property value, public revenue programs, and public expenditure categories. It also makes explicit the litany of terms used almost exclusively with fiscal impact analysis, e.g., "school-age children," "per capita multipliers," etc. By clarifying the language, the glossary serves as a valuable aid to both the novice and the more seasoned fiscal impact practitioner. The index enables the user to locate general as well as detailed topics in the handbook and specific references to particular authors, studies, court cases, revenue systems, expenditure categories, types of multipliers, etc.

Analyst's Guide

The fiscal impact analyst should first review Chapters 1 and 8; Calculating Costs and Calculating Revenues (Parts 1 and 2). They serve as a crucial introduction to the subject matter, laying down basic terms, introducing the overall framework of fiscal impact analysis and suggesting which cost-revenue strategies may be best for a given situation. They also mention the limitations of the methods — constraints which the analyst should bear in mind when using one or another of the methods for his specific case.

The user's objectives and his experience and expertise will govern further use of the handbook. Those who wish actually to undertake one or more of the fiscal impact analyses should focus mainly on Parts 1 (Calculating Costs) and 2 (Calculating Revenues) and Part 4 (Supplementary Data). A practitioner interested in the derivation of demographic or income multipliers and their variations should turn specifically to Part Four, Chapters 13 through 16 (Demographic and Gross Income Multipliers). An analyst who wants to review a fiscal impact analysis should concentrate on the Introduction and Part 3 (General Applicability) and use portions of Parts 1 and 2 only as they deal with specific procedures used in the analysis under review. A sponsor who wants to commission a fiscal impact analysis may be interested in viewing the extent of comparable work and should review Part 3, Chapter 12 (Field Experience).

This handbook has been developed through an extensive survey of the needs of local officials and planners. It is specifically addressed to municipal and school district planners, managers, and budget administrators. The manual is also useful, with slight variations, in analyzing the fiscal impact problems of county, regional, and state levels of government.

PART 1

CALCULATING COSTS: METHODS OF PROJECTING MUNICIPAL AND SCHOOL DISTRICT COSTS

The part which follows provides methods for determining the direct public costs associated with residential and/or nonresidential growth. It contains seven chapters. The first introduces the reader to the components and dynamics of costs while the six succeeding chapters detail six fiscal impact projection methods (Per Capita Multiplier—Chapter 2, Case Study — Chapter 3, Service Standard — Chapter 4, Comparable City — Chapter 5, Proportional Valuation — Chapter 6 and Employment Anticipation — Chapter 7).

Each method specifies operating and capital costs to both municipality and school district. Further, methods are presented in a standard format: Background, Application, Basic Assumptions, Procedures, Data Requirements, Sophistication of User, Advantages and Disadvantages and Interpreting Results.

The first few steps within each method walk the user through the analyses necessary to determine costs; the remaining few summarize the revenue calculation and ultimately present a cost revenue comparison. Detailed procedures for determining revenues (the same for each method) are contained in the next part. Most data resources, as well as specific references to augmenting material, are found in each method.

Part 1: Calculating Costs

Four methods detail procedures to calculate costs associated with residential growth; two methods provide means to determine costs associated with nonresidential growth. The applicability of one or another method to a specific fiscal impact situation is covered generally in the following chapter and specifically within the "Application" portion of the six succeeding chapters.

When initiating a fiscal impact analysis the user should review all sections of the method before moving to the "Procedures" portion. This will provide an overview of assumptions, advantages/disadvantages, required user sophistication and necessary data specific to each method. These all bear directly or indirectly on the method's effectuation and outcome. Further, until the user is confident with the employment of one or another method, it is very important to set up schedules or chart-form exhibits almost identical to the ones found in the text. This will lead to an orderly and predictable presentation of results and additionally offer the opportunity to compare results with those of the example at interim stages of the analysis.

Most methods presented here represent both a culling of existing field practice and necessary refinement to provide standardization within each method. The user, at his discretion, may introduce procedural variations or data alternatives which may be more amenable to or better reflect the local fiscal context.

An important point to remember throughout the analysis is that nothing replaces common sense. With a basic knowledge of the local fiscal context (i.e., "it costs $200 per person to provide municipal services or $2,000 per student to provide school services) a reasonable estimate of cost based on the magnitude of the new population may be inferred. This "sense of cost" is essential to avoid the arithmetic errors which plague many fiscal impact analyses. All fiscal impact methods presented here are capable of being carried out by the practicing planner and should pose few substantive or procedural problems to this level of user.

1

RELATING METHODS TO TASKS AND CONTEXTS OF FISCAL IMPACT ANALYSIS

Introduction

The purpose of this chapter is to direct the planning practitioner to specific fiscal impact cost calculation methods, given both the kind of development situation he is attempting to evaluate fiscally and the type of community in which the evaluation is taking place. The first portion of the chapter lists, by individual method, the more appropriate applications of a method both in terms of the problematical alternatives demanding analysis and the fiscal context of the analysis.

While there definitely appear situations where one or another method may seem more appropriate, there are also instances of fiscal impact evaluation where the use of multiple methods concurrently, or any one of several methods individually, may also serve the practitioner's needs.

It is thus the province of the fiscal impact analyst, after careful reading of the assumptions, data requirements and situational preferability associated with each of the several methods, to choose one or more of these approaches for the pending fiscal impact evaluation.

While the guides which follow link methods to various geographical settings and problematical contexts, other factors, such as available resources and sophistication of staff personnel, also weigh heavily in the choice of method.

What Methods Are Used, Where, When?

There are six fiscal impact methods: Per Capita Multiplier, Case Study, Service Standard, Comparable City, Proportional Valuation and Employment Anticipation. The axes of Exhibit 1-1 list the tasks for (top) and contexts of (side) fiscal impact analysis. Within the body of the exhibit are found methods which are conceptually more appropriate to a given task-context grouping.

Per Capita Multiplier Method

The Per Capita Multiplier Method, the most widely used of average costing techniques, is employed in situations where service infrastructure bears a close relationship to service demand such that the average costs of providing services to current users is a reasonable approximation of the costs to provide similar services to future users. It is most typically employed in contexts of mid-size, established, suburban areas or second-order cities experiencing slow to moderate growth (Exhibit 1-1, rows 3 and 4). In these situations, it is an excellent tool for analyzing development proposals, zoning changes, land use alternatives, annexations and the economic portion of the EIS requirement.

The versatility of the Per Capita Multiplier Method is a function of its assumptions. It assumes that tomorrow's costs are not unlike today's. Service underutilization in a particular municipal function may be balanced by service overutilization in another, or a certain pattern of deficient or excess service capacity exists which is identifiable as a local average and can be extended as such into the future.

The Per Capita Multiplier Method is particularly useful because it provides a fast approximation of the costs of new development based on readily-available, historical, local data. New residential single family or multi-family subdivisions and small-to-average planned residential developments, being developed in communities with a relatively established service infrastructure, represent the mode of application for this method.

Because this method is relatively inexpensive to apply it may also be used when a community posits *alternative* development scenarios for the future. A local decision to zone for single family versus townhouses or garden apartments may require three separate fiscal impact analyses. To undertake these analyses using the depth probes of the Case Study Method would incur significant extra cost for a possibly more accurate projection which may not be necessary at this early stage of development choice.

Case Study Method

The Case Study Method is ideally suited for the types of fiscal impact activity likely to be undertaken in large or second order, stable/declining cities or small, rapidly growing rural-fringe areas. These are areas with significant over-used or under-used service capacities, respectively, such that if development takes place it does so either at minimal or substantial local operational or capital expenditures (Exhibit 1-1, rows 1-2, 5-6). Thus the average of yesterday's costs per capita multiplied by the population to be added is *not* the best indication of future costs. This type of situation calls for a method sensitive to existing excess or deficient service capacity. In the large city, experiencing slow growth or decline, municipal and educational service infrastructures are well established and may contain excess service capacity. In this context the Case Study Method may accurately depict a situation of local growth which occasions little, if any, expansion of the service system. Growth takes place as a result of development, yet no additional operational

Relating Methods to Analysis

EXHIBIT 1-1
RELATING METHODS TO CONTEXTS AND TASKS OF FISCAL IMPACT ANALYSIS

ROW: Status of Community's Existing Service Capacity	Community Most Typifying Service Capacity	Development Proposals (Residential)	Development Proposals (Nonresidential)	Land Use Alternatives	Rezonings/ Variances	Annexations/ Boundary Changes	EIS's	Urban Renewal/ Community/ Redevelopment
1. Significant excess capacity [a]	Central city— declining moderately or slightly	CS	CS	CS/CC	CS/CC	CS	CS	CS
2. At capacity, [b] slight excess capacity	Second order city— stable growth or declining slightly	CS/CC	CS/EA	CS/CC	CS/CC	CS	CS/CC	CS
3. At capacity	Suburb—stable growth or slightly increasing	M/SS	PV/EA	M/SS	M/SS	M/SS	M/SS	CS
4. At capacity, slight deficient capacity [c]	Suburb—moderately increasing growth	M/SS	PV/EA	M/SS	M/SS	M/SS	M/SS	
5. Moderate deficient capacity	Exurban—moderately increasing growth	CS/CC	CS	CS/CC	CS/CC	M/SS	CS/CC	
6. Significant deficient capacity	Exurban—rapidly increasing growth	CS/CC	CS	CS	CS/CC	CS	CS	

Applicable Methods:
M = Per Capita Multiplier
CS = Case Study
SS = Service Standard
CC = Comparable City
PV = Proportional Valuation
EA = Employment Anticipation

Notes:
a. Excess Capacity — The service system is underutilized and exhibits room for service expansion without significant additional operational or capital expenditures.
b. At Capacity — The service system is operating at its most efficient level; most service categories exhibit neither over nor underutilization.
c. Deficient Capacity — The service system is overutilized; the slightest form of additional service demand will occasion significant operational or capital expenditures.

personnel are hired nor are new capital facilities provided. The size of patrol areas or beats may be increased, classroom size may grow slightly and rescue calls per hour may rise; the scale of the service system however, remains essentially unchanged. The typical task for this method, in an excess capacity context, is an evaluation of the impact of a convenience shopping center in a redevelopment area or a proposal for subsidized housing in the same type of area.

The Case Study Method is also employed at the other end of the growth-population spectrum. In small, rapidly growing areas with minimal operating services and capital facilities, the Case Study more accurately portrays the immediate and usually significant impact of proposed growth than the two average costing techniques (Per Capita Multiplier, Service Standard). For instance, a small municipality which must review a development proposal in the midst of existing overspent services and probable significant future additional demand, may opt to build a large elementary school while the development itself would occasion only the addition of several classrooms. A tipping point has been reached because of this specific development increment and a local decision is made to build a new school. This, in fact, is the real world of municipal decision making. If development had not occurred, the existing level of services would probably have been maintained. Growth occasioned the necessity for the new school. The costs of this new school are assigned to the growth increment which necessitated the move. In the previous, excess capacity case minimal costs were assigned; in this deficient capacity case substantial costs are assigned. This is the essence of the residential case study.

The Case Study Method is also invaluable for the large nonresidential or public facility development or redevelopment. A coliseum, civic center, large shopping center, hotel, office or industrial complex are the types of facilities which require depth analyses of the service capacities of existing systems. These types of facilities may place unique demands on specific services, public safety or public works for instance, such that an average projection of comparable previous growth is essentially inappropriate as a projection of future impact.

The Case Study (due to its specificity of projection, i.e., number of personnel needed by service category, required capital facilities by type and size, etc.) is further appropriate for analysis of the one-of-a-kind defense or energy facility, or plant *openings* or *closings*, particularly in large rural areas. In this case, impact is so far ranging and proposed municipal/school district servicing facilities so critical, that the "average costing" specification of impact is too general to be of significant utility. In the case of large defense or energy plant *openings,* most service systems must be significantly expanded or replaced. In many cases an existing utility system which has unused service capacity must be totally replaced even though it may have as much as 50 to 60 percent system capacity remaining. A plant *closing* may make such an indentation on a particular local elementary school as to require its withdrawal from the existing capital plant. In both of these instances the costs incurred or costs saved may be far in excess of what average costing projections would reveal.

Service Standard Method

The Service Standard Method, another average costing procedure, is typically employed when moderately growing suburbs or cities contemplate a population increment and would like a detailed estimate by service category of the manpower, equipment and capital facility requirements of such a population change. Estimates are derived, using U.S. Census of Governments' tabulations of service manpower per thousand population or pupils, for "common municipal functions" and education. The Service Standard Method frequently is used in situations where there exist only gross approximations of future service demand; for instance, total population to be added rather than detailed tallies of the number of forthcoming dwelling units and the bedroom distribution of these units. While applicable to a similar range of tasks as the Per Capita Multiplier Method (Exhibit 1-1, rows 3-4), this method is almost always used in annexation analyses, as there is usually a desire in such situations for both manpower and capital facilities estimates by service function, information which is largely unavailable from the Per Capita Multiplier Method.

The Service Standard Method may also be used as a necessary frame of reference when undertaking a Case Study. Municipal officials may, either in their zeal or conservatism, tend to over- or underestimate, the impacts of proposed growth. A projection of likely impact, based on manpower utilization levels of cities of a similar size and geographical location, (the type of detail provided by the Service Standard Method) is an excellent comparative tool to evaluate the responses given by the interviewee in the Case Study Method.

The Service Standard Method, because it presents manpower levels by population size and geographic region is further sensitive to both economies of scale and geographic differentials in the quantity of public services provided. Thus this method is most appropriate where there are significant changes in planned population, particularly in the long run, or where development is being undertaken in a geographic location noted for an absence or presence of a particular service. The fiscal implications of long-range or "horizon plans" of counties or states (end-state population projections) have been undertaken using the Service Standard Method. Similarly, school servicing cost estimates in the western portions of the United States (noted for significant education expenditures) have been frequently completed, using educational service manpower standards which are specific to this region.

Comparable City Method

The Comparable City Method, another marginal costing fiscal impact procedure, is employed in similar fiscal and geographic situations as the Case Study (Exhibit 1-1, rows 1-2, 5-6). This method, relying on expenditure ratios by population size and growth rate, is sensitive to economies and diseconomies of scale in local expenditures as well as expenditure variations which are a function of both the direction and pace of growth.

The Comparable City Method should be employed in instances where there is believed excess or deficient service system capacity and it is felt that the experience of other comparably sized and similarly growing communities would be of assistance in providing insight to this system capacity as it relates to the impact projection.* The versatility of the Comparable City Method is providing expenditure information for growth taking place in locations of population and growth extreme — very large or very small cities gaining or losing population at significant rates. Large, declining cities have expenditure traits which differ from large, stable or slow-growing cities; small, declining cities exhibit expenditure patterns dissimilar to small growing cities. These differences can be interpreted using the expenditure ratios of different size/growth rate communities found within the Comparable City Method. This is one of the few methods sensitive to these expenditure variations without specific, depth case analysis.

An example of the use of this method is the situation in which a very large development is planned for a relatively small community — a new town in a rural, undeveloped geographic area.

---

*As the Case Study Method, the Comparable City Method may also be used in situations of minimal excess or deficient service capacity; results in these instances will be similar to what would be obtained by applying the Per Capita Multiplier or Service Standard Methods. The application of these average costing methods to the type of situation where marginal costing methods could be used, ignores the strengths of interpretation of the marginal approaches.

The community projects future population growth and arrives at both a new future population base and annual growth rate enroute to this new population level. Using this information to obtain the correct set of expenditure ratios, new per capita and per pupil expenditures are derived which, when applied to the future population estimate, yield future expenditure levels, a portion of which are assignable to the new development.

The Proportional Valuation Method

The Proportional Valuation Method is used only in evaluations of the fiscal impact of nonresidential (commercial or industrial) facilities (Exhibit 1-1, rows 3-4). Other, more accurate, average costing methods are available to evaluate the impact of residential uses. The proportional technique assumes that a share of costs are assigned to a development in proportion to that development's share of local property value. In terms of context, it is employed in many of the same areas and situations as the Per Capita Multiplier and Service Standard methods — locations of minimal excess or deficient service capacity such that a share of today's costs is a reasonable approximation of the costs to be incurred in the future.

The Proportional Valuation Method is least appropriate for a situation where a large nonresidential development is contemplated for a rural area with an unsophisticated service system. The service demands of this scale of facility, relative to what is in-place, may be so great that a simple proportion of existing costs as an index of future costs bears no relationship to the expenditures which must be undertaken locally to provide services to this new facility. This type of situation is uniquely the province of the Case Study Method.

The obvious usefulness of the Proportional Valuation Method is that it provides an extremely fast and inexpensive gauge of the fiscal impact of nonresidential facilities. The technique is further sensitive to the economies of scale of larger versus smaller nonresidential facilities locating in a similar size community. The assignment of costs takes place using refinement coefficients. These coefficients are sensitive to the nonlinearity of impact as the scale of facility increases, and service requirements tended to be internalized and handled privately rather than publicly (security, garbage collection, etc.). The method may be used for either commercial or industrial activities — with differences in impact for similarly valued facilities shown at the specific municipal service level.

The Employment Anticipation Method

The Employment Anticipation Method relies on regression coefficients to specify expenditure impact to a particular service category based on a nonresidential facility's introduction of additional employees to a geographic service area.

In similar fashion to the Proportional Valuation Method, the use of this technique enables a quick and inexpensive estimate of nonresidential development impact. Since it views municipal costs in direct relationship to the number of new local employees generated, the method is more appropriately applied to those nonresidential development instances that are typified by an unusually large or small number of employees per unit of nonresidential space (Exhibit 1-1, rows 2-5).

This method provides differing impacts according to the size of city involved. It is thus sensitive to the incremental level of expenditure relative to the scale of the community in which the new nonresidential use is being developed.

Method Choice/Employment
And The Interpretation of Results

During the course of this study the various methods to specify cost which are detailed in subsequent chapters were taken to the field and tested in multiple locations to answer: What were the differences in projected cost-revenue impacts when (1) alternative methods were employed at the same site, (2) the same method was applied at alternative sites?

Viewing results in pursuit of the first question, the variations occurred, as anticipated, between classes of methods, i.e., differences between average versus marginal cost projections of future public expenditures with the development. Thus, marginal costing, Case Study and Comparable City Methods usually provided a somewhat different impact estimate than was the case for the average costing, Per Capita Multiplier and Service Standard Methods, applied in a similar development situation and fiscal context. The difference in result was always predictable, however, given detailed information about the community for which impact was being projected and allowing this information to affect the selection of the impact method. In other words, the differences noted were not peculiar to a method's operation but rather due to an anticipated, less than appropriate pairing of class of method and context. For instance, for a potential annexation contemplated by the City of Richmond, Virginia, the Comparable City Method proved to be a more appropriate method to evaluate fiscal impact than was the Service Standard Method. In this case, the Service Standard Method appeared to overstate fiscal impact. Richmond, as other, large, declining* central cities, had significant unused capacity in the school system and in its municipal public safety and public works departments. Taking into account this excess capacity, using the economies of scale inherent in the future-to-current service multipliers of the Comparable City Method for 100,000–500,000 population size, declining cities, produced a smaller specification of potential impact than was observed via the Service Standard Method using a different set of employment standards for southern cities of 200,000–300,000 population size. In this case, the marginal economies of declining cities, interpreted by the Comparable City Method, better represented the reality of local impact.

On the other hand, when these classes of methods (average costing — Per Capita Multiplier, Service Standard; marginal costing — Case Study Comparable City) were applied to East Windsor, New Jersey, a mid-size municipality of moderate growth, all four of the methods produced essentially similar results with considerable savings of time evidenced in the employment of both average costing techniques versus the marginal costing, Case Study Method.**

Applying the same method at alternative sites also yielded predictable results. Differences observed in the cost-revenue balance for a similar development interpreted with the same method at different geographical locations were almost entirely related to staffing levels/wage scales and revenue structure at a particular site rather than differences brought about by the internal operations of the method. Differing results of the Service Standard or Per Capita Multiplier Methods applied to Barrington, Illinois, versus Fresno, California, for instance, had to do with more reliance on the property tax/other own source revenues or state/federal inter-governmental transfers at one or the other location as well as differences in manpower levels or accompanying wage scales/benefit packages peculiar to location. Again, this is in opposition to significant

---

*Prior to annexation.

**Both average and marginal costing techniques can be applied with essentially similar results in situations which clearly call for average costing techniques. In most instances, however, it is more time consuming to employ the marginal technique and accuracy is not significantly improved.

differences observed as a result of an inappropriate pairing of a method and a specific geographical context. Thus an apartment development might show a reduced surplus in cost-revenue impact in Fresno, California, versus Barrington, Illinois. Both service levels per 1,000 population and wage rates are higher in the California community (more costs) and incoming revenues are reduced (less revenues) as a function of greater state assistance in school support. In addition, these revenues change less on development impact (via the operations of transfer formulas) than would be the case for a similar share of locally generated revenues.

In sum, if differences were found either in the employment of different methods at the same site or the same methods at different sites, these differences were predictable in the first case, given the selection of a particular method and its associated strengths of interpretation, or in the second, given the quality of service peculiar to a particular region and the associated revenue system of that region.

The Use of Multiple Methods in Pursuit of A Single Fiscal Impact Solution

There are situations when there is less than complete knowledge concerning the context of the fiscal impact evaluation. Excess and deficient service capacity may either be confused or lack interpretation due to other, uncharted, simultaneous development pressures impacting on the city or an absence of data which adequately describe current service conditions. In these cases, it may be appropriate, if not obligatory, to project alternative fiscal impacts based on the differing assumptions of each class of method, or method variation. It is entirely conceivable, for instance, for a fiscal impact analysis of a central city annexing an adjacent, moderately developed, unincorporated area that the Case Study, Comparable City and Service Standard Methods be employed and the differing impact specified by each of these methods be interpreted for the client before a conclusion on most appropriate impact is reached.

The mix and match of methods may also take place within particular service categories. Public safety services for instance, in which police manpower is allocated fairly consistently across all but the largest population categories at the rate of two per thousand population, lends itself very nicely to average costing, Per Capita or Service Standard interpretation. Library service, in which a relatively significant level of unfulfilled demand is necessary to support even the smallest of self-contained facilities, is an area of municipal service where depth analyses or techniques sensitive to excess or deficient service capacity are more appropriate. Public works capital improvements also lend themselves to marginal analysis. It makes little sense to apply an average costing approach to a development situation when there are no utilities at the site. In this case, the depth analysis of the Case Study, which would reveal the actual marginal cost of developing such utilities, may be a much more appropriate index of assignable cost for this service subsector.

Finally, mix and match is already inherent to one method — the Per Capita Multiplier — which in developing per capita costs assigned to the residential sector initially factors off a portion of municipal costs to nonresidential uses.

Field practice already reflects the use of multiple methods in fiscal impact solutions. According to a survey of practitioners, the second most popular "method," after the Per Capita Multiplier, is the use of multiple methods in the fiscal impact evaluation. Most typically, as noted previously, the specific advantages of the Per Capita Multiplier and the Case Study are linked to different categories of municipal service.

EXHIBIT 1-2
GEOGRAPHICAL AND PROBLEMATICAL CONTEXTS OF FISCAL IMPACT COST CALCULATION DEMONSTRATIONS

HYPOTHETICAL PROBLEM DEMONSTRATED	GEOGRAPHICAL SETTING	METHOD USED	SPECIFICS OF DEVELOPMENT OR DEVELOPMENT ALTERNATIVE

I. Large, single, mixed-use development (residential and nonresidential)	New Jersey / Illinois	Per Capita Multiplier / Case Study	Residential — 3000 unit PUD
			  Townhouses (1500)
			    1 Bedroom 250
			    2 Bedrooms 1000
			    3 Bedrooms 250
			  Garden Apartments (1000)
			    1 Bedroom 700
			    2 Bedrooms 300
			  Single Family House (500)
			    3 Bedrooms 250
			    4 Bedrooms 250
			Nonresidential — 100,000 Ft^2 Community Shopping Center

II. Alternative zoning classifications for a 1,000 acre land tract (residential)	Georgia / California	Service Standard / Comparable City	Alternative #1 — 2000 units of single-family housing at 2 units per acre
			Residential
			Alternative #2 — 5000 units of mixed residential development at 5 units per acre
			Residential 30% single family (1500)
			    50% townhouses (2500)
			    20% condominiums (1000)
			Alternative #3 — 7000 garden apartments at 10 units per acre
			Residential

III. Large, single, nonresidential development (commercial and industrial)	Texas	Proportional Valuation / Employment Anticipation	Nonresidential — 100,000 Ft^2 Commercial Development Nonresidential — 100,000 Ft^2 Industrial Development

Source: Rutgers University, Center for Urban Policy Research, Spring 1978.

The Settings For The Demonstrated Cost Calculations

In the chapters which follow the methods to calculate projected municipal and school district expenditures are purposely demonstrated in alternative *geographical* settings. Geographic variation is sought to demonstrate both expenditure variation due to manpower and wage variation, and revenue resource differentials which become evident as a function of location. Methods of cost calculation are further demonstrated in different *problematical* settings — the three classic land development situations facing the fiscal impact practitioner: (1) a large, single, mixed-use development including both residential and nonresidential land uses, (2) multiple residential zoning alternatives for a land tract, and (3) a moderate-size, free-standing, nonresidential facility. In the first case, the practitioner is provided with a reasonable amount of detail concerning the proposed development, i.e., the number of housing units of various kinds, the proportion of residential to nonresidential uses and the sales price/rental levels of inclusive dwelling units and commercial/industrial properties. In the second and third cases, again reflecting "real world," the practitioner is given only very general information about forthcoming development — the number and type of residential units or the proposed size of the nonresidential units. Fiscal impact estimates must be made for alternative residential zoning classifications for a tract of land usually with only gross estimations of the future population available, and for free-standing, nonresidential facilities with only gross estimates of the intended square footage of the building or the future number of employees. The geographical settings reflect the expenditure emphases and revenue resources characteristic of the Northeast, North Central, Southern and Western regions of the United States. They are represented respectively by the States of New Jersey, Illinois, Georgia, Texas and California. The large single, mixed-use development hypothetical is posited for New Jersey and Illinois, whereas the alternative residential development scenario is examined in California and Georgia settings. Finally, the free-standing, nonresidential development is viewed in a Texas community.

Exhibit 1–2 lists the locations, types of fiscal impact problem considered, methods employed to illustrate the impact calculation, and the specifics of the development involved.

2

PER CAPITA MULTIPLIER FISCAL IMPACT METHOD

Background

The Per Capita Multiplier Method is the classic average costing approach for projecting the impact of population change on local municipal and school district costs and revenues.[1] Due to its simplicity and ease of operation, the method has been applied to almost every type of fiscal impact situation in which an estimate of the impact of residential growth is desired.

The Per Capita Multiplier Method of estimating municipal costs is largely a product of the 1950s. Per capita multipliers had their origins in the first large-scale statistical manipulations of data to predict municipal expenditures.[2] They were subsequently employed in classic studies to determine whether certain types of housing fiscally "pay their own way."[3] These studies introduced per pupil multipliers to estimate the costs of education. Thus a method for analyzing fiscal impact came to include both per capita and per pupil multipliers. It was not until the late 1960s and early 1970s, however (when statistical analyses linked municipal and school district costs and dwelling unit size/configuration), that the technique emerged in the form we know it today.[4] During this period extensive field surveys were undertaken to develop demographic profiles of residents and school children associated with different housing types. Linking this demographic information with average municipal operating costs per person and school district operating costs per pupil provided a simple, straightforward means of assigning local costs to a proposed population change. Embraced as an indispensable planning tool by the private planning consultant, the technique became established as the leading device for estimating local fiscal impact.

The availability of more and more refined data and its rise in popularity, not unsurprisingly insured the Per Capita Multiplier Method as a basic element of the bulk of fiscal impact projection models of the early 1970s.[5] It is currently the foundation of the two most widely distributed computerized fiscal impact models (MUNIES and PROMUS) and appears in noncomputerized form, either alone or linked with other techniques (principally the Case Study Method) in approximately *two-thirds* of the fiscal impact analyses surveyed in this handbook. (See Appendix 2.)

The Per Capita Multiplier Method relies on detailed demographic information by housing type (total household size and number of schoolage children) and the average cost, per person and per pupil, of municipal and school district operating expenses (including the amortization of capital expenditures) to project an annual (operating/capital) cost assignable to a particular population change. Using the Proportional Valuation Method (see Chapter 6), the technique begins by sifting off the local costs assigned to nonresidential uses. Then it expresses all local municipal costs per person and school district costs per pupil. These per capita and per pupil costs, multiplied by an estimate of the population shift resulting from growth (partitioned by pupils and adults) are the incremental costs assigned to the specific growth generator.

To illustrate, assume that a midwestern municipality is attempting to analyze the local fiscal impact of 100 garden apartments (80 percent - one bedroom; 20 percent - two bedroom). Units in the proposed development will rent for an average of $250 and $300 monthly and are estimated to be valued at $15,000 and $21,000 per unit, respectively. Demographic profiles of garden apartments for the area indicate that an average 1.686 residents and 0.036 school-age children may be expected to reside in one bedroom units and 2.685 residents and 0.232 school-age children in two bedroom units. Information obtained from the city manager and superintendent of schools tabulates current total municipal operating costs per person at $250 annually and total school district costs per pupil at $1,500 annually. The development is assigned $33,720 (80 units × 1.686 persons per unit × $250 per person) in municipal costs and $4,320 (80 units × 0.036 children per unit × $1,500 per child)* in school district costs for the local fiscal impact of one-bedroom units, and $13,425 in municipal costs (20 × 2.685 × $250), and $6,960 in school district costs (20 × 0.232 × $1,500)* for two-bedroom units. The total cost to the municipality and school district for operations and capital additions for the 100 unit garden apartment development is thus estimated at approximately $58,000 annually ($33,720 + $4,320 + $13,425 + $6,960).

Revenues, determined by procedures detailed in Part 2, include municipal and school district own source funds and intergovernmental transfers. They total approximately $110,000 annually. The development, in terms of its cost-revenue posture, thus produces almost twice as much total annual revenue as it occasions in total annual costs.

Over the last several years the Per Capita Multiplier technique has received considerable attention from fiscal impact practitioners. Due to its versatility and favorable local acceptance, practitioners have sought continued refinement of the building blocks of the technique — the demographic multipliers. Questions about the regional and temporal variations of multipliers are addressed in Chapter 13 of this handbook. Briefly, multipliers for standard configurations of common housing types have been found not to vary across *regions,* reflecting similar housing demand/supply relationships; they also appear to remain relatively stable over *time.* Detailed summaries of demographic multipliers for standard housing types by region of the United States, and a discussion of their derivation, are included in this chapter.

Application

The Per Capita Multiplier Method, in similar fashion to the Service Standard Method, is most applicable in communities where the demand for local services is directly reflected in the scale and scope of current local services; that is those situations in which the local instance of excess or deficient service capacity is minimal. Communities of significant excess service capacity cannot be expected to maintain their excess in the face of new demand. On the other hand, communities with existing service deficiencies also probably will find it necessary to correct the deficiencies when

---

*It will be shown later in this method that this cost must be reduced to reflect solely the *public* school burden.

plans for increased service population are underway. In the former case municipalities may not be required to expand services and a projection of service increase based on current averages would overstate local reaction. In the latter case they may significantly expand some local services to accommodate the increase, and a projection based on previous averages might severely understate local reaction. The type of communities described above are typically suburban metropolitan area municipalities or free standing, nonmetropolitan cities of 10,000 to 50,000 people and a 2 to 3 percent annual growth rate. (See Chapter 1.)

The Per Capita Multiplier Method provides a reasonably accurate analysis without a significant expenditure of time or an intimate knowledge of the site-specific service system. The technique operates most easily, however, with detailed information on the size and type of proposed residential units. The method is ideally suited to evaluating the fiscal impact of residential development proposals, land use alternatives within a proposed growth strategy, annexation or rezoning decisions, and fiscal segments of suburban environmental impact statements. It has been used most frequently in the past for development proposals; its future role will lean heavily towards evaluating the fiscal effects of alternative land uses.

The Per Capita Multiplier Method is not suited to analyze the fiscal effects of redevelopment or exclusively nonresidential development. Redevelopment frequently occurs in communities with an overabundance of system capacity so that future service demand is not an accurate reflection of past "average" expenditures. Nonresidential development typically does not directly foster the local growth of either residents or students. It is thus not suited to a fiscal impact method which expresses local service costs on a per capita or per pupil base. (Nonresidential facilities should be examined via the Proportional Valuation or Employment Anticipation strategies.)

The use of the Per Capita Multiplier Method also reflects the type of fiscal impact practitioner. Private planning consultants have traditionally favored this strategy because the only data the analyst must secure from the community being investigated are current total municipal and school district expenditures and per capita and per pupil local demographic multipliers, if they are available. Extensive knowledge of the details of municipal or school district operations is not required. The local public staff planner, on the other hand, is usually familiar with or has direct access to information regarding planned increases or decreases in municipal services. He thus (given sufficient time and resources) would probably use a method that would more accurately reflect local conditions, such as the Case Study Method.

Basic Assumptions

A basic assumption of the Per Capita Multiplier Method is that over the long run, *current* average operating costs per capita and per student are the best estimates of *future* operating costs occasioned by growth. A second assumption is that current *local* service levels are the most accurate indicators of future service levels and that they will continue on the same scale in the future. A further premise is that the current composition of the population occasioning costs and the population contributing to future costs are sufficiently similar that the above scenario will remain unaltered.

A fourth assumption is that the number of residents and students introduced locally varies primarily with the size of the dwelling unit (i.e., number of bedrooms) and secondarily with the type of dwelling unit. Thus the most accurate estimate of future service population is obtained from information on expected residences presented by number of bedrooms or rooms and by type or configuration.

A fifth and final premise is that the current distribution of expenditures among the various sectors of municipal service will remain constant in the short run and will serve as the primary indicator of the way in which additional expenditures will be subsequently allocated.

To the extent that existing knowledge about the community provokes evidence that one or more of the foregoing premises lacks validity, or is subject to question, the basis for using the Per Capita Multiplier technique thereby is weakened.

Procedures

Exhibit 2-1 displays the sequence of steps to be followed when using the Per Capita Multiplier Method. Each will be described in one of the following sections.

Step 1 *Obtain Information on Budgets, Current Population and Assessments.*

Contact key local administrators, i.e., the city manager and the superintendent of schools, to obtain copies of the most current published annual municipal and school district operating budgets. The general information in the published official budgets, rather than more detailed data of the unpublished working budget, will suffice because the only information which will be extracted from these documents is total annual operating expenses.

The latest population estimates for the municipal jurisdiction and school district must also be obtained. Municipal population estimates are usually available from the local planning office;

EXHIBIT 2-1

PER CAPITA MULTIPLIER FISCAL IMPACT METHOD: SUMMARY OF PROCEDURES

Step Number	Analysis/Actions
1	Contact the office of the city manager and superintendent of schools to obtain local municipal and school district budgets and the latest estimates of municipal/school district populations.
2	Categorize local expenditures into five municipal service categories plus the school district function.
3	Obtain total annual municipal expenditures by summing the annual costs, including debt service for capital facilities, for each of the five service categories. Obtain total annual school district expenditures.
4	Assign a share of total annual municipal costs to existing local nonresidential facilities based on the proportion of their value to total local real property valuation. Subtract this share from the total annual municipal costs.
5	Calculate the *net* (residentially induced) annual costs of the five municipal functions on a per capita basis and the annual costs of education on a per pupil basis.
6	Calculate anticipated total resident and school populations by housing type.
7	Calculate residentially induced total annual municipal and school district expenditure increases by multiplying per capita/per pupil municipal and school district expenditures by the projected number of residents/pupils.
8	Calculate municipal costs for any nonresidential uses if they are an inclusive element of the growth increment; assign a share of local costs to the nonresidential facility based on the facility's share of total local nonresidential property valuation.
9	Determine total annual public costs and refine the projection by allocating total costs by service category.
10	Project total annual public revenues.
11	Calculate the cost-revenue surplus or deficit by comparing total costs incurred and total revenues generated.

Per Capita Multiplier

they may be either a straight-line projection or a summation of building permits or certificates of occupancy from the latest census. School district population estimates are obtained from the school district's most recent year-end financial report; it will contain the total average daily attendance (ADA) for all local primary and secondary schools. The example used to illustrate the Per Capita Multiplier Method (a township in New Jersey) uses 16,000 as the existing municipal population and 2,400 as the existing school district population. (For a full description, see Chapter 1.)

Other items of information that should be obtained at this juncture are: (1) total local equalized real property value — the aggregate local real property tax base, including all residential, commercial, industrial, vacant properties, etc.; (2) the local equalized nonresidential real property value — the market value of only commercial and industrial tax paying parcels; (3) total number of taxable land parcels — the sum of all real property taxable parcels, including residential, industrial, commercial, vacant, etc.; (4) total residential land parcels — the sum of solely commercial and industrial properties; and (5) where applicable, the equalized real property value of the nonresidential facility (in this case, the local shopping center) in the residential development being examined. These data are needed to calculate the share of municipal expenditures assignable to inclusive nonresidential uses.

For a discussion of the sources of the values and parcel information see Chapter 6. A summary of this and other required information that should be obtained in this step takes the following form:

EXHIBIT 2-2
GENERAL PARAMETERS OF A NEW JERSEY TOWNSHIP, 1976

1.	Total local assessed real property value	$232,264,500
2.	Total local real property value for nonresidential properties	$ 83,120,250
3.	Local equalization ratio	.86
4.	Total local equalized real property value (1 ÷ 3)	$270,075,000
5.	Total local equalized nonresidential real property value (2 ÷ 3)	$ 96,651,453
6.	Total number of taxable land parcels	4,524
7.	Total number of nonresidential land parcels	296
8.	Average equalized real property value per parcel (4 ÷ 6)	$ 59,698
9.	Average equalized nonresidential real property value per parcel (5 ÷ 7)	$ 326,525
10.	Market value of nonresidential facility (100,000 square foot shopping center) (see page 36)	$ 2,646,000

Any local information (surveys, census tallies, etc.) containing estimates of total household size and/or school-age children by housing type should also be sought. Frequently, local demographic characteristics have been surveyed for other studies, and the analyst must be aware of the information's availability.

Step 2 Categorize Local Expenditures into Five Municipal Service Categories Plus the School District Function.

Categorizing local expenditures ensures that costs are assigned by manageable and recognizable subcategories of municipal and school district service. This is a much more useful approach than either simply indicating a single, aggregate municipal expenditure or at the other extreme subdividing into a myriad of lower level subcategories of municipal service. The categorizing of costs is accomplished in the following manner. Using the local budgets obtained in the previous step, group municipal public services into the broad service functions of *general government, public safety, public works, health and welfare, and recreation and culture.* Use Exhibit 4-7 of the Service Standard Method as a guide to classify four of the municipal services and the school district function. Health and welfare* should include at least the following subcategories: health services except environmental; welfare-public assistance; animal, insect, and rodent control; other welfare services, etc.

While municipal and school district statutory expenditures (pensions, FICA, employee fringe benefits, etc.) are included within the operating statement of each functional service category, debt service typically is not. The aggregated debt service figures for the municipality and the school district must be used.

Step 3 Obtain Total Annual Municipal (by service category) and School District Expenses (including operating and debt service costs).

This total is determined by summing the salaries and wages, other expenses, and statutory expenditures for each governmental subfunction (i.e., highways, sewage, sanitation, etc.) to arrive at a total annual operating expenditure figure for each of the five categories of municipal services (general government, public safety, public works, etc.) and the school district function. Exhibit 2-3 shows these tallies by municipal and school district services.

EXHIBIT 2-3
MUNICIPAL AND SCHOOL DISTRICT EXPENDITURES BY SERVICE CATEGORY,
_____ TOWNSHIP NEW JERSEY, 1976

	Salaries & Wages/ Other Expenses	Percent of Total
MUNICIPAL		
Operating (including statutory)		
General Government	$ 355,000	11.0
Public Safety	1,136,744	35.0
Public Works	725,904	22.0
Health and Welfare	81,516	2.0
Recreation and Culture	223,819	7.0
Debt Service	743,188	23.0
TOTAL	$3,266,171	100.0
SCHOOL DISTRICT		
Operating (including statutory)	3,996,000	90.0
Debt Service	444,000	10.0
TOTAL	$4,440,000	100.0

---

*The Census of Governments includes health and welfare as a "variable" rather than a "common" municipal function. Since the census provides only manpower estimates for "common" municipal functions, it is not included as a local service in the Service Standard Method. Health and welfare are included here, however, since a considerable proportion of municipalities and townships, especially larger ones, offer health-related services as part of their local public services.

Per Capita Multiplier

The dollar totals shown in Exhibit 2-3 are also expressed as percentages of total municipal or school district costs. These percentages will be used in step 7 to assign the incremental costs resulting from growth to the respective municipal service categories and to operating versus capital functions (expressed as debt service) for both municipal and school district services.

Step 4 Assign a Share of Annual Municipal Expenditures to Existing Nonresidential Uses.

The existing local residentially induced per capita cost must be used as a base to assign a true portion of expenditures to an incoming residential facility. To employ the total per capita expenditure would overstate expected costs since this total is generated by local residential as well as nonresidential uses. A Proportional Valuation technique is utilized to derive the residential per capita cost (for a full discussion see Chapter 6). This strategy segregates and assigns a share of the total municipal service costs to existing nonresidential uses; the remaining expenditures are then divided by the existing local population to yield the true residentially generated per capita outlay. Procedurally, the Proportional Valuation technique assigns costs based on the relationship of incoming to existing real property values. This simple relationship is modified by using refinement coefficients whose magnitude depends on the relationship of the mean value of nonresidential parcels to the mean value of all parcels (for a step by step explanation see Chapter 6).

The first step in isolating the nonresidentially induced municipal expenditure is to determine the nonresidential share of total local real property value. Using the information obtained in step 1, the analyst divides equalized nonresidential real property value by total local taxable equalized real property value.

$$\frac{\$ 96,651,453}{\$270,075,000} = 0.36$$

In this case, nonresidential uses (commercial and industrial) comprise 36 percent of the value of all locally taxable real property. Using the number of nonresidential land parcels and the total number of locally taxable land parcels (both obtained in step 1), the analyst can then determine that the average value of a local nonresidential property exceeds the average value of all local property (residential and nonresidential) by a factor of 5.47.

$$\frac{\text{Nonresidential Real Property Value}}{\text{Nonresidential Land Parcels}} \quad \frac{\$ 96,651,453}{296} = \$326,525 \text{ per parcel}$$

$$\frac{\text{Total Local Real Property Value}}{\text{Total Local Land Parcels}} \quad \frac{\$270,075,000}{4,524} = \$ 59,698 \text{ per parcel}$$

$$\text{Ratio of nonresidential to average parcel value} \quad \frac{\$326,525}{\$ 59,698} = 5.47$$

Note that average nonresidential value per parcel is significantly higher than the average value of all properties. In this case the straight Proportional Valuation Method would overstate costs assigned to nonresidential uses. (See the Proportional Valuation Method.) Consequently, the analyst employs Exhibit 6–3 of that method to obtain a coefficient to refine the assignable costs. When the average value of local nonresidential property exceeds the average value of all local property by a magnitude of 5.5, the coefficient is 1.02. Thus local nonresidential uses would be assigned (.36 × 1.02) of total local municipal service costs or 0.3672 of total outlays (0.367 × 1.02). As total annual municipal service costs were found to be $3,266,171 (Exhibit 2–3), the share of costs assigned to the nonresidential sector is $1,199,338.

Total Existing Municipal Expenditures Attributable to Nonresidential Uses		Total Municipal Expenditures	×	Simple Proportion of Nonresidential to Total Local Real Property Value	×	Refinement Coefficient
	=	$3,266,171	×	(0.36	×	1.02)
$1,199,338	=	$3,266,171	×	.3672		

Step 5 Calculate Net Annual Per Capita and Per Pupil Expenditures.

The analyst at this step divides the net annual total residential expenditures for municipal services by the number of people currently residing in the jurisdiction and the annual total school district outlays by the number of children attending local public schools. This calculation yields the current per capita and per pupil costs for existing residential uses and the future costs to be assigned to new residental uses.

Net annual municipal total expenditures are the share of municipal operating expenditures which have not been assigned to nonresidential uses. In step 4, $1,199,338 of the $3,266,171 annual municipal total costs was assigned to existing nonresidential uses. The remaining portion, $2,066,833, is assigned to the residential sector. This figure, divided by the latest local population estimate (16,000), represents current municipal per capita costs ($129) borne by the residential sector.

Current school district costs per pupil are determined by dividing total annual school district costs, (including debt service) determined in step 3, by the latest school district population estimate, obtained in step 1. In this case, the per student cost is $4,440,000 ÷ 2,400 or $1,850.

Annual per Capita Costs for Municipal Services to Residential Properties	Annual per Pupil Costs for School District Services
$129	$1,850

Step 6 Calculate Anticipated Total Resident and School Populations by Housing Type.

Total resident and school populations by housing type are determined by multiplying the expected number of housing units by the appropriate demographic multiplier for the specific size (number of bedrooms or rooms) and type of dwelling (single family homes, townhouse, garden apartment, etc.) being examined.

Demographic multipliers by housing type and for various regions are shown in Exhibit 2-4. They have been derived using the 1970 U.S. Census Public Use Sample. Multipliers for *standard configurations of common housing types,* do not vary appreciably by region. Multipliers for specialized housing types do vary by region of the country, primarily because the people who occupy these units, either by choice or circumstance, exhibit different demographic characteristics. For example, due to the lack of an adequate supply of townhouses in the Northeast, or because Northeasterners, according to market preference, do not demand townhouses in the same proportion as they do in the Southeast, those who by the standards of other regions would normally occupy this type of unit in the Northeast, given the equivalent supply as in other regions, occupy another housing type, i.e., possibly a single-family home. Variation of occupant demographic profiles will affect the multipliers of the housing they do not occupy as well as the housing they do occupy.

Multipliers do not appear to vary significantly over time. Multipliers for housing built from 1950 to 1960 tabulated in 1960 and again in 1970 are essentially similar. Also, multipliers for housing built from 1950 to 1960 tabulated in 1960 are similar to multipliers of comparable housing built from 1960 to 1970 and tabulated in 1970. (For a full discussion of these issues see Chapter 13.)

The multipliers are simple to use. Total resident population is projected by multiplying the anticipated number of incoming housing units by the appropriate household multiplier for the size and type of residence in a particular region of the country. Total school population is predicted similarly with one additional step. First, the expected number of residential units is multiplied by the appropriate school-age children multiplier for the size and type of unit being examined. This calculation yields the total expected school-age population. Since some of the total school-age population will not attend public educational institutions but rather will go to parochial or other private schools, the analyst must factor off from the total school-age children projection, the expected percentage of non-public school children, as follows: public school-age children = total school-age children × percentage of local children attending public school. The private school attendance share may be roughly estimated by interviewing local public school officials, who monitor public versus private school attendance ratios for their own planning purposes. The figure could also be obtained by comparing the number of census defined school-age children to school district enrollees for a comparable year.

Exhibit 2-5 shows how to calculate the fiscal impact of a proposed development, in this case a 3,000 unit planned unit development. Column 2 shows the multipliers which pertain to single family homes, townhouses, and garden apartments in the Middle Atlantic region. Column 3 lists the expected residents and students for each housing type; these numbers are the product of columns 1 and 2. Total expected residents for the 3,000 unit PUD is 8,154; total expected school-age children is 1,456. Since 15 percent of the local school-age children attend private schools, expected public school children is 1,238 (1,456 × 0.85).

Step 7 *Calculate Residentially Induced Total Annual Municipal and School District Expenses.*

Residentially induced total annual municipal and school district expenditures are obtained for municipal services by multiplying the total projected resident population (step 6) by the average municipal costs per capita (step 5). For school district operations, they are derived by multiplying the total estimated public school-age children (step 6) by the existing average outlay per pupil. Exhibit 5, columns 3 and 4 show the population and cost data that are multiplied, while column 5 lists the product of this multiplication (residentially-induced costs) for both the municipality and school district by housing type. The impact of the residential portion of the 3,000 unit PUD is $1,051,866 in annual municipal expenditures and $2,290,300 in school district outlays.

EXHIBIT 2-4A

REGIONAL AND NATIONAL DEMOGRAPHIC MULTIPLIERS FOR COMMON CONFIGURATIONS OF STANDARD HOUSING TYPES[1]
TOTAL HOUSEHOLD SIZE BY HOUSING TYPE AND SIZE
(U.S. CENSUS PUBLIC USE SAMPLE – 1970)[3]

	SINGLE FAMILY				GARDEN APARTMENTS				HOUSING TYPES — HIGH RISE				TOWN HOUSES				MOBILE HOMES			
	Two Bedroom	Three Bedroom	Four Bedroom	Blended[5]	One Bedroom	Two Bedroom	Blended[5]	Studio	One Bedroom	Two Bedroom	Three Bedroom	Blended[5]	One Bedroom	Two Bedroom	Three Bedroom	Blended[5]	One Bedroom	Two Bedroom	Three Bedroom	Blended[5]
REGION																				
NORTHEAST[4]																				
New England	2.485	3.940	4.965	3.931	1.500	2.430	2.114	1.071	1.470	2.270	1.700	—	2.200	—[2]	—	2.390	3.588	2.595
Middle Atlantic	2.536	3.776	4.655	3.831	1.722	2.525	2.190	1.077	1.436	2.523	1.790	1.885	2.630	4.110	3.933	1.556	2.441	3.928	2.700
NORTH CENTRAL																				
East North Central	2.595	3.892	4.909	3.911	1.719	2.576	2.285	1.070	1.432	2.570	2.357	1.364	2.727	4.129	3.588	1.647	2.450	3.835	2.620
West North Central	2.517	3.714	4.840	3.697	1.584	2.479	2.195	—	1.386	—	1.515	—	2.833	3.500	3.015	1.757	2.402	3.877	2.654
SOUTH																				
South Atlantic	2.960	3.819	4.485	3.775	1.686	2.685	2.632	—	1.208	—	1.417	—	2.778	—	—	1.955	2.560	3.680	2.807
East South Central	2.823	3.683	4.550	3.608	1.576	2.622	2.418	—	1.367	2.385	1.619	—	2.600	4.000	2.844	2.065	2.697	3.793	2.910
West South Central	2.995	3.758	4.680	3.754	1.690	2.652	2.246	—	1.282	1.867	1.483	1.783	2.720	3.735	2.741	2.070	2.592	4.089	2.951
WEST																				
Mountain	2.865	3.716	4.486	3.983	1.667	2.570	2.216	1.050	1.333	2.000	1.443	—	2.154	—	2.846	1.739	2.551	4.013	2.960
Pacific	2.745	3.687	4.561	3.826	1.596	2.530	2.149	1.159	1.338	2.220	1.585	1.768	2.735	4.033	2.965	1.746	2.133	3.807	2.113
NATIONAL (All Area Average)	2.673	3.752	4.665		1.653	2.560		1.112	1.435	2.270		1.859	2.731	4.073		1.754	2.431	3.865	

Notes: [1] Units built from 1960–1970.
[2] Less than 1,000 units in this category (insufficient sample size).
[3] See Chapter 13 for definitions and instructions on how to use these tables.
[4] See Chapter 13 for inclusive states.
[5] All unit average.

Source: U.S. Census Public Use Sample, 1970.

EXHIBIT 2-4B

REGIONAL AND NATIONAL DEMOGRAPHIC MULTIPLIERS FOR COMMON CONFIGURATIONS OF STANDARD HOUSING TYPES[1]
SCHOOL-AGE CHILDREN BY HOUSING TYPE AND SIZE
(U.S. CENSUS PUBLIC USE SAMPLE – 1970)[3]

	SINGLE FAMILY				GARDEN APARTMENTS				HOUSING TYPES HIGH RISE				TOWN HOUSES				MOBILE HOMES			
	Two Bedroom	Three Bedroom	Four Bedroom	Blended[5]	One Bedroom	Two Bedroom	Blended[5]	Studio	One Bedroom	Two Bedroom	Blended[5]	One Bedroom	Two Bedroom	Three Bedroom	Blended[5]	One Bedroom	Two Bedroom	Three Bedroom	Blended[5]
REGION																			
NORTHEAST[4]																			
New England	0.246	1.130	2.068	1.212	0.038	0.150	0.174	0.000	0.015	0.081	0.033	—	0.000	—[2]	0.640	—	0.268	0.324	0.396
Middle Atlantic	0.288	1.111	1.911	1.211	0.011	0.200	0.156	0.000	0.015	0.318	0.125	0.115	0.304	1.311	1.187	0.048	0.177	1.022	0.375
NORTH CENTRAL																			
East North Central	0.355	1.173	2.102	1.249	0.036	0.232	0.219	0.000	0.013	0.290	0.483	0.000	0.409	1.371	1.078	0.078	0.208	1.148	0.360
West North Central	0.361	1.099	2.063	1.142	0.023	0.165	0.173	0.000	0.068	—	0.136	—	0.389	0.750	0.544	0.135	0.233	1.169	0.430
SOUTH																			
South Atlantic	0.553	1.121	1.760	1.130	0.009	0.269	0.358	—	0.000	—	0.083	—	0.556	—	0.838	0.136	0.194	0.906	0.367
East South Central	0.443	1.066	1.728	1.024	0.035	0.306	0.323	—	0.000	—	0.021	0.000	0.267	1.500	0.656	0.323	0.262	0.928	0.422
West South Central	0.604	1.109	1.988	1.161	0.052	0.298	0.274	—	0.000	0.200	0.050	0.087	0.400	1.265	0.570	0.239	0.239	1.207	0.513
WEST																			
Mountain	0.404	1.081	1.825	1.364	0.034	0.246	0.245	0.000	0.000	0.000	0.000	—	0.231	—	0.577	0.043	0.283	1.158	0.565
Pacific	0.445	1.106	1.842	1.255	0.040	0.307	0.290	0.023	0.000	0.098	0.069	0.015	0.322	1.333	0.617	0.031	0.159	1.433	0.192
NATIONAL																			
(All Area Average)	0.401	1.104	1.924		0.043	0.271		0.012	0.017	0.182		0.103	0.345	1.331		0.074	0.207	1.076	

Notes: [1] Units built from 1960-1970.
[2] Less than 1,000 units in this category (insufficient sample size).
[3] See Chapter 13 for definitions and instructions on how to use these tables.
[4] See Chapter 13 for inclusive states.
[5] All unit average.

Source: U.S. Census Public Use Sample, 1970.

36 THE FISCAL IMPACT HANDBOOK

EXHIBIT 2-4C

REGIONAL DEMOGRAPHIC MULTIPLIERS FOR COMMON CONFIGURATIONS OF SPECIALIZED HOUSING TYPES
TOTAL HOUSEHOLD SIZE BY HOUSING TYPE AND SIZE (FIELD SURVEYS, 1970–1975)

		HOUSING TYPES										
	VACATION HOMES[3]				CONDOMINIUMS (Low Rise/Garden)[C] (Single Family Attached)[D] (High Rise)[E]				ELDERLY RESIDENCES (High Rise)[F] (Low Rise)[G]		SINGLES RESIDENCES (Low Rise/Garden)	
	(Single Family)											
REGIONS	Rooms[A] Lot Size[B]	1 Room 5000 Ft^2	2 Room 5000-9999	3 Room 10000-19999	4 Room 20000-29999	One Bedroom	Two Bedroom	Three Bedroom	Four Bedroom	Studio	One Bedroom	Two Bedroom	Studio	One Bedroom	Two Bedroom
NORTHEAST New England[4] Middle Atlantic		3.085[A]	3.039[A] 2	3.198[A]	3.244[A]					—	1.699[G] 1	1.898[G]			
NORTH CENTRAL East North Central		3.637[B]	3.626[B]	3.699[B]	3.514[B]								—	1.163	1.947
SOUTH South Atlantic										1.380[F]	1.650[F]	1.850[F]			
WEST Pacific													1.089	1.282	—
NATIONAL						2.714[C] — 2.368[E]	2.614[C] 3.133[D] 2.966[E]	3.735[D]	4.731[D]						

EXHIBIT 2-4D

REGIONAL DEMOGRAPHIC MULTIPLIERS FOR COMMON CONFIGURATIONS OF SPECIALIZED HOUSING TYPES
SCHOOL-AGE CHILDREN BY HOUSING TYPE AND SIZE (FIELD SURVEYS, 1970–1975)

REGIONS	1	2	3	4	One Bdrm	Two Bdrm	Three Bdrm	Four Bdrm	Studio	One Bdrm	Two Bdrm	Studio	One Bdrm	Two Bdrm
NORTHEAST New England Middle Atlantic	0.780[A]	0.703[A]	0.794[A]	0.915[A]					—	0.000[G]	0.000[G]			
NORTH CENTRAL East North Central	1.510[B]	1.354[B]	1.454[B]	1.378[B]								—	0.000	0.000
SOUTH South Atlantic									0.000[F]	0.000[F]	0.000[F]			
WEST Pacific												0.000	0.000	—
NATIONAL					1.190[C] — 1.000[E]	0.982[C] 1.308[D] 1.225[E]	1.804[D]	2.615[D]						

Notes: [1]New units.
[2]No surveys at this location.
[3]See Chapter 13 for definitions.
[4]See Chapter 13 for inclusive states.

Source: Survey Samples at various locations — See Chapter 13.

Step 8 *Calculate Municipal Costs for Inclusive Nonresidential Uses.*

Since the proposed 3,000 unit PUD contains 100,000 square feet of commercial space for a community shopping center, municipal costs must also be assigned to this proposed facility. (For a full discussion, see Chapter 6.) Again a Proportional Valuation approach will be employed. The value of the facility may be estimated using the gross income multipliers for community shopping centers found in Chapter 16.

$$\text{Value} = \text{Size (Ft}^2\text{)} \times \text{Annual Rent per Ft}^2 \times \text{Gross Income Multiplier}$$

$$\$2{,}646{,}000 = 100{,}000 \text{ Ft}^2 \times \$4.50/\text{Ft}^2 \times 5.88$$

Per Capita Multiplier

The estimated market or equalized value of the community shopping center is $2,646,000. The shopping center's proportion of local nonresidential real property value is 2.7 percent($2,646,000 ÷ $96,651,453). The equalized real property value of the shopping center, which occupies one land parcel, is 8.1 times the local nonresidential average equalized property valuation ($2,646,000/326,525 = 8.1); the coefficient to be applied to straight-line proportional valuation to refine the municipal cost assignment is 0.38 (See Exhibit 6-3). Annual total municipal costs assigned to the new community shopping center are thus $12,353.

Shopping Center's Annual Municipal Costs		Total Municipal Expenditures Assigned to the Nonresidential Sector		Simple Proportional Valuation of the Shopping Center to Total Local Nonresidential Real Property Value		Refinement Coefficient
	=	$1,199,338	×	(.027	×	0.38)
$12,353	=	$1,199,338	×	.0103		

Step 9 Determine Total Annual Public Costs and Distribute Costs Both by Municipal Service and by Municipal and School District Operating Versus Debt Service Expenditures.

Total annual public expenditures assignable to the PUD are obtained by summing the individual costs for municipal and school district purposes for all examined residential and nonresidential facilities. (See Exhibit 2-5.) To project impact by municipal service category and municipal and school district operations and debt service, the analyst merely arrays total assignable expenditures by the percentage distribution of existing expenditures obtained in step 3. (See Exhibit 2-6 below.)

Total costs assignable to the PUD are thus $3,354,519, about 70 percent of which goes to supporting school district expenditures, 30 percent for municipal purposes. Of school district expenditures approximately 90 percent is reserved for operations; for municipal purposes approximately 77 percent is set aside for operating expenses.

Step 10 Project Total Annual Public Revenues.

Local revenue increases occasioned by development consist of those which increase as a direct function of local levies and charges (own source revenues) and those which change as a result of larger fiscal flows from other levels of government (intergovernmental transfers). The analyst should employ Chapters 9 and 10 for detailed revenue projection instructions.

Exhibit 2-7 shows anticipated revenues, by source, resulting from the 3,000 unit PUD in a New Jersey community. Of obvious importance in this area of the country is real property tax revenue for both municipal and school district purposes. It is fully 54 percent of municipal revenues and 71 percent of school district revenues. Other important municipal revenues are utility gross receipts, utility franchise taxes and revenue from fees and permits. Other key school district revenues are state flat grants and categorical aid as well as charges and miscellaneous funds.

THE FISCAL IMPACT HANDBOOK

EXHIBIT 2-5

USING THE PER CAPITA MULTIPLIER METHOD TO EVALUATE THE FISCAL IMPACT OF A DEVELOPMENT PROPOSAL

3,000 Unit Planned Unit Development	Number of Dwelling Units (1)	Demographic Multipliers Household (2)	Demographic Multipliers Students (2)	Total Residents[1] (3)	Students[1] (3)	Annual Expenditure Per Capita/ Municipal[2] (4)	Annual Expenditure Per Pupil/ School District[2] (4)	Total Annual Expenditures Municipal[4] (5)	Total Annual Expenditures School District[4] (5)	Total Annual Public (Municipal and School District) Expenditures (6)
RESIDENTIAL										
Townhouses (1,500)										
1 bedroom (elderly)	250	1.699	0.000	425	—	$129	$1,850	$ 54,825	$ —	$ 54,825
2 bedroom	1,000	2.630	0.304	2,630	304	129	1,850	339,270	562,400	901,670
3 bedroom	250	4.110	1.311	1,028	328	129	1,850	132,612	606,800	739,412
Garden Apartments (1,000)										
1 bedroom	700	1.722	.011	1,205	8	129	1,850	155,445	14,800	170,245
2 bedroom	300	2.525	.200	758	60	129	1,850	97,782	111,000	208,782
Single Family Homes (500)										
3 bedroom	250	3.776	1.111	944	278	129	1,850	121,776	514,300	636,076
4 bedroom	250	4.655	1.911	1,164	478	129	1,850	150,156	884,300	1,034,456
Total Residential	3,000	—	—	8,154	1,238 (1,456)[3]	—	—	1,051,866	2,290,300[5] (2,693,600)[6]	3,342,166[7] (3,745,466)[8]
NONRESIDENTIAL										
Community Shopping Center (100,000 Ft[2])	3,000 (100,000 Ft[2])	—	—	—	—	—	—	12,353[9]	—	12,353
TOTALS				8,154	1,456			$1,064,219	$2,290,300[10]	$3,354,519[10]

Notes:
[1] Equals the demographic multipliers shown in column (2) multiplied by the number of units shown in column (1).
[2] Includes operating and debt service for capital facilities.
[3] The figure in parentheses is the actual subtotal of column (3) for projected pupils. Since the multipliers in column (2) are total school-age children rather than public school-age children and in this particular locale 15 percent of school-age children attend public schools, projected local pupils has been multiplied by 85 percent to reflect the actual anticipated public school burden.
[4] Equals total residents/students multiplied by cost per resident/student.
[5] Equals total *public* school-age children (1,238) multiplied by the cost per pupil ($1,850). This is the figure the analyst is interested in because it indicates actual generated public costs.
[6] Equals total school-age children (1,456) multiplied by the cost per pupil ($1,850). It is also equal to the sum of the shown subtotals.
[7] Equals $1,051,866 + $2,290,300.
[8] Equals $1,051,866 + $2,693,600.
[9] See page 51.
[10] Totals include only public school-age children school district costs ($2,290,300).

Per Capita Multiplier

EXHIBIT 2-6

MUNICIPAL AND SCHOOL DISTRICT EXPENDITURES BY SERVICE CATEGORY
ASSIGNABLE TO THE 3,000 UNIT PUD

	PUD – Generated Costs by Service Category	Percent of Total PUD – Generated Costs ($1,064,219)	
MUNICIPAL			
Operating			
General Government	$ 117,064	11.0	
Public Safety	372,473	35.0	
Public Works	234,128	22.0	
Health and Welfare	21,284	2.0	
Recreation and Culture	74,495	7.0	
Debt Service	244,770	23.0	
TOTAL	$1,064,219*	100.0	(31.7)
SCHOOL DISTRICT			
Operating	2,061,270	90.0	
Debt Service	229,030	10.0	
TOTAL	$2,290,300	100.0	(68.3)
TOTAL PUBLIC COSTS (Municipal and School District)	$3,354,519		(100.0)

* Totals and subtotals may differ due to rounding.

Step 11 Calculate the Cost-Revenue Surplus or Deficit.

As indicated below, the 3000 unit PUD will produce a deficit of revenues over costs to the New Jersey municipality where development is contemplated.

Public Body	Total Annual Public Cost	Total Annual Public Revenue	Total Annual Net Fiscal Impact
Municipality	$1,064,219	$1,209,736	$ + 145,517
School District	2,290,300	2,068,886	– 221,414
TOTAL	$3,354,519	$3,278,622	$ – 75,897

Data Requirements

The most important data for the Per Capita Multiplier method are current local per capita municipal and per pupil school district operating costs. They are obtained from operating budgets published annually by municipalities and school districts (steps 1 through 3). Other significant data are the demographic multipliers by housing type which have been summarized in Exhibit 2-4 and are found in detail in Chapter 13. Exhibit 2-8 lists additional data requirements by procedural step.

EXHIBIT 2-7

COMPUTATION SHEET FOR REVENUE PROJECTION*

REVENUE SOURCES

MUNICIPAL

I. Own Source Revenues
    A. Taxes
        1. Real Property $ 654,298
    TOTAL TAXES $ 654,298

    B. Charges/Miscellaneous
        1. Interest earnings $ 27,876
        2. Fees and permits   52,500
        3. Fine and forfeitures   15,330
        4. User charges — special services   10,193
        5. User charges — sanitation   64,000
    TOTAL CHARGES/MISCELLANEOUS $ 169,899
TOTAL OWN SOURCE REVENUE $ 824,197

II. Intergovernmental Transfers
    A. State
        1. Utility franchise $ 38,985
        2. Utility gross receipts   310,500
        3. Business personal property   1,040
        4. Motor fuels   2,104
    TOTAL STATE $ 352,629

    B. Federal
        1. Revenue sharing $ 13,910
        2. CETA   12,000
        3. Anti-recession   7,000
    TOTAL FEDERAL $ 32,910
TOTAL INTERGOVERNMENTAL TRANSFER $ 385,539
TOTAL MUNICIPAL REVENUE $1,209,736

SCHOOL DISTRICT

I. Own Source Revenues
    A. Taxes
        1. Property taxes $1,472,170
    TOTAL TAXES $1,472,170

    B. Charges/Miscellaneous
        1. Charges/miscellaneous   90,374
    TOTAL CHARGES/MISCELLANEOUS   90,374
TOTAL OWN SOURCE REVENUE $1,562,544

II. Intergovernmental Transfers
    A. State
        1. Flat grants $ 189,414
        2. Categorical aid   247,600
        3. State redistributed federal   69,328
    TOTAL STATE $ 506,342

    B. Federal
        1. 0 $ 0
    TOTAL FEDERAL $ 0
TOTAL INTERGOVERNMENTAL TRANSFERS $ 506,342

TOTAL SCHOOL DISTRICT $2,068,886

TOTAL MUNICIPAL AND SCHOOL DISTRICT REVENUE $3,278,622

*For detailed calculations, see Exhibits 10-1 and 10-2 in Chapter 10.

EXHIBIT 2-8
PER CAPITA MULTIPLIER METHOD: DATA REQUIREMENTS AND SOURCES

Step Number	Data Requirements	Source(s)	Comments
2 – Categorize local expenditures into five municipal service categories plus the school district function	Local published municipal and school district budget	Municipal administrator superintendent of schools	
		Exhibit 2-2 of Case Study Method	
3 – Obtain total municipal and school district annual operating expenditures (including debt service)	Municipal and school district expenditures by service category	Local published municipal and school district budget	
4 – Assign share of total municipal costs to existing nonresidential facilities	Total assessed value of existing nonresidential facilities; total assessed value of all local real property	Tax assessor	Also obtain local equalization ratio.
5 – Calculate the net municipal costs and school district costs on a per capita and per pupil basis	Existing population estimates for municipality and school district	Latest U.S. census for area Local planning office School administration office	
6 – Calculate anticipated resident and school populations by housing type	Demographic multipliers by housing type	Exhibit 13-4 of this method Handbook, Chapter 13	Heed strengths and weaknesses of multipliers as detailed in Chapter 13.
8 – Calculate municipal costs for any nonresidential uses	Market value of inclusive nonresidential facilities; total assessed value of all properties;	See Step 4	
9 – Distribute total costs to service categories	Local equalization ratio; percentage distribution of costs by service categories	See Step 2	
10 – Project total annual public revenues	Municipal and school district real property tax rates; state and federal intergovernmental transfers For other data, see Chapters 9 and 10	Part 2, Calculating Revenues	

EXHIBIT 2-9

TIME ESTIMATES TO USE THE PER CAPITA MULTIPLIER METHOD

Step Number	Activities	Time
1	Obtain local financial and demographic data	8 hours
2	Categorize local expenditures	4 hours
3	Obtain total annual municipal and school district expenditures	6 hours
4	Assign a share of annual municipal costs to existing nonresidential uses	2 hours
5	Calculate net annual per capita and per pupil costs	2 hours
6	Calculate anticipated total residential and school populations by housing type	2 hours
7	Calculate residentially-induced local expenditures	2 hours
8	Calculate municipal costs for inclusive nonresidential uses	2 hours
9	Determine total annual public costs	2 hours
10	Project total annual public revenues	10 hours
11	Calculate the cost revenue impact	2 hours
Report Preparation	Prepare and reproduce final report (optional)	10 hours
		52 hours

Sophistication of User

The Per Capita Multiplier Method of projecting cost-revenue impact may be undertaken by a relatively unsophisticated user. Junior or project level planners under the supervision of principal or midrange superiors could easily use the method.

The arithmetical operations of the Per Capita Multiplier Method should pose few substantive problems. The selection of demographic multipliers and the method's procedures are extremely straightforward. Interpreting results, however, does require some level of sophistication. The analyst must be cognizant of the type of locale he is analyzing; he must consider both existing service levels and community wealth and how they could influence the results of the impact analysis. He must further realize that the method's assumptions — that today's costs are indicative of tomorrow's, and that the service demands of the existing user population are equivalent to those of the future population — are inherent parts of the conclusions.

Advantages and Disadvantages

Advantages

Simplicity/Low Cost   The Per Capita Multiplier Method is comparable to the Comparable City and Service Standard Methods in terms of ease of implementation. The analysis may be undertaken in about 50 man hours (see Exhibit 2-8) and yields relatively accurate, long-term, fiscal impact predictions.

Operational Utility   The information generated by the Per Capita Multiplier Method provides both educational and noneducational costs related to a proposed development, zone change, annexation, etc. It employs information which reflects existing local service levels and extends this service level into the future. Its value is its frank appraisal of local fiscal impact generated by new growth relative to that generated by existing local land uses.

Acceptability   The Per Capita Multiplier Method is the most widely accepted fiscal impact procedure available, particularly for the private planning consultant. Current per capita and per pupil operating expenses are readily available, and it is no longer necessary to undertake local field surveys to obtain site-specific demographic multipliers. Chapter 13 of this handbook tabulates demographic multipliers by region and further provides the analyst with a simple procedure to obtain similar site specific multipliers, if so desired, using the Public Use Sample. (See Chapter 14.)

Disadvantages

Richness of Detail   Probably the single greatest disadvantage of this method is the detail to which results are available. Its most accurate indication of costs is only to the level of municipal and school district services. Although the procedures outlined here tabulate municipal service cost by functional category (e.g., public safety, public works, general government, etc.), this result is only a reallocation of gross noneducational impact by the percent distribution of the municipal service dollar prior to impact evaluation. Even if the allocations to the service function level were essentially current, the Per Capita Multiplier Method does not provide the level of accuracy of estimates of personnel hiring costs or required new capital facility estimates that can be achieved with the use of the Case Study technique.

Long-Term versus Short-Term Impact   As opposed to the Case Study Method, the Per Capita Multiplier approach projects only long-term, average impact costs. It neither reflects the decisions that must take place immediately after the development approval nor does it take into account existing service slack or deficiency. During public presentations, the analyst must constantly attempt to relate general costs to contemplated actions resulting from this level of expenditure. Since he is usually not as intimately familiar with the local service system as is the Case Study analyst, the answers he provides to the questions of the local citizenry concerning actual service responses are not nearly as specific nor as definitive.

Interpreting Results

The analyst who uses the Per Capita Multiplier Method must exercise caution in interpreting statements of cost-revenue surplus or deficit. Given an observed surplus, the analyst concludes that over the long run, given existing local financial parameters, the growth increment will impose less local costs than the revenues it generates. Given a deficit, the reverse conclusion is appropriate.

Significant pitfalls are inherent in this apparently straightforward approach, however. Existing financial parameters are so woven into the Per Capita Multiplier Method that results are extremely site specific. In states which rely heavily on the property tax, for example, it is highly probable that a middle-income development in a relatively poor community will be a fiscal asset, whereas in a more affluent community the same development may well be a fiscal charge. The latter scenario characterizes the PUD example in this chapter. The development has an average unit real property valuation of approximately $30,000; the existing average local real property valuation is slightly over $50,000. This disparity in part explains why the PUD generates a $76,000 deficit. The Per Capita Multiplier Method, in relying so much on local information, becomes encumbered with a relative rather than an absolute picture of fiscal impact. This is a much different situation than employing the Service Standard technique whose manpower estimates are essentially neutral to location. The analyst must point out this characteristic to those who attempt to mold land use policy based on cumulative analyses using the Per Capita Multiplier Method.

NOTES

1. See Chapter 12, Field Experience, and Appendix 2.
2. Ruth L. Mace, *Municipal Cost-Revenue Research in the United States* (Chapel Hill, N.C.: University of North Carolina Press, 1961).
3. Ruth L. Mace and Warren J. Wicker, *Do Single Family Homes Pay Their Way?* Research Monograph 15 (Washington, D.C.: Urban Land Institute, 1968).
4. See George Sternlieb, et al., *Housing Development and Municipal Costs* (New Brunswick, N.J.: Rutgers University Center for Urban Policy Research, 1972).
5. See Chapter 17; Models for Cost Revenue Analysis.

3

CASE STUDY FISCAL IMPACT METHOD

Background

The Case Study Method is the classic marginal cost approach to project the effect of population change on municipal and school district costs. In its traditional unstructured form it has been employed in the early cost-revenue investigations of declining areas in the 1930s, public housing fiscal impact studies of the 1940s, HUD-701 assisted master plans in suburban expansion areas of the 1950s, projections of new community capital facility requirements of the 1960s, and the fiscal impact of growth-no-growth alternatives of the 1970s.[1] The Case Study Method elicits, through interviews with knowledgeable public officials, information about immediate plans to expand or maintain local services. It is a detailed, especially time consuming, and frequently costly approach. Its accuracy depends on the ability of local officials to predict the public consequences of growth of a specified size and location; it is important to note that some have questioned whether such future projections can be accurately made by public officials. On the plus side is the Case Study's ability to offer insight into the immediacies of cost-revenue impact that other methods may not supply.

In brief, the Case Study Method employs intensive site-specific investigations to determine categories of *excess* or slack public service capacity (capacity beyond that needed to accommodate the existing service or target population at current public service levels) or *deficient* or overage capacity (capacity below that needed to accommodate the existing service or target population). The excess or deficient service capacities are subtracted from or added to best estimates of the operating and capital demands posed by growth for each service category. (Estimated changes in service population is the measure by which public officials gauge future operating and capital reactions.) The result of population-imposed need, mitigated by existing excess capacity or worsened by deficient capacity, is projected future service demand based upon known service categories where expansion may or may not be necessary.

For example, during an interview, the superintendent of schools reveals that both number of students per classroom and pupil-teacher ratios are significantly lower than in the past. He estimates that constructing a housing development will cause classroom size and pupil-teacher ratios to increase to previous levels but will not require new teachers to be hired or capital facilities to be expanded. In this case of obvious excess capacity, the new development is charged a minimal cost. In another example, however, new development requires that a rescue station must immediately be built, and additional firemen hired to serve an area already partially developed. In the case of existing deficient capacity, the new development is charged the *full* extent of these additional expenditures, even though previous development has contributed to the cost and will benefit from both the new facility and the additional personnel.

Revenues are obtained by adding increases in municipal and school district own source and intergovernmental revenues resulting from growth. In the former area, direct revenues from local taxes and charges (local real property tax, sales tax, sanitation charges, etc.) are tabulated. In the latter, changes in fiscal flows from upper levels of government are calculated. The sum of these revenue changes is then compared with previously projected costs. The resulting surplus or deficit represents the best estimate of this new growth's impact on local municipal and school district expenditures.

Application

The Case Study approach takes three to four times longer and costs commensurately more than other fiscal impact projection techniques. It should thus be used only for those situations where other strategies are not suited or cannot provide the analyst with as much detailed information. Specifically, the Case Study Method is most applicable in certain localities for specific categories of cost revenue tasks and to certain types of study practitioners.

The technique is most useful in communities at the extreme ends of the service capacity spectrum — those suspected of having either considerable service excess or deficient service capacity. In such "end of spectrum" areas, other cost-revenue techniques may often yield a distorted picture of fiscal impact, at least in the short term. A community with extensive slack capacity — a central-city with declining population, for example, may be able to accommodate a public housing development without having to expand either its capital infrastructure or hire additional staff; in sum, without significantly increasing local expenditures. The Case Study Method takes into account this local elasticity and projects minimal costs generated by the proposed new growth, in effect, the expected short run impact.

In contrast, if a community's existing services are strained to capacity (a small city experiencing rapid growth), the Case Study Method projects considerable expenditures resulting from growth — a scenario that accurately depicts the actual, immediate effect of population change in this type of locality. Most other fiscal impact techniques are not sensitive to either the absorption capacity or immediate expansive nature of service systems and may project outlays considerably above or below what is actually the case.

The Case Study Method provides a detailed view of the operating and capital impact of growth. It is therefore very useful to municipal administrators for general budget projections and to other city officials for insight into the immediate effects of growth, such as a public works department wishing to project short-term capital facility demand or a municipal commissioner, the titular head of a department, needing specific information on operating and capital impact in order to respond adequately to an anticipated population change. In contrast, other methods, which translate growth pressures into gross public dollar costs per service category, yield less detailed data. A Per Capita Multiplier or Proportional Valuation approach, for example, may predict that a particular planned unit development or shopping center will, on average, generate considerable cost-revenue surpluses over time; this is not of direct use to public department heads or officials concerned with analyzing specifically how they must respond with manpower and equipment to answer the service needs of the development.

Case Study

Whether or not to use the Case Study Method also depends on the type of study practitioner and sponsor. The method requires the time and cooperation of public officials and relies upon accurate, firsthand knowledge of a department's operations. As such, it is ideal for studies conducted by city analysts. The internal planner, although not neutral, knows the biases of fellow department officials and can use this information to temper his evaluation. Local officials understand local operations best.

The amount of time and money involved in the Case Study Method also affects the decision to use it. The technique requires meeting with a broad range of public employees (school district, public safety, public works, general government, etc.), sometimes for more than one interview, to acquire information, which must then be carefully tabulated. In one case, analyzing the impact of a 3,000 unit PUD, which added 10,000 residents to a township's existing population of 12,000, required sixteen in-depth interviews of approximately one to two hours each and four hours of scheduling appointments before sufficient information could be obtained to begin the analysis.[2] The analysis itself consumed sixty hours and report preparation another ten hours. Assuming standard salary and overhead scales for a planner, municipal department head, and clerical employees, personnel costs for analysis were almost $13,000. The cost for the Case Study Method, because it requires more time, may thus be as much as ten times the expense of other methods.

The Case Study approach has been used satisfactorily to estimate the impact of traditional nonresidential facilities — a shopping center, for example — on municipal services. The fiscal impact of this land use cannot readily be projected by using common population-based methods (Per Capita Multiplier or Comparable City Methods), because the use generates no *direct* additional residents. The Proportional Valuation approach, while often used as a short cut to provide a rough gauge of impact, needs continuous calibration to ensure its reliability. Local officials' estimates of added police to handle traffic, additional street maintenance and additional auditing and tax monitoring are accurate enough to project immediate local costs.

The Case Study Method is also useful for evaluating the impact of exceptional nonresidential uses, the "one of a kind" phenomena such as a proposal for a sports complex or convention center. Other fiscal impact projection methods simply cannot be utilized because the scope of impact or scale of planned activity is so substantially different from what has occurred previously, locally or in comparison with other communities, that a whole new situation is created.

Basic Assumptions

The Case Study approach is based on four assumptions. The first assumption is that communities differ in the degree to which they exhibit excess or deficient service capacity which significantly affects the level of local service extensions. The second assumption is that marginal changes in providing municipal and school district services, as a reaction to excess or deficient service capacity, are the most accurate indications of future local servicing costs. Thus, what is actually contemplated in terms of local service additions are the costs to be assigned to the growth increment. As stated by one author:

> There is no point in allocating some portion of the cost of the City Council and Clerk to residential areas, putting these on a per capita or per (000) population basis, and including this as a cost of additional population, unless there is a real reason to believe that added population will increase the expense in this account. If there is reason to believe that there will be an increase in expense in this account, this should itself be estimated directly.[3]

The third premise is that while current local service levels may be altered slightly, they, and not national standards, represent the criteria against which local excess and deficient capacity are calculated.

The fourth and final assumption is that local department heads, intimately familiar with the service delivery capacity of their departments, when properly approached and provided with comparative information, provide the most accurate gauge of future expenditure extensions in a particular category of municipal or school district service.

Procedures

The Case Study approach has been critized for being unstructured. One author notes that "The specific method of the case study depends upon the wit, common sense, and imagination of the person doing the investigation. The investigator makes up his procedure as he goes along because he purposely refuses to work within any set of categories or classifications."[4] There is no denying that the Case Study Method has frequently been less structured and less formal than other fiscal impact methods. Few have discussed which officials were or were not approached, what types of questions were asked and why, and general procedures followed to undertake the analysis.[5]

At another extreme is a very detailed Case Study procedure, *Cost-Revenue Impact Analysis for Residential Developments*,[6] recently prepared by the Connecticut Development Group Inc., and the Research Corporation of Connecticut. This approach suggests the utilization of over seventy information probes or "schedules" to be administered to or completed by public officials. The schedules elicit a wide range of data — existing community population, population change over time, the number of persons and students currently being served by various public agencies, the amount of excess or deficient capacity, and the incremental cost of serving the additional population generated by a residential project.

This handbook proposes a Case Study approach that is more structured than what has previously been used but far less structured than this first attempt by the Connecticut group to formalize the Case Study process. The major steps in the analysis are summarized in Exhibit 3-1.

EXHIBIT 3-1

CASE STUDY FISCAL IMPACT METHOD: SUMMARY OF PROCEDURES

Step Number	Analysis/Actions
1	Contact "key" public officials, e.g., city manager, municipal administrator, superintendent of schools.
2	Categorize public service functions and delineate responsibilities by local municipal and school district services.
3	Determine presence or absence, and magnitude of any existing public operating and capital excess or deficient capacity for various public services.
4	Project population and student increases through the use of appropriate multipliers. Estimate population-induced service demand, using primarily service standards and capital ratios.
5	Interview local public officials to determine how their respective departments will respond to growth (given identified areas of existing service excess or deficiency and the rough gauge of population-induced demand) in terms of expanding or not expanding their operating and capital capacities.
6	Project the costs that will be incurred by different public jurisdictions as a consequence of the manpower and facility expansions pinpointed in step 5.
7	Project total annual public revenues.
8	Determine cost-revenue surplus or deficit by comparing projected total revenues to projected total costs.
9	Submit draft report to local officials for review and comment.

Case Study 49

Step 1 Contact Local Officials.

The most important input to an effective Case Study analysis is the information derived through the cooperation of local officials. Consequently, it is crucial to contact "key" officials — the city manager or business administrator, and the school district superintendent — to inform them of the study's objective and to elicit their support. The city manager and superintendent of schools may assign a knowledgeable administrative assistant (familiar with the workings and staff of operating departments) to assist the Case Study analyst in determining municipal and school district costs. It is important to work closely with these supervisory people in order to establish initially a mutually agreeable approach for contacting and interviewing line and staff department heads. Senior public officials can also prove to be invaluable resources for informing the analyst of their impressions of local slack or overage service capacity and the presence or absence of similar studies.

The importance of this first step cannot be overemphasized. If the analyst has not approached the most knowledgeable local officials or if he has not established a solid working relationship with the individuals to be interviewed, then the Case Study Method will not be effective.

The Case Study analyst will spend most of his time with the staff suggested by his municipal contact persons. Optimally, this will enable him to work with individuals who are experienced and thoroughly familiar with the service levels, resources, capabilities and operation of the different departments. Both staff and line personnel should be interviewed; the former can best offer background information while the latter are more sensitive to daily operational needs and expenditures of resources.

This handbook will not provide a series of structured questions to elicit information from department heads but rather emphasizes the interview approach. Advance scheduling is very important; the Case Study analyst must be flexible and adjust his schedule to that of the person questioned. The interviews should be as short, concise and focused as possible. It would be helpful to send, in advance, a list of written questions to those who will be contacted in order to make the verbal interview more efficient. One point requires further emphasis. In interviews with public officials it is important to describe accurately the *location* of the proposed site as there may be certain geographic characteristics such as proximity to feeder roads and sewer lines which will significantly influence whether or not existing service excess capacity can be used.

Step 2 Categorize Public Service Functions and Delineate Responsibilities.

To organize the interviews, cost assignments, and revenue calculations, the analyst should categorize public functions and delineate responsibilities for providing these services by different levels of government. This classification could take the form of very broad categories — general government, public safety, public works, etc., — without finer detailing. Such a strategy, while relatively easy, is too general for pinpointing the consequences of growth. It is not very meaningful, for example, to predict that a certain population increase will require the hiring of five general government employees, nine public safety workers, etc. Such projections are hard to translate into costs because they do not relate to specific departments. Categorizing public functions and responsibility department by department (as listed in a line-item budget), on the other hand, is much too cumbersome, for there are often numerous operating agencies. The U.S. Census of Governments offers a compromise classification system. It divides municipal and school district services into six major groupings (general government, public safety, public works, health and welfare, recreation and culture, and education), and several subcategories (police, fire, etc.).[7] This categorization has already been utilized in the cost-revenue analysis field and Service Standard

Method of this handbook.* The specific U.S. Census of Governments delineation and the relationship of this categorization to typical line-item budget entries are shown in Exhibit 3-2.

The analyst must remember that all local government activities are linked to basic public services and must be categorized. This classification serves two functions. It indicates current emphasis on expenditures by service category and provides initial indications of excess or deficient capacity.

Step 3 *Determine Excess and Deficient Service Capacity.*

The next step is to determine whether excess or deficient service capacity exists, and if it does to what extent. The analyst must evaluate whether the municipality and school district service capacity is *above* or *below* that needed to accommodate the existing resident population. To evaluate the situation, the analyst must first ascertain local standards, or desired service levels, for operating and capital services.** For example, the desired service level for local schools may be one teacher per twenty-five students, and one classroom per thirty-five students.

In a few localities, municipal personnel will know locally desired service levels and use them regularly in their planning — especially for school district functions. When local staff members do not know desired service levels, however, the analyst will have to work with municipal and school district staff and line personnel to determine best estimates of the levels to which service provision is adequate locally.

It is fundamental, but important, to stress that desired service levels are not determined simply by dividing the existing population by the various operating and capital public service units (e.g., teachers, classrooms, policemen, etc.). This procedure yields merely *current* service levels. If the analyst uses current rather than desired service levels, he will never be able to determine excess and deficient capacity; the analyst probes for the community's long term accepted service standards.

After he determines desired local service levels, the analyst determines and measures excess or deficient capacity by interviewing municipal and school district officials. These individuals are specifically asked:

> Is there any excess capacity in terms of capital facilities or operational resources, with reference to the service you are responsible for, so that an acceptable service quality could be provided if existing facilities and manpower served a larger user population? If yes, please indicate the exact level of slack.

These individuals are also asked:

> Is there any deficient capacity in terms of capital facilities or operational resources, with reference to the service you are responsible for, so that the services provided to your existing population are below desired public levels? If yes, please indicate the exact level of deficient capacity.

Responses to these questions should be quantified in the same units used to project demand for the service item.

---

*The Census of Governments provides manpower estimates only for "common" municipal functions and does not include health and welfare services. The category is included in the Case Study Method, however, because numerous localities, especially the larger ones, provide this service.

**Operating expenses consist primarily of public personnel expenditures (including statutory costs), although it also includes nonpersonnel outlays for equipment and supplies. Capital expenses consist of outlays for the public physical plant, e.g., a new school or sewage treatment plant. To illustrate, the physical construction of a new road is a capital outlay, the manpower needed to maintain the road is a personnel operating expense, and the materials (e.g., asphalt, tar, stone) used for upkeep is a nonpersonnel operating expenditure.

Case Study 51

EXHIBIT 3-2
RELATIONSHIP OF CENSUS OF GOVERNMENTS SERVICE CATEGORIES AND LINE – ITEM CLASSIFICATIONS

Census of Governments Service Category	Typical Line – Item Budget Classification	Census of Governments Service Category	Typical Line – Item Budget Classification
MUNICIPAL			
GENERAL GOVERNMENT		Sewerage:	Department/Division/Office of: Sewers, Sewage Treatment, Sewage Disposal
Financial Administration:	Department/Division/Office of: Administration, Purchasing, Finance, Disbursements, Tax Collection, Assessment, Accounts Control Licenses and Permits	Sanitation:	Department/Division/Office of: Sanitation Disposal, Leaf Collection
		Water Supply:	Department/Division/Office of: Water Engineering, Water Accounting, Water Operating, Water Purchasing
General Control:	Department/Division/Office of: Township Clerk, Personnel, Law, Real Estate, Zoning Board. Also includes Municipal Court, Office of the Mayor, and Municipal Council	HEALTH & WELFARE	
		Public Welfare:	Department/Division/Office of: Public Assistance
		Hospitals:	Department/Division/Office of: Hospitals, Public Clinic
PUBLIC SAFETY		Health:	Department/Division/Office of: Public Health Inspectors, Inspections (Sanitary)
Police Protection:	Department/Division/Office of: Police, Traffic Control and Maintenance		
Fire Protection:	Department/Division/Office of: Fire Protection, Fire Prevention	RECREATION & CULTURE	
Housing & Urban Renewal	Department/Division/Office of: Public Housing, Redevelopment, Urban Renewal	Parks & Recreation:	Department/Division/Office of: Parks, Recreation, Water Safety
		Libraries:	Free Public Library, Bookmobile
PUBLIC WORKS		*SCHOOL DISTRICT*	
Highways:	Department/Division/Office of: Streets, Highway Engineering, Highway Maintenance	PRIMARY AND SECONDARY SCHOOLS	Department/Division/Office of: Superintendent, Finance, Personnel, Buildings and Grounds, Special Pupils, Pupil Services
(Continued in cols 3 and 4)			

Source: U.S. Department of Commerce, *Classification Manual, Government Finances* (Washington, D.C.: Government Printing Office, 1972) and selected sample of local budget worksheets.

To illustrate, a chief engineer might reveal excess capacity by responding that an existing sewage treatment plant can serve not only the existing population but also another 750 single-family homes or 100,000 gallons per day. A police commissioner might indicate deficient capacity by responding that the existing force of twenty-five uniformed personnel is inadequate for a community of 30,000, given the desired local service level of two uniformed personnel per 1,000 residents.

The interviewing should proceed on a step-by-step basis to encompass all public services, both school district and the various municipal subcategories. This series of interviews will indicate whether or not there is excess or deficient capacity in the public delivery system. The exact operating and capital excess and deficient capacity in an Illinois community of 16,000 population and 4,000 pupils in which a 3,000-unit PUD (1,500 townhouses, 1,000 garden apartments, 500 single family homes and a 100,000 square foot shopping center)* is proposed is shown in Exhibit 3–3, column 2 and Exhibit 3–4, column 2, respectively. This locality has, for example, an excess of seven teachers and one social service worker, and a deficiency of two reading specialists and two police patrolmen.

The key to successfully pinpointing excess or deficient capacity is *detailed and careful interviewing of public officials.* Officials may sometimes hesitate to admit the existence of excess capacity for fear it may justify reduced operating or capital funding. They may also hesitate to admit the exact magnitude of deficient capacity, because it may appear to be poor planning. The cost revenue analyst must be aware of these factors when he considers officials' responses. The analyst should balance numbers and need. For example, it may not make sense to hire two additional patrolmen to cover an unmanned area unless an entire patrol shift can be created.

Step 4 Project Population Increases and Population Induced Demand.

Thus far, the analysis has focused on examining the existing local service delivery system in terms of categorizing public functions and determining their excess and deficient capacity. Now that the status quo is defined, it is possible to analyze what effect growth will have on municipal and school district units of government. The analyst must project the exact increase in total and school-age population and the gross demands these groups impose. Population may be estimated via the employment of demographic multipliers. Briefly, since this procedure is detailed in Per Capita Multiplier Method, household and population projections are accomplished by multiplying the expected variations in size and type units by appropriate household size and school-age children multipliers. (See Chapter 13 for multipliers for your area.) Summarizing the products of these processes for all units yields the total number of people and pupils that will be generated by a specific form of residential growth or residential zoning change. This analysis is a basic element of the Case Study Method, because it indicates the magnitude of the population increase expected from growth and because the increase will exert immediate pressures on services. Except in declining areas, this increase will almost always also increase local service expenditures.

After he determines the amount of population increase, the analyst's next step is to generate population-induced service demand. This estimate uses regional public employee service levels and capital-to-operating expenditure ratios** (these are presented by municipal and school district population size groupings in the Service Standard Method) to project the number of employees

---

*For a full description, see Chapter 1.
**For a full discussion, see Chapter 4, Service Standard Method.

Case Study 53

EXHIBIT 3-3

USING THE CASE STUDY METHOD TO EVALUATE THE OPERATING FISCAL IMPACT OF A DEVELOPMENT PROPOSAL

Governmental Functions (1)	Step 3 Capacity Determination Excess[1] (2)	Step 3 Capacity Determination Deficient[1] (2)	Step 4 Population-Induced Demand[2] (Employees) (3)	Step 5 Local Service Response (4)	Step 6 Local Operating Service Cost per Unit[3] (5)	Step 6 Cost of Local Response[4] (6)
MUNICIPAL						
GENERAL GOVERNMENT						
FINANCIAL & ADMINISTRATIVE	+1 Accountant	−1 Clerk	2.5	5 Clerks	$ 9,800	$ 49,000
GENERAL CONTROL/PUBLIC BUILDINGS	+2 Engineers	−2 Custodians	4.8	4 Custodians/3 Clerks	9,100/9,400	64,600
PUBLIC SAFETY						
POLICE PROTECTION	+1 Dispatcher	−2 Patrolmen	14.4	16 Patrolmen	16,100	257,600
FIRE PROTECTION	+1 Lieutenant	−1 Fireman	7.8	8 Firemen	15,900	127,200
HOUSING & URBAN RENEWAL[5]	+2 Planners	−2 Secretaries	5.0	5 Laborers	8,000	40,000
PUBLIC WORKS						
HIGHWAYS	+1 Traffic Engineer	−1 Laborer	6.8	10 Laborers /5 Clerks	10,100/5,901	130,505
SEWERAGE	+1 Chemist	−1 Engineer	3.3	4 Engineers	16,900	67,600
SANITATION	+1 Supervisor	−2 San. Workers	3.5	4 San. Workers	15,100	60,400
WATER SUPPLY	+1 Engineer	−3 Technicians	4.7	2 Technicians	13,000	26,000
HEALTH AND WELFARE[5]						
PUBLIC WELFARE	+1 Case Worker	−1 Clerk	6.0	8 Clerks	8,800	70,400
HOSPITALS	+1 Supervisor	−4 Orderlies	6.2	7 Orderlies	8,100	56,700
HEALTH	+1 Orderly +1 Sanitary Aide	−1 Nurse	3.0	1 Nurse	12,495	12,495
RECREATION AND CULTURE						
PARKS AND RECREATION	+1 Supervisor	−1 Rec. Spec.	2.6	6 Rec. Specialists	8,000	48,000
LIBRARIES	+1 Clerk	−1 Librarian	1.3	2 Librarians/4 Clerks	10,000/9,000	56,000
	TOTAL +17	TOTAL −23	TOTAL MUNICIPAL 71.9	TOTAL 94		
				TOTAL MUNICIPAL OPERATING EXPENDITURES		1,066,500
SCHOOL DISTRICT				70 Teachers	15,700	1,099,000
LOCAL PRIMARY & SECONDARY SCHOOL DISTRICT	+7 Teachers	−2 Reading Spec.	TOTAL SCHOOL DISTRICT 106.2 employees	4 Reading Spec.	15,900	63,600
	+2 Supervisors	−1 A-V Aide		3 A-V Aides	13,800	41,400
	+1 Librarian	−2 Clerks		8 Clerks	10,500	84,000
	TOTAL +10	TOTAL −5		15 Aides	8,900	133,500
				5 Administrators	18,400	92,000
				20 Other Personnel	9,000	180,000
				TOTAL 125		
				TOTAL SCHOOL DISTRICT OPERATING EXPENDITURES		1,693,500
				TOTAL MUNICIPAL AND SCHOOL DISTRICT OPERATING EXPENDITURES		2,760,000

Notes:
[1] A plus (+) indicates excess capacity while a minus (−) indicates deficient capacity.
[2] Development-generated population and public school-age children multiplied by the service standards shown in Chapter 4, Exhibits 2 through 5.
[3] Includes salaries, statutory expenditures and material costs per employee. See page 110 for derivation.
[4] Equals column 4 multiplied by column 5.
[5] Population induced demand for these services estimated from national service standards since Chapter 4 does not list standards for these services.

and amount of capital expenditure a population increment of a certain magnitude will generate.* Although this procedure is somewhat difficult, it will increase the method's reliability. The analyst must be aware of the subjective nature of officials' estimates of cost induced by growth. If he can show officials what population-induced demand (based on average public employee levels and

---

*Chapter 4 does not include service standards and capital-to-operating ratios for housing and urban renewal, public welfare, and hospital and health services, because these are not "common" municipal functions for which the Census of Governments provides information on average manpower servicing levels. The analyst will therefore have to estimate operating and capital population-induced demand in these four areas by using recommended service levels published by trade associations, unions, equipment, suppliers, e.g., International Association of Fire Chiefs. For an excellent compilation of service standards see: Joseph DeChiara and Lee Koppelman, *Manual of Housing, Planning and Design Criteria* (Englewood Cliffs, N.J.: Prentice Hall, 1975).

EXHIBIT 3-4

USING THE CASE STUDY METHOD TO EVALUATE THE CAPITAL FISCAL IMPACT OF A DEVELOPMENT PROPOSAL

Step 2	Step 3		Step 4	Step 5	Step 6	Step 6
Governmental Functions (1)	Capacity Determination		Population-Induced Demand (dollars) (3)	Local Service Response (4)	Local Service Cost per Unit (5)	Local Cost of Local Response (6)
	Excess[3] (2)	Deficient[3]				
MUNICIPAL						
GENERAL GOVERNMENT						
FINANCIAL & ADMINISTRATIVE	+8,000 ft^2 ofc. space			No response		
GENERAL CONTROL/PUBLIC BUILDINGS		−3,500 ft^2 ofc. space		No response		
PUBLIC SAFETY						
POLICE PROTECTION	+4,000 ft^2 ofc. space	−3,000 ft^2 garage space	$6,440	Police station annex	$500,000	$ 46,560[1]
FIRE PROTECTION	+1 fire truck	−1 pumper	4,834	1 pumper	60,000	6,473[2]
HOUSING & URBAN RENEWAL[4]	—	—		No response		
PUBLIC WORKS						
HIGHWAYS	+1 steamroller	−1 street paver	30,930	1 street paver	50,000	5,394[2]
SEWERAGE	+500,000 gal. treatment	−1 sweeper	6,760	No response		
SANITATION	+3 dump trucks	−1 sweeper	—	No response		
WATER SUPPLY	—	—	2,262	No response		
HEALTH & WELFARE[4]						
PUBLIC WELFARE	+3,600 ft^2 ofc. space		2,500	No response		
HOSPITALS	+20 bed wing	−1 X ray machine	5,000	No response		
HEALTH	+3,000 ft^2 treatment area	−1 X ray machine	3,500	Clinic annex	300,000	27,936[1]
RECREATION & CULTURE						
PARKS	+10 acres of parks	−4 acres playground	3,936	No response		
LIBRARIES	+2,000 linear ft. shelf space			No response		
			TOTAL MUNICIPAL 55,162	TOTAL MUNICIPAL CAPITAL EXPENDITURES		$ 86,363
SCHOOL DISTRICT						
LOCAL PRIMARY & SECONDARY SCHOOL DISTRICT	+15 classrooms	−3,000 ft^2 ofc. space	TOTAL SCHOOL DISTRICT 89,756	New School	3,000,000	$279,360[1]
				TOTAL SCHOOL DISTRICT CAPITAL EXPENDITURES		$279,360
				TOTAL MUNICIPAL AND SCHOOL DISTRICT CAPITAL EXPENDITURES		$365,723

Notes:
[1] Amortized at 7% interest rate over 20 years.
[2] Amortized at 7% interest rate over 15 years.
[3] A plus (+) indicates excess capacity, while a minus (−) indicates deficient capacity.
[4] Figure projected from national service standards since Chapter 4 does not list standards for these services.

capital expenditures per given population increment) can be expected, however, the estimate based on levels of service helps provide a more reliable base for accurate projections of the consequences of growth.

Exhibit 3-5 illustrates the procedure used to estimate the population and school-age children in the 3,000 unit PUD; a total of 8,360 residents and 1,416 public school children is predicted. Exhibits 3-2 and 3-3 contain a column (column 3) which itemizes the analyst's estimates of both operating and capital population-induced service demand. These are based on average manpower service levels and median capital to operating cost ratios for North Central communities of population size 10,000 to 24,999, and North Central school districts with more than 3,000 pupils — the appropriate size cohorts for the hypothetical Illinois community. (See Exhibits 4-3 and 4-10.) To illustrate, midwestern localities in this size range employ, on the average, 1.72 policemen per 1,000 residents while such size school districts hire 75 school district personnel per 1,000 students. The projected increase — 8,360 residents and 1,416 *public* school-age children — in such a locality would thus require fourteen additional policemen (8.360 × 1.72) and 106 school district staff (1.416 × 75). Capital costs are calculated the same way by using the capital-to-operating expenditure ratios. Thus, in police service, there is a population induced capital demand of $6,440 ($257,600 [projected operating cost] × .025 = $6,440).

Case Study

EXHIBIT 3-5

PROJECTION OF RESIDENT AND SCHOOL-AGE POPULATION

Housing Type	Number of Dwelling Units (1)	Household Size Multipliers[1] (2)	School-Age Children Multipliers (3)	Total Resident Population[2] (4)	Total School-Age Population[3] (5)
Townhouses (1,500)					
1 bedroom (elderly)	250	1.699	- - -	425	- - -
2 bedroom	1,000	2.727	0.409	2,727	409
3 bedroom	250	4.129	1.371	1,032	343
				4,184	752
Garden Apartments (1,000)					
1 bedroom	700	1.719	0.036	1,203	25
2 bedroom	300	2.576	0.232	773	70
				1,976	95
Single Family Houses (500)					
3 bedroom	250	3.892	1.173	973	293
4 bedroom	250	4.909	2.102	1,227	526
				2,200	819
		TOTAL		8,360	1,416 (1,666)[4]

Notes: [1] From Exhibit 2-4.
[2] Column (1) times column (2).
[3] Column (1) times column (3).
[4] The figure in parentheses is the actual subtotal of number of school-age students. Since the school-age children multipliers which are used are total school-age children rather than public school-age children and in this community 85 percent of all school-age children attend private schools, the projection of local students has been multiplied by 85 percent to reflect the actual anticipated *public school* burden.

Step 5 Determine Anticipated Local Service Response.

Steps 3 and 4 yield the raw data about excess and deficient capacity and the population-induced demand of the proposed development. With this information, the analyst then *reinterviews local officials to determine how their respective departments will respond to projected growth in terms of expanding or not expanding their operating and capital capacity* (e.g., hiring new teachers, adding firemen, building new capital facilities).

Specifically, the staff and line officials of the different departments are asked "What is the expected reaction to accommodate a population change of _____ (specify projected total and student population changes); induced by _____ (specify development proposal, zoning change, annexation, redevelopment, etc.); at _____ (specify location)? Will any additional staff be hired? If so, how many and of what type? Will capital facilities be added or expanded? If so, exactly what additions and expansions are anticipated?"

In a nonresidential situation, a similar approach would be taken except that staff and line officials would be asked the following question: "What is the expected reaction to accommodate a

_____ (specify the general type and size of nonresidential facility, i.e., community shopping center of 100,000 FT^2 GLA); induced by _____ (specify development proposal, zoning change, redevelopment, etc.): at _____ (specify location, especially in reference to existing roads and highways and utility and sewerage service networks)? Will any additional staff by hired? If so, what type of personnel? Will capital facilities be built or expanded? If so, exactly what additions and/or expansions are anticipated?"

The analyst's task in this step is to determine the *immediate* local response to growth — what the jurisdiction intends to do in the near future to accommodate growth. Postponed decisions, such as building a school five years hence, are not charged to the current growth generator. It is assumed that postponed decisions are a "wash transaction," i.e., that the proportion of immediate decisions resulting from past postponed actions will equal the proportion of current decisions that are postponed.

Procedurally, the analyst, in soliciting anticipated service response from the department head should refresh him with both the desired service levels and the excess and deficient capacity in each service category determined in step 3, and the population-induced demand determined in step 4. The public official must consider these data carefully before he can estimate his department's probable reaction. A more intensive response may be anticipated if there is minimal excess capacity or if deficient capacity exists than if considerable excess is present.

The analyst must remember, however, that these data are only one basis for the public official to consider in estimating his department's response. A jurisdiction may not immediately correct deficient capacity, nor is it true that it will take no action if most growth can be accommodated with existing excess capacity. The municipal service system is not governed by desired service levels; other factors, economic and locational, play an important role.

The jurisdiction's *current financial capacity* is one such critical consideration: a community experiencing a severe budget crunch, having just increased local taxes, is likely to forego incurring major additional expenditures even if this expenditure is sorely needed to alleviate a situation of existing service over-utilization. In contrast, a jurisdiction experiencing a favorable financial climate may decide to increase its operating services or capital plant even if short-term growth could be accommodated largely by existing excess capacity.

The *site* where growth is anticipated also influences a jurisdiction's response. There may be excess capacity in a system which, because of the location of a development, cannot be drawn upon. A decision may be made to build another link of a sewer system or a new waste treatment plant, despite a general municipal-wide surplus in these services, if the particular growth catalyst is located in an area *not* currently serviced by these facilities. Conversely, a school district may decide that a development will not necessitate the hiring of new teachers, despite a community deficient capacity in the desired elementary student-teacher ratio, because the posed development will be fortuitously located near an elementary school with a surplus of teachers.

Exhibit 3-3, column 4, summarizes the increases in operating services expected to be added as a result of the PUD's 3,000 residential units and 100,000 square feet of commercial space; Exhibit 3-4, column 4, pinpoints the extent of new capital additions that would be required. Estimates are presented by the various subcategories of municipal and school district services. To illustrate, for school district services alone, development would require, over and above excess capacity absorption, the hiring of seventy teachers and four reading specialists and the construction of a new local elementary school.

Case Study 57

Step 6 Project Total Annual Public Costs.

The analyst must then convert manpower and capital facility projections to public expenditures. He determines operating outlays by first calculating the salaries (including statutory costs*) for those employees who are expected to be hired and the material costs (equipment, supplies, etc.) that will be generated by the new employees. These cost figures can be obtained from the appropriate local officials and/or the municipal and school district working budgets. These documents contain a formal compilation of expenditures (differentiated into salaries, statutory expenditures and miscellaneous or material expenses) by service function as well as by the number and type of employees for each service category. Dividing total operating outlays (salaries, statutory and material expenditures) per service function by the total number of employees in that service category yields average operating costs per employee. (For a full discussion see Page 77, Service Standard Fiscal Impact Method.) Operating outlays per employee for the Illinois community are shown in Exhibit 3-3, column 5.

After operating costs per employee are determined, it is easy to calculate future operating expenditures by multiplying the unit costs by the number of employees expected to be added as the result of planned municipal service expansions. To illustrate, the community where the 3,000 unit PUD is proposed has a $16,100 cost per patrolman. Since there is an anticipated service response of adding sixteen patrolmen, police operating expenditure will amount to $257,600 ($16,100 × 16). Similarly, at a $15,900 average salary per reading specialist, the school district will incur $63,600 ($15,900 × 4) in costs for hiring such individuals. Expenditures for other services are calculated in a like manner and are shown in Exhibit 3-3, column 6.

Capital outlays to accommodate the 3,000 unit PUD are illustrated in Exhibit 3-4, column 5. Capital costs are not charged as one lump sum (i.e., $500,000 for a school, $1,000,000 for a road extension); instead they are expressed in an annual amortized amount. To illustrate, the PUD is expected to require the construction of $3,000,000 in new school facilities. The amortized cost of these buildings will be about $280,000 annually.** This procedure is used because public jurisdictions pay for capital facilities by selling bonds, a portion of which they repay each year with interest; their true costs then are an annual amortized amount.*** Additionally, this yearly calculation of capital costs enables us to add capital outlays to operational costs, which are recurring annual expenses. The annual outlay as a common denominator for operating and capital costs is important — when costs are linked to revenues (the bulk of which are annual) there must be a direct means of comparison.

It is also important to note that the entire cost of projected hiring, purchasing, and building to accommodate the population change is charged to the specific development proposal, zoning change, or annexation that occasions the action. This is illustrated in the Case Study example by charging the new development the full cost of a new elementary school even though children from both existing and future developments will benefit from this facility. This 100 percent costing

---

*FICA, unemployment compensation, etc.
**The entire amount is charged here. It is assumed that the new facility, after it has been paid for, has no residual value.
***The colloquial version of the term amortization is used here to represent scheduled principal repayment *including* interest.

procedure is one of the distinguishing features of the Case Study Method. Once the tipping point is reached at which growth necessitates a series of operating and capital responses, the particular growth generator is assigned all costs of these activities.

In the example of the 3,000 unit PUD, the operating costs assigned to the development are $1,066,500 for local municipal expenses and $1,693,500 for school district outlays. When the annual amortized bonding amount of capital facilities (Exhibit 3-4) for municipal and school district services is added to operating costs, total impact costs attributable to the proposed development are $1,152,863 and $1,972,860, respectively.

Public Body	Total Annual Operating Cost	Total Annual Capital Cost	Total Annual Public Cost
Municipality	$1,066,500	$ 86,363	$1,152,863
School District	1,693,500	279,360	1,972,860
Total	$2,760,000	$365,723	$3,125,723

Step 7   Project Total Annual Public Revenue.

In step 7 the analyst turns from examining expenditures to considering revenues. Revenues obtained by the municipality are summed first. These include own source revenues, both taxes (real property tax, sales and gross receipts tax, property transfer tax, etc.) and charges and miscellaneous revenues (interest earnings, fees and permits, user charges, etc.). Changes in state and federal intergovernmental transfers (sales tax, CETA, Revenue Sharing, Community Development Block Grants etc.) are then projected and when added to own source revenues yield the total municipal revenues induced by a population change. School district revenues are calculated in a similar fashion; total own source revenues, both taxes and charges and miscellaneous funds, are estimated, followed by a projection of state and federal intergovernmental assistance. Total revenues equal the sum of the total municipal and school district revenue subtotals. (Revenue projection procedures are explained in detail in Chapters 9 and 10.)

In the Illinois PUD example a number of revenues stand out as being extremely significant. Real property tax revenues are most important; they constitute almost 60 percent and over 80 percent of municipal and school district own source revenues respectively. Revenues from the state sales and motor fuels taxes are the most important element of municipal intergovernmental revenues while state foundation aid dominates school district intergovernmental transfers. These and other revenue resources are detailed in Exhibit 3-6.

Step 8   Calculate the Cost Revenue Impact.

The final calculation is to determine the cost-revenue impact by comparing public costs obtained in step 6 to the public revenues derived in step 7. The cost-revenue impact must be a comparison of either all public costs to all public revenues (if total impact is desired), or real property tax costs to real property tax revenues (if only real property tax impact is opted for). A common mistake of fiscal impact analysis is to attempt to view costs and revenues from two different bases. The most typical error is to compare total costs to real property tax raised revenues. This, in effect, is an incorrect pairing of total public costs and local taxpayer supported revenues. It either overstates costs or understates revenues. The base of comparison must always be similar — either all costs and revenues or some commonly agreed upon portion (i.e., real property tax supported).

Case Study

EXHIBIT 3-6

COMPUTATION SHEET FOR REVENUE PROJECTION*

REVENUE SOURCES			
MUNICIPAL			
I. *Own Source Revenues*			
A. Taxes			
1. Real Property		$ 444,045	
TOTAL TAXES			$ 444,045
B. Charges/Miscellaneous			
1. Interest earnings		$ 92,474	
2. Fees and permits		58,500	
3. Fines/forfeitures		29,929	
4. User charges — specific services		15,717	
5. User charges — sanitation		47,100	
6. User charges — sewerage		96,000	
TOTAL CHARGES/MISCELLANEOUS		$ 336,720	
TOTAL OWN SOURCE REVENUE			$ 780,765
II. *Intergovernmental Transfers*			
A. State			
1. Sales tax		$ 155,977	
2. Income tax		75,900	
3. Motor fuels		100,878	
TOTAL STATE			$ 332,755
B. Federal			
1. Revenue sharing		$ 41,796	
2. CETA		4,300	
3. Anti-recession		2,400	
4. LEAA		4,825	
TOTAL FEDERAL			$ 53,321
TOTAL INTERGOVERNMENTAL TRANSFERS			$ 386,076
TOTAL MUNICIPAL REVENUE			$1,166,841
SCHOOL DISTRICT			
I. *Own Source Revenues*			
A. Taxes			
1. Property tax		$ 846,975	
TOTAL TAXES			$ 846,975
B. Charges/Miscellaneous			
1. Charges/miscellaneous		$ 141,600	
TOTAL CHARGES/MISCELLANEOUS			$ 141,600
TOTAL OWN SOURCES REVENUE			$ 988,575
II. *Intergovernmental Transfers*			
A. State			
1. Foundation aid		$ 531,000	
2. Categorical aid		203,904	
3. State redistributed federal		127,440	
TOTAL STATE			$ 862,344
B. Federal			
1. 0		$ 0	
TOTAL FEDERAL			$ 0
TOTAL INTERGOVERNMENTAL REVENUES			$ 862,344
TOTAL SCHOOL DISTRICT REVENUE			$1,850,919
TOTAL MUNICIPAL/SCHOOL DISTRICT REVENUE			$3,017,760

*For detailed calculations, see Exhibits 10-1 and 10-2 in Chapter 10.

The cost-revenue impact of the PUD example is shown below. The municipality experiences a surplus while the school district exhibits a deficit. Overall, the project incurs a $107,963 deficit because it generates $3,125,723 in total public costs while occasioning $3,017,760 in total public revenues.

Public Body	Total Annual Public Cost	Total Annual Public Revenue	Total Annual Net Fiscal Impact
Municipality	$1,152,863	$1,165,841	$+13,978
School District	1,972,860	1,850,919	-121,941
Total	3,125,723	3,016,760	-107,963

Step 9 Review Draft Report.

Because the Case Study Method relies on local officials' estimates, the analyst should present a copy of the draft fiscal impact analysis to both "key" officials and department heads before it is published or disseminated. This is far from a courtesy step. Staff members can check to see that their estimates of how the locality will respond to growth have been interpreted correctly. Senior officials, such as the city manager, business administrator and the school district superintendent can screen staff estimates and alert the analyst to those projections that are financially or politically unrealizable. The review also allows a final check to make certain all sources of revenue have been included.

Data Requirements

The Case Study Method uses demographic multipliers for school-age children and household size that are available elsewhere in this handbook (Chapter 13). The basic data needed to implement the method — estimates of excess or deficient service capacity and expected local service responses — come from local municipal employees, however. These factors are specific to each locality; they must be obtained through on-site interviews. The inability to rely on national or local averages to project local costs is unique to the Case Study Method. It is the reason for the method's substantial demands of time and cost. The specific data requirements and data sources for each step of the procedure are summarized in Exhibit 3-7.

Sophistication of User

The Case Study Method requires a reasonably sophisticated user. Local staff planners and private planning consultants should, however, be able to use this strategy without major difficulties. Steps 1 through 5 involve basically straightforward interviewing procedures; steps 6 through 8 require simple arithmetic calculations.

A caveat is in order, however. While the Case Study Method can be applied by a user with only moderate quantitative skills, it does take a certain amount of experience, patience, and shrewdness to obtain maximum results. The analyst should be aware of certain potentially serious problems. Identifying all revelant operating and capital services cannot be done simply and quickly. The unsophisticated user may fail to consider the range of local services provided, which could lead to a serious underestimation of cost and an invalid skewing of the cost-revenue projection. This is the reason the initial categorization of municipal functions (step 2) is so important. Another danger is that the novice, by not spending sufficient time with knowledgeable

Case Study

EXHIBIT 3-7
CASE STUDY METHOD: DATA REQUIREMENTS AND SOURCES

Step Number	Data Requirements	Source(s)	Comments
2 – Categorize/delineate public service functions and responsibilities	General scope and nature of local service operations	Municipal administrator or city manager and superintendent of schools	This is a key step for organizing and structuring the Case Study analysis.
	Functional responsibility for providing different services for local municipal and school district services	Municipal administrator or city manager and superintendent of schools	See Exhibit 3-2 for suggested service categorization.
3 – Determine excess and deficient capacity	Excess and deficient capacity in various government services	Municipal and school district department heads	Information on local service standards will likely be more readily available for school district services. Careful, sensitive interviewing is crucial in this step.
4 – Project population and population induced demand	Existing community and school district population (The data are required to determine the correct local service standards and capital-to-operating expenditure ratios, because they are differentiated by community and school district size. The existing population determines the population group for which standards are obtained.)	U.S. Census; local/regional planning department; local school superintendent or business manager	Exact school enrollment data should be available. Try to obtain current local community population estimate.
		Chapter 4, Service Standard Method	
	Multipliers for household size and school age children for different types and size of residential units	Handbook, Chapter 13.	
	Service standards for different public functions differentiated by community size and region	Handbook, Chapter 4.	Be sure to use appropriate standards (by region and by size of locality/school district).
	Capital-to-operating expenditures ratios differentiated by community size and region.	Handbook, Chapter 4.	Use same region/size groups as those utilized to select personnel service standards.

EXHIBIT 3-7
CASE STUDY METHOD: DATA REQUIREMENTS AND SOURCES (Cont'd.)

Step Number	Data Requirements	Source(s)	Comments
5 – Determine anticipated local service response	Projected local reaction to population change in terms of hiring personnel and constructing capital facilities	Municipal and school district department heads	Determine immediate responses of local municipal and school district governments.
6 – Project total annual public costs	Public cost of providing operating and capital services	Local business administrator/town manager, town clerk, school district superintendent, school district or business manager	Obtain line item budget which lists employee salaries, statutory expenditures, and material outlays.
7 – Project total annual public revenues	Municipal and school district real property tax rates	Local tax assessor's office or clerk's office	
	Property assessment procedures	Local -- county tax assessor's offices	
	Federal and state intergovernment revenue	See Part 2	Part 2, Calculating Revenues, contains detailed information about where to obtain data on intergovernmental transfers as well as other sources of revenue.
	For other revenues, see Chapters 9 and 10.		

public officials, may not accurately be able to obtain a feeling for realizable local services levels. Determining local excess and deficient capacity may thus be meaningless, leaving the projection unrefined by local conditions.

Experience and patience are crucial requisites for a successful case study. The method requires a skilled, persistent interviewer who knows exactly which data he seeks and who is aware of the many demands on a public official's time. Such a person can most accurately and effectively conduct a fiscal impact analysis by using the Case Study Method.

Advantages and Disadvantages

Advantages

Richness of Detail   The other fiscal impact analysis methods omit the detailing of manpower and capital facility needs as a prerequisite for assigning costs. The Case Study Method, however, not only predicts the financial consequences of growth, but also assigns the costs of growth to operating and capital facilities by component service category..

Operational Utility   The results of the Case Study, describing the impact of growth in considerable (almost line item) detail, can prove invaluable for public officials who must make certain local services can meet anticipated population changes. Using the Case Study Method, the analyst can reasonably project the number of teachers to be hired, the number of police cars to be purchased, and whether or not a new municipal building is needed — considerations of immense interest to public officials.

Acceptance   The Case Study Method is not nearly as prevalent as the Per Capita Multiplier Method as a fiscal impact technique, due primarily to cost and time considerations. It is, however, extremely well received by both local officials and residents. It deals in the terms and references that they are accustomed to hearing. The school must be expanded, the volunteer fire squad must be upgraded to a small fire department, garbage collection must become a municipal rather than privately provided service, etc. It does not describe fiscal impact only in terms of dollars and cents, derived from unfamiliar per capita or per pupil averages.

Disadvantages

Time and Cost   The Case Study Method is complex and costly. Exhibit 3-8 displays cost requirements for the 3,000 unit PUD example. The method requires extensive interviews and other field work. It is more expensive than the other fiscal impact analysis methods described in this handbook. The Per Capita Multiplier, Comparable City, Proportional Valuation, and Employment Anticipation techniques can be quickly applied at very modest costs, with reasonable estimates of local impact. The Service Standard approach is also easier to undertake, provided certain service ratios are made available to the analyst. (See Chapter 4 of the handbook.) The relative ease and simplicity of these methods stand in contrast to the considerable time and cost necessary to undertake the Case Study Method.

The Accuracy of Public Official Projections   Thomas Muller and others have criticized the Case Study Method as depending on inadequate sources of information.

> A drawback of this [case study] approach is that the estimates may reflect short-term estimates, rather than long-term expenditures. The use of estimates by local officials and department heads to project future service costs has been shown to be inaccurate in a retrospective analysis of the fiscal impact of a large development. Local officials, even taking inflationary pressures into account, significantly underestimated the increase in the community budget.[8]

EXHIBIT 3-8

TIME ESTIMATES TO USE THE CASE STUDY METHOD

Step Number	Activities	Time
1	Meet with local leaders; determine service functional responsibilities	25 hours
2	Categorize and delineate public service functions and responsibilities	10 hours
3	Meet with department heads; determine excess and deficient service capacities and local service levels	80 hours
4	Project population and population-induced demand	6 hours
5	Meet with department heads to determine service response	80 hours
6	Convert manpower/capital facility responses to dollar costs	60 hours
7	Calculate revenues	10 hours
8	Compare costs to revenues to derive impact	2 hours
9	Review draft report	15 hours
Report Preparation	Prepare and reproduce final report	15 hours
		303 hours

The Case Study procedure, proposed here by requiring the analyst to calculate a rough gauge of population-induced demand attempts to mitigate the prescriptive underestimation of local officials. When the analyst interviews public officials the second time he brings with him not only the tallies of service excess or insufficiency but also his estimate of the anticipated service response. The analyst works jointly with the department head to achieve a mutually acceptable prediction of local reaction. It is the multiple interview and the dual effort of analyst and department head which serves to forestall criticism of department predictive weaknesses.

The Case Study Method, properly executed, is the most accurate short-term gauge of fiscal impact available to the analyst. There is currently no better technique to obtain an estimate of short-term public service response, given certain existing conditions of service excess or deficient service capacity than the Case Study Method.

Interpreting Results

The Case Study Method in the example of the 3,000 unit PUD found local service excesses of twenty-seven employees, 63 percent of them in municipal functions. It also uncovered service deficiencies of twenty-eight employees, 82 percent of them in municipal services. Thus, while gross total local personnel excesses equalled deficiencies, excess and deficient capacity was unevenly distributed among various municipal service categories as well as between the municipal and school district functions.

In addition, exclusive use of service standards (population-induced demand) would have shown a local addition of 178 employees after considering excess or deficient capacity. Approximately 40 percent of the additional personnel would have been allocated for municipal purposes. The Case Study Method, in contrast, projects that 20 percent more employees, a total of 219, will be hired and also indicates that about 45 percent of the total will be allocated to municipal services.

The analyst, when he uses the Case Study Method, thus becomes intimately aware not only of excess and deficient local service capacity but also of local priorities for service delivery. While those who commission the analysis pay a significant amount more than most methods for its effectuation, its sensitivity to local service operations is unparalleled.

When he interprets results, the analyst must also be aware of local biases toward growth. Officials in anti- or slow-growth areas could easily exaggerate deficient service capacity and the expected response to population change (in terms of employees hired, capital facilities constructed, etc.) to show that new development will not only be expensive but also will "change the nature of the community." The analyst must be sensitive to such possible biases and should question local estimates of excess and deficient capacity and anticipated service responses that appear inaccurate based on national service standards or his own experience and common sense. He should be wary, for example, of a school superintendent's projection that a new twenty-classroom school will be built to handle seventy-five additional school children. The analyst obviously should not attempt to force what he believes to be the "truth" but he should probe and question where he feels that the data provided are suspect.

NOTES

1. See Chapter 4 of this Handbook.
2. Robert W. Burchell, *Planned Unit Development: New Communities American Style* (New Brunswick, N.J.: Rutgers University Center for Urban Policy Research, 1972).
3. Connecticut Development Group, Inc., *Cost-Revenue Impact Analysis for Residential Developments* (Hartford, Conn.: Connecticut Development Group - Research Corporation of Connecticut, 1975).
4. Julian Simon, *Basic Research Methods in Social Science: The Art of Empirical Investigations* (New York: Random House, 1969), p.298.
5. See Chapter 4 and Appendix II of this Handbook.
6. Connecticut Development Group, Inc., *Cost-Revenue Impact Analysis for Residential Developments*.
7. U.S. Department of Commerce, Bureau of the Census, *1972 Census of Governments* (Washington, D.C.: Government Printing Office, 1974).
8. Thomas Muller, *Fiscal Impacts of Growth* (Washington, D.C.: Urban Institute, 1972).

4

SERVICE STANDARD FISCAL IMPACT METHOD

Background

The Service Standard Method uses average costing to project the impact of population change on local municipal and school district costs and revenues. The method has been used since the efficiency and time-motion studies of the 1940s; more recently it has been utilized to predict the local fiscal impact of proposed development, land use alternatives, and annexation[1] (See Chapter 1). Although it has been used in one form or another for three decades, it has never been as prevalent as either the Per Capita Multiplier or Case Study Methods. The primary reason is that there is no simple way to obtain and manipulate national standards for different service categories of municipal and school district operating and capital expenditures.

Estimates of ideal service levels are available from multiple sources[2] — trade associations, unions, equipment suppliers, etc. — for various aspects of service operations from manpower commitments and capital facilities to the smallest detail of service equipment. This handbook avoids the endless stream of standards and relies instead on the reporting source for municipal operations, the U.S. Census of Governments, to obtain general averages of manpower and capital facility service levels for municipalities and school districts of similar size and geographic location.

The Service Standard Method, as presented here, relies on average employment levels and a relationship of annual capital-to-operating expenditures to estimate the expected increment in local municipal and school district expenditures. These ratios, drawn from a national sample and expressed per thousand population, differ for communities of varying size* and by region.**

---

*(Less than 2,500; 2,500 to 4,999, 5,000 to 9,999, 10,000 to 24,999, 25,000 to 49,999, 50,000 to 99,999, 100,000 to 499,999, 500,000 to 999,999 and 1,000,000 and over.) U.S. Department of Commerce, Bureau of the Census, *Census of Governments — Public Employment* (Washington, D.C.: Government Printing Office, 1972).

**Northeast, North Central, South and West.

In brief, this technique, as the Case Study approach, determines the total number of additional employees by service function (financial administration, general control, police, fire, highways, sewerage, sanitation, water supply, parks and recreation, and libraries*) that will be required as the result of growth. The analyst determines the local operating cost for additional personnel adding local operating outlays (salary, statutory and equipment expenditures) per employee by service function (e.g., $14,500 per policeman, $13,900 per fireman) to an annual expenditure for capital facilities specific to the service function. The annual capital expenditure is obtained through the use of capital-to-operating service ratios, derived from Census information, and applied to the local total operating cost per employee.

To illustrate, a Northeastern city of 33,000 residents will grow to 38,000 as a result of a new 1,600-unit single-family subdivision. Using service ratios of 2.33 policemen and 1.88 firemen per 1,000 population^3 (for Northeastern municipalities of 25,000 — 49,999), if the community follows average service patterns specific to its population size and location, a service demand for 11.7 policemen (2.33 × 5.0) and 9.4 firemen (1.88 × 5.0) will be created locally as a result of the development. At the previously stated local average operating cost per policeman ($14,500) and fireman ($13,900), the operating costs assignable to the development for just these two functional areas is $300,310 ($169,650 [$14,500 × 11.7] + $130,660 [$13,900 × 9.4]). Using a 0.025 capital-to-operating ratio (Northeastern municipalities of 25,000 - 49,999 population) for police capital expenditures and applying this to the product of the number of policemen to be added locally and the average local operations cost per policeman will add $4,241 ($169,650 × 0.025); a 0.005 capital-to-operations ratio for fire protection capital expenditures, similarly applied to the product of the additional firemen, and the average local operations cost per firemen will add an additional $653 ($130,660 × 0.005). The total assignable cost (operating plus capital debt service) to the growth increment for these two functions is $305,204. This procedure is repeated for each functional area listed above to ascertain total costs assignable.

Revenues are obtained in a similar manner for all fiscal impact prediction techniques. (See Chapters 9 and 10). Municipal own source revenues, including both taxes (real property, business franchise) and charges/miscellaneous revenues (fines, sanitation user charges, interest earnings, etc.) are estimated, followed by a projection of both state (state sales and income tax revenues, etc.) and federal (revenue sharing, CETA, etc.) intergovernmental transfers. Adding all municipal own source revenues and intergovernmental transfers yields total municipal revenues. School district revenues are similarly projected: first, determining own source revenues, then projecting intergovernmental transfers. Combining the two subcategories yields total school district revenues. The sum of total municipal and school district revenues is total public revenues. When revenues are matched against costs, a surplus or deficit is derived indicating whether the new growth will be a financial plus or drain on the municipality and school district.

Application

The decision to use the Service Standard Method depends on several local conditions: the type of community where the analysis is undertaken, the study's objectives, the type of analyst (a private consultant or a public staff planner), and the resources available to the analyst.

The Service Standard approach is most useful in communities where the existing service capacity is closely related to existing service demand so that there exists neither considerable excess or deficient capacity. Mid-size (10,000 to 50,000 population), moderately growing suburban areas or slower growing second-order cities are the "middle of the road" locations for which this

---

*The "common" municipal functions, according to the U.S. Census of Governments. See Glossary.

technique is most suited.[4] The Service Standard approach uses mean employment levels and median capital-to-operating service ratios for communities of varying size to analyze fiscal impact. More data are available about mid-sized, moderately growing communities than about the extreme cases so that the mean service standards and median capital-to-operating service ratios are more reliable. Small communities with rapidly growing populations and large cities of declining size are likely to experience significant positive or negative cost responses to growth.

These fluctuations do not readily lend themselves to the averaging of the Service Standard approach. Thus, even though average service levels are provided here for extreme size municipalities, the specific response for a particular small/high growth or large/slow growth community may differ substantially from the indicated average for the group. As in all cases, however, desired results and resources dictate method deployment. If sufficient resources are not available to employ the Case Study Method in communities at the extreme ranges of population size and growth rate, or greater detailing is desired than is available from the Comparable City Method, the Service Standard Method may be applied. The analyst must realize, however, that at the extremes, the basic service standards data are at their weakest.

The objective of the fiscal impact analysis will also influence whether or not to use the Service Standard approach. This method *cannot* be used for investigating the fiscal impact of solely nonresidential proposals because there are simply no accepted personnel service ratios — number of policemen per 1,000 square feet of commercial space, number of sanitation workers per 10,000 square feet of industry — pertaining to exclusively nonresidential use. The Service Standard Method assumes that the costs to service nonresidential uses accompanying residential growth are included within the residential segment's assigned costs. Inherent in the average manpower levels for each service category by community size and regional location are manpower increments for the level of nonresidential use which would normally accompany residential development of a certain magnitude.

On the other hand, the Service Standard technique is particularly useful for general fiscal planning and for projecting the fiscal impact of annexation for two reasons. First, personnel costs are the largest share of public service expenditures, and if an estimate of future personnel commitments is available, the analyst also has a reasonable idea of future gross expenditures. Second, pinpointing the number and type of employees that must be hired gives the fiscal planner insight into specific future expenditures by service function — i.e., $100,000 for policemen, associated equipment and capital expenditures; $250,000 for teachers, associated equipment and capital expenditures. Except for the Case Study Method, which is much more costly and time-consuming, no other fiscal impact projection method generates information on public personnel requirements. The Per Capita Multiplier or Comparable City Methods, for example, may project that a 1,000 unit single-family development will cause a $100,000 annual operating deficit, but the information is of little use to the fiscal planner who wants to know how the deficit is distributed between municipal and school district services.

The Service Standard Method is also very useful in situations where the amount and composition (particularly school children) of the additional population that will be generated by growth is only generally known or must be estimated. This type of data insufficiency is most frequently found in the annexation, land use alternative or general fiscal planning situations where often only general information is known about the population to be annexed or the growth alternatives to be decided upon. The analyst might be told, for example, that the potential annexation site will contain five square miles and will add approximately 8,000 residents to a community of 16,000. To project the number of school children in the annexation, the analyst would have to employ the last U.S. Census to obtain for the geographical area to be annexed, the proportion of residents aged 5 to 18 of the total (8,000) population and use this as a rough estimate of forthcoming school-age children. The Service Standard technique can be used with these types of data, because it demands only rough approximations of the anticipated municipal population and school district size. (The rough projections suffice as relatively wide bands of community and school district populations are used to group service standards.) Using such imprecise data is in contrast to the requirements of other methods, particularly the Per Capita Multiplier and Case Study approaches.

The type of practitioner also influences whether or not the Service Standard approach is employed. Unlike the Case Study Method which may best be carried out by public staff planners with firsthand knowledge of local service operations, the Service Standard strategy may readily be used by someone who is not familiar with local operations. The method does not require special data or information that may be difficult to obtain. In this respect it is similiar to the Comparable City and Per Capita Multiplier approaches, which may be undertaken from afar at modest expenditures of both time and money.

Basic Assumptions

A fundamental assumption of the Service Standard approach is that, over the long run average *existing* service levels for both manpower and capital facilities of comparable cities can be used to assign costs to future development. (The strategy further assumes that appropriate groups of comparable cities can be identified.)

Another premise of the technique is that service levels for both manpower and capital facilities vary according to the community's population. This has long been established in cost-revenue analysis literature — first by Fabricant, then successively by Brazer, Booms, Gabler and Weicher.[5] Each has found that both small and very large communities expend more per capita than is the case for their mid-size counterparts. So distinctive are these variations in expenditure patterns that in assigning "standards" of service, the analyst must be sensitive to changes in service levels as a function of population size.

A further assumption is that after population size, geographic location also affects public service levels. Again in the cost-revenue analysis literature this has been well documented, first in an essay by Horowitz and more recently in the writing of Libera, using a national single equation regression model.[6] This latter factor of location is on a par with growth rate, and both fall second to population size in explaining the variation surrounding local expenditure patterns. The choice of geographical location in the Service Standard Method as an accompaniment to population size is prompted by the availability of service standards listed in the U.S. Census of Governments and differentiated by municipal and school district size and region.

A fourth and final premise is that the average servicing levels of the population group appropriate for the local municipality and school district *at the time* of development, annexation, zone change, etc., are those that should be used to assign the service load to the new development. This basically follows the average costing view of development impact and states, in effect, that if servicing levels are to be assigned to a future population increment, current costs expressed on a per unit base are the most accurate description of future burden.

Procedures

As stated above, previous analyses using the Service Standard approach have relied on service ratios suggested by various national professional groups,[7] but this handbook uses employment and capital-to-operating ratios actually in effect and reported by the 1972 U.S. Census of Governments. Professional standards were not used for a number of reasons. First, they are based on what the national groups think are *desirable* levels of service; these suggested ratios may or may not reflect actual conditions. Since we are interested in potential local response it is the *actual* performance ratio (as indicated by the Census) rather than the *suggested* standard that should pertain. Second, different professional groups may suggest different standards for the same service category. Third, professional groups may not suggest standards for infrequently used services (housing and urban renewal personnel, for example). In contrast, service ratios available from the U.S. Census of Governments offer three distinct advantages. First, these service levels reflect the *actual* commitment of manpower to different services by communities throughout the country. Second, service levels for different functions can be refined according to size of community and regional location. Third, the Census service ratios are updated every four years. Communities may opt for different levels of service from the "norms" presented here. However, as a first measuring stick they are most useful. The step-by-step procedures of the Service Standard approach is summarized in Exhibit 4-1 and are elaborated in the following sections.

Step 1   Determine Population and Student Increase Resulting from Growth.

It is important to obtain at least a rough idea of the increase of total population and school children that will result from growth. This information is basic to the determination of the number of employees to be added as well as the annual commitment for capital expenditures.

The rough population and student increases employed as the demand segment of the Service Standard approach can be approximated by using the general demographic multipliers or the more specialized multipliers of Chapter 13. Since in the situations in which the Service Standard Method is employed (land use alternatives, general fiscal planning) specific data on exact bedroom configuration of housing units that will be developed or exist on land to be annexed (i.e., 100 three-bedroom single-family homes, 200 one-bedroom garden apartments, etc.) are usually not provided, the analyst must employ the blended (for all bedroom configurations) household size and school-age children multipliers for generic types of housing (e.g., single-family houses, garden apartments, townhouses).

EXHIBIT 4-1

SERVICE STANDARD FISCAL IMPACT METHOD: SUMMARY OF PROCEDURES

Step Number	Analysis/Actions
1	Using general multipliers for household and school-age children, determine population and student increase resulting from growth.
2	Using service ratios for communities of different regions and sizes project number of incremental public employees resulting from growth.
3	Calculate average operating expenses per employee by service category by dividing total operating expenses per service category by the total number of employees in that function attributable to growth.
4	Project total annual operating costs by multiplying average operating expenses per worker by the number of employees attributable to growth.
5	Project total annual capital costs by multiplying capital-to-operating expenditure ratios by total annual operating cost.
6	Project total annual public costs by adding total annual operating expenses to total annual capital expenses.
7	Project total annual public revenues.
8	Calculate the cost-revenue surplus or deficit by comparing projected total revenues to projected total costs.

To illustrate, the current resident population of a Georgia community is 16,000; school population is 4,200.* Three possible development schemes are being contemplated for a 1,000 acre area in the community. The first alternative is to continue the existing zoning of single-family homes on one-half acre lots (allowing 2,000 units). The second alternative is mixed-use development at five units per acre according to the following distribution: 30 percent single-family houses (1,500 units), 50 percent townhouses (2,500 units), 20 percent condominiums (1,000 units). The third alternative is to keep 300 acres for open space and build garden apartments at ten units per each remaining acre (7,000 units). The calculation below shows the projections needed to estimate resident and student populations generated by each of the three alternatives. They are based on the blended demographic multipliers for a given housing type.

Development Alternative	Number/Type Housing (1)	Household Size Multiplier (2)	School-Age Children Multiplier (3)	Total Residents[1] (4)	Total School-Age Children[2] (5)
1	2,000 single-family homes	3.775	1.130	7,550	1,989 (2,260)[3]
2	2,500 townhouses	3.027	.838	7,568	2,095
	1,500 single-family homes	3.775	1.130	5,663	1,695
	1,000 condominiums	2.614	.982	2,614	982
				15,845	4,199 (4,772)[3]
3	7,000 garden apartments	2.632	.358	18,424	2,205 (2,506)[3]

Notes: [1] Column (1) times column (2).
[2] Column (1) times column (3).
[3] The figure in parentheses is the actual subtotal of the number of students projected. Since in this particular area, 12 percent of the school-age children attend private schools, projected total pupils are multiplied by 88 percent to reflect the anticipated burden on the public schools.

Step 2   *Project Number of Public Employees Resulting From Growth.*

To estimate the future number of public employees by public service category, the analyst must utilize the service ratios for different size communities in various regions of the county. These base data are tabulated for the analyst by municipal and school district service functions in Exhibits 4-2 through 4-5. Each displays ratios for service functions by region, i.e., Northeast, North Central, South and West.** Service functions are displayed vertically; the municipal and school district size grouping appear horizontally. Both the functional categories of public service and the jurisdictional population groupings are synonymous with reporting categories used by the U.S. Census of Governments.

---

*For a full description, see Chapter 1.
**The states which comprise each region are listed in Exhibit 13-3 and are indicated in Exhibits 4-2 through 4-5.

Service Standard

EXHIBIT 4-2
FULL-TIME PUBLIC EMPLOYEES PER 1,000 POPULATION AND PUPILS FOR MUNICIPAL AND SCHOOL DISTRICT SERVICES, BY MUNICIPAL/SCHOOL DISTRICT SIZE AND REGION OF THE UNITED STATES[1] (NORTHEAST REGION[2])

Municipal Population Size (Number of Residents)	(Use for Municipal[3] Functions)	Less Than 2,500	2,500 to 4,999	5,000 to 9,999	10,000 to 24,999	25,000 to 49,999	50,000 to 99,999	100,000 to 199,999	200,000 to 299,999	300,000 to 499,999	500,000 to 999,999	1,000,000 And Over
MUNICIPAL FUNCTIONS												
GENERAL GOVERNMENT												
Finance Administration		0.50	0.36	0.33	0.45	0.48	0.49	0.58	0.29	0.48	0.73	0.55
General Control		0.63	0.66	0.62	0.61	0.59	0.57	0.65	0.73	0.79	1.27	1.36
PUBLIC SAFETY												
Police		1.26	1.77	1.86	2.08	2.33	2.45	3.02	3.09	4.13	4.11	4.26
Fire		0.09	0.15	0.28	0.99	1.88	2.33	2.68	2.49	2.70	2.73	1.81
PUBLIC WORKS												
Highways		1.29	1.22	1.97	1.15	1.07	0.95	0.98	0.57	0.26	0.97	0.82
Sewerage		—	0.32	0.28	0.32	0.30	0.39	0.40	0.18	0.41	0.09	0.29
Sanitation		—	0.31	0.41	0.59	0.67	0.75	0.91	0.97	1.80	0.62	1.60
Water Supply		—	0.34	0.29	0.40	0.54	0.57	0.58	0.58	0.75	0.53	0.41
RECREATION AND CULTURE												
Parks and Recreation		—	0.15	0.14	0.34	0.75	0.59	0.88	0.76	0.83	1.00	0.85
Libraries		—	0.04	0.09	0.26	0.33	0.39	0.47	0.87	0.35	1.08	0.45

SCHOOL DISTRICT FUNCTION						
Primary and Secondary Schools		86		81		85
School District Enrollment (Number of Students)	(Use for Education[4])	Less than 1,200		1,200–2,999		3,000 and over

Notes: [1]These figures are read as follows: In a municipality whose population falls between 2,500 and 4,999, there are, on the average, 1.77 full-time employees in the police department per 1,000 population. In a school district whose enrollment (pupils) falls between 1,200 and 2,999, there are, on the average, 81 full-time employees in primary, secondary, and special education services per 1,000 pupils.
[2]Includes Connecticut, Maine, Massachusetts, New Hampshire, New Jersey, New York, Pennsylvania, Rhode Island, Vermont.
[3]Use the multipliers above the dotted line for municipal functions.
[4]Use the multipliers below the dotted line for school district functions.

Source: U.S. Census of Governments, 1972.

EXHIBIT 4-3

FULL-TIME PUBLIC EMPLOYEES PER 1,000 POPULATION AND PUPILS FOR MUNICIPAL AND SCHOOL DISTRICT SERVICES, BY MUNICIPAL/SCHOOL DISTRICT SIZE AND REGION OF THE UNITED STATES[1] (NORTH CENTRAL REGION[2])

Municipal Population Size (Number of Residents)	(Use for Municipal[3] Functions)	Less Than 2,500	2,500 to 4,999	5,000 to 9,999	10,000 to 24,999	25,000 to 49,999	50,000 to 99,999	100,000 to 199,999	200,000 to 299,999	300,000 to 499,999	500,000 to 999,999	1,000,000 And Over
MUNICIPAL FUNCTIONS												
GENERAL GOVERNMENT												
Finance Administration		0.22	0.35	0.34	0.30	0.29	0.29	0.34	0.38	0.34	0.42	0.34
General Control		0.83	0.74	0.74	0.57	0.49	0.48	0.54	0.72	0.68	0.70	0.48
PUBLIC SAFETY												
Police		1.16	1.83	1.88	1.72	—	1.72	1.95	2.03	2.35	3.24	4.27
Fire		0.89	0.49	0.61	0.93	1.26	1.32	1.56	1.51	1.62	1.58	1.37
PUBLIC WORKS												
Highways		1.06	1.07	0.98	0.81	0.74	0.74	0.70	0.94	1.25	0.85	0.82
Sewerage		0.01	0.45	0.39	0.40	0.36	0.31	0.43	0.57	0.60	0.41	0.20
Sanitation		0.01	0.33	0.38	0.42	0.55	0.47	0.44	0.82	0.70	0.89	1.11
Water Supply		0.01	0.62	0.63	0.56	0.48	0.50	0.59	1.08	0.77	0.83	0.89
RECREATION AND CULTURE												
Parks and Recreation		0.01	0.22	0.31	0.31	0.44	0.59	0.74	0.82	1.05	0.85	0.48
Libraries		—	0.14	0.17	0.15	0.26	0.22	0.23	0.18	0.34	0.28	0.42

SCHOOL DISTRICT FUNCTION						
Primary and Secondary Schools		81		74	75	
School District Enrollment (Number of Students)	(Use for Education)[4]	Less than 1,200		1,200–2,999	3,000 and over	

Notes: [1]These figures are read as follows: In a municipality whose population falls between 2,500 and 4,999, there are, on the average, 1.83 full-time employees in the police department per 1,000 population. In a school district whose enrollment (pupils) falls between 1,200 and 2,999, there are, on the average, 74 full-time employees in primary, secondary and special education services per 1,000 pupils.
[2]Includes Illinois, Indiana, Iowa, Kansas, Michigan, Minnesota, Missouri, Nebraska, North Dakota, Ohio, South Dakota, Wisconsin.
[3]Use the multipliers above the dotted line for municipal functions.
[4]Use the multipliers below the dotted line for school district functions.

Source: U.S. Census of Governments, 1972.

Service Standard

EXHIBIT 4-4
FULL-TIME PUBLIC EMPLOYEES PER 1,000 POPULATION AND PUPILS FOR MUNICIPAL AND SCHOOL DISTRICT SERVICES,
BY MUNICIPAL/SCHOOL DISTRICT SIZE AND REGION OF THE UNITED STATES[1] (SOUTHERN REGION[2])

Municipal Population Size (Number of Residents)	(Use for Municipal[3] Functions)	Less Than 2,500	2,500 to 4,999	5,000 to 9,999	10,000 to 24,999	25,000 to 49,999	50,000 to 99,999	100,000 to 199,999	200,000 to 299,999	300,000 to 499,999	500,000 to 999,999	1,000,000 And Over
MUNICIPAL FUNCTIONS												
GENERAL GOVERNMENT												
Finance Administration		0.33	0.46	0.43	0.46	0.52	0.57	0.44	0.70	0.38	0.57	0.22
General Control		0.67	0.81	0.77	0.58	0.53	0.55	0.49	0.48	0.51	1.04	0.25
PUBLIC SAFETY												
Police		1.54	1.96	2.14	2.01	2.01	2.17	2.32	2.28	2.29	3.83	2.03
Fire		0.41	0.62	0.91	1.24	1.64	1.75	1.76	1.72	1.76	1.91	1.69
PUBLIC WORKS												
Highways		0.80	1.09	1.25	1.12	1.00	0.95	0.92	0.97	0.78	0.87	0.53
Sewerage		—	0.42	0.42	0.53	0.53	0.52	0.41	0.70	0.56	0.56	0.35
Sanitation		0.02	1.38	1.51	1.47	1.44	1.44	1.55	1.35	1.25	1.49	0.63
Water Supply		0.01	0.78	0.83	0.94	0.99	0.95	0.90	0.72	1.02	1.06	0.78
RECREATION AND CULTURE												
Parks and Recreation		—	0.16	0.37	0.58	0.82	1.00	0.96	1.29	1.12	1.22	0.56
Libraries		—	0.05	0.08	0.12	0.17	0.20	0.26	1.33	0.31	0.51	0.27
SCHOOL DISTRICT FUNCTION												
Primary and Secondary Schools			77				78				78	
School District Enrollment (Number of Students)[4]	(Use for Education)[4]		Less than 1,200				1,200–2,999				3,000 and over	

Notes: [1]These figures are read as follows: In a municipality whose population falls between 2,500 and 4,999 there are, on the average, 1.96 full-time employees in the police department per 1,000 population. In a school district whose enrollment (pupils) falls between 1,200 and 2,999 there are, on the average, 78 full-time employees in primary, secondary and special education services per 1,000 pupils.
[2]Includes Alabama, Arkansas, Delaware, Florida, Georgia, Kentucky, Louisiana, Maryland, Mississippi, North Carolina, Oklahoma, South Carolina, Tennessee, Texas, Virginia, Washington, D.C., West Virginia.
[3]Use the multipliers above the dotted line for municipal functions.
[4]Use the multipliers below the dotted line for school district functions.

Source: U.S. Census of Government, 1972.

EXHIBIT 4-5

FULL-TIME PUBLIC EMPLOYEES PER 1,000 POPULATION AND PUPILS FOR MUNICIPAL AND SCHOOL DISTRICT SERVICES, BY MUNICIPAL/SCHOOL DISTRICT SIZE AND REGION OF THE UNITED STATES[1] (WESTERN REGION[2])

Municipal Population Size (Number of Residents)	(Use for Municipal[3] Functions)	Less Than 2,500	2,500 to 4,999	5,000 to 9,999	10,000 to 24,999	25,000 to 49,999	50,000 to 99,999	100,000 to 199,999	200,000 to 299,999	300,000 to 499,999	500,000 to 999,999	1,000,000 And Over
MUNICIPAL FUNCTIONS												
GENERAL GOVERNMENT												
Finance Administration		0.46	0.37	0.41	0.43	0.37	0.31	0.48	0.41	0.29	0.56	0.25
General Control		1.00	1.06	0.84	0.65	0.50	0.45	0.56	0.54	0.43	0.98	0.68
PUBLIC SAFETY												
Police		2.00	2.27	2.14	1.83	1.73	1.69	2.08	2.39	2.24	2.68	3.47
Fire		0.85	0.60	0.81	1.12	1.10	1.14	1.51	1.57	1.51	1.62	1.18
PUBLIC WORKS												
Highways		1.48	1.14	0.94	0.76	0.66	0.66	0.87	0.46	0.98	0.98	0.60
Sewerage		—	0.38	0.32	0.28	0.21	0.18	0.22	0.40	0.30	0.32	0.22
Sanitation		0.01	0.58	0.53	0.38	0.33	0.24	0.46	1.16	0.25	0.70	0.43
Water Supply		0.01	0.65	0.73	0.45	0.45	0.37	0.63	0.72	0.45	1.01	1.15
RECREATION AND CULTURE												
Parks and Recreation		—	0.45	0.50	0.72	0.70	0.83	1.01	1.33	1.40	1.36	0.99
Libraries		—	0.13	0.20	0.21	0.29	0.30	0.45	0.46	0.35	0.42	0.38

SCHOOL DISTRICT FUNCTION	(Use for Education)[4]								
Primary and Secondary Schools		81		Less than 1,200		80	1,200–2,999	70	3,000 and over
School District Enrollment (Number of Students)									

Notes: [1]These figures read as follows: In a municipality whose population size falls between 2,500 and 4,999, there are, on the average, 2.27 full-time employees in the police department per 1,000 population. In a school district whose enrollment (pupils) falls between 1,200 and 2,999, there are, on the average, 80 full-time employees in primary, secondary and special education services per 1,000 pupils.
[2]Includes Alaska, Arizona, California, Colorado, Hawaii, Idaho, Montana, Nevada, New Mexico, Oregon, Utah, Washington, Wyoming.
[3]Use the multipliers above the dotted line for municipal functions.
[4]Use the multipliers below the dotted line for school district functions.

Source: U.S. Census of Government, 1972.

Service Standard

The exhibits which list manpower levels by category of municipal and school district service are easy to use. First, the exhibit pertaining to the region being studied is selected. In the land use alternative example, since the study area is Georgia, the exhibit containing service characteristics for the Southern region should be selected. (Exhibit 4-4.) Second, the appropriate community size grouping must be chosen. In the land use alternative case, growth is being considered in a community with a current population of 16,000 and a school enrollment of 4,200. The analyst therefore uses the municipal service employment standards for the 10,000 to 24,999 category and school district employment ratios for the over-3,000 group. Thus, for municipal services the following employee ratios per 1,000 population are used: 0.46 financial administration staff members, 2.01 policemen, 1.24 firemen, etc. For school district services the ratio of 78 employees per 1,000 pupils is used. The same manpower ratios are used for all land use alternatives being considered. The differential burden which pertains to one land use alternative versus another is based on the different mix of residents/students each alternative introduces to the community.

After he finds the correct ratios, the analyst projects the additional employees required to accommodate the various development alternatives by *multiplying the service ratios by the added population increments.* To do so, the service standards and the additional population must be expressed in the same increments, in thousands (000) of additional residents and students. To illustrate, development alternative 1 adds 7,550 new residents locally. Consequently, the service standards shown in column 3, Exhibit 4-6, which are the ratios per thousand additional population, are multiplied by 7.550 to obtain the projected number of full-time employees by functional public service needed to accommodate the 2,000 single-family houses. For instance, the analyst determines that 3.47 financial administration staff members will be needed (0.46 × 7.550). development alternative 1 also adds 1,989 public school-age children; at a ratio of 78 school district employees per 1,000 students, an additional 155.14 school district employees (78 × 1.989) are needed. The remaining manpower estimates (in column 4 of Exhibit 4-6) are derived in the same way.

These calculations, while simple, should not be followed blindly. The analyst must make certain that the community provides basically the same range of services for which service ratios are presented. Small localities often fail to offer a local library, yet ratios for them are presented in the exhibits. A community may support a health department, yet ratios for this service are not included. For most examples, the Census of Governments information may be followed without augmentation or deletion. It provides an estimate of individual impact and certainly is sufficient for relative comparisons. The analyst can modify the ratios to suit a specific community as the need arises.

The analyst must also categorize line-item functions within the confines of the Census of Governments definitions of the commonly provided municipal functions. An example of such categorization is shown in Exhibit 4-7. The analyst should use these broad functional definitions, because they are the categories for which service ratios are being provided. This use is particularly important for the next step, determining average operating expenditures per employee by the standard categories of municipal service. Average salary and expense slotting must parallel Census manpower reporting categories.

Step 3 *Calculate Average Operating Expenses (Salary, Statutory and Material Costs) per Employee.*

In this step, the analyst converts the incremental personnel projections derived in step 2 into operating costs by calculating the average salary, the statutory and material costs per employee, by service function. He then multiplies these expenditures by the total estimated number of additional

EXHIBIT 4-6

USING THE SERVICE STANDARD METHOD TO PROJECT THE FISCAL IMPACT OF LAND USE ALTERNATIVES: LAND USE ALTERNATIVE 1

	Step 1	Step 1	Step 2	Step 2	Step 3	Step 4	Step 5	Step 5	Step 6
	Anticipated Population and Public School-Age Children[1] (1)	Governmental Functions (2)	Manpower Ratios for Population Size Group and Region[2] (3)	Estimated Number of Future Employees[3] (4)	Operating Expenses Per Future Employee[4] (5)	Total Annual Operating Costs by Function[5] (6)	Capital-to Operating Ratios for Population Size Group and Region[6] (7)	Total Annual Capital Costs by Function[7] (8)	Total Annual Public Costs (Operating + Capital) by Function[8] (9)
LAND USE ALTERNATIVE 1	7,550 Population 1,989 Public School-Age Children								
		MUNICIPAL FUNCTIONS							
		GENERAL GOVERNMENT							
		Finance Administration	.46	3.47	$14,333	$ 49,736	.000	- - -	$ 49,736
		General Control	.58	4.38	9,736	42,644	.000	- - -	42,644
		PUBLIC SAFETY							
		Police	2.01	15.18	13,737	208,528	.054	$ 11,261	219,789
		Fire	1.24	9.36	14,205	132,959	.026	3,457	136,416
		PUBLIC WORKS							
		Highways	1.12	8.46	12,942	109,489	.199	21,788	131,277
		Sewerage	.53	4.00	13,267	53,068	.147	7,801	60,869
		Sanitation	1.47	11.10	11,580	128,538	.078	10,026	138,564
		Water Supply	.94	7.10	12,904	91,618	.226	20,706	112,324
		RECREATION AND CULTURE							
		Parks and Recreation	.58	4.38	8,883	38,908	.097	3,774	42,682
		Libraries	.12	.91	9,282	8,447	.000	- - -	8,447
		Total Municipal				863,935		78,813	942,748
		SCHOOL DISTRICT							
		Primary/Secondary Schools	78	155.14	11,800	1,830,652	.073	133,638	1,964,290
		Total School District				1,830,652		133,638	1,964,290
		TOTAL MUNICIPAL AND SCHOOL DISTRICT				2,694,587		212,451	2,907,038

Notes:
[1] See page 72.
[2] See Exhibit 4-4.
[3] Anticipated population (7,550) and (1,989) public school-age children (expressed in 000s as 7.550 and 1.989, respectively) multiplied by service ratios shown in column 3.
[4] See Exhibit 4-8.
[5] Column 4 multiplied by column 5.
[6] See Exhibit 4-11.
[7] Column 6 multiplied by column 7.
[8] Column 6 plus column 8.

Source: U.S. Census of Governments, 1972.

Service Standard 79

EXHIBIT 4-6 (Cont'd.)

USING THE SERVICE STANDARD METHOD TO PROJECT THE FISCAL IMPACT OF LAND USE ALTERNATIVES: LAND USE ALTERNATIVE 2

	Step 1	Step 1	Step 2	Step 2	Step 3	Step 4	Step 5	Step 5	Step 6
	Anticipated Population and Public School-Age Children[1] (1)	Government Functions (2)	Manpower Ratios for Population Size Group and Region[2] (3)	Estimated Number of Future Employees[3] (4)	Operating Expenses Per Future Employee[4] (5)	Total Annual Operating Costs by Function[5] (6)	Capital-to-Operating Ratios for Population Size Group and Region[6] (7)	Total Annual Capital Costs by Function[7] (8)	Total Annual Public Costs (Operating + Capital by Function[8] (9)
LAND USE ALTERNATIVE 2	15,845 Population 4,199 Public School-Age Children	*MUNICIPAL FUNCTIONS*							
		GENERAL GOVERNMENT							
		Finance Administration	.46	7.29	$14,333	$ 104,488	.000	- - -	$ 104,488
		General Control	.58	9.19	9,736	89,474	.000	- - -	89,474
		PUBLIC SAFETY							
		Police	2.01	31.85	13,737	437,523	.054	$ 23,626	461,149
		Fire	1.24	19.65	14,205	279,128	.026	7,257	286,385
		PUBLIC WORKS							
		Highways	1.12	17.75	12,942	229,721	.199	45,714	275,435
		Sewerage	.53	8.40	13,267	111,443	.147	16,382	127,825
		Sanitation	1.47	23.29	11,580	269,698	.078	21,036	290,734
		Water Supply	.94	14.89	12,904	192,141	.226	43,424	235,565
		RECREATION AND CULTURE							
		Parks and Recreation	.58	9.19	8,883	81,635	.097	7,919	89,554
		Libraries	.12	1.90	9,282	17,636	.000	- - -	17,636
		Total Municipal				1,812,887		165,358	1,978,245
		SCHOOL DISTRICT							
		Primary/Secondary Schools	.78	327.52	11,800	3,864,736	.073	282,126	4,146,862
		Total School District				3,864,736		282,126	4,146,862
		TOTAL MUNICIPAL AND SCHOOL DISTRICT				5,677,623		447,484	6,125,107

Notes: [1] See page 104.
[2] See Exhibit 4-4.
[3] Anticipated (15,845) population and (4,199) public school-age children (expressed in 000s as 15.845 and 4.199 respectively) multiplied by service ratios shown in column 3.
[4] See Exhibit 4-8.
[5] Column 4 multiplied by column 5.
[6] See Exhibit 4-11.
[7] Column 6 multiplied by column 7.
[8] Column 6 plus column 8.

Source: U.S. Census of Government, 1972.

EXHIBIT 4-6 (Cont'd.)

USING THE SERVICE STANDARD METHOD TO PROJECT THE FISCAL IMPACT OF LAND USE ALTERNATIVES: LAND USE ALTERNATIVE 3

	Step 1	Step 1	Step 2	Step 2	Step 3	Step 4	Step 5	Step 5	Step 6
	Anticipated Population and Public School-Age Children[1] (1)	Government Functions (2)	Manpower Ratios for Population Size Group and Region[2] (3)	Estimated Number of Future Employees[3] (4)	Operating Expenses Per Future Employee[4] (5)	Total Annual Operating Costs by Function[5] (6)	Capital-to-Operating Ratios for Population Size Group and Region[6] (7)	Total Annual Capital Costs by Function[7] (8)	Total Annual Public Costs (Operating + Capital) by Function[8] (9)
LAND USE ALTERNATIVE 3	18,424 Population 2,205 Public School-Age Children	**MUNICIPAL FUNCTIONS**							
		GENERAL GOVERNMENT							
		Finance Administration	.46	8.48	$14,333	$ 121,544	.000	---	$ 121,544
		General Control	.58	10.69	9,736	104,078	.000	---	104,078
		PUBLIC SAFETY							
		Police	2.01	37.03	13,737	508,681	.054	$ 27,469	536,150
		Fire	1.24	22.85	14,205	324,584	.026	8,439	333,023
		PUBLIC WORKS							
		Highways	1.12	20.63	12,942	266,993	.199	53,132	320,125
		Sewerage	.53	9.76	13,267	129,486	.147	19,034	148,520
		Sanitation	1.47	27.08	11,580	313,586	.078	24,460	338,046
		Water Supply	.94	17.32	12,904	223,497	.226	50,510	274,007
		RECREATION AND CULTURE							
		Parks and Recreation	.58	10.69	8,883	94,959	.097	9,211	104,170
		Libraries	.12	2.21	9,282	20,513	.000	---	20,513
		Total Municipal				2,107,921		192,255	2,300,176
		SCHOOL DISTRICT							
		Primary/Secondary Schools	78	171.99	11,800	2,029,482	.073	148,152	2,177,634
		Total School District				2,029,482		148,152	2,177,634
		TOTAL MUNICIPAL AND SCHOOL DISTRICT				4,137,403		340,407	4,477,810

Notes: [1] See page 72.
[2] See Exhibit 4-4.
[3] Anticipated (18,424) population and (2,205) public school-age children (expressed in 000s as 18.424 and 2.205 respectively) multiplied by service ratios shown in column 3.
[4] See Exhibit 4-8.
[5] Column 4 multiplied by column 5.
[6] Exhibit 4-11.
[7] Column 6 multiplied by column 7.
[8] Column 6 plus column 8.

Source: U.S. Census of Governments, 1972.

EXHIBIT 4-7
RELATIONSHIP OF CENSUS OF GOVERNMENTS SERVICE CATEGORIES AND LINE-ITEM BUDGET CLASSIFICATION

Census of Governments Service Category	Typical Line-Item Budget Classification	Census of Governments Service Category	Typical Line-Item Budget Classification
MUNICIPAL			
GENERAL GOVERNMENT		Sanitation:	Department/Division/Office of: Sanitation, Disposal, Leaf Collection
Financial Administration:	Department/Division/Office of: Administration, Purchasing, Finance, Disbursements, Tax Collection, Assessment, Accounts Control, Licenses and Permits	Water Supply:	Department/Division/Office of: Water Engineering, Water Accounting, Water Operating, Water Purchasing
		RECREATION AND CULTURE	
General Control:	Department/Division/Office of: Township Clerk, Personnel, Law, Real Estate, Zoning Board. Also includes Municipal Court, Office of the Mayor, and Municipal Council	Parks & Recreation:	Department/Division/Office of: Parks, Recreation, Water Safety
		Libraries:	Free Public Library, Bookmobile
		SCHOOL DISTRICT	
PUBLIC SAFETY		*PRIMARY & SECONDARY SCHOOLS*	Department/Division/Office of: Superintendent, Finance, Personnel, Buildings and Grounds, Special Pupils, Pupil Services
Police Protection:	Department/Division/Office of: Police, Traffic Control and Maintenance		
Fire Protection:	Department/Division/Office of: Fire Protection, Fire Prevention		
PUBLIC WORKS			
Highways:	Department/Division/Office of: Streets, Highway Engineering, Highway Maintenance		
Sewerage:	Department/Division/Office of: Sewers, Sewage Treatment, Sewage Disposal		

Source: U.S. Department of Commerce, *Classification Manual, Government Finances* (Washington, D.C.: Government Printing Office, 1972) and selected samples of local budget worksheets.

employees. This operating expenditure projection for each service category is made following the procedures described below.

The analyst first obtains a copy of the *working* (usually *not the published*) line-item budget for both the municipality and the school district. This document may be referred to by various titles such as "budget worksheets," "budget breakouts," etc. but, by whatever title, it must consist of (1) a formal compilation of expenditures (salaries, statutory costs, and material expenses) by service function and (2) the number of employees for each service category. Number of employees usually is not available in published budgets but the necessary information is generally available in the working line-item budgets for both the municipality and school district. These can be obtained from the municipal business administrator, town clerk and superintendent of schools. Municipalities and school districts have detailed working budget documents (frequently in mimeographed form), for this is their basic guide for determining what is authorized to be spent in the upcoming year and is also used for other functions, such as for general fiscal planning, and for projections of civil service employees.

After he has grouped the line-item budget into the Census of Governments service categories, the analyst can then determine average operating expenses per employee. He first adds the individual line-item salaries, statutory expenses, and material expenditures for each grouped service function to determine the respective totals for each service category. In the Georgia community in the example, the municipal budget shows for the financial administration service category $108,909 for wages, $17,478 for statutory expenses, and $2,610 for material costs. Total expenditures are $128,997. The analyst next determines the total number of employees in each service category by adding the employees in each of the line-item expenditure functions. In the Georgia municipality, nine people are employed in the local financial administration office. The analyst then divides total wages, statutory expenses, and equipment costs for each service category by the total number of employees in that service category. In this case, dividing the $108,909 in salaries, $17,478 in statutory outlays and $2,610 in material costs by the total number of employees, (9) yields an average of $12,101 (salaries) $1,942 (statutory expenses), and $290 (material expenses) per financial administration worker (See Exhibit 4-8). The average total operating cost per financial administration employee is $14,333 ($128,997/9). Costs per employee for other service functions are derived in the same way (See Exhibit 4-8) and are summarized in Exhibit 4-6, column 5.

Although somewhat comparable expenditure information is available from the Census of Governments, the analyst should use *local* salaries and other operating expenses because they most accurately reflect *current, local, dollar commitments* per employee. While inflation will alter expenditures considerably the Census service ratios should remain reasonably stable over time, especially due to the level of partitioning involved (population and region). Thus, if the analyst uses both Census service ratios and local operating costs, two problems — using information from a specific time to project long-term costs and using salary information that rapidly becomes dated — are somewhat mitigated.

Step 4 Project Total Annual Operating Costs.

At this point, it is now possible to calculate the yearly operating outlays by service category, using the data obtained in the previous two steps. The analyst multiplies the number of employees attributable to growth by service category (obtained in step 2) by operating costs per employee (obtained in step 3) to determine the operating expenses per employee.

To illustrate, alternative 1 will require 3.47 additional financial administration workers, alternative 2 adds 7.29 such employees while alternative 3 potentially adds 8.48 such employees.

EXHIBIT 4-8

SALARY, STATUTORY AND MATERIAL, AND TOTAL OPERATING COSTS PER EMPLOYEE BY SERVICE FUNCTION

PUBLIC SERVICE FUNCTIONS	Total Salaries (1)	Total Statutory Cost (2)	Total Material Cost (3)	Total Operating Cost [1] (4)	Total Existing Public Employees (5)	Average Salary Cost per Employee [2] (6)	Average Statutory Cost per Employee [3] (7)	Average Material Cost per Employee [4] (8)	Average Operating Cost per Employee [5] (9)
MUNICIPAL									
GENERAL GOVERNMENT									
Financial Administration	$ 108,909	$ 17,478	$ 2,610	$ 128,997	9	$ 12,101	$ 1,942	$ 290	$ 14,333
General Control	33,604	3,556	1,784	38,944	4	8,401	889	446	9,736
PUBLIC SAFETY									
Police	367,535	56,000	57,260	480,795	35	10,501	1,600	1,636	13,737
Fire	250,128	43,200	47,592	340,920	24	10,422	1,800	1,983	14,205
PUBLIC WORKS									
Highways	125,025	13,665	55,440	194,130	15	8,335	911	3,696	12,942
Sewerage	58,884	6,419	27,566	92,869	7	8,412	917	3,938	13,267
Sanitation	209,256	22,488	46,176	277,920	24	8,719	937	1,924	11,580
Water Supply	133,335	13,860	46,365	193,560	15	8,889	924	3,091	12,904
RECREATION & CULTURE									
Parks & Recreation	107,016	9,800	7,546	124,362	14	7,644	700	539	8,883
Libraries	41,055	4,000	1,355	46,410	5	8,211	800	271	9,282
SCHOOL DISTRICT									
Primary and Secondary Level	3,322,968	328,328	219,104	3,870,400	328	10,131	1,001	668	11,800

Notes: [1] Column 1 plus column 2 plus column 3.
[2] Column 1 divided by column 5.
[3] Column 2 divided by column 5.
[4] Column 3 divided by column 5.
[5] Column 4 divided by column 5 — also column 6 plus column 7 plus column 8.

Source: Expenditure columns 1 through 3 and employment figures (column 5) are derived from the local working budget.

(See Exhibit 4-6, column 4.) The average operating expense per financial administration worker for the municipality in Georgia is $14,333 (Exhibit 4-6, column 5). Consequently, potential future operating costs for financial administration personnel are $49,736 for the first development alternative (3.47 × $14,333), $104,488 (7.29 × $14,333) for the second, and $121,544 (8.48 × $14,333) for the third (Exhibit 4-6, column 6). Annual operating expenditures for the remaining municipal functions are derived in a similar fashion (Exhibit 4-6, column 6). The total costs for the three development alternatives are indicated below.

Development Alternative	Total Annual Municipal Operating Cost	Total Annual School District Operating Cost	Total Annual Municipal and School District Operating Cost
1	$ 863,935	$1,830,652	$2,694,587
2	1,812,887	3,864,736	5,677,623
3	2,107,921	2,029,482	4,137,403

Step 5   Project Total Annual Capital Costs.

After he determines annual operating costs, the analyst can then determine annual capital costs in the form of annual debt service.

The Service Standard Method uses median* annual capital-to-operating expenditure ratios derived from Census of Governments data to project anticipated annual capital expenditures. These ratios are multiplied by annual operating outlays determined in the previous step. Exhibits 4-9 through 4-12 present capital-to-operating ratios by community size and region in similar fashion to the way in which manpower ratios have been presented earlier. The interpretation of these exhibits also parallels the previous discussion. To illustrate, Exhibit 4-11 indicates that the ratio for fire protection for Southern communities in the 10,000 to 24,999 population group is 0.026. This means that, on the average, capital expenditures in the form of annual debt service for fire protection in this type of municipality equal approximately 2.6 percent of annual fire service operating outlays (See Exhibit 4-11).

As with manpower ratios, capital to operating ratios may be applied with considerable ease. The analyst first locates the appropriate data slot. He employs the capital-to-operating ratios for the same municipal and school district population group and region of the country that were identified previously (step 2). To illustrate, for the Georgia municipality, manpower ratios for municipalities in the 10,000 to 24,999 group and school districts in the over-3,000 group were used. The same population and pupil groups are utilized to enter the chart for the Southern region to obtain capital-to-operating service ratios for various service functions.

After identifying the correct series of capital-to-operating ratios, the analyst can then use the annual operating cost estimations (calculated in step 4) to project annual capital expenditures. The analyst multiplies the annual operating outlays for each service category (determined in step 4) by the respective capital-to-operating ratio. The capital-to-operating ratio indicates the fraction of annual operating expenses represented by annual capital expenses. By multiplying total operating expenditures by the ratio, the analyst can reasonably estimate likely annual capital expenditures attributable to growth.

---

*Median capital-to-operating expenditure ratios are used because they are the best estimates of central tendency.

Service Standard

EXHIBIT 4-9

ANNUAL CAPITAL-TO-OPERATING EXPENDITURE RATIOS FOR MUNICIPAL AND SCHOOL DISTRICT SERVICES,
BY MUNICIPAL/SCHOOL DISTRICT SIZE AND REGION OF THE UNITED STATES[1] (NORTHEAST REGION[2])

Municipal Population Size (Number of Residents)	(Use for Municipal[3] Functions)	Less Than 2,500	2,500 to 4,999	5,000 to 9,999	10,000 to 24,999	25,000 to 49,999	50,000 to 99,999	100,000 to 199,999	200,000 to 299,999	300,000 to 499,999	500,000 to 999,999	1,000,000 And Over
MUNICIPAL FUNCTIONS												
GENERAL GOVERNMENT												
Finance Administration		.000	.000	.000	.000	.000	.001	.003	.004	.011	.010	.002
General Control		.000	.000	.000	.000	.000	.001	.003	.001	.039	.008	.039
PUBLIC SAFETY												
Police		.000	.000	.029	.028	.025	.020	.026	.001	.021	.003	.044
Fire		.091	.000	.000	.000	.005	.006	.015	.002	.026	.014	.039
PUBLIC WORKS												
Highways		.269	.159	.153	.176	.161	.234	.276	.136	.417	.649	.479
Sewerage		.783	.052	.007	.048	.224	.898	.698	.583	.657	.772	.476
Sanitation		.033	.000	.000	.000	.000	.000	.040	.227	.210	.003	.076
Water Supply		.242	.217	.136	.168	.180	.115	.263	.045	.352	.312	.627
RECREATION AND CULTURE												
Parks and Recreation		.181	.000	.000	.032	.055	.094	.325	.214	.564	.687	.397
Libraries		.000	.000	.000	.000	.000	.000	.001	.049	.010	.141	.135
SCHOOL DISTRICT FUNCTION												
Primary and Secondary Schools			.019			.017		.016				
School District Enrollment (Number of Students)	(Use for Education)[4]		Less than 1,200			1,200–2,999		3,000 and over				

Notes: [1]These figures are read as follows: In a municipality whose population falls between 2,500 and 4,999, median capital expenditures (annual debt service costs) in the highway department amount to 15.9 percent of total highway department operating expenses. In a school district whose enrollment (pupils) falls between 1,200 and 2,999, median capital expenditures amount to 1.7 percent of total school district operating expenses.
[2]Includes Connecticut, Maine, Massachusetts, New Hampshire, New Jersey, New York, Pennsylvania, Rhode Island, Vermont.
[3]Use the ratios above the dotted line for municipal functions.
[4]Use the ratios below the dotted line for school district functions.

Source: U.S. Census of Governments, 1972.

EXHIBIT 4-10
ANNUAL CAPITAL-TO-OPERATING EXPENDITURE RATIOS FOR MUNICIPAL AND SCHOOL DISTRICT SERVICES, BY MUNICIPAL/SCHOOL DISTRICT SIZE AND REGION OF THE UNITED STATES[1] (NORTH CENTRAL REGION[2])

Municipal Population Size (Number of Residents)	(Use for Municipal[3] Functions)	Less Than 2,500	2,500 to 4,999	5,000 to 9,999	10,000 to 24,999	25,000 to 49,999	50,000 to 99,999	100,000 to 199,999	200,000 to 299,999	300,000 to 499,999	500,000 to 999,999	1,000,000 And Over
MUNICIPAL FUNCTIONS												
GENERAL GOVERNMENT												
Finance Administration		.000	.000	.000	.000	.000	.001	.007	.004	.002	.014	.012
General Control		.000	.000	.000	.000	.000	.000	.001	.005	.003	.004	.009
PUBLIC SAFETY												
Police		.000	.000	.011	.025	.029	.028	.030	.016	.019	.050	.016
Fire		.154	.034	.050	.038	.025	.026	.027	.032	.037	.035	.007
PUBLIC WORKS												
Highways		.261	.236	.236	.237	.319	.532	.659	1.104	1.154	0.916	0.515
Sewerage		1.136	.084	.104	.100	.346	.581	1.350	.697	1.848	1.207	4.201
Sanitation		.043	.000	.000	.000	.000	.005	.031	.055	.028	.030	.090
Water Supply		.328	.153	.171	.087	.128	.171	.238	.100	.460	.516	.905
RECREATION AND CULTURE												
Parks and Recreation		.250	.000	.060	.082	.174	.112	.182	.167	.536	.331	.111
Libraries		.000	.000	.000	.000	.018	.014	.012	.155	.030	.103	.027

School District Enrollment (Number of Students)	(Use for Education)[4]	Less than 1,200	1,200–2,999	3,000 and over
SCHOOL DISTRICT FUNCTION				
Primary and Secondary Schools		.039	.044	.053

Notes: [1]These figures are read as follows: In a municipality whose population falls between 2,500 and 4,999 median capital expenditures (annual debt service costs) in the highway department amount to 23.6 percent of total highway department operating expenses. In a school district whose enrollment (pupils) falls between 1,200 and 2,999, median capital expenditures amount to 4.4 percent of total school district operating costs.
[2]Includes Illinois, Indiana, Iowa, Kansas, Michigan, Minnesota, Missouri, Montana, Nebraska, North Dakota, Ohio, South Dakota, Wisconsin.
[3]Use the ratios above the dotted line for municipal functions.
[4]Use the ratios below the dotted line for school district functions.

Source: U.S. Census of Governments, 1972.

EXHIBIT 4-11
ANNUAL CAPITAL-TO-OPERATING EXPENDITURE RATIOS FOR MUNICIPAL AND SCHOOL DISTRICT SERVICES, BY MUNICIPAL/SCHOOL DISTRICT SIZE AND REGION OF THE UNITED STATES[1] (SOUTH[2])

Municipal Population Size (Number of Residents)	(Use for Municipal[3] Functions)	Less Than 2,500	2,500 to 4,999	5,000 to 9,999	10,000 to 24,999	25,000 to 49,999	50,000 to 99,999	100,000 to 199,999	200,000 to 299,999	300,000 to 499,999	500,000 to 999,999	1,000,000 And Over
MUNICIPAL FUNCTIONS												
GENERAL GOVERNMENT												
Finance Administration		.000	.000	.000	.000	.008	.006	.004	.012	.005	.016	.036
General Control		.000	.000	.000	.000	.008	.011	.010	.009	.007	.010	.009
PUBLIC SAFETY												
Police		.000	.058	.056	.054	.051	.047	.058	.052	.064	.037	.062
Fire		.099	.018	.050	.026	.022	.029	.063	.047	.043	.049	.074
PUBLIC WORKS												
Highways		.196	.094	.162	.199	.284	.452	.777	1.090	.733	.830	1.890
Sewerage		.888	.000	.071	.147	.345	.485	1.936	1.581	1.291	1.313	.068
Sanitation		.093	.000	.049	.078	.064	.104	.114	.047	.039	.068	.149
Water Supply		.413	.168	.217	.226	.386	.406	.572	1.206	1.012	.466	1.759
RECREATION AND CULTURE												
Parks and Recreation		.269	.000	.031	.097	.124	.148	.245	.345	.471	.317	.320
Libraries		.001	.000	.000	.000	.000	.031	.000	.034	.040	.044	.407

School District Enrollment (Number of Students)	(Use for Education)[4]	Less than 1,200	1,200–2,999	3,000 and over
SCHOOL DISTRICT FUNCTION				
Primary and Secondary Schools		.056	.057	.073

Notes: [1] These figures are read as follows: In a municipality whose population falls between 2,500 and 4,999 median capital expenditures (annual debt service costs) in the highway department amount to 9.4 percent of total highway department operating expenses. In a school district whose enrollment (pupils) falls between 1,200 and 2,999, median capital expenditures amount to 5.7 percent of total school district operating costs.
[2] Includes Alabama, Arkansas, Delaware, Florida, Georgia, Kentucky, Louisiana, Maryland, Mississippi, North Carolina, Oklahoma, South Carolina, Tennessee, Texas, Virginia, Washington, D.C., West Virginia.
[3] Use the ratios above the dotted line for municipal functions.
[4] Use the ratios below the dotted line for school district functions.

Source: U.S. Census of Governments, 1972.

EXHIBIT 4-12

ANNUAL CAPITAL-TO-OPERATING EXPENDITURE RATIOS FOR MUNICIPAL AND SCHOOL DISTRICT SERVICES, BY MUNICIPAL/SCHOOL DISTRICT SIZE AND REGION OF THE UNITED STATES[1] (WEST[2])

Municipal Population Size (Number of Residents) (Use for Municipal[3] Functions)	Less Than 2,500	2,500 to 4,999	5,000 to 9,999	10,000 to 24,999	25,000 to 49,999	50,000 to 99,999	100,000 to 199,999	200,000 to 299,999	300,000 to 499,999	500,000 to 999,999	1,000,000 And Over
MUNICIPAL FUNCTIONS											
GENERAL GOVERNMENT											
Finance Administration	.000	.000	.000	.005	.007	.010	.009	.006	.008	.006	.014
General Control	.000	.000	.000	.006	.006	.006	.011	.007	.007	.006	.005
PUBLIC SAFETY											
Police	.000	.046	.043	.036	.025	.018	.014	.113	.032	.052	.050
Fire	.077	.060	.061	.030	.020	.027	.019	.037	.036	.038	.030
PUBLIC WORKS											
Highways	.255	.147	.363	.367	.408	.715	.845	1.139	.851	1.308	1.127
Sewerage	.400	.046	.143	.212	.248	.466	.214	1.143	1.609	2.017	2.422
Sanitation	.400	.046	.143	.212	.248	.466	.124	1.143	1.609	2.017	2.422
Water Supply	.165	.167	.249	.362	.318	.352	.411	1.115	.565	.652	.899
RECREATION AND CULTURE											
Parks and Recreation	.292	.053	.101	.127	.174	.155	.290	.906	.184	.534	.313
Libraries	.059	.000	.012	.011	.017	.026	.017	.206	.003	.088	.022

School District Enrollment (Number of Students) (Use for Education)[4]	Less than 1,200	1,200–2,999	3,000 and over
SCHOOL DISTRICT FUNCTION			
Primary and Secondary Schools	.040	.042	.049

Notes: [1]These figures are read as follows: In a municipality whose population falls between 2,500 and 4,999, median capital expenditures (annual debt service costs) in the highway department amount to 14.7 percent of total highway department operating expenses. In a school district whose enrollment (pupils) falls between 1,200 and 2,999, median capital expenditures amount to 4.2 percent of total school district operating costs.
[2]Includes Alaska, Arizona, California, Colorado, Hawaii, Idaho, Montana, Nevada, New Mexico, Oregon, Utah, Washington, Wyoming.
[3]Use the ratios above the dotted line for municipal functions.
[4]Use the ratios below the dotted line for school district functions.

Source: U.S. Census of Governments, 1972.

Service Standard   89

   For the Georgia municipality in the example, annual capital costs for fire protection for the first of the development strategies is calculated by multiplying $132,959 (annual operating costs for fire service) by .026 (the median capital-to-operating ratio) yielding $3,457 in annual capital debt service expenditures. Capital fire outlays for the second development alternative are derived by multiplying $279,128 by .026 yielding $7,257; for the third development alternative the procedure is the same ($324,584 × .026) producing $8,439 in annual capital debt service expenditures. Annual capital expenditures for other municipal as well as for school district services are calculated using similar procedures (see Exhibit 4-6, columns 7 and 8).

Development Alternative	Total Annual Municipal Capital Cost	Total Annual School District Capital Cost	Total Annual Municipal and School District Capital Cost
1	$ 78,813	$133,638	$212,451
2	$165,358	$282,126	$447,484
3	$192,255	$148,152	$340,407

Step 6 Project Total Annual Public Costs.

Total annual public costs equals total annual operating costs (determined in step 4) plus total annual capital debt service expenditures (determined in step 5). Operating and capital outlays are first grouped horizontally by service category and then summed vertically to obtain total annual public costs (Exhibit 4-6, column 9).

Development Alternative	Total Annual Municipal Operating Cost	Total Annual Municipal Capital Cost	Total Annual Municipal Public Cost	Total Annual School District Operating Cost	Total Annual School District Capital Cost	Total Annual School District Public Cost	Total Annual Municipal and School District Public Cost
1	$ 863,935	$ 78,813	$ 942,748	$1,830,652	$133,638	$1,964,290	$2,907,038
2	1,812,887	165,358	1,978,245	3,864,736	282,126	4,146,862	6,125,107
3	2,107,921	192,255	2,300,176	2,029,482	148,152	2,177,634	4,477,810

Step 7 Project Total Annual Public Revenues.

   Thus far, the analyst, in projecting the public expenditures that are generated by the several growth alternatives, has performed the bulk of the labor yet only one half of the cost-revenue calculation. As a prerequisite to obtaining a *net* fiscal impact, the other side of the equation, public revenues derived from each of the alternatives are examined. The full gamut of public revenues flowing to the local municipal and school district jurisdictions as a result of development, rezoning, annexation, etc., must be included. These revenues, and methods for their projection, are discussed in detail in Chapters 9 and 10.
   To summarize briefly, the analyst first estimates municipal own source revenues occurring from growth. These include both taxes, almost universally the real property tax, but encompassing other taxes (property transfer, plus various franchise or employment based taxes), and charges and miscellaneous revenue including recreation or sewerage charges and fees and permit earnings.

Municipalities also receive both federal intergovernmental aid (Revenue Sharing, Comprehensive Employment Training Assistance [CETA] grants, etc.) and state intergovernmental support such as utility gross receipts and shares of the locally generated income and sales taxes. These upper level intergovernmental transfers, when added to municipal own source revenue, yield total municipal revenues. The analyst follows a similar procedure for calculating school district revenues. First, own source revenues, predominately the real property tax, are calculated, followed by charges and miscellaneous revenues including such miscellaneous items as athletic facility/school lunch income. The sum of own source plus charges and miscellaneous revenues equal total school district own source revenue. Intergovernmental transfers, which are extremely important to the school district, are then projected. These include both state intergovernmental transfers (i.e., flat grants, foundation and categorical aid) and federal assistance (i.e., aid to federally impacted areas). Total school district revenues equal the sum of district own source plus intergovernmental transfers. Adding total municipal plus total school district revenues yields the total public revenues generated by the growth increment being studied.

The revenue calculations for the three land use alternatives in the Georgia community are shown in Exhibit 4-13. Total revenues are $3,217,455 for alternative 1, $6,511,363 for alternative 2, and $4,279,346 for alternative 3. Of note in this particular example is the number and amount of local charges as a share of municipal own source revenues. Income from user charges, for example, is almost double the sum raised from real property taxes; the user charge for water alone is more than the revenue derived from the real property tax. Another distinguishing characteristic is the breakdown of school district revenues: Intergovernmental transfers are twice the amount of school district own source revenues. This ratio is common in the South where states pay a large share of educational costs.

Step 8 *Calculate the Cost-Revenue Surplus or Deficit.*

The final step of the fiscal impact analysis is to compare projected costs and projected revenues. The analyst subtracts total public costs (determined in step 6) from total public revenues (calculated in step 7). Total costs (personnel, statutory and material) must be compared to total revenues (municipal and school district own source and intergovernmental transfers).

In the land use alternative example, three final fiscal impacts are obtained, one for each development alternative. As is indicated below, two produce surpluses; alternative 1 yields a $310,417 gain while alternative 2 generates a similar $386,256 surplus. The third development alternative results in a $198,464 deficit.

Development Alternative	Total Annual Municipal Cost	Total Annual Municipal Revenue	Total Annual Municipal Net Fiscal Impact	Total Annual School District Cost	Total Annual School District Revenue	Total Annual School District Net Fiscal Impact	Total Annual Municipal and School District Net Fiscal Impact
1	$ 942,748	$1,210,310	+$ 267,562	$1,964,290	$2,007,145	+$ 42,855	+$ 310,417
2	$1,978,245	$2,284,268	+$ 306,023	$4,146,862	$4,227,095	+$ 80,233	+$ 386,256
3	$2,300,176	$1,994,790	-$ 305,386	$2,177,634	$2,284,556	+$ 106,922	-$ 198,464

Service Standard

EXHIBIT 4-13

COMPUTATION SHEET FOR REVENUE PROJECTION*

REVENUE SOURCES	ALTERNATIVE 1		ALTERNATIVE 2		ALTERNATIVE 3	
MUNICIPAL						
I. Own Source Revenues						
A. Taxes						
1. Real property	$ 340,000		$ 595,000		$ 411,264	
2. Personal Property	51,000		87,550		73,484	
3. Utility franchise	36,000		67,500		73,500	
4. Alcohol excise	98,150		205,985		239,512	
5. Cable TV franchise	2,160		5,400		7,560	
TOTAL TAXES		$ 527,310		$ 961,435		$ 805,320
B. Charges/Miscellaneous						
1. Interest earnings	$ 6,288		$ 11,040		$ 7,608	
2. Fees and permits	5,000		12,500		17,500	
3. Fines/forfeitures	29,143		61,162		71,117	
4. User charges – special services	31,106		65,281		75,907	
5. User charges – sanitation	12,000		30,000		42,000	
6. User charges – sewerage	136,000		255,000		140,000	
7. User charges – water	400,000		750,000		700,000	
TOTAL CHARGES/MISCELLANEOUS		$ 619,537		$1,184,983		$1,054,132
TOTAL OWN SOURCE REVENUE		$1,146,847		$2,146,418		$1,859,452
II. Intergovernmental Transfers						
A. State						
1. Urban/rural aid	$ 27,200		$ 50,000		$ 53,000	
2. Road/road lighting aid	8,250		15,000		18,000	
TOTAL STATE		$ 35,450		$ 65,000		$ 71,000
B. Federal						
1. Revenue sharing	$ 18,000		$ 37,500		$ 16,800	
2. CETA	5,200		25,520		34,200	
3. Anti-recession	0		0		1,050	
4. LEAA	4,813		9,830		12,288	
TOTAL FEDERAL		$ 28,013		$ 72,850		$ 64,338
TOTAL INTERGOVERNMENTAL TRANSFER		63,463		137,850		135,338
TOTAL MUNICIPAL REVENUE		$1,210,310		$2,284,268		$1,994,790
SCHOOL DISTRICT						
I. Own Source Revenues						
A. Taxes						
1. Taxes	$ 560,000		$ 980,000		$ 677,376	
TOTAL TAXES		$ 560,000		$ 980,000		$ 677,376
B. Charges/Miscellaneous						
1. Charges/miscellaneous	$ 95,472		$ 201,552		$ 105,840	
TOTAL CHARGES/MISCELLANEOUS		$ 95,472		$ 201,552		$ 105,840
TOTAL OWN SOURCE REVENUE		655,472		1,181,552		783,216
II. Intergovernmental Transfers						
A. State						
1. Foundation aid	$1,148,795		$2,617,245		$1,276,430	
2. Categorical aid	103,428		218,348		114,660	
3. State redistributed federal	99,450		209,950		110,250	
TOTAL STATE		$1,351,673		$3,045,543		$1,501,340
B. Federal						
1. 0	$ 0		$ 0		$ 0	
TOTAL FEDERAL		$ 0		$ 0		$ 0
TOTAL INTERGOVERNMENTAL TRANSFERS		$1,351,673		$3,045,543		$1,501,340
TOTAL SCHOOL DISTRICT REVENUE		$2,007,145		$4,227,095		$2,284,556
TOTAL MUNICIPAL/SCHOOL DISTRICT REVENUE		$3,217,455		$6,511,363		$4,279,346

*For detailed calculations, see Exhibits 10-1 and 10-2 in Chapter 10.

Data Requirements

The basic data needed to implement the Service Standard Method consist of multipliers for household size and school-age population for different types of housing; population estimates for municipalities, and school districts; public employee service standard, by service category; average operating costs per employee; annual capital-to-operating expenditure ratios by service category; and information about revenues such as real property assessed value, property tax rate, sales tax rate, intergovernmental transfer formulas, etc. Except for specific local information, such as average salaries and tax rates, and amounts of intergovernmental transfers, all of the required data are available elsewhere in this handbook. Specific data requirements for each of the method's steps and the sources of this information are summarized in Exhibit 4-14.

Sophistication of User

The Service Standard approach may be employed by a modestly sophisticated user who has had an average amount of experience with fiscal impact analysis. Local staff planners and private planning consultants should be able to use the method relatively easily.

The analyst must be careful to select the appropriate household and children multipliers for a given housing type and the appropriate manpower and capital-to-operating expenditure ratios, by population size and regional location. He must also be careful when categorizing the local line item expenditures into the Census of Governments service categories. Experience is not a prerequisite for using the Service Standard Method, but persistence, accuracy, and meticulousness are.

Advantages and Disadvantages

Advantages

Richness of Detail   The Service Standard Method is second only to the Case Study Method in the amount of detail it provides. The other fiscal impact analysis techniques generate net fiscal impact in terms of expenditures but do not provide any clue to actual local response in terms of personnel to be hired, capital facility commitments, etc. The Service Standard technique not only predicts the financial consequences of population change but also traces specific growth-induced responses for each public service category.

Operational Utility   Information derived by using the Service Standard approach, especially detailed number of employees and amount of capital expenditures by service category, is useful for public officials anticipating future growth. While the projection of future employees needed to accommodate growth is not as detailed as in the Case Study Method, it is still one of only two methods that yield operational data by *service* category. In addition, it is far easier, quicker, and less expensive to use than the Case Study Method.

Acceptance   While this method is not as prevalent as the Per Capita Multiplier approach, it has been used for many years. It is accepted as a legitimate technique to project the fiscal impact of growth. Refining the method to avoid the use of standards from a variety of sources and to varying levels of detail should make the technique even more versatile. Like the Case Study Method, the Service Standard Method uses terms that public officials and local citizenry understand — the necessity to hire ten policemen or $250,000 for highway department capital costs, etc.

Simplicity/Low Cost   The Service Standard technique is straightforward and inexpensive to use. Time commitments to use the Service Standard approach, as applied to the Georgia community, are shown in Exhibit 4-15.

Service Standard 93

EXHIBIT 4-14
SERVICE STANDARD METHOD: DATA REQUIREMENTS AND SOURCES

Step Number	Data Requirements	Source(s)	Comments
1 – Determine resident and student increases resulting from growth	School-age children and household size multipliers for various housing types	Handbook, Chapter 13.	If detailed data on types of housing to be included are available, use appropriate multipliers for housing units of different bedroom configuration. Multiply total school-age children by the local percentage of public school enrollment to obtain public school-age children.
2 – Project number of public employees resulting from growth	Existing community and school district size	U.S. Census; local/regional planning department, local school, superintendent or business manager's office	Exact data on school district size should be available. Try to obtain updated Census information on local community size.
	Service standards for different public service functions differentiated by community size and region of the country	Exhibits 4-2 through 4-5	Be sure to use service standards for appropriate community and school district size group. The analyst should use the size of the municipality and school district *at the time of the study*.
3 – Calculate average operating expenses per employee	Municipal and school district working budgets	Local business administrator, town manager, town clerk, school district superintendent, school district business manager	Obtain line-item budgets that list total number of employees, total salaries, total statutory expenditures, and total equipment and material expenses for different services.
5 – Project total annual capital costs	Capital-to-operating expenditure ratios	Exhibits 4-9 through 4-12 in this method	Use same region and community size group as used in step 2.
7 – Project total annual public revenues	Municipal and school district real property tax rates	Local tax assessor's office or clerk's office	For other data requirements see Part 2.
	Property assessment procedures	Local-county tax assessor's office	
	State and federal intergovernmental transfers	Part 2	

EXHIBIT 4-15

TIME ESTIMATES TO USE THE SERVICE STANDARD METHOD

Step Number	Activities	Time
1	Determine resident and student increases resulting from growth	2 hours
2	Project number of public employees resulting from growth	2 hours
3	Calculate average operating expenses per employee	8 hours
4	Project total annual operating costs	2 hours
5	Project total annual capital costs	2 hours
6	Project total annual public costs	1 hour
7	Project total annual public revenues	10 hours
8	Calculate the cost-revenue impact	2 hours
Report Preparation	Prepare and reproduce final report (optional)	10 hours
		39 hours

Disadvantages

The Service Standard strategy assumes that local performance (the hiring of employees and committing funds for capital facilities in response to growth) will, in the long run, be similar to the existing expenditure patterns of cities of similar size and location. This relationship allows the analyst to use average service standards and median capital-to-operating expenditure ratios partitioned by population size and regional location. To the extent that actual local performance differs from the average (due to variance in local wealth, excess or deficient service capacity situations, labor rules or traditions, public service emphases) the projection will either overestimate or underestimate true local expenditures. It is assumed, however, that service overemphases in certain areas will balance underemphases in others so that average expenditures in comparable communities are an adequate first estimate of future costs for a specific community.

Interpreting Results

In the Georgia community in the example, only the alternatives of the relatively more expensive, single-family homes and mixed development produce positive fiscal impacts; the garden apartment alternative imposes substantially more local costs than revenues. Fiscal criteria are by no means the *only* input to be used for establishing local land use policy, however. Local demand for public services to accommodate a *variety* of housing options must also be considered. In this instance it may make much more sense, in terms of local housing need, to choose the garden apartment development alternative, acknowledging its negative fiscal impact, than to zone exclusively for expensive single-family homes or the mixed development when most of the area's residents may never be able to afford them.

The analyst should be aware of several points in interpreting the results of the Service Standard Method. Like the Per Capita Multiplier technique, this approach uses average costing. Consequently, its projections are best estimates of the long-term consequences of growth, rather than specific responses to immediate need. (Those interested in the immediate aftermath should utilize the Case Study Method for detailed impact and the Comparable City Method technique for general impact.)

The analyst must also be aware that the Service Standard strategy, as presented here, does not project expenditures for health and welfare services. The analyst must interpret his results with that information in mind.

NOTES

1. See Chapter 12.
2. For an excellent compilation of standards, see Joseph DeChiara and Lee Koppelman, *Manual of Housing/Planning and Design Criteria* (Englewood Cliffs, N.J.: Prentice Hall, 1975).
3. These are ratios reported in Bureau of the Census, *Census of Governments — Public Employment*.
4. See Chapter 1.
5. Solomon Fabricant, *The Trend of Government Activity in the United States Since 1900* (New York: National Bureau of Economic Research, 1952); Harvey E. Brazer, *City Expenditures in the United States* (New York: National Bureau of Economic Research, 1959); Bernard Booms, "City Governmental Form and Public Expenditure Levels," *National Tax Journal* (June 1966); L.R. Gabler, "Economies and Diseconomies of Scale in Urban Public Sectors," *Land Economics* (November 1969); John C. Weicher, "Determinants of Central City Expenditures: Some Overlooked Factors and Problems," *National Tax Journal* (December 1970).
6. Julian Horowitz, "Municipal Fiscal Structure in a Metropolitan Region," *Southern Economics Journal* (June 1972); Charles J. Libera, *An Investigation of the Determinants of Municipal Expenditures in the United States* (unpublished Ph.D. dissertation, University of Maryland, 1971).
7. For a sampling of standards, see DeChiara and Koppelman, *A Manual of Housing/Planning and Design Criteria*.

5

COMPARABLE CITY FISCAL IMPACT METHOD

Background

The Comparable City Method is used to project marginal fiscal impact. It relies upon relationships between community size and growth rate and local expenditure levels to project the effect of population *change* on municipal and school district costs and revenues.[1] It is the most recent of all the fiscal impact analysis methods; practical application was during the mid-1970s.

A variation of the Comparable City Method was first used approximately fifteen years ago when analysts first considered the common expenditure traits of communities of similar *size*.[2] Others were quick to point out that the direction and *rate* at which population size was attained also had a potential effect on the profile of public expenditures.[3] They questioned whether the characteristic expenditure figure occurred during increases or decreases in the service infrastructure, at what rate the increase or decrease would occur, and what the implication of the increase or decrease would be on future expenditure levels. In 1973, the Rutgers University Center for Urban Policy Research and the Institute for Urban Studies at the University of North Carolina, Charlotte, using expenditure data for New Jersey communities, first summarized the expenditure patterns of a significant number of communities of different size and growth rate.[4]

The information on the Comparable City Method in this handbook marks the first time that a national profile of cities and their accompanying expenditure patterns has been generally available to practicing planners. While the fiscal impact analysis method which follows is relatively new, it has immense potential due to its simplicity, ease of comprehension and relatively modest implementation costs.

The Comparable City Method relies on expenditure multipliers that vary by size and growth rate of community or school district. The multipliers, presented in chart form, represent a proportional relationship of the average expenditures of cities of various size and growth rates to the average expenditures of cities of the most common population size and growth rate.* As a community grows or declines at a certain pace, and in so doing changes population categories, its expenditure pattern is characterized by a different multiplier. The ratio of the new multiplier to the old multiplier is multiplied by existing per capita expenditures to determine new local municipal and school district costs resulting from change. The expenditure multipliers have been derived from data compiled by the U.S. Census of Governments and are available in sixteen increments for community size and growth rate.[5] Briefly, the method projects increases or decreases in future gross expenditures for the five basic municipal functions (general government, public safety, public works, health and welfare, recreation and culture) and school district services (primary and secondary education) by comparing the products of a community's expenditure ratios, per capita costs, and service populations before and after a projected growth increment.

To illustrate, a municipality with a population of 49,000 and a historical annual growth rate of 0.4 percent rezones land to accommodate a large planned development. This development will house 10,000 residents and be built over a five-year period. The community will thus grow to a level of 59,000 with a 4 percent annual growth rate over the period of its construction (10,000/49,000 = .20/5 yrs. = .04/yr). Its pregrowth general government operating expenditure ratio is .97 (from Exhibit 5-2 — communities of 25,001 to 50,000 population and 0 to .5 percent annual growth rate); its postgrowth operating expenditure ratio is 1.21 (communities of 50,000 to 100,000 population and over 2 percent annual growth rate). Assuming that before development the community exhibited a $20 per capita general government operating expenditure, then if this community behaves in a fashion similar to other communities of this post-growth population size and growth rate, it may anticipate that future expenditures for general government purposes will be $25 per person ($20 × 1.21/.97 = $25).

Multiplying this figure by the present plus the increment in service population, the community will experience (based on historic trends of the similar communities) $1,475,000 in total general government operating expenditures (59,000 × $25). Since prior to development it spent $980,000 annually for this service (49,000 × $20), the general government operating expense engendered by the large planned development, and thus assignable to this growth, is $495,000 annually ($1,475,000 minus $980,000).

General government *capital* costs would be calculated in a similar fashion using the product of expenditure ratios and per capita debt service costs for both the new and old service populations and assigning the difference to the growth increment. This projection procedure for operating and capital expenditures is repeated for each of the basic municipal and school district functions (i.e., public safety, public works, health/welfare, recreation/culture) to determine total costs assignable to future growth.

Revenues are obtained by adding increases in municipal and school district own source and intergovernmental revenues resulting from the growth. The sum of these revenue changes is then compared with previously projected costs. The resulting surplus or deficit represents the best estimate of the new growth's impact on local municipal and school district income and expenditures.

The Comparable City Method, like the Case Study Method, is a marginal costing technique. Changes in the cost of serving the existing as well as the new population are assigned to the new population. While the Case Study Method yields greater insight into the types of personnel hirings that are necessary and the specific, planned capital additions occasioning future costs, the

---

*Community expenditure patterns are expressed in relation to a common base so that absolute dollar expenditures over time remain useful and are not dated because of inflation. It is assumed that the relationship between communities will remain relatively constant, at least over the four-year intercensal period.

Comparable City Method, admittedly more general, is simpler, easy to use and understand and, thus, less expensive to implement. Analysts who do not need the Case Study's exactness but still prefer a projection technique which is sensitive to the marginal expenditure effects of growth should use the Comparable City approach.

Application

The Comparable City Method may be used in several ways. It is intended primarily, however, for situations where a new population size and/or growth rate is expected because of future, large scale development or municipal/school district boundary changes. The method is thus ideal for annexations, horizon planning, land use alternatives for the same geographic area, and/or major rezonings.

The method's strength is its provision of information about the expenditure behavior of communities similar to the one in which the analyst is operating. In communities of average size and growth rate there is a large data base from which to draw — the information is strongly reliable. At the extremes, less information on comparable cities is available — the information is admittedly weaker yet this is one of the few techniques for which information is available for unique growth situations. The sample of large, rapidly growing or small declining communities may be small, but the existing data are made available to the analyst for comparison and interpretation.

The Comparable City fiscal impact method is to be used in situations where the analyst feels that the experience of other communities undergoing population change will support the anticipated variations in the community being analyzed. (The reliance on excess capacity in rapid growth situations and the resulting expenditure conservativeness, as well as continued expenditure in situations of deficient capacity resulting in excessive outlays, presented as an average for a number of communities is the type of information made available by this technique.) If service standards were used in the former case they would likely overstate future expenditures; in the latter case, use of service standards would understate reality.

The Comparable City strategy is especially appropriate for considering the effects of population decline, because its multipliers take into account both population increases and decreases. Population loss often occurs in central cities and in smaller cities or towns in regions experiencing employment/population outmigration. Other fiscal impact methods are insensitive to the relatively slow pace of service cutbacks accompanying losses in population and tend to overstate the magnitude of decreases in expenditures. When costs continue to increase as population decreases, only the Comparable City and the Case Study assess future expenditure reality reasonably.

The purpose of the fiscal impact analysis also helps determine the application of the Comparable City Method. The technique cannot be used for considering solely nonresidential uses because the multipliers have been derived using public service expenditures expressed per person or per pupil. People and students are usually not introduced to the community as the *direct* result of commercial or industrial development. It is assumed that the costs to serve nonresidential uses induced by residential growth are included in the assigned costs of the residential growth. The local outlays for the level of nonresidential development which would usually be found in communities of certain size and growth rates are included in the expenditure multipliers for each category of community population size/growth rate.

The Comparable City Method may be used for local budget planning, but other methods are better. The Case Study approach yields far greater detail on the specific personnel who must be hired, the operating materials that must be purchased, and the capital facilities that must either be constructed or acquired. The Service Standard technique yields a more general view than the Case Study but still provides the analyst with reasonably detailed data on personnel needs and associated costs for *common* municipal functions. The Comparable City Method, in contrast, considers neither specific personnel requirements nor the exact nature of capital facilities; instead, it projects gross operating and capital costs for aggregated municipal and school district functions.

Finally, the Comparable City Method may be used when the analyst can expend only a limited amount of time on the analysis; it makes similar resource demands as the Service Standard strategy, slightly more than the Per Capita Multiplier Method, but far less time than the Case Study Method.

Basic Assumptions

A basic assumption of the Comparable City Method is that public service expenditures vary significantly according to a community's *size* and *growth rate*. The influence of size has been studied and confirmed by numerous economists and planners including Brazer, Bahl, Beaton, Baumol, Sternlieb, *et al.*, and Weicher.[6] Their empirical analyses have shown that both very small and very large communities spend more per capita to service their populations' needs than mid-size communities.

The second basic assumption is that a city's growth rate also affects local service expenditures. While the impact of growth has not been as widely studied as the influence of size, analyses by Maslin and Quindry, Bahl, Netzer, Feinberg, Beaton, Sternlieb, *et al.*, and Miller have demonstrated that both the direction and rate of growth affects the future level of public expenditures.[7] In general, rapidly growing and declining areas will be forced to spend more per capita for services than moderately growing communities. Service infrastructure and distribution costs are high for rapidly growing areas and the current population on which the services are spent is relatively small. In declining communities, the cost of the service infrastructure and service distribution remains even after a significant portion of the service population has left the city. This situation also results in relatively high per capita costs. In mid-size, moderate growth areas, the population is better able to bear current service costs.

The third basic assumption of the Comparable City Method is that the expenditure pattern of the municipality or school district *after* growth is the best indication of future local expenditures. *Further, any increases or decreases in the existing local expenditure profile as well as the costs to service the new population increment are the costs assigned to the specific growth catalyst.* This assumption reflects the marginal cost view of the Comparable City Method. It focuses on a changed future expenditure pattern rather than projecting from the current cost basis. It attributes the change in expenditure profile and the cost to service the new population to the growth that occasioned it.

Procedural Steps

The step-by-step procedures to implement the Comparable City Method are summarized in Exhibit 5-1.

Step 1. *Determine Population/Student Growth*

The analyst must obtain an estimate of both the magnitude of additional community population/student enrollment and the period over which growth will take place. These data are necessary for selecting the appropriate multipliers for future expenditures which are categorized by size/growth rate.

Increases in population and students based on anticipated residential development of a certain

Comparable City

EXHIBIT 5-1

COMPARABLE CITY FISCAL IMPACT ANALYSIS METHOD: SUMMARY OF PROCEDURES

Step Number	Analysis/Actions
1	Using blended multipliers for household size and school-age children, determine the magnitude and rate of population/student growth.
2	Using the population projected in step 1, select appropriate expenditure multipliers and determine the rate of change in these multipliers.
3	Divide total operating and capital outlays for each service category by the existing local population to calculate current average operating and capital expenditures per capita.
4	Project future per capita costs by service category by multiplying the per capita expenditures determined in step 3 by the multiplier rate-of-change ratios calculated in step 2.
5	Determine future net annual costs by multiplying the future expenditures per person and per pupil by the community's future population and then subtracting the costs that would be incurred even if there were no growth.
6	Project total annual public revenues.
7	Calculate the cost-revenue surplus or deficit by comparing total revenues generated and total costs incurred.

type and configuration are projected by using the demographic multipliers found in Chapter 13. Household size and school-age children multipliers for types of housing (i.e., single-family, garden apartment, townhouses, high rise, etc.) *not* shown by number of bedrooms will usually have to suffice. These "blended" multipliers are often used out of necessity; the analyst is rarely given exact numbers or exact configurations of housing (i.e., 1,000 three-bedroom townhouses, 500 four-bedroom townhouses, etc.) to be planned or zoned for, or to be anticipated as a result of annexation.

Three alternative development strategies in a moderate size California community are used to illustrate the Comparable City Method. The community has a total population of 16,000 residents and 5,500 pupils.* The development plans affect an area of 1,000 acres. The first alternative which follows present zoning allows the construction of 2,000 single-family homes on half-acre lots (2,000 units). The second alternative permits a mixed use development at five units per acre distributed as follows: 50 percent townhouses (2,500 units), 30 percent single-family homes (1,500 units), and 20 percent condominiums (1,000 units). The third alternative is restricted entirely to garden apartments. Three hundred of the 1,000 acres will be maintained as privately held open space. At ten units per acre, 7,000 garden apartments are thus proposed. All three alternatives are to be completed within a five-year period. The population and student size projections for the three alternatives, using blended multipliers for household size and school-age children, are shown in the following exhibit.

---

*For a full description see Chapter 1.

Development Alternative	Number/Type Housing (1)	Household Size Multiplier (2)	School-Age Children Multiplier (3)	Total Population[1] (4)	Total School-Age Children[2] (5)
1	2,000 single family homes	3.826	1.255	7,652	2,259 (2,510)[3]
2	2,500 townhouses	2.965	0.617	7,413	1,389 (1,543)[3]
	1,500 single family homes	3.826	1.255	5,739	1,695 (1,883)[3]
	1,000 condominiums	2.614	0.982	2,614	884 (982)[3]
			TOTAL	15,766	3,968 (4,408)[3]
3	7,000 garden apartments	2.149	0.290	15,043	1,827 (2,030)[3]

Notes: [1] Column (1) times column (2).
[2] Column (1) times column (3).
[3] The figure in parentheses is the actual number of pupils. Since in this community 10 percent of all school-age children attend private schools, the projected numbers of local pupils have been multiplied by 90 percent to reflect the actual anticipated burden on the public school.

The projected increases in residents and pupils are then added to the community's existing population and the school district's average daily enrollment to yield the size of both the community and the school district following growth. The three development alternatives would have the following impacts on the California community.

Development Alternative	Current Community Population	Current School District Size	Projected Population Increase	Projected Student Increase	Total Future Municipal Population[1]	Total Future School District Population[2]
1	16,000	5,500	7,652	2,259	23,652	7,759
2	16,000	5,500	15,766	3,968	31,766	9,468
3	16,000	5,500	15,043	1,827	31,043	7,327

Notes: [1] Current community size plus projected population increase.
[2] Current school district size plus projected student increase.

Comparable City

Step 2. Obtain Appropriate Expenditure Multipliers and Calculate the Rate of Change in the Multipliers

At the heart of the Comparable City Method are expenditure multipliers. The analyst must take care to select the most appropriate multipliers for the community being examined. Expenditure multipliers for communities of different sizes and growth rates are presented in Exhibits 5-2 and 5-3. The former are multipliers for operating expenditures (salaries, statutory outlays and materials); the latter for capital expenditures.

The multipliers represent the ratio of per capita expenditures for communities of a particular size and growth rate to the per capita outlays for the largest group of mid-sized cities, i.e., those mid-sized communities whose size and growth rate are most common. To develop the expenditure multipliers found within Exhibits 5-2 and 5-3 the following procedure was used. First, the median annual expenditure per person, by service category, was tabulated for the largest group of mid-sized communities. This was found to be communities with a population of 25,000 to 50,000 and an annual growth rate of 2 percent or more. For general government services, this group of cities

EXHIBIT 5-2

MUNICIPAL AND SCHOOL DISTRICT MEDIAN OPERATING EXPENDITURE MULTIPLIERS BY POPULATION SIZE AND GROWTH RATE

Municipal Population (Number of Residents)	(Use for Municipal Functions)	(1) 1,000– 10,000	(2) 10,001– 25,000	(3) 25,001– 50,000	(4) 50,001– 100,000	(5) 100,001– 500,000	(6) 500,001– 1,000,000	(7) Over 1,000,000
0% to 0.5% increase	General Government	0.80	0.87	0.97	1.47	1.90	N/A*	N/A
	Public Safety	0.63	0.98	1.25	1.70	1.95	N/A	N/A
	Public Works	1.16	1.23	1.18	1.16	1.20	N/A	N/A
	Health/Welfare	0.07	0.68	1.26	2.69	2.26	N/A	N/A
	Recreation/Culture	0.52	0.77	1.20	1.59	1.89	N/A	N/A
	Education	1.02	0.99	1.00	1.03	1.08	1.04	1.07
0.5% to 1.0% increase	General Government	0.77	0.92	1.27	1.06	1.59	N/A	N/A
	Public Safety	0.62	0.98	1.35	1.21	1.50	N/A	N/A
	Public Works	1.14	1.33	1.16	1.05	0.99	N/A	N/A
	Health/Welfare	0.04	0.41	1.45	1.04	2.35	N/A	N/A
	Recreation/Culture	0.46	0.73	1.10	1.29	1.06	N/A	N/A
	Education	1.02	0.99	1.00	1.03	1.08	1.04	1.07
1.0% to 1.5% increase	General Government	0.73	0.91	1.00	1.07	0.98	N/A	N/A
	Public Safety	0.59	0.95	1.22	1.25	1.37	N/A	N/A
	Public Works	1.14	1.08	1.14	0.99	1.14	N/A	N/A
	Health/Welfare	0.04	0.54	0.45	0.86	0.45	N/A	N/A
	Recreation/Culture	0.45	0.91	1.13	1.02	1.99	N/A	N/A
	Education	1.02	0.99	1.00	1.03	1.08	1.04	1.07
School District Enrollment (Number of Students)	(Use for Education)	Less than 1,200	1,200– 2,499	2,500– 4,999	5,000– 9,999	10,000– 24,999	25,000– 99,999	100,000 And Over

*Data not available.

Source: U.S. Census of Governments, 1972. These figures are to be read as follows: In a municipality whose size falls between 10,001 and 25,000 and has a growth gain between .5% and 1.0%, the appropriate median general goverment operating expenditure multiplier is 0.92. In a school district whose enrollment (pupils) falls at less than 1,200, the appropriate median operating expenditure multiplier is 1.02.

EXHIBIT 5-2 (Cont'd)
MUNICIPAL AND SCHOOL DISTRICT MEDIAN OPERATING EXPENDITURE MULTIPLIERS BY POPULATION SIZE AND GROWTH RATE

Municipal Population (Number of Residents)	(Use for Municipal Functions)	(1) 1,000–10,000	(2) 10,001–25,000	(3) 25,001–50,000	(4) 50,001–100,000	(5) 100,001–500,000	(6) 500,001–1,000,000	(7) Over 1,000,000
1.5% to 2.0% increase	General Government	0.82	0.96	1.22	1.01	1.37	N/A*	N/A
	Public Safety	0.61	0.82	1.21	1.41	1.28	N/A	N/A
	Public Works	1.14	1.19	1.14	1.22	1.28	N/A	N/A
	Health/Welfare	0.04	0.58	0.77	1.63	3.16	N/A	N/A
	Recreation/Culture	0.48	0.77	0.95	1.11	1.51	N/A	N/A
	Education	1.02	0.99	1.00	1.03	1.08	1.04	1.07
over 2.0% increase	General Government	0.81	0.86	1.00	1.21	1.19	1.30	N/A
	Public Safety	0.62	0.82	1.00	1.24	1.39	1.47	N/A
	Public Works	1.05	1.05	1.00	0.98	1.04	1.06	N/A
	Health/Welfare	0.04	0.58	1.00	0.20	0.54	2.98	N/A
	Recreation/Culture	0.44	0.64	1.00	1.37	1.50	1.76	N/A
	Education	1.02	0.99	1.00	1.03	1.08	1.04	1.07
0% to 0.5% decrease	General Government	0.69	0.97	1.23	1.59	1.47	2.35	N/A
	Public Safety	0.58	0.94	1.09	1.40	1.61	3.38	N/A
	Public Works	1.10	1.21	1.26	1.21	1.20	1.51	N/A
	Health/Welfare	0.04	0.32	0.86	1.48	3.97	4.44	N/A
	Recreation/Culture	0.40	0.89	1.02	1.13	1.51	3.11	N/A
	Education	1.02	0.99	1.00	1.03	1.08	1.04	1.07
School District Enrollment (Number of Students)	(Use for Education)	Less than 1,200	1,200–2,499	2,500–4,999	5,000–9,999	10,000–24,999	25,000–99,999	100,000 And Over

*Data not available.

Source: U.S. Census of Governments, 1972. These figures are to be read as follows: In a municipality whose size falls between 10,001 and 25,000 and has a growth rate between 1.5% and 2.0%, the appropriate median general government operating expenditure multiplier is 0.96. In a school district whose enrollment (pupils) falls at less than 1,200, the appropriate median operating expenditure multiplier is 1.02.

spent $21.50 per capita.* All other groups of communities were given a multiplier that reflected the ratio of their general government expenditures to those of the "common" group cities. For instance, localities in the 1,000 to 10,000 size category, exhibiting a population loss of 2 percent or more annually, exhibited a median annual per capita general government expenditure of $15.00. The ratio of this figure to the previous $21.50 for the "common group" cities, 0.70 ($15.00/21.50), is the expenditure multiplier for this group of cities' general government services. Multipliers for population size/growth rate groups within other service categories are calculated in the same way — using median expenditures of the 25,000 to 50,000 population cell and over 2 percent growth rate as the standard upon which to base expenditures.

The analyst must consider two sets of expenditure multipliers: (1) multipliers appropriate to the community without the growth catalyst (referred to as "current multipliers") and (2) multipliers applicable to the locality after population growth (referred to as "future multipliers"). In each case, the multipliers pertain to particular community sizes/growth rates evident at distinct times.

---

*U.S. Census of Governments, 1972.

Comparable City

EXHIBIT 5-2 (Cont'd)
MUNICIPAL AND SCHOOL DISTRICT MEDIAN OPERATING EXPENDITURE MULTIPLIERS
BY POPULATION SIZE AND GROWTH RATE

Municipal Population (Number of Residents)	(Use for Municipal Functions)	(1) 1,000-10,000	(2) 10,001-25,000	(3) 25,001-50,000	(4) 50,001-100,000	(5) 100,001-500,000	(6) 500,001-1,000,000	(7) Over 1,000,000
.5% to 1.0% decrease	General Government	0.72	1.07	1.16	1.22	2.18	3.30	2.63
	Public Safety	0.60	0.98	1.31	1.51	1.85	2.86	2.83
	Public Works	1.13	1.18	1.18	1.08	1.10	1.35	1.38
	Health/Welfare	0.04	0.26	2.03	2.98	3.66	2.19	6.00
	Recreation/Culture	0.40	0.79	0.87	0.85	1.65	2.11	1.54
	Education	1.02	0.99	1.01	1.03	1.08	1.04	1.07
1.0% to 2.0% decrease	General Government	0.73	0.97	1.19	2.00	1.73	1.63	N/A*
	Public Safety	0.58	1.02	1.36	1.69	2.23	2.34	N/A
	Public Works	1.05	1.14	1.33	1.35	1.38	1.23	N/A
	Health/Welfare	0.14	0.63	0.95	0.99	2.03	4.79	N/A
	Recreation/Culture	0.38	0.70	0.98	1.12	1.45	1.88	N/A
	Education	1.02	0.99	1.00	1.03	1.08	1.04	1.07
Over 2.0% decrease	General Government	0.70	0.71	1.09	N/A	N/A	N/A	N/A
	Public Safety	0.68	1.18	1.44	N/A	N/A	N/A	N/A
	Public Works	0.92	1.10	1.19	N/A	N/A	N/A	N/A
	Health/Welfare	0.04	0.41	0.09	N/A	N/A	N/A	N/A
	Recreation/Culture	0.26	0.41	0.67	N/A	N/A	N/A	N/A
	Education	1.02	0.99	1.00	1.03	1.08	1.04	1.07
School District Enrollment (Number of Students)	(Use for Education)	Less than 1,200	1,200-2,499	2,500-4,999	5,000-9,999	10,000-24,999	25,000-99,999	100,000 And Over

*Data not available.

Source: U.S. Census of Governments, 1972. These figures are to be read as follows: In a municipality whose size falls between 10,001 and 25,000 and has a growth loss between 0.5% and 1.0%, the appropriate median general government operating expenditure multiplier is 1.07. In a school district whose enrollment (pupils) falls between at less then 1,200, the appropriate median operating expenditure multiplier is 1.02.

The analyst must know *current* community size before he can determine the magnitude and rate of population change. The *current* annual growth rate is obtained by comparing the community's current population estimate with its population determined in the latest decennial census and dividing the difference by the decennial population. This process yields the total percentage change since the latest census; annual change or growth rate is determined by dividing this total by the number of years between the census and the current estimate. To illustrate, the California community chosen for analysis had an estimated population of 16,000 in 1976. In 1970 its recorded census population was 14,500. Its total growth rate over the six-year period was thus 10.3 percent $(1,500/14,500 = .103)$; its annual growth rate was 1.7 percent $(.103/6 = .017)$.

Determining future community size/growth rate is a more intricate calculation. Like the former operation, however, it is a basic arithmetic calculation. The community's *future* size equals the sum of two population components: (1) current residents and (2) the population added by the specific growth proposal under study. Both the current size of the community and the population introduced by the proposed growth were obtained in step 2. Dividing the development population increase expressed as a percentage of current population by the number of years into the future for which it is projected yields the *future* annual growth rate.

EXHIBIT 5-3

MUNICIPAL AND SCHOOL DISTRICT MEDIAN CAPITAL EXPENDITURE MULTIPLIERS
BY POPULATION SIZE AND GROWTH RATE

Municipal Population (Number of Residents)	(Use for Municipal Functions)	(1) 1,000–10,000	(2) 10,001–25,000	(3) 25,001–50,000	(4) 50,001–100,000	(5) 100,001–500,000	(6) 500,001–1,000,000	(7) Over 1,000,000
0% to 0.5% increase	General Government	0.17	0.31	0.49	1.50	0.75	N/A*	N/A
	Public Safety	1.01	1.03	1.61	3.63	4.18	N/A	N/A
	Public Works	0.48	0.44	0.62	0.92	1.15	N/A	N/A
	Health/Welfare	0.50	0.83	1.33	2.67	4.17	N/A	N/A
	Recreation/Culture	0.04	0.35	0.46	1.05	1.05	N/A	N/A
	Education	1.01	1.05	1.00	1.19	1.60	2.64	2.07
0.5% to 1.0% increase	General Government	0.09	0.31	0.95	0.51	2.68	N/A	N/A
	Public Safety	0.91	1.11	0.87	1.48	2.80	N/A	N/A
	Public Works	0.44	0.58	0.62	1.17	1.59	N/A	N/A
	Health/Welfare	0.50	1.50	1.17	3.17	12.50	N/A	N/A
	Recreation/Culture	0.04	0.55	0.64	0.68	0.36	N/A	N/A
	Education	1.01	1.05	1.00	1.19	1.60	2.64	2.07
1.0% to 1.5% increase	General Government	0.15	0.25	0.33	0.83	1.38	N/A	N/A
	Public Safety	0.87	1.00	1.18	0.97	2.54	N/A	N/A
	Public Works	0.44	0.60	0.67	0.83	2.05	N/A	N/A
	Health/Welfare	0.33	1.17	1.17	1.83	5.00	N/A	N/A
	Recreation/Culture	0.40	0.53	0.95	0.86	1.50	N/A	N/A
	Education	1.01	1.05	1.00	1.19	1.60	2.64	2.07
School District Enrollment (Number of Students)	(Use for Education)	Less than 1,200	1,200–2,499	2,500–4,999	5,000–9,999	10,000–24,999	25,000–99,999	100,000 And Over

*Data not available.

Source: U.S. Census of Governments, 1972. These figures are to be read as follows: In a municipality whose size falls between 10,001 and 25,000 and has a growth rate between 0.5% and 1.0%, the appropriate median general government capital expenditure multiplier is 0.31. In a school district whose enrollment (pupils) falls at less than 1,200, the appropriate median capital expenditure multiplier is 1.01.

After he determines the appropriate current and future community sizes and growth rates for the jurisdiction being studied, the analyst can then select the correct expenditure multipliers by service category from Exhibits 5-2 and 5-3.

To illustrate, the California community has a current population of 16,000 and an annual growth rate of 1.7 percent. The school district has 5,500 pupils. The appropriate current operating expenditure multiplier for general government services for a community of this size and growth rate is 0.96 (Exhibit 5-2); the corresponding capital expenditure multiplier is 0.21 (Exhibit 5-3). The appropriate school district operating and capital expenditure multipliers are 1.03 and 1.19, respectively.

Alternative 1 increases the community's population size to 23,652 over a five-year period, thus increasing population at an over 2 percent annual growth rate.* The community's new general government expenditure multiplier is 0.86 for operating and 0.49 for capital expenditures. (These

---

*Actually the change from 16,000 to 23,652 population over a 5-year period results in an annual simple population increase of almost 10 percent per year. In this method, however, the largest growth rate grouping is over 2 percent annually.

Comparable City

EXHIBIT 5-3 (Cont'd)

MUNICIPAL AND SCHOOL DISTRICT MEDIAN CAPITAL EXPENDITURE MULTIPLIERS
BY POPULATION SIZE AND GROWTH RATE

Municipal Population (Number of Residents)	(Use for Municipal Functions)	(1) 1,000– 10,000	(2) 10,001– 25,000	(3) 25,001– 50,000	(4) 50,001– 100,000	(5) 100,001– 500,000	(6) 500,001– 1,000,000	(7) Over 1,000,000
	General Government	0.23	0.21	0.39	0.71	2.13	N/A*	N/A
1.5%	Public Safety	0.85	0.81	2.07	1.69	2.37	N/A	N/A
to	Public Works	0.56	0.42	1.20	0.85	2.05	N/A	N/A
2.0%	Health/Welfare	0.33	0.67	2.50	2.00	16.67	N/A	N/A
increase	Recreation/Culture	0.05	0.36	0.77	0.82	5.27	N/A	N/A
	Education	1.01	1.05	1.00	1.19	1.60	2.64	2.07
	General Government	0.25	0.49	1.00	1.97	1.18	3.31	N/A
Over	Public Safety	1.08	1.00	1.00	1.78	2.83	3.13	N/A
2.0%	Public Works	0.60	0.75	1.00	1.48	1.87	2.88	N/A
increase	Health/Welfare	0.40	0.83	1.00	1.50	3.67	16.67	N/A
	Recreation/Culture	0.05	0.56	1.00	1.95	2.59	13.18	N/A
	Education	1.01	1.05	1.00	1.19	1.60	2.64	2.07
Population	General Government	0.11	0.37	0.40	0.79	1.66	1.82	N/A
Decline	Public Safety	0.77	1.06	1.56	1.44	3.00	4.40	N/A
0%	Public Works	0.41	0.57	0.96	0.80	1.69	4.26	N/A
to	Health/Welfare	0.33	0.83	2.33	2.33	10.33	26.66	N/A
0.5%	Recreation/Culture	0.04	0.39	0.86	1.11	2.57	4.16	N/A
decrease	Education	1.01	1.05	1.00	1.19	1.60	2.64	2.07
School District Enrollment (Number of Students)	(Use for Education)	Less than 1,200	1,200– 2,499	2,500– 4,999	5,000– 9,999	10,000– 24,999	25,000– 99,999	100,000 And Over

*Data not available.

Source: U.S. Census of Governments, 1972. These figures are to be read as follows: In a municipality whose size falls between 10,001 and 25,000 and has a growth gain between 1.5% and 2.0%, the appropriate median general government capital expenditure multiplier is 0.21. In a school district whose enrollment (pupils) falls at less than 1,200, the appropriate median capital expenditure multiplier is 1.01.

are the appropriate multipliers for municipalities of 10,001 to 25,000 population with a 2 percent plus annual growth rate.) The development alternative increases school enrollment to 7,759; school district operating and capital expenditure multipliers of 1.03 and 1.19 are appropriate. (These are multipliers for school districts of 5,000 to 9,999 enrollment.)

Multipliers for the other municipal and school district services are presented in Exhibit 5-4. This exhibit also contains the full set of current and future multipliers for alternatives 2 and 3. To illustrate, the former development increases the California community's population from 16,000 to 31,766 over a five-year period, thus increasing local population at an over 2 percent annual rate. The future general government operating expenditure multiplier is 1.00 while the capital multiplier is likewise 1.00 — the appropriate multipliers for communities with a 25,001 to 50,000 population and over 2 percent annual growth rate. This development expands school enrollment to 9,468. An operating expenditure multiplier of 1.03 and a capital multiplier of 1.19 (for school district size 5,000 to 9,999) is used.

Once the above operations have been completed, the analyst determines the future-to-current expenditure ratio by *dividing the post-growth by the pre-growth expenditure multipliers*. The division is done for all of the general municipal and school district services for both operating and capital expenditures. The post to pre-growth expenditure ratios *are central to this method for they*

EXHIBIT 5-3 (Cont'd)

MUNICIPAL AND SCHOOL DISTRICT MEDIAN CAPITAL EXPENDITURE MULTIPLIERS
BY POPULATION SIZE AND GROWTH RATE

Municipal Population (Number of Residents)	(Use for Municipal Functions)	(1) 1,000– 10,000	(2) 10,001– 25,000	(3) 25,001– 50,000	(4) 50,001– 100,000	(5) 100,001– 500,000	(6) 500,001– 1,000,000	(7) Over 1,000,000
0.5% to 1.0% decrease	General Government	0.03	0.39	0.83	1.34	1.62	5.45	5.45
	Public Safety	0.71	0.87	1.31	1.10	3.00	4.50	2.50
	Public Works	0.43	0.53	0.39	0.70	1.57	1.20	2.55
	Health/Welfare	0.50	0.83	1.83	3.50	16.67	20.00	1.75
	Recreation/Culture	0.04	0.31	0.27	0.52	3.05	16.50	1.23
	Education	1.01	1.05	1.00	1.19	1.60	2.64	2.07
1.0% to 2.0% decrease	General Government	0.09	0.18	0.36	1.26	2.33	1.58	N/A
	Public Safety	0.79	0.60	0.80	3.00	1.80	1.60	N/A
	Public Works	0.28	0.28	0.50	0.76	1.55	1.15	N/A
	Health/Welfare	0.05	11.00	2.50	22.50	10.00	15.00	N/A
	Recreation/Culture	0.04	0.15	0.29	0.30	10.68	2.36	N/A
	Education	1.01	1.05	1.00	1.19	1.60	2.64	2.07
Over 2.0% decrease	General Government	0.21	0.24	0.08	N/A*	N/A	N/A	N/A
	Public Safety	0.66	0.59	9.64	N/A	N/A	N/A	N/A
	Public Works	0.48	0.01	0.23	N/A	N/A	N/A	N/A
	Health/Welfare	2.67	5.50	0.00	N/A	N/A	N/A	N/A
	Recreation/Culture	0.04	0.23	0.27	N/A	N/A	N/A	N/A
	Education	1.01	1.05	1.00	1.19	1.60	2.64	2.07
School District Enrollment (Number of Students)	(Use for Education)	Less than 1,200	1,200– 2,499	2,500– 4,999	5,000– 9,999	10,000– 24,999	25,000– 99,999	100,000 And Over

*Data not available.

Source: U.S. Census of Governments, 1972. These figures are to be read as follows: In a municipality whose size fall between 10,001 and 25,000 and has a growth loss between 0.5% and 1.0%, the appropriate median general government capital expenditure multiplier is 0.39. In a school district whose enrollment (pupils) falls at less than 1,200, the appropriate median capital expenditure multiplier is 1.01.

foretell the effect of the growth-induced change on future per capita operating and capital expenditures.

To illustrate, the community's current general government operating expenditure multiplier is .96 while its future operating multiplier under alternative 1 would be .86. Its general government operating expenditure ratio of future to current expenditures is therefore .90 (.86/.96). Its per capita operating outlays for this municipal service may thus be expected to decrease by approximately 10 percent by moving to the new population size/growth rate. The change ratio for general government capital costs is 2.33 (.49/.21). The remaining ratio calculations for municipal (public safety, public works, health and welfare, recreation/culture) and school district (primary and secondary education) services due to the new servicing requirements engendered by alternative 1 are displayed in Exhibit 5-4. Servicing costs related to alternative 2 and 3 are also shown in this exhibit.

Step 3 Calculate Current Average Operating and Capital Expenditures Per Capita.

Ratios obtained in step 2 must be applied to estimates of existing per capita operating and capital expenditures for the five municipal services and the educational function. To estimate existing per

Comparable City

EXHIBIT 5-4
USING THE COMPARABLE CITY METHOD TO EVALUATE THE FISCAL IMPACT OF LAND USE ALTERNATIVES

Step 1	Step 2	Step 2	Step 2	Step 2	Step 2	Step 3	Step 4	Step 5	Step 5	Step 5	Step 5
Anticipated Increments of Population and School-Age Children (1)	Governmental Functions (2)	Current Expenditure Multipliers Operating (3)	Current Expenditure Multipliers Capital (3)	Future Expenditure Multipliers Operating (4)	Future Expenditure Multipliers Capital (4)	Future-Current Expenditure Multiplier Ratio Operating (5)	Future-Current Expenditure Multiplier Ratio Capital (5)	Current Annual Expenditures per Person and per Pupil Operating (6)	Current Annual Expenditures per Person and per Pupil Capital (6)	Future Annual Expenditures per Person and per Pupil Operating (7)	Future Annual Expenditures per Person and per Pupil Capital (7)	Future Total Annual Expenditures Operating (8)	Future Total Annual Expenditures Capital (8)	Current Total Annual Expenditures Operating (9)	Current Total Annual Expenditures Capital (9)	Net Annual by Function Operating (10)	Net Annual by Function Capital (10)	Total Operating and Capital Costs

LAND USE ALTERNATIVE 1

2000 single-family homes (average market value — $50,000)

7,652 Population
2,259 School-age children

MUNICIPAL
	General government	0.96	0.21	0.86	0.49	0.90	2.33	$15.54	$1.93	$13.99	$4.50	$330,891	$106,434	$248,640	$30,880	$82,251	$75,554	$157,805
	Public safety	0.82	0.81	0.82	1.00	1.00	1.23	38.52	5.15	38.52	6.33	911,075	149,717	616,320	82,400	294,755	67,317	362,072
	Public works	1.19	0.42	1.05	0.75	0.88	1.79	48.80	13.49	42.94	24.15	1,015,617	571,196	780,800	215,840	234,817	355,356	590,173
	Health and welfare	0.58	0.67	0.58	0.83	1.00	1.24	4.10	0.65	4.10	0.81	96,973	19,158	65,600	10,400	31,373	8,758	40,131
	Recreation and culture	0.77	0.36	0.64	0.56	0.83	1.56	5.50	0.81	4.57	1.26	108,090	29,802	88,000	12,960	20,090	16,842	36,932
	TOTAL MUNICIPAL											$2,462,646	$876,307	$1,799,360	$352,480	$663,286	$523,827	$1,187,113

SCHOOL DISTRICT
| | Primary/secondary schools | 1.03 | 1.19 | 1.03 | 1.19 | 1.00 | 1.00 | $1,217.00 | $80.00 | $1,217.00 | $80.00 | $9,442,720 | $620,720 | $6,693,500 | $440,000 | $2,749,203 | $180,720 | $2,929,923 |
| | ***TOTAL MUNICIPAL AND SCHOOL DISTRICT*** | | | | | | | | | | | | | | | | | |

LAND USE ALTERNATIVE 2

Mixed-use development (2500 townhouses, 1500 single-family homes, 1,000 condominiums) (average market value — $35,000)

15,652 Population
3,968 School-age children

MUNICIPAL
	General government	0.96	0.21	1.00	1.00	1.04	4.76	$15.54	$1.93	$16.16	$9.19	$513,339	$291,930	$248,640	$30,880	$264,699	$261,050	$525,749
	Public safety	0.82	0.81	1.00	1.00	1.22	1.23	38.52	5.15	46.99	6.33	1,492,684	201,079	616,320	82,400	876,364	118,679	995,043
	Public works	1.19	0.42	1.00	1.00	0.84	2.38	48.80	13.49	40.99	32.11	1,302,088	1,020,006	780,800	215,840	521,288	804,166	1,325,454
	Health and welfare	0.58	0.67	1.00	1.00	1.72	1.49	4.10	0.65	7.05	0.97	223,950	30,813	65,600	10,400	158,350	20,413	178,763
	Recreation and culture	0.77	0.36	1.00	1.00	1.30	2.78	5.50	0.81	7.15	2.25	227,127	71,474	88,000	12,960	139,127	58,514	197,641
	TOTAL MUNICIPAL											$3,759,188	$1,615,302	$1,799,360	$352,480	$1,959,828	$1,262,822	$3,222,650

SCHOOL DISTRICT
| | Primary/secondary schools | 1.03 | 1.19 | 1.03 | 1.19 | 1.00 | 1.00 | $1,217.00 | $80.00 | $1,217.00 | $80.00 | $11,522,556 | $757,440 | $6,693,500 | $440,000 | $4,829,056 | $317,440 | $5,146,496 |
| | ***TOTAL MUNICIPAL AND SCHOOL DISTRICT*** | | | | | | | | | | | | | | | | | $8,369,146 |

LAND USE ALTERNATIVE 3

7000 garden apartments (average rental $250/Mo.)

15,043 Population
1,827 School-age children

MUNICIPAL
	General government	0.96	0.27	1.00	1.00	1.04	4.76	$16.00	$1.93	$16.16	$9.19	$501,655	$285,285	$248,640	$30,880	$253,015	$254,405	$507,420
	Public safety	0.82	0.81	1.00	1.00	1.22	1.23	38.52	5.15	46.99	6.33	1,458,711	196,502	616,320	82,400	842,391	114,102	956,493
	Public works	1.19	0.42	1.00	1.00	0.84	2.38	48.80	13.49	40.99	32.11	1,272,453	996,791	780,800	215,840	491,653	780,951	1,272,604
	Health and welfare	0.58	0.67	1.00	1.00	1.72	1.49	4.10	0.65	7.05	0.97	218,853	30,112	65,600	10,400	153,253	19,712	172,965
	Recreation and culture	0.77	0.36	1.00	1.00	1.30	2.78	5.50	0.81	7.15	2.25	221,957	69,847	88,000	12,960	133,957	56,887	190,844
	TOTAL MUNICIPAL											$3,673,629	$1,578,537	$1,799,360	$352,480	$1,874,269	$1,226,057	$3,100,326

SCHOOL DISTRICT
| | Primary/secondary schools | 1.03 | 1.19 | 1.03 | 1.19 | 1.00 | 1.00 | $1,217.00 | $80.00 | $1,217.00 | $80.00 | $8,916,959 | $586,160 | $6,693,500 | $440,000 | $2,223,459 | $146,160 | $2,369,619 |
| | ***TOTAL MUNICIPAL AND SCHOOL DISTRICT*** | | | | | | | | | | | | | | | | | $5,469,945 |

Notes: Column (3) and (4) Data for these columns are derived from Exhibits 5-2 and 5-3.
Column (5) equals column (4) divided by column (3).
Column (6) data derived from Exhibit 5-5.
Column (7) equals column (6) multiplied by column (5).
Column (8) equals column (7) multiplied by total *future* population.
Column (9) equals column (6) multiplied by total *current* population.
Column (10) equals column (8) minus column (9).

capita outlays, the analyst divides total annual operating and capital debt service expenditures in each municipal service category by the total number of local residents. He obtains per pupil outlays by dividing school district expenditures by number of local public school children.

The analyst should first obtain a copy of the latest published municipal and school district budgets. He should then group the service subfunctions into the broader service categories of general government, public safety, public works, health/welfare, recreation/culture and education. Exhibit 5-2 in the Case Study Method may be employed as a grouping guide.

After services are classified the analyst calculates total operating and capital expenditures for each of the service categories. He determines total operating costs by summing the salaries, statutory outlays and material expenses for each subfunction. To illustrate, public works operating expenditures consist of the salaries and wages, benefit packages and miscellaneous expenses listed for the highways, sewer, sanitation, water supply departments, etc. Total capital expenditures in the form of debt service are calculated in the same way — combining the capital sums listed for each component service into the more encompassing municipal or school district category.

The analyst then divides the totals for operating and capital expenditures by service category by the latest estimate of local population (for the municipal functions) and school enrollment (for school district services) to obtain operating and capital costs per capita and per pupil. The latest municipal population estimate usually is available from the local planning department or city manager's office. Existing school enrollment is available from the research department of the local school district; it is often also contained in annual reports published by the state department of education.

Per capita cost calculations are illustrated in Exhibit 5-5. Per capita/pupil expenditures represent the best indication of current, local costs. Historical expenditure patterns of a particular community or school district are maintained as such into the future. They are subsequently modified by rate-of-change ratios that reflect economies or diseconomies of scale and a different growth rate, but previous patterns of under- or overexpenditure, as reflected in local per capita expenditure levels, remain essentially unchanged.

Step 4 Calculate Future Average Operating and Capital Expenditures Per Capita

The analyst can now calculate future per capita operating and capital expenditures by utilizing the data obtained in the previous two steps. Multiplying the current per capita outlays obtained in step 3 by the multiplier rate-of-change ratios derived in step 2 yields the projected future per capita/pupil expenses. To illustrate, the California community facing a choice between three growth alternatives had a $15.54 current general government per capita operating expenditure and spent $1.93 in capital outlays for this municipal service (See Exhibit 5-5). Under alternative 1 the community's change ratios are .90 and 2.33 for operating and capital expenditures. (See Exhibit 5-4.) Its future general government per capita operating expense is therefore $13.99 ($15.54 × .90) while its future per capita capital expenditure is $4.50 ($1.93 × 2.33). Future per capita costs for the other municipal functions and per pupil outlays by the school district are shown in Exhibit 5-4. This exhibit also shows the calculations for the remaining two alternatives.

This step permits the analyst a glimpse of the future local cost environment. It yields a detailed picture of which per capita costs will increase, and which will decrease, and what the exact magnitude of per capita and per pupil costs for the different municipal and school district services will be.

Comparable City

EXHIBIT 5-5

PER CAPITA/PER STUDENT COST CALCULATIONS BY SERVICE FUNCTION

Public Service Functions	Total Operating Cost	Total Capital Cost	Existing Municipal/ School District Populations	Operating Cost Per Capita/Student[1]	Average Per Capita/ Student Capital Cost[2]
MUNICIPAL					
General government	$248,640	$30,880	16,000	$15.54	$1.93
Public safety	616,320	82,400	16,000	38.52	5.15
Public works	780,800	215,840	16,000	48.80	13.49
Health and welfare	65,600	10,400	16,000	4.10	.65
Recreation and culture	88,000	12,900	16,000	5.50	.81
SCHOOL DISTRICT					
Primary & secondary education	6,693,500	440,000	5,500	1,217.00	80.00

Notes: [1] Equals total operating costs divided by the existing municipal/school district populations.

[2] Equals annual capital debt service costs divided by the existing municipal/school district populations.

Source: Costs were derived from local municipal and school district published budgets; population and student figures were provided by the municipal planning department and the research department of the local school district.

Step 5 Determine Net Costs Attributable to Growth

Step 5 uses the data obtained in steps 3 and 4 to project future local municipal and school district operating and capital costs directly attributable to growth. Multiplying the estimated future municipal per capita operating and capital outlays by the size of the community following the population change being studied yields the future total annual municipal operating and capital expenditures. This is done for all the categories of municipally-provided services. For school district services, future per capita operating and capital expenditures are multiplied by the future school population. The analyst must also perform the same operations to derive costs for current conditions. The product of the current operating and capital per capita/pupil expenditures and the current user or service populations is then subtracted from future estimates of servicing expenditures, and the difference is assigned as costs (both operating and capital) attributable to growth.

The California community considering alternative 1 would incur future aggregate general government operating costs of $13.99 \times 23,652$ or $330,891; future general government capital costs are $106,434 ($4.50 × 23,652). Current operating costs* for the same municipal service are $15.54 × 16,000 or $248,640; current capital expenditures are $30,880 ($1.93 × 16,000). The net costs assignable to the growth increment are $82,251 ($330,891 − $248,640) and $75,554 ($106,434 minus $30,880) for operating and capital expenditures. This procedure, repeated for each municipal service category, yields a total net annual cost assignable to alternative 1 of $1,187,113.

School district cost projections are derived following a similar strategy. The future annual gross school district expenditure equals the school district's future student body size (7,759) multiplied by the estimated future per pupil cost ($1,217) or $9,442,703 under alternative 1. Without the 2,000 single-family homes added by this land use strategy, the school district would provide services for 5,500 students; at a cost of $1,217 per pupil, the expected student outlay would be $6,693,500.* Aggregate school district capital costs for a projected future with alternative 1 are $620,720; current capital costs total $440,000. Thus, the net school district expenditures attributable to the first development alternative are the sum of $2,749,203 for operating costs ($9,442,703 minus $6,693,500) and $180,720 for capital expenditures ($620,720 minus $440,000) or $2,929,923. Combining this figure with the previous one for municipal costs yields a total of $4,117,036 attributable to growth from alternative 1.

Exhibit 5-4, columns (8), (9), and (10), show future and current operating and capital expenditures for municipal service and school district functions for the three development alternatives. Totals for all three development alternatives are summarized below. Marginal costs of public services are being assigned to the development whose impact is being evaluated. Thus, both the cost to serve the new population increment and the change in costs associated with serving che existing population are borne by the new development.

Development Alternative	Total Annual Municipal Cost	Total Annual School District Cost	Total Annual Municipal and School District Costs
1	$1,187,113	$2,929,923	$4,117,036
2	3,222,650	5,146,496	8,369,146
3	3,100,326	2,369,619	5,469,945

Step 6 Project Total Annual Public Revenue

The analyst must now project revenues resulting from each of the proposed alternatives. (Detailed instructions about how to calculate revenues are contained in Part 2.) He must consider all sources of both municipal and school district revenues: taxes (real property, sales, gross receipts, property transfers etc.); charges and miscellaneous fees (interest earnings, fees and permits, user charges etc.); and intergovernmental transfers (sales tax, income tax, revenue sharing, etc.). Exhibit 5-6 shows revenues for each of the three development alternatives for the California community.

---

*These costs can also be obtained from Exhibit 5-5.

Comparable City

EXHIBIT 5-6

COMPUTATION SHEET FOR REVENUE TABULATION*

REVENUE SOURCES	DOLLARS					
	Development Alternative #1		Development Alternative #2		Development Alternative #3	

MUNICIPAL

I. Own Source Revenues

A. Taxes
1. Real property	$ 480,000		$ 840,000		$ 545,328	
2. Personal property	24,000		42,000		27,266	
3. Property transfer	200,000		350,000		227,220	
4. Utility franchise	9,000		16,875		18,375	
5. Business franchise	2,000		2,000		2,000	
6. Cable T.V. franchise	8,640		21,600		30,240	
TOTAL TAXES		$ 723,640		$1,272,475		$ 850,429

B. Charges/Miscellaneous
1. Interest earnings	$ 25,461		$ 44,690		$ 28,946	
2. Fees and permits	63,035		157,586		220,621	
3. Fines/forfeitures	23,262		47,929		45,734	
4. User charges	76,673		157,975		150,731	
TOTAL CHARGES/MISCELLANEOUS		$ 188,431		$ 408,180		$ 446,032
TOTAL OWN SOURCE REVENUE		$ 912,071		$1,680,655		$1,296,461

II. Intergovernmental Transfers

A. State
1. Sales tax	$ 116,250		$ 203,438		$ 244,125	
2. Motor fuels	25,236		33,600		33,300	
3. Cigarettes/Alcohol	22,400		38,700		45,000	
4. Motor vehicle	49,500		74,250		84,600	
TOTAL STATE		$ 213,386		$ 349,988		$ 407,025

Federal
1. Revenue sharing	$ 28,500		$ 60,000		$ 22,500	
2. CETA	5,000		30,800		38,160	
3. Anti-recession			0		1,000	
TOTAL FEDERAL		$ 33,500		$ 90,800		$ 61,660
TOTAL INTERGOVERNMENTAL		$ 246,886		$ 440,788		$ 468,685
TOTAL MUNICIPAL		$1,158,957		$2,121,443		$1,765,146

SCHOOL DISTRICT

I. Own Source Revenues

A. Taxes
1. Real property	$1,250,000		$2,187,500		$1,420,125	
TOTAL TAXES		$1,250,000		$2,187,500		$1,420,125
B. Charges/Miscellaneous	$ 205,569		$ 361,088		$ 166,257	
TOTAL CHARGES/MISCELLANEOUS		$ 205,569		$ 361,088		$ 166,257
TOTAL OWN SOURCE REVENUE		$1,455,569		$2,548,588		$1,586,382

II. Intergovernmental Transfers

A. State
1. Foundation aid	$ 591,853		$ 876,928		$ 321,552	
2. Categorical aid	399,843		702,336		323,379	
3. State distributed federal Intergovernmental	185,238		325,376		149,814	
TOTAL STATE		$1,176,934		$1,904,640		$ 794,745

B. Federal
1. Federal aid	$ 0		$ 0		$ 0	
TOTAL FEDERAL		$ 0		$ 0		$ 0
TOTAL INTERGOVERNMENTAL		$1,176,934		$1,904,540		$ 794,745
TOTAL SCHOOL DISTRICT		$2,632,503		$4,453,228		$2,381,127
TOTAL MUNICIPAL/SCHOOL DISTRICT		$3,791,460		$6,574,671		$4,146,273

*For detailed calculations, see Exhibits 10-1 and 10-2 in Chapter 10.

Step 7 Calculate the Cost-Revenue Impact

The final step is to compare the costs incurred (from step 5) with the revenues produced (from step 6) by the growth alternatives under study. Net fiscal impact is obtained by comparing total costs generated with all derived revenues, i.e., the full array of operating and capital costs versus both own source and intergovernmental transfers. A summary of the fiscal impact for each alternative is shown below. Each alternative shows a projected loss to the municipality.

Development Alternative	Total Annual Municipal Cost	Total Annual Municipal Revenue	Total Annual Municipal Fiscal Impact	Total Annual School District Cost	Total Annual School District Revenue	Total Annual School District Fiscal Impact	Total Annual Municipal School District Fiscal Impact
1	$1,187,113	$1,158,957	$ -28,156	$2,929,923	$2,632,503	$-297,420	$ -325,571
2	3,222,650	2,121,443	-1,101,207	5,146,496	4,453,228	-693,268	-1,794,475
3	3,100,326	1,765,143	-1,335,183	2,369,619	2,381,127	+11,508	-1,323,675

Data Requirements

The most important data to implement the Comparable City Method are the expenditure multipliers for municipal and school district services, by community size and growth rate. These are shown in Exhibits 5-2 and 5-3. Other important data are household size and school age children for different types of housing, population estimates for the municipality and school district, and information about local revenues. Data requirements and sources for each step of the Comparable City Method are summarized in Exhibit 5-7.

Sophistication of User

The Comparable City Method should be used by a reasonably sophisticated analyst who has had some fiscal impact experience. Local staff planners and private planning consultants can use this technique. The method's assumptions are clear, data requirements are not excessive, arithmetic operations are straightforward, and the interpretation of results is very basic. These characteristics make the technique extremely attractive.

The novice must take care to select appropriate expenditure multipliers for the different municipal and school district services, use correct multipliers for household size and school-age children, and group local services according to the municipal service categories in the Case Study Method.

Advantages and Disadvantages

Advantages

Time and Cost The Comparable City Method is relatively inexpensive to effect. Time requirements to employ this method for the land use alternative example are shown in Exhibit 5-8.

Comparable City

EXHIBIT 5-7
COMPARABLE CITY METHOD: DATA REQUIREMENTS AND SOURCES

Step	Data Requirements	Source(s)	Comments
1 – Determine population and student growth	Multipliers for household size and school-age children for various housing types, i.e., single family homes, townhouses, etc.	Handbook, Chapter 13.	Use blended multipliers if detailed data on the exact types of housing to be included are unavailable.
	Existing community and school district size	U.S. Census, local/regional planning department; local school district superintendent's or business manager's office	Exact data on school district size should be available. Try to obtain updated information from previous census on local community size.
2 – Obtain appropriate expenditure multipliers and calculate the rate-of-change	1970 local population current local population; population/student growth attributable to growth, additional future population	Population data obtained in step 1. Local planning department or analyst's projections	
	Expenditure multipliers for different public functions differentiated by community size and growth rate	Exhibits 5-2 and 5-3	Make sure that expenditure multipliers for appropriate community and school district size/growth rate groups are used.
3 – Calculate current per capita expenditures	Municipal and school expenditures by service category	Local published municipal and school district budget available from local business administrator, town manager, town clerk, tax assessor, school district, superintendent or business manager (step 1)	The unpublished line item budget is not required.
	Existing population estimates for municipality and school district		
4 – Calculate future per capita expenditures	Current per capita expenditures	Step 3 in this method	
	Expenditure multiplier rate-of-change ratios	Step 2 in this method	
5 – Calculate costs attributable to growth	Future and current per capita expenditures	Steps 3 and 4 in this method	Be sure to subtract carefully the costs that would be incurred without the added population.
	Future and current population and student body size	Step 1 in this method	
6 – Project total annual public revenues	Municipal school district property tax rates	Local tax assessor's office or clerk's office	Part 2, Calculating Revenues, contains detailed information about where to obtain data on intergovernmental transfers as well as local sources of revenue.
	Property assessment procedures	Local/county tax assessor's office	
	Existing local real property tax base	Local/county tax assessor's office	
	State and federal intergovernmental transfer regulations.		
	For other data requirements, see Chapters 9 and 10		

Comparing this exhibit to similar exhibits for other *residential* fiscal impact strategies reveals the Comparable City Method is slightly less time consuming than both the Per Capita Multiplier and Service Standard Methods.

Availability of Required Data   The information required to use the Comparable City Method is readily available. Most of the information is found in this handbook; the remainder is available locally, usually in published form.

EXHIBIT 5-8

TIME ESTIMATES TO USE THE COMPARABLE CITY METHOD

Step Number	Activities	Time
1	Project population/student growth	2 hours
2	Obtain appropriate expenditure multiplier and calculate the rate-of-change in the multiplier	4 hours
3	Calculate current average operating and capital costs per capita	2 hours
4	Calculate future average operating and capital costs per capita	4 hours
5	Determine net annual costs attributable to growth	4 hours
6	Project total annual public revenues	10 hours
7	Calculate the cost revenue impact	2 hours
Report Preparation	Prepare and reproduce final report (optional)	10 hours
		38 hours

Disadvantages

Validity of the Expenditure Multipliers   The Comparable City Method assumes that local operating and capital expenditures attributable to growth will, in the long run, emulate the expense patterns of communities of comparable size and growth rate. This assumption allows the analyst to use the operating and capital expenditure multipliers shown in Exhibits 5-2 and 5-3. If local costs differ from the patterns indicated by the expenditure multipliers of comparable cities because there has been: (1) private or on-site assumption of typically public service functions, or (2) a significant change in the scope or scale of local public services provided by the municipality, average expenditure multipliers used to predict local response to population change, may tend to either under- or overestimate the true reaction.

Detail   While the Comparable City Method provides more detailed results than the Per Capita Multiplier Method, it gives the analyst considerably less specific information than other fiscal impact analysis methods. The Service Standard Method projects the personnel needs and capital costs for each of several local service departments. The Case Study Method yields an entire series of information about excess or deficient service capacity.

Acceptance   The Comparable City Method is not as prevalent nor as accepted as other fiscal impact procedures. In part, this is due to the newness of the technique and additionally to the fact that it has not been employed previously in a standardized fashion. The refining of this strategy by the introduction of national expenditure multipliers should make the method much more versatile and thus more accepted.

Interpreting Results

Each of the three development alternatives for the California community will occasion a net fiscal burden. The combined operating and capital cost-revenue deficit for the various alternatives varies from about $300,000 to about $1.8 million annually. Alternative 1 poses significantly less burden than either of the other two alternatives. Although alternative 1 introduces more people and pupils per unit, it also introduces significantly fewer dwelling units and thus a much smaller increment in municipal and school district service population than either of the other two alternatives.

The Comparable City Method can accentuate the level of local costs if operating or capital service costs per person increase with larger service populations. The Service Standard Method extends current service infrastructure characteristics into the future. The Comparable City Method, however, uses the service infrastructure costs of the size and growth rate to which the community will grow. This use can result in a significant increase in assignable costs. For instance, the municipal capital expenditure multiplier for the future population size and growth rate can be, on the average, two to three times the current level. In addition, each development alternative, in pushing the community to a new service threshold, bears the change in local service costs to current residents — again occasioning a severe test of fiscal impact.

The analyst must thus be sensitive to the size and scale of the proposed development alternative relative to existing conditions. If significant change in population size and/or growth rate will occur, then the analyst should use the Comparable City Method, because it assigns the cost of these changes to the growth which occasioned them. If however, population increase is slight and the community continues to grow at its present rate, then the Service Standard or Per Capita Multiplier Methods may be a more accurate gauge of costs.

NOTES

1. See pages 141–142.
2. See Harvey E. Brazer, *City Expenditures in the United States* (New York, National Bureau of Economic Research, 1959).
3. John T. Maslin and Kenneth E. Quindry, "A Note on City Expenditures Determinants," *Land Economics,* Vol. 16 February 1970).
4. W. Patrick Beaton, "Analyzing Municipal Expenditures: A Cross City Approach" (unpublished paper), Institute for Urban Studies and Community Service, University of North Carolina at Charlotte; George Sternlieb et al., *Housing Development and Municipal Costs* (New Brunswick, N.J.: Rutgers University Center for Urban Policy Research, 1973).
5. U.S. Department of Commerce, Bureau of Census, *Government Finances: Finances of Municipalities and Township Governments* (Vol. 4-4). *Finances of School Districts* (Vol. 4-3) (Washington, D.C.: U.S. Government Printing Office, 1974).
6. Brazer, *op. cit.;* Sternlieb *et al., op. cit.;* W. Patrick Beaton, "The Determinants of Police Protection Expenditures," *National Tax Journal* (June 1974); Roy W. Bahl, *Metropolitan City Expenditures: A Comparative Analysis* (Lexington, Ky.: University of Kentucky Press, 1969); William J. Baumol, "Urban Services: Interactions of Public and Private Decisions," in *Public Expenditure Decisions in the Urban Community,* ed. Howard G. Schaller (Washington, D.C.: Resources for the Future, 1963); John C. Weicher, "Determinants of Central City Expenditures: Some Overlooked Factors and Problems," *National Tax Journal* (December 1970).
7. Maslin and Quindry, *op. cit.;* William Miller, *Revenue-Cost Ratios of Rural Townships with Changing Land Uses* (Trenton, N.J.: New Jersey Department of Agriculture, 1965); Dick Netzer, "Financing Suburban Development," in *Studies of the Nassau-Suffolk* Planning Region, ed. Deiter K. Zschock (Stony Brook, 1969); Mordecai Feinberg, "The Implications of Core-City Decline for the Fiscal Structure of the Core-City," *National Tax Journal,* Vol. XVII (September 1964); Bahl, *op. cit.;* Beaton, *op. cit.;* Sternlieb *et al., op. cit.*

6

PROPORTIONAL VALUATION FISCAL IMPACT METHOD

Background

The Proportional Valuation Method is an average costing approach used to project the impact of *nonresidential (industrial and commercial)* development on local costs and revenues. Because data on real property value are almost universally maintained, analysts have regularly used this method, like the Case Study, to assess the municipal fiscal implications of commercial and industrial growth.

The Proportional Valuation Method assigns costs attributable to the share of the real property value that a nonresidential use adds to a community's real property tax base. Early nonresidential analyses conducted in the 1950s and 1960s by Margolis,[1] Bagby[2] and others[3] used either the Case Study or the Proportional Valuation Methods. These pre-1960 projections were concerned primarily with the question of whether nonresidential development as a class was a local fiscal benefit.

Studies undertaken in the late 1960s and early 1970s by Muller and Dawson, Fleck/Sterling, Gladstone Associates, Lowenstein, and the Miami Valley Regional Planning Commission[4] also have employed similar Case Study or Proportional Valuation methods. These analyses have gone beyond the "class" orientation of nonresidential fiscal impact and instead have focused on analyzing the impact of "categories" of industrial or commercial growth[5] as well as the impact of nonresidential growth within various fiscal contexts.[6] Parallel research during this time explored the possibility of using multivariate analysis to project the impact of nonresidential facilities on municipal costs; this approach is just beginning to gain acceptance.[7] (See the Employment Anticipation Method.)

The Proportional Valuation Method employs a two-step process to assign a share of municipal costs to a new commercial or industrial establishment. First, a share of total municipal costs is given to all local nonresidential uses. Second, a portion of these nonresidential costs is allocated to the incoming nonresidential facility. The method assumes that relative real property values represent shares of municipal costs. Experience has shown, however, that while the direction of this cost assignment procedure is relatively accurate, as the value of nonresidential property significantly differs from the average value of existing local property, the direct proportional assignment of costs tends either to overstate or understate the magnitude of assignable costs. Thus, the analyst must use refinement coefficients to compensate for this over- or understatement of costs, and to modify the direct proportional relationship in the allocation of municipal costs.

To illustrate, a local shopping center, valued at $5,000,000, is proposed for a Texas community whose total property valuation is $100,000,000 ($80,000,000 residential, farm, and vacant land, and $20,000,000 for commercial and industrial property). Annual municipal operating expenditures, including statutory and capital debt service costs, are $3,500,000.

The analyst using the Proportional Valuation Method first assigns a share of the $3,500,000 annual municipal operating expenditures to all local nonresidential uses. To do so, he multiplies all municipal costs by the product of local nonresidential real property valuation to total local real property valuation (in this example $20,000,000/$100,000,000 or 0.20) and a refinement coefficient (1.38).* The resulting share is $966,000. He next assigns a share of these costs to the incoming nonresidential facility by multiplying total nonresidential costs by the product of the real property valuation of the new facility to total local nonresidential valuation ($5,000,000/ $20,000,000 or 0.25) and a refinement coefficient (0.18). The result is $43,470. Costs are ten partitioned into the six categories of municipal service, using percentage distributions which have been derived from case studies, of other industrial and commercial fiscal impact.

Revenues are tabulated by municipal and school district own source revenues and intergovernmental transfers. The sum is compared with a projection of municipal costs to yield a statement of net fiscal impact.

Application

The application of the Proportional Valuation Method may best be described by comparing it with another long standing method for evaluating the fiscal impact of nonresidential uses, the Case Study, and to a new multivariate approach, the Employment Anticipation Method. The Proportional Valuation Method is a quick, straightforward technique to be used when the employment level of the nonresidential use being evaluated is neither very substantial nor comparatively low.

The analyst who wants a detailed picture of the effect of nonresidential growth, including a projection of personnel requirements and intended capital facility improvements, should use the Case Study Method. The intricate mosaic of municipal service response to a proposed nonresidential use may be best deciphered through this method's interviews of local public officials and intensive on-site analysis. Department heads, sensitive to local service excess or deficiency and familiar with the response pattern of the community, usually are able to project the local incremental reaction to industrial or commercial development. This method usually results in an extremely detailed projection of future service response. Neither the Proportional Valuation nor the Employee Anticipation Methods, both based on data which are not as sensitive to specific local conditions, can yield the specific, site bound analysis of the Case Study.

The Case Study Method, however, demands numerous interviews and should be undertaken only when there is considerable economic resource commitment to the proposed study. In situations where a reasonable estimate is desired and/or where there are inadequate resources for

---

*The range of refinement coefficients and their varations with real property valuation are discussed in Step 2 of this method.

Proportional Valuation 121

effectively completing the Case Study, the Proportional Valuation or Employment Anticipation techniques should be used. The two methods are particularly useful in examining a single nonresidential, multistage use or several alternative nonresidential land uses for a particular site since it would strain the capacity of most organizations to embark on individual case studies when so many projections are required.

The Proportional Valuation and the Employee Anticipation Methods require similar resource allocations. The Employment Anticipation Method may be more appropriate than the Proportional Valuation Method, however, if the employment situation is unusual. A commercial or industrial use with relatively few employees compared to its valuation (a power station or mechanized storage facility, for example) is likely to generate less municipal cost than indicated if its incremental-to-total local real property valuation is used as a gauge. The Proportional Valuation Method is likely to overstate true costs in this instance. In contrast, a nonresidential use with many workers relative to its property value (a restaurant or amusement park, for example) may cause larger expenditures than might be indicated if costs are assigned in the simple proportion of their property values. Using the Proportional Valuation Method is likely to understate true costs.

Basic Assumptions

A basic assumption of the Proportional Valuation Method is that municipal costs increase with the intensity of land use, and change in real property value is a reasonable substitute for change in intensity of use. Further, as nonresidential real property value departs significantly from the average* local real property value, the direct proportional relationship must be refined to avoid either overstating (where incremental or average nonresidential real property value significantly exceeds average local property value) or understating costs (where incremental or average nonresidential real property value is significantly less than average local property value).

A third assumption is that the *aggregate* impacts of commercial and industrial land uses on municipal services are sufficiently similar to group these land uses in a single nonresidential category. The method does not distinguish between basic and service industries, companies that hire semiskilled versus highly skilled workers, and nonresidential uses with varying environmental consequences. Finally, it is assumed that nonresidential development primarily affects municipal functions rather than school district services, which may thus be ignored.

Procedures

The Proportional Valuation Method may be undertaken in six basic steps (See Exhibit 6-1). To overview, base data are collected in step 1. Costs are determined in steps 2 and 3 and allocated to specific service areas in step 4. Revenues are estimated in step 5 and net fiscal impact is obtained in step 6.

Step 1 *Assemble and Prepare Base Data*

The first step in completing the Proportional Valuation Method is to obtain local financial data. The range of information required to analyze the impact of a 100,000 square foot shopping center in a Texas community** is shown in Exhibit 6-2. It consists primarily of municipal expenditures, real property values, and land parcel characteristics in the locality where the analysis is being

---

*See Exhibit 6-2, items 6, 7, and 8.
**For a full description see Chapter 1.

EXHIBIT 6-1

PROPORTIONAL VALUATION FISCAL IMPACT METHOD: SUMMARY OF PROCEDURES

Step Number	Analysis/Actions
1	Obtain basic data including municipal expenditures, real property valuation, and land parcel characteristics of the locality where the cost revenue analysis is being conducted.
2	Assign a share of existing municipal expenditures to existing total nonresidential uses by using proportional valuation and refinement coefficients applied toward total local municipal expenditures.
3	Project future total annual nonresidential costs induced by the nonresidential facility being studied by using proportional valuation and refinement coefficients applied toward total local municipal expenditures induced by growth.
4	Assign total annual nonresidential facility costs to service categories (general government, public safety, public works, etc.).
5	Project total annual public revenues.
6	Calculate the cost-revenue surplus or deficit by comparing total revenues generated with total costs incurred.

conducted. Both municipal and school district real property tax rates must be obtained. Municipal expenditures may be found within the published summary budget available at the town clerk's, finance or local business administrator's office. The same offices can supply information about equalized tax rates for both the municipality and the school district.

Assessment information, both local assessed real property value (total and nonresidential) and the assessed value of the nonresidential property under study must also be obtained. To ensure that a common base is used to express value, the analyst should convert assessed value to equalized values* for segments of existing tax base and use the market value of the subject nonresidential facility. The analyst must also know the total number of land parcels in the community as well as the number of nonresidential land parcels. The best source of information about real property value and the number of land parcels is the local tax assessor's office. Other sources of similar data are the city manager, business administrator, finance director, and/or town clerk.

Definitions are extremely important in this step. Total local equalized real property value is the aggregate community market value of all local tax-paying properties—residential, farm, vacant, commercial, industrial, etc.—on which taxes are assessed. *Nonresidential real property value* is the market value solely of commercial and industrial tax-paying properties. *Total number of land parcels* is the sum of all local properties on which taxes are assessed. *Total nonresidential land parcels* is the sum of commercial and industrial tax-paying properties.

Step 2 Assign a Share of Existing Municipal Expenditures to Total Local Nonresidential Uses

Both nonresidential and residential land uses incur local municipal costs. To pinpoint the share of expenditures that a nonresidential facility will generate, the analyst must first determine the proportion of municipal outlays assignable to the nonresidential sector of the community. This method assumes that costs can be allocated based on the proportion of nonresidential to total local real property value. Since the relationship is nonlinear, it must be scaled to reflect this

---

*They can be readily derived by dividing the assessed or nonequalized real property value by a local equalization (assessment/sales) ratio. If a community has a tax base of $50,000,000 and a 50 percent equalization ratio, then its equalized real property value is $100,000,000 ($50,000,000/0.50).

Proportional Valuation

EXHIBIT 6-2

BASIC DATA REQUIRED TO IMPLEMENT THE PROPORTIONAL
VALUATION METHOD IN A TEXAS COMMUNITY

1.	Municipal annual operating expenditures (including statutory expenses and debt service)	$ 2,692,051
2.	Total local equalized real property value	$134,734,888
3.	Total number of land parcels	7,451
4.	Total nonresidential equalized real property value	$ 41,841,111
5.	Total number of nonresidential land parcels	637
6.	Average equalized real property value per parcel (2 ÷ 3)	$ 18,083
7.	Average nonresidential equalized real property value per parcel (4 ÷ 5)	$ 65,685
8.	Real property (market) value of 100,000 square foot shopping center (See Chapter 16 for derivation)	$ 4,000,000
9.	Equalized real property value average nonresidential parcel to average local parcel (7 ÷ 6)	3.6
10.	Real property value of facility to average nonresidential real property value (8 ÷ 7)	60.9

deviation through the application of a refinement coefficient. This process yields the dollar share of existing municipal expenditures attributable to local nonresidential uses. Expressed in formula terms:

Total Existing
Municipal
Expenditures   Proportion of
Attributable   Total   Nonresidential
to Nonresidential = Municipal   ×   Value to   × Refinement
Uses   Expenditures   Total Local Real   Coefficient
                                          Property Value

To illustrate, a fiscal impact analysis is being completed for a 100,000 square foot shopping center in a hypothetical Texas community. To assign a share of all municipal costs to the nonresidential sector of the community, the analyst first divides the community's nonresidential equalized real property value ($41,841,111) by total local equalized real property value ($134,734,888). This calculation yields the simple proportion of nonresidential to total local real property value, in this case 0.31.

The analyst must then select a refinement coefficient from Exhibit 6-3.

There are two curves in Exhibit 6-3. They are upper and lower bands of a third (not shown) which depicts the relationship of the real property value of a nonresidential facility undergoing fiscal impact analysis to the average value of all local real property. This third curve has been derived from detailed case studies of actual nonresidential municipal costs compared with what would have been assigned to them had a simple proportion of total local real property value been used. Upper and lower bands of this curve should be used because it is more efficient to assign first a share of costs to the nonresidential sector and then a component of these costs to the facility being examined. To read the graph, the analyst proceeds as follows. The x (horizontal) axis shows a relationship between valuation of properties—either average nonresidential to average local real property value (the upper band) or facility real property value to average nonresidential real property value (the lower band). The refinement coefficient is found on the y (vertical) axis, horizontally opposite the intersection of the relationship between valuation of properties and the appropriate upper or lower band.

EXHIBIT 6-3

REFINEMENT COEFFICIENTS FOR THE PROPORTIONAL VALUATION FISCAL IMPACT METHOD

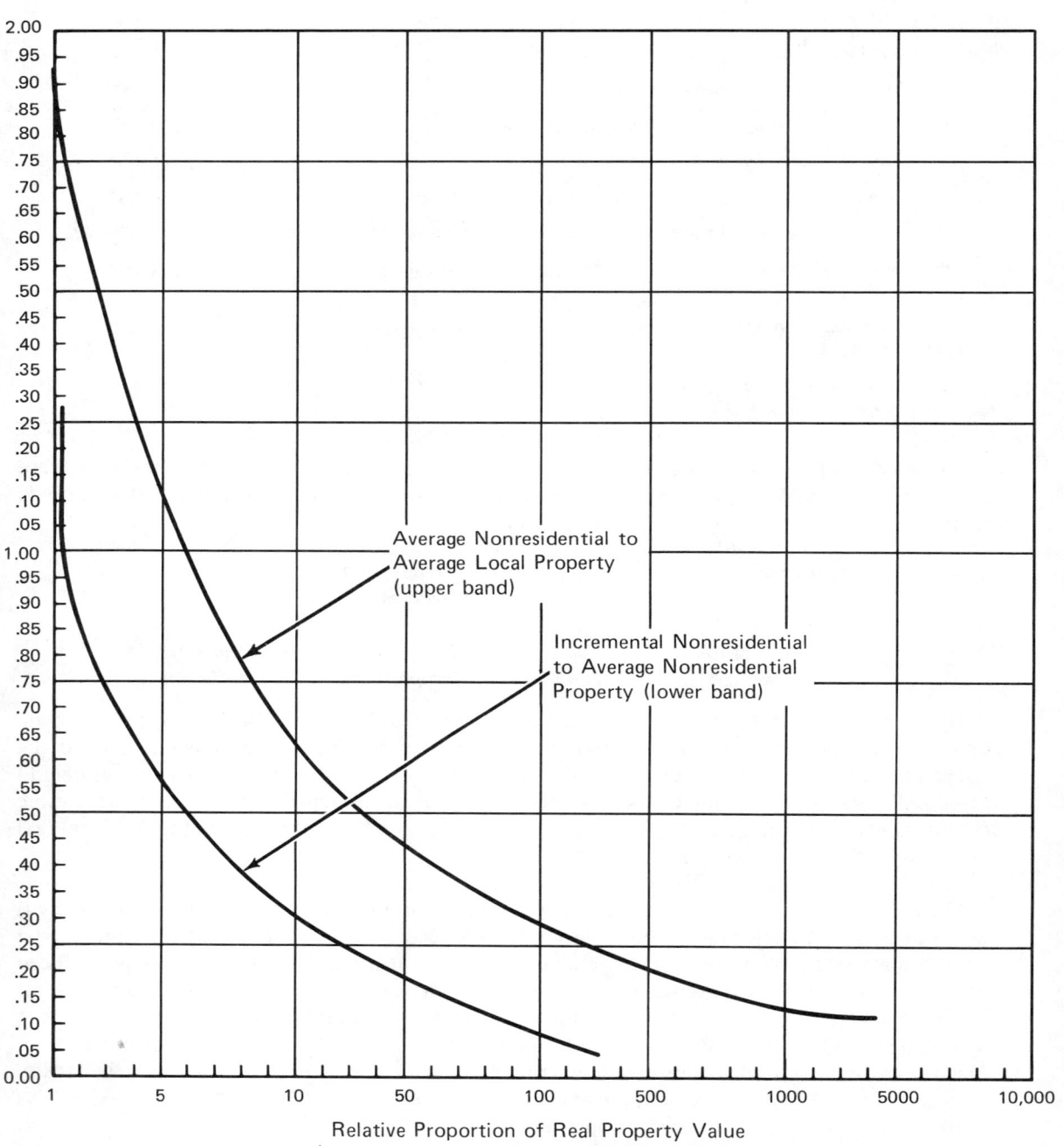

Source: Case Studies of Nonresidential Impact—Rutgers University, Spring, 1977.

Proportional Valuation 125

To select the first refinement coefficient the analyst must derive the relationship of average nonresidential to average local real property value. To do so, he divides nonresidential equalized real property value by the number of nonresidential land parcels and total real property value by the total number of land parcels. These two quotients are then divided by each other. For the Texas example, the procedure may be summarized as follows:

$$\frac{\text{Nonresidential Equalized Real Property Value}}{\text{Number of Nonresidential Land Parcels}} \qquad \frac{\text{Total Equalized Real Property Value}}{\text{Total Number of Land Parcels}} \qquad \frac{\text{Average Nonresidential Real Property Value}}{\text{Average Local Real Property Value}}$$

$$\frac{\$41{,}841{,}111}{637} = \$65{,}685 \qquad \frac{\$134{,}734{,}888}{7{,}451} = \$18{,}083 \qquad \frac{\$65{,}685}{\$18{,}083} = 3.6$$

Thus, the average nonresidential property is valued at 3.6 times the average local property. The analyst uses this figure to enter Exhibit 6-3 (x-axis, 3.60) and picks from the *upper* curve a refinement coefficient (y-axis, 1.30). When the average nonresidential property is valued at 3.6 times the average local property an insufficient share of local costs is being assigned via the simple proportion of aggregate real property value. Empirical evidence has shown that this cost should be increased. The vehicle which accomplishes this is the refinement coefficient. Applying the refinement coefficient to the simple proportion of value and multiplying by total municipal operating costs results in an increased share of total municipal operating costs assigned to aggregate local nonresidential uses.

$$\begin{array}{c}\text{Total Existing Municipal Expenditures Attributable to Nonresidential Uses}\end{array} = \begin{array}{c}\text{Total Local Municipal Expenditures}\end{array} \times \begin{array}{c}\text{Proportion of Nonresidential Value to Total Local Real Property Value}\end{array} \times \begin{array}{c}\text{Refinement Coefficient}\end{array}$$

$$\$1{,}084{,}897 = \$2{,}692{,}051 \times (.31) \times (1.30)$$

Step 3 Project the Future Total Municipal Operating Costs Induced by the Future Nonresidential Use.

Having isolated total municipal expenditures assignable to existing nonresidential development, the analyst must now project the share of this total that is expected to be generated by the incoming nonresidential facility. He uses a procedure similar to the one described for step 2. First, he divides the market value of the nonresidential facility by the average nonresidential parcel value to determine a simple proportion of value. He then multiplies by a refinement coefficient. The product of this multiplication carves out, from total local nonresidential expenditures, a share of costs which would be assigned to the nonresidential facility if it were to locate in the community. This estimate of the magnitude of assignable costs is then transferred to the new facility. Again language plays an important part here. A portion of *existing* costs is not being assigned to the new facility. Rather, a portion of existing costs is being used to gauge what the servicing cost of the new facility might be. If the new facility is developed locally these costs would be *in addition* to current local costs. The formula is as follows:

Costs Assignable to the Incoming Nonresidential Facility = Total Municipal Expenditures Assigned to the Nonresidential Sector × Proportion of the Incoming Nonresidential Facility to Total Local Nonresidential Real Property Value × Refinement Coefficient

In the Texas example the market value of the incoming shopping center is estimated at $4,000,000. (Exhibit 6-2.) If the value of the property is not known, it may be estimated using the information contained in Chapter 16.

Total nonresidential equalized real property value is $41,841,111 (Exhibit 6-2). The simple proportion of facility equalized real property value to average nonresidential real property value is thus 0.096 ($4,000,000/$41,841,111). The analyst then uses this relationship to select a refinement coefficient—this time from the lower band.

Dividing facility real property value ($4,000,000) by the average nonresidential real property value ($65,685) per parcel indicates that the real property value of the new nonresidential facility is 60.9 times the average nonresidential real property value. The analyst then finds this figure on the x-axis and picks a refinement coefficient where the lower curve intersects the y-axis (0.15). In other words, when a facility is valued at sixty times the average value of local nonresidential properties, the simple proportion overstates actual municipal costs. Applying the refinement coefficient to the simple proportion of value and multiplying this figure by municipal expenditures attributable to nonresidential uses yields the percentage share of nonresidential costs assigned to the new facility.

Municipal Costs Allocated to the Nonresidential Facility = Total Existing Municipal Expenditures Attributable to Nonresidential Uses × Proportion of Facility to Total Local Nonresidential Real Property Value × Refinement Coefficient

$15,623 = $1,084,897 × (.096) × (.15)

Step 4 Assign Total Annual Nonresidential Facility Costs to Component Service Categories.

To project the specific impact of a nonresidential facility on various local services, the analyst must use information obtained through retrospective case studies. Case studies of several industrial and commercial developments in New Jersey municipalities, confirmed by case studies of nonresidential facilities elsewhere, indicate that commercial uses affect primarily public safety expenditures, whereas, industrial land uses share this heavy public safety impact with a public works component. Commercial uses require traffic control services, regular vehicle patrols and occasionally require site visits for investigations of petty larceny, street disturbances, etc. Industrial development, while on occasion heavily using public safety traffic services during the "working day," infrequently requires weekend or evening public safety services. It does, however, draw regularly on public works, road repair and maintenance services and occasionally is charged its share of on-site street lighting services.

The other areas of municipal service are impacted minimally. For general government, the new

Proportional Valuation

nonresidential facility is just one of many land parcels on which records are maintained. For recreation and culture, service costs involve primarily the extension of municipal library activities to nonresident workers or shoppers; for health and welfare they comprise the provision of health inspection services to on-site eating or rest room facilities.

The analyst must therefore temper his distribution of aggregate municipal costs with the kinds of services provided locally. He must also take into account the potential assumption of typically public services by the private facility. The distribution of services shown in Exhibit 6-4 is, however, a reasonable gauge of the order of magnitude of likely impact, by service category.

EXHIBIT 6-4

TYPICAL IMPACT OF NONRESIDENTIAL USES ON VARIOUS LOCAL PUBLIC SERVICE CATEGORIES

	NONRESIDENTIAL USE Percentage Distribution			
	Industrial		Commercial	
Service Category *	Mid - Point	Range	Mid - Point	Range
General Government	6	4 - 8	6	4 - 8
Public Safety	45	35 - 55	75	60 - 90
Public Works	45	35 - 55	15	10 - 20
Health and Welfare	3	2 - 4	2	1 - 3
Recreation and Culture	1	0 - 2	2	1 - 3
TOTAL	100	-	100	-

*Includes statutory and capital debt service costs

Source: Case studies conducted by the Rutgers University Center for Urban Policy Research, spring 1977.

In Exhibit 6-5 the multiple steps of the calculation process are repeated for the example Texas community.

Step 5 Project Total Annual Public Revenue

The analyst must now project revenues resulting from the proposed shopping center. (Detailed instructions about how to calculate revenues are contained in Part II.) He must consider all sources of both municipal and school district revenues: taxes (real property, sales, gross receipts, property transfers, etc.); charges and miscellaneous fees (interest earnings, fees and permits, user charges, etc.); and intergovernmental transfers (sales tax, income tax, revenue sharing, etc.). Exhibit 6-6 shows revenue sources for the Texas community in the example.

As indicated in Exhibit 6-6 for this example, municipal own source revenue equals $34,820 while municipal intergovernmental aid is $98,050; total municipal revenues are thus $132,870. School district own source revenues are tabulated to be $37,600; there are no projected school district intergovernmental flows. Total revenues accruing locally are $170,470.

Step 6 Calculate the Cost Revenue Impact

The final step in this as in other methods is to project the costs incurred versus revenues produced by the development under study. This is accomplished by comparing the results obtained in step 4 to those of step 5. Actual net fiscal impact is obtained by comparing total municipal costs to total derived revenues.

In this example, the community shopping center would produce a surplus of $154,847 since it would generate $15,623 in costs, compared to $170,470 in derived revenues.

EXHIBIT 6-5

USING THE PROPORTIONAL VALUATION METHOD TO PROJECT THE FISCAL IMPACT
OF A PROPOSED NONRESIDENTIAL DEVELOPMENT

LOCAL NONRESIDENTIAL USE COST PROJECTION (Step 2)

Total Existing Municipal Expenditures Attributable to Nonresidential Uses	=	Total Municipal Expenditures	X	Proportion of Nonresidential Value to Total Local Real Property Value[1]	X	Refinement Coefficient[2]
		$2,692,051	X	($ 41,841,111 / 134,734,889)	X	1.30)
$1,084,897		$2,692,051	X	(.31	X	1.30)

INCOMING NONRESIDENTIAL USE COST PROJECTION (Step 3)

Municipal Costs Allocated to the Incoming Nonresidential Facility	=	Total Existing Municipal Expenditures Attributable to Nonresidential Uses	X	Proportion of Facility to Total Local Nonresidential Real Property Value[3]	X	Refinement Coefficient[4]
		$1,084,897	X	($ 4,000,000 / 41,841,111)	X	.15)
$ 15,623		$1,084,897	X	(.096	X	.15)

INCOMING NONRESIDENTIAL USE COST DISTRIBUTION (Step 4)

Distribution of Total Costs

Municipal Service Category*	Percentage[5]	Dollars
General Government	6	$ 937
Public Safety	75	11,717
Public Works	15	2,343
Health and Welfare	2	313
Recreation and Culture	2	313
TOTAL	100	$15,623

* Includes statutory and capital debt service costs

[1] Simple Proportional Valuation = $\dfrac{\text{Existing Total Local Nonresidential Real Property Value}}{\text{Total Local Real Property Value}}$

[2] The value multiplier for the refinement coefficient is determined by comparing the average value of nonresidential parcels to the average value of all parcels.

[3] Simple Proportional Valuation = $\dfrac{\text{Subject Nonresidential Real Property Value}}{\text{Existing Total Nonresidential Real Property Value}}$

[4] The value multiplier for the refinement coefficient is determined by comparing the value of the new nonresidential facility to the average value of local nonresidential parcels.

[5] Percentage distribution for commercial nonresidential uses. See Exhibit 6-4.

Proportional Valuation

EXHIBIT 6-6
COMPUTATION SHEET FOR REVENUE TABULATION *

REVENUE SOURCES			
MUNICIPAL			
I. Own Source Revenues			
A. Taxes			
1. Real Property		$ 30,000	
2. Utility Franchise		$ 2,820	
TOTAL TAXES			$ 32,820
B. Charges/Miscellaneous			
1. User Charges (sanitation)		$ 2,000	
TOTAL CHARGES/MISCELLANEOUS			$ 2,000
TOTAL OWN SOURCE REVENUE			$ 34,820
II. Intergovernmental Transfers			
A. State			
1. Sales Tax		$100,000	
TOTAL STATE			$100,000
B. Federal			
1. CDBG		$ -1,950	
TOTAL FEDERAL			$ -1,950
TOTAL INTERGOVERNMENTAL REVENUE			$ 98,050
TOTAL MUNICIPAL REVENUE			$132,870
SCHOOL DISTRICT			
I. Own Source Revenues			
A. Taxes			
1. Real Property		$ 37,600	
TOTAL TAXES			$ 37,600
B. Charges/Miscellaneous			
1. No revenues		$ 0	
TOTAL CHARGES/MISCELLANEOUS			$ 0
TOTAL OWN SOURCE REVENUE			$ 37,600
II. Intergovernmental Transfers			
A. State			
1. No revenues		$ 0	
TOTAL STATE			$ 0
B. Federal			
1. No revenues		$ 0	
TOTAL FEDERAL			$ 0
TOTAL INTERGOVERNMENTAL REVENUE			$ 0
TOTAL SCHOOL DISTRICT REVENUE			$ 37,600
TOTAL MUNICIPAL/SCHOOL DISTRICT REVENUE			$170,470

*For detailed calculations, see Exhibits 10-1 and 10-2 in Chapter 10.

Data Requirements

The Proportional Valuation Method requires a limited amount of data; most of it readily available. The most important segment of information is the equalized real property value—for the new nonresidential facility, for all nonresidential real property, and for all local real property. This information is available from the local tax assessor. Refinement coefficients, to scale the costs to all nonresidential property and to the new nonresidential facility, are found in Exhibit 6-3. Information about local revenues can be obtained from the local business administrator or town clerk. Data requirements and sources of these data for each step of this method are summarized in Exhibit 6-7.

Sophistication of User

Of the three nonresidential cost revenue methods, the Proportional Valuation Method requires the least amount of user sophistication. Local staff planners and private planning consultants with limited fiscal impact experience should encounter few problems in implementing this method. The assumptions are few and clear, there are limited data requirements, calculations are simple and interpretation of results is relatively straightforward.

Advantages and Disadvantages

Advantages

Time and Cost The Proportional Valuation Method may be completed quickly and inexpensively. Exhibit 6-8 illustrates the time commitments necessary to implement this approach. Approximately thirty hours are required. This time factor, while comparable to the Employee Anticipation Method, is far less than the time required to complete a Case Study.

Availability of Required Data Information needed for the Proportional Valuation Method is not very extensive. The refinement coefficients are found in Exhibit 6-3 and most of the raw data can be obtained in a single visit to the offices of the local tax assessor and business administrator. These data requirements, while more than those of the Employee Anticipation Method, are far less than those required for the Case Study approach.

Acceptance The Proportional Valuation Method, with the Case Study Method, has traditionally been used to assess the impact of nonresidential facilities. Both are accepted in the field as reasonable fiscal impact methods. While it is true that the Proportional Valuation Method, as with the refinement coefficients presented here, differs from the simple proportional strategy used in the past, the basic approach and reliance on real property value are continued.

Disadvantages

Validity of the Refinement Coefficients Two sets of refinement coefficients are employed to improve the accuracy of the Proportional Valuation Method. They are derived from retrospective analyses which compared the actual expenditures generated by nonresidential facilities to those projected using a simple proportional valuation strategy. To obtain widely applicable coefficients, these comparisions were made in communities which differ in tax base, size, maturity of development and the residential/nonresidential composition of total real property value. As with all information derived from case study, however, the refinement coefficients shown in 6-3 should be expanded considerably through additional research. The retrospective case study is an excellent tool to analyze fiscal impact results; yet infrequently employed. To upgrade constantly this method's accuracy these types of analyses must continue to be undertaken. The refinement coefficients contained here are thus initial approximations which must be significantly expanded in the future.

EXHIBIT 6-7
PROPORTIONAL VALUATION METHOD: DATA REQUIREMENTS AND SOURCES

Step Number	Data Requirements	Source(s)	Comments
1 – Obtain basic data	Municipal expenditures Total local value Total nonresidential value Total number of land parcels Total nonresidential parcels Equalization ratio	Local tax collector or assessor, business administrator, town clerk, etc.	Nonresidential parcels are defined as those classified as industrial or commercial and not farm, vacant or multifamily.
2 – Project nonresidential share of total municipal expenditures	Refinement coefficient Value and parcel data Municipal expenditures	Exhibit 6-3 and step 1 in this chapter	
3 – Project costs of nonresidential use under study	Refinement coefficient Value and parcel data Local expenditures attributable to new nonresidential facility	Exhibit 6-3 and step 1	
4 – Assign costs to municipal services	Percentage distribution of nonresidential costs into different service categories	Exhibit 6-4 in this chapter	
5 – Project total annual public revenues	Municipal and school district property tax rates Property assessment procedures Existing local property tax base State and federal intergovernmental transfer regulations	Local tax assessor's office Local or county tax assessor office Local or county tax assessor office	Part 2, Calculating Revenues, contains detailed information about where to obtain data on intergovernmental transfers as well as other sources of revenue

Detail The Employee Anticipation and the Proportional Valuation Methods yield similar levels of detail. Both project the total expenditures generated by development and subsequently disaggregate the expected outlays by service category, i.e., public safety, public works, etc. The Employee Anticipation is more accurate than the Proportional Valuation Method for in the former specific coefficients are developed for each service category, whereas, in the latter, allocations are made to specific services by a rough gauge of the experiences of other instances of documented nonresidential impact. The Case Study technique yields far greater detail. Costs are estimated for each individual municipal department, i.e., police, fire, highways, sanitation, water supply, etc.

EXHIBIT 6-8

TIME ESTIMATES TO EMPLOY THE PROPORTIONAL VALUATION METHOD

Step Number	Activities	Time
1	Obtain basic data	6 hours
2	Project nonresidential share of total municipal expenditures	2 hours
3	Project costs of nonresidential facility under study	1 hour
4	Assign costs to municipal service categories, i.e., Public safety, Public Welfare, etc.	1 hour
5	Project total annual public revenues	10 hours
6	Calculate the cost-revenue impact	2 hours
Report Preparation	Prepare and reproduce final report (optional)	10 hours
		32 hours

Interpreting Results

Employing the Proportional Valuation Method in this example yielded $15,623 in costs versus $170,470 in revenues, thereby producing a net surplus of $154,847. The relatively high revenue and therefore the consequent large positive balance is a function of both the available revenue sources in the jurisdiction and the particular type of facility being examined. The largest share of revenues for the shopping center in this example occurred from a locally levied sales tax. Absent this revenue, either because the community did not impose a sales tax or the nonresidential facility under study did not produce taxable sales, the cost-revenue surplus would be considerably lower.

In interpreting the results of this method, the analyst must keep in mind that only the direct effects of development impact are being analyzed. These are the costs of the specific municipal service extensions versus the increased revenue flows to both municipality and school district. Due to the typically large magnitude of the school versus municipal tax rates and their joint applicability to all classifications of property, if a land use is not generating direct educational costs yet is contributing to educational revenues, a reasonably large fiscal surplus should be in evidence.

NOTES

1. H. Margolis, *Nonresidential Fiscal Analysis* (unpublished report submitted to Los Angeles Planning Department: 1953).

2. Scott Bagby, *A Comprehensive Plan for the Borough of Morris Plains, N.J.* (Montclair, N.J.: Bagby Associates, 1948).

3. See Ruth Mace, *Municipal Cost-Revenue Research in the United States* (Chapel Hill: University of North Carolina Press, 1961).

4. See Appendix 2 of this Handbook for annotations of these studies.

5. See Appendix 2 of this study and Thomas Muller, *Fiscal Impacts of Land Development* (Washington, D.C.. The Urban Institute, 1973).

6. *Ibid.*

7. See W. Patrick Beaton, "Multivariate Nonresidential Cost-Revenue Analysis" (Unpublished paper), Institute for Urban Studies and Community Service, University of North Carolina at Charlotte, 1976.

7

EMPLOYMENT ANTICIPATION FISCAL IMPACT METHOD

Background

The Employment Anticipation Method is a recently developed marginal costing technique for projecting the impact of *nonresidential (industrial and commercial)* growth on local municipal costs and revenues. The method was developed in 1976 at the Institute for Urban Studies, Charlotte, North Carolina, and refined in 1977 by the Center for Urban Policy Research at Rutgers University.[1] It builds on information drawn from earlier multivariate analyses of municipal costs and nonresidential development undertaken by Scott and Feder (1957), Brazer (1959), Carroll and Sacks (1962), Sunley (1968), Bowman (1974), Beaton (1974), and Ladd (1975).[2] The method relies on relationships between local commercial and industrial employment levels and per capita municipal costs. It predicts a change in municipal costs based on an anticipated change in local commercial or industrial employment. Coefficients for the five categories of municipal service (general government, public safety, public works, health/welfare, recreation/culture) and for statutory/unclassified expenses and debt service have been developed using multivariate regression analysis to predict the change in municipal expenditures related to local employment variation. The coefficients may be read as "a change of one commercial or industrial employee will produce an increase in per capita local public service expenditures of X percent."

To illustrate, assume that a new industrial plant with 1,000 employees will be built in a growing community whose current population is 16,000 and whose current per capita public safety cost is $50.00. The cost for this service generated by the new facility is calculated by first multiplying the percentage increase per employee for public safety (0.00162*) by the number of employees (1,000), which yields an increase in the per capita costs of public safety of 1.62 percent. Per capita outlays will therefore rise by $.81 ($50.00 X 0.0162 = $.81); from $50.00 to $50.81. Multiplying the resident population by the increase in costs (16,000 X $.81) yields the total increase in operating

---

*In this chapter percentages under one percent are always presented in their decimal form. For example, 0.00162 percent will be used in the text; 0.0000162 will be used in the exhibits.

costs ($12,960) for public safety assignable to the new industrial plant. This procedure is repeated for each of the remaining categories of municipal service and for aggregate statutory and capital (debt service) expenditures to determine total annual municipal costs related to growth. Revenues are tabulated in the same way as for the other methods and compared with costs to determine net fiscal impact.

The Employment Anticipation Method is the first serious inquiry into the relationship of employment generating facilities and municipal costs. Several sources* tabulate numbers of employees by Standard Industrial Classification (SIC) for various categories of industrial and commercial activities, and analysts are beginning to search actively for a way to express changes in local public service costs as a function of changes in the local employment base. While the empirical data upon which this method is based may expand in the future, the method itself should remain essentially unchanged. Its position as one of the most versatile fiscal impact analysis methods for evaluating the impact of nonresidential uses will undoubtedly become more important.

Application

The Employment Anticipation Method is applicable in situations where the analyst wants to know the impact of exclusively nonresidential (commercial or industrial) facilities on municipal costs. It is particularly useful if a facility has relatively few employees for the amount of nonresidential space (a large bank) or many employees for the amount of space (a manufacturing plant). The costs assigned via this method take into account this sensitivity to differing employment levels. The Proportional Valuation Method, in contrast, would assign a lower cost to a bank and a higher cost to a manufacturing plant.

This method, like the Proportional Valuation Method, is ideal in instances where a "fast approximation" of impact is desired. As such, it is an excellent tool for evaluating alternative nonresidential land uses (the fiscal impact of zoning for industrial rather than commercial purposes) or for large nonresidential development that will be built in stages over several years and may require recurring fiscal impact projections.

The Employment Anticipation and the Proportional Valuation Methods may be used when resources for impact analysis are limited. The time required to undertake either method is a fraction of that required for the Case Study Method. Rough estimates of fiscal impact may be made in less than a day.

Basic Assumptions

The Employment Anticipation Method is based on three assumptions: (1) the level of local commercial or industrial employment directly affects the magnitude of local municipal expenditures[3]; (2) the relationship viewed is the impact of commercial or industrial employment on municipal expenditures within a multivariate context, controlling for the confounding effects of other social, political, and economic factors[4]; (3) the impact of additional employment will vary for communities of differing population size and direction of growth. This distinction arises from the assumptions of the Comparable City Method (see Chapter 5).[5]

---

*U.S. Census of Retail Trade, U.S. Census of Selected Service Industries, U.S. Census of Manufacturing, U.S. Census of Business.

Employment Anticipation

Procedures

Exhibit 7-1 lists the sequence of steps necessary to undertake the Employment Anticipation Method.

Step 1 Determine Per Capita Municipal Expenditures By Service Category

Using the local published municipal operating budget (available from the office of the township administrator or city manager) categorize all local services into five broad public service categories following the guide presented in the Case Study Method. Segregate costs by service category (general government, public safety, public works, health/welfare, recreation/culture) and group all statutory and capital expenditures (debt service) into two additional categories. The latter is necessary as percent increases in statutory and debt service costs related to predicted employment are presented as single, aggregate items.

From the local planning office obtain the most recent population estimate and divide the costs within each of the service categories and those for statutory and debt service by this figure. To illustrate, in a Texas municipality of 16,000 total public safety costs (excluding statutory costs and debt service) are $726,400 annually. Dividing this by current population yields a per capita cost of $45.40. This procedure is repeated for each of the service functions and for statutory costs and debt service.

EXHIBIT 7-1

EMPLOYMENT ANTICIPATION FISCAL IMPACT METHOD: SUMMARY OF PROCEDURES

Step Number	Analysis/Actions
1	Using information from the published local budget and the most recent population estimate, determine per capita municipal expenditures by service category.
2	Obtain anticipated employment for the new commercial or industrial facility from developer estimates or by multiplying the square footage of the new facility by the average number of employees per square foot for a comparable facility.
3	Using the known direction of growth over the previous decade and current population size, choose the applicable percentage increase per employee, by service category, for municipal service costs (Exhibit 7-2 or 7-3).
4	Multiply the new employment increment by the percentage increase in costs per employee to determine total percentage increase for each service.
5	Multiply the percentage increase in per capita expenditures by service category by the existing per capita expenditure in that service category to determine the dollar increase per capita for each service.
6	Multiply the increase in per capita expenditures for each service category by the existing population to determine the cost increase assignable to the new nonresidential facility for each service. Total the expenditure increases for each service category to obtain the aggregate assignable costs.
7	Project total annual public revenues.
8	Determine the cost-revenue surplus or deficit by comparing projected total revenues to projected total costs.

Step 2 Obtain Anticipated Employment for the New Commercial or Industrial Nonresidential Facility from Developer Estimates or by Multiplying the Square Footage of the New Facility by the Average Number of Employees Per Square Foot for a Comparable Facility

Frequently, if a commercial or industrial facility is being proposed, the developer will have an idea of the type of client that will occupy the space. Comparisons may then be made to similar local or regional facilities to obtain an estimate of the anticipated number of future employees.

If this information is not available, the analyst, knowing the size of the facility, can estimate the number of future employees by using a standard of employees per square foot developed for various subcategories of industrial or commercial establishments. In general, however, this information is difficult to secure. Most of the Census sources listed previously report income or sales by type of facility and by number of paid full-time employees. They do *not* provide any other gauge of the facility's size (square feet, for example). Several industry reporting guides, ULI's *Dollars and Cents of Shopping Centers, Industrial Development Handbook*[6]; National Research Bureau's *Shopping Center Directory*[7]; and BOMA's *Office Building Experience Exchange Report*,[8] report size in square feet and sales/income. Using both types of sources simultaneously, it is possible, *for a similarly covered period of time,* to derive employees per square foot from sales per employee and sales per square foot. Since these two factors have a common numerator (sales in dollars), dividing one by the other will yield employees per square foot.

$$\frac{\text{Sales/Income (\$)}}{\text{Ft}^2} \div \frac{\text{Sales/Income (4)}}{\text{Employees}} = \frac{\text{Employee}}{\text{Ft}^2}$$

If information from either source is not available, the analyst can use several gross rules of thumb to relate facility size to number of employees. They are extremely general measures and should be used only in situations where rough approximations are desired.[9] *Shopping centers employ about one worker for each 500 square feet of gross leasable area (GLA).*

Large offices have approximately one employee for each 250 square feet of net leasable area (NLA). (One employee for each 165 square feet [administrative centers]; one employee for each 337 square feet [corporate headquarters]).

Industrial plants have approximately one employee for each 300 square feet of net leasable area.
Warehouses have about one employee for each 750 square feet of gross leasable area.

In the example community in Texas, 110,000 gross square feet of industry (100,000 square feet of NLA) is planned for an I-3 (light industry) zone. Dividing the 100,000 square feet of anticipated net leasable space by the general estimate of 300 square feet per employee yields approximately 333 anticipated new employees (Exhibit 7-4 column 4).

Step 3 Using Known Direction of Growth Over the Previous Decade and Current Population Size, Choose the Applicable Percentage Increase Per Employee, by Service Category, in Per Capita Municipal Costs.

Over the period 1960 to 1970, as reported by the Census of Housing, the community under study in Texas increased in population by 1 percent annually. From 1970 to 1976, interim population estimates showed a continuation of the 1960 to 1970 trend. The community, which in 1977 was estimated at approximately 16,000 population, may be categorized according to the definitions

Employment Anticipation

contained in Exhibits 7-2 and 7-3 as a growing community of 10,000 to 24,999. Since the analyst is interested in predicting the impact of industrial employment growth, he would employ the percent changes* in municipal expenditures found in Exhibit 7-3 for "Industrial Activities" under the headings "growing, 10,000 to 24,999." For public safety services, each additional industrial employee will increase existing per capita general government costs by .00162 percent. Column 4 of Exhibit 7-4 contains each of the percent changes for the remaining areas of municipal service and for statutory and capital facility, debt service costs.

Step 4 Multiply the New Employment Increment by the Percentage Increase in Per Capita Costs Per Employee to Obtain Total Percentage Increase for Each Service

The analyst next multiplies the expenditure changes per employee, by service category, by the anticipated employment change introduced by the new nonresidential facility. This calculation provides the per capita percentage increase related to the aggregate local employment growth generated by that facility. For instance, it was found in step 2 that a new local industry of 100,000 feet^2 NLA will generate 333 new employees. The percentage change (increase) in public safety service costs per additional industrial employee is 0.00162 percent. Thus a new industrial facility locating in a large growing community would occasion an increase in per capita public safety service costs of 0.5395 percent (333 × .0000162). Column 6 of Exhibit 7-4 presents the total percentage change by service function in per capita expenditures occasioned by the new facility.

Step 5 Multiply the Percent Increase in Per Capita Expenditures Per Service Category by the Existing Per Capita Dollar Expenditure in That Service Category to Obtain the Per Capita Dollar Increase for Each Service

To determine the per capita dollar increase of service costs attributable to nonresidential growth, the analyst multiplies the percentage increase in per capita costs in each service category (step 4) by the existing per capita expenditures in that service category (step 1). The results are column 8 of Exhibit 7-4. In the previous example, for the Texas community of 16,000, the percent increase in per capita public safety costs was found to be 0.5395 percent. Since existing costs are currently $45.40 per capita annually, the addition of 333 new employees by the industrial plant would increase local per capita public safety expenditures by $.24 (.005395 × $45.40).

Step 6 Multiply Dollar Per Capita Expenditure Increase in Each Service Category by the Existing Population to Obtain the Municipal Cost Increase for Each Municipal Service Assignable to the Nonresidential Facility

The analyst next obtains the aggregate dollar impact of the new development for each municipal service category. The dollar increment in per capita costs by service category (step 5) is multiplied by the existing community population (Exhibit 7-4, column 9). The impact of the industrial facility in Texas will increase local public safety costs by approximately $3,919 annually. This is obtained by multiplying the per capita increase of $.24 in public safety costs by the current population (16,000). After this process is repeated for each service category the results are summed. In this example, total costs, including statutory costs and debt service, are slightly over $15,000.

---

*Expressed as a decimal. For a full discussion of the expenditure multipliers, see W. Patrick Beaton, "The Impact of Commercial and Industrial Development upon the Municipal Budget" (unpublished paper), Institute for Urban Studies and Community Service, University of North Carolina at Charlotte.

EXHIBIT 7-2
EXPENDITURE MULTIPLIERS MEASURING THE DEMAND GENERATED IMPACT OF
COMMERCIAL ACTIVITY UPON SEVEN CATEGORIES OF PER CAPITA MUNICIPAL EXPENDITURES

City Size	Growing Cities[1] Category of Municipal Service							Declining Cities Category of Municipal Service						
	General Government	Public Safety	Public Works	Health and Welfare	Recreation and Culture	Statutory and Unclassified Expenses	Debt Service	General Government	Public Safety	Public Works	Health and Welfare	Recreation and Culture	Statutory and Unclassified Expenses	Debt Service
Less than 2,500	0.0000076	0.0000702	0.0000134	0.0000186	0.0001845	0.0001561	0.0001079	0.0001176	0.0000004	0.0000000	0.0000105	0.0000091	0.0000606	0.0000197
2,500-4,999	0.0000061	0.0000686	0.0000132	0.0000199	0.0001710	0.0001461	0.0000882	0.0001243	0.0000004	0.0000000	0.0000080	0.0000050	0.0000545	0.0000137
5,000-9,999	0.0000065	0.0000655	0.0000183	0.0000168	0.0001978	0.0001537	0.0000726	0.0001243	0.0000003	0.0000000	0.0000080	0.0000034	0.0000347	0.0000059
10,000-24,999	0.0000048	0.0000453[2]	0.0000120	0.0000103	0.0000817	0.0000880	0.0000516	0.0001053	0.0000027	0.0000000	0.0000033	0.0000012	0.0000189	0.0000029
25,000-49,999	0.0000027	0.0000056	0.0000052	0.0000031	0.0000319	0.0000305	0.0000305	0.0000734	0.0000000	0.0000000	0.0000029	0.0000009	0.0000083	0.0000009
50,000-99,999	0.0000015	0.0000023	0.0000022	0.0000000	0.0000129	0.0000099	0.0000078	0.0000332	0.0000000	0.0000000	0.0000000	0.0000000	0.0000035	0.0000004
100,000-150,000	0.0000005	0.0000007	0.0000004	0.0000000	0.0000014	0.0000007	0.0000006	0.0000018	0.0000000	0.0000000	0.0000000	0.0000000	0.0000004	0.0000038

Notes: [1] Growing and declining cities refer to the direction of population change over the past five to ten years.
[2] Numbers are read as follows: One additional commercial employee in a growing city whose current population is between 10,000 and 24,999 will increase per capita public safety expenditures by 0.00453 percent.

Source: Rutgers University, Center for Urban Policy Research, spring 1977; University of North Carolina (Charlotte), Institute for Urban Studies, 1977.

EXHIBIT 7-3

EXPENDITURE MULTIPLIERS MEASURING THE DEMAND GENERATED IMPACT OF
INDUSTRIAL ACTIVITY UPON SEVEN CATEGORIES OF PER CAPITA MUNICIPAL EXPENDITURES

	Growing Cities[1] Category of Municipal Service							Declining Cities Category of Municipal Service						
City Size	General Government	Public Safety	Public Works	Health and Welfare	Recreation and Culture	Statutory and Unclassified Expenses	Debt Service	General Government	Public Safety	Public Works	Health and Welfare	Recreation and Culture	Statutory and Unclassified Expenses	Debt Service
Less than 2,500	0.0000022	0.0000181	0.0000337	0.0000465	0.0000518	0.0000925	0.0000607	0.0000161	0.0000564	0.0000689	0.0000280	0.0000182	0.0001042	0.0000380
2,500-4,999	0.0000015	0.0000180	0.0000332	0.0000398	0.0000503	0.0000865	0.0000444	0.0000014	0.0000523	0.0000655	0.0000201	0.0000166	0.0001025	0.0000267
5,000-9,999	0.0000026	0.0000187	0.0000461	0.0000279	0.0000577	0.0000900	0.0000366	0.0000014	0.0000397	0.0000620	0.0000120	0.0000188	0.0001016	0.0000207
10,000-24,999	0.0000018	0.0000162[2]	0.0000299	0.0000104	0.0000403	0.0000496	0.0000272	0.0000008	0.0000168	0.0000471	0.0000033	0.0000006	0.0000540	0.0000136
25,000-49,999	0.0000001	0.0000109	0.0000002	0.0000031	0.0000244	0.0000157	0.0000099	0.0000004	0.0000032	0.0000148	0.0000000	0.0000027	0.0000106	0.0000037
50,000-99,999	0.0000005	0.0000043	0.0000007	0.0000000	0.0000009	0.0000046	0.0000046	0.0000000	0.0000013	0.0000064	0.0000000	0.0000007	0.0000041	0.0000017
100,000-150,000	0.0000000	0.0000002	0.0000004	0.0000000	0.0000014	0.0000001	0.0000006	0.0000000	0.0000003	0.0000007	0.0000000	0.0000006	0.0000007	0.0000004

Notes: [1] Growing and declining cities refer to the direction of population change over the past five to ten years.
[2] Numbers are read as follows: One additional industrial employee in a growing city whose current population is between 10,000 and 24,999 will increase per capita public safety expenditures by 0.00162 percent.

Source: Rutgers University, Center for Urban Policy Research, spring 1977; University of North Carolina (Charlotte), Institute for Urban Studies, 1977.

EXHIBIT 7-4

USING THE EMPLOYMENT ANTICIPATION METHOD TO EVALUATE THE FISCAL IMPACT OF A DEVELOPMENT PROPOSAL

	STEP 1	STEP 2	STEP 3		STEP 4		STEP 5		STEP 6	
	Determine Per Capita Municipal Expenditures	Determine Number of Expected Employees	Choose Appropriate Per Capita Change Per Employee		Multiply by Number of Employees		Multiply by Existing Per Capita Expenditures		Multiply by Existing Population	
	Column 1	Column 2	Column 3	Column 4	Column 5	Column 6	Column 7	Column 8	Column 9	
General Government	$236,800 / 16,000 = $14.80	100,000 FT² NLA ÷ 1 Employee/ 300 FT² = 333 Employees	General Government	0.0000018 ×	333	= 0.000599	× $14.80	= 0.008865	× 16,000	= $ 142
Public Safety	$726,400 / 16,000 = $45.40		Public Safety	0.0000162 ×	333	= 0.005395	× $45.40	= 0.244933	× 16,000	= $ 3,919
Public Works	$488,000 / 16,000 = $30.50		Public Works	0.0000299 ×	333	= 0.009957	× $30.50	= 0.303689	× 16,000	= $ 4,859
Health and Welfare	$ 22,400 / 16,000 = $ 1.40		Health and Welfare	0.0000104 ×	333	= 0.003463	× $ 1.40	= 0.004848	× 16,000	= $ 78
Recreation and Culture	$ 75,200 / 16,000 = $ 4.70		Recreation and Culture	0.0000403 ×	333	= 0.013420	× $ 4.70	= 0.063074	× 16,000	= $ 1,009
Statutory and Unclassified	$230,400 / 16,000 = $14.40		Statutory and Unclassified	0.0000496 ×	333	= 0.016517	× $14.40	= 0.237845	× 16,000	= $ 3,806
Debt Service	$172,800 / 16,000 = $10.80		Capital Facilities Debt Service	0.0000212 ×	333	= 0.007060	× $10.80	= 0.076248	× 16,000	= $ 1,220
Total			Total Operating and Capital							= $15,033

Employment Anticipation

Step 7   Project Total Annual Public Revenues

The analyst must now project the revenues that will accrue to the municipality due to the arrival of the new industrial facility. Exhibit 7-5 shows the anticipated revenues by source for the Texas community. This exhibit lists revenues from own sources and intergovernmental flows both to the municipality and school district. Essentially the new plant will pay both municipal and school district real property taxes, a local utility tax, based on consumption, and a user charge for special sanitation services. In addition, it will occasion a small decrease in the current CDBG allocation as a smaller percentage of local workers will be below the poverty level due to the local employment opportunities of the new manufacturing facility. In total, $70,470 will be generated in local revenues.

Step 8   Calculate the Cost-Revenue Impact

The final step is to compare costs and revenues to determine the net fiscal impact. The new facility in this community will generate a net annual surplus of approximately $55,000; $15,000 in costs will be offset by $70,000 in revenues.

The analyst must keep in mind that only directly assignable costs are included. They do not include secondary revenues such as employee retail purchases and thus growth of sales tax revenue, or employee decisions to reside in new local housing, thus possibly contributing to an increase in both local servicing costs and revenues, etc.

Data Requirements

Data required for the Employment Anticipation Method consists of four elements: (1) existing per capita expenditures by service category, (2) coefficients of per capita percent change per employee, (3) projections of future employees by nonresidential type; and (4) current municipal population estimates. Items 1 and 4 are obtained from municipal administrative offices, item 2 is found within Exhibits 7-2 and 7-3, item 3 may be obtained from either the developer, industrial/commercial data reporting sources or from the general guidelines in this chapter. Data requirements and specific sources of information are summarized in Exhibit 7-6.

Sophistication of User

To undertake the Employment Anticipation Method requires a relatively modest level of skills. The method certainly can be undertaken by the entry level practicing planner or an assistant municipal city manager/business administrator. Most required information is found within the method itself and procedural steps flow clearly and logically. An important procedure to keep in mind, especially for the novice to fiscal impact analysis, is to set up the calculation tabulations as indicated in the illustrative exhibits. Confusion is minimized if the structure of the exhibits is employed almost verbatim. Another point of potential confusion is the use of decimal points. As each of the coefficients must be subsequently multiplied by projected employees and current population, they are small, in some cases carried seven places beyond the decimal point. If the analyst is not careful it is quite easy to make an error in the placing of the decimal point. An error of this type can obviously have a significant effect on the fiscal impact conclusion.

Understanding the model and multivariate analyses used to obtain results as well as the statistical manipulations used to derive coefficients may require more than entry level sophistication.[10] An excellent primer to augment the general discussion contained here is found in Nie: *et al, Statistical Package for the Social Sciences* (SPSS), (1971).[11]

EXHIBIT 7-5

COMPUTATION SHEET FOR REVENUE TABULATION *

REVENUE SOURCES		
MUNICIPAL		
I. Own Source Revenues		
A. Taxes		
1. Real Property	$ 30,000	
2. Utility	$ 2,820	
TOTAL TAXES		$ 32,820
B. Charges/Miscellaneous		
1. Sanitation	$ 2,000	
TOTAL CHARGES/MISCELLANEOUS		$ 2,000
TOTAL OWN SOURCE REVENUE		$ 34,820
II. Intergovernmental Transfers		
A. State		
1. None	$ 0	
B. Federal		
1. CDBG	$ −1,950	
TOTAL FEDERAL/TOTAL INTERGOVERNMENTAL		$ −1,950
TOTAL MUNICIPAL REVENUE		$ 32,870
SCHOOL DISTRICT		
I. Own Source Revenues		
A. Taxes		
1. Real Property	$ 37,600	
TOTAL TAXES		$ 37,600
B. Charges/Miscellaneous		
1. None	$ 0	
TOTAL CHARGES/MISCELLANEOUS		$ 0
TOTAL OWN SOURCE REVENUES		$ 37,600
II. Intergovernmental Transfers		
A. State		
1. None	$ 0	
TOTAL STATE		$ 0
B. Federal		
1. None	$ 0	
TOTAL FEDERAL/TOTAL INTERGOVERNMENTAL		$ 0
TOTAL SCHOOL DISTRICT REVENUE		$ 37,600
TOTAL MUNICIPAL/SCHOOL DISTRICT REVENUE		$ 70,470

*For detailed calculations, see Exhibits 10-1 and 10-2 in Chapter 10.

Advantages

Operational Utility   An obvious advantage of the Employment Anticipation Method is that it expresses future municipal costs as a function of expected employees—the direct local product of nonresidential growth. The intensity of use of a facility which is believed to affect directly the magnitude of costs is employed to specify fiscal impact. The level of future municipal expenditures thus relates directly to the projected level of employment the new commercial or industrial facility will generate. Employment data, which are now more readily available, are some

EXHIBIT 7-6
EMPLOYMENT ANTICIPATION METHOD: DATA REQUIREMENTS AND SOURCES

Step Number	Data Requirements	Source(s)	Comments
1 – Determine per capita municipal expenditures by service category	Municipal operating expenditures by service category; current estimate of municipal population	Published municipal operating budget Local planning office, office of city manager/business administrator	See text of method.
2 – Obtain projected employment for the new nonresidential facility	Number of employees per square foot by type of facility or SIC	General information listed within this chapter. Various U.S. Censuses in conjunction with: 1. Dollars and Cents of Shopping Centers. 2. Industrial Development Handbook. 3. Office Building Experience Exchange Report.	
3 – Choose applicable percentage increase in service costs per employee	Percentage increase (expressed as a decimal) in per capita costs per employee by type of nonresidential facility.	Exhibits 7-2 and 7-3	For derivation of these exhibits see footnote 10.
7 – Project total annual public revenues	Municipal/school district equalized property tax rates. Current own source and intergovernmental revenues. Formulas for own source and intergovernmental revenues.	Local tax assessors office Published municipal operating budget Part 2 of this handbook	Consult applicable state statutes.

of the few items of information (other than real property value) that are known in the early development stages or that may be obtained from the historical experience of other facilities.

The impact of the new commercial or industrial development is projected differently for cities of different sizes and directions of growth. Thus, it is sensitive to nonresidential impact on cities both small and large, with expanding or contracting public service bases.

Detail   The Employment Anticipation Method projects percent increase in per capita municipal expenditures for each category of municipal service, statutory costs and debt service. Specific information is on hand for the locality to anticipate impact not only in the aggregate but also by category of local service. Impact on specific services is only indirectly available in the Proportional Valuation Method and available only at significant expense via the Case Study approach. This method offers reasonably detailed projections at a modest budget.

Simplicity/Cost   The Employment Anticipation Method is inexpensive to use. It is similar in scope to the Proportional Valuation Method, taking approximately four person-days to implement (Exhibit 7-7).

EXHIBIT 7-7
TIME ESTIMATES TO EMPLOY THE EMPLOYMENT ANTICIPATION METHOD

Step Number	Activities	Time
1	Determine per capita municipal expenditures by service category	4 hours
2	Obtain anticipated employment for the new facility	2 hours
3	Choose applicable coefficients for percentage increase	2 hours
4	Determine total percentage increase for each service	2 hours
5	Determine the dollar increase per capita for each service	2 hours
6	Determine the total cost increase assignable to the new facility	1 hour
7	Project total annual public revenues	10 hours
8	Calculate the cost-revenue impact	2 hours
Report Preparation	Prepare and reproduce final report (optional)	10 hours
		35 hours

Disadvantages

This method relies on coefficients to express changes in per capita municipal expenditures for categories of cities defined by population size and direction of growth. In so doing, a single multiplier is used for all cities within a particular population group. Since cities may vary by populations of close to 50,000 for the larger groups, the same nonresidential facility in a city of 149,000 may be shown to be significantly more costly than one in a city of 100,000. Obviously this is not the case. It is the grouping technique that limits the result. Yet population groups for larger city sizes may not be made smaller as the sample within each group is insufficient. This situation is not intolerable and does not detract significantly from the accuracy of the method. It should be kept in mind, however, when interpreting impact results for larger cities.

The Employment Anticipation Method is further limited in that it does not provide coefficients for cities over 150,000. This is due to the data base that was used (New Jersey municipalities), which contained only a few cities in excess of 150,000 and these were subsequently eliminated for insufficiency of sample. If nonresidential development is contemplated for cities over 150,000, the Case Study Method will probably be the most effective method to use.

Interpret Results

Percentage increases in per capita municipal costs are derived from regression equations which attempt to explain the expenditure variation within each service category, using commercial and industrial employment as a surrogate of local demand. The regression coefficient yields a dollar increase in service expenditure per employee which, when divided by the mean per capita service expenditure, is translated to percentage increase.

The resulting statement of cost is interpreted to mean that (after viewing the municipal expenditure patterns and employment levels in close to 600 cities) these are the types of expenditure changes which occur as the employment level of a city changes. Changes in a city's employment are viewed sinultaneously with other changes taking place in city structure (i.e. income, wealth, tax base, etc.). The specific effect of employment change on municipal expenditures is then segregated from other internal socioeconomic changes and specified as to magnitude. The analyst should interpret new local levels of municipal expenditure as similar to those experienced by other cities.

NOTES

1. W. Patrick Beaton, "The Municipal Cost Revenue Implications of Proposed New Business Activity: Method and Analysis," *National Tax Journal* (forthcoming).

2. Stanley Scott and Edward L. Feder, *Factors Associated with Variations in Municipal Expenditure Levels* (Berkeley, Calif.: Bureau of Public Administration, University of California at Berkeley, 1957); Harvey E. Brazer, *City Expenditures in the United States* (New York: National Bureau of Economic Research, 1959) (Occasional Paper 66); John J. Carroll and Seymour Sacks, "The Property Tax Base and the Pattern of Local Government Expenditures: The Influence of Industry," in *Papers and Proceedings of the Regional Science Association,* Vol. 9 (Philadelphia: Regional Science Association, 1962); Emil McKee Sunley Jr., *The Determinants of Government Expenditures within Metropolitan Regions,* Unpublished Ph.D. dissertation, University of Michigan, 1968; John H. Bowman, "Tax Exportability, Intergovernmental Aid and School Finance Reform," *National Tax Journal,* Vol. 27 (June 1974); W. Patrick Beaton, "The Determinants of Police Protection Expenditures," *National Tax Journal,* Vol. 27 (June 1974); Helen F. Ladd, "Local Education Expenditures, Fiscal Capacity and the Composition of the Property Tax Base," *National Tax Journal,* Vol. 28 (June 1975).

3. Woo Sik Kee, "Industrial Development and its Impact on Local Finance," *Quarterly Review of Economics and Business* (April 1968); and Helen F. Ladd. *op.cit.*

4. See Stanley Scott and Edward L. Feder, *op.cit.*

5. See Harvey E. Brazer, *op.cit;* Bernard Booms, "City Governmental Form and Public Expenditure Levels," *National Tax Journal* (June, 1966); John C. Wecher, "Determinants of Central City Expenditures: Some Overlooked Factors and Problems," *National Tax Journal* (December 1970).

6. Urban Land Institute, *The Dollars and Cents of Shopping Centers* (Washington, D.C.: Urban Land Institute, 1974); Urban Land Institute, *Industrial Development Handbook* (Washington, D.C.: Urban Land Institute, 1972) (Community Builders Handbook Series).

7. National Research Bureau, *Shopping Center Directory* (Chicago. National Research Bureau, 1976).

8. Building Officials Management Association, *1975 Office Building Experience Exchange Report* (Washington, D.C.: Building Officials Management Association, 1976).

9. See Harvey S. Moskowitz, *Useful Planning Standards* (New Brunswick, N.J.: Rutgers University, *Bureau of Government Research, 1976);* F. Stuart Chapin, Jr., *Urban Land Use Planning* (Urbana, Ill.: University of Illinois, 1965); James H. Boykin, *Industrial Potential of the Central City* (Washington, D.C.: Urban Land Institute, Research Report #21, 1973); Robert Moore Fisher, *The Boom in Office Buildings: An Economic Study of the Past Two Decades* (Washington, D.C.: Urban Land Institute, Technical Bulletin #58, 1967); J. Ross McKeever, *Business Parks, Office Parks, Plazas and Centers* (Washington, D.C.: Urban Land Institute, Technical Bulletin #65, 1970). For current information (unpublished) write to Society of Industrial Realtors, 925 15th St. N.W., Washington, D.C. 20005; National Association of Industrial Parks, 1901 N. Ft. Myer Drive, Suite 1110, Arlington, Va. 22209; Shopping Center Directory, 1200 State Street, Chicago, Illinois.

10. See Beaton, "The Municipal Cost Revenue Implications of Proposed New Business Activity," *op.cit.*

11. Norman H. Nie *et al., Statistical Package for the Social Sciences* (New York: McGraw-Hill, 1975).

PART 2

CALCULATING REVENUES: METHODS OF FISCAL IMPACT REVENUE PROJECTION

This part provides detailed procedures to tabulate local revenues resulting from residential and nonresidential growth. It contains three chapters, with the last (Chapter 10) divided into two sections. Chapter 8 describes trends in local revenues over time as well as geographic concentrations of certain types of revenue raising mechanisms. Chapter 9 and Chapter 10 (Section II) present methods to calculate municipal and school district own source revenues (locally raised) and intergovernmental transfers (funds flowing from state and federal levels). The procedural guides in these chapters detail first, how to calculate own source revenues such as:

taxes — real property, personal property, income, sales, property transfer, occupation and business privilege, per capita, transient occupancy.

charges/miscellaneous revenues — interest earnings, fees and permit revenue, fines, forfeitures and penalties.

and second, how to project intergovernmental transfers from:

state — sales tax redistribution, income tax redistribution, motor fuels tax, cigarette and alcohol tax, educational basic assistance, educational categorical aid, etc.

federal — Revenue Sharing, CETA, CDBG, Public Works Countercyclical, and Federal Impact School Assistance, etc.

Part 2: Calculating Revenues

The revenue tabulation procedures presented in Chapters 9 and 10 have been drawn from the cost-revenue studies assembled in Appendix 2 of the Handbook as well as from the state statutes and federal assistance program guidelines specific to the type of revenue being considered. As such, they represent the most typical types of allocation mechanisms. Although procedures for allocation differ by locale, the generic form pertaining to a class of revenues is what is presented here. Thus, the user must check the revenue allocation measures specific to his geographic area and incorporate local variations within each procedure.

Section II of Chapter 10 contains example revenue tabulations which have been completed for the revenue side of the cost-revenue example contained in each cost projection method (Chapters 2 through 7). These summaries, with detailed footnotes, follow the procedural form recommended for calculating each potential revenue resource and are tabulated using different fiscal settings in the United States.

The material in this part is organized to provide for the analyst both familiarity with and procedures for revenue calculation. Chapter 8, an overview, may be read initially, digested, and reread occasionally, if necessary. Chapter 10, Section II example calculations are for use in referencing the specific results of an inclusive cost projection method. Chapters 9 and 10 (Section I) are the heart of this part and are to be used by the analyst at the outset of each fiscal impact analysis.

An important caveat is that in undertaking the revenue calculation, the user should be aware of the time involved to tabulate revenues and the potential return (in terms of percent of local revenues) associated with calculating each revenue alternative. Very frequently the most time consuming revenue calculations are those associated with tabulating intergovernmental transfers. In locales which are heavily dependent on own source or local revenue these types of calculations may prove to be expensive with little value in unearthing additional revenue streams.

8

REVENUE TRENDS

This chapter introduces the user to the array of revenues which must be considered in a fiscal impact analysis. It covers the types of revenue resources, the ways in which they vary geographically, and their emphasis and deemphasis over time.

The point that must be stressed at the outset is that the cost-revenue equation has two sides — the *costs* of development, redevelopment, zone change or annexation (these were covered in the cost part of the handbook), and the *revenues* associated with the same kinds of municipal actions. (These are covered in the revenue part.) The procedures outlined in this handbook for calculating fiscal impact consider *all direct costs*. Thus, the revenue half of the calculation must also delve deeply into the array of local fiscal resources. Typically, however, when the user attempts to project revenues, the number of alternative local resources with which he is confronted is staggering. Two important segments of information help to mitigate the arduous task of revenue tabulation. The first is a determination of which of these revenues will be impacted by growth. This type of information is included within the narrative of the projection procedure which is demonstrated for each revenue resource (Chapters 9 and 10). Information of this type permits the elimination of several categories of revenue from consideration — making the quantity of revenues with which the analyst must deal more manageable.

More important is a firm grasp by users on how revenues are generated locally. This may be obtained from close scrutinization of local municipal and school district operating budgets. The user will find, for instance, that the locality may depend heavily on the property tax or a locally levied income tax, or for that matter be supported to an extensive degree by intergovernmental transfers, i.e., from either the state or federal governments. This knowledge of local revenue distribution permits the analyst to segregate those types of revenues which are important and, therefore, must undergo detailed calculations from those which are unimportant, capable of grouping and only worthy of estimation.

Familiarity with revenue types, emphases and calculations is a critical prerequisite for fiscal impact analysis. This chapter introduces the reader to the components and dynamics of municipal and school district revenues.

Municipal and School District Revenue Resources

The U.S. Census Bureau recognizes four major types of revenue sources: general revenue, utility revenue, liquor store revenue, and insurance trust revenue.[1] This handbook confines its interest to *general revenue* because the other sources are not major contributors to a local government's general fund. Utility revenue — the receipts from sales of water, electric service, transit service and gas, is often a large part of a municipality's gross revenues but an insignificant portion of net revenues. User charges (except for transit which is usually a fiscal drain) typically reflect the unit cost of utility operations and do not provide significant local revenue outside the general fund. Similarly, insurance trust revenue, which comes from both contributions from employers and earnings on assets, and which provides income for social insurance and employee retirement benefits, usually can be used only to increase the insurance trust fund. Therefore, this type of revenue is also excluded from the discussion. Finally, liquor store revenues (in states that operate public liquor stores) provide such a small proportion of local revenues that they too have been excluded.[2]

This handbook considers the two primary components of general revenue: (1) own source revenue (raised by the locality itself) consisting of taxes and charges/miscellaneous revenue; and (2) intergovernmental transfers, contributed by both the state and the federal governments. Taxes include real personal and corporate income (franchise) taxes; charges include receipts for specific services or commodities sold; miscellaneous revenue includes such items as special assessments, sales of property, and interest earned on cash balances. Intergovernmental transfers include grants, shared taxes, and contingent loans and advances for specific functions.

All discussions will be in terms of two functional types of local governments:* educational and noneducational jurisdictions. For the sake of simplicity, school districts[3] are considered educational bodies; municipalities are considered noneducational bodies.** The discussion will also center on above-mentioned categories of revenues — own source and intergovernmental.

Exhibit 8-1 shows each type of government's reliance on the two broad categories of revenue sources. Municipalities rely more on own source revenue rather than intergovernmental transfers. Seventy percent of municipal revenues are raised by the locality itself. The predominant municipal revenue source is tax monies (46.4 percent). For school districts, the pattern is quite different. Intergovernmental transfers, typically from the state rather than the federal government, account for a much larger percentage — almost half of the revenues received (44.4 percent). The percentage of revenue based on taxes is similar to that for municipalities (46 to 48 percent), but income from charges and miscellaneous revenue is almost nonexistent (6.8 percent).

There is, however, a steady and growing trend toward diversification of local (municipal and school district) revenue sources.[4] As Exhibit 8-2 shows, since 1942, there has been a move towards greater reliance on intergovernmental transfers and less on own source revenues (particularly from local property taxes). The percentage of local income from both other taxes and charges and miscellaneous revenues has increased slightly.

---

*Special districts, or those geographic areas in which particular local public services are provided, are not considered here. Most districts levy user charges for consumption of services on a per unit basis. Use charges reflect, almost exclusively, the cost of district operations. Thus only minor positive or negative cash flows occur with growth; the expansion of services usually follows closely the existing rate.

**The data which follow for noneducational purposes has been tabulated from information presented for Census-defined townships and municipalities. For the remainder of this section, the term "municipality" will be used when information is discussed for this aggregate data set.

Revenue Trends

EXHIBIT 8-1

RELIANCE ON REVENUE SOURCES BY MUNICIPALITIES AND SCHOOL DISTRICTS, UNITED STATES (1972)

	Percent of General Revenue	
REVENUE SOURCE	Townships & Municipalities	School Districts
Own Source	70.1	55.6
Taxes	46.4	48.8
Charges and miscellaneous	23.7	6.8
Intergovernmental	29.9	44.4
TOTAL	100.0	100.0

Source: U.S. Census of Governments, 1972.

EXHIBIT 8-2

CHANGE IN REVENUE SOURCES WITHIN MUNICIPALITIES AND SCHOOL DISTRICTS (COMBINED)

(1942–1972)

	Percent of General Revenue		Percent Change (Simple)
REVENUE SOURCE	1972	1942	
Own Source	61.6	77.3	−20.3
Tax Revenue	49.5	69.5	−28.8
Property Tax	41.0	63.2	−35.1
Other Taxes	8.5	6.3	+34.9
Charges and Miscellaneous	12.1	7.8	+55.1
Intergovernmental	38.4	22.7	+69.2
TOTAL	100.0	100.0	—

Source: U.S. Census of Governments, 1972.

Exhibit 8-3 shows that the general trend toward diversification of local government revenue is a phenomenon more of municipalities than of school districts. Intergovernmental transfers accounted for 18 percent of municipal revenues in 1957; in 1972 they were 30 percent, a relative change of 67 percent. This increase exactly parallels the trend for *total* local revenues (both municipal and school district) shown in Exhibit 8-2. During the same 15-year period, intergovernmental transfers for school districts increased only about 4 percent, primarily because of the reduced emphasis on school district property tax levies. The critical and changing nature of intergovernmental transfers prompts a detailed evaluation of this revenue source.

Intergovernmental Transfers

Overview

In 1972 intergovernmental transfers accounted for nearly 30 percent of revenues for municipalities, and more than 44 percent of revenues for school districts. This type of revenue comes to the local jurisdiction from state and federal governments for use in performing specific functions or for general financial support.

Direct federal grants to municipal governments come in the form of federal-local funding of selected public works projects of joint interest (waste treatment facilities, pollution control), unconditional or general revenue grants such as the State and Local Fiscal Assistance Act of 1972 (Revenue Sharing), manpower grants such as the Comprehensive Employment Training Act of

---

*Five states (Alaska, Hawaii, Maryland, North Carolina, Virginia) and the District of Columbia are omitted from the analyses of school district finances which follow. In these jurisdictions school district finances are wholly *dependent* on those of another level of government — state, county or city.

156   THE FISCAL IMPACT HANDBOOK

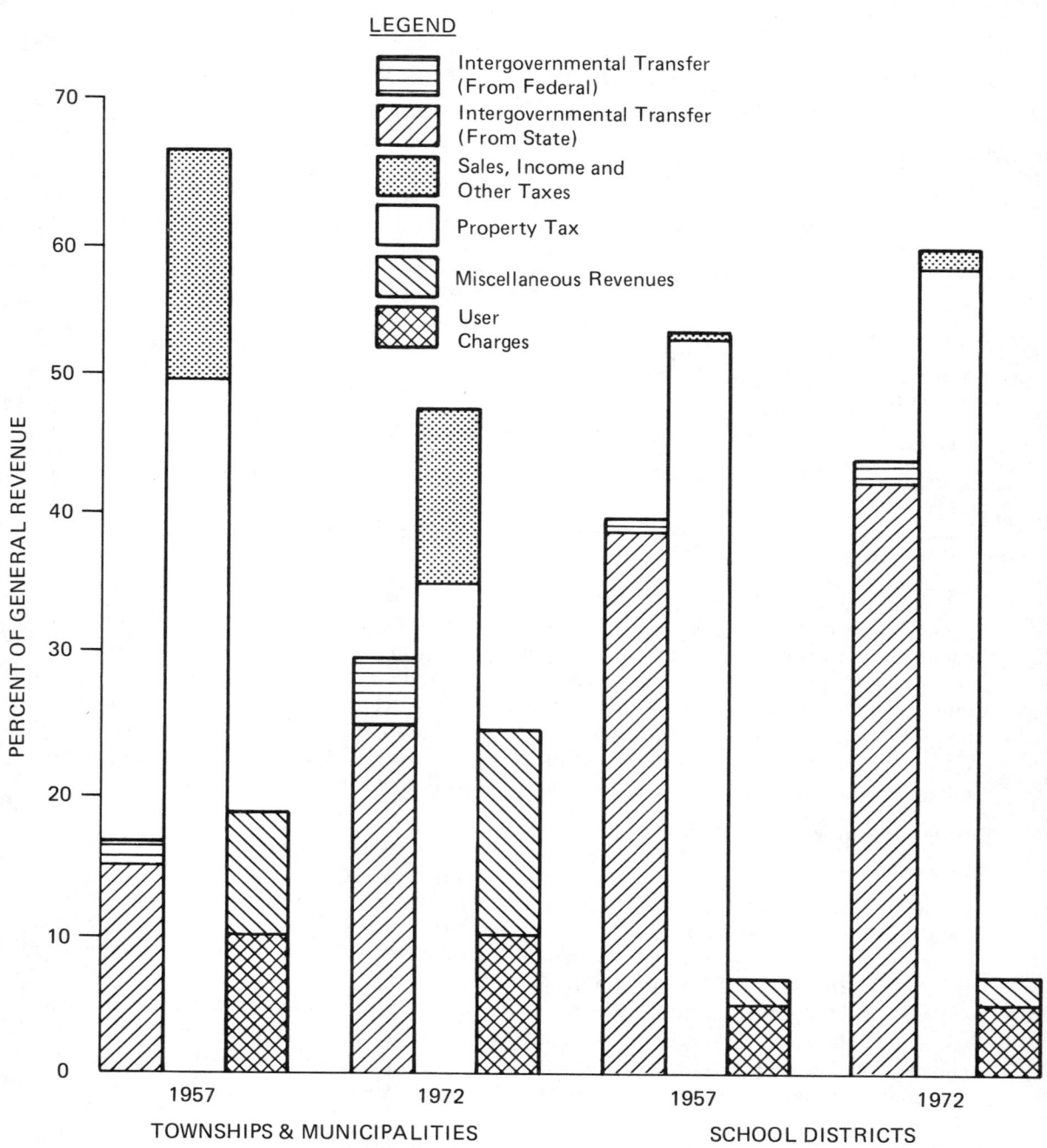

EXHIBIT 8-3
CHANGE IN REVENUE SOURCE DEPENDENCY IN MUNICIPALITIES AND SCHOOL DISTRICTS
(1957-1972)

Source: U.S. Census of Governments, 1972.

Revenue Trends 157

1973 (CETA), and housing and community redevelopment assistance such as the Housing and Community Development Act of 1974 authorizing community development block grants — CDBG). Grants for school districts are generally for federally designated impact areas.[5] State government transfers are by far the more important source of intergovernmental transfers for local governments. They consist of two basic types: grants and state-levied, locally shared taxes. As with federal government grants, state grants are also generally for public works, manpower assistance, redevelopment, and education. They are usually for specific activities of joint state-local interest. Shared taxes are based on the premise that some taxes can be collected more efficiently at the state rather than at the local level. Local governments surrender their option to levy a tax in return for a share of the state collections via some agreed upon and uniform basis.[6] In terms of general local revenue, state sharing is important for state-levied income taxes, gasoline taxes, sales, tobacco taxes and pari-mutuel taxes. Shared revenues enter the general fund of municipalities and school districts with minimal earmarking and are essentially general purpose funds.

Regional Patterns

Exhibits 8-1 through 8-3 have been based on national figures. More insight into local revenue resources is gained by showing sources of intergovernmental transfers by region. It may be that the use of one revenue source over another is in some measure determined by cultural preferences that follow geographic configurations. Exhibit 8-4 shows the reliance on intergovernmental transfers for municipalities and for school districts by region. (See Exhibit 13-3 for a listing of inclusive states within each region.) In every region municipalities receive more funds from the federal government, and school districts receive more funds from the state government.

In the regions encompassing Southern states (South Atlantic, East South Central), the state frequently contributes substantially more than in other regions to both municipalities and school districts.* States where municipalities rely significantly on state transfers are Maryland, Virginia, Delaware, Tennessee, and Mississippi; states where school districts depend heavily on intergovernmental transfers are Alabama, Delaware, Mississippi, West Virginia, South Carolina, Georgia, and Kentucky. (See Exhibit 8-5) Other states outside the South Atlantic and East South Central region include New Mexico (both municipalities and school districts), New York (municipalities), and Maine (school districts).

The reader should be aware that when revenues are tabulated for fiscal impact analyses in the states listed above, intergovernmental transfers and thus the federal- or state-issued formulas for local apportionments assume utmost importance.

Own Source Revenues

Taxes

Local jurisdictions use three primary types of taxes: property tax, sales tax, and income tax. Exhibit 8-6 shows the contribution of these and all other taxes to both municipal and school district revenues.

---

*Substantial dependence on intergovernmental transfers to support municipal functions is defined as revenues financing more than 30 percent of local operations; for school districts, it is revenues financing more than 60 percent of local operations.

158　THE FISCAL IMPACT HANDBOOK

EXHIBIT 8-4
INTERGOVERNMENTAL TRANSFERS IN MUNICIPALITIES AND SCHOOL DISTRICTS BY REGION
(1972)

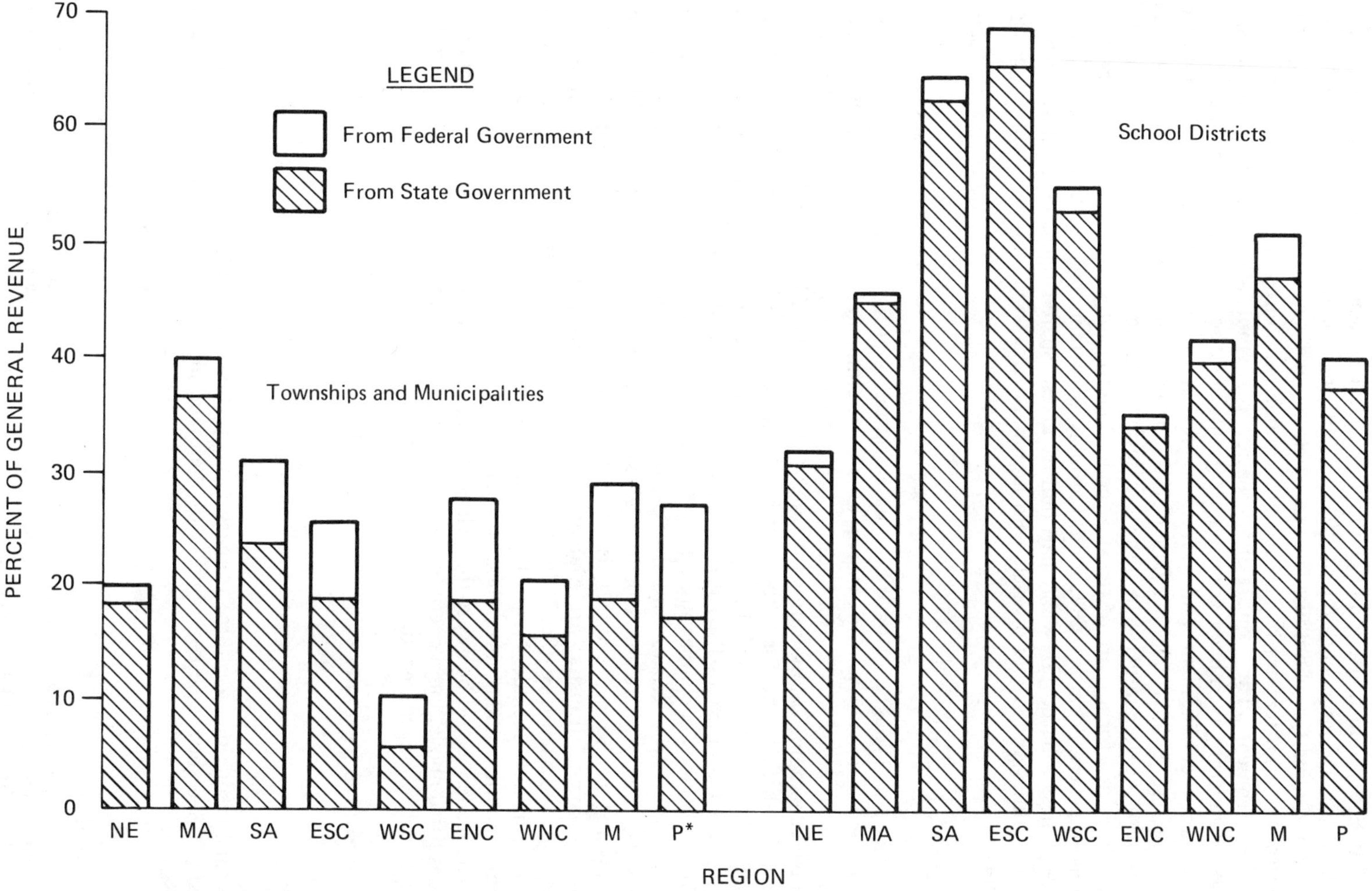

* For subregion abbreviation key see Chapter 13, Exhibit 13-3.

Source: U.S. Census of Governments, 1972.

Revenue Trends

EXHIBIT 8-5

RANK ORDER OF STATES FOR INTERGOVERNMENTAL (STATE AND FEDERAL) SUPPORT OF MUNICIPAL AND SCHOOL DISTRICT OPERATIONS — 1972

Townships and Municipalities			School Districts		
% General Revenue From Intergovernmental Transfers	State	Region	% General Revenue From Intergovernmental Transfers	State	Region
57.4%	Maryland	SA	76.5%	New Mexico	M
49.0	New Mexico	M	74.9	Alabama	ESC
44.2	New York	MA	74.1	Maine	NE
40.7	Wisconsin	ENC	71.6	Delaware	SA
40.2	Virginia	SA	69.4	Mississippi	ESC
39.2	Delaware	SA	65.6	Louisiana	WSC
37.4	Wyoming	M	64.9	West Virginia	SA
36.9	Tennessee	ESC	64.7	South Carolina	SA
33.8	Mississippi	ESC	62.1	Tennessee	ESC
32.8	Rhode Island	NE	61.0	Georgia	SA
				Kentucky	ESC
				Nevada	M[1]

[1] For subregion abbreviation key, see Chapter 13, Exhibit 13-3.
Source: U.S. Census of Governments, 1972.

EXHIBIT 8-6

CONTRIBUTION OF TAXES TO LOCAL REVENUE (1972)

Government	Taxes (in 1,000s)	As Percent of General Revenue	As Percent of Own Source Revenue
Townships and Municipalities	$17,244,806	46.4	66.2
School Districts	18,946,679	48.8	87.8

Source: U.S. Census of Governments, 1972.

This exhibit indicates that school districts rely more heavily on taxes than do municipalities, in terms of the percentage of both general revenues and own source revenues.

Property Tax

Overview

The property tax is by far the most heavily used type of tax for local revenue (Exhibit 8-7).

Property tax is a levy on wealth held in the form of property. Property is divided into two main categories — real and personal.* Real property consists of land and the improvements on it, including structures. All other property is considered personal property. Personal property is classified as either tangible or intangible. Tangible personal property includes machinery, equipment, inventory, furniture, motor vehicles, etc. Intangible personal property includes stocks,

---

*The practical problems of identifying and tabulating personal property (especially intangible personal property) are causing personal property taxes to be deemphasized nationally.

EXHIBIT 8-7

CONTRIBUTION BY PROPERTY TAX TO LOCAL REVENUE

Government	Property Taxes (in 1,000s)	As Percent of General Revenue	As Percent of Own Source Revenue
Townships and Municipalities	$13,305,260	35.8	51.1
School Districts	18,558,427	47.8	86.0

Source: U.S. Census of Governments, 1972.

bonds, notes, mortgages, and money.[7] Legally, the property tax base in a particular state may include all or some of these property categories. Practically, however, the tax base is almost always significantly composed of real property.

There are four reasons for the heavy reliance on the real property tax. First, it is a significant revenue raiser. Second, the receipts are stable and predictable, and allow governments to budget well in advance. Third, the tax is hard to evade, since real property, the major component of the tax base, is difficult to conceal. Finally, by reasoning that local public services enhance a community and thereby raise property values, it can be concluded that the tax to some extent charges those who benefit from the services it provides.[8] Despite these reasons, the property tax has been criticized as regressive, uneven, discriminatory and insufficient.[9] The recent trend therefore has been toward *diversification of revenue sources and away from predominant dependence on property tax.* Exhibit 8-8 demonstrates this trend.

While the dependence on the property tax has declined for municipalities, its use has not decreased significantly for school districts. In spite of all the criticism, court cases, etc., it remains a significant source of funds for local educational services.

Regional Patterns

Exhibit 8-9 shows percentages of both total general revenue and own source revenue that the property tax provides for both municipalities and school districts in various regions. This exhibit shows quite dramatically the different emphasis on the property tax these two jurisdictions place. Except in New England, where both types of government rely almost exclusively on the property tax, school districts depend on the levy much more heavily than do municipalities.

The New England and the East North Central regions dominate in terms of property tax support of both municipal and school district functions. Connecticut, New Hampshire, Vermont and Wisconsin fund significant amounts of *both* municipal and school district expenditures from property taxes. Rhode Island, Maine, and Massachusetts rely heavily on the property tax to fund municipal expenditures; Illinois and Ohio follow a similar pattern for the funding of school expenditures. New Jersey and California are two major states that are mavericks to their respective regions in terms of property tax reliance since both fund a very high share of both municipal and school district expenditures from property tax revenuesrelative to the averages of other inclusive states.

Significant property tax support* for both municipalities and school districts occurs most frequently in the New England and East North Central regions, and in New Jersey and California.

---

*Significant dependence on property tax rather than other own source revenues to support municipal functions is defined as revenues financing more than 60 percent of operations supported by own source revenues. For school districts, it is financing more than 90 percent of own source-supported operations.

Revenue Trends

EXHIBIT 8-8

RELIANCE ON PROPERTY TAX (1942–1972)

Revenue Source	Townships and Municipalities			School Districts		
	1942	1972	Percent Change	1942	1972	Percent Change
Property Tax						
Percent of general revenue	64.9	35.8	−44.8	49.9	47.8	−4.2
Percent of own source revenue	77.5	51.1	−34.1	92.3	86.0	−6.8

Source: U.S. Census of Governments, 1972.

EXHIBIT 8-9

REGIONAL RELIANCE ON PROPERTY TAX BY TYPE OF GOVERNMENT (1972)

Type of Government, Region	As Percent of General Revenue	As percent of Own Source Revenue
TOWNSHIPS AND MUNICIPALITIES		
New England	68.5	85.9
Middle Atlantic	31.7	52.9
South Atlantic	30.3	43.8
East South Central	21.8	29.5
West South Central	31.2	34.6
East North Central	35.3	48.4
West North Central	31.7	39.9
Mountain	20.0	28.2
Pacific	26.9	36.5
SCHOOL DISTRICTS		
New England	60.9	89.0
Middle Atlantic	47.0	84.5
South Atlantic	28.9	75.1
East South Central	20.2	62.5
West South Central	35.3	76.7
East North Central	58.3	89.6
West North Central	50.0	85.6
Mountain	42.8	86.1
Pacific	55.2	91.5

Source: U.S. Census of Governments, 1972.

Sales Tax, Income Tax, and Other Taxes

Overview: Sales Tax

By fiscal year 1972, local governments obtained 4.5 percent of their local tax revenues from sales taxes. A sales tax is a tax on goods or services usually levied at the point of final transaction (i.e., at the retail rather than the wholesale level). It's usually expressed in percentage terms. A general sales tax is one broadly applicable to the purchase of a wide range of goods and services. Food is often excluded from a general sales tax; clothing is occasionally excluded. A selective sales tax, in contrast, is limited by law to only a few items (motor fuel, alcoholic beverages, tobacco products, and public utilities).[10] As of 1976 retail sales taxes were imposed by local governments in twenty-eight states and authorized but unused in one other (See Exhibit 8–11). Geographic coverage in the various states differs greatly — from universal in California and Virginia to the use by only one

EXHIBIT 8-10

RANK ORDER OF STATES FOR PROPERTY TAX SUPPORT OF
MUNICIPAL AND SCHOOL DISTRICT OPERATIONS — 1972

Townships and Municipalities			School Districts		
Percent of Own Source Revenue	State	Region	Percent of Own Source Revenue	State	Region
91.0	Connecticut	NE	95.9	New Hampshire	NE
90.9	Rhode Island	NE	94.8	New Jersey	MA
89.6	Maine	NE	93.3	Vermont	NE
88.5	Massachusetts	NE	92.8	Wisconsin	ENC
85.3	New Hampshire	NE	92.5	California	P
83.8	Vermont	NE	91.8	Nevada	M
75.2	Wisconsin	ENC	91.3	Illinois	ENC
73.4	Indiana	ENC	90.8	Oregon	P
72.0	New Jersey	MA	90.4	Ohio	ENC
64.8	Hawaii	P	90.2	Connecticut	NE*

Source: U.S. Census of Governments, 1972.

city in Minnesota and Arkansas.[11] The sales tax accounted for approximately one dollar in ten of the revenue of municipal governments in 1970; it amounted to 20 to 25 percent of the total revenue in half of all cities with more than 100,000 population.[12] A local sales tax may be locally administered, or state administered or both. State administrations impose varying fees on local governments for collecting the tax (from 1 to 4 percent except Ohio, Virginia, and Colorado where this service is performed free). In areas where the local sales tax is locally administered, there is a great variation in *substantive coverage;* when state administered, local levies are almost identical in coverage to the state levies. The same basic principle is true for sales tax *rate* variation.

Income Tax

An income tax is a levy on the net income of individuals or households. The local income tax is typically a flat rate tax, most often around 1 percent. It applies typically at different rates, to those who work in the city whether or not they reside there. Usually coverage is narrower than federal income tax — primarily wages and salaries, not capital gains or other dividends. For most localities the local income tax is thus an earned income tax. Another dissimilarity between most locally imposed income taxes and the federal income tax is frequent lack of personal exemptions, deductions, and employee business expense allowances.

As of 1976, *local* income taxes existed in eleven states (Exhibit 8-12). All of the Indiana and Maryland Counties, almost all Pennsylvania localities and many Ohio cities impose local income taxes. Kentucky and Michigan jurisdictions imposed local income taxes extensively. Alabama, California, Delaware, Missouri, and New York used them in isolated cases. Fifteen of the forty-eight largest cities in the central states received revenue from local income taxes by the first fiscal year of the 1970s. Several of these cities received more than half their tax revenue from local income taxes.[13] As with the sales tax, local income taxes may be state, locally or jointly administered.

---

*For subregion abbreviation key, see Chapter 13, Exhibit 13-3.

Revenue Trends 163

EXHIBIT 8-11
SALES TAXES IMPOSED BY LOCAL JURISDICTIONS, BY STATE (1976)

STATE AND TYPE OF LOCAL GOVERNMENT	Statutory Authority	Number Using	Scope	Rate Limits	Voter Approval	Administration
Alabama						
Municipalities	Business and occupational license	240	Sales & use	None	No	Local option[1]
Counties	Specific[2]	25	Do	2%	Yes[2]	State[1]
Alaska						
Municipalities	Specific	80	Do	3%	No[3]	Local
Boroughs	Do	6	Do	3%	Yes	Do
Arizona						
Municipalities	Business and occupational license	38	Sales	None	No	Do
Arkansas						
Municipalities	Specific	1	Do	1%	Yes	State
California						
Municipalities	Specific	394	Sales & use	1%[4]	No	State
Counties	Do	58[5]	Do	1¼%[4]	Do	Do
Special districts	Do	1	Do	0.25% or 0.5%	Do	Do
Colorado						
Municipalities	Home rule[6]	106	Both[6]	None[6]	Do[6]	25 Local 81 State[6,7]
Counties	Specific	14	Sales & use	[6]	Yes	State
Special district[8]	Do	1	Sales	0.5%	Do	Do
Georgia[9]						
Municipalities[9]	Do	2	Sales & use	1%	Yes	State
Counties[9]	Do	12	Do	1%	Do	Do
Special district[10]	Do	2[10]	Sales & use	1%[10]	No	Do
Illinois						
Municipalities	Do	1,240	Do	1%	Do	State
Counties	Do	102	Do	1%	Do	Do
Kansas						
Municipalities	Do	3	Sales & use	0.5%	Yes	Do
Counties	Do	4	Do	0.5%	Do	Do
Kentucky						
Transit districts	Do	....	Sales	½%	Yes	State
Louisiana[11]						
Municipalities	Do	112	Sales & use	1½%	Yes	Local
Parishes	Do	19	Do	1%	Do	Do
School districts	Do	52	Do	1%	Do	Do
Minnesota						
Municipality	Do	1	Do	None	Yes	Do

EXHIBIT 8-11

SALES TAXES IMPOSED BY LOCAL JURISDICTIONS, BY STATE (1976) (Cont'd)

STATE AND TYPE OF LOCAL GOVERNMENT	Statutory Authority	Number Using	Scope	Rate Limits	Voter Approval	Administration
Missouri						
Municipalities	Do	149	Sales	0.5% or 1%	Yes	State
Transit districts		3	Do	0.5%	No	Do
Nebraska						
Municipalities	Do	3	Sales & use	0.5% or 1%	No	Do
Nevada						
Counties	Specific	12	Sales & use	0.5%	No	State
New Mexico						
Counties	Do	3	Sales	0.25% or 0.5%[12]	Yes[12]	State
Municipalities[13]	Do	29	Gross receipts	0.25%	No	Do
New York						
Municipalities	Do	24	Sales & use	3%	No	State
Counties	Do	44	Do	3%	Do	Do
North Carolina						
Counties	Do	96	Do	1%	No[14]	Local option (State)
Ohio						
Counties	Do	32	Do	0.5%	[14]	State
Regional transit authorities	Do	1	Do	0.5%; 1%; 1.5%	Yes	State
Oklahoma						
Municipalities	Do	356	Sales	[15]	Yes	Local[16]
Oregon						
Municipalities[17]	Do	....	Do	None	No	Local
South Dakota						
Municipalities	Do	18	Sales & use	None	Do	State
Tennessee						
Municipalities	Do[18]	25	Sales & use	2¼%[19]	Yes	State[20]
Counties	Do[18]	90	Do	2¼%[19]	Do	Do[20]
Texas						
Municipalities	Do	854	Do	1%	Do	State
Utah						
Municipalities	Do	175	Sales	0.75%	No	State
Counties	Do	29	Do	0.75%[21]	Do	Do
Virginia						
Cities	Specific	38[22]	Sales & use	1%	No	State
Counties	Do	96[22]	Do	1%	Do	Do

Revenue Trends 165

EXHIBIT 8-11

SALES TAXES IMPOSED BY LOCAL JURISDICTIONS, BY STATE (1976) (Cont'd)

STATE AND TYPE OF LOCAL GOVERNMENT	Statutory Authority	Number Using	Scope	Rate Limits	Voter Approval	Administration
Washington						
Municipalities	Do	262	Sales & use	0.5%[23]	Do	Do
Counties	Do	38	Do	0.5%[23]	Do	Do
Wisconsin						
Counties	Do[24]	....	Sales	0.5%	No	Do
Wyoming						
Counties	Do[25]	5	Do	0.5% or 1%	Yes	Do

Notes:

[1] The State Department of Revenue is authorized, on request by a municipality, to collect local sales and use taxes. The municipal tax must parallel the State tax except for the rate. The Department of Revenue presently administers 209 of the 240 municipal sales taxes. The statutes applicable to individual counties usually (in 21 counties) require State administration.

[2] Specific statutory authority is given to individual counties (22); voter approval is required in most cases; and counties enabling act (3 counties).

[3] Home rule and first class general law cities may levy a sales and use tax without voter approval.

[4] A city tax may be at any rate up to 1% and must be credited against the countywide 1¼% tax so that in effect cities usually receive 80% of the collections.

[5] Includes the city-county of San Francisco.

[6] Home rule cities only. H.B. 1141, Laws 1967 provides that counties, second class cities and incorporated towns, with voter approval, may also levy sales taxes but the total State and county, city or town rate cannot exceed 7%. Such taxes must begin either January 1 or July 1 of any year and are administered by the Director of Revenue. The director must be notified at least 120 days prior to the effective date. The law does not affect or limit the power of home rule cities to levy local sales and use taxes.

[7] Home rule cities may contract with the State for administration and collection, without charge, if local tax conforms to certain specifications (one requirement is that home rule cities do not impose a use tax).

[8] Regional Transportation District, consisting of the city and county of Denver, the counties of Jefferson, Boulder and Douglas; and parts of Adams and Arapahoe Counties.

[9] Counties are authorized to impose 1% sales and use taxes, subject to voters' approval, to be administered and collected by the State Revenue Commissioner. If the governing authority at either of the two most populous municipalities in a county requests the county to levy a sales and use tax and the county does not initiate a referendum within 90 days, or if the referendum is defeated by the voters, the governing authority of any municipality in such county is authorized to call for a referendum election on the question of whether to levy the tax. If a county or municipality levies a local income tax it is prohibited from levying a sales and use tax. Effective July 1, 1975.

[10] Governing bodies which enter into rapid transit contracts with the Metropolitan Atlanta Rapid Transit Authority may levy sales and use taxes at the rate of 1% for the first 10 years, and ½ of 1% thereafter if the tax is also imposed in Fulton and DeKalb Counties. Taxes must parallel state tax except for rate, and are state collected. Fulton and DeKalb county tax effective April 1, 1972.

[11] The rate limits shown apply generally; several taxing jurisdictions are authorized to levy a higher rate of tax. The maximum combined local rate cannot exceed three percent.

[12] The general limit is ¼%; certain specific counties are authorized to levy a ½% rate without voter approval.

[13] Any ordinance imposing the tax must take effect, or be repealed, on either January 1 or July 1 occurring first after the expiration of at least five months from the date the taxing ordinance is adopted or repealed. Effective 4/10/75.

[14] Not required unless a specified percentage of voters petition.

[15] Incorporated cities and towns are authorized to levy and collect taxes (except property taxes) to the same extent as the State legislature. The State sales tax is currently 2 percent. A 3% tax may be levied by municipalities having adopted a sales tax ordinance providing that the proceeds of a 1% sales tax levy are dedicated exclusively to the support of an educational or health institution.

[16] Municipalities and the State Tax Commission are authorized to enter into contractual agreement for State collection (all municipal sales taxes are presently State collected). Municipalities are required to enforce their own sales tax laws, even if the Commission collects the tax.

[17] Cities with population of 9,000 – 10,500 only, but none is presently using this authority.

[18] Where the county elects to levy such tax, half the proceeds originating in a city or town are shared with such city or town, and any city or town is pre-empted from enacting such tax unless it does not reach the maximum rate in which case the city or town may levy the difference between the rate established by a county and the maximum rate allowed.

[19] The rate is limited to ½ of the State sales tax rate until 6/30/77 and may not exceed ¾ of the State rate thereafter, and the maximum tax on a single transaction is limited to $7.50 if the local rate exceeds 1%.

[20] Optional.

[21] Counties located in transit districts may levy an additional ¼ percent tax (subject to voter approval) to fund a public transportation system.

[22] The local sales tax is levied by every county and "independent" city in the state.

[23] County rates must be ½ of 1%, city rates may not exceed ½ of 1%. If the county in which the city is located imposes a tax, the rate of the city tax may not exceed 0.425%. County tax must allow credit for full amount of any city tax. Class A counties, or cities and municipal corporations within such counties, may impose additional sales and use taxes of 1/10, 2/10, or 3/10 of 1% subject to voter approval to finance public transportation systems.

[24] S.B. 95 approved August 27, 1969 authorized counties to levy ½ of 1% sales taxes on same items subject to the State sales tax. If enacted, taxes will become operative on January 1 of the year following enactment.

[25] Ch. 183 (H.B. 261), effective 7/1/73, authorized counties to impose a ½% or 1% sales tax on same items subject to State tax if voters approve.

Source: Advisory Commission on Intergovernmental Relations, *Significant Features of Fiscal Federalism 1976-1977* (Washington, D.C. ACIR, March 1977) pp. 188-189.

EXHIBIT 8-12

INCOME TAXES IMPOSED BY LOCAL JURISDICTIONS, BY STATE (1976)

State and Local Government	Rate July 1, 1976 (percent)	Municipal Tax Collections, 1973-74 (Cities with over 50,000 population in 1970) (in thousands)		Income Tax Collections
		Total Tax Collections	Amount	As a Percent of Total Collections
Alabama:				
Auburn	1.0	—	—	—
Birmingham	1.0	$ 37,546	$ 11,143	29.7
Gadsden	2.0	6,313	3,554	56.3
Montgomery	1.0	—	—	—
Opelika	1.0	—	—	—
Rainbow City	2.0	—	—	—
California:				
Oakland[1]	1.0	1	1	1
Delaware:				
Wilmington	1.25	24,384	7,755	31.8
Indiana (counties):[2]				
Bartholomew	1.0	—	—	—
Benton	0.5	—	—	—
Blackford	0.5	—	—	—
Brown	0.5	—	—	—
Carroll	1.0	—	—	—
Cass	0.5	—	—	—

Revenue Trends 167

EXHIBIT 8-12

INCOME TAXES IMPOSED BY LOCAL JURISDICTIONS, BY STATE (1976) (Cont'd)

		Municipal Tax Collections, 1973-74 (Cities with over 50,000 population in 1970)		
	Rate July 1, 1976 (percent)	Total Tax Collections	Income Tax Collections	
State and Local Government			Amount	As a Percent of Total Collections
Clinton	1.0	—	—	—
Decatur	1.0	—	—	—
DeKalb	1.0	—	—	—
Elkhart	1.0	—	—	—
Fountain	0.5	—	—	—
Hancock	1.0	—	—	—
Hendricks	0.5	—	—	—
Huntington	1.0	—	—	—
Jasper	0.5	—	—	—
Jay	1.0	—	—	—
Johnson	0.5	—	—	—
Kosciusko	0.5	—	—	—
Lawrence	1.0	—	—	—
Marshall	1.0	—	—	—
Morgan	0.5	—	—	—
Newton	0.5	—	—	—
Noble	1.0	—	—	—
Ohio	0.5	—	—	—
Pulaski	1.0	—	—	—
Randolph	1.0	—	—	—
Ripley	0.5	—	—	—
Rush	0.75	—	—	—
Starke	0.5	—	—	—
Steuben	0.5	—	—	—
Tipton	0.5	—	—	—
Union	1.0	—	—	—
Wabash	1.0	—	—	—
Warren	1.0	—	—	—
Washington	0.5	—	—	—
Wayne	1.0	—	—	—
Wells	0.5	—	—	—
White	1.0	—	—	—
Kentucky:				
Ashland	1.5	—	—	—
Auburn	1.0	—	—	—
Benton	0.5	—	—	—
Berea	1.5	—	—	—
Bowling Green	1.5	—	—	—
Burkesville	0.5	—	—	—
Cadiz	1.0	—	—	—
Catlettsburg	1.0	—	—	—
Covington	2.5	5,787	3,511	60.7
Cynthiana	1.5	—	—	—
Danville	1.0	—	—	—
Dawson Springs	1.0	—	—	—
Elizabethtown	0.8	—	—	—
Flemingsburg	1.0	—	—	—
Frankfort	1.0	—	—	—

EXHIBIT 8-12

INCOME TAXES IMPOSED BY LOCAL JURISDICTIONS, BY STATE (1976) (Cont'd)

	Rate July 1, 1976 (percent)	Municipal Tax Collections, 1973-74 (Cities with over 50,000 population in 1970)		
			Income Tax Collections	
State and Local Government		Total Tax Collections	Amount	As a Percent of Total Collections
Fulton	1.0	—	—	—
Gamaliel	1.0	—	—	—
Glasgow	1.0	—	—	—
Harrodsburg	0.75	—	—	—
Hazard	1.0	—	—	—
Hickman	1.0	—	—	—
Hopkinsville	1.0	—	—	—
Leitchfield	1.0	—	—	—
Lexington-Fayette Urban County	2.0	19,967	10,810	54.1
Louisville	1.45	43,711	25,241	57.7
Jefferson County[3]	2.2	—	—	—
Ludlow	1.0	—	—	—
Madisonville	1.0	—	—	—
Marshall County	0.5	—	—	—
Mayfield	1.0	—	—	—
Maysville	1.5	—	—	—
Middlesboro	2.0	—	—	—
Morgantown	1.0	—	—	—
Newport	2.5	—	—	—
Nicholasville	1.5	—	—	—
Owensboro	1.0	3,694	1,611	43.6
Paducah	1.25	—	—	—
Pikeville	1.5	—	—	—
Prestonburg	1.0	—	—	—
Princeton	1.0	—	—	—
Richmond	1.0	—	—	—
Russellville	1.0	—	—	—
Shirley	0.5	—	—	—
Springfield	1.0	—	—	—
Versailles	1.0	—	—	—
Wilder	0.25	—	—	—
Wilmore	1.0	—	—	—
Woodford County	0.5	—	—	—
Approx. 12 other local jurisdictions (with less than 50,000 population)	0.5-1.5	—	—	—
Maryland:				
Baltimore City	50	$246,718	$ 40,323	16.3
20 Counties	50	—	—	—
Queen Anne's County	40	—	—	—
Talbot County	35	—	—	—
Worcester County	20	—	—	—
Michigan[4]				
Albion	1.0	—	—	—
Battle Creek	1.0	—	—	—
Big Rapids	1.0	—	—	—
Detroit	2.0[5]	304.931	108,511	35.6
Flint	1.0	22,104	11,292	51.1

EXHIBIT 8-12

INCOME TAXES IMPOSED BY LOCAL JURISDICTIONS, BY STATE (1976) (Cont'd)

		Municipal Tax Collections, 1973-74 (Cities with over 50,000 population in 1970)		
	Rate July 1, 1976 (percent)	Total Tax Collections	Income Tax Collections	
State and Local Government			Amount	As a Percent of Total Collections
Grand Rapids	1.0	18,564	9,119	49.1
Grayling	1.0	—	—	—
Hamtramck	1.0	—	—	—
Highland Park	1.0	—	—	—
Hudson	1.0	—	—	—
Jackson	1.0	—	—	—
Lansing	1.0	14,991	7,272	48.5
Lapeer	1.0	—	—	—
Pontiac	1.0	14,976	5,620	37.5
Port Huron	1.0	—	—	—
Saginaw	1.0	10,288	4,788	46.5
Missouri:				
Kansas City	1.0	92,245	33,190	36.0
St. Louis	1.0	139,150	37,817	27.2
New York:				
New York City	0.9-4.3[6]	4,324,366	804,729	18.6
Ohio:				
Akron	1.5	30,685	22,357	72.9
Canton	1.5	11,046	9,231	83.6
Cincinnati	2.0	81,023	50,749	62.6
Cleveland	1.0	86,677	46,042	53.1
Cleveland Heights	1.0	5,180	2,023	39.1
Columbus	1.5	57,421	45,561	79.3
Dayton	1.75	28,446	17,461	61.4
Elyria	1.0	4,339	3,069	70.7
Euclid	1.0	10,738	3,816	35.5
Hamilton	1.5	5,518	4,201	76.1
Kettering	1.0	5,429	2,846	52.4
Lakewood	1.0	5,057	1,941	38.4
Lima	1.0	3,119	2,416	77.5
Lorain	1.0	6,539	4,295	65.7
Mansfield	1.0	5,182	3,436	66.3
Parma	1.0	6,937	4,213	60.7
Springfield	1.5	6,558	5,345	81.5
Toledo	1.5	37,289	29,471	79.0
Warren	1.0	4,518	3,480	77.0
Youngstown	1.5	14,314	10,047	70.2
365 cities and villages (with less than 50,000 population)	0.25-1.7	—	—	—
Pennsylvania:[7]				
Abington Township	1.0[8]	57	25	43.9
Allentown	1.0[8]	9,949	2,114	21.2
Altoona	1.0[9]	3,402	841	24.7
Bethlehem	1.0[8]	7,121	1,467	20.6
Chester	1.0[10]	5,301	2,244	42.3
Erie	1.0[8]	9,346	2,075	22.2

170 THE FISCAL IMPACT HANDBOOK

EXHIBIT 8-12

INCOME TAXES IMPOSED BY LOCAL JURISDICTIONS, BY STATE (1976) (Cont'd)

Municipal Tax Collections, 1973-74
(Cities with over 50,000 population in 1970)

State and Local Government	Rate July 1, 1976 (percent)	Total Tax Collections	Income Tax Collections Amount	As a Percent of Total Collections
Harrisburg	1.0^8	5,141	980	19.1
Lancaster	1.0^8	4,251	781	18.4
Penn Hills Township	1.0^8	3,190	1,032	32.4
Philadelphia	4.3125^{11}	451,333	303,417	67.2
Pittsburgh	1.0^8	66,525	3,949	5.9
Reading	1.0^8	6,279	1,159	18.5
Scranton	2.0^{12}	7,628	2,437	31.9
Wilkes-Barre	1.0^8	4,386	791	18.0
York	1.0^8	4,617	704	15.2
Approx. 3,500 other local jurisdictions (including over 1,000 school systems)	0.25-1.0	—	—	—

Note: Excludes Washington, D.C., which has a graduated net income tax that is more closely akin to a state tax than to the municipal income taxes (see State tables). Also excludes the Denver Employee Occupational Privilege Tax of $2 per employee per month, which applies only to employees earning at least $250 per month; the Newark 1% payroll tax imposed on employers, profit and nonprofit, having a payroll over $2,500 per calendar quarter; the San Francisco 1.1% payroll expense tax; the 4/10 of 1% (5/10 of 1%—1/1/76 to 6/30/77) quarterly payroll tax on employers imposed in the Tri-county Metropolitan Transit District (encompassing all of Washington, Clackamas and Multnomah counties, Oregon); the 0.54 percent payroll tax imposed on employers in the Lane County Oregon Mass Transit District and the Portland business license tax of 2.3% of net income.

— Signifies a county, or a city under 50,000 population.
n.a. - "not available."

[1] The Oakland employees' quarterly license fee of 1 percent on all salaries, wages, bonuses, and commissions in excess of $1,625. Efective July 1, 1976.
[2] The tax rate on nonresidents for all counties is 1/4 of 1%.
[3] A taxpayer subject to the 1.45 percent tax imposed by the City of Louisville may credit this tax against the 2.2 percent levied by Jefferson County.
[4] Under the Michigan "Uniform City Income Tax Act," the prescribed rates are 1.0 percent for residents and 0.5 percent for nonresidents. A resident is allowed credit for taxes paid to another city as a nonresident.
[5] The rate for residents in Detroit was increased from 1 percent to 2 percent effective October 1, 1968.
[6] New York City residents' rate ranges from 0.9 percent on taxable income of less than $1,000 to 4.3 percent on taxable income in excess of $25,000. An earnings tax of 0.45 percent of wages or 65/100 of 1 percent on net earnings from self-employment, not to exceed that which would be due if taxpayer were a resident, is levied against nonresidents. A 4% tax is imposed on unincorporated businesses carried on in the city.
[7] Except for Philadelphia, Pittsburgh, and Scranton, the total rate payable by any taxpayer is limited to 1 percent. For coterminous jurisdictions, such as borough and borough school district, the maximum is usually divided equally between the jurisdictions unless otherwise agreed. However, school districts may tax only residents. Thus, if a borough and a coterminous school district each have a stated rate of 1 percent, the total effective rate for residents is 1 percent (1/2 of 1 percent each to the borough and school district) and the tax on nonresidents is 1 percent, the stated rate imposed by the borough.
[8] The school district rate is the same as the municipal rate.
[9] The school district rate is 0.5 percent.
[10] There is no school district income tax.
[11] The Philadelphia school district imposes a 4.3125% tax on investment income.
[12] Combined city and school district rate may not exceed 2.0 percent. The city rate is 2%, the school district rate is 1%.

Source: Advisory Commission on Intergovernmental Relations, *Significant Features of Fiscal Federalism 1976-1977* (Washington, D.C. ACIR, March 1977) pp. 225-228.

Revenue Trends

A significant aspect of both the sales tax and the income tax is that, although a different rate structure may exist, they can be levied on nonresidents who otherwise do not pay for the service benefits they receive. The income tax in particular may place some burden for supporting services rendered at the place of employment on the commuter.

Other Taxes

Several other taxes are often mentioned as potential sources of local revenue. They represent only 2.4 percent of all local (municipal and school district) revenues. They include per capita taxes, occupation and business privilege taxes, licenses, real estate transfer fees, etc.

Per Capita Tax — (Delaware, Pennsylvania and Vermont) Small lump sum tax levied on resident adults ages 18 to 65 with exemptions for disabilities (i.e., deafness, blindness, or insanity).

Occupation and Business Privilege Tax — (most states) Taxes commonly regarded as licenses levied on individuals engaged in particular occupations, on owners of businesses, and on corporations either at a flat amount or at a variable amount such as a percentage of gross receipts.

Real Estate Transfer Tax — (California, Delaware, District of Columbia, Maryland, New York, Ohio, Pennsylvania, South Carolina, Virginia, Washington, West Virginia) A tax on the turnover of real property, usually based on market value and taxed at the rate of 1 percent of the sales price, although considerable rate variation does exist.

Exhibit 8-13 shows the national changes in reliance on all types of taxes since 1942 by municipalities and school districts. Obviously, the change in amount of one tax does not equal another over time. As noted earlier, growth in various categories of intergovernmental transfers has occurred over the thirty-year period at the expense of all tax revenues. Exhibit 8-13 also clearly points out that sales, income, and other tax increases largely support municipal rather than school district functions. Municipalities, except in New England, use taxes other than property taxes for approximately 15 to 20 percent of their own source revenues. While the use of taxes other than property taxes has changed most drastically for school districts, these taxes still account for less than 2 percent of their own source revenues.

Regional Patterns

Exhibit 8-14 shows the regional patterns in use of sales, income, and other taxes by municipalities and school districts. Except in New England, where the property tax is the dominant tax for municipal purposes, municipalities' dependence on sales, income, and other taxes is consistent throughout the country. Municipalities in the Mountain and Pacific regions — particularly

EXHIBIT 8-13

RELIANCE ON TAXES BY MUNICIPALITIES AND SCHOOL DISTRICTS (1942-1972)

	Percentage of General Revenue					
	Townships and Municipalities			School Districts		
Type of Tax	1942	1972	Percent Change (Simple)	1942	1972	Percent Change (Simple)
All taxes	74.3	46.4	−37.6	60.0	48.8	−18.7
Property tax	64.9	35.8	−44.8	49.9	47.8	−4.2
Sales, income, other	9.4	10.6	+12.8	0.1	1.0	+900
	Percentage of Own Source Revenue					
All taxes	88.8	66.2	−25.5	92.4	87.8	−5.0
Property tax	77.5	51.1	−34.1	92.3	86.0	−6.8
Sales, income, other	11.3	15.1	+33.6	0.1	1.8	+1700

Source: U.S. Census of Governments, 1972.

172   THE FISCAL IMPACT HANDBOOK

EXHIBIT 8-14
REGIONAL PATTERN OF USE OF SALES, INCOME, AND OTHER TAXES
IN MUNICIPALITIES AND SCHOOL DISTRICTS
(1972)

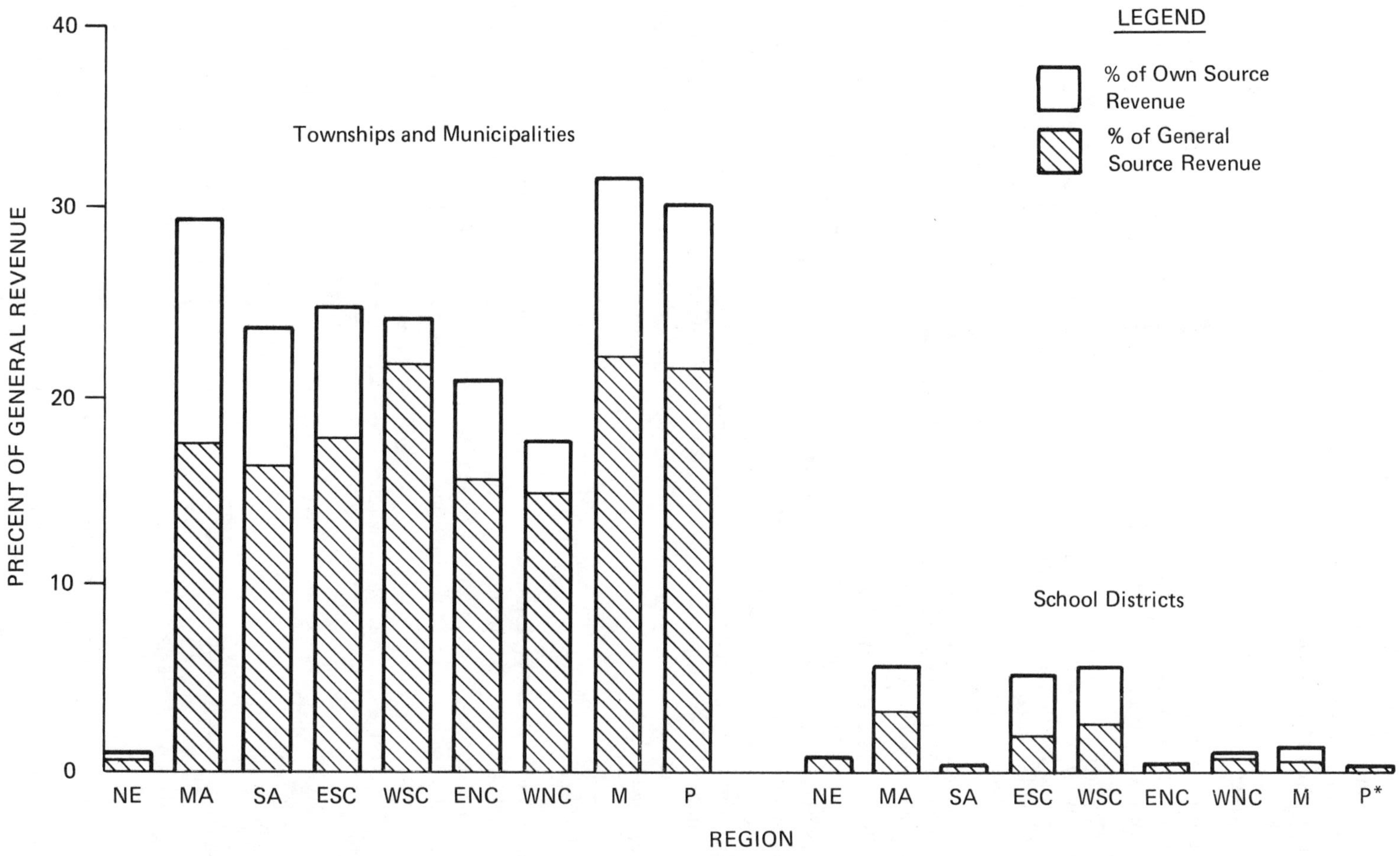

* For subregion abbreviation key see Chapter 13, Exhibit 13-3

Source: U.S. Census of Governments, 1972.

Revenue Trends   173

Arizona, Colorado, Montana, and California — rely more heavily on sales, income, and other taxes. School districts in the West South Central, East South Central, and Middle Atlantic regions — particularly Louisiana, Tennessee, Kentucky, Oklahoma, and Pennsylvania — rely on taxes other than property taxes more than other regions.

Charges and Miscellaneous Revenue

Overview

In 1972, charges and miscellaneous revenue accounted for 23.7 percent of all general revenues for municipalities and 6.8 percent for school districts. They accounted for 33.8 percent of own source revenue for municipalities and 12.3 percent for school districts.

User charges are charges received for the performance of a service or provision of a product. They include municipal court fees, charges for sewage disposal, and fees for school lunches. Charges for educational (23 percent) and hospital (28 percent) services and sewage disposal (11 percent) dominate this category. Recreation fees and parking fees are significantly lower. Miscellaneous revenues come from special assessments, sales of property, interest earned on idle cash balances, fines and forfeitures, etc. Interest earnings and fines/forfeitures represent 70 percent of miscellaneous revenues. User charges contribute approximately 16.4 percent to local revenues, while miscellaneous revenues contribute approximately 7.2 percent.

Exhibit 8-15 shows the changes in the reliance on these revenue sources from 1942 to 1972. The patterns are familiar. Municipalities are increasing their reliance on these revenue sources; while school districts are also increasing their dependence on these sources, their use is still small.

Regional Patterns

Exhibit 8-16 ranks the top ten states in their use of charges and miscellaneous revenues. The western regions of the United States — Wyoming, Alaska, New Mexico, North Dakota, Oklahoma, Minnesota, and Arizona — particularly rely on charges and miscellaneous revenues to fund municipal expenditures.* Using charges and miscellaneous revenues to support educational

EXHIBIT 8-15

CHANGES IN USE OF CHARGES AND MISCELLANEOUS REVENUES FOR MUNICIPALITIES AND SCHOOL DISTRICTS (1942-1972)

ITEM	Townships and Municipalities			School Districts		
	1942	1972	Percent Change (Simple)	1942	1972	Percent Change (Simple)
Charges and miscellaneous as percentage of general revenue	9.4	23.7	+152.1	4.9	6.8	+38.8
Charges and miscellaneous as percentage of own source revenue	11.2	33.8	+201.8	7.6	12.3	+61.8

Source: U.S. Census of Governments, 1972.

---

*Heavy dependence on charges and miscellaneous revenues (versus other own source revenues) to support municipal functions is defined as revenues financing more than 50 percent of operations supported by own source revenues. For school districts, it is revenues financing more than 20 percent of operations supported by own source revenues.

expenditures is a southern phenomenon, however; the use is concentrated most heavily in Alabama, Tennessee, Mississippi, Florida, Kentucky, Delaware, and Georgia. (See Exhibit 8-17.)

Summary — The Revenue Systems of Municipalities and School Districts

This chapter has pointed out the relative importance and geographic concentration of components of local sources of revenue. The fiscal impact analyst must be aware of which sources of revenue

EXHIBIT 8-16

RANK ORDER OF STATES IN USING CHARGES AND MISCELLANEOUS REVENUES TO SUPPORT MUNICIPAL OPERATIONS (1972)

Percent of Own Source Revenue	Townships and Municipalities State	Region
66.6	Wyoming	M
61.8	Alaska	P
57.8	New Mexico	M
53.0	North Dakota	WNC
51.4	Oklahoma	WSC
50.8	West Virginia	SA
50.6	Alabama/Kentucky	ESC/ESC
50.3	Mississippi	ESC
50.1	Minnesota	WNC
50.0	Arizona	M*

*For subregion abbreviation key, see Chapter 13, Exhibit 13-3.
Source: U.S. Census of Governments, 1972.

EXHIBIT 8-17

RANK ORDER OF STATES IN USING CHARGES AND MISCELLANEOUS REVENUES TO SUPPORT SCHOOL DISTRICT OPERATIONS (1972)

PERCENTAGE OF OWN SOURCE REVENUE	School Districts State	Region
44.6	Alabama	ESC
38.5	Tennessee	ESC
32.7	Mississippi	ESC
30.2	New Mexico	M
28.8	Florida	SA
25.9	Maine	NE
25.4	Massachusetts	NE
23.8	Kentucky	ESC
22.5	Delaware	SA
22.1	Georgia	SA*

*For subregion abbreviation key, see Chapter 13, Exhibit 13-3.
Source: U.S. Census of Governments, 1972.

Revenue Trends

are emphasized in the locale where he is working so he can properly project local resources. He must also be aware of the general nature of revenue systems used elsewhere so he can correctly interpret the results of fiscal impact analyses undertaken at several locations. For example, a housing development may have a favorable local cost-revenue impact in an essentially residential area which depends heavily on the real property tax for local revenues. Its impact may be unfavorable, however, in a locality which relies upon a state-levied sales tax for local revenues.

Exhibits 8-18, 8-19, and 8-20 summarize the information presented thus far. Exhibit 8-18 clearly shows that school districts and municipalities fund expenditures differently. School districts rely heavily on intergovernmental transfers (for about 45 percent of total revenues), and 96 percent of that source comes from the state. Municipalities, on the other hand, rely much less on intergovernmental transfers, and a smaller share (80 percent) of these revenues comes directly from the state.

Municipalities and school districts differ significantly in their dependence on various categories of own source revenue. School districts depend more heavily on property tax revenues to finance expenditures, but municipalities emphasize sales, income, and other taxes; user charges; and miscellaneous revenue.

Exhibit 8-19 shows municipalities' reliance on sources of revenue by region. Intergovernmental transfers are an important source of funds for municipalities in the South, particularly the East South Central and the South Atlantic regions. In New England, the property tax is the dominant source of local revenues. Sales, income, and other taxes as a percentage of local revenues, are relatively even across most of the United States, except New England. The Western portion of the United States, especially the West South Central, Mountain and Pacific regions, relies heavily on user charges and miscellaneous revenues.

Exhibit 8-20 shows school districts' reliance on sources of revenue by region. Intergovernmental transfers constitute more than 60 percent of school district revenues in the South, specifically in the South Atlantic and East South Central regions. The New England, Middle Atlantic, East North Central, and Pacific regions rely most heavily on property taxes for school district revenues. Sales, income and other taxes are significant contributors in the East South Central and West South Central regions. Finally, charges and miscellaneous revenue concentrations parallel those of intergovernmental transfer.

EXHIBIT 8-18
REVENUE SOURCES OF MUNICIPALITIES AND SCHOOL DISTRICTS (1972)

REVENUE SOURCE	Townships and Municipalities		School Districts	
Own source revenue	70.1%		55.6%	
Property tax		35.8		47.8
Sales, income and other taxes		10.6		1.0
Current charges		10.1		5.4
Miscellaneous revenues		13.6		1.4
Intergovernmental Revenue	29.9		44.4	
From state		24.1		42.6
From federal		5.8		1.8
TOTAL	100.0%		100.0%	

Source: U.S. Census of Governments, 1972.

176 THE FISCAL IMPACT HANDBOOK

EXHIBIT 8-19
MUNICIPALITIES RELIANCE ON VARIOUS SOURCES OF REVENUE, BY REGION
(1972)

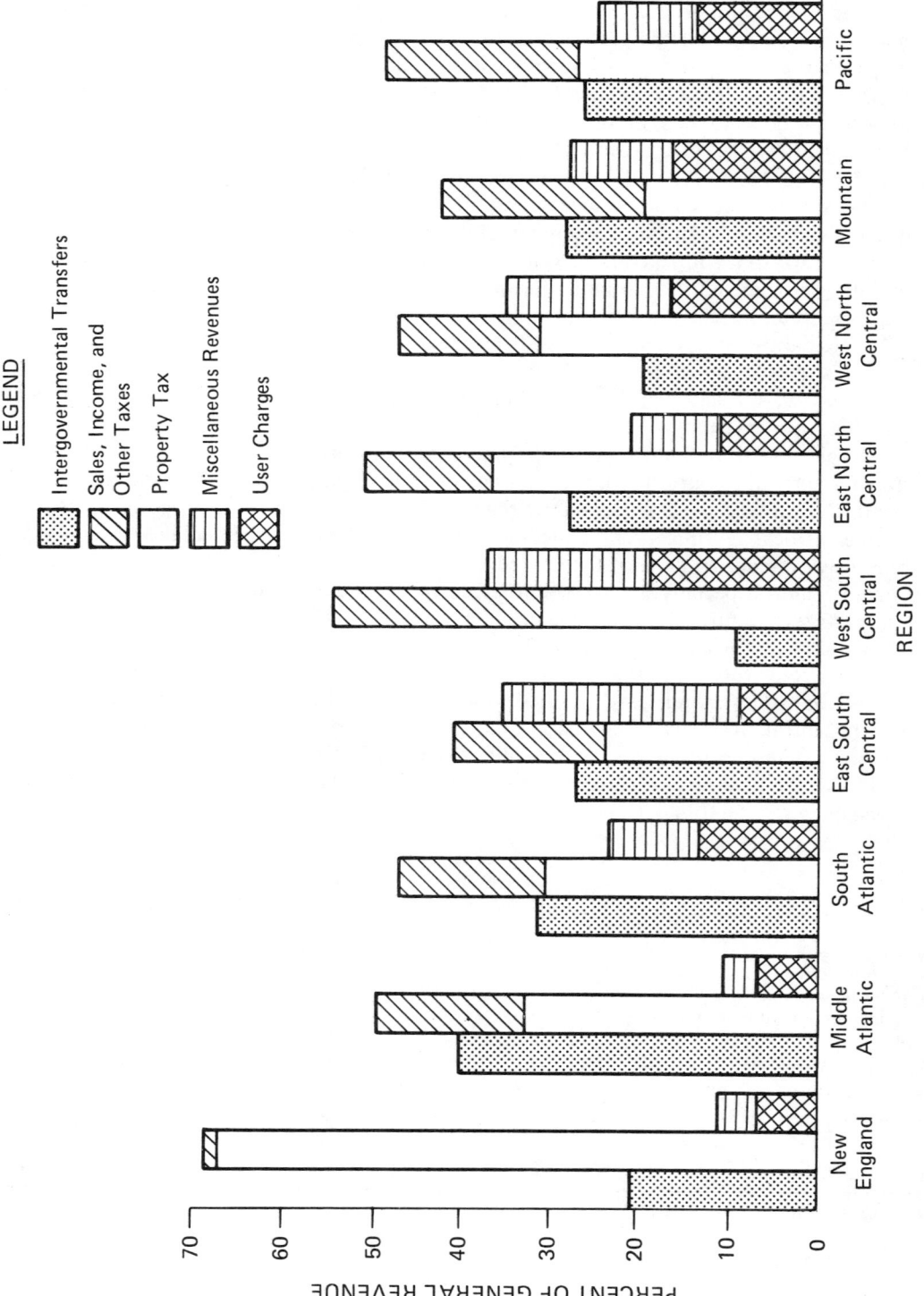

Source: U.S. Census of Governments, 1972.

Revenue Trends 177

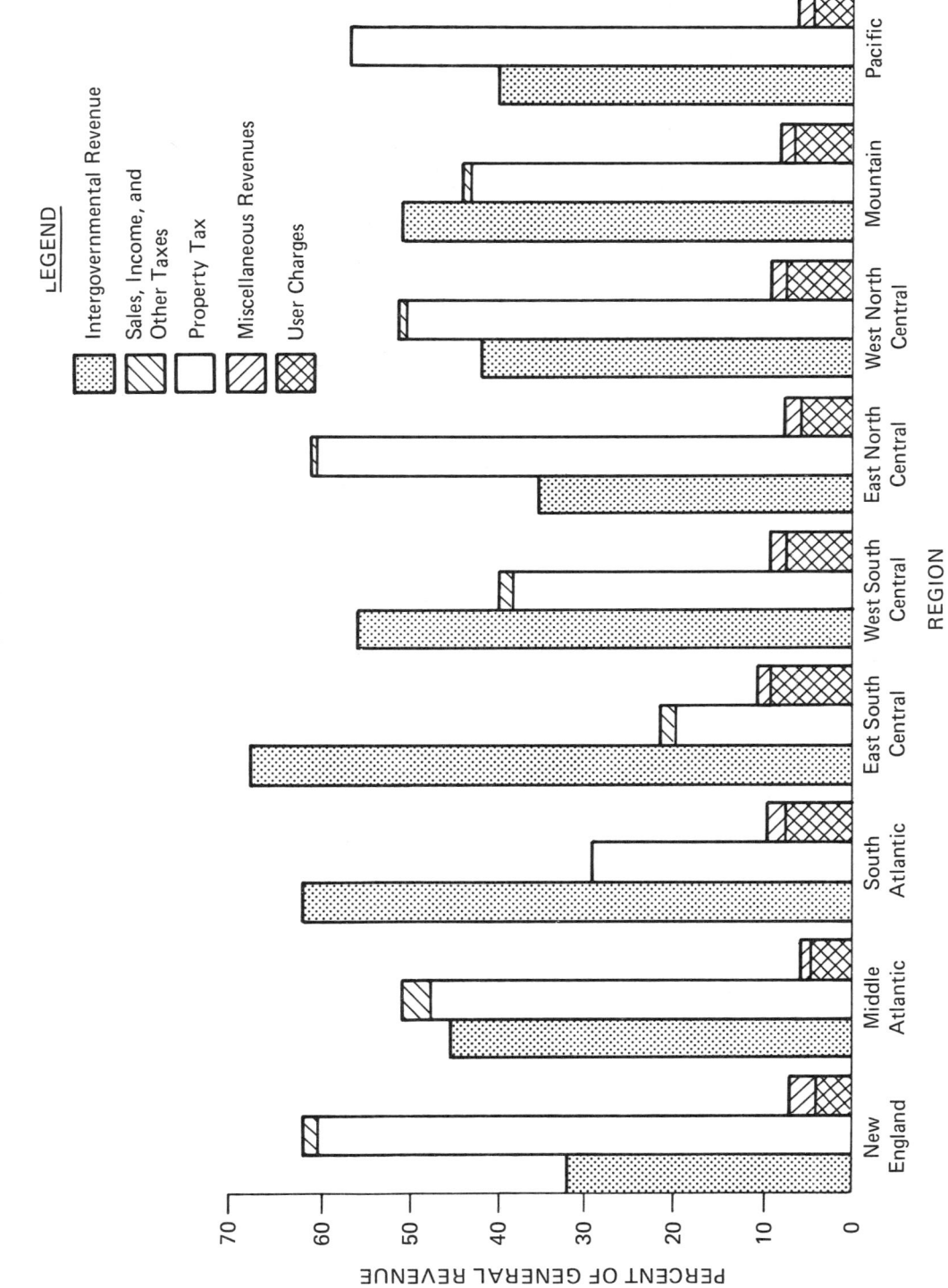

EXHIBIT 8-20
SCHOOL DISTRICTS RELIANCE ON VARIOUS SOURCES OF REVENUE, BY REGION
(1972)

Source: U.S. Census of Governments, 1972.

NOTES

1. U.S. Department of Commerce, Bureau of the Census. *Classification Manual, Government Finances.* (Washington, D.C.; Government Printing Office, 1971), p. 19.

2. *Ibid* p. 20.

3. Independent school districts have been chosen to represent local educational jurisdictions; municipalities and townships to represent local non-educational jurisdictions.

4. U.S. Advisory Commission on Intergovernmental Relations (ACIR), *Federal-State-Local Finances: Significant Features of Fiscal Federalism* (1974–1975 [Washington, D.C. ACIR], 1977). Introduction.

5. U.S. Management and Budget Office *Catalog of Federal Domestic Assistance — 1975* (Washington, D.C.; Government Printing Office, 1975).

6. Henry S. Reuss, *Revenue Sharing* (New York, Praeger Publishers, 1970) Chapter 1.

7. *The Prentice Hall Encyclopedic Dictionary of Business Finance* (Englewood Cliffs, New Jersey, Prentice Hall, 1960).

8. University of Oregon, Bureau of Governmental Research and Service, *Taxation of Business by Local Governments* (Eugene, Oregon, Bureau of Governmental Research, 1971).

9. Robert D. Reischauer and Robert W. Hartman, *Reforming School Finance.* (Washington, D.C.; The Brookings Institute, 1973); Richard Netzer, *The Economics of the Property Tax* (Washington, D.C.; The Brookings Institute, 1970).

10. William Davis, *The Language of Money* (Boston, Houghton-Mifflin Company, 1973).

11. Richard Aronson and Eli Schwartz (eds.) *Management Policies in Local Government Finance* (Washington, D.C.; International City Managers Association [ICMA], 1975) p. 122.

12. *Ibid.* p. 123.

13. *Ibid.* p. 138.

9

PROJECTING MUNICIPAL AND SCHOOL DISTRICT OWN SOURCE REVENUES

The next two chapters describe the procedures the fiscal impact practitioner should use to project revenues for municipalities and school districts. Chapter 9 focuses on local, own source revenues, and Chapter 10 emphasizes revenues granted by upper levels of government/intergovernmental revenues.

Exhibit 9-1 shows the local revenues for which illustrative calculations are shown in these two chapters. They are categorized in exactly the same fashion as has been developed in Chapter 8. A local jurisdiction will rarely receive funds from *all* of these sources. But Exhibit 9-1, based on studies by the International City Managers Association and the Advisory Commission on Intergovernmental Relations, lists the spectrum of the revenue sources available to municipalities and school districts in the United States. It is possible, however, that a unique school district or locality may have sources of revenue for which estimation procedures have not been included. These must be projected on site, via procedures developed by the analyst himself.

The procedures presented to estimate revenues reflect the general structure and form of revenue alternatives applicable to most localities. The analyst should consult state statutes and local ordinances to determine the specific procedures for reallocation or for taxing/charging which pertain to a specific geographic area. It is especially important in calculating intergovernmental revenues that the aid formulas at the time of the analysis be checked, for the basis and procedures surrounding intergovernmental assistance may occasionally change.

To project revenues that will be generated *locally* as a function of growth, the analyst should employ a two step process:

First, consult the local municipal and school district annual operating budgets. They list both the type and magnitude of various revenue resources. The analyst can then determine which revenue sources the local jurisdiction emphasizes. He can quickly tell, for instance, whether the municipality depends heavily on property taxes, or federal or state school aid, or on user charges.

EXHIBIT 9-1

LOCAL REVENUES FOR WHICH CALCULATION PROCEDURES ARE ILLUSTRATED

Revenue Source	Revenue Most Often Flows Principally To:
I. OWN SOURCE REVENUES	
Property, Income and Sales Taxes	
1. Real Property Tax	Municipality/School District
2. Personal Property Tax	Municipality/School District
3. Income Tax	Municipality/School District
4. Sales Tax	Municipality/School District
Other Taxes	
5. Property Transfer Tax	Municipality/School District
6. Occupation and Business Privilege Tax	Municipality
7. Per Capita Tax	Municipality
8. Transient Occupancy Tax	Municipality
Miscellaneous Revenues	
9. Interest Earnings	Municipality
10. Fees and Permit Revenue	Municipality
11. Fines, Forfeitures and Penalty Revenue	Municipality
User Charges	
12. Recreation, Health and Property Services	Municipality/School District
13. Water, Sewerage and Solid Waste Charges	Municipality
II. INTERGOVERNMENTAL TRANSFERS	
State	
1. Sales Tax Redistribution	Municipality
2. Income Tax Redistribution	Municipality
3. Motor Fuels Tax Redistribution	Municipality
4. Cigarette and Alcohol Tax Redistribution	Municipality
5. Incorporated/Unincorporated Business or Business Income Tax Redistribution	Municipality
6. Road and Road Lighting Aid	Municipality
7. Public Utilities Franchise Tax Redistribution	Municipality
8. Aid to Urban or Rural Areas	Municipality
9. Homestead and Foregone Tax Rebate	Municipality
10. Educational Basic Support Via Flat Grants	School District
11. Educational Assistance Via Variable Guarantees	School District
12. Educational Categorical Aid	School District
13. Elementary and Secondary Education Act Subsidies (ESEA Titles I-IV)	School District
Federal	
14. State/Local Fiscal Assistance Act (Federal Revenue Sharing)	Municipality
15. Comprehensive Employment Training Act (CETA)	Municipality
16. Public Works Employment Act (Anti-Recession Aid)	Municipality
17. Community Development Block Grants (CDBG)	Municipality
18. Educational Assistance in Federal Impact Areas (P.L.815,874)	School District

Source: U.S. Census of Governments, 1972.

This "prioritizing" of potential revenue flows according to existing emphases is an important step for it assists the analyst in allocating his time among various revenue calculations. He will be able to concentrate his efforts on those revenues which provide most of the locality's income.

Second, after the analyst has familiarized himself with both the sources of and emphasis on local revenues, he should calculate own source and intergovernmental revenues according to the individual methods shown in the next two chapters. Each revenue source shown in Exhibit 9–1 is described, and procedures for its estimation are illustrated. The results of the computations can be

Projecting Own Source Revenues

summarized on a sheet like the one shown in Exhibit 9-2.* This sheet, when properly completed, will represent the aggregate revenues attributable to the proposed development, zone change, annexation, etc.

It is important to stress that the amount of attention paid to a specific revenue source should be commensurate with its local importance. The analyst should also use all information available; state offices of local fiscal assistance, and the state divisions of treasury are superb sources of information which are often not used. If these points are kept in mind, the revenue portion of the fiscal impact analysis is as simple to project as costs.

Own Source Revenues: Property, Income, Sales and Other Taxes

Real Property Tax

The real property tax is frequently the most significant source of local revenues. It is a percentage levy on the value of land and improvements. In most states, the municipality and the school district each levy a separate tax, even though the municipality often collects both revenues. The real property tax rate is expressed either in mills (one thousandth of a dollar) or as a dollar amount per hundred dollars of assessed valuation. A rate of forty mills thus equals a local tax rate of $40.00 per thousand or $4.00 per $100 of assessed valuation.

To project revenues from the real property tax, the analyst multiplies the expected assessed valuation by the local tax rate (expressed as a decimal). If the *value* of real property is not known but figures are available on *gross rent* or *income*, the analyst applies a multiplier to annual gross rent/income to estimate property value (see Chapter 16, "Gross Income Multipliers for Residential and Commercial Properties").

The local tax rate multiplied by the expected assessed valuation should always produce the same estimate of revenue as the product of the equalized tax rate and the market or true value of the property. Equalization is a process of estimating true value of a property by applying a sales/assessment ratio to its assessed valuation. County or state governments often use this process because local municipalities often assess at different percentages of true values and frequently have dated assessments. In both cases the assessed value of a property is thus less than its true or market value.

The analyst can usually obtain information about the current municipal and school district tax rates and equalization rates from the municipal tax assessor's office. If equalization information is not available locally, it can be obtained from county or state offices.

The following examples demonstrate how to calculate the real property tax in a New Jersey** community using several variations of locally obtained information. Hypothetical developments of 1,000 single family homes, 500 garden apartments, and 10 specialty stores are alternatively used.

Residential Units for Sale (1,000 single-family homes),
Given Market Value and Equalized Tax Rate

	Market Value/Unit	X	Equalized Tax Rate	X	No. of Units	=	Total Revenues
Municipality	$50,000	X	$0.75/$100	X	1,000	=	$ 375,000
School District	$50,000	X	$2.25/$100	X	1,000	=	$1,125,000

---

* This is the format for revenue tabulation in which the examples of Chapter 10, Section II are presented.

**This chapter shows illustrative examples of revenue calculations in different states—New Jersey, Ohio, Pennslyvania, etc.

Residential Units for Sale (1,000 single-family homes),
Given Assessed Value and Local Tax Rate

	Assessed Value/Unit	X	Local Tax Rate	X No. of Units	= Total Revenues
Municipality	$40,000	X	$0.94/$100	X 1,000	= $ 376,000
School District	$40,000	X	$2.81/$100	X 1,000	= $1,124,000

Residential Units for Sale (1,000 single-family homes),
Given Market Value, Equalization Ratio and Local Tax Rate

	Market Value/Unit	X	Equalization Ratio*	X	Local Tax	X No. of Units	=	Total Revenues
Municipality	$50,000	X	0.80	X	$0.94/$100	X 1,000	=	$ 376,000
School District	$50,000	X	0.80	X	$2.81/$100	X 1,000	=	$1,124,000

Residential Units for Rent (500 garden apartments),
Given Monthly Rent (Excluding Utilities), Gross Income Multiplier, and Equalized Tax Rate

	Monthly Rent/ Unit	X	(Annual) 12	X	Gross Income Multiplier	X	Equalized Tax Rate	X	No. of Units	=	Total Revenues
Municipality	$300	X	12	X	5.88	X	$0.75/$100	X	500	=	$ 79,380
School District	$300	X	12	X	5.88	X	$2.25/$100	X	500	=	$238,140

Nonresidential Structures for Rent (ten specialty stores),
Given Rent/Ft^2/Year, Gross Income Multiplier, and Equalized Tax Rate

	Annual Rent per Ft^2	X	Number of Ft^2	X	Gross Income Multiplier	X	Equalized Tax Rate	X	No. of Units	=	Total Revenues
Municipality	$4.50	X	10,000	X	6.50	X	$0.75/$100	X	10	=	$21,938
School District	$4.50	X	10,000	X	6.50	X	$2.25/$100	X	10	=	$65,813

Personal Property Tax (Household and Business)

Localities in a significant number of states levy taxes on household and business personal property. Municipalities and school districts frequently share the revenue equally.** Household personal property subject to taxation may include automobiles, aircraft, boats, furs and jewelry. Business personal property may include a variety of tangible assets such as machinery, equipment, inventory, and office furniture.

---

*See glossary for definition of this term.
**For sharing procedure see the subsequent *Property Transfer Tax* calculation.

Projecting Own Source Revenues 183

EXHIBIT 9-2
COMPUTATION SHEET FOR REVENUE PROJECTION

Revenue Sources	Dollars

MUNICIPAL

I. Own Source Revenues
   A. Taxes
      1. _____   1. $ _____
      2. _____   2. _____
      3. _____   3. _____
      4. _____   4. _____
         TOTAL TAXES
   B. Charges/Miscellaneous
      1. _____   1. $ _____
      2. _____   2. _____
      3. _____   3. _____
      4. _____   4. _____
         TOTAL CHARGES/MISCELLANEOUS
         TOTAL OWN-SOURCE REVENUES

II. Intergovernmental Transfers
   A. State
      1. _____   1. $ _____
      2. _____   2. _____
      3. _____   3. _____
      4. _____   4. _____
         TOTAL STATE
   B. Federal
      1. _____   1. $ _____
      2. _____   2. _____
      3. _____   3. _____
      4. _____   4. _____
         TOTAL FEDERAL
         TOTAL INTERGOVERNMENTAL TRANSFERS

Total Municipal Revenue

SCHOOL DISTRICT

I. Own Source Revenues
   A. Taxes
      1. _____   1. $ _____
      2. _____   2. _____
      3. _____   3. _____
      4. _____   4. _____
         TOTAL TAXES
   B. Charges/Miscellaneous
      1. _____   1. $ _____
      2. _____   2. _____
      3. _____   3. _____
      4. _____   4. _____
         TOTAL CHARGES/MISCELLANEOUS
         TOTAL OWN-SOURCE REVENUES

EXHIBIT 9-2
COMPUTATION SHEET FOR REVENUE PROJECTION (Continued)

Revenue Sources	Dollars
SCHOOL DISTRICT (Continued)	
II. *Intergovernmental Transfers*	
A. State	
1. _____	1. $ _____
2. _____	2. _____
3. _____	3. _____
4. _____	4. _____
TOTAL STATE	_____
B. Federal	
1. _____	1. $ _____
2. _____	2. _____
3. _____	3. _____
4. _____	4. _____
TOTAL FEDERAL	_____
TOTAL INTERGOVERNMENTAL TRANSFERS	_____
Total School District Revenue	$ _____
TOTAL MUNICIPAL/SCHOOL DISTRICT REVENUE	$ _____

Note: Format for placing column totals and subtotals is shown in the Computation Sheets for Revenue Projection exhibits found in Chapters 2 through 7.

In states where the personal property tax is used as a source of local revenue, detailed data are usually available on average value of personalty for both residential (by owner/renter) and nonresidential (by category of business) uses. If information to this level of detail is not available, the analyst may project personal property taxes using automobiles as an indicator for household personal items and machinery/inventory per square foot for businesses. Assessed value is often assumed to be one half of the original retail cost of the item for its projected life.

Residential (1,000 single-family homes)

Average Number of Automobiles per Unit		Average Assessed Value per Automobile		Household Property Tax Rate		Average Household Personal Property Tax Revenue per Dwelling Unit
1.5* (Suburban)	X	$2,000	X	.05**	=	$150
.75* (in-city)	X	$2,000	X	.05	=	$ 75

    *These figures are for illustration only; the average number of automobiles per unit is available by locality from the decennial *U.S. Census of Population*.

    **Very frequently local real and personal property are taxed at a similar rate. If they are not, the personal property tax rate is available from the assessor's office.

Average Household Personal Property Tax Revenue per Dwelling Unit		Number of Units		Total Revenues
	×		=	
$150(suburban)	×	1,000†	=	$150,000
$ 75(in-city)	×	1,000	=	$ 75,000

Noneresidential (10 specialty stores)

Value per ft² of Inventory/Equipment		Size in (Ft²) of Nonresidential Facility		Business Personal Property Tax Rate		Business Personal Property Tax per Facility
	×		×		×	
$15*		2,000		.05		$1,500

Business Personal Property Tax per Facility		Number of Facilities		Total Revenues from Business Personal Property Tax Attributable to Growth
$1,500	×	10	=	$15,000

The local tax assessor is the primary source of information for the personal property tax. Information on the number of automobiles per household is available from the U.S. Census of Population and from the Bureau of Labor Statistics.[1] Data on inventory/machinery in dollars per square foot are available from Urban Land Institutes *Dollars and Cents of Shopping Centers*,[2] the U.S. Census of Retail Trade, and the U.S. Census of Manufacturing and Business.[3]

Earned Income Tax

A significant number of localities throughout the country levy a tax on earned income. The levy is usually shared by municipalities and school districts. Typically the levy is on resident family *earned* income, without allowances for deductions. To project revenues from this source, the most frequent procedure is to convert estimated monthly housing costs (taxes, debt service, and insurance) or contract rental costs to family income. The procedure outlined below assumes that a family spends 20 percent of its monthly income on housing. To obtain monthly income, the analyst multiplies monthly housing costs by 5; to obtain annual income he further multiplies that product by 12. To convert monthly housing costs directly to annual earned income, he multiplies by 60. Other methods can be used to estimate annual income — detailed information from market analyses of residents' projected incomes, or from tabulations of mortgage applications, for example.

The analyst then multiplies family income by the local income tax rate and the number of units in the development to estimate total revenue from this source.

---

* In states where localities levy personal or business property tax the state government division of local finance, or its equivalent, frequently tabulates estimates of business personal property per square foot by type of establishment.

Information on the local income tax rate, the nature of the income taxes, and any permissible deductions is available from the local tax assessor's office if locally administered, and from the state treasurer's office if state administered.

The example below projects municipal and school district revenues from 1,000 single family houses and 500 garden apartments in an Ohio locality. The local income tax rate is 0.5 percent.

Residential (1,000 single-family homes)

Average Monthly Housing Cost (Taxes, Debt Service, Insurance)	×	60	=	Average Annual Family Income (Homeowners)
$500	×	60	=	$30,000

Residential (500 garden apartments)

Average Monthly Rent (Contract Rent)	×	60	=	Average Annual Family Income (Renters)
$250	×	60	=	$15,000

Residential (combined)

Annual Family Income	×	Income Tax Rate	×	No. of Units	=	Total Revenues from Local Income Tax Attributable to Growth
$30,000		0.005		1,000*	=	$150,000*
$15,000		0.005		500	=	$ 37,500*

Sales Tax

As of 1977, 26 states imposed locally levied sales taxes. The tax most often applies to tangible personal property at the rate of 1 percent of the retail sales price. The tax is almost exclusively a source of municipal** revenue, except in Louisiana, where school districts are also allowed to tax consumer durables.

Residential Development

Revenue from the local sales tax may be estimated for new residential development as follows:

New Development *** Aggregate Family Income Pre-Development Local *** Aggregate Family Income	×	Current Revenues from Local Sales Tax	×	Resident Proportion of Total Local Sales †	=	Additional Revenues from Local Sales Tax Attributable to Growth
$ 30,000,000 or .15 $200,000,000	×	$200,000	×	.25	=	$ 7,500

---

* Assumes 100 percent occupancy.

** In this Ohio community local distribution is based on 30 percent for the municipality, 70 percent for the school district. The municipal portion would thus be $56,250, the school district $131,250.

*** Income from retirees should be included here.

† This information may be obtained from comparable existing facilities in the local area.

Projecting Own Source Revenues

The assumption in using a ratio of new to existing aggregate income by which to multiply prior sales tax revenues is that new residents will have similar incomes and expenditure patterns as current residents.*

A new development's aggregate family income may be tabulated using a multiplier of anticipated monthly housing costs as illustrated in the local income tax calculation. (See *Locally Levied Income Tax*.) Local aggregate family income is determined by multiplying the *current estimate* of median or mean family income by the number of local households. Household data are available from *the community planning office* or its planning consultant. Estimates of current revenues from the local sales tax are available from the local tax collector's office.

Nonresidential Development

Projections of local sales tax revenues from new nonresidential uses may be obtained by first estimating gross additional, local sales income generated by such uses and multiplying this figure by the local sales tax rate. This two-step process begins by obtaining average sales per square-foot (from published data) by category of retailer or wholesaler. This figure, multiplied by the size of the facility, yields total annual sales income.

Discount Store

Gross Annual Sales per Square Foot	X	Size of Facility (Ft.^{2})	=	Gross Additional Sales Income
$100/Ft.^{2}		20,000		$2,000,000

The next step is to estimate how this new business will affect or be affected by existing businesses—whether it will cause local income to suffer or will suffer because of local competition. Both situations would decrease projections of forthcoming local sales revenue. This estimate is obtained by multiplying the new facility's projected gross annual sales income by a coefficient representing new business drawn to a local area rather than business taken from it.

Gross Annual Sales	X	Assumed New Business Factor	=	Additional Gross Income Subject to Sales Tax
$2,000,000		0.80		$1,600,000

This coefficient is very difficult to estimate. The analyst must assess the local competition as well as the capacity of the local population to support the new facility. For instance, a freestanding discount store developed without significant, planned residential growth has to depend heavily on capturing a significant proportion of existing similar business. Thus, the net or new local sales income and the tax revenue based on this income will be significantly less than tax revenue based entirely on gross sales of which all were assumed to be new.

After determining additional gross sales income subject to the sales tax, the analyst must calculate the additional sales tax revenue by multiplying the additional sales income generated by the existing local sales tax rate.

---

*This assumption probably understates slightly the income of new residents and thus derivative sales tax revenues because new home buyers are frequently more affluent than existing residents.

Total Additional Local Sales Generated in $	X	Local Sales Tax Rate (1%)	=	Additional Sales Tax Revenue Attributable to Growth
$1,600,000	X	0.01	=	$16,000

Sales dollars per square foot for convenience and nonconvenience goods are available from the Urban Land Institute's *Dollars and Cents of Shopping Centers* and from *Sales Management Magazine* (Annual Compendium).[4] The new business factor is best obtained from combined opinions of the local tax assessor and the manager of the new nonresidential facility.

Real Property Transfer Tax

Many municipalities levy a tax on the transfer of real property. This tax is often equally shared by municipality and school district. To project revenues from this source, the analyst multiplies the unit's sales price or market value by the transfer tax rate, the number of units, and the average frequency of unit transfer. A common mistake is to ignore the turnover factor and credit too large a revenue to the development as a result of applying the transfer tax rate to all new units rather than to the estimated annual portion of these units that will change ownership. The turnover figure in the example below is based on 1972 Census data, which indicate that, in general, homeowners move once every five years. Put another way, 20 percent of the owner-occupied housing stock is transferred annually.

Information on the transfer tax rate is available from the local tax assessor; the total number of annual property transfers may be obtained from the county registry of deeds. Dividing this number by the latest estimate of the total number of owned dwelling units in the county yields the percentage of transfers. The county transfer rate may then be used as a local index of property transfer. The rate for several years should be added and the average annual transfer rate used to project revenue from this source.

In the example below, a development of 1,000 single-family houses in a Pennsylvania community contributes $100,000 annually to the local treasury based on a transfer tax rate of 1 percent and a property turnover rate of 20 percent.

Residential (1,000 single-family homes)

Market Value/Unit	X	Transfer Tax Rate*	X	No. of Units	X	Percent of Housing Turnover/Year	=	Total Revenues
$50,000	X	.0100	X	1,000	X	0.20 (National Figure)	=	$100,000

Occupation and Business Privilege Tax
(Including business franchises, professional licenses, cable TV franchise, etc.)

Many states allow both municipalities and school districts to levy annual taxes on residents who are gainfully employed or employed in certain occupations. These taxes are usually flat fees. They also allow municipalities to levy taxes on businesses or corporations located within their bounds. They are usually based on a percentage of gross receipts.

---

* In Pennsylvania, the municipal/school district share is 50/50. Thus $50,000 is for municipal revenues, and $50,000 is for school district revenues.

Projecting Own Source Revenues

The occupational privilege tax, levied equally on all job holders who live within district boundaries, may be estimated for a development of 1,000 single-family homes as follows:

Residential (1,000 single-family homes)

Number of Adults per Unit (Household Size - School Age Children) for Specific Dwelling Types		Male & Female Labor Force Participation Rates / 2		Number of New Job Holders per Unit
4.3 − 1.6	×	(0.98 (males)* + 0.62 (females)) / 2	=	
2.7	×	.80	=	2.2

Number of New Job Holders per Unit		Occupational Privilege Tax per Job Holder		Number of Units		Total Revenue from the Occupational Privilege Tax Attributable to Growth
2.2	×	$10.00	×	1,000**	=	$22,000

The number of adults per unit multiplied by the labor force participation rates (male and female) yields an estimate of the number of job holders per unit. The number of job holders per unit multiplied by the occupational privilege tax per job holder and the number of new dwelling units yields the projected additional revenue from the occupational privilege tax attributable to growth.

In the example above, household size and school-age children demographic multipliers are taken from this handbook. (See Chapter 13.) Labor force participation rates are available from the U.S. Census; the occupational privilege tax levy is available from the local tax assessor.

The business privilege tax, an annual levy on businesses, corporations, and professionals doing business within the city's bounds, is usually based on a percentage of their gross receipts.*** It is a municipal levy, frequently in addition to statewide licensing fees. It may be estimated for new nonresidential facilities as follows:

Nonresidential

	Estimated Taxable Gross Receipts		Business Privilege Tax Rate		No. of Businesses		Total Revenue from Business Privilege Tax Attributable to Growth
Supermarket (20,000 Ft.²)	$1,000,000	×	0.005	×	1	=	$ 5,000
Specialty Stores (2,000 Ft.²)	$ 120,000	×	0.005	×	10	=	$ 6,000
Office Space (1,000 Ft.²)	$ 75,000	×	0.005	×	5	=	$ 1,875
					TOTAL		$12,875

---

* Assumes 98 percent male (over 18 years of age) labor participation rate for new developments.
** Assumes 100 percent occupancy.
*** Physicians, dentists, attorneys and other professionals maintaining a local office are often included in this category rather than in the same category for the occupational privilege tax.

Estimated annual gross receipts by class of business and the local business privilege tax rate are available from the local tax assessor. Estimated annual gross receipts per square foot by category of business are available by region from the annual compendium of *Sales Management* and from the Urban Land Institute's *Dollars and Cents of Shopping Centers*.[5] Annual gross receipts per square foot for office space are available by type of occupant from the Building Owners and Managers Association's *Office Space Guide*[6] (See Chapter 16 for further detailing of information contained in these sources.)

Per Capita Tax

The per capita tax is a lump sum tax levied on adults aged 18 to 65. It may be levied by municipalities and/or school districts. Revenues derived from new development are estimated by first subtracting dwelling unit estimates of school-age children (SAC) from similar estimates of total household size (HHS). This figure, the estimate of the adult resident population, is multiplied by the per capita tax and by the number of anticipated occupied dwelling units. If information is not available on the type of dwelling unit but rather only on the expected population, the analyst may use the U.S. Census of Population to estimate the proportion of the total population aged 18 to 65 in the immediate area of development. This proportion multiplied by the total expected population increase yields the new resident adult population. This figure, multiplied by the per capita tax levy, yields the anticipated additional local revenue from this source.

The per capita tax yield from a development of 1,000 single family homes in a Pennsylvania community is shown below. The per capita tax in this community is $10.

Residential (1,000 single-family homes)

Number of Adults (18 Years and Over) Per Unit (Household Size Minus School-Age Children)		X Per Capita Tax	X No. of Units	=	Total Revenues from Per Capita Tax Attributable to Growth
3.91 – 1.01 = 2.90	X	$10	X $1,000*	=	$29,000

Transient Occupancy Tax

A considerable number of cities levy a tax on the occupancy of a room in any lodging. It is strictly a source of municipal revenue. The levy may be in the form of a tax included in the room fee (1 percent is common) or an annual tithe ($50) on the room itself. Increases in local revenues from this tax may be anticipated when nonresidential development includes plans for a motel or hotel. Revenues from this levy are estimated as follows:

Nonresidential (50 unit motel)

Number of New Motel/ Hotel Rooms		Annual Flat Fee Occupancy Tax per Room		=	Revenues from Transient Occupancy Tax Attributable to Growth	or
50	X	$50		=	$2,500	

---

* Assumes 100 percent occupancy.

Projecting Own Source Revenues

Number of New Motel/ Hotel Rooms		Daily Motel/ Hotel Occupancy Rate				Number of Rooms Rented Daily
50	X	.60	=			30

Number of Rooms Rented Daily		Daily Rate Per Room		Transient Occupany Tax		No. of Days		Revenues from Transient Occupancy Tax Attributable to Growth
30	X	$20.00	X	0.01	X	365	=	$2,190

Information on the transient occupancy tax is available from the local tax assessor. Daily occupancy rates for motels are available from chains' national headquarters or from the local manager of a comparable facility. The developer can usually also supply an estimate, since banks, before financing a new hotel or motel, may require a study which would have to include the expected occupancy rate or at least a range of possible rates.

Own Source Revenues: Miscellaneous Revenues and User Charges

Interest Earnings

Nationally, for units of local government, the largest single category of miscellaneous revenues is interest on investments. Many states allow municipalities to invest a share of their unused revenues during fertile cash flow periods (immediately after taxes are collected) in short-term marketable securities.

As population increases, general revenues increase and more tax money is available for investment. The per capita amount of revenues resulting from investment remains essentially the same, however. The reverse is also true. As a city begins to decline, the tax base diminishes; it is not able to issue as many tax anticipation notes and instead must rely on its own cash revenues for lean periods, thus limiting short-term investment potential. The per capita amount also remains relatively constant. The additional revenue resulting from interest on investment may be projected as follows:

Residential (1,000 single-family homes)

Current Estimate of Annual Interest on Earnings, Public Property Rentals and Sales*		Total Assessed Valuation of the New Development** ————————————— Total Assessed Valuation of all Local Properties		Increment on Investment on Earnings Attributable to Growth
$90,000	X	$ 40,000,000 / $200,000,000		
$90,000	X	0.20	=	$18,000

---

* These additional revenues may be lumped in this category for estimation purposes.
** Minus the value of the assessment on the existing vacant land.

Market valuation for the new development may be obtained from the developer; total local property valuation and an estimate of the new development's future assessed valuation are available from the local tax assessor.

Fees and Permits

Most revenue from fees and permits is the result of building, occupancy, electrical, explosive and landfill permissions or assurances. (A minor amount of revenue is obtained from animal licenses, marriage licenses, birth or death certificates, etc.) This resource is almost exclusively municipal. Most income from fees and permits represents money paid by local property owners for services extended to both existing and newly developed real property. Fees from developed properties, except in rural developing communities, far exceed those from undeveloped property. Additional revenue accruing from this source can be estimated via a two step process. First, the current total annual revenue from this source is divided by the current estimate of the number of local dwelling units. This quotient represents the annual permit fee revenue per dwelling unit. Multiplying this figure by the estimated number of incoming dwelling units yields a projection of future development generated revenue from fees and permits.

Information on annual revenues obtained from fees and permits is found in the local budget. Estimated current dwelling units is available from the local building inspector's office or the planning department.

Residential (1,000 single-family homes)

Revenue Obtained from Fees and Permits per Year	÷	Number of Current Dwelling Units Available	=	Fee/Permit Revenue per Dwelling Unit
$64,000	÷	4,000	=	$16.00

Permit/Fee Revenue per Dwelling Unit	X	Number of Anticipated Additional Dwelling Units	=	Total Additional Revenues from Fees and Permits Attributable to Growth
$16.00	X	1,000	=	$16,000

Fines, Forfeitures and Penalties

Fines are levied locally for violation of traffic, safety (fire), building code and health ordinances. Penalties include payments for tax and library fund delinquency. This revenue resource is almost exclusively a municipal one. It may be estimated on a per capita basis as shown in the following example:

Residential (1,000 single-family homes)

Total Annual Revenues Collected from Fines and Forfeitures	÷	Current Estimated Population	=	Per Capita Revenue from Fines and Forfeitures
$64,000	÷	16,000	=	$4.00

Per Capita Revenue from Fines and Forfeitures	X	Anticipated Development Population	=	Total Revenue from Fines and Forfeitures Attributable to Growth
$4.00	X	4,300	=	$17,200

Projecting Own Source Revenues

Information on current fines and forfeitures is available from the local municipal budget; population estimates may be obtained from the local planning office or from the municipal business administrator.

User Charges for Special Services

Municipalities and school districts levy user charges for specific rather than general services. Examples are school lunches, recreation fees, use of public buildings, curb cuts, city fire hydrant/sprinkler rentals, municipal parking (nonauthority). Except for school lunches, almost all of them support municipal purposes.

Revenues from this source may be estimated on a per capita basis as shown in the following example:

Residential (1,000 single-family homes)

Total Annual Revenues from User Charges (Excluding Sanitation, Water, and Sewerage)	÷	Current Estimated Population	=	Per Capita Revenue from User Charges
$320,000	÷	16,000	=	$20.00

Per Capita Revenue from User Charges	×	Anticipated Development Population	=	Total Revenue from User Charges Attributable to Growth
$20.00	×	4,300	=	$86,000

User charges to nonresidents and other municipalities should be eliminated from the annual figure before revenue from this source is expressed on a per capita basis. New population in a community is not likely to cause revenues obtained from nonresidents to vary significantly. Information on user charges is available from the local budget; local population estimates may be obtained from the local planning office, the town clerk, or city manager.

User Charges for Water, Sewerage and Sanitation Services

Contrary to the Census definition, municipalities frequently provide water, sewerage, and sanitation services which are neither operated as a distinct segregable authority (in which costs are assumed to equal revenues and thus the general treasury is unaffected) nor are they privately operated (again the assumption is that general treasury remains unchanged). Frequently a municipality provides water, sewerage and sanitation services using public works personnel and the taxes levied or flat fees charged enter the general treasury. The example below pertains to such a case.

Water and Sewerage

Daily Water Consumption by Type of Facility (gallons/day)		Number of Days		Number of Dwelling Units		Total Annual Water Consumption for Domestic Purpose (gallons)
250 (single family homes)	×	365	×	1,000	=	91,250,000
200 (apartments)	×	365	×	500	=	36,500,000

Total Annual Water Consumption	X	Water Rate + Sewer Rate	=	Total Revenue from Water and Sewerage Charges Attributable to Growth
91,250,000	X	$1.50/1,000 Gal. + .50/1,000 Gal.	=	$182,500
36,500,000	X	$1.50/1,000 Gal. + .50/1,000 Gal.	=	$ 73,000

Sanitation

Sanitation Charge per Household (or per Commercial Facility)	X	Number of Households (Number of Commercial Facilities)	=	Total Revenue from Sanitation Charges Attributable to Growth
$48/yr (single family home)	X	1,000	=	$48,000
$200/yr (specialty shops)	X	10	=	$ 2,000

Water consumption rates by type of dwelling may be obtained from the appropriate state department. Public user charges for scavenger or carting services are available from the municipal business administrator.

NOTES

1. U.S. Department of Labor, Bureau of Labor Statistics (BLS), *Consumer Expenditure Survey Series Diary Data — Report 448-1* (Washington, D.C.: Government Printing Office, 1976).
2. Urban Land Institute (ULI), *Dollars and Cents of Shopping Centers* (Washington, D.C.: ULI, 1975).
3. U.S. Department of Commerce, Bureau of Census, *U.S. Census of Retail Trade*; *U.S. Census of Business and Manufacturing* (Washington, D.C.: Government Printing Office, 1972)
4. *Sales Management: The Marketing Magazine* (New York: Sales Management, Inc., 1976).
5. *Dollars and Cents of Shopping Centers* (Appendix I); *Sales Management Magazine* (by region and states within regions).
6. Building Owners and Managers Association, *International Office Building Experience Exchange Report: 1975* (Washington, D.C.: BOMA, 1975).

10

SECTION I:

PROJECTING MUNICIPAL AND SCHOOL DISTRICT INTERGOVERNMENTAL REVENUES

This chapter consists of two sections. The first continues the detailing of revenue calculations, focusing on the second major component of local revenues—intergovernmental assistance. The same format is followed: important intergovernmental revenue sources are first described, followed by a description of the computational procedure through an example in an actual jurisdiction. These step-by-step examples walk the reader through the required calculations. The chapter's second section contains revenue tabulations which have been completed for the revenue side of the cost-revenue example contained in each cost projection method (Chapters 2 through 7).

Intergovernmental revenues are often more difficult to project than own-source funds: the allocation formulas are more complicated; eligibility for assistance changes as local wealth, unemployment or other indicators move upward or downward; and there are frequent overall community effects that must be considered. To illustrate, state school aid is granted inversely to local wealth. Thus, a development that significantly altered local affluence would affect not only the level of state assistance granted to the students coming from the specific housing under scrutiny, but to all the existing pupils in the locality. The analyst must calculate this overall, community-wide net change, as well as the immediate project impact, if he is to obtain a true count of incoming intergovernmental revenue.

A further caveat concerns the significance of intergovernmental assistance. While this revenue has become more important in recent years, not all communities receive large amounts of state/federal aid. To avoid unnecessary work, it is especially important for the analyst to obtain a copy of the local budget before commencing any intergovernmental revenue calculations. With the budget in hand, it is possible to see quickly not only the overall local importance of intergovernmental revenue as a group but the specific significance of individual state/federal aids, i.e., revenue sharing versus CDBG assistance.

Intergovernmental Transfers: State

State Levied Sales Tax Redistribution

Sales tax levied by a state for the privilege of selling or renting tangible personal property at retail rates typically is returned to local governments as a flat and uniform percentage of the locality's taxable retail sales. The reapportionment rate is frequently less than 10 percent of total state taxes collected in a locality. This revenue flows almost exclusively to the general fund of municipalities. The key to predicting additional revenue from this source is to project the additional sales which will take place in the locality.* Patterns of the new population's convenience** and non-convenience goods (or shopping goods)*** purchases and the proportions of income new residents will spend on taxable items in each of these categories are the basic data necessary for the calculation.

Several studies have documented that the great majority of shopping trips by automobile take no more than 7 minutes travel time (one way) for convenience goods nor 15 minutes for shopping goods.[1] Consumer surveys report that, on average, residents commit 75 percent of their expenditures for convenience goods to local vendors (local is defined as within the area covered by the seven-minute shopping trip) but only 25 percent of their expenditures for shopping goods to local vendors. In addition, according to the Bureau of Labor Statistics, approximately 20 percent of family income is spent on convenience goods and approximately 10 percent on shopping goods.[2] Other studies have estimated that, nationally, approximately 50 percent of consumer expenditures for convenience goods are for taxable goods; approximately 10 percent of consumer expenditures for shopping goods are for taxable items.

To calculate the state sales tax redistribution requires four steps. The analyst must first estimate the new increment of gross sales. From this figure, he must then project the dollar amount of locally captured sales. Third, he applies a tax rate to this figure to obtain the gross amount of additional taxes sent to the state. Finally, multiplying this figure by the state-calculated or legislated reapportionment percentage, yields the state redistributed sales tax increment to the locality. The calculation for a development of 1,000 single-family homes is as follows:

---

*This procedure is an alternative to using the increase in aggregate income of local residents as a surrogate for the increase in local sales tax revenue. (See locally levied *Sales Tax* in Chapter 9).

**Convenience goods — goods from grocery, drug, liquor, and hardware stores, beauty, barber and baking shops, and laundry and cleaning stores.

***Shopping goods — goods from variety, department, general merchandise stores — toys, hobbies, sporting goods, small appliances, household, textile, garden and lawn supplies, luggage and leather, music, books, housewares, children's apparel, candy, radios and televisions, and gasoline[4].

Sect. I: Projecting Intergovernmental Revenues

Residential (1,000 single-family homes)

New Development Aggregate Family Income	X	Percentage Spent on Goods	=	Amount Spent on Goods
$30,000,000	X	0.20 (convenience)	=	$6,000,000
	X	0.10 (shopping)	=	$3,000,000

Amount Spent on Goods	X	Taxable Share	=	Taxable Share of Goods
$6,000,000	X	0.50 (convenience)	=	$3,000,000
$3,000,000	X	0.90 (shopping)	=	$2,700,000

Value of Taxable Convenience Goods	X	Percentage Captured Locally	=	Value of Taxable Goods Purchased Locally
$3,000,000	X	0.75	=	$2,250,000

Value of Taxable Shopping Goods				
$2,700,000	X	0.25	=	$675,000

Value of Taxable Goods Purchased Locally (Convenience plus Shopping)	X	Sales Tax Rate	=	Sales Tax Amount Sent to State
$2,925,000	X	0.05	=	$146,250

Sales Tax Amount Sent to State	X	Legislated or State Determined Percentage of Local Return*	=	Additional State Sales Tax Revenues Flowing to the Locality
$146,250	X	0.10	=	$14,625

To estimate aggregate family income from a proposed development, multipliers are applied to estimated sales prices and rents of the housing offered in the development (See Chapter 9, locally levied *Income Tax.*)

Proportion of income spent on convenience and shopping goods is available by region and income classification from the Bureau of Labor Statistics' *Survey of Consumer Expenditures.* Consumer expenditure patterns, including which items are or are not purchased locally, purchase trip travel times, etc., have been surveyed by Rutgers University Center for Urban Policy Research and reported in *Housing Development and Municipal Costs* and by the Institute for Survey Research at the University of Michigan.[5] These surveys indicate approximate percentages of convenience and shopping goods purchased locally. The convenience/shopping goods share of items subject to sales tax is available from publications issued by the Advisory Commission on Intergovernmental Relations. Information is updated every four years.[6]

---

* This figure is frequently found in the state statute pertaining to the sales tax levy.

State-levied tax from nonresidential development is calculated the same way as a locally levied sales tax (See Chapter 9, locally levied *Sales Tax—Nonresidential Uses*). Expected gross annual sales per square foot multiplied by the size of the facility yields gross annual sales income. This figure, first multiplied by the taxable share and then by the state sales tax rate, yields additional revenues sent to the state from the locality. The additional revenues multiplied by the local reapportionment rate yields the projected additional local revenue from nonresidential development.

Nonresidential (Discount Store)

Gross Annual Sales per Square Foot (discount store)	×	Size of Facility	=	Gross Additional Sales Income
$100	×	20,000 ft^2	=	$2,000,000

Gross Additional Sales Income	×	Taxable Share	=	Taxable Share of Gross Additional Sales Income
$2,000,000*	×	0.90	=	$1,800,000

Taxable Share of Gross Additional Sales Income	×	State Sales Tax Rate	=	Additional State Revenues from the Locality
$1,800,00	×	.05	=	$90,000

Additional State Revenues from Locality	×	Local Reapportionment Percentage	=	Additional Revenues Flowing to Locality from State-Levied Sales Tax
$90,000	×	0.10	=	$9,000

Information on gross annual sales per square foot by type of facility is included in Chapter 9, locally levied *Sales Tax*. Information on local reapportionment rates is typically available from the state treasurer's office.

Redistribution of State-Levied Income Tax

Several states redistribute state-levied income tax to local jurisdictions. In most cases, the direct fiscal flow is to the municipality rather than to the school district. Less than 5 percent of total state income tax is typically returned directly to municipalities. Most state imposed income taxes are based on family earned income with few, if any, allowances for deductions. A growing number of states use a percentage of federal income taxes paid.

The local reapportionment formula in the majority of cases is based strictly on the proportion of state population and seldom bears any relation to the amount of taxes collected locally. The analyst must remember certain important aspects about any redistribution formula which does not relate to a percentage share of revenues paid directly by the locality to the state but rather distributes a "pool" of revenues according to an ever changing share of population, road miles or other criteria: (1) the gross amount of money to be apportioned is changing; (2) other localities

---

* The procedure to reduce taxable income from initial local computation may also be used here. See Chapter 9, locally levied *Sales Tax*.

Sect. I: Projecting Intergovernmental Revenues

within the state are changing their demands on the overall amount via population and/or apportionment criteria variation and (3) changes in population and/or other apportionment criteria are taking place within the locality other than the development itself. Gross income for a new housing development may be estimated in exactly the same fashion as was demonstrated for own source revenues from the local income tax (See Chapter 9, locally levied *Income Tax*.) Changes in the gross amount of state resources available for allocation must be taken into account, as well as changes in state and community population; each ultimately affect the local share.

Residential (1,000 single family-homes)

Current Estimate of Statewide Income Tax to be Redistributed × Current Estimate of Local Population (Including Proposed Development) / Current Estimate of State Population = Local Revenue from State Income Tax

$24,000,000 × 15,000/7,500,000 or .002 = $48,000

Local Revenue from State Income Tax × Proposed Development Population / Current Local Population (Including Proposed Development) = Additional in State Income Tax Attributable to Growth

$48,000 × 4300/15,000 or .29 = $13,920

Information on the gross amount of income tax to be reapportioned is available from the state treasurer's office. Community population estimates may be obtained from the local planning office.

Redistribution of State Levied Motor Fuels Tax

Many states redistribute a share of the revenues raised from motor fuels taxes to localities. The tax usually applies to sales of gasoline, diesel fuel and liquefied petroleum gas, and compressed natural gas used in motor vehicles on public highways. Usually this revenue flows exclusively to the municipality and not to the school district. Distribution frequently is based on an equally weighted share of the locality's proportion of population and road mileage to total state population and road mileage.

The analyst uses a two-step process to estimate new local revenues from the motor fuels tax attributable to development. First, he must estimate the new local revenue share* and then the development's portion of this new amount. To estimate the new local revenue share, he must first obtain an estimate of the new total revenues from the motor fuels tax to be apportioned locally as well as estimates of both local and state population and local and state road mileage. He then multiplies the statewide total amount to be apportioned by the equally weighted proportion of new

---

* The new local revenue share is defined as the most current estimate of the municipality's share of state funds according to the most recent official application of allocation criteria.

total local population/road mileage to new total state population/road mileage (including population and mileage added by the development). This product is the new local share of funds to be apportioned.

The second step is to assign a share of the new local motor fuels tax revenue to the proposed development. The analyst uses the same formula. He multiplies the local share of statewide motor fuels tax revenue by the equally weighted proportion of the development's population/road mileage to the new local population/road mileage (including population and road mileage added by the development). The resulting figure is the amount of new local revenues from the motor fuels tax which will flow to the municipality as a result of the development.

Information on the current statewide amount of revenues raised through the motor fuels tax to be apportioned to localities* is available from the state treasurer's office. The estimate of current state population and road mileage can also be obtained there, but it should be compared with figures from the U.S. Census—*Federal-State Cooperation for Population Estimates*,[7] for population, and with the state department of transportation's estimate for current road mileage. Local population and road mileage data are available from the local planning office and department of traffic.

Residential Development (1,000 single-family homes)

$$\text{Current Estimate of Statewide Motor Fuels Tax to be Distributed to Localities} \times \frac{\frac{\text{New Local Population (Including Development)}}{\text{New State Population}} + \frac{\text{New Local Road Mileage (Including Development)}}{\text{New State Road Mileage}}}{2} = \text{Total Local Revenues from Motor Fuel Tax}$$

$$\$1{,}000{,}000 \times \frac{\frac{15{,}000}{225{,}000} + \frac{30}{1500}}{2}$$

$$\$1{,}000{,}000 \times \frac{.007 + .020}{2}$$

$$\$1{,}000{,}000 \times .044 = \$44{,}000$$

$$\text{Total Local Revenues from Motor Fuel Tax} \times \frac{\frac{\text{Development Population}}{\text{New Local Population (Including Development)}} + \frac{\text{Development Road Mileage}}{\text{New Local Road Mileage (Including Development)}}}{2} = \text{Total Local Motor Fuel Tax Revenues Attributable to Growth}$$

$$\$44{,}000 \times \frac{\frac{4300}{15{,}000} + \frac{20}{30}}{2}$$

$$\$44{,}000 \times \frac{.286 + .667}{2}$$

$$\$44{,}000 \times .477 = \$20{,}988$$

---

* In states where reallocation is based on the locality where motor fuels were purchased, the formula in *Redistribution of State Levied Cigarette and Alcohol Taxes* should be used.

Redistribution of State-Levied Cigarette and Alcohol Taxes

Typically, half of the tax on cigarettes and alcoholic beverages collected by the state is redistributed to municipalities. The redistribution is based on a joint proportion (equally weighted) of municipal-to-total collections from sales taxes and municipal-to-total state population.*

The analyst uses the same principle to determine revenue from these taxes as that used to determine redistribution of the motor fuels tax. The analyst must remember that the gross amount of money to be apportioned by the state is changing, that other localities in the state are changing their demands on the aggregate sum, and that the municipality itself is undergoing change other than that caused by the proposed development. The two step estimation process is shown below:

Residential (1,000 single-family homes)

Current Estimate of Statewide Cigarette and Alcohol Tax to be Distributed to Localities		$\dfrac{\text{New Local Population}}{\text{New State Population}} + \dfrac{\text{Additional Local State Sales Tax Collections}}{\text{Total Local State Sales Tax Collections}}$ $\overline{\qquad\qquad 2 \qquad\qquad}$	=	Total Local Revenues from Cigarette and Alcoholic Beverage Taxes
$1,000,000	×	$\dfrac{\dfrac{15,000}{225,000} + \dfrac{70,000}{1,400,000}}{2}$		
$1,000,000	×	$\dfrac{.067 + .050}{2}$		
$1,000,000		.059	=	$59,000

Total Local Revenues from Cigarette and Alcoholic Beverage Taxes		$\dfrac{\text{Development Population}}{\text{New Local Population}} + \dfrac{\text{Development's Local State Sales Tax Collections}}{\text{Additional Local State Sales Tax Collections}}$ $\overline{\qquad\qquad 2 \qquad\qquad}$	=	Total Revenues from Cigarette and Alcohol Taxes Attributable to Growth
$59,000	×	$\dfrac{\dfrac{4,300}{15,000} + \dfrac{34,650}{70,000}}{2}$		
$59,000	×	$\dfrac{.287 + .495}{2}$		
$59,000	×	.391	=	$23,069

---

* Where the state distributes alcoholic beverages (ABC stores or the equivalent), a portion of revenues collected by the state flows to municipalities, usually in proportion to their percentage of state population.[8]

Information on the current aggregate amount of cigarette and alcohol taxes to be redistributed is available from the state treasurer's office. Data on increases in local sales may be obtained from the state treasurer's office and confirmed by the local tax collector or the city manager.

Redistribution of Incorporated/Unincorporated Business Tax

A considerable number of states impose a 3 to 5 percent franchise tax on the net worth or gross receipts* of a business for the privilege of having or exercising a corporate charter or doing business, employing or owning capital or property, or maintaining an office in the state.** Funds typically are returned to municipalities by a small override (1 to 1.5 percent) included within the state tax rate. Except for Philadelphia and several other large cities which distribute funds to school districts, the tax is returned exclusively to the municipality. This source provides considerable revenue for municipalities; in many cases, it is the single largest transfer of state-local funds. The examples below show how to project revenue from both incorporated and unincorporated businesses.

Nonresidential
Incorporated (Pharmaceutical Corporation)

Estimated Annual Corporate Gross Receipts	X	Guaranteed Municipal Share of State-Levied Corporate Business Tax	=	Amount of Revenue from State-Levied Corporate Business Tax Attributable to Growth
$5,000,000	X	.0125 (total tax .033)	=	$62,500

Unincorporated (Rental 50 Offices in an Office Park)

Estimated Annual Business Income per Unit Rented	X	Guaranteed Municipal Share of State-Levied Unincorporated Business Tax	=	Amount of Revenue per Unit from State-Levied Unincorporated Business Tax Attributable to Growth
$150,000	X	.0025 (total tax .0125)	=	$375

Amount of Revenue per Unit Returned from State-Levied Unincorporated Business Tax	X	No. of Units	=	Total Revenues from Unincorporated Business Tax Attributable to Growth
$375	X	50	=	$18,750

State Road/Street Lighting Aid

This state assistance supports the municipalities in their road construction, maintenance/repair, and street lighting programs. Funds may be used to construct, reconstruct, maintain or repair roads; remove snow and ice; purchase street lights; or upgrade equipment.

---

* Gross receipts is the more common base to which the tax is applied.
** A somewhat smaller rate is frequently levied on the gross receipts of unincorporated businesses under the same principal and local redistribution formula.

Sect. I: Projecting Intergovernmental Revenues 203

Allocations to localities for roads and street lighting are frequently based on a locality's equally weighted proportion of state road mileage and total population. The calculation, therefore, usually parallels that for distribution of the state motor fuels tax.

Residential (1,000 single-family homes)

Current Estimate of Statewide Road/Street Lighting Aid to be Distributed to Localities	×	(New Local Population (Including Development) / New State Population + New Local Road Mileage (Including Development) / New State Road Mileage) / 2	=	Total Local Revenues From State Road/Street Lighting Aid
$1,000,000	×	(15,000/225,000 + 30/1,500) / 2		
$1,000,000	×	(.067 + .020) / 2		
$1,000,000	×	.044	=	$44,000

Total Local Revenues from State Road or Street Lighting Aid	×	(Development Population / New Local Population (Including Development) + Development Road Mileage / New Local Road Mileage (Including Development)) / 2	=	Total Local Road Aid/Street Lighting Revenues Attributable to Growth
$44,000	×	(4,300/15,000 + 20/30) / 2		
$44,000	×	(.287 + .667) / 2		
$44,000	×	.477	=	$20,988

Information on total current road mileage is available from the state department of transportation; current population is available from the division of state and regional planning. Local total road mileage and population estimates are available from the municipal planner or planning consultant.

Redistribution of Public Utilities Franchise/Gross Receipts Tax

Many states levy a franchise tax on a proportion of the gross receipts of specific public utilities (telegraph, telephone, or cable companies) in lieu of property taxes on these utilities. A gross receipt tax is similarly levied on the remaining utilities (street, railway, traction, sewerage, water, gas, electric, light, heat and power corporations). In states, for taxation purposes, the distinction between telegraph/telephone/cable and other utilities may not be made. In some cases, the utility levy may be in the form of a local, rather than state-redistributed, revenue source. Funds are returned exclusively to the municipality; they often represent a considerable share of the local general fund.

The municipality receives a percentage of the aggregate taxes the utility pays. The percentage is based on the municipality's share of the mains/lines. The locality receives the entire reapportionment share of the tax when the utility's operations are located entirely within its boundaries.

Development would occasion a local increase in state-returned utility franchise or gross receipts taxes if additional mains or lines were constructed in a municipality to service that development. The potential impact is greatest in sparsely serviced rural areas. The additional revenues attributable to growth may be estimated as follows:

Residential (1,000 single-family homes)

$$\frac{\text{Current Estimate of Statewide Utility Taxes to be Distributed to Municipalities}}{} \times \frac{\text{Current Local Utility Valuation (Including Development)}}{\text{Total Statewide Utility Valuation}} = \text{Total Local Revenues from State Utility Tax}$$

$$\$80{,}000{,}000 \times \frac{\$8{,}000{,}000}{\$1{,}600{,}000{,}000} \text{ or } .005 = \$400{,}000$$

$$\frac{\text{Total Local Revenues from State Utility Tax}}{} \times \frac{\text{Development Utility Valuation}}{\text{Current Local Utility Valuation (Including Development)}} = \text{Local Revenues from State Utility Tax Attributable to Growth}$$

$$\$400{,}000 \times \frac{\$1{,}000{,}000}{\$8{,}000{,}000} \text{ or } .125 = \$50{,}000$$

Information on current local utility valuation and valuation by municipality is available from the state public utilities commission; estimates of current gross utility revenue may be obtained from the state treasurer's office.

State Aid to Urban or Rural Areas

State grants to urban or rural areas are designed to assist localities in depressed areas, which have been defined as such by location, amount of population, and/or population characteristics.

A municipality is qualified to receive aid, usually based exclusively on amount of population (large or small). In New Jersey, cities above 50,000 receive urban aid; in Georgia, municipalities under 5,000 receive rural assistance. Once the required population level is reached, grants are made on a per capita basis.

In rural areas, a new large development could slightly decrease a municipality's total aid; in urban areas, the same development would most likely occasion a slight increase in state assistance. The calculation for an urban area parallels the procedures to redistribute income tax. (See *Redistribution of State-Levied Income Tax*.)

Sect. I: Projecting Intergovernmental Revenues

Residential (1,000 townhouses)

Current Estimate of Statewide Urban Aid to be Redistributed	×	Current Estimate of Local Population (Including Development) / Current Estimate of Aggregate Population of Cities Receiving Aid	=	Local Revenues from Urban Aid
$40,000,000	×	50,000 / 2,000,000 or .025	=	$1,000,000

Local Revenues from Urban Aid	×	Development Population / Current Local Population (Including Development)	=	Additional Revenue from Urban Aid Attributable to Growth
$1,000,000	×	4,300 / 50,000 or .086	=	$86,000

For a rural area* that has been pushed above a population threshold and may lose state assistance, the calculation is as follows:

Residential (1,000 single-family homes)

Existing Population	×	Current Rural Aid per Capita	=	Existing Rural Assistance Revenue
4,900	×	$4.00	=	$19,600
New Population (Including Development)	×	New Rural Aid per Capita	=	New Rural Assistance Revenue
9,200	×	$2.00	=	$18,400
Existing Rural Assistance	−	New Rural Assistance	=	Net Rural Assistance Revenue Attributable to Growth
$19,600	−	$18,400	=	$1,200

Information on state urban or rural aid is available from the state treasurer's office. This office can also provide information about the existence of any hold harmless clauses. (See *Basic Support Via Flat Grants and Foundation Aid/Variable Guarantees*.)

State Homestead and Property Tax Relief Reimbursement

This revenue is allocated to localities as reimbursement for loss of property tax due to homestead provisions or special circumstance (housing for the elderly, for example) property tax relief.

---

* This calculation is based on a Georgia community whose current population is 4,000. In this state cities under 10,000 receive special state assistance. If population is less than 5,000, the per capita aid is double that if their population is between 5,000 and 10,000. No hold harmless clause exists.

Redistribution is based on the reported magnitude of prior years' foregone taxes.

Under homestead provisions, the state returns to the municipality a certain proportion of property taxes lost due to resident-owner property tax credits for homeownership. Almost all of the states that have this provision use an "initial full property tax payment and subsequent refund" procedure. Therefore, for the purposes of the cost-revenue calculation, in most states where a homestead provision is operative or where circuit breaker or property tax relief programs exist, the analyst can merely assume that full property taxes are paid by the owner. The state rebate is not tallied as a separate item flowing to the municipality.

Educational Support

There are three major types of state aid to education—basic support, categorical aid and intergovernmental subsidies. Basic support, the most important subsidy, is a block grant designed to assist overall local educational funding. (Basic support consists of flat grants and/or foundation and variable guarantee assistance). It is usually supplemented by categorical aid programs slotted to help specific types of students (the physically and mentally handicapped, for example) or certain school activities (vocational education, language and media instruction, for example). States also distribute many federal intergovernmental subsidies for culturally deprived and other students. (The Census of Governments classifies this federally funded but state-administered assistance as state aid.)[10] Dividing state programs into the basic support, categorical and intergovernmental categories organizes literally hundreds of disparate subsidies into more meaningful and manageable groups. The following paragraphs discuss how the fiscal impact analyst can project revenues from the different programs. Before commencing it is important to note that educational assistance programs often have complicated, changing formulas that affect both entitlement and the amount of assistance granted. Care must be exercised in computing educational support.

Educational Basic Support Via Flat Grants

In many jurisdictions basic support amounts to 90 percent or more of all state school aid and is the most significant intergovernmental subsidy that the analyst must consider. Basic support is granted through flat grants, and/or foundation grants or variable guarantee programs. The simplest form is the flat grant: The state gives a local school district a specified fixed sum, usually based on a standard unit of measurement such as the average daily pupil membership or number of classrooms or teachers. In some instances (North Carolina and Delaware), the flat grant is the major basic state subsidy, while in others (Nebraska, New York, and California), it is substantially supplemented by other categorical aids. The total flat grant subsidy attributable to growth can be calculated by using the following formula:

Residential (1,000 single-family homes)

Flat Grant in Dollars per Pupil		Expected Number of Pupils* (In New Development)		Anticipated Flat Grant Aid
	X		=	
$125 (California)		1,600		$200,000
$200 (New York)		1,600		$320,000

---

* All school children in this section are assigned equal weights.

The flat grant calculation is simple and demands data that the analyst should already have access to via sections of this handbook (expected number of pupils by bedroom and dwelling type) or can obtain from the state department of education or the local school district business administrator (current level of flat grant assistance per pupil). Several questions, however, must be answered prior to proceeding with these calculations. First, does the state give flat grants to all districts or only to affluent or other local educational agencies not receiving large amounts of other basic support? Second, does the state count pupils in a particular manner? For instance, the assignment of a weighting factor to particular types of students; 1.5 for vocational students, 1.25 for high school students, 0.75 for elementary, etc. If a weighting scheme is used, the analyst will have to convert *actual* pupils into *total* pupils for allocation purposes. An additional question for which an answer must be secured is the unit upon which allocation is based. The two principal alternatives are per pupil or per teacher (with a given ratio of students per teacher). This variation does not change the revenue calculation. To illustrate, North Carolina grants certain districts a flat $15,372 *per teacher* with an allowed ratio of about one teacher per 29 students. The *per pupil* flat grant would therefore equal $530 ($15,372/29 = $530) and the flat grant assistance generated by growth equals $530 multiplied by the expected number of additional pupils.

Education Basic Support
Via Foundation Aid

Almost all states have basic support programs in addition to simple flat grants. One type is the foundation program: The state establishes an acceptable expenditure figure per pupil (foundation amount) and grants shares of this sum inversely according to wealth. State aid is distributed as follows:*

1. The state designates a foundation amount per student, which may vary for different types of pupils (kindergarten, high school, vocational, for example).
2. The state establishes a property tax rate that must be imposed by localities if they wish to receive foundation assistance. This tax is called the required local tax effort (RLTE).
3. The state distributes aid equal to the foundation amount per pupil minus the amount raised locally from the RLTE.

To estimate foundation aid, the analyst must first determine the number of pupils generated by growth, a projection illustrated in each of the cost revenue methods. He must also know the foundation amount and RLTE. These data are supplied in the triennial federal publication, *Public School Finance Programs,*[11] though the analyst should check with the state department of education or local school district to obtain the most current program allocation details. He should also determine the local equalized valuation per pupil by: (1) adding the current, total, local, equalized valuation of real property to the equalized valuation being added by growth; (2) adding the expected number of students attributable to growth to the existing local enrollment; and (3) dividing the combined valuation by the combined number of students.

It is imperative to calculate the overall, net change in local foundation assistance occasioned by growth and not limit the analysis only to the foundation aid granted to the incoming students. Because of the way this state support is granted, a large development can markedly affect not only the level of foundation subsidy, but threshold eligibility. (If local wealth increases so that valuation per pupil × RLTE is greater than the foundation amount, then no aid will be for-

---

*For a detailed view of the impact of annexation on state aid to education, see Appendix 2, study number 131.

thcoming.) In general, if growth results in an increase in local wealth (valuation per pupil), then total local foundation grants will decrease, while conversely, construction that decreases local affluence will increase foundation support. These overall net changes must be traced.

The example below illustrates the effect of a development of 1,000 single-family houses (valued at $50,000 each) on foundation assistance in Iowa. This state has allowed a foundation amount of $857 per pupil with a .0054 RLTE. A district with an existing total property valuation of $250,000,000, a $62,500 equalized property valuation per pupil, and an existing school enrollment of 4,000 that accepted the 1,000 units would now have a $300,000,000 ($250,000,000 plus $50,000,000) total property tax base, 5,600 (4,000 plus 1,600) students, and a $53,571 equalized property valuation per pupil. Net state foundation aid equals the *total* amount of foundation assistance granted after the introduction of new pupils (taking into account the attendant change in enrollment, local wealth per pupil, and assistance per student) minus the *total* foundation subsidy that would have been given without this change. The Iowa school district in this example will thus receive a net increase of $1,104,800 in state foundation aid.

Residential (1,000 single-family homes)

Property Valuation per Pupil	×	RLTE	=	Amount Raised per Pupil by the RLTE
$62,500 (Existing)	×	.0054	=	$338
$53,571 (Future)	×	.0054	=	$289
Foundation Amount	−	Amount Raised per Pupil by the RLTE	=	Foundation Aid per Pupil
$857	−	$338 (Existing)	=	$519
$857	−	$289 (Future)	=	$568
Foundation Aid per Pupil	×	Total Pupils	=	Total Foundation Aid
$519 (Existing)	×	4,000	=	$2,076,000
$568 (Future)	×	5,600	=	$3,180,800
Total Future Foundation Aid	−	Existing Foundation Aid	=	Net Foundation Aid
$3,180,800	−	$2,076,000	=	$1,104,800

The impact to the school district of a development's *increasing* valuation does not have to be considered if the state has a permanent hold harmless clause—meaning that no district can be given less aid in one year than it received in a previous year, even if its local valuation has increased significantly. Although many states have hold harmless or similar guarantee provisions, most hold harmless clauses have a maximum time frame of one to two years so that the desired equalizing can occur. The analyst should thus assume that any hold harmless or equivalent provisions have only an interim effect (unless they have been specifically designed as permanent provisions—a not unusual occurrence prompted by political considerations) and that existing local school aid will be adjusted as a result of changes in local wealth associated with new development. The calculations shown above (and those for variable guarantee support) can be used to project revenues attributable to growth if growth has decreased the local valuation or if it has increased local valuation* and hold harmless clauses are nonexistent or operate with a short time frame.

As in the case with the flat grant, in calculating foundation aid the analyst should determine whether the state uses a special student weighting strategy. If it does, then the students generated by growth will have to be counted according to this specified weighting system. Another check is whether the state provides for different foundation amounts in various types of districts, i.e., urban versus rural, large versus small, etc. A final consideration, again paralleling the flat-grant program, is the cases where the foundation amount is expressed per teacher (with a given student-teacher ratio) rather than per student. The previously discussed conversion process to pupils should be undertaken.

Educational Basic Support Via Variable Guarantees

Programs of state aid which guarantee a *variable* dollar amount to school districts are the chief alternatives to foundation aid. A school district might receive a flat grant plus *either* foundation aid or a variable guarantee. Unlike foundation aid, where a state sets the guaranteed level, variable guarantees are based on local school district decisions about spending, tax effort (within certain prescribed constraints), and wealth.

There are three principal variable guarantee programs: average valuation, guaranteed valuation and the guaranteed state yield. Net variable guarantee aid equals the total amount of this support granted after the addition of new students (taking into account the subsequent change in local wealth and assistance per pupil) minus the existing amount of variable guarantee assistance.

Variable guarantee aid is more difficult to project than foundation aid, but it should not present a problem provided the assistance formulas are carefully calibrated and utilized. The analyst must remember that the state average valuation, guaranteed valuation, or guaranteed yield is always changing. Current figures, and preferably the advance estimates of the figures to be used for the next year's allocation, should be sought. The analyst must also determine whether minimum and maximum state guarantees exist.

The data required to project revenues using guarantee formulas are available from the triennial publication *Public School Finance Programs*[12] as well as from the school district superintendent and state department of education.

---

* Where local wealth has increased and a strong hold harmless clause exists, then foundation assistance could be calculated by examining the program assistance just for the new entering pupils as follows:

Foundation Amount per Pupil − Local Equalized Valuation per Pupil × RLTE Following Growth = Foundation Aid per Pupil

Foundation Aid per Pupil × Number of Incoming Students = Total Increment Foundation Aid

AVERAGE VALUATION APPROACH*

Residential (1,000 single-family homes)

100 Percent	−	Local Property Valuation per Pupil / State Average Property Valuation per Pupil	=	State Aid (Percent)
100 Percent	−	$78,000 / $80,000 or 98 Percent (Existing)	=	2 Percent
100 Percent	−	$75,000 / $80,000 or 94 Percent (Future)	=	6 Percent
State Aid (Percent)	×	Total Local Expenditure per Pupil	=	Variable Guarantee Aid per Pupil
2 Percent (Existing)	×	$1,400	=	$28
6 Percent (Future)	×	$1,400	=	$84
Variable Guarantee Aid per Pupil	×	Number of Pupils	=	Total Variable Guarantee Aid
$28 (Existing)	×	3,500 (Existing)	=	$98,000 (Existing)
$84 (Future)	×	3,750 (Future)	=	$315,000 (Future)
Total Future State Aid	−	Existing State Aid	=	Net State Aid
$315,000	−	$98,000	=	$217,000

GUARANTEED VALUATION APPROACH

Residential (1,000 single-family homes)

100 Percent	−	Local Property Valuation per Pupil / State Guaranteed Property Valuation per Pupil	=	State Aid (Percent)
100 Percent	−	$73,000 / $78,000 or 94 Percent (Existing)	=	6 Percent
100 Percent	−	$74,500 / $78,000 or 96 Percent (Future)	=	4 Percent
State Aid (Percent)	×	Local Cost per Pupil	=	Variable Guarantee per Pupil
6 Percent (Existing)	×	$1,400	=	$84
4 Percent (Future)	×	$1,400	=	$56
Variable Guarantee Aid per Pupil	×	Number of Pupils	=	Total Variable Guarantee Aid
$84 (Existing)	×	2,100 (Existing)	=	$176,400
$56 (Future)	×	2,500 (Future)	=	$140,000
Total Future State Aid	−	Existing State Aid	=	Net State Aid
$140,000	−	$176,000	=	−$36,000

* Three different communities and development scenarios are used to illustrate the three forms of variable guarantee assistance. The reader must also realize that variations to these basic approaches are possible.

Sect. I: Projecting Intergovernmental Revenues

GUARANTEED STATE YIELD APPROACH

Residential (1,000 single-family homes)

Guaranteed State Yield per Pupil	−	Actual Local Yield per Pupil	=	Variable Guarantee Aid per Pupil
$900	−	$857 (Existing)	=	$43
$900	−	$686 (Future)	=	$214
Variable Guarantee Aid per Pupil	×	Number of Pupils	=	Variable Guarantee Aid
$43	×	3,500 (Existing)	=	$150,500
$214	×	5,100 (Future)	=	$1,091,400
Total Future State Aid $1,091,400	−	Existing State Aid $150,500	=	Net State Aid $940,900

Educational Assistance Via Categorical Aid

Scores of categorical aid programs exist to assist special pupils (the handicapped, prekindergarten, vocational students, for example), different activities (transportation, driver education, luncheon, health and guidance programs, for example), and special situations (culturally deprived or bilingual students, or school districts defined as either urban or rural). Almost all states provide at least some of these categories of aid. Categorical aid usually represents a relatively small percentage of total school district revenues and may be projected on a per pupil basis.

Total Existing State Categorical Aid per School District	÷	School District Enrollment	=	Average Categorical Aid per Pupil
$1,000,000	÷	1,000	=	$100
Average Categorical Aid per Pupil	×	Expected Number of Pupils	=	Categorical Aid Generated by Growth
$100	×	100	=	$10,000

In most cases, projecting categorical aid with detailed formulas is unnecessary. First, the percentage of total local educational revenues that is categorical aid is usually small. Second, the representation of the physically and mentally handicapped in the population (the group receiving the largest amount of categorical aid) is much more a function of statistical probability than it is of local indices of earned income, education, or community capital assets. Third, for poverty-impacted areas (the group receiving the second largest amount of categorical aid), a requirement defining need usually exists (the locality's population, the percentage of students requiring bilingual instruction). Revenues allocated to areas meeting such requirements are based almost exclusively on the areas' proportion of the special population. Some cases, however—the addition of a large public housing project, for example—will substantially affect net local revenues, and the analyst should use the applicable categorical aid formula to project revenues resulting in this case.

The primary sources for data on categorical aid programs are HEW's *Public School Finance Programs*, the school district superintendent, and the state department of education.[13]

Educational Assistance Via State Apportioned Federal Programs

The federal government transfers subsidies for special educational assistance to states for further redistribution to localities. Federal intergovernmental support consists primarily of the various Elementary and Secondary Education Act (ESEA) subsidies.

ESEA	Title I (assistance to the educationally disadvantaged)
ESEA	Title II (general support and school libraries)
ESEA	Titles III, IV (supplementary services and bilingual education)
ESEA	Title V (grants and special projects)

Title I aid to assist culturally deprived children constitutes about 75 percent of all authorized ESEA grants. Title I grants are allocated according to a formula that is sensitive to the number of local poverty families, the ratio of children from local AFDC families and current state average expenditures per student. The other titles distribute aid according to a number of specialized factors, i.e., on a per student basis, or according to the quality and nature of the local educational offering.

In most school districts, federal subsidies constitute only a minor share of total educational revenues; frequently it is less than the amount from categorical aid. Because intergovernmental subsidies are a minor part of school district revenues, the analyst can use average per pupil assistance to project revenues. (He should, however, check the average figure for stability over time.)

Residential (1,000 single-family homes)

Total Existing State Distributed Federal Intergovernmental Aid		Total Existing Enrollment		Average State Distributed, Federal Intergovernmental Aid per Pupil
	X		=	
$105,000	÷	3,500	=	$30
Average State Distributed Federal Intergovernmental Aid per Pupil	X	Expected Number of Pupils	=	Total State Distributed Federal Intergovernmental Aid Generated by Growth
$30	X	1,600	=	$48,000

Sect. I: Projecting Intergovernmental Revenues 213

Data for these calculations are available in this handbook (number of pupils by housing type and number of bedrooms), from the local school district budget (total intergovernmental support), or from the local school district's superintendent of schools (existing enrollment). These calculations, while simple, should not be done blindly. If the housing being examined is atypical, (a large public housing project, for example), the analyst must project state distributed federal intergovernmental support by examining the formulas that govern these programs. Program guidelines are available from the division in the state department of education that handles Title I educational programs. It should also be available from the school district superintendent's or business administrator's office.

Intergovernmental Revenue: Federal

State-Local Fiscal Assistance Act of 1973 (Federal Revenue Sharing)
Public Law 92-512; 86 STAT 919

The Treasury Department administers funds authorized by this Act. Funds are allocated directly to states and units of local government. Allocation of funds to local governments (two-thirds of the total collected) is based on the local government population, multiplied by the general tax effort (adjusted taxes collected divided by aggregate personal income), multiplied by the relative income factor (per capita income for the local government divided by the per capita income for the county-municipality). Those municipalities with more people, more tax money per dollar of personal income, and larger shares of impoverished residents will receive more money. (No jurisdiction in a state will receive more than 145 percent of the statewide per capita revenue sharing average, however.) The impact of a large development on revenue sharing funds for a large city is comparatively small. For annexations, border changes, significant rezonings, or changes in land use, the detailed calculation may prove worthwhile; for most developments, per capita estimates based on the prior year's allocation may be much more reasonable.

If the analyst wishes to use the detailed calculation, he must first estimate current local revenue sharing funds. To do so, he multiplies the latest estimate of the aggregate statewide revenue-sharing funds to be apportioned locally by the locality's ratio (relative to state averages) of population, tax effort, and per capita income. He then projects the amount of locally received revenue-sharing funds resulting from growth. To project this amount, the analyst multiplies the most current estimate of the *local* amount of revenue-sharing funds by the growth's ratio (relative to local averages) of population, tax effort, and per capita income. The example below illustrates the procedure for a city involved in annexing areas in which 45,000 people reside.*

Information on the current estimate of statewide federal revenue-sharing funds to be distributed to localities is available from the state treasurer's office.* Some states have developed a simple, iterative computer program which allows state finance personnel to gauge local changes in revenue sharing as a function of annual changes in indices of local entitlement. Several states distribute to municipalities an estimate of all future intergovernmental transfers in November of each year to be used in budget calculations for the following March. This information (relative population, wealth, tax effort, etc.) is often available from the state treasurer's office.

---

* For this program and *Anti Recession Aid,* if information is not available at the state level, contact the U.S. Department of Treasury, Division of Revenue Sharing.

Residential (annexation)

Current Estimate of Statewide Federal Revenue-Sharing Funds to be Distributed to Localities		New Local Population (Including Annexed Area) / New State Population		New Local Tax Effort (Including Annexed Area) / New State Tax Effort		New State per Capita Income / New Local per Capita Income (Including Annexed Area)		Total Local Revenues from Federal Revenue-Sharing Funds
$40,000,000	×	415,000 / 8,300,000	×	.05 / .04	×	$4,350 / $5,000		
$40,000,000	×	.050	×	1.250	×	.870	=	$2,175,000
Current Estimate of Local Revenues Sharing	×	Annexed Area's Population / New Local Population (Including Annexed Area)	×	Annexed Area's Tax Effort / New Local Tax Effort (Including Annexed Area)	×	New Local per Capita Income (Including Annexed Area) / Annexed Area's Per Capita Income	=	Total Local Revenues from Revenue Sharing Attributable to Growth
$2,175,000	×	45,000 / 415,000 or .108	×	$5,000 / $8,000 or .63				
$2,175,000					×	.0351	=	$76,343

Comprehensive Employment and Training Act (CETA) of 1972
Public Law 93–203; 87 STAT 839

The Department of Labor administers CETA. Its central purpose is to provide job training and employment opportunities for economically disadvantaged, unemployed, and underemployed persons (and to ensure that training and other services lead to the maximum employment opportunities and enhance self-sufficiency by establishing a flexible and decentralized system of federal, state, and local programs).

Local governmental units with at least 100,000 people or consortia of local governments, at least one of which has a total population of 100,000 or more, are eligible for this program. The allocation formula is based on three unequally weighted elements: proportion of manpower funds obligated in the prior fiscal year (50 percent); total number of unemployed residents (37.5 percent), and number of resident adults in low-income families (12.5 percent). Cities with historically high manpower payments, current high unemployment, and large numbers of poor people will receive more money. Cities cannot, however, receive more than 150 percent nor less than 90 percent of the previous year's manpower funds.

Sect. I: Projecting Intergovernmental Revenues 215

A typical proposed private residential development probably will not affect revenues from this program because of the size of the jurisdiction to which the program applies, the number of poverty indices involved, and the hold harmless provision. A large public housing project or annexation which significantly changes a city's economic profile, however, will have a major impact. The following example illustrates how to project CETA funds in this case.

Residential (1,000 3 bedroom subsidized apartments)

$$\text{Current Year's Estimate of Statewide CETA Funds to be Apportioned to Localities} \times (3)^* \frac{\text{Total Local Unemployment}}{\text{Total Statewide Unemployment}} + (1)^* \frac{\text{Local Total Number of Adults in Low-Income Families (Including Development)}}{\text{Statewide Total Number of Adults in Low-Income Families}} \Bigg/ 4 = \text{Current Year's Estimate of Local CETA Funds}$$

$$\$40{,}000{,}000 \times (3)^* \frac{60{,}000}{830{,}000} + (1)^* \frac{100{,}000}{1{,}660{,}000} \Bigg/ 4$$

$$\$40{,}000{,}000 \times (3)^* (.072) + (1)^* (.060) \Bigg/ 4$$

$$\$40{,}000{,}000 \times \frac{.216 + .060}{4}$$

$$\$40{,}000{,}000 \times \frac{.276}{4} \text{ or } .069 = \$2{,}760{,}000$$

$$\frac{\text{Prior Year's Allocation of Local CETA Funds} + \text{Current Year's Estimate of Local CETA Funds}}{2} = \text{Current Actual Local Share of CETA Funds}$$

$$\frac{\$3{,}500{,}000 + \$2{,}760{,}000}{2} = \$3{,}130{,}000$$

---

* Weights applied to different indices.

Current Actual Local Share of CETA Funds		Estimated Total Development Unemployment / Total Local Unemployment (Including Development)		Development Total Number of Adults in Low-Income Families / Local Total Number of Adults in Low-Income Families (Including Development)		Local CETA Funds Attributable to Growth
	× (3)*		+ (1)*		=	
		4				
$3,130,000	× (3)*	120 / 60,000	+ (1)*	500 / 100,000		
		4				
$3,130,000	×	3(.002) + 1(.005)				
		4				
$3,210,000	×	.006 + .005				
		4				
$3,210,000	×	.011 / 4 or .003			=	$9,630

Information on local CETA funding for prior and current years, statewide and local unemployment figures, and number of adults in poverty families may be obtained from regional offices of the Bureau of Labor Statistics.

Public Works Employment Act of 1976
(Anti-recession or Countercyclical Aid) — Public Law 94-369; 90 STAT 999

The Public Works Employment Act of 1976 is administered by the Department of Commerce. The Act's purpose is to alleviate national high unemployment by assisting local governments to build and maintain necessary public facilities. Title I provides 100 percent lump-sum grants for public works capital construction; Title II provides annual antirecession stipends to rehire employees who have been laid off.**

At least 5 percent but not more than 10 percent of the pool of funds is allocated to any one state. Local jurisdictions are designated CETA and non-CETA municipalities; a CETA municipality is one which the Department of Labor has designated as having an unemployment rate of at least 4.5 percent for the previous three quarters. Allocations are made to localities on the basis of a joint index of unemployment severity and their final revenue sharing allocation.

The aggregate funds set aside nationally for lower level disbursement are divided into two sections: allocations reserved for states (one-third of total); allocations reserved for localities (two-thirds of total). Within the funds set aside for localities there are funds for CETA and funds for

---

* Weight applied to different indices.

** Procedures for estimating Title II disbursements, the most prevalent of these two local resources, will be illustrated here.

non-CETA municipalities. The amount which flows to a specific municipality is determined as follows (assume the area is a CETA-designated municipality): First, the aggregate CETA-municipalities' share of total local funds (both CETA and non-CETA municipalities) must be determined. This figure is available from the U.S. Department of Treasury, Division of Revenue-Sharing. It is derived by multiplying the aggregate disbursable local funds by a fraction whose numerator is the summed product of all CETA localities' excess unemployment rates (above 4.5 percent) times their annual revenue-sharing allocation, and whose denominator is this figure plus a similar figure for non-CETA areas. (The sum of the product of their excess unemployment rate times their total annual revenue-sharing allocation.)

Once the aggregate CETA-municipalities' share of Public Works Act funds is determined, the analyst can then estimate the portion for one CETA city. This process employs a similar relationship. It is the aggregate CETA-municipalities' share of funds multiplied by a fraction whose numerator is the product of the specific city's excess employment rate times the total annual revenue-sharing allocation and whose denominator is the sum of the product of these two indices for all designated CETA areas. (The same number the numerator determined in the previous step to tabulate aggregate CETA-municipalities' share).

The portion of locally received funds assignable to a specific development, zoning change or annexation is obtained by multiplying the local aggregate amount by the fraction in the step above, substituting development for local information in the numerator and local for national information in the denominator.

As with all federal redistribution programs, this calculation is useful only for extremely large developments or annexations, or specialized developments with high rates of unemployment or severe poverty. The illustration below demonstrates the process for a city of 400,000 annexing an area of 43,000.

Current National Annual Total of Public Works Act Funds Distributed to both CETA and Non-CETA Areas (2/3 of total for lower level redistribution)		Summed Products of Excess Unemployment Rate Times Revenue-Sharing Allocation for all CETA-Designated Areas				Amount of Public Works Act Funds Reserved for CETA Areas
	X	Summed Products of Excess Unemployment Rate Times Revenue Sharing Allocation for all CETA-Designated Areas	+	Summed Products of Excess Unemployment Rate Times Revenue-Sharing Allocation for all Non-CETA Areas	=	
$200,000,000	X	$\dfrac{120,000,000}{120,000,000 + 60,000,000}$		or .67	=	$134,000,000
Amount of Public Works Act Funds Reserved for CETA Areas	X	Product of Excess Unemployment Rate Times Revenue-Sharing Allocation of the Local Area			=	Amount of Public Works Act Funds Reserved for Local Area
		Summed Products of Excess Unemployment Rate Times Revenue-Sharing Allocation for all CETA-Designated Areas				
$134,000,000	X	$\dfrac{80,000}{120,000,000}$		or .00067	=	$89,780

Amount of Public Works Act Funds Reserved for Local Area	×	Product of Excess Unemployment Rate Times Revenue-Sharing Allocation of the Annexed Area / Product of Excess Unemployment Rate Times Revenue-Sharing Allocation of the Specific City	=	Amount of Public Works Act Funds Attributable to Growth
$89,780	×	$\frac{12,000}{80,000}$ or .15	=	$13,467

Community Development Block Grants (CDBGs) (Title I of the Housing and Community Development Act of 1974) — Public Law 93-382, 88 STAT 633

The Department of Housing and Urban Development administers this Act, which is a consolidation of several earlier programs: Urban Renewal; Rehabilitation Loans; Open Space; Neighborhood Facilities; Advanced Land Acquisition; Water and Sewer Facilities and Model Cities.

Cities in Standard Metropolitan Statistical Areas (SMSAs) whose populations exceed 50,000 ("urban counties" as defined in the Act) and cities in SMSAs with populations under 50,000 are eligible to receive funds determined by a statutory formula. Localities which received grants under the former urban renewal and model cities programs receive hold harmless grants based on their level of prior participation in those programs. The formula to determine the amount of funds is based on three principal indices—population, housing overcrowding, and poverty level. Larger, poorer areas, containing more overcrowded housing receive proportionately more revenue than smaller, more affluent, and less crowded municipalities. The Department of Housing and Urban Development provides a five year forecast of forthcoming revenues to affected communities.

The poverty requirements for receiving funds under this program are so pervasive that private residential development serving the middle class, even though it adds population, is therefore unlikely to result in increased revenue for the locality.

This program can effectively be ignored for a reasonably sized, new development. For annexation or the addition of a large public housing project, the analyst should use the formula to project revenue attributable to growth. The example below demonstrates the calculation for a low-income (10 percent of the occupants below the poverty level), high density (0.95 persons per room) area of 45,000 population which is to be annexed to a city whose population is 415,000.

Residential (annexation)

Current Estimate of CDBG Funds to be Allocated Statewide to Local Governments	×	New Local Population (Including Annexation) / New State Population	×	Average Persons per Room for Locality (Including Annexation) / Average Persons per Room for State	×	Local Proportion of Population Beneath Poverty Level (Including Annexation) / State Proportion of Population Beneath Poverty Level	=	Total Local Revenues from CDBG
$10,000,000	×	$\frac{460,000}{8,300,000}$	×	$\frac{1.10}{0.90}$	×	$\frac{.30}{.15}$		
$10,000,000	×	.06	×	1.22	×	2.0	=	$1,400,000

Total Local Revenues from CDBG	×	Annexation's Population / New Local Population (Including Annexation)	×	Average Persons per Room for Annexation / Average Persons per Room (Including Annexation)	×	Annexation's Proportion of Population Beneath Poverty Level / Local Proportion of Population Beneath Poverty Level (Including Annexation)	=	Revenues from CDBG Attributable to Annexation
$1,200,000	×	45,000 / 460,000	×	0.95 / 1.10	×	.10 / .30		
$1,200,000	×	.98	×	0.86	×	.33	=	$333,749

Information on local apportionment of CDBGs is available from the local community development office and the HUD area office. Iterative computer programs for allocation adjustments based on administrative guidelines or estimates of existing hold harmless provisions may be available at the HUD area office.

Educational Assistance in Federal Impact Areas
Public Law 81-874; 64 STAT 1100

One major program—School Assistance to Local Educational Agencies in Federally Affected Areas—provides *direct* federal aid to local school districts. This subsidy, commonly called, impact aid, is given to "local educational agencies upon which the United States has placed financial burdens" by virtue of the fact that:

1. The revenue available to such agencies has been reduced as the result of the government's acquisition of real property; or
2. Such agencies provide education for children residing on federal property; or
3. Such agencies provide education for children whose parents are employed on federal property; or
4. There has been a sudden and substantial increase in school attendance as the result of federal activities.

The analyst should determine whether the housing he is examining is in an impacted school district as defined above. (This information is available from the state department of education or the local school district.) If the housing is in a defined impacted area and if the units he is considering are likely to contain children:

1. Who reside on federal property;
2. Who have a parent employed on federal property;
3. Who have a parent currently on active duty in the uniformed services and working on federal property; or
4. Who have a parent who was on active duty in the uniformed servies;

then the analyst should project federal impact assistance. It is difficult to pinpoint which type of housing will contain such children, but likely candidates include units near a military base or near an employment facility or complex on federally owned land (e.g., a naval shipyard, a munitions plant or a space base).

The analyst should check with the local school district superintendent and the state department of education (federal grants office) to help determine how many children in the housing being constructed are likely to qualify for impact aid. Federal impact aid per pupil typically equals the per student revenue derived from *local* sources in a comparable nonimpacted district.* This figure is determined by personnel in the state commissioner of education's office (following federal guidelines). The analyst should check with the commissioner's office to determine the exact amount of impact assistance per pupil. The *total* impact aid generated by growth is calculated as shown in the following example.

Residential (1,000 single-family homes)

Number of Pupils Eligible for Impact Aid		Impact Aid per Pupil		Total Impact Aid Attributable to Growth
1,600	X	$700	=	$1,120,000

---

* Impact aid calculations follow detailed guidelines that change annually. One important determinant is the Local Contribution Rate (LCR). At minimum, the LCR is equal to no less than 50 percent of the national average per pupil cost in the second year preceding the application for aid or 50 percent of the state average, whichever is greater. The LCR can be higher than these 50 percent thresholds, provided either the state or local district submits evidence to the Department of Defense that certain groups of districts (state application) or at least five comparable districts (local application) have higher expenditures than the national/state averages.

Once the LCR is determined, impact aid roughly equals:

$ADA \times \% LCR \times Adjustment \% = Impact\ Assistance$

where *ADA* is the average daily attendance; *percent LCR* is a share of the LCR where the percent varies by category of child, namely, his/her "federal connection," i.e., parent resides on federal property, parent currently on active duty, etc.; *Adjustment percent* is a proration of the ADA × LCR product. This percent varies by type of pupil and the amount of impact aid funding available.

NOTES

1. Connecticut Development Group, Inc., and the Research Corporation of Connecticut, *Cost Revenue Impact Analysis for Residential Developments* (Hartford, Conn.: Connecticut Development Group, 1975).

2. U.S. Department of Labor, Bureau of Labor Statistics, *Consumer Expenditure Survey Series Diary Data – Report 448-1* (Washington, D.C.: Government Printing Office, 1976).

3. U.S. Advisory Commission on Intergovernmental Relations (ACIR), *Federal-State-Local Finances: Significant Features of Fiscal Federalism 1974-1975* (Washington, D.C.: ACIR, 1977).

4. Urban Land Institute (ULI), *Dollars and Cents of Shopping Centers* (Washington, D.C.: ULI, 1975).

5. George Sternlieb *et al.*, *Housing Development and Municipal Costs* (New Brunswick, N.J.: Rutgers University, Center for Urban Policy Research, 1975); John B. Lansing and Nancy Barth, *Residential Location and Urban Mobility: A Multivariate Analysis* (Ann Arbor, University of Michigan Institute for Social Research, 1964).

6. ACIR, *Significant Features of Fiscal Federalism, op. cit.*

7. U.S. Department of Commerce, Bureau of Census, *Federal-State Cooperation for Population Estimates* (Washington, D.C.: Government Printing Office, Series P-26).

8. ACIR, *op. cit.*

9. James W. Hughes and Kenneth D. Bleakly, *Urban Homesteading* (New Brunswick, N.J.: Rutgers University, Center for Urban Policy Research 1975).

10. U.S. Department of Commerce, Bureau of Census, *Finances of School Districts* (Vol. 4-3) (Washington, D.C.: Government Printing Office, 1972).

11. U.S. Department of Health, Education and Welfare, *Public School Finance Programs* (Washington, D.C.: Government Printing Office, 1975).

12. *Ibid.*

13. *Ibid.*

SECTION II:

EXAMPLE REVENUE CALCULATIONS FOR ALTERNATIVE FISCAL IMPACT METHODS

Exhibits 10-1 and 10-2 illustrate revenue projections for several locations. They provide more detailed calculations than the summary information presented in prior descriptions of each fiscal impact method (Chapters 2-7). The format of Exhibits 10-1 and 10-2 exactly parallels that of Exhibit 9-2 (Chapter 9) — the Revenue Computation Sheet. Notes and additional exhibits follow which further specify assumptions, necessary adjustments of procedure and the basic data employed.

Own source revenues and intergovernmental transfers for each particular location reflect the revenue alternatives available to a community of 16,000 as of 1976-1977. Information on current revenues was obtained from the business administrator or financial officer of a representative community in each location. Local tax rates, assessed valuation per capita, equalization ratios, etc., reflect the 1975-1976 experience of these localities. Revenues from intergovernmental transfers represent the level of state and federal participation in local funding of municipal and school district services characteristic of a particular region. Specific formulas for federal/state municipal/school district revenue transfers have been obtained from applicable state statutes or federal guidelines and regulations.

The analyst must keep in mind that the procedures for projecting revenues described in this handbook are for *general* application only. It is unlikely that any specific situation will exactly parallel the procedures given here. States will vary in their emphasis on different resources and their distribution formats. The analyst must therefore obtain information from state and local sources to augment the general instructions in this handbook.

The analyst should also keep in mind that each of these examples projects a fairly large population increment when compared to the population of the community where development is to take place and that calculations are therefore rather detailed. When the additional population attributed to growth is small relative to community size, the same level of detail may not be appropriate.

EXHIBIT 10-1

MUNICIPAL REVENUES BY SOURCE
(FISCAL IMPACT EXAMPLES)*

	PER CAPITA MULTIPLIER NEW JERSEY (Single Development— 3,000 Unit PUD)	CASE STUDY ILLINOIS (Single Development— 3,000 Unit PUD)	PROPORTIONAL VALUATION EMPLOYMENT ANTICIPATION TEXAS (Nonresidential Development)	Alternate #1 (2,000 Single Family Houses)
OWN SOURCE REVENUE				
TAXES				
Real Property Tax	$81,787,200 × .0080[1] = $654,298	$82,230,600 × .0054[1] = $444,045	$4,000,000 × .0075[1] = $30,000	$100,000,000 × .0048[1] = $480,000
Personal Property Tax				
Tangible	Not Applicable	Not Applicable	Not Applicable	$5,000,000 × .0048[2] = $24,000
Intangible	Not Applicable	Not Applicable	Not Applicable	Not Applicable
Property Transfer Tax	Not Applicable	Not Applicable	Not Applicable	400 × $500,000 × .01[5] = $200,000
Utility Franchise Tax	Not Applicable	Not Applicable	Not Applicable	2000 × $600 × .0075[6] = $9,000
			$141,000 × .02[6] = $2,820	
Business Franchise Tax	Not Applicable	Not Applicable	Not Applicable	20 businesses × $100/yr[7] = $2,000
Alcohol Excise Tax	Not Applicable	Not Applicable	Not Applicable	Not Applicable
Cable TV Franchise Tax	Not Applicable	Not Applicable	Not Applicable	1200 × $120 × .06[9] = $8,640
TOTAL TAXES	$654,298	$444,045	$32,820	$723,640
CHARGES/MISCELLANEOUS				
Interest Earnings	$92,000 × $81,787,200[10] / $270,075,000 = $27,876	$174,150 × $82,230,600[10] / $155,000,000 = $92,474	Not Applicable	$41,000 × $100,000,000[10] / $161,000,000 = $25,461
Fees & Permits	$70,000 × 3000[11] / 4000 = $52,500	$78,000 × 3000[11] / 4000 = $58,500	Not Applicable	$126,069 × 2000[11] / 4000 = $63,035
Fines/Forfeitures	$30,000 / 16,000 = $1.88[12]	$57,200 / 16,000 = $3.58[12]	Not Applicable	$48,616 / 16,000 = $3.04[12]
	$1.88 × 8154 = $15,330	$3.58 × 8360 = $29,929	Not Applicable	$3.04 × 7652 = $23,262
User Charges (Special Services)	$20,000 / 16,000 = $1.25[13]	$30,000 / 16,000 = $1.88[13]	Not Applicable	$160,270 / 16,000 = $10.02[13]
	$1.25 × 8154 = $10,193	$1.88 × 8360 = $15,717	Not Applicable	$10.02 × 7652 = $76,673
User Charges (Sanitation)	$20 × 3,000 (residential)[14] = $60,000	$13.50 × 3,000 (residential)[14] = $40,500	Not Applicable	Not Applicable
	$200 × 20 (nonresidential)[15] = $4,000	$180 × 20 (nonresidential)[15] = $3,600	$100 × 20[15] = $2,000	
User Charges (Sewerage)	Not Applicable	$30 × 3,000 (residential)[16] = $90,000	Not Applicable	Not Applicable
		$300 × 20 (nonresidential) = $6,000		
User Charges (Water)	Not Applicable	Not Applicable	Not Applicable	Not Applicable
TOTAL-CHARGES/ MISCELLANEOUS	$169,899	$336,720	$2,000	$188,431
TOTAL OWN SOURCE REVENUE	$824,197	$780,765	$34,820	$912,071

*Totals may vary slightly due to rounding.

Sect. II: Example Revenue Calculations

EXHIBIT 10-1 (Cont'd)
MUNICIPAL REVENUES BY SOURCE
(FISCAL IMPACT EXAMPLES)*

	COMPARABLE CITY CALIFORNIA (Three Land Use Alternatives)		SERVICE STANDARD GEORGIA (Three Land Use Alternatives)		
	Alternative #2 (5,000 Unit Mixed Use Development)	Alternative #3 (7,000 Garden Apartments)	Alternative #1 (2,000 Single Family Homes)	Alternative #2 (5,000 Unit Mixed Use Development)	Alternative #3 (7,000 Garden Apartments)
OWN SOURCE REVENUE					
TAXES					
Real Property Tax	$175,000,000 × .0048[1] = $ 840,000	$113,610,000 × .0048[1] = $ 545,328	$100,000,000 × .0034[1] = $ 340,000	$175,000,000 × .0034[1] = $ 595,000	$120,960,000 × .0034[1] = $ 411,264
Personal Property Tax Tangible	$ 8,750,000 × .0048[2] = $ 42,000	$ 5,680,500 × .0048[2] = $ 27,266	$2000 × 1.5 × 2000 × .0034[3] = $ 20,400	$2000 × 1.0 × 5000 × .0034[3] = $ 34,000	$2000 × .75 × 7000 × .0034[3] = $ 35,700
Intangible	Not Applicable	Not Applicable	$9,000,000 × .0034[4] = $ 30,600	$1,575,000 × .0034[4] = $ 53,550	$11,113,200 × .0034[4] = $ 37,784
Property Transfer Tax	1000 × $35,000 × .01[5] = $ 350,000	$113,610,000 × .20 × .01[5] = $ 227,220	Not Applicable	Not Applicable	Not Applicable
Utility Franchise Tax	5000 × $450 × .0075[6] = $ 16,875	7000 × $350 × .0075[6] = $ 18,375	2000 × $600 × .03[6] = $ 36,000	5000 × $450 × .03[6] = $ 67,5000	7000 × $350 × .03[6] = $ 73,500
Business Franchise Tax	20 businesses × $100/yr[7] = $ 2,000	20 businesses × $100/yr[7] = $ 2,000	Not Applicable	Not Applicable	Not Applicable
Alcohol Excise Tax	Not Applicable	Not Applicable	7550 × $13[8] = $ 98,150	15,845 × $13[8] = $ 205,985	18,424 × $13[8] = $ 239,512
Cable TV Franchise Tax	3000 × $120 × .06[9] = $ 21,600	4200 × $120 × .06[9] = $ 30,240	1200 × $60 × .03[9] = $ 2,160	3000 × $60 × .03[9] = $ 5,400	4200 × $60 × .03[9] = $ 7,560
TOTAL TAXES	= $1,272,475	= $ 850,429	= $ 527,310	= $ 961,435	= $ 805,320
CHARGES/MISCELLANEOUS					
Interest Earnings	$ 41,000 × $175,000,000[10] / $161,000,000 = $ 44,690	$ 41,000 × $113,610,000[10] / $161,000,000 = $ 28,946	$ 8,000 × $100,000,000[10] / $127,200,000 = $ 6,288	$ 8,000 × $175,000,000[10] / $127,200,000 = $ 11,040	$ 8,000 × $120,960,000[10] / $127,200,000 = $ 7,608
Fees & Permits	$126,069 × 5000 / 4000[11] = $ 157,586	$126,069 × 7000 / 4000[11] = $ 220,621	$ 10,000 × 2000 / 4000[11] = $ 5,000	$ 10,000 × 5000 / 4000[11] = $ 12,500	$ 10,000 × 7000 / 4000[11] = $ 17,500
Fines/Forfeitures	$ 48,616 / 16,000 = $3.04[12] $3.04 × 15,766 = $ 47,929	$ 48,616 / 16,000 = $3.04[12] $3.04 × 15,043 = $ 45,731	$ 61,760 / 16,000 = $3.86[12] $3.86 × 7550 = $ 29,143	$ 61,760 / 16,000 = $3.86[12] $3.86 × 15,845 = $ 61,162	$ 61,760 / 16,000 = $3.86[12] $3.86 × 18,424 = $ 71,117
User Charges (Special Services)	$160,270 / 16,000 = $10.02[13] $10.02 × 15,766 = $ 157,975	$160,270 / 16,000 = $10.02[13] $10.02 × 15,043 = $ 150,731	$ 65,920 / 16,000 = $4.12[13] $4.12 × 7550 = $ 31,106	$ 65,920 / 16,000 = $4.12[13] $4.12 × 15,845 = $ 65,281	$ 65,920 / 16,000 = $4.12[13] $4.12 × 18,424 = $ 75,907
User Charges (Sanitation)	Not Applicable	Not Applicable	$6.00 × 2,000[14] = $ 12,000	$6.00 × 5,000[14] = $ 30,000	$6.00 × 7,000[14] = $ 42,000
User Charges (Sewerage)	Not Applicable	Not Applicable	$34 × 2 × 2,000[16] = $ 136,000	$34 × 1.5 × 5,000[16] = $ 255,000	$20 × 1.0 × 7,000[16] = $ 140,000
User Charges (Water)	Not Applicable	Not Applicable	$200 × 2,000[17] = $ 400,000	$150 × 5,000[17] = $ 750,000	$100 × 7,000[17] = $ 700,000
TOTAL CHARGES/ MISCELLANEOUS	$ 408,180	$1,146,029	$ 619,537	$1,184,983	$1,054,132
TOTAL OWN SOURCE REVENUE	$1,680,655	$1,296,458	$1,146,847	$2,146,418	$1,859,452

*Totals may vary slightly due to rounding.

EXHIBIT 10-1 (Cont'd)

MUNICIPAL REVENUES BY SOURCE
(FISCAL IMPACT EXAMPLES)*

	PER CAPITA MULTIPLIER NEW JERSEY (Single Development— 3,000 Unit PUD)	CASE STUDY ILLINOIS (Single Development— 3,000 Unit PUD)	PROPORTIONAL VALUATION EMPLOYMENT ANTICIPATION TEXAS (Nonresidential Development)	Alternate #1 (2,000 Single Family Houses)
INTERGOVERNMENTAL TRANSFERS				
STATE				
Sales Tax	None Redistributed	3,000 x $12,650 x .20 x .75 x .90 x .01[18] = $ 51,232 (C-R)* 3,000 x $12,650 x .10 x .25 x .50 x .01[18] = $ 4,745 (NC-R)* 100,000 x $100 x .01 = $ 100,000 (NR)*	100,000 x $100 x .01 = $ 100,000 (NR)	2,000 x $30,000 x .20 x .75 x .90 x .0125[18] = $ 101,250 (C-R) 2,000 x $30,000 x .10 x .25 x .80 x .0125[18] = $ 15,000 (NC-R)
Income Tax	None Redistributed	$37,950,000 x .0020[18] = $ 75,900	Not Applicable	Non Redistributed
Utility Franchise	.15 x $259,900[20] = $ 38,985	Not Applicable	Not Applicable	Not Applicable
Utility Gross Receipts	.30 x $1,035,000[21] = $ 310,500	Not Applicable	Not Applicable	Not Applicable
Business Personal Property	$8,000 x .50 x .0130 x 20 (NR)[22] = $ 1,040	Not Applicable	Not Applicable	Not Applicable
Urban/Rural Aid	Not Applicable	Not Applicable	Not Applicable	Not Applicable
Road/Road Lighting Aid	None Redistributed	Not Applicable	Not Applicable	Not Applicable
Motor Fuels	$6,375 x .33[25] = $ 2,104	$197,800 x .51[25] = $ 100,878	Not Applicable	.36 x $70,100[25] = $ 25,236
Cigarettes/Alcohol	None Redistributed	None Redistributed[26]	Not Applicable	$80,000 x .28[26] = $ 22,400
Property Tax Relief	Not Applicable	Not Applicable	Not Applicable	$0[27]
Motor Vehicle In-lieu	Not Applicable	Not Applicable	Not Applicable	$150,000 x .33[28] = $ 49,500
TOTAL STATE	$ 352,629	$ 332,755	$ 100,000	$ 213,386
FEDERAL				
Revenue Sharing	$107,000 x .13[29] = $ 13,910	$278,640 x .15[29] = $ 41,796	Not Applicable	$190,000 x .15[29] = $ 28,500
CETA	$100,000 x .12[30] = $ 12,000	$43,000 x .10[30] = $ 4,300	Not Applicable	$50,000 x .10[30] = $ 5,000
Anti-Recession	$70,000 x .10[31] = $ 7,000	$30,000 x .08[31] = $ 2,400	Not Applicable	Not Applicable
CDBG	Not Applicable	Not Applicable	$30,000 x .065[32] = $ -1,950	Not Applicable
LEAA	Not Applicable	$9,460 x .51[33] = $ 4,825	No Change	Not Applicable
TOTAL FEDERAL	$ 32,910	$ 53,321	$ -1,950	$ 33,500
TOTAL INTERGOVERNMENTAL TRANSFER	$ 385,539	$ 386,076	$ 98,050	$ 246,886
TOTAL MUNICIPAL REVENUES	$1,209,736	$1,166,841	$ 132,870[34]	$1,158,957

*Totals may vary slightly due to rounding.

Sect. II: Example Revenue Calculations

EXHIBIT 10-1 (Cont'd)
MUNICIPAL REVENUES BY SOURCE
(FISCAL IMPACT EXAMPLES)*

	COMPARABLE CITY CALIFORNIA (Three Land Use Alternatives) Alternative #2 (5,000 Unit Mixed Use Development)	Alternative #3 (7,000 Garden Apartments)	Alternative #1 (2,000 Single Family Homes)	SERVICE STANDARD GEORGIA (Three Land Use Alternatives) Alternative #2 (5,000 Unit Mixed Use Development)	Alternative #3 (7,000 Garden Apartments)
INTERGOVERNMENTAL TRANSFERS					
STATE					
Sales Tax	5,000 × $21,000 × .20 × .75 × .90 × .0125[18] = $ 177,188 (C-R)*	7,000 × $18,000 × .20 × .75 × .90 × .0125[18] = $ 212,625 (C-R)*	None Redistributed	None Redistributed	None Redistributed
	5,000 × $21,000 × .10 × .25 × .80 × .0125[18] = $ 26,250 (NC-R)*	7,000 × $18,000 × .10 × .25 × .80 × .0125[18] = $ 31,500 (NC-R)*			
Income Tax	None Redistributed	None Redistributed	None Redistributed	None Redistributed	None Redistributed
Utility Franchise	Not Applicable	Not Applicable	Not Applicable	Not Applicable	Not Applicable
Utility Gross Receipts	Not Applicable	Not Applicable	Not Applicable	Not Applicable	Not Applicable
Business Personal Property	Not Applicable	Not Applicable	Not Applicable	Not Applicable	Not Applicable
Urban/Rural Aid	Not Applicable	Not Applicable	$85,000 × .32[23] = $ 27,200	$100,000 × .50[23] = $ 50,000	$100,000 × .53[23] = $ 53,000
Road/Road Lighting Aid	Not Applicable	Not Applicable	$25,000 × .33[24] = $ 8,250	$30,000 × .50[24] = $ 15,000	$30,000 × .60[24] = $ 18,000
Motor Fuels	80,000 × .42[25] = $ 33,600	90,000 × .37[25] = $ 33,300	None Redistributed	None Redistributed	None Redistributed
Cigarettes/Alcohol	$90,000 × .43[26] = $ 38,700	$100,000 × .45[26] = $ 45,000	None Redistributed	None Redistributed	None Redistributed
Property Tax Relief	$0[27]	$0[27]	Not Applicable	Not Applicable	Not Applicable
Motor Vehicle In-lieu	$165,000 × .45[28] = $ 74,250	$180,000 × .47[28] = $ 84,600	Not Applicable	Not Applicable	Not Applicable
TOTAL STATE	$ 349,988	$ 407,025	$ 35,450	$ 65,000	$ 71,000
FEDERAL					
Revenue Sharing	$240,000 × .25[29] = $ 60,000	$225,000 × .10[29] = $ 22,500	$200,000 × .09[29] = $ 18,000	$250,000 × .15[29] = $ 37,500	$280,000 × .06[29] = $ 16,800
CETA	$70,000 × .44[30] = $ 30,800	$72,000 × .53[30] = $ 38,160	$52,000 × .10[30] = $ 5,200	$58,000 × .44[30] = $ 25,520	$60,000 × .57[30] = $ 34,200
Anti-Recession	Not Applicable	$25,000 × .04[31] = $ 1,000	Not Applicable	Not Applicable	$30,000 × .035[31] = $ 1,050
CDBG	Not Applicable	Not Applicable	Not Applicable	Not Applicable	Not Applicable
LEAA	Not Applicable	Not Applicable	$10,240 × .47[33] = $ 4,813	$10,240 × .96[33] = $ 9,830	$10,240 × 1.2[33] = $ 12,288
TOTAL FEDERAL	$ 90,800	$ 61,660	$ 28,013	$ 72,850	$ 64,338
TOTAL INTERGOVERNMENTAL TRANSFER	$ 440,788	$ 468,685	$ 63,463	$ 137,850	$ 135,338
TOTAL MUNICIPAL REVENUES	$2,121,442	$1,765,143	$1,210,310	$2,284,268	$1,994,790

*Totals may vary slightly due to rounding.

EXHIBIT 10-1 (Cont'd)
MUNICIPAL REVENUES BY SOURCE

Notes:

[1] Market value of the real property within the proposed development or land use alternative multiplied by the equalized municipal property tax rate.

[2] Estimated market value[a] of tangible personal property (excluding automobiles) multiplied by the equalized municipal property tax rate.

[3] Automobile value is used as a surrogate for tangible personal property. One half of the original retail cost of an automobile multiplied by (1) an estimate of the number of automobiles per unit, (2) the number of units per development or land use alternative and (3) the municipal property tax rate.

[4] Estimated market value[a] of intangible personal property multiplied by the equalized municipal property tax rate.

[5] Twenty percent of the number of owned units[b] multiplied by (1) their market value and (2) the local real property transfer tax rate.

[6] The number of residential units multiplied by (1)[c] an estimated average utility consumption figure and (2) the local utility gross receipts tax.

[7] Number of new commercial establishments multiplied by the average licensing fee for small convenience goods outlets.

[8] Projected development or land use alternative population multiplied by the per capita alcohol revenue in dollars.

[9] Number of residential units (assuming a 60 percent user rate) multiplied by (1) the average annual user charge and (2) the gross receipts tax rate levied on cable TV companies.

[10] Current interest earnings multiplied by the ratio of development or land use alternative equalized valuation to total local equalized valuation.

[11] Current fees and permit revenue multiplied by the ratio of development or land use alternative residential units to total existing local dwelling units.

[12] Fines/forfeitures per capita multiplied by the projected development or land use alternative population.

[13] User charges for miscellaneous services per capita multiplied by the projected development or land use alternative population.

[14] Annual household user charge for sanitation multiplied by the projected number of dwelling units.

[15] For businesses the annual commercial sanitation charge for small convenience goods outlets is multiplied by the projected number of businesses in the development.

[16] Average annual sewer charge per household multiplied by the projected number of residential units.[d] In Georgia the sewerage levy is based on the number of commodes. In this case the commode fee is multiplied by (1) an assumed number of commodes per residential unit and (2) the number of residential units per development or land use alternative.

[17] Average annual water charge by type of residential unit multiplied by the projected number of units in the development.

[18] For residential development—number of residential units[e] multiplied by (1) the average annual income per household, (2) the percentage of income spent on convenience or shopping goods, (3) the percentage of convenience or shopping goods purchases made locally (4) the percentage of those purchases taxable, and (5) the sales tax return rate to the locality. For commercial development—size of facility in square feet multiplied by (1) estimated annual sales per square foot and (2) local sales tax rate. (This revenue does not apply for the industrial development example.) All sales taxes shown here are locally levied—they are included as intergovernmental transfers because they are state administered.

[19] Estimated aggregate development income multiplied by the state return rate to the locality.

[20] The ratio of additional utility valuation (telegraph, telephone, cable) necessitated by development to new local utility valuation multiplied by the projected estimate of local revenues from the utility franchise tax.

[21] The ratio of additional utility main length (railway, sewerage, water, gas, electric) necessitated by development to new[f] local utility main length multiplied by the projected estimate of revenues from the utility gross receipts tax.

[22] One half of the average estimated retail cost of business personnal property for small convenience goods outlets multiplied by (1) the percentage return rate of the business personal property tax to localities and (2) the number of businesses.

[23] Projected local urban or rural aid multiplied by the ratio of development to new local population.

[24] Projected local road aid multiplied by the ratio of development road miles to new[f] total road mileage.

[25] Projected local motor fuels tax return multiplied by an equally weighted ratio of development population to new local population plus development road mileage to new[f] local road mileage.

[26] Projected local cigarette or alcohol tax return multiplied by an equally weighted ratio of development population to new[f] local population plus development generated sales tax revenue to new local sales tax revenue.

[27] Full property tax payment assumed under own-source revenues; no additional credit given here.

[28] Projected local motor vehicle in-lieu tax return multiplied by the ratio of development vehicles to new[f] local vehicles (1.5 vehicles for single family, 1.00 for mixed use, .75 for garden apartments).

[29] Projected local Revenue Sharing amount multiplied by the equally weighted ratios of (1) development population to new[f] local populations, (2) development tax effort to new[f] local tax effort and (3) new[f] local per capita income to development per capita income.

[30] Projected local CETA amount multiplied by unequally weighted ratios of (1) development unemployment to new[f] local unemployment and (2) development adults in low-income families to new[f] local adults in low-income families.

[31] Projected local Anti-Recession aid multiplied by the ratio of the product of the development's excess unemployment rate times its revenue sharing increment to the new[f] local unemployment rate times the new[f] local revenue sharing amount.

[32] Projected local CDBG grant multiplied by equally weighted ratios of (1) development population to new[f] local population, (2) development crowding index to new[f] local crowding index and (3) development poverty index to new local poverty index.

[33] Projected LEAA grant multiplied by a simple ratio of development population to local population.

[34] This total is $100,000 less for the industrial example in the Employment Anticipation method due to the lack of inclusion of the sales tax revenue.

[a] Estimated by using the current ratio of tangilbe or intangible personal property to real property value in the municipality.

[b] For rental units 20 percent of the aggregate market value multiplied by the local real property transfer tax rate.

[c] For non-residential development in Texas the ratio of the additional utility mains to existing utility mains multiplied by the current local utility income.

[d] For businesses, the average annual commercial sewerage charge multiplied by the projected number of businesses in the development.

[e] For businesses, the size of the establishment (in square feet) multiplied by (1) estimated annual sales (in dollars per square foot) and (2) the sales tax return rate to the locality.

[f] "New", in this note and all the following ones where it is used, includes existing plus development and other growth generated.

*Abbreviations for state redistributed sales tax:
- (C-R) = Convenience goods, residential projection
- (NC-R) = Nonconvenience or shopping goods, residential projection
- (NR) = Nonresidential projection

Sect. II: Example Revenue Calculations

EXHIBIT 10-2
SCHOOL DISTRICT REVENUES BY SOURCE
(FISCAL IMPACT EXAMPLES)*

	PER CAPITA MULTIPLIER NEW JERSEY (Single Development— 3,000 Unit PUD)	CASE STUDY ILLINOIS (Single Development— 3,000 Unit PUD)	PROPORTIONAL VALUATION EMPLOYMENT ANTICIPATION TEXAS (Nonresidential Development)	Alternative #1 (2,000 Single Family Homes)	COMPARABLE CITY CALIFORNIA (Three Land Use Alternatives) Alternative #2 (5,000 Unit Mixed Use Development)
OWN SOURCE REVENUE					
TAXES	$81,787,200 × .0180[1] = $1,472,170	$82,230,600 × .0103[1] = $846,975	$4,000,000 × .0094[1] = $37,600	$100,000,000 × .0125[1] = $1,250,000	$175,000,000 × .0125[1] = $2,187,500
TOTAL TAXES	$1,472,170	$846,975	$37,600	$1,250,000	$2,187,500
CHARGES/MISCELLANEOUS	$175,000 ÷ 2400[2] = $73	$400,000 ÷ 4000[2] = $100	Not Applicable	$500,000 ÷ 5500[2] = $91	$500,000 ÷ 5500[2] = $91
	$73 × 1238[3] = $90,374	$100 × 1416[3] = $141,600		$91 × 2259[3] = $205,569	$91 × 3,968[3] = $361,088
TOTAL CHARGES/MISCELLANEOUS	$90,374	$141,600	0	$205,569	$361,088
TOTAL OWN SOURCE REVENUE	$1,562,544	$988,575	$37,600	$1,455,569	$2,548,588
INTERGOVERNMENTAL TRANSFERS					
STATE					
Basic Support Flat Grants	$153 × 1238[4] = $189,414	Not Applicable[12]	Not Applicable	Not Applicable[10]	Not Applicable[10]
Foundation Aid/Variable Guarantee[5]	Not Applicable	$531,000[9]	Not Applicable	$33,638 × .0223[11] = $750	$35,488 × .0223[11] = $791
				$1,012 − $750[12] = $262	$1,012 − $791[12] = $221
				$262 × 2,259 = $591,858	$221 × 3,968 = $876,928
Categorical Aid	$480,000 ÷ 2400[6] = $200	$575,000 ÷ 4000[6] = $144	Not Applicable	$975,000 ÷ 5500[6] = $177	$975,000 ÷ 5,500[6] = $177
	$200 × 1238 = $247,600	$144 × 1416 = $203,904		$177 × 2259 = $399,843	$177 × 3,968 = $702,336
State Distributed Federal Intergovernmental Aid	$135,000 ÷ 2400[7] = $56	$360,000 ÷ 4000[7] = $90	Not Applicable	$450,000 ÷ 5500[7] = $82	$450,000 ÷ 5,500[7] = $82
	$56 × 1238 = $69,328	$90 × 1416 = $127,440		$82 × 2,259 = $185,238	$82 × 3,968 = $185,238
TOTAL STATE	$506,342	$862,344	0	$1,176,939	$1,904,640
FEDERAL	Not Applicable[8]	Not Applicable[8]		Not Applicable[8]	Not Applicable[8]
TOTAL FEDERAL	0	0	0	0	0
TOTAL INTERGOVERNMENTAL TRANSFERS	$506,342	$862,344	0	$1,176,939	$1,904,640
TOTAL SCHOOL DISTRICT REVENUES	$2,068,886	$1,850,919	$37,600	$2,632,508	$4,453,228

*Total may vary slightly due to rounding.

EXHIBIT 10-2 (Cont'd)

SCHOOL DISTRICT REVENUES BY SOURCE
(FISCAL IMPACT EXAMPLES)*

	Alternative #3 (7,000 Garden Apartments)	Alternative #1 (2,000 Single Family Homes)	SERVICE STANDARD GEORGIA (Three Land Use Alternatives) Alternative #2 (5,000 Unit Mixed Use Development)	Alternative #3 (7,000 Garden Apartments)
OWN SOURCE REVENUE				
TAXES	$113,610,000 x .0125[1] = $1,420,125	$100,000,000 x .0056[1] = $ 560,000	$175,000,000 x .0056[1] = $ 980,000	$120,960,000 x .0056[1] = $ 677,376
TOTAL TAXES	$1,420,125	$ 560,000	$ 980,000	$ 677,376
CHARGES/MISCELLANEOUS	$500,000 ÷ 5,500[2] = $ 91	$200,000 ÷ 4,200[2] = $ 48	$200,000 ÷ 4,200[2] = $ 48	$200,000 ÷ 4,200[2] = $ 48
	$ 91 x 1,827[3] = $ 166,257	$ 48 x 1,989[3] = $ 95,472	$ 48 x 4,199[3] = $ 201,552	$ 48 x 2,205[3] = $ 105,840
TOTAL CHARGES/MISCELLANEOUS	$ 166,257	$ 95,472	$ 201,552	$ 105,840
TOTAL OWN REVENUE	$1,586,382	$ 655,472	$1,181,552	$ 783,216
INTERGOVERNMENTAL TRANSFERS				
STATE				
Basic Support Flat Grants	Not Applicable[10]	Not Applicable[13]	Not Applicable[13]	Not Applicable[13]
Foundation Aid/Variable Guarantee[5]	$ 37,479 x .0223[11] = $ 836	$1,392,300 − $243,505[14]* = $1,148,795[25]	$2,939,300 − $322,055[14] = $2,617,245[25]	$1,543,500 − $267,070[14] = $1,276,430[25]
	$1,012 − $836[12] = $ 176			
	$ 176 x 1,827 = $ 321,552			
Categorical Aid	$975,000 ÷ 5,500[6] = $ 177	$220,000 ÷ 4,200[6] = $ 52	$220,000 ÷ 4,200[6] = $ 52	$220,000 ÷ 4,200[6] = $ 52
	$ 177 x 1,827 = $ 323,379	$ 52 x 1,989 = $ 103,428	$ 52 x 4,199 = $ 218,348	$ 52 x 2,205 = $ 114,660
State Distributed Federal Intergovernmental Aid	$450,000 ÷ 5,500[7] = $ 82	$210,000 ÷ 4,200[7] = $ 50	$210,000 ÷ 4,200[7] = $ 50	$210,000 ÷ 4,200[7] = $ 50
	$ 82 x 1,827 = $ 149,814	$ 50 x 1,989 = $ 99,450	$ 50 x 4,199 = $ 209,950	$ 50 x 2,205 = $ 110,250
TOTAL STATE	$ 794,745	$1,351,673	$3,045,543	$1,501,340
FEDERAL	Not Applicable[8]	Not Applicable[8]	Not Applicable[8]	Not Applicable[8]
TOTAL FEDERAL	0	0	0	0
TOTAL INTERGOVERNMENTAL TRANSFERS	$ 794,745	$1,351,673	$3,045,543	$1,501,340
TOTAL SCHOOL DISTRICT REVENUES	$2,381,127	$2,007,145	$4,227,095	$2,284,556

*Totals may vary slightly due to rounding.

Sect. II: Example Revenue Calculations 231

EXHIBIT 10-2 (Cont'd)
SCHOOL DISTRICT REVENUES BY SOURCE

Notes:
[1] PUD, land use alternative, or nonresidential use, total equalized valuation multiplied by the local school district equalized tax rate.

[2] Existing or pregrowth total existing charges and miscellaneous revenue divided by the existing or pregrowth total pupils.

[3] State aid per pupil multiplied by PUD or land use alternative generated students.

[4] District is too wealthy to qualify for resource equalization aid, but rather receives 10 percent ($153) of the K-12 minimum flat support per pupil ($1,528). Flat support multiplied by generated pupils, equals total flat support assistance.

[5] States have had hold harmless provisions.

[6] Existing or pregrowth total categorical aid to local district divided by existing pupils.

[7] Total state distributed federal intergovernmental aid to local district divided by existing pupils.

[8] Neither district nor housing is considered "impacted."

[9] In Illinois basic support equals the subsidy from the largest of four programs: equalization aid, flat grant, resource equalizer, and alternate method. In this district, the maximum aid was generated by the resource equalizer program, which operates as follows: (guaranteed valuation per pupil—actual valuation per pupil) x operating tax rate = aid per pupil. Pupils have not been weighted, and it is assumed that all PUD-generated pupils not attending parochial school will attend the local public elementary school.

[10] District qualifies for equalization assistance and therefore does not receive basic aid.

[11] Post-growth valuation per pupil (See Exhibit 10-5) multiplied by the computational tax rate for elementary school districts (As in Illinois example, it is assumed that all PUD-generated pupils will attend the local elementary schools) equals the amount raised locally for participation in the foundation program.

[12] Foundation amount minus the amount raised locally equals foundation assistance per pupil (California's equalization aid formula is a foundation program. Flat grants are given only to districts not qualifying for foundation assistance).

[13] Georgia distributes basic support, Adequate Program for Education in Georgia (APEG), according to the following formula: state aid = APEG approved costs − local share, where the local share is determined by a property valuation adjustment formula. In this district, the local share is .0031 under alternative development #1, .0041 under alternative development #2 and .0034 under alternative development #3.

[14] Total APEG-approved items (see footnote 13) minus the local share: Local share: .0031 x $78,550,000 = $243,505
.0041 x $78,550,000 = $322,055
.0034 x $78,550,000 = $267,070

EXHIBIT 10-3

MARKET VALUE OF REAL PROPERTY FOR 3,000 UNIT PUD (NEW JERSEY AND ILLINOIS)

RESIDENTIAL/ NONRESIDENTIAL DEVELOPMENT	Number of Dwelling Units	Valuation/ Rent per Unit	TOTAL VALUATION New Jersey	TOTAL VALUATION Illinois
Residential				
Townhouses (1,500)				
1 Bedroom (elderly)	250	$25,000	$ 6,250,000	$ 6,250,000
2 bedroom	1,000	30,000	30,000,000	30,000,000
3 bedroom	250	35,000	8,750,000	8,750,000
		Total	$45,000,000	$45,000,000
Garden Apartments (1,000)				
1 bedroom	700	$250	$10,164,000[1]	$10,332,000[1]
2 bedroom	300	300	5,227,200[2]	5,313,600[2]
		Total	$15,391,200	$15,645,600
Single Family Houses (500)				
3 bedroom	250	$35,000	$ 8,750,000	$ 8,750,000
4 bedroom	250	40,000	10,000,000	10,000,000
			$18,750,000	$18,750,000
Nonresidential				
Community Shopping Center	100,000 Ft.	$4.50 per square foot	$ 2,646,000[3]	$ 2,835,000[3]
		Total	$81,787,200	$82,230,600

Notes: For appropriate multipliers, see Chapter 16 (Gross Income Multipliers Residential and Commercial Properties).

[1] Generates $2,100,000 in annual rent roll ($250 x 12 = $3,000, $3,000 x 700 = $2,100,000). Applying a 4.84 gross income multiplier yields a $10,164,000 value. Applying a 4.92 gross income multiplier yields a $10,332,000 value.

[2] Generates $11,080,000 in annual rent roll ($300 x 12 = $3,600, $3,600 x 300 = $1,080,000). Applying a 4.84 gross income multiplier yields a $5,227,200 value. Applying a 4.92 gross income multiplier yields a $5,313,600 value.

[3] Generates $450,000 in annual rent roll ($4.50 x 100,000 = $450,000). Applying a 5.88 gross income multiplier yields a $2,646,000 value. Applying a 6.30 gross income multiplier yields a $2,835,000 value.

EXHIBIT 10-4

MARKET VALUE OF REAL PROPERTY FOR DEVELOPMENT ALTERNATIVES
(CALIFORNIA AND GEORGIA)

DEVELOPMENT ALTERNATIVE	Number of Dwelling Units	Valuation/ Rent per Unit	TOTAL VALUATION California	TOTAL VALUATION Georgia
1 (single family)	2,000	$50,000	$100,000,000	$100,000,000
2 (mixed use)	5,000	$35,000	$175,000,000	$175,000,000
3 (garden apartments)	7,000	$250	$113,610,000[1]	$120,960,000[1]

Note: [1] Generates $21,000,000 annual rent roll ($250 x 12 x 7,000 = $1,750,000, $1,750,000 x 12 = $21,000,000). Applying a 5.41 gross rent multiplier yields a $113,610,000 value. Applying a 5.76 gross income multiplier yields a $120,960,000 value.

EXHIBIT 10-5
PRE- AND POST-GROWTH PROPERTY VALUATION AND STUDENT POPULATION

FINANCIAL/ EDUCATIONAL PARAMETERS	New Jersey (PUD)	Illinois (PUD)	California (Land Use Alternatives)	Georgia (Land Use Alternatives)
1. Existing district valuation	$270,075,000	$155,000,000	$161,000,000	$127,000,000
2. Existing district enrollment	2,400	4,000	5,500	4,200
3. Existing valuation per pupil	$ 112,531	$ 38,750	$ 29,272	$ 30,238
4. PUD/Alternative Development Valuation	$ 81,787,200[4]	$ 82,230,600[4]	$100,000,000[1] $175,000,000[2] $113,610,000[3]	$100,000,000[1] $175,000,000[2] $120,960,000[3]
5. PUD/Alternative Development Students	1,238[4]	1,416[4]	2,259[1] 3,968[2] 1,827[3]	1,989[1] 4,199[2] 2,205[3]
6. Combined valuation (1 + 4)	$351,862,200[4]	$237,230,600[4]	$261,000,000[1] $336,000,000[2] $274,610,000[3]	$227,000,000[1] $302,000,000[2] $247,960,000[3]
7. Combined students (2 + 5)	3,638[4]	5,416[4]	7,759[1] 9,468[2] 7,327[3]	6,189 8,399 6,405
8. Combined valuation per pupil (6 ÷ 7)	$ 96,719[4]	$ 43,802[4]	$ 33,638[1] $ 35,488[2] $ 37,479[3]	$ 36,678 $ 35,957 $ 38,714

Notes: [1]Alternative 1. See Exhibit 10-4
[2]Alternative 2. See Exhibit 10-4
[3]Alternative 3. See Exhibit 10-4
[4]PUD

PART 3

GENERAL APPLICABILITY: ARE FISCAL IMPACT CONSIDERATIONS ACCEPTABLE MUNICIPAL ACTIVITIES OR REQUIREMENTS?

It is the purpose of this part to acquaint the user with the substantive areas in which fiscal impact analysis *may* concern itself and then the specific issues and tasks that it *has* focused on. Consisting of two chapters, the first (Chapter 11) details the potential universe of legally required or allowed fiscal impact activities, while the second (Chapter 12) shows the precise field level application and emphasis.

Chapter 11 has two basic sections: (1) an examination of why and in what instances fiscal impact considerations are legally justified, (2) an analysis of the substantive involvement of fiscal impact considerations in land use planning over time, and the courts' acceptance or rejection of such participation. In a sense, what is provided here is a legal roadmap charting both areas of accepted roles for fiscal impact considerations as well as those which violate the rights of individuals and thus may not be followed.

In pursuit of these goals, Chapter 11 presents a national survey of state enabling legislation for local zoning, subdivision regulation, comprehensive planning, annexation, rezoning/variances and planned developments/cluster provisions. Summarized for the user, by state, are the authorizations for fiscal impact considerations as a part of each of these regulatory processes. Further, the user is familiarized with the case law* surrounding fiscal impact practice over the last decade and trends in the law are summarized for specific regions of the country. The reader is introduced, for instance, to the pitfalls of allowing fiscal impact considerations to be used as a form of local exclusionary zoning.

The importance of this chapter to the user is to show him the many possible areas of cost-revenue inquiry, and to assure him that fiscal impact considerations are part and parcel of a number of land use activities nationally — the technique is recognized as a component element of multiple land use regulatory forms throughout the country. It further cautions the user that if fiscal impact considerations are not employed judiciously, land use decisions which reflect their input will be closely scrutinized by the courts.

Chapter 12 turns from the discussion of where fiscal impact analysis may and should be employed to where it has been used. It summarizes the cost revenue field experience nationally, covering such inclusive elements as general purposes for which cost-revenue studies are used, typical practitioners, methods employed, general ranges of costs and revenues considered, geographic concentrations, and current levels of user satisfaction with different types of methods.

The national review is based on 136** cost-revenue studies sponsored by various groups and conducted by different types of authors. The analyses had a wide range of tasks (i.e., examining a development, land use alternative, annexation, etc.) that were conducted in both small and large localities throughout the country. The reports provide the groundwork for considering the following field level cost-revenue concerns and emphases.

1. Subject, jurisdictional focus, method and land use analyzed.
2. Geographical and fiscal context
3. Scope of study and data resources
4. Author, audience and significance of the study.

---

*A national summary of case law relating to fiscal impact analysis is contained in Appendix 1 of this handbook.
**The 136 studies are detailed in a matrix annotation in Appendix 2 of this handbook.

11

CURRENT LEGAL STANDING

The purpose of this chapter is to present to the user of this handbook a detailed summary of the current legal standing of fiscal impact considerations as a foundation upon which to base local land use decisions. This is the context within which one must view the emergence of impact analysis and its application to local questions of the costs versus revenues of various municipally-permitted, private realty developments.

Fiscal responsibility is an important local issue. Yet in the process of maintaining fiscal stability, the potential for violation of a citizen's rights is nonetheless always present. This chapter explains the careful line that must be made between municipal efficiency and individual equity.

The information presented here has been obtained from legal searches of the enabling legislation and case law of the fifty states, Washington, D.C., and Puerto Rico. This type of research is important for two reasons. In the first case, it acknowledges the fact that even though a Standard Zoning Enabling Act has been adopted by fifty states and is still in effect in forty-seven, varying judicial attitudes have had such an enormous influence on state legal systems that there are now fifty individual state systems of land use law with little in common. To say fiscal impact analysis is an acceptable development accompaniment to be required of the developer or to be undertaken by the municipality as part of a local approval process is a statement which cannot be made for all localities in every state. The police power is a state power delegated to localities within specified limits, and each state defines these limits through enabling legislation. Further, each state interprets the legitimacy of local practice through judicial review, resulting in its case law.

Second, the legal searches contained here have pointed out that, to become a part of local regulations, planning objectives (such as fiscal impact considerations) (1) must be tied to a discernable municipal need (fiscal stability) and (2) must be employed in a fashion which accomplishes their purpose without infringing upon the constitutional rights of those who live within the bounds of that municipality. Both of these are locally-determined rather than nationwide issues.

This chapter clearly shows that fiscal impact considerations are either legally authorized or that there are fertile grounds for authorization within the confines of numerous planning or planning related tasks. Economy and efficiency in the land development process have long been basic planning objectives. Fiscal impact calculations could thus easily be a part of a comprehensive planning process. The comprehensive plan could well include a fiscal impact statement similar to the currently required environmental impact statement.

Fiscal impact analysis further can be used in cases of special exception or permitted use (for instance, as part of the PUD approval process) to assure local fiscal stability throughout the multiple stages of a large development. It may be used in variances or rezonings to provide documentation that undue hardship to an individual property owner is mitigated by general community economic benefit or that the fiscal situation has so changed in a community that the existing zoning bears no relationship to reality and, in fact, is counterproductive to orderly growth. These are key questions in granting these forms of relief.

Fiscal impact considerations are similarly useful in annexations. They assess the likely financial outcome of convergence to both jurisdictions and prevent annexations which would be especially beneficial to the residents of one jurisdiction at the expense of the residents of the other. Impact considerations are within the purview of state land use laws, which attempt to coordinate the often conflicting objectives of smaller units of government.

Yet the user must realize, however, that every land use cannot be a municipal benefit, and while we may assess relative fiscal merit, it does not follow that those land uses that either are not as beneficial as others or impose a liability can then necessarily be excluded.

Where fiscal impact analysis has had some history, the courts have in part specified its role. Fiscal considerations, while the concern of local land use policy, are neither the sole concern, nor may they be the basis on which to exclude totally a category of land use. Fiscal impact analysis is a local accounting mechanism which provides insight to the fiscal effect of land use decisions. Analyses will inform local authorities, for instance, that certain forms of residential development will not be "profitable" while others will, and that generally, nonresidential uses will be more "profitable" than residential. The courts have said then that localities may indeed use this information to plan for the future; however, the fiscal implications of particular development are only one element within the planning process. Courts have recognized that municipalities also have to provide housing for those who work nearby, answer regional as well as local needs, and provide housing opportunities for those who are economically or racially disadvantaged.

In sum, there are many tasks for which fiscal impact considerations are authorized, but there are also areas for potential misuse. Fortunately, there is legal precedent in both instances to assist the user in the correct application of fiscal impact analysis as a planning tool.

Fiscal Impact Considerations: Are They Permissible Municipal Concerns?

Fiscal impact analysis provides planning officials with a potentially powerful tool, a method whereby they can estimate the net impact of existing and future development on the fiscal well-being of their communities. Questions must be answered, however, before this analytical device can hope to gain broad professional acceptance. To begin, fiscal impact analysis must live up to its promise. It must show that it can be used to project correctly the costs and revenues of the various types and configurations of land use. This is the general subject matter of the introduction of this handbook and related to specific methods in Chapter 1.

Yet, even if as a planning device fiscal impact analysis does successfully meet the test, a second test awaits the larger conceptual issue. Are fiscal impact considerations legitimate components of local land use policy? Although more than fifty years have passed since the U.S. Supreme Court recognized that zoning was a proper exercise of the police power,[1] the exact limitations of a locality's ability to regulate land use within its borders are yet to be defined. In fact, with the constantly increasing trend toward more numerous and more sophisticated methods of land use control, the boundaries of the police power in this area are becoming increasingly open to speculation.

Since the first decisions established zoning as a legal device for the control of land development, a myriad of techniques for land use regulation has emerged. They include subdivision regulation and site plan review, planned unit development, planned residential (commercial/industrial) development, and cluster development. Additionally, the complex notions of the transfer of development rights and of a site's "holding capacity" have recently become potential factors in a locality's policy for land use control. Yet, persistent legal questions remain about the extent to which these techniques may be utilized by land use regulatory agencies. One noted authority in his treatise on land use states, in fact, that we are quickly moving to a realization that local regulations are not by definition beneficial and in the public interest but rather may serve a nonlegitimate purpose, be the product of parochial vision, be unduly harsh with little compensating public benefit or merely be inept.[2]

Added to these numerous issues concerning the extent of the police power as it applies to land use control is the critical question, presently raised, of whether fiscal impact considerations may properly be included in land use planning. This question is of utmost significance given several jurisdictions' recent identification of "exclusionary zoning." At issue is whether fiscal considerations, albeit accurate and made in good faith, are to be so weighted as to justify land use regulations which are exclusionary. Does a municipality, for example, have the right to limit either minimum building lot size or a dwelling unit's maximum number of bedrooms and thereby deny entrance to families who because of lower income or larger size receive more local services than they pay for in taxes? From this perspective, land use regulation based on fiscal impact considerations clearly involves serious social questions.

Courts may therefore be asked to resolve this conflict between local fiscal responsibility and the need for housing, typically for low and moderate income families. Many traditional land use devices will consequently be taken to task, including large-lot zoning, prohibitions on multi-family dwellings, bedroom restrictions, minimum floor space requirements, low income housing exclusions, building moratoria, mobile home prohibitions, environmental impact requirements, and, often as common as these others, municipal refusals to provide services to new developments. The courts will have to balance responsible municipal planning with exclusionary zoning practices.

Nonetheless, presently in all but a few jurisdictions the question as to the applicability of fiscal impact considerations as a basis for the administration of land use regulations remains very much unresolved. And, as noted, in those jurisdictions where fiscal impact considerations have been reviewed, the courts often base their decisions on ethical considerations raised by exclusionary zoning.[3] In these jurisdictions, moreover, and in New Jersey in particular, where land use decisions which are based on a project's impact on the *local tax rate* have been held invalid, the question may be open as to whether a local regulatory agency may consider other public health and safety constraints such as a proposal's impact on existing local sewerage facilities or drainage capabilities, absent massive capital improvements, as a reason for municipal rejection.[4] Consequently, the use of fiscal impact considerations as an element of local land use policy is often related to the specific facts under review, and no general statement about the validity of fiscal impact considerations has yet emerged from the courts.

Scope of Survey

What then are the legally acceptable roles for the application of the cost-revenue techniques listed elsewhere in this handbook? A survey of state enabling legislation is a first step in answering that question. Only by beginning with the state enabling statutes, from which local and county governments derive their planning and zoning powers, can the very nature and scope of those powers be delineated.

The areas examined by a survey of state enabling legislation were selected with the understanding that they represent the steps within the planning process most amenable to the application of fiscal impact analysis. Sections of state enabling legislation authorizing zoning, variances, comprehensive and master plans, subdivision controls, annexation, planned unit developments, and state land use laws were examined in an effort to determine if they required, permitted, or prohibited the application of fiscal impact analysis.

Enabling Legislation and Its Specification of the Ability to Undertake Fiscal Impact Analysis

Comprehensive Planning

The enabling legislation authorizing the formulation of a comprehensive plan serves primarily to initiate the planning process. The function of such a plan is to provide a rational basis for future growth. Although not legally binding by itself, its impact is based on the requirement that zoning ordinances "be made in accordance with a comprehensive plan."[5] Consequently, a zoning ordinance that is not in accordance with a comprehensive plan would probably be declared invalid.

The survey indicates that there exist three basic models for an enabling statute. Fourteen states[6] have passed a basic statute essentially providing only that the plan include a proposal for the physical development of the community. Nothing specific is said about policy recommendations or planning goals. A typical example of such an authorization is the South Dakota Statute (*S.D. COMPILED LAWS ANN.* §11-6-14) which simply states that the comprehensive plan shall include "recommendations for the said physical development" of the municipality.

The secnd group of statutes, found in eleven jurisdictions,[7] tends to build upon the premise of the first. Not only do they encourage physical considerations to be contained in the plan, they also require a public facilities component, i.e., how the municipality will provide for necessary public services. Arizona (*ARIZ. REV. STAT.* §9-461) and Arkansas (*ARK. STAT. ANN.* §19-2827) are typical examples; i.e., the physical development plan "must (shall) include a public facilities component."

The third group, which includes twenty-seven states,[8] notes that a comprehensive planning program must have as one of its purposes the promotion of "efficiency and economy" in the land development process. An example is the New Mexico Statute (*N.M. STAT. ANN.* §14-8-9) dealing with the purposes of a master plan:

> The plan shall be made with the general purpose of guiding and accomplishing a coordinated, adjusted, and harmonious development of the municipality, which will, in accordance with existing and future needs best promote health, safety, morals, order, convenience, prosperity or the general welfare as well as efficiency and economy in the process of development.

Or, as a further example, reference may be made to Vermont's enabling legislation (VT. STAT. ANN. TITLE 24, §4382 et seq.):

> A utility and facility plan showing present and prospective services; for rural towns the plan shall state the appropriate timing or sequence of land development activities in relation to the provision of necessary community facilities and services.

The extent to which fiscal impact considerations are authorized under these statutes is still unanswered. It can be inferred from twenty-seven states' requirement for "efficiency and economy in the process of development," however, that fiscal impact considerations are emerging as an important factor in determining future growth.

In addition, the Virginia statute refers specifically to the cost of public services and its relationship to the tax burden. In Idaho, Missouri and Virginia the growth of public facilities must be related directly to the community's financial resources.[9] In New Jersey, the master plan is to provide for public improvement so as not to impose an excessive financial burden on the taxpayer; and land use regulation has among its goals:

1. To promote the establishment of appropriate population densities and concentrations that will contribute to the well-being of persons, neighborhoods, communities and regions and preservation of the environment;
2. To encourage the appropriate and efficient expenditure of public funds by the coordination of public development with land use policies; and
3. To encourage coordination of the various public and private procedures and activities shaping land development with a view of lessening the cost of such development and to the more efficient use of land.[10]

In general, then, it can be concluded that fiscal impact considerations are particularly applicable to comprehensive planning. It is during this stage of planning that the overall implications of alternative developments may best be gauged. Analyzing the fiscal impact of proposed alternatives appears to comply with the intent of both long-standing and newly drawn enabling legislation.

Zoning

The enabling statutes authorizing zoning usually include authorization to regulate physical aspects of developments, such as the height, bulk and density of the use of land and structures thereon. Further, such enabling legislation authorizes regulation over the nature and purpose for which land may be used. Significantly, the extent of the powers thus granted determines whether fiscal impact considerations are within the scope of the zoning prerogatives in any specified jurisdiction.

In construing these statutes, it is important to note that zoning is inherently based on the police power (i.e., the state's power to act so as to promote the public health, safety, and welfare). In the *Standard State Zoning Enabling Act,* for example, it is found that among the relevant purposes of zoning are "[the promotion] of health and general welfare...to facilitate the adequate provision of transportation, water, sewerage, schools, parks, and other public requirements." The scope of the police power, however, has not been definitely established by the courts, nor is it likely that a final limit will be assigned to the actions coming within this rather broad judicial concept. Instead, it becomes necessary to examine within the context of each state's case law the nature of the interpretations given to the police power. While a more complete attempt at this is made in the following section on fiscal zoning case law, at this point it is noted that *the zoning power is authorized through the police power, and only if fiscal impact considerations are ruled to be a proper activity within the scope of that power will they be accepted by the courts as proper constituents of local policy.*

In several instances this problem of judicial interpretation is diminished by the specific statutory inclusion of phrases referring to: "the protection of the tax base," found in the Utah statute (UTAH CODE ANN. §17-21-13) authorizing zoning powers for counties; "In the interest of prosperity" in Ohio (OHIO REV. CODE ANN. §713.06 *et seq.*) and Tennessee (TENN. CODE ANN. §13-701); and finally, "[to] facilitate economic and adequate provision of [public services]" in the Georgia statutes (GA. CODE ANN. §69-801). Thus zoning based on fiscal impact considerations would appear to be authorized in these jurisdictions.

Notwithstanding such general police power authorization, however, an implicit restraint upon the zoning power deals with the assurance of adequate provisions for public facilities. This must also be analyzed in light of its cost-revenue potential. If a fiscal impact analysis showed that without augmentation at extraordinary taxpayer cost, existing facilities were inadequate to meet the needs of future development, would this fiscal reason alone be an acceptable basis upon which to base local zoning? Not surprisingly, convincing arguments can be made on both sides of the issue. One might suggest that the inadequacy of public facilities is a valid criterion upon which to base zoning because if such premature development were allowed it would threaten "the health, safety and general welfare" of the community. Moreover, an important reason for zoning is to promote the efficient and economical provision of public services and this can only be accomplished if development is closely regulated.

On the other hand, others might argue that inadequate public service falls outside the scope of the zoning power. They might argue that zoning must look to the future and that the current absence of such facilities is no justification for depriving someone of the desired use of his/her land.[11] Moreover, such an action would, in fact, penalize an individual property owner for the shortcomings of the entire community. Such criteria would have an exclusionary impact. A locality without adequate public services would often be fiscally justified in excluding housing; it could thereby effectively prevent unwanted growth. Finally, those arguing against this use of zoning would point out that other powers such as safety and health regulations exist and are more directly related to preventing potentially harmful development.

It is evident that substantial questions remain for judicial review and interpretation. Yet, at least on one side of the argument, zoning to ensure adequate public facilities or to protect the tax base is a reasonable interpretation of the intent of the police power. If this is true, fiscal impact considerations and cost-revenue analysis, the planning tool to estimate the extent of fiscal disparity, may be required of those who wish to develop according to the desired fiscal posture of the community.

Having examined the origins of the basic zoning power, we now look at legislation defining more specific powers. In the great majority of states the language used for authorizing a local board of adjustment to grant a variance was again drawn, at least in part, from the Standard State Zoning Enabling Act. Section 7 (3) of that model statute lists as a power of the local board:

> To authorize upon appeal in specific cases such variance from the terms of the ordinance as will not be contrary to the public interest, where, owing to special conditions a literal enforcement would result in unnecessary hardship and so that the spirit of the ordinance shall be observed and substantial justice be done.

A key criterion in granting a variance involves the definition of those exceptions that would be "contrary to the public interest." In addition, the petitioner must be able to demonstrate that the existing ordinance engenders "unnecessary hardship" or "special reasons" and that just relief can be granted within the "spirit of the ordinance."

Any use of fiscal impact considerations in deciding the fate of a variance must be framed within the scope of the language used in the enabling legislation. The following issues will, in all likelihood, arise:

> Can preservation of the tax rate be included within the meaning of protection of the public interest?
>
> At what point does a single property owner's pecuniary hardship outweigh any financial gains to an entire community?
>
> How can the ordinance be changed and still preserve the spirit of the law?
>
> May a municipality deny an application for a variance on the grounds that it does not have the infrastructure and utilities necessary to serve such development?

Fiscal impact considerations could easily be used to demonstrate significant community economic gain at only minor loss of individual property rights, or, in the reverse case, such economic loss to the community as to be contrary to the public interest. Three states, for example, have chosen a set of criteria upon which to base their variance determinations. California (GOV'T CODE §65903 et seq. [West]), Kentucky (KY. REV. STAT. ANN. §100.217 [Baldwin]), and Alaska (ALASKA STAT. §29.33) all authorize the granting of a variance in situations where the petitioner would otherwise be deprived of reasonable capacity to use the land in a manner equivalent to that permitted other landowners in the same zone. Fiscal impact analysis could thus effectively be one gauge of "equivalent use."

Also worth noting is the statute in Puerto Rico (P.R. LAWS ANN. Title 23, §627).[12] It serves to turn the tables on an application for development which is otherwise in accordance with the zoning ordinance. If special circumstances exist that "make impracticable the application of the regulations. . .due to factors such as economy. . ., lack of facilities or public improvements" the project approval may be denied. The potential exists for fiscal impact analysis to be used as a basis to determine what is not practical as authorized by the enabling legislation.

Subdivision Controls

In several respects subdivision controls go hand in hand with fiscal impact considerations. Both require that at some point the cost of supplying municipal services to a new development must be determined. To the extent that subdivision controls require a builder to provide specified public services and facilities, the fiscal well-being of that community may be improved. The magnitude as well as the developer/municipal share must still be estimated — the role of fiscal impact considerations in land use policy.

In forty-two of the jurisdictions examined, subdivision controls explicitly include the right to require various public utilities to be provided by the subdivision and dedicated to the city for future use. In most cases, a bond e.g., Mississippi (MISS. CODE ANN. §2890.5, §3374-123), New York (N.Y. TOWN LAWS §216 [McKinney]), North Carolina (N.C. GEN. STAT. §160A-372), Virginia (VA. CODE §15.1-465 et seq.), and Wisconsin (WIS. STAT. ANN. §62.23 [West] is required to insure the future provision of these services. In others, e.g., Louisiana (LSA-R.S. §33:112), Vermont (VT. STAT. ANN. Title 24, §4411) there is a requirement of a fee in lieu of direct provision of utilities. In several instances there is a land dedication requirement for parks e.g., Hawaii (HAW. REV. STAT. Title 13, §46-4), New York (N.Y. TOWN LAWS §276 [McKinney]), South Carolina (S.C. CODE §53-40), or schools e.g., Illinois (ILL. ANN. STAT. C. 24, §11-12-8), Washington (WASH. REV. CODE ANN. §58.17).

Although the general rule is that undesired and municipally burdensome fiscal impact is not directly stated as the reason behind subdivision controls (because the developer "gains" buildable lots and block and lot property descriptions, and is "joined" to the community by submitting to standard division of his property), interesting exceptions to this are found in the Montana and New Hampshire Statutes. Section 11-38 of the Montana Statute (MONT. REV. CODES ANN. §11-38) specifically requires that the *"burden on the tax rate of a proposed development in terms of the cost to provide it with municipal services should be weighed against the expected tax revenues to be generated by that development"* (emphasis added) — the very basis of fiscal impact considerations. The New Hampshire Statute (N.H. REV. STAT. ANN. §36:19) requires that subdivision regulations provide against: "injury to health, safety or prosperity by reason of the lack of water supply, drainage, transportation, schools, fire department or other public services, or *necessitate an excessive expenditure of public funds for the supply of such services"* (emphasis added).

Moreover, under the new Municipal Land Use Law of New Jersey N.J.S.A. 40:551)-1 *et seq.*, a subdivider may be required to pay his "pro-rata share" of the cost of those *off-tract* "street improvements and water, sewerage and drainage facilities, and easements therefor [which have been] necessitated or required by construction or improvements within such subdivision or development." Estimating the pro-rata share is certainly within the confines of fiscal impact considerations.[14] The conditions observed here leave no question as to a very definite role for fiscal impact considerations, and thus the tool fiscal impact analysis, in molding local land use policy. In Montana and New Hampshire it's an obvious one — an evaluation of cost versus revenues to provide local services and the resulting impact on the "tax rate" or "prosperity" of the community.

In those states whose subdivision regulations require dedication of land for schools as part of the approval process the role of fiscal impact analysis, while not as explicit, is nonetheless a potentially powerful one. If a developer can demonstrate significant municipal and school cost-revenue surpluses can he not be relieved of his land dedication requirements? In the reverse case, if educational costs so outweigh revenues, is land dedication for schools a sufficient fiscal exaction?

Indeed, fiscal impact considerations are in the very nature of the subdivision process. As all local capital improvements appear in the operating budget of a community as annual debt service, the effect of subdivision development on the municipal fisc is properly a matter for local concern.

Planned Unit Developments

Several states, in recognizing the inflexibility of existing zoning and subdivision regulations, particularly where large scale development is concerned, have recently passed Planned Unit Development (PUD) legislation to facilitate "more efficient use of land."[13] These authorizations, while providing a more comprehensive regulatory device than subdivision controls, still tend to concentrate on insuring the adequate provision of public utilities. An example is an Ohio statute (OHIO REV. CODE ANN. §519.02.1) which authorizes the use of PUD to promote "greater efficiency in providing public and utility services."

The Idaho statute, however, goes significantly beyond the scope of the other states and, in fact, authorizes a fiscal impact approach. Section 67-6515 of the Idaho Statute (IDAHO CODE §67-6515) permits PUD applications to be dealt with under the special use permit. Under that procedure studies may be required of the "social, market, *fiscal* and environmental effects of the proposed special use." (emphasis added).

Applying fiscal impact considerations to the approval of planned developments serves a basic purpose to assure a local jurisdiction that a development, very frequently one which is larger than any they have previously experienced, will not be a severe financial strain. Fiscal impact analysis as a modern planning tool has made perhaps its greatest inroad through this particular application to land use control.

Annexation

The final type of land use control examined was the statute permitting municipalities to extend their existing boundaries. In this situation fiscal impact analysis could be productively used both in estimating the short run fiscal effect of such an extension as well as its long-term implications.

Not surprisingly, our survey found that for this type of municipal action fiscal impact considerations were *explicitly* required more often than in the specification of any other *land use regulation*. In most instances, due to the size of the acquisition, the potential for financial error is enormous. Although gross annexation figures are muddied by the inclusion of small boundary changes, between 1970 and 1973 annexations of ten square miles or more occurred in seventeen states. Approximately the same number of states (18) have statutes which make reference to the necessity of evaluating the magnitude and developing a plan for financing the extension of public services to the annexed territory before approval of annexation is granted.[15] This is almost the exact wording of the Florida (FLA. STAT. ANN. §171.021), Indiana (IND. CODE ANN. §185-5-10-21), Maryland (MD. ANN. 23 A §19), Mississipi (MISS. CODE ANN. §3374-10), Missouri (MO. ANN. STAT. §71.015), Montana (MONT. REV. CODES ANN. §11-514 et seq.), Nebraska (NEB. REV. STAT. §16-117), Nevada (NEV. REV. STAT. §268.596 *et seq.*), New

Mexico (N.M. STAT. ANN. §14-7-1 *et seq.*), North Carolina (N.C. GEN. STAT. §160-453.3) and North Dakota (N.D. GEN. CODE §40-51.1-01 *et seq.*) statutes.

In several states the enabling statutes closely control the fiscal solvency of the annexing area at the expense of the annexed area. The intent is to prevent premature annexation for purely selfish local reasons. In Iowa (IOWA CODE ANN. 362.7) a precondition to annexation is a demonstration that the community is capable of extending services to an area and that it is not "annexing territory merely for the purpose of increasing tax revenues." In Michigan (MICH. STAT. ANN. §5.2246 [West]) and Minnesota (MINN. STAT. ANN. §414.01 [West]) preconditions require showing that the increase in taxes in the areas to be annexed bear some relation to the expected benefits which will be received by residents. In Oregon (OR. REV. STAT. §222.111), following the same reasoning, limitations are placed on the maximum tax rate that may be levied on the annexed area relative to the annexing jurisdiction.

The potential role for fiscal impact analysis is thus considerable. In Washington (WASH. REV. CODE ANN. §35.13), it is perhaps clearest of all. A review board is authorized to determine whether annexation is in the public interest. Its deliberations must include an examination of the immediate and potential revenues that would be derived by the city as a result of annexation, and their relation to the cost of providing service to the area.

Statewide Land Use Plans

Twenty-one states have enacted statewide planning statutes.[16] These authorizations serve primarily to provide for a coordinated statewide development plan emphasizing the economic and efficient provision of public facilities.

Our survey shows two basic models of statewide planning; each represents a different level of state involvement. The simplest prototype authorizes state boards to develop plans for the future physical development of the state and to explore how planned statewide public expenditures will be financed. This authorization attempts to expand to the state the same underlying purpose of the local comprehensive plan, that of achieving efficient and orderly development of land. There is, however, *no direct state regulatory power*. An example is the "Advisory Comprehensive Planning and Research" statute in Alabama (ALA. CODE Title 37, §154) which has as one of its purposes the preparation of:

> a guide for long-range development of advisory physical plans with respect to the pattern and intensity of land use and the provision of public facilities including transportation facilities with *long-range fiscal plans for such development* [emphasis added].

Other states with similar provisions are Colorado (COL. REV. STAT. §24-65-101), Delaware (DEL. CODE ANN. Title 29, §9101), Georgia (GA. CODE ANN. §40-290), North Carolina (N.C. GEN. STAT. §160-453.3), Pennsylvania (PA. STAT. ANN. Title 53, §66945 [Purdon]) and Nevada (NEV. REV. STAT. §268.596 *et seq.*).

The second basic model permits the state to review local plans and exert *direct state control* if local plans are not in harmony with upper level governmental objectives. Frequently, the legislation authorizes a fiscal impact approach to examining proposed growth. In Vermont, the "State Land Use and Development Plan" (VT. STAT. ANN. Title 10, §6001) establishes district commissions to review development plans. According to the law they are to take into account whether or not the proposed development will significantly affect..."*existing and potential financial capacity to reasonably accommodate both the total growth and the rate of growth otherwise expected for the town and region* which would result from the development if approved" [emphasis added]. Similar considerations are found in the land use laws of Florida (FLA. STAT. ANN. §23.00), Hawaii (HAW. REV. STAT. Title 38 §481), Minnesota (MINN. STAT. ANN. §562.381) and Oregon (OR. REV. STAT. §53.100).

As state land use laws continue to be passed on an incremental basis and as the second and more powerful of the two models dominates recent state approvals, fiscal considerations and the tool of fiscal impact analysis will also grow.

The state is, in effect, not only asking local units to be fiscally responsible in planning for the future, they are also asking that comparative analyses be performed with and without a proposed development or among land use alternatives.

State land use and economic development plans are on a par with annexations in terms of their explicitness in specification of fiscal considerations as an element of land use planning and derivative zoning.

Interpreting Enabling Legislation

Now that the legal constraints in the form of state enabling legislation have been identified, the next and perhaps the most critical step in determining the legal standing of fiscal impact considerations in land use policy is to discern the courts' interpretations of these statutes. The next half of this chapter addresses this basic question, but some general guidelines are useful here.

One prominent land use attorney provides an outline of the rules of the game used by the judicial branch. The tests used for determining the validity of a land use regulation based on the police power are:[17]

1. Any public restriction of private rights must be based upon considerations of the broad public welfare and not involve a favor to some individual or group.
2. The goal of the ordinance must be a legitimate subject for public regulation under the police power.
3. The means chosen to achieve this policy must be an appropriate way to proceed toward that goal.
4. Any regulation adopted by the appropriate agency of government is presumed to be valid except (in some states) in the case of a few specially favored activities and land uses.
5. Under the adopted regulation, a landowner must have some reasonable opportunity to derive income from it, now or in the reasonably near future.
6. A regulation does not have to permit either the best or the highest use of land.
7. Sacrifice required of the landowner must not be out of proportion to the public benefits to be derived.
8. All regulations must be clear and definite.
9. Regulations which discriminate between classes must be related to goals appropriate under the police power.
10. Appropriate regulations may be modified to some extent to facilitate administrative simplicity and convenience.

Summary

Land use regulations generally are based on the broad authorization of local government's use of the police power. Despite a lack of specific authorization for fiscal impact considerations, the language of such planning enabling legislation often appears to permit implicitly this type of analytic input. This recurs in the procedures surrounding comprehensive plans, zoning ordinances, variances, subdivision controls, planned unit developments and annexations. While planning practice will determine under which aegis fiscal impact considerations may best be applied, it is clear that there are numerous areas under which they can be used. The situations for, and exact nature of, these kinds of considerations will, however, come directly from the courts, unless legislatures amend their existing statutes and address the issue directly.

Fiscal Impact Considerations: Are They An Authorized Use of the Police Power?

Having recognized that a locality's authority to regulate land use derives from the state's delegation of the police power by means of enabling legislation, one must now review the judiciary's interpretation and application of these statutes. Only through court action can the nature and extent of this delegated authority be properly understood. Therefore, one must examine existing case law throughout the states to draw reasonable conclusions about the applicability of fiscal impact considerations as a means to plan for and control land use development.

Initially, however, a survey of the case law raises a recurring difficulty. Since the idea of basing land use policy, at least in part, on fiscal considerations is a relatively new planning endeavor, there exists little if any precedent which specifically considers the question at issue. As with much legal hypothesis and review, analogy to related concepts and phraseology is necessary. Consequently, reference may be properly directed to the fact that the basic tenet at issue, the degree to which a municipality can regulate land use within its borders on the basis of fiscal impact, has been examined within the context of fiscal zoning and exclusionary zoning cases.

Methodology

The goal of this survey was to identify existing case law that provides insight into the judicial response to the use of fiscal impact considerations as an input to land use regulations, either through its interpretation of state enabling legislation or through its scrutiny of more fundamental precepts such as the impact of exclusionary zoning. To achieve this goal, it was necessary to review the zoning decisions for each state, Washington, D.C. and Puerto Rico. Secondary sources such as the zoning treatises of Anderson and Williams were also examined.[18]

Preliminary Results

The most striking conclusion, although it was anticipated, is the predominant absence of judicial decisions addressing the issue of a municipality's ability to control land use solely on the basis of a development's local fiscal impact. Significantly, in at least twenty-two states, the case law on zoning did not address this issue.[19] Although the reasons for this finding vary, depending on the characteristics of the state and its courts, several possible explanations exist:

1. Substantial areas in many states are totally without zoning laws, so there is a relatively low volume of land use cases.
2. In many states, zoning laws are not strictly enforced.
3. Most courts still attach a presumption of validity both to zoning regulations and to the administration of such regulations.
4. Fiscal considerations will only stir controversy where growth pressures exist.
5. Lower level courts are unsophisticated and thus choose to avoid planning issues.

Implicit in these suggested explanations, however, is the assumption that they inevitably will come before the courts.[20] As zoning laws spread, as government control of individual land use decisions becomes more pervasive, as growth pressures increase, and finally, as planners and judges become more sophisticated, the issues involved will undoubtedly be closely scrutinized by those who referee the land development process.

This trend can already be discerned. Forty percent of all decisions addressing basic zoning laws were handed down in only the last five years. Litigation on related issues may also reasonably be expected to increase.

The Setting

In the courts of several states, the issue of fiscal impact as related to zoning has been considered, although even in these jurisdictions there has been only a minimal number of such decisions. Yet it is from these opinions that insight may be drawn as to the legal applicability of fiscal impact considerations as a basis for municipal land use decisions.

Our survey found that zoning cases give rise to a great variety of legal issues ranging from narrow questions of statutory interpretation to complex matters of due process and equal protection. It also found, however, that questions about fiscal impact considerations were raised primarily in one type of prototypical litigation involving property owners and the municipality.

There are two versions of this litigation. In the first situation a zoning board's decision to grant a variance in order to permit a more intense land use is challenged by nearby property owners on the basis that the resultant increased density would overburden the existing municipal facilities and therefore be harmful to the community's health and general welfare.

The second version is almost a mirror image of the first, but from the municipality's point of view. Here the property owner challenges a decision either to rezone his property for a more restricted use, or challenges a zoning board's decision to deny a variance permitting a higher density use. In either case the decision is purportedly based on the lack of adequate municipal services.

Not surprisingly, the courts throughout the country are widely split as to whether the availability of municipal services and its concomitant burdening of the tax base is a valid purpose underlying the zoning power. Of the thirty states where courts have addressed this issue, a wide divergence of opinion has emerged (including intrastate differences). The federal courts, with only a few decisions handed down, apparently affirm the validity of fiscal impact analysis.

Fiscal Impact: A Valid Consideration

The states which permit zoning decisions based on the adequacy of public facilities are: Alabama, Georgia, Washington, Tennessee, Kentucky, Ohio, North Carolina, Mississippi, Minnesota, Kansas, Connecticut, Maryland, Nebraska, New Hampshire, Louisiana and New York. In the federal courts, this view has also been endorsed. A typical decision is *Steel Hill Development Inc.* v. *Town of Sanbornton* 469F 2d 956 (1st Cir. 1972), in which the court wrote:

> We recognize, as within the general welfare, concerns relating to the construction and integration of hundreds of new homes which would. . .*pose substantial financial burdens on the town for police, fire, sewer and road service.*

Another argument which the judiciary has accepted stops short of the pronouncement in *Sanbornton* and states merely that the provision of adequate public facilities particularly with regard to water and sewerage falls within promoting the "health" component of the zoning power. The courts have tactitly approved the validity of these considerations in their refusal to question the judgment of the local board on these matters.

In an Ohio case, *Willott* v. *Village of Beachwood*,[21] which denied a challenge to the validity of a zoning amendment to permit a shopping center, the court asks:

> where the council of a municipality makes a determination of land use policy which involves the control of traffic, the burden of traffic. . ., the municipal revenue which will be produced for the city, and the land use consistent with the best interests of the general welfare and prosperity and development of the community as a whole, does the court have the authority to invalidate such an ordinance in the absence of a showing that such power has been exercised in such an arbitrary, confiscatory and unreasonable manner as to be in violation of constitutional guarantees?

Its answer is that "the courts are without authority to interfere." See also, *Hukle* v. *City of Kansas City,* 512 P2d 457 (1973).

One of the more recent and most publicized cases which approved the use of zoning based in part on the availability of public services was the New York Case of *Golden* v. *Planning Board of the Town of Ramapo.*[22] The highest court in New York upheld the validity of a zoning ordinance which tied future residential development to the availability of public facilities as determined by an eighteen-year capital budget plan. The court accepted the underlying purpose of the ordinance: "to phase residential development to the town's ability to provide the facilities or services." Fiscal impact considerations were the major items upon which the decision turned. A similar attempt at capital facilities phasing in Petaluma, California, was sustained on appeal, again due to the presence of fiscal impact documentation.

Fiscal Impact: Not a Valid Consideration

Among the states in which there are significant rulings prohibiting the consideration of the adequacy of public facilities or its impact on the tax base are Michigan, California, Colorado, Missouri, Virginia, Pennsylvania, Florida, Washington, D.C., Nevada, Massachusetts, Illinois and Arkansas. The courts have accepted two distinct arguments as the logic for invalidating zoning determinations based on these economic considerations. In the first set of holdings the courts have reasoned that the unavailability of municipal services, while definitely a public concern, should be dealt with by powers other than those of land use regulations. In the Maryland case of *Crowther, Inc.* v. *Johnson,*[23] for example, while upholding a denial of a special permit for a mobile home park, the court stated that "the health threat could not in itself preclude the appellant from acquiring the special permit. . .; any problem [as to] a health hazard could easily be alleviated and controlled by the Health Department authorities."[24]

An equally strong pronouncement limiting use of the zoning power was handed down by the Pennsylvania Supreme Court in the case of *National Land and Investment* v. *Easttown Twp.*[25] The court held unconstitutional a four acre minimum lot requirement for single family residential development. It stated, "A zoning ordinance whose primary purpose is to prevent the entrance of newcomers in order to avoid future burdens, economic and otherwise, upon the administration of public services and facilities can not be held valid." Hence, in this fashion, the courts have linked the question of fiscal zoning with the complexities inherent in the question of exclusionary land use regulation. The reasoning of *National Land* has surfaced in decisions in several other state courts: Washington, D.C., Virginia, Nebraska, Rhode Island, and Michigan. Control of the rate of growth by withholding public utilities to outlying areas has also been disapproved. See *Robinson* v. *Boulder,* 547 P. 2d 228 (Colo. 1976).

Moreover, in both New Jersey and Rhode Island a third aspect of this problem has arisen.[26] For, although the courts there have indicated that fiscal zoning may not be utilized to stabilize the tax rate (i.e. by overzoning for industry), the question has been left open as to whether a zoning board could properly consider, among other elements, a project's impact on the municipality's ability to provide utilities and services to its present and prospective citizenry. Thus, in these decisions, the applicability of fiscal impact analysis has not been totally foreclosed.

The New Jersey Story

The question of the degree to which the zoning power implicitly authorizes the examination of fiscal impact can be traced most clearly in New Jersey. As fiscal impact considerations more regularly become part of the local planning process their role is increasingly narrowed. In 1959, in rebuking a challenge to a revised zoning ordinance, the court in the case of *Ward* v. *Township of Montgomery* held that

> . . .the conclusion is inescapable that the township was hungry for tax revenue. Manifestly, its fiscal picture was such that a new source of income would serve the general economic welfare. Pursuit of that objective was entirely worthy of the attention of the municipal fathers.

This decision underwent a slight modification three years later when the court, in *Gruber* v. *Mayor and Township Commission of Raritan Township,* approved a reclassification of land use from residential to nonresidential. The court cited as its justification that this type of fiscal zoning was duly authorized by the state enabling act when *"done reasonably as part of and in furtherance of a legitimate comprehensive plan for the zoning of the entire municipality."* [Emphasis added.]

The New Jersey courts thus guardedly sanctioned municipal consideration of a project's fiscal implications. Yet, this judicial language was so inexact as to leave doubt concerning the extent to which fiscal considerations were "in furtherance of a legitimate comprehensive plan." It did not answer the question as to whether a proposed development could be denied primarily because of its effect on the local tax base, or due to its need for additional utilities and services. Essentially, the right to consider a project's fiscal impact was sustained, but the scope of this power remained undefined. This latter element of the problem was the next to be addressed by the New Jersey courts.

In the first lower court decision in *Oakwood at Madison, Inc.* v. *Township of Madison,* however, the court attempted to define the scope of this power. The court issued a forceful denunciation of exclusionary zoning. Among its concerns was the question of fiscal zoning:

> The underlying objective of the ordinance under attack was fiscal zoning, zoning as a device to avoid school construction and other governmental costs incident to population expansion. Housing needs of the region were not taken into consideration in its enactment, according to several members of the township council and planning board.
>
> Fiscal zoning *per se* is irrelevant to the statutory purpose of zoning. But the Supreme Court in *Gruber v. Mayor, etc., Raritan Tp.,* 39 N.J. 1,9(1962), recognized that "alleviating the tax burden and the harmful school conjestion" was a permissible zoning purpose if done reasonably and in furtherance of a comprehensive zoning plan. *Gruber* and the antecedent *Newark, etc., Cream Corp.* v. *Parsippany-Troy Hills Twp.,* 47 N.J. Super. 306 (Law Div. 1957), may be distinguished because they dealt with the pursuit of tax revenues through zoning for new industry, not the stabilization of the tax rate through zoning to exclude new low and moderate income housing.
>
> In any event, the Madison Township zoning ordinance must stand or fall not as fiscal zoning. The test must be whether it promotes a reasonably balanced and well ordered plan for the entire municipality.[27]

The court, therefore, implied that fiscal considerations may be deemed valid if their focus is to provide zoning districts for industrial growth. *But, by way of subtle distinction, the court further implied that such zoning for industry, and therefore for tax revenues, cannot have the effect of excluding housing.* Such a result, the court implied, would not be in furtherance of a legitimate comprehensive plan. The same court's most recent decision in *Urban League of New Brunswick* v. *Borough of Carteret,* 142 N.J. Super. 11 (Land Div. 1976), upholds this principle. If a municipality zones for industry, it must also zone for housing to accommodate a fair share of the present and prospective employees.

To zone for industry, then, to attract tax ratables is permissible. But, to zone to exclude housing, by overzoning for industry, and then base this latter policy on insuring a stable local fiscal posture, is not permitted.

Significantly, the New Jersey Supreme Court has emphasized this point:

> We have previously held that a developing municipality may properly zone for and seek industrial ratables to create a better economic balance for the community vis-a-vis educational and governmental costs engendered by residential development, provided that such was "done reasonably as part of and in furtherance of a legitimate comprehensive plan for the zoning of the entire municipality." *Gruber* v. *Mayor and Township Commission of Raritan Township,* 39 N.J. 1, 9–11 (1962). We adhere to that view today. *But we were not there concerned with, and did not pass upon, the validity of municipal exclusion by zoning of types of housing and kinds of people for the same local financial end* [emphasis

added]. We have no hesitancy in now saying, and do so emphatically, that, considering the basic importance of the opportunity for appropriate housing for all classes of our citizenry, *no municipality may exclude or limit categories of housing for that reason or purpose* [emphasis added]. While we fully recognize the increasingly heavy burden of local taxes for municipal governmental and school costs on homeowners, relief from the consequences of this tax system will have to be furnished by other branches of government. It cannot legitimately be accomplished by restricting types of housing through the zoning process in developing municipalities. *Certainly when a municipality zones for industry and commerce for local tax benefit purposes, it without question must zone to permit adequate housing within the means of the employees involved in such uses* [emphasis added]. The amount of land removed from residential use by allocation to industrial and commercial purposes must be reasonably related to the present and future potential for such purposes. In other words, such municipalities must zone primarily for the living welfare of people and not for the benefit of the local tax rate. *So. Burlington Co. N.A.A.C.P. v. Mt. Laurel Tp., 67 N.J.* 151, 184, 186, 187, 188 (1975).[28]

The state Supreme Court has also dealt with additional similarly complex facets of the fiscal zoning issue. In affirming the lower court decision in *Oakwood, supra,* for example, the Supreme Court expressly reviewed the relationship between certain fiscal impact considerations and the validity of zoning based on them [72 N.J. 481 (1977)]. Specifically, a developer and several individual plaintiffs had challenged the township's zoning ordinance, alleging it to be exclusionary and invalid under the precepts of *So. Burlington County N.A.A.C.P. v. Mt. Laurel Tp.,* 67 N.J. 151, app. dim. & cert. den. 423 U.S. 808, 96 S. Ct. 18, 46 L. Ed 2d 2028 (1975). Among plaintiffs' contentions was the claim that the requirements for planned unit development in the township had an exclusionary effect.

The ordinance required that a PUD developer provide roads, water, and sewerage facilities. The area zoned for PUD, however, was two miles removed from existing utilities. (72 N.J. 521). The PUD developer was required to extend these existing facilities so as to reach and service the PUD. The Court noted that:

> the record clearly shows that the sites were deliberately chosen in order to force the PUD developers and their customers to carry the burden of developing these remote areas. The township planner testified that the 'decision was made that two PUDs would be the incentive to complete and bring around the water system. . .to provide a main system that would rationally service one-third of the township.' (72 N.J. 522)

Based on these proofs, the court determined that such provisions "add sufficiently to final costs as to tend to have an exclusionary impact." Since the township could not justify such requirements, these provisions were invalid pursuant to the principles of *Mt. Laurel, supra* (72 N.J. 522, 523). The municipality was therefore directed to (1) eliminate the requirements or revise them so they would not be exclusionary; (2) require proportionate donation by other property holders; or (3) relocate these on PUD tracts nearer to utility hookups.

Essentially, the township's PUD requirements reflected complex fiscal impact considerations — how to locate the PUD so the necessary utility installation and road development would benefit the entire community. The most significant portion of the Supreme Court's *Oakwood* decision, therefore, as regards fiscal impact considerations, is that the subtle, fiscally-related technique of site selection through zoning is not permissible if it has an exclusionary effect and cannot otherwise be justified by the municipality, i.e., no other available land.

The New Jersey courts have rendered a series of decisions limiting a municipality's ability to zone for fiscal reasons. From their early affirmation of a municipality's relative freedom to apply fiscal reasoning, through their reliance on the statutory requirements of rational planning, to their recognition of the complex ethical implications of fiscal impact considerations, New Jersey courts have confronted and attempted to answer many of the questions associated with the legality of fiscal impact considerations. Zoning based on fiscal well-being may be considered locally, but it may be neither the sole basis for zoning nor a means for individual exclusion.

Summary

The review of the case law throughout the states leads unavoidably to the realization that the legal acceptability of land use controls to promote fiscal stability on a national scale is in various stages of acceptance. In many jurisdictions, the issue is novel, never having been considered. Other courts expressly declare such considerations to be appropriate. Some states permit these deliberations to serve as one among several bases for local land use decision making. Several additional jurisdictions would permit fiscal considerations to serve as an element in the decision-making process, but only in determining the weight of evidence regarding the overall reasonableness of a proposal for development. Finally, in several states, including New Jersey, Pennsylvania and Michigan, fiscal considerations as an input to zoning are frowned upon. Here the issue involves constitutional implications concerning a municipality's power to exclude "newcomers," including low and moderate income persons, from its borders.

Essentially, therefore, the answer may ultimately be found in the validity of fiscal impact considerations as a planning endeavor. For if the value of fiscal impact considerations can be demonstrated and their relationship to planning established, then one may anticipate increasingly wider judicial affirmation as a reasonable component of responsible land use control. In any case there are two fronts on which the issue will be fought and these are the focus of the previous material. Knowledge of the issues involved in both areas is of vital importance to planning practitioners and elected officials who are concerned with the complex task of incorporating fiscal responsibility into local land use policy.

NOTES

1. *Euclid* v. *Ambler,* 272 U.S. 365 (1926).
2. Norman Williams, "The Future of Land Use Controls" in *Future Land Use,* eds. Robert W. Burchell and David Listokin (New Brunswick, N.J.: Rutgers University, Center for Urban Policy Research, 1975), p.30.
3. See *Green* v. *Twp. of Lima,* 40 Mich. App. 655 (1972); *Snookler* v. *Twp. of Wheatfield,* 46 Mich. App. 162 (1973); *National Land and Investment Co.* v. *Kohn,* 419 Pa. 504 (1965); *Twp. of Williston* v. *Chesterdale Farms, Inc.,* 7 Pa. Commonwealth 453 (1973), aff'd. 462 Pa. 445 (1975); Appeal of *Girsch,* 437 Pa. 237 (1970).
4. See *Southern Burlington Co. N.A.A.C.P.* v. *Mt. Laurel Tp.,* 67 N.J. 151 (1975); *Oakwood at Madison* v. *Madison Twp.,* 117 N.J. Super. 11, 18 (Law Div. 1971), on remand, 128 N.J. Super. 438, aff'd 72 N.J. 481 (1977); *Town of Gloucester* v. *Divio's Mobile Home Ct., Inc.,* 111 R.I. 120 (1973).
5. Standard State Zoning Enabling Act, §.3.
6. ALASKA STAT. §29.33.085; DEL. CODE ANN. Title 22, §702 et seq.; GA. CODE ANN. §69-802; KAN. STAT. ANN. §12-704; ME. REV. STAT. ANN. Title 30, §4952; MINN. STAT. ANN. §462.355 (West); MISS. CODE ANN. §28905, §3374-123; OKLA. STAT. ANN. Title 11, §423 (West); OR. REV. STAT. §227.090; PA. STAT. ANN. Title 53, §12129 (Purdon); S.D. COMPILED LAWS ANN. §11-6-14; TEX. CIV. CODE ANN. Title 28, §1011m.; UTAH CODE ANN. §10-9-20; WASH. REV. CODE ANN. §35.63.100.
7. ARIZ. REV. STAT. §9-461; ARK. STAT. ANN. §19-2827; CAL. GOV'T CODE §65301 et seq. (West); HAW. REV. STAT. Title 13, §201-23; ILL. ANN. STAT. Chp. 24, §11-12-5 (Smith-Hurd); IND. CODE ANN. §18-7-5-32 (Burns); MASS. ANN. LAWS Chp. 41, §81D (Michie-Law Co-op); N.Y. TOWN LAWS §272-a (McKinney); OHIO REV. CODE ANN. §713.02 (Dage's); D.C. CODE §1-163; P.R. LAW'S ANN. Title 23, §8.
8. ALA. CODE Title 27, §791; CONN. GEN. STAT. ANN. §8-23 (West); FLA. STAT. ANN. §163.160 (West); IDAHO CODE §67-6502; IOWA CODE ANN. §368.7; KY. REV. STAT. ANN. §100.83 (Baldwin); LSA-R.S. §33:106; MD. Art. 66B CODE ANN. §3.05; MICH. STAT. ANN. §5.2996 (West); MO. ANN. STAT. §89.340 (Vernon) or V.A.M.S. §89.340; MONT. REV. CODES ANN. §11-38.01; NEB. REV. STAT. 19-903; NEV. REV. STAT. §278.150; N.H. REV. STAT. ANN. §36:13; N.J.S.A. §40:55-1.10 et

seq.; N.M. STAT. ANN. §14-8-9; N.C. GEN. STAT. §160A-360; N.D. GEN. STAT. §40-48-08; R.I. GEN. LAWS §45-22-6; S.C. CODE §5-3-40; TENN. CODE ANN. §13-503; VT. STAT. ANN. Title 24, §4382; VA. CODE §15.1-446.1; W.VA. CODE §8-24-16; WIS. STAT. ANN. §62.23 (West); WYO. STAT. §15.1-73.

9. IDAHO CODE §67-6502; V.A.M.S. §89-340; VA. CODE §15.1-446.1.

10. N.J.S.A. 40:550-1.10 et seq.; N.J.S.A. 40:55d-2(e)(f)(m).

11. See, for example, *National Land and Investment Company v. Kohn* 419 Pa. 504 (1965), where the Court states: "Zoning is a means by which a governmental body can plan for the future — it may not be used as a means to deny the future."

12. P.R. LAWS ANN. Title 23, §627.

13. NEV. REV. STAT. §280A.010; KAN. STAT. ANN. §12-725; PA. STAT. ANN. Title 53, §10711 [Purdon] CONN. GEN. STAT. ANN. §8-13b [West]; IDAHO CODE §67-6515; COLO. REV. STAT. §24-67-101; N.J.S.A. §40:55-54 et seq.; VT. STAT. ANN. Title 24, §4407.

14. See also *Divan Bldg. v. Wayne Tp.*, 66 N.J. 582 (1975).

15. ALA. CODE Title 27, §154; ARK. STAT. ANN. §19-317; FLA. STAT. ANN. §171.021 [West]; COLO. REV. STAT. §31-8-102; IND. CODE ANN. §18-5-10-21 [Burns]; MD. Art. 23A CODE ANN. §19; MISS. CODE ANN. §3374-10; MO. ANN. STAT. §71.015; N.C. GEN. STAT. §160-453.3; MONT. REV. CODES ANN. §11-514; NEB. REV. STAT. §16-117; NEV. REV. STAT. §268.596; N.M. STAT. ANN. §14-7-1; N.D. GEN. STAT. §40-51.1-01 et seq.; S.C. CODE 5-3-40; TENN. CODE ANN. §6-310; VA. CODE §15.1-1032 et seq.; WYO. STAT. §15.1-54.

16. Council of State Governments (COG), Lexington, Kentucky, *Land: State Alternatives for Planning and Management* (Lexington, Ky.: COG, 1975), pp. 10-11, Figure 1.

17. Norman Williams, *American Land Planning Law* (Chicago: Callaghan & Company, 1974), Volume 1.

18. Norman Williams, *American Land Planning Law;* Robert M. Anderson, *American Law of Zoning: Zoning, Planning, Subdivision Control;* (Rochester, N.Y.: Lawyers Cooperative Publishing Company, 1968), 4 Volumes.

19. These states were Alaska, Arizona, Wyoming, West Virginia, Utah, Oregon, Vermont, Texas, Iowa, Montana, Delaware, Indiana, Hawaii, Idaho, Oklahoma, New Mexico, Maine, N. Dakota and S. Dakota, S. Carolina, Wisconsin and Puerto Rico.

20. See, for example: *Cedar-Riverside Environmental Defense Fund et al. v. Hills,* 422 F. Supp. 294 (D. Minn. 1976), wherein the environmental impact statement for a high-rise, high-density project was invalidated due, in part, to its failure to analyze governmental revenue increases resulting from this type of development (as opposed to lower density alternatives). See also *Construction Industry Association, Sonoma County v. City of Petaluma,* 552 F. 2d 897, cert. den. 424 U.S. 934, 96 S. Ct. 1148, 47 L. Ed. 2d 342).

21. 175 Ohio St. 447 (1964).

22. 324 N.Y.S. 2d 178 (1971) revised 30 N.Y. 2d 559 (1972), cert. denied 409 U.S. 1003 (1972). *Construction Industry Association of Sonoma County v. City of Petaluma,* 522 F. 2d 897 (9th Cir. 1975), cert. denied, 424 U.S. 934 (1976).

23. 225 Md. 379, 384 (1961).

24. See also: *Sundance Hill Homeowners Assoc. v. Bd. of Commissioners,* 188 Col. 321 (1975).

25. 419 Pa. 504, 532 (1966).

26. *So. Burlington Co. N.A.A.C.P. v. Mt. Laurel Tp.,* 67 N.J. 151 (1975); *Town of Gloucester v. Divio's Mobile Home Ct., Inc.* 111 R.I. 120 (1973).

27. 39 N.J. 1, 9 (1962) 117 N.J. Super 11, 18 (Law Div. 1971), aff'd. 72 N.J. 481 (1977), on remand 128 N.J. Super. 438 (Law Div. 1974).

28. In a footnote the court also stated:

> This case does not properly present the question of whether a developing municipality may time its growth and, if so, how. See, e.g., *Golden v. Planning Board of the Town of Ramapo,* 30 N.Y. 2d 359, 334 N.Y.S. 2d 138, 285 N.E. 2d 291 (1972), appeal dismissed 409 U.S. 1003, 93 S. Ct. 436, 440, 34 L. Ed. 2d 294 (1972); *Construction Industry Association of Sonoma County v. City of Petaluma,* 375 F. Supp. 574 (N.D. Cal. 1974), appeal pending (citation of these cases is not intended to indicate either agreement or disagreement with their conclusions). We now say only that, assuming some type of timed growth is permissible, it cannot be utilized as an exclusionary device or to stop all further development and must include early provision for low and moderate income housing.

12

FIELD EXPERIENCE: FISCAL IMPACT ANALYSIS IN THE UNITED STATES

Fiscal impact analyses are by no means a new phenomenon. As reported by Ruth Mace, in a now classic literature summary, fiscal impact analyses have been a part of the planning profession for over forty years.[1] Planners first employed this type of evaluation in the early 1930s' public housing efforts to justify the replacement of obviously deteriorated housing due to negative local fiscal effects.[2] In the early 1940s it was used in the urban renewal process to demonstrate the local fiscal advantages of the new land use which would replace the old.[3] During the 1950s it was employed during the massive suburbanization movement to gauge the impact of single-family homes on the local school district.[4] In the 1960s, supported by HUD 701 planning assistance funding, it was used to evaluate the economic effects of the master plan.[5] Also during this period there was evidence of a quest for fiscal stability of declining areas through annexation of peripheral growing jurisdictions. Fiscal impact analysis was sought to weigh the cost versus revenues of annexation to both jurisdictions.[6] During the 1970s the technique emerged as an almost universal large scale development accompaniment — either volunteered by the developer or required by the municipality.[7] This period also bore witness to the rise of fiscal impact models reflecting the growth of regional government and the need of these jurisdictions and their inclusive localities for a fiscal impact approach which would replicate a simple calculation numerous times — the basic role of a computer assisted strategy. The history of fiscal impact analysis is reflected in the nature of post-1970 fiscal impact studies. The bulk of the studies, influenced by the two most recent "eras," are concerned with evaluating the effects of either development proposals or alternative land use plans. Fewer studies are concerned with the fiscal consequences of public housing or the economic effects of alternative urban renewal proposals.

In terms of methodological emphases, the early periods (1930s, 1940s, 1950s) were characterized by almost exclusive use of the Case Study. The Service Standard approach, whose origins date to the time-motion studies of the 1940s, has been used sporadically in fiscal impact analysis since that time. The Per Capita Multiplier and Proportional Valuation Methods originated in the mid-1960s and continue strong today. The Comparable City and Employment Anticipation methods are the product of the mid-1970s and have little or no field experience.

In an effort to obtain a better feeling for local practice, over 21,000 requests for information about studies conducted in their jurisdiction were sent to planners, developers and planning program administrators throughout the country. From this mailing approximately 140 cost-revenue studies were selected from slightly over 200 replies. The selected studies represent a national sample of fiscal impact analyses completed over the period 1970 to 1976. It is from this sample that the following description of current practice is drawn.

This chapter's analysis of current practice concentrates on the last and most active period of fiscal impact growth. It provides both an overview of cost-revenue experience as well as a glimpse at the state of the art of fiscal analysis of this period. The text first considers the focus of fiscal impact analyses and the application of specific cost-revenue methods within the context of these substantive concerns. Second, there is a summary of where fiscal impact analyses have been undertaken nationally with an emphasis on geographical, fiscal and legal context. Next, the scope and sophistication of the analyses are examined. Finally, the section explores the reactions of sponsors of fiscal impact analyses to determine their level of satisfaction and overall evaluation of the analyses conducted within their jurisdictions.

Fiscal Impact Analysis: Use and Method Application

For What is Fiscal Impact Analysis Used?

Exhibit 12-1 details the focus of cost-revenue studies and the differing popularity of various projection strategies. Obviously there are multiple substantive concerns of fiscal impact analyses. Fiscal impact studies are undertaken in conjunction with general fiscal planning and budgeting efforts, others concern the cost versus revenues of annexations or municipal boundary changes, while still other investigations do not focus on a particular case but rather attempt to improve the state of the art by summarizing trends or suggesting refinements to existing procedures and data resources. For the most part these applications of the procedure or its refinements are atypical, however. *Fiscal impact analysis is most often used to assess the economic impact of either residential/mixed use development proposals or land use alternatives.* About two-thirds of the investigations undertaken over the most recent period fall into these latter two categories (see Exhibit 12-1). And the core of current practitioner concern is new, typically suburban and exurban development rather than redevelopment strategies or proposals in the center city. Some examples include the Abt Associates' evaluation of high-rise development in Boston (Mass.) [001],* the Barton-Aschman study of alternative single family development strategies in Barrington (Ill.) [013] and the University of California and Rutgers University planned unit development studies in Fremont (CA.) [126] and East Windsor (N.J.) [109], respectively.

Fiscal impact review is identified with the more complex development types. The practitioner is most frequently called upon to evaluate combined residential-nonresidential development of various forms. (See Exhibit 12-1). Studies of solely single-family or industrial/commercial facilities are relatively rare though projections of the impact of apartment developments (residential and nonresidential) or alternative scenarios of residential versus nonresidential development are increasing in number. These patterns reflect the preponderance of residential over nonresidential development proposals as well as a methodological bias which seems to concentrate effort on the local impact of residential rather than nonresidential land uses. This tendency is related to the assumption that nonresidential uses do not directly affect school district costs.

---

*Numbers in brackets refer to the identification number of the study as reported in the detailed matrix annotation in Appendix 2.

EXHIBIT 12-1
SUBJECT, JURISDICTIONAL FOCUS, METHOD, LAND USE TYPE, AND LAND USE FORM ANALYZED

Subject	Number	Percent	Jurisdictional Focus	Number	Percent	Method	Number	Percent
Residential/Mixed Use Proposal	38	27.9	Local	98	72.1	Per Capita Multiplier	39	28.7
Land Use Alternatives	44	32.4	County	34	25.0	Case Study	20	14.7
Zone Variance or Rezoning	7	5.1	Regional	1	0.7	Per Capita Multiplier/Case Study	23	16.9
Annexation or Boundary Change	10	7.4	State	3	2.2	Service Standard	7	5.1
Fiscal Planning/Budgeting	17	12.5				Proportional Valuation	3	2.2
Redevelopment/Public Facility	7	5.1				Model/Regression	2	1.5
Method/Procedural Guide	13	9.6				Multiple Methods	42	30.9
Total	136	100.0		136	100.0		136	100.0

Land Use Type	Number	Percent	Land Use Form	Number	Percent
Single Family Residential	7	5.1	Standard Subdivision Site Plan	92	67.6
Multifamily Residential	12	8.8	PUD/New Community	30	22.1
Single Family and Multifamily Residential	22	16.2	Retirement/Vacation Homes	5	3.7
Industrial/Commercial	12	8.8	Mobile Homes	4	2.9
Residential & Nonresidential	52	38.2	Multiple Alternatives	5	3.7
Multiple Alternatives	31	22.8			
Total	136	100.0		136	100.0

Source: Rutgers University Center for Urban Policy Research, Field Survey, Spring 1976.

Further, fiscal impact studies most often consider standard development patterns. About two-thirds of the current field experience considers traditional single family subdivisions or multifamily site plans, i.e., the 100 unit tract development on a rectangular grid, the garden apartment complex at six units to the acre, etc. Again, due to their propensity, these are the type of development modes that occasion requests for fiscal impact analysis and thus form the bulk of the activity for the public planner or private consultant. New towns, planned unit developments, cluster developments or specialized housing (singles complexes, retirement communities, condominiums, mobile home parks, etc.), while frequently occasioning fiscal impact analyses, represent such a small proportion of current development that analysis of these development types also represent only a minor share of the aggregate analyses.

What Fiscal Impact Analysis Methods Are Used?

Exhibit 12-1 also shows which fiscal impact analysis methods are more widely used. The practitioner must bear in mind that the universe of methods considered here does not include either the Comparable City or the Employment Anticipation Methods. These are essentially new techniques introduced to field practice for the first time in this Handbook. The Per Capita Multiplier approach is the single most popular strategy; it is used several times more often than any other individual method. This technique is simple to use, easy to understand and can quickly be implemented, factors which provide an explanation of why it is often the first choice of both private and public practitioners. Next in usage is the Case Study, followed by the Service Standard approach. The former is attractive for the extreme local insight it yields and because it is one of the few approaches which relates cost analysis to existing concentrations of excess or deficient service capacity; the latter strategy has not seen a great deal of field use due to the impracticability of amassing detailed standards for the multiple categories of local public services.

Exhibit 12-1 further reveals the extent to which methods are combined to perform analyses. Fully 30 percent of the extant analyses used two or more methods, while an additional 17 percent opted for the specific joint application of the Per Capita Multiplier and Case Study approaches. The Ann Arbor (MI) Growth Study [007] for instance, employed jointly the Per Capita Multiplier, Case Study and Service Standard techniques while the Quincy (MA) projection of the economic impact of residential development [101] relied on a Per Capita Multiplier/Case Study combination. Why the popularity of the multiple approaches? Comprehensive coverage of a diverse development proposal or choosing among one of several land use alternatives are the types of situations which may demand the employment of more than one technique. The Per Capita Multiplier Method may be used for the residential portion of a mixed use development; the Proportional Valuation Method for the nonresidential segment. Garden apartments, as one zoning alternative for a locale, may be evaluated with the Service Standard Method; a shopping center for the same tract of land may be used further as a means of sorting or prioritizing development strategies. The Ann Arbor Growth Study [007] mentioned above used the Per Capita Multiplier Method to yield a rough prediction of the cost consequences of several potential growth alternatives. After this initial shift, the growth strategies that were most realistic in terms of fiscal impact were then examined in detail via Case Study and Service Standard approaches.

In-depth analysis of current field applications evidences a definite pairing of specific fiscal impact methods with different types of fiscal impact tasks. For instance, residential or mixed use development proposals and land use alternative problems are evaluated most frequently via the Per Capita Multiplier technique. This method's cost and time benefits make it ideal for the arduous fiscal impact task of undertaking the multiple calculations associated with the land use alternative problem or the detailed calculations of a single, large scale development.

The Case Study Method is a key approach for the redevelopment studies or new public facilities as well as for atypical nonresidential development. The Fleck/Sterling analysis of the Hampton

(VA) convention center [038] and the HOK Associates study of the feasibility of a downtown mall in Midland (MI) [051] are examples of the former. The nonresidential impact analysis completed by personnel from the Urban Institute for Albemarle County (VA) [129] and a similar analysis undertaken by the Pasadena Research Institute for Carson (CA) [093] are examples of the latter. The Case Study is sensitive to the slack capacity found in many communities undertaking redevelopment and can ultimately yield more accurate predictions of the impact of change in such environments. The unique service demands of the one-of-a-kind public facility, e.g., convention center, sports complex, coliseum, etc., can only be handled through this kind of detailed, site specific examination. The Proportional Valuation strategy is another cost prediction technique of reasonable field experience. It is most frequently used for impact projections of nonresidential uses where first approximations are the acceptable level of tolerance, i.e., typically those situations where financial constraints do not permit the detailed view of the Case Study (see Barton Aschman Associates' Tax Impact Study for Dupage County (IL) [020]).

The Service Standard Method is often used for general fiscal planning and budgeting, because it provides an estimate of overall impact as well as public personnel hiring needs by service function. This service disaggregation is crucial for the local budget officer or city manager who is directly concerned with correctly allocating limited public resources to future demands on public services. The Service Standard strategy is also used in the examination of large scale annexation proposals (or land use alternatives) where data on the projected housing types are sufficiently incomplete (i.e., lacks type and size of future residential accommodations) that demographic multipliers and per capita costs are inappropriate and rather service personnel commitments per 1,000 population are the more appropriate measures of future service costs (see Booz, Allen Hamilton study of alternative growth plans for Tucson (AZ) [022]).

Fiscal Impact Analysis:
Geographic, Fiscal and Legal Context

Regional Incidence of Cost-Revenue Analysis

Exhibit 12–2 reveals a fairly even distribution among the Northeastern, North Central, Southern and Western regions of the country. Estimating the costs of future development is becoming a local priority in most regions of the country. There are slight differences in regional emphases however, due, for the most part, to variation in ongoing land use activity. Annexation evaluations are concentrated primarily in the West and North Central regions (see studies [058], [060], [062], [069], [096], [120], [123], and [131]). Also in the West, perhaps because of recurring efforts to channel and control population movement (for example, the Petaluma and Boulder growth plans, etc.) there is a growing emphasis on fiscal impact analysis which dealt with the economic implications of alternative land uses. Redevelopment cost-revenue projections are most frequently found in the Northeast and North Central regions (see studies [008], [051], [088] and [118]); these areas also have proportionally more fiscal impact analyses related to special exceptions and rezoning petitions. Finally, in the North Central region, there is a slight emphasis on fiscal impact analysis for favoring of planning and budgeting purposes.

While there is a fairly even distribution of fiscal impact incidence *among* regions, *within* regions most analyses are conducted in several key states. In the Northeast, New Jersey and Pennsylvania dominate; in the South, Virginia, Maryland and Florida; in the North Central region, Illinois and Michigan; finally in the West, California and Colorado. The following circumstances help to explain why activity is concentrated in these areas:

1. Most of the states, especially New Jersey, Virginia and California are growth nuclei within their respective regions.

EXHIBIT 12-2
GEOGRAPHICAL AND FISCAL CONTEXT

Region	Number	Percent		1970 Population Base	Number	Percent		Annual 1960-1970 Growth Rate	Number	Percent
Northeast	27	19.9		<10,000	17	12.5		Decline	11	8.1
North Central	30	22.1		10,000–24,999	20	14.7		0–2%	57	41.9
South	37	27.2		25,000–49,999	18	13.2		3–4%	23	16.9
West	35	25.7		50,000–99,999	26	19.1		5–6%	20	14.7
Canada	3	2.2		100,000–499,999	27	19.9		7% and over	21	15.4
Not Applicable	4	2.9		500,000 and over	24	17.6		Not applicable	4	2.9
				Not applicable	4	2.9				
Total	136	100.0		Total	136	100.0		Total	136	100.0

School District Revenue Sources*	Number	Percent		Municipal Revenue Sources*	Number	Percent		Case Law	Number	Percent
Over 50% from local taxes	33	24.3		Over 40% from property taxes	18	13.2		Limited case law permits fiscal impact	16	11.8
Over 50% from state aid	14	10.3		Over 20% from sales and gross receipts	14	10.3		Limited case law prohibits fiscal impact	36	26.5
Over 10% from federal aid	12	8.8		Over 10% from other taxes	9	6.6		Significant case law permits fiscal impact	22	16.2
				Over 15% from other revenue	21	15.4		Significant case law prohibits fiscal impact	44	32.4
				Over 15% from inter-governmental transfer	15	11.0		No case law	14	10.3
								Not applicable	4	2.9
Total	—	—			—	—			136	100.0

*No response to this information subset is possible; 136 is the base upon which percentages are tabulated so columns do not add to 136 or 100 percent.

Source: Rutgers University Center for Urban Policy Research, Field Survey, Spring 1976.

2. Growth in these jurisdictions is supported by local taxes; therefore, citizens are more aware of the fiscal impacts of population change.
3. There are many small local units of government, thereby heightening the competition for "profitable" versus "unprofitable" land uses.
4. Fiscal impact analyses beget more fiscal impact analyses; completing one analysis stimulates demand for others.

Fiscal Impact Analysis and Local/County Community Characteristics

The focus of fiscal impact analyses in about 75 percent of the cases is local impact — the dollar effect on the municipality and/or local school district (Exhibit 12-1). An additional 25 percent of the current studies have a county orientation. They are often undertaken only in rural or agricultural areas where the smallest governing body providing public services is the county, or in areas of the United States where counties have strong growth management policies desires (such as Virginia, Maryland and California).

As shown in Exhibit 12-2 fiscal impact analyses are conducted in a variety of size areas ranging from under 10,000 to over 500,000. Localities interested in fiscal impact analyses most frequently fall in the 10,000 to 25,000 size category while counties are found in the larger 100,000 to 500,000 population cohorts. The types of analyses undertaken in various jurisdictions often parallel the size of the areas. Development proposals are most often clustered in the smaller jurisdictions. Land use alternative analyses are more common in municipalities of 25,000-50,000 population which are still growing or in similarly growing counties of 500,000 to 1,000,000 population. Public facility analyses are found in mid size to larger communities (i.e., 50,000-100,000); redevelopment proposals are concentrated in the largest cities — those of 500,000 population or more.

Fiscal impact analyses are conducted most frequently in those local/county jurisdictions that are growing the fastest and those that must bear the fiscal consequences of such growth directly. Almost one-third of current fiscal impact practice takes place in areas whose population is increasing at a rate of 50 to 70 percent per decade; twice as many fiscal impact analyses are undertaken in areas where school costs are paid mostly from local taxes than in those areas where the county or state has assumed this role.

Exurban and rural fringe areas are confronted by the largest number of development proposals, many of which require either initial zoning or a more appropriate rezoning to reflect the current situation. Besieged by growth proposals and spiraling costs, the fast growth jurisdictions turn to fiscal impact analysis as a way to forestall growth, to provide time to monitor better and channel local expenditures. The Nicholas and Blowers study of the Marco Island Development (FL) [083] and the Hammer, Siler and George study of Cherokee Village (AZ) [047] are classic analyses of proposed developments for undeveloped areas. Declining or static population jurisdictions, in contrast, experience much less cause for cost-revenue projections for, by definition, they exhibit minimal population or employment increases; and in addition, can often rely on existing service slack to accommodate an isolated incoming project (see for instance the Carr study for the Washington (D.C.) West End Plan [088]).

The burden of paying for public services also helps determine the incidence of fiscal impact analyses; the heavier the local burden, the more frequent the fiscal impact projection. The closer and more obvious the responsibility of paying for future growth the greater the local cost-revenue consciousness. This is a prime reason why fiscal impact analysis is so entrenched in New Jersey and Illinois which traditionally have called upon local units of government to pay their own way. In Hawaii and North Carolina, most public costs are paid directly by the state and fiscal impact analysis is a novelty.

Fiscal Impact Analysis and the Legal Environment

As discussed in the chapter on General Applicability, there is an evolving case law influencing where and how fiscal impact considerations will be allowed to affect land use policy. Exhibit 12-2 shows that about 60 percent of the fiscal impact analyses are being conducted in areas where the case law currently limits such practice. At first this relationship appears illogical; it is precisely in areas of high local service support (the location of the largest amount of unfavorable case law) that fiscal impact analysis should flourish because there is greater significance in projecting the tax implications of growth, casting them to other municipalities if negative, welcoming them if positive. Yet, it is in just such areas that individuals' rights have been violated under the guise of municipal fiscal responsibility (i.e., not approving certain configurations of residential development proposals because they did not generate cost-revenue surpluses). In turn, courts in these locations have responded with provisions to limit the role of fiscal criteria in planning. New Jersey is a prime example. Fiscal impact considerations have influenced land use policy there since the 1940s. In turn, the State Supreme Court has sharply constrained how cost-revenue projections are to be interpreted and used, a move generated by its concern that a focus on fiscal impact considerations would enhance or perpetuate existing restrictive suburban zoning.

Fiscal Impact Analysis: Scope of Study and Data Resources

Fiscal Impact Analysis *Costs:* Scope Considered, Data Bases Drawn Upon

Exhibit 12-3 summarizes many of the important technical features of the current sample of field practice. Most are self explanatory and this section notes only their highlights. The immediate, local impact focus of fiscal impact analyses in terms of the government jurisdiction to which cost is predicted, is again demonstrated. Not only are all of the fiscal impact analyses performed by locals concerned with the local fisc, but also about one-third of the county-initiated studies focus on impacts solely to local jurisdictions.

Further, regardless of geographic location of a proposed project within a community's bounds, i.e., direct center or towards its edges, the majority of studies predict only costs to the jurisdiction in which the project is primarily located. Spillover effects, even if the project were to be developed on a municipality's border, are rarely considered. In a related vein, current practice almost universally traces only direct costs. Secondary or induced outlays, even to the principal public body being impacted, are not assigned because (1) of the difficulty to predict secondary consequences and (2) even greater difficulty in assigning appropriate shares of these second tier costs to the specific project, zone changes, etc., occasioning this growth.

At the heart of fiscal impact analyses are the data employed. In terms of the supply side of the equation, services and their costs are most often expressed in simple averages of the per capita experience; a second source of similar information are estimates of consumption and associated costs provided by local officials. These are much less frequently employed by practitioners. Per capita costs are directly incorporated into the Per Capita Multiplier, Comparable City and Employment Anticipation Methods. Information from local officials is the principal ingredient of the Case Study Method.

On the demand side of the equation, demographic multipliers, specifically household size and school age children multipliers, are used most frequently by the practitioner. These are essential for predicting the specific population and pupil load generated by a particular development. There are a number of approaches for obtaining multipliers:

Field Experience 265

EXHIBIT 12-3
SCOPE OF STUDY AND DATA RESOURCES

Number of Projection Points	Number	Percent	Impact Breadth	Number	Percent	Impact Scope	Number	Percent	Data Resources*	Number	Percent
At full development	69	50.7	Direct costs	117	86.0	Jurisdictional	116	85.3	Published HHS and SAC multipliers	79	58.1
At full development plus interim projection	67	49.3	Direct plus Induced Costs	19	14.0	Jurisdictional plus extra-jurisdictional	20	14.7	School district SAC multipliers	83	61.0
									U.S. Census HHS multipliers	35	25.7
									SAC/HHS multipliers resident survey	30	22.1
									Per Capita Expenditure Data	126	92.6
									Expenditure Data from Public Officials	110	80.9
Total	136	100.0		136	100.0		136	100.0		--	--

Revenues Considered*	Number	Percent	Costs Considered	Number	Percent	Means of Analysis Procedure	Number	Percent	Cost-Revenue Impact	Number	Percent
Property tax	136	100.0	Education Aggregated	6	4.4	Computer	14	10.3	Positive	52	38.2
Sales and Gross receipts tax	80	58.8	Education Detailed	4	2.9	Manual	122	89.7	Negative	23	16.9
Other taxes	84	61.8	Non-Education Aggregated	6	4.4				Mixed	43	31.7
Other revenues	94	69.1	Non-Education Detailed	27	19.9				No conclusion	18	13.2
Intergovernmental transfers	73	53.7	Ed. Aggregated/Non-Ed. Detailed	75	55.2						
			Ed. Aggregated/Non-Ed. Aggregated	18	13.2						
Total	--	--		136	100.0		136	100.0		136	100.0

*Multiple selections possible; 136 is the base upon which percentages are tabulated.

Source: Rutgers University Center for Urban Policy Research, Field Survey, Spring 1976.

1. Using published survey figures for both household size and school-age children
2. Relying on secondary school district data for estimates (for school age children multipliers) and Census data for total household size
3. Using the Public Use sample of the U.S. Census to derive multipliers for total household size and school-age children
4. Conducting local surveys to develop local multipliers

In the majority of the cases, about 60 percent, practitioners rely on published multipliers, figures provided by school district officials, published Census material, or a combination of these three. The latter two approaches for obtaining demographic multipliers, even though the most accurate, are avoided due to the time and expense involved in their undertaking. In a subsequent chapter of this handbook guides are provided to estimate demographic multipliers both using the Census Public Use Sample and from field survey to encourage the use of information from these two sources.

Fiscal Impact Analysis *Revenues:*
Scope Considered, Data Bases Drawn Upon

As with costs there is little variety in field experience to the scope of revenues considered. Real property tax revenues are almost always calculated in fiscal impact analyses. Standardizing for locations in which they are not present, there is a sharp decrease in the tabulation of revenues other than the property tax. Sales, gross receipts, and other taxes were examined in only two-thirds of the analyses in locations where they represented a significant share of local revenues. The situation is worse for intergovernmental transfers. They were projected in only one-half the analyses in locations where they too played a sizable role in financing local expenditures. Practitioners tend to concentrate on revenues generated by the real property tax because they are understood by local taxpayers and they are conceptually and procedurally the easiest to deal with. This emphasis is true even in areas where other revenues and intergovernmental transfers have a large funding role. Information on both local revenues and intergovernmental transfers is almost always obtained from the published local budget and the latter projected "straight line" into the future. Very rarely, if ever, are the state and federal offices which originate intergovernmental transfers contacted for allocation formulas or program guidelines.

Other Fiscal Impact Characteristics

The majority of fiscal impact analyses report the aggregate educational costs to the school district but assign future municipal costs in disaggregate form, i.e., by service category — police, fire, highways, etc. Even though the magnitude of school district costs may exceed municipal costs by as much as five to one, locals most often relate public services to those which are municipally provided and are much more interested in what portion of the dollar is being spent on police versus welfare costs than they are on the cost of primary versus secondary education or administrative versus teaching priorities, etc.

The calculations for fiscal impact analyses are overwhelmingly performed manually. Computerized fiscal impact techniques have been available since 1970, but because they were too expensive, data hungry and difficult to understand, many have been shelved. While there are currently attempts to market models which provide cheap, easily understood, first approximations, fiscal impact practice, at least for the near future, will reflect slow growth in models, in part related to initial implementation difficulties.

A last observation concerns the results obtained in current cost-revenue practice. More than two-thirds of the analyses sampled showed either a positive effect or at least a mixed impact, e.g., in a land use alternative example, one case results in a net loss while another may prove to be profitable. Fiscal impact is often used as evidence by those who wish to show the positive financial aftereffects of a project or land use alternative they support. It is the advocate who is most willing to make the time and financial commitment required to volunteer an analysis or to proceed with subdivision or site plan review where such an analysis is a precondition to project approval.

Fiscal Impact Analysis: Author, Audience and Significance of Study

Author and Time Commitments

There is an approximately even split between private and public fiscal impact practitioners. Private planners tend to concentrate on fiscal impact analyses dealing with development proposals. Public planners typically conduct fiscal impact analyses dealing with land use alternatives or the economic impacts of a proposed plan.

Planning consultants are the single most important cost-revenue practitioners in terms of the share of studies which involve their participation. (See Exhibit 12-4.) They have the expertise and experience that many developers and public jurisdictions lack; they thus are sought by each. Public staff planners at the local level participate in fiscal impact analyses twice as frequently as county planners and three times as frequently as regional/state planners. Universities and research centers have also become active in the field. They usually become involved in one-of-a-kind or large public projects. Corporations perform fiscal impact analyses on large private developments usually with which they are directly involved.

Whoever does the fiscal impact projection should know that the belief that it can be completed over a short period of time is not borne out by the facts. Exhibit 12-4 shows that about three-quarters of the analyses completed over the period 1970–1976 consumed at least two months to one year. This is not to say that the actual calculation required this time input but rather gathering data, attending public meetings, and obtaining a "sign-off" for the analysis contributed to the time frame indicated above. The methods, data and revenue tabulation formulas should greatly shorten the time required, at least for the analysis.

Practitioner Reaction to Current Practice

The practitioner of a particular method influences its style content and flow. Analyses vary in completeness, both in terms of the range of costs and revenues considered as well as the documentation of what has been done. As documented by practitioners, the latter situation is even more disturbing than the former. The absence of key steps or insufficient explanations of how a projection of costs or revenues was determined, was found to be present in a substantial proportion (over 25 percent) of fiscal impact analyses. This type of omission affects both the ability to judge these studies' accuracy and the desire to initiate other studies. In fact, in over half of the locations of the sample studies, the analysis of fiscal impact could not be judged as to accuracy by the presiding local official. Further, in one-third of the cases even though there was a demand for additional analyses they were not being commissioned due to practitioner dissatisfaction with the prior effort. It is interesting to note that the simplest and those most easy to effectuate are the methods most preferred by practitioners and are those which are given the highest ratings as to both accuracy and completeness. As such, the Per Capita Multiplier Method is most preferred and most believed in terms of the results it produces. The Case Study, due to time consumption, and fiscal impact models, generally due to conceptual complexity, appear to be least preferred.

EXHIBIT 12-4
AUTHOR AUDIENCE AND SIGNIFICANCE OF STUDY

Author	Number	Percent	Quality	Number	Percent	Logical Sequence	Number	Percent	Accuracy	Number	Percent
Planning consultant	52	38.2	Significant	26	19.1	Yes, complete	84	61.8	Substantially accurate	35	25.7
Municipality	33	24.3	Average	75	55.2	Yes, incomplete	35	25.7	Reasonably accurate	31	22.8
County	18	13.2	Modest	35	25.7	No	17	12.5	Rough gauge	10	7.4
State/regional	11	8.1							Not able to determine	60	44.1
Institute/university/ corporation	22	16.2									
Total	136	100.0		136	100.0		136	100.0		136	100.0

Duration	Number	Percent	Complexity	Number	Percent	User Sophistication	Number	Percent	Follow-up Study	Number	Percent
1 month or less	21	15.4	Simple	43	31.6	Low Level	40	29.4	Yes	36	26.5
2-5 months	47	34.6	Moderate	82	60.3	Medium	81	59.6	No	100	73.5
6 months – 1 year	36	26.5	Difficult	11	8.1	High Level	15	11.0			
1 year +	32	23.5									
Total	136	100.0		136	100.0		136	100.0		136	100.0

Source: Rutgers University Center for Urban Policy Research, Field Survey, Spring 1976.

Field Experience 269

Summary

Field practice, as viewed through an analysis of fiscal impact studies undertaken post 1970, reflects the ambivalence of the state of the art. Demand for fiscal impact analysis is ever increasing. There are competing demands to move forward with techniques yet to obtain a better understanding of techniques and their inputs before initiating movement. The latter is reflected in two principal concerns of practitioners. The first is a desire to check the reliability of and augment existing input data. The second is to promulgate and standardize fiscal impact methods. Additional demographic data on specialized housing types, a test of the reliability of demographic multipliers for standard housing types, a compilation of service standards for municipal and school services, and income to value multipliers for nonresidential uses are some types of information which have been sought since 1970, but they are as yet largely unavailable.

In addition, there has been a quest for a basic statement on the methods used to undertake fiscal impact analyses as well as their assumptions, strengths/weaknesses and situational deployment. To date, there have been only limited attempts to catalog the work of the field enroute to compiling methods. There have been further half-hearted attempts to describe an individual method in an orderly and standardized fashion. A minimal number of unrelated tests of method accuracy have been performed. This handbook is thus a response to these inadequacies; it attempts to fulfill those needs.

NOTES

1. Ruth L. Mace, *Municipal Cost-Revenue Research in the United States* (Chapel Hill: University of North Carolina Press, 1961), p.1.

2. Boston City Planning Board, *Report on the Income and Cost of Six Districts in the City of Boston* (Boston: Boston City Planning Board, 1934).

3. It should be noted, however, that the fiscal impact analysis of deteriorated neighborhoods has been done sporadically until today. Variations on this type of study, such as the property tax burden shared by different areas, are still being effected.

4. Scott Bagby, *A Comprehensive Plan for the Borough of Morris Plains, N.J.* (Montclair, N.J.: Bagby Associates, 1948); Morrow Planning Associates, *The Master Plan of Florham Park* (Ridgewood, N.J.: Morrow Planning Associates, 1965); Homer Hoyt Associates, *Economic Survey of Land Uses of Evanston* (Larchmont, N.Y.: Homer Hoyt Associates, 1949); Walter Isard and Robert E. Coughlin, *Municipal Costs and Revenues Resulting from Community Growth* (Wellesley, Mass.: Chandler Davis, 1955); William Wheaton and Morton J. Schussheim, *The Cost of Municipal Services in Residential Areas* (Washington, D.C.: Government Printing Office, 1955).

5. See U.S. Department of Housing and Urban Development, *701 Comprehensive Planning Assistance Statutes, Regulations and Pertinent Excerpts from Selected House and Senate Reports* (Washington, D.C.: Government Printing Office, 1975).

6. See Appendix 2 to this handbook.

7. See Appendix 2 to this handbook.

8. See Chapter 17. For further discussion of the fiscal impact analysis context, see Thomas Muller, *Fiscal Impacts of Land Development* (Washington, D.C.: The Urban Institute, 1973); Contra Costa County, California, *East County/Delta Cost Effectiveness Study* Part I (Contra Costa, Calif.: Contra Costa County Planning Board, 1975); John F. Kain, "Urban Form and the Cost of Services," Program on Regional and Urban Economics, Discussion Paper No. 6 (Cambridge, Harvard University, 1967); Thomas Muller and Grace Dawson, *The Fiscal Impact of Residential and Commercial Development: A Case Study* (Washington, D.C.: Urban Institute, 1972); Robert W. Burchell, *Planned Unit Development: New Communities American Style* (New Brunswick, N.J.: Rutgers University, Center for Urban Policy Research, 1972); Sternlieb *et al.*, *Housing Development and Municipal Costs;* (New Brunswick, N.J.: Rutgers University, Center for Urban Policy Research, 1972); Connecticut Development Group, Inc., *Cost-Revenue Impact Analysis for Residential Developments* (Hartford, Conn.: Connecticut Development Group, 1972); Tara Ellman, "Fiscal Impact Analysis," unpublished paper prepared for Resources for the Future, Washington, D.C., 1975.

PART 4

ADDITIONAL DATA: MULTIPLIERS AND MODELS USED IN FISCAL IMPACT ANALYSIS

It is the purpose of this part to present basic data for fiscal impact analysis and to look closely into the "black boxes" of the automated fiscal impact approaches. Consisting of five chapters, this part contains information on demographic and gross income multipliers which serve as input to fiscal impact analyses, as well as models which have been developed to undertake such studies. The first three chapters of the part consider demographic multipliers, the next presents gross income multipliers, while the last summarizes fiscal impact models.

Chapter 13 presents demographic multipliers for various areas of the country and discusses the use of these multipliers in fiscal impact analyses as well as their geographic variations and variations over time. Chapters 14 and 15 are two procedural guides for the user if he should find it necessary to calculate demographic multipliers using (1) Census-prepared information or (2) survey sampling. In the first case, definitions which classify housing types, age groupings which are

Part 4: Additional Data

necessary to predict kindergarten, elementary school, and high school impact, as well as the specific programming, are provided. In the second case, such information as a sample questionnaire and methods to determine sample size are provided.

Chapter 16 presents gross income multipliers by type and location of residential and nonresidential facilities. The multipliers are used to estimate the real property value of residential and commercial properties. They are invaluable as guides when rental level, rather than property value, is the information provided by the developer to the fiscal impact analyst. The chapter demonstrates for the user the procedures necessary to develop and employ income multipliers used to determine property value for certain categories of real property. In addition, gross income multipliers are derived for classes of residential and commercial property by region of the country.

Chapter 17 summarizes the dozen or so cost-revenue models which have been used for fiscal impact analysis over the last decade and the current status of each. The models are described briefly in terms of origins and sites of application and then compared across several common variables:

1. Cost revenue method(s) used
2. Data base/resources required
3. Range of costs/revenues considered
4. Sophistication of user required.

13

DEMOGRAPHIC MULTIPLIERS FOR STANDARD AND SPECIALIZED HOUSING TYPES: ORIGINS, USES, DERIVATIONS

Demographic multipliers are used to predict the municipal and school populations that will result from new housing development. When the number, type and configuration of incoming housing units and therefore the magnitude of the new population are known, estimates of public service requirements and costs (i.e., police, fire, public works, personnel/equipment, etc.) can easily be projected. The multipliers which describe the two principal users of local services (people for municipal services and school-age children for school services) are frequently expressed by number of rooms or bedrooms. The example below illustrates such multipliers.

Demographic Characteristics Northeast/New England	Single Family Homes Number of Bedrooms			Garden Apartments Number of Bedrooms	
	Two	Three	Four	One	Two
Total household size*	2.485	3.940	4.965	1.500	2.430
School-age children	0.246	1.130	2.068	0.038	0.150

*Total household size is the total number of persons, both related and unrelated, residing in a housing unit. School-age children includes all persons aged 5 to 18 residing in the housing unit.

These multipliers are developed from household surveys or from data found in the U.S. Census public use samples for recently constructed housing. The example above is interpreted: "An average of 3.94 residents and 1.13 school age children live in a three-bedroom, single family home in New England. An average of 1.50 residents and 0.038 school-age children are found to live in one-bedroom garden apartments in the same area. If three-bedroom, single family homes or one-bedroom, garden apartments are proposed to be developed locally, the product of demographic multipliers and the number of forthcoming housing units provide an estimate of the magnitude of new residents and school-age children for whom municipal and school services must be provided.

Assume, for example, that one hundred, one-bedroom garden apartments are being considered for an area. Assume also that locally it costs $200 per person to provide municipal (general government, public safety, public works, health/welfare, recreation) services and $2,000 per pupil to provide school (primary and secondary education) services. Using the demographic multipliers shown above, one hundred, one bedroom garden apartments would, on the average, generate 150 people (1.500 × 100) and four school-age children (.038 × 100). Multiplying these population estimates by per capita and per pupil servicing costs indicates that roughly $38,000 will be the cost to provide public services to the new apartments (150 × $200) plus (4 × $2000).

Background

Early in the 1960s survey samples of specific types of dwelling units were taken to estimate both household size and numbers of school-age children. Published results of demographic multipliers obtained in these surveys by housing type were adopted by planning practitioners nationally in their local fiscal impact analyses. For high rise units, studies were undertaken by Del Guidice of the Urban Land Institute (1963) and by Fairfax (Va.) and Montgomery (Md.) Counties (1965, 1966).[1] For garden apartments, studies were completed by Sternlieb of Rutgers University (1964) and the Rolde Company for the National Association of Homebuilders (1962).[2] Most were summarized by Holley for the American Society of Planning Officials in 1966.[3]

These studies became the classics for demographic multipliers. All were conducted at specific sites, and all involved survey research of reasonable quality. Yet most did not report total household size multipliers or disaggregate school-age children multipliers by dwelling unit size. After the early reports, Stuart and Teska of Barton-Aschman Associates studied single family homes (1971) and Burchell of Rutgers University surveyed townhouses.[4] These surveys and most subsequent work reported both total household size and school-age children multipliers, and they presented the multipliers by housing type and by number of bedrooms.

Demographic multipliers were again summarized and supplemented via an extensive sample by Rutgers University published as a monograph in *Housing Development and Municipal Costs* (1973) and in periodical form, "The Numbers Game: Forecasting Household Size" (1974).[5] Since early 1974 these latter summaries have received widespread distribution and appear in one form or another in many of the fiscal impact studies which have been conducted nationally.

In the course of the last Rutgers University survey, a number of parallel studies were undertaken. They used multivariate statistical analyses to find linkages between household size/school-age children and a number of variables describing the socioeconomic profiles of those who occupied housing of certain types as well as other housing structure and development characteristics. The variables included dwelling unit size (measured by number of bedrooms or rooms), rent or value of the dwelling unit, tenant race, development size and age, unique development features (density, access to recreational amenities, quality of the neighborhood) and geographical location. The researchers found that for garden, high-rise apartments, single family homes and townhouses the dominant factor impacting on the number of people/pupils per unit was the physical size of the dwelling unit.[6] The best indication of the number of occupants a dwelling unit would have was its number of bedrooms or rooms. Further, the size variable was so robust that it dominated the housing type as an index of household composition. The number of people or pupils who occupied a dwelling unit was more similar for different housing types of the same size that it was between the same housing type of different sizes. Simply put, if the practitioner desired to know the number of people or school children that would reside in the locality because of proposed new housing, he must also know the size of the dwelling units. This variable, expressed in either rooms or bedrooms, was the best index of the population to be introduced by this new housing.

Calculating Demographic Multipliers

Until recently practitioners have depended on demographic multipliers determined from local field surveys to project future population. Often sample sizes, procedures, specific characteristics of occupants, etc., allowed the results of the surveys to be applicable in only limited areas. One of the larger samples was the previously mentioned 1973 Rutgers University survey—results were reported for four structure types (garden apartments, high-rise apartments, single-family homes and townhouses). The procedural guide following this section draws largely on the methods and instruments used in this survey and explains how and when to sample for demographic multipliers. It covers such matters as questionnaire design, sample size, survey efficiency, and survey costs. It further lists basic references for undertaking survey research. Due to the cost and complexity of survey sampling, the practitioner should definitely consult these pages before planning a field survey to determine demographic characteristics.

A better procedure for determining demographic multipliers has also begun to emerge, however. This procedure uses U.S. Census Public Use Samples to estimate demographic multipliers by housing type. The analyst can obtain an appropriate state or county group Census tape for an area, use certain programming to define housing types and convert age group distributions to school-age children, and thus estimate the number of people and pupils by housing type. Due to the rising costs of sample surveys and the possibility of bias due to sample design or administration, employment of the U.S. Census Public Use Samples is receiving increasing attention. Recent articles in the *Journal of the American Institute of Planners* by James and Windsor, formerly of Rutgers University (1975) and Archer of the University of Florida (1977) attest to the increasing use of this data resouce.[7] The procedural guide following this section details the necessary steps to develop demographic multipliers from the Public Use Samples.

Public Use Samples and Demographic Multipliers: Standard Housing Types

Samples

The Public Use Samples constitute a superior data base for calculating demographic multipliers. They offer a national overview, comprehensive coverage of a variety of housing types, and unparalleled accuracy stemming from large sample sizes. The Public Use Samples provides a one-in-a-hundred sample of complete household records. Each record contains all census population and housing information for every member of the household (except name, address, and detailed geographic location, which are withheld for reasons of confidentiality).

The availability of a complete record on a case-by-case basis allows detailed analysis of individual and household characteristics by housing unit and by structure type. As such it is an excellent resource for information on demographic characteristics and resultantly, demographic multipliers. Total household size and the number of school-age children are calculated first, by categorizing the total number of housing units by housing type and size of unit (number of bedrooms); second, by obtaining a count of household size and school-age children for each housing unit in each type/size subsample; and third, by averaging household size and school-age children counts for each type/size subsample. (For a complete description of the steps involved, see the procedural guide in chapter 14 directly following this section.)

In 1977, the Center for Urban Policy Research, using the county group Public Use Sample, derived average household size and average number of school-age children per housing unit for various housing types. Public Use data for nine states found to be representative* of the nine regional subdivisions recognized by the Census were analyzed. Multipliers were calculated for all recently built units (those constructed between 1960 and 1970.) in these states. Recently built units were used because they provide baseline data most similar to the expected characteristics of units that will be built in the near future.

The data base used to calculate the multipliers was quite comprehensive. The total sample of housing units for the states selected was 297,952 units. Since this figure constitutes a one-in-a-hundred sample, the data base represents a total of 29,795,200 housing units, or nearly 50 percent of the nation's 1970 total of 63.4 million occupied housing units. Of this total, multipliers were calculated for units built during the period 1960 to 1970. The state sample consisted of 79,065 units, representing 7,906,500 units or again nearly 50 percent of the 16.9 million units built nationally from 1960 to 1970.

Definitions

Housing types are identified in the Public Use Samples by using Census codes to specify number of units and/or number of stories and/or the presence of an elevator.

	Housing Type	Definition
1.	Single family homes	Single detached structures of one unit
2.	Garden apartments	Single structures of more than three housing units and three or fewer stories
3.	Townhouses	Single attached structures of one unit
4.	High-rise apartments	Housing units in structures with seven or more stories serviced by an elevator
5.	Mobile homes	Mobile homes other than those used only for business or vacation

Multipliers are presented in Exhibits 13-1 and 13-2 for common configurations of standard housing types (the five categories shown above). Common configurations are their more usual size forms as determined by the most significant concentrations within the distribution of all units of a given type, i.e., two-, three-, or four-bedroom single family homes; one- or two-bedroom garden apartments; studio, one- and two-bedroom high-rise units; one-, two- and three-bedroom townhouses; and one-, two- and three-bedroom mobile homes.

---

*This selection was made by considering six variables: three socioeconomic characteristics (median family income, years of school completed, percent employed in manufacturing) and three housing unit characteristics (median value/contract rent, vacancy rate, presence of plumbing facilities).

Demographic Multipliers

EXHIBIT 13-1
REGIONAL AND NATIONAL DEMOGRAPHIC MULTIPLIERS FOR COMMON CONFIGURATIONS OF *STANDARD* HOUSING TYPES[1] FOR *TOTAL HOUSEHOLD SIZE* BY HOUSING TYPE AND NUMBER OF BEDROOMS

HOUSING TYPES[3]

REGION	SINGLE-FAMILY HOMES			GARDEN APARTMENTS			HIGH-RISE APARTMENTS				TOWN HOUSES				MOBILE HOMES			
	Two Bedroom	Three Bedroom	Four Bedroom	Blended[5]	One Bedroom	Two Bedroom	Blended[5]	Studio	One Bedroom	Two Bedroom	Blended[5]	One Bedroom	Two Bedroom	Three Bedroom	Blended[5]	One Bedroom	Two Bedroom	Three Bedroom	Blended[5]
NORTHEAST[4]																			
New England	2.485	3.940	4.965	3.931	1.500	2.430	2.114	1.071	1.470	2.270	1.700	—	2.200	—[2]	—	—	2.390	3.588	2.595
Middle Atlantic	2.536	3.776	4.655	3.831	1.722	2.525	2.190	1.077	1.436	2.523	1.790	1.885	2.630	4.110	3.933	1.556	2.441	3.928	2.700
NORTH CENTRAL																			
East North Central	2.595	3.892	4.909	3.911	1.719	2.576	2.285	1.070	1.432	2.570	2.357	1.364	2.727	4.129	3.588	1.647	2.450	3.835	2.620
West North Central	2.517	3.714	4.840	3.697	1.584	2.479	2.195	—	1.386	—	1.515	—	2.833	3.500	3.015	1.757	2.402	3.877	2.654
SOUTH																			
South Atlantic	2.960	3.819	4.485	3.775	1.686	2.685	2.632	—	1.208	—	1.417	—	2.778	—	—	1.955	2.560	3.680	2.807
East South Central	2.823	3.683	4.550	3.608	1.576	2.622	2.418	—	1.367	2.385	1.619	—	2.600	4.000	2.844	2.065	2.697	3.793	2.910
West South Central	2.995	3.758	4.680	3.754	1.690	2.652	2.246	—	1.282	1.867	1.483	1.783	2.720	3.735	2.741	2.070	2.592	4.089	2.951
WEST																			
Mountain	2.865	3.716	4.486	3.983	1.667	2.570	2.216	1.050	1.333	2.000	1.443	—	2.154	—	2.846	1.739	2.551	4.013	2.960
Pacific	2.745	3.687	4.561	3.826	1.596	2.530	2.149	1.159	1.338	2.220	1.585	1.768	2.735	4.033	2.965	1.746	2.133	3.807	2.113
NATIONAL (All Area Average)	2.673	3.752	4.665		1.653	2.560		1.112	1.435	2.270		1.859	2.731	4.073		1.754	2.431	3.865	

Notes: [1] Units built from 1960-1970. [2] Less than 1,000 units in this category (insufficient sample size). [3] See text for definitions and instructions on how to use these tables. [4] See Exhibit 13-3 for inclusive states. [5] All unit average.

Source: U.S. Census Public Use Sample, 1970.

EXHIBIT 13-2

REGIONAL AND NATIONAL DEMOGRAPHIC MULTIPLIERS FOR COMMON CONFIGURATIONS OF *STANDARD* HOUSING TYPES[1] FOR *SCHOOL-AGE CHILDREN* BY HOUSING TYPE AND NUMBER OF BEDROOMS

	SINGLE-FAMILY HOMES			GARDEN APARTMENTS			HOUSING TYPES[3] HIGH-RISE APARTMENTS				TOWN HOUSES			MOBILE HOMES		
	Two Bedroom	Three Bedroom	Four Bedroom	Blended[5]	One Bedroom	Two Bedroom	Blended[5]	Studio	One Bedroom	Two Bedroom	Blended[5]	One Bedroom	Two Bedroom	Three Bedroom	Blended[5]	One Bedroom	Two Bedroom	Three Bedroom	Blended[5]
REGION																			
NORTHEAST[4]																			
New England	0.246	1.130	2.068	1.212	0.038	0.150	0.174	0.000	0.015	0.081	0.033	—	0.000	—[2]	0.640	—	0.268	0.824	0.396
Middle Atlantic	0.288	1.111	1.911	1.211	0.011	0.200	0.156	0.000	0.015	0.318	0.125	0.115	0.304	1.311	1.187	0.048	0.177	1.022	0.375
NORTH CENTRAL																			
East North Central	0.355	1.173	2.102	1.249	0.036	0.232	0.219	0.000	0.013	0.290	0.483	0.000	0.409	1.371	1.078	0.078	0.208	1.148	0.360
West North Central	0.361	1.099	2.063	1.142	0.023	0.165	0.173	0.000	0.068	—	0.136	—	0.389	0.750	0.544	0.135	0.233	1.169	0.430
SOUTH																			
South Atlantic	0.553	1.121	1.760	1.130	0.009	0.269	0.358	—	0.000	—	0.083	—	0.556	—	0.838	0.136	0.194	0.906	0.367
East South Central	0.443	1.066	1.728	1.024	0.035	0.306	0.323	—	0.000	—	0.021	0.000	0.267	1.500	0.656	0.323	0.262	0.928	0.422
West South Central	0.604	1.109	1.988	1.161	0.052	0.298	0.274	—	0.000	0.200	0.050	0.087	0.400	1.265	0.570	0.239	0.239	1.207	0.513
WEST																			
Mountain	0.404	1.081	1.825	1.364	0.034	0.246	0.245	0.000	0.000	0.000	0.000	—	0.231	—	0.577	0.043	0.283	1.158	0.565
Pacific	0.445	1.106	1.842	1.255	0.040	0.307	0.290	0.023	0.000	0.098	0.069	0.015	0.322	1.333	0.617	0.031	0.159	1.133	0.192
NATIONAL (All Area Average)	0.401	1.104	1.924		0.043	0.271		0.012	0.017	0.182		0.103	0.345	1.331		0.074	0.207	1.076	

Notes: [1] Units built from 1960-1970. [2] Less than 1,000 units in this category (insufficient sample size). [3] See text for definitions and instructions on how to use these tables. [4] See Exhibit 13-3 for inclusive states. [5] All unit average.

Source: U.S. Census Public Use Sample, 1970.

Household Size and School-Age Children Multipliers: Standard Housing Types

Exhibits 13-1 and 13-2 summarize multipliers for total household size and school-age children. Each segment of information is presented both by type and size of housing unit. Although regional variation is fairly insignificant for standard housing types, multipliers are presented by region for consistency with specialized housing types. For those instances where the practitioner does not have information on the size of forthcoming housing units but only on type, "blended" multipliers are presented. They are weighted averages for all size configurations of a particular type of housing.

To illustrate, assume that a developer in Virginia is planning to build 100, one-bedroom garden apartments. He must file a fiscal impact analysis of the municipal and school district costs this development will impose locally. He must first estimate both municipal and school district service *demand*. One approach would be to use the demographic multipliers in Exhibits 13-1 and 13-2. To project municipal service demand the analyst would begin Exhibit 13-1 at the extreme left-hand column, first under "South" for region and then under the portion of this region in which Virginia falls, i.e., South Atlantic. To obtain the applicable region and subregion for each state the analyst should consult Exhibit 13-3.

Once the correct region or row of this exhibit is obtained, the analyst proceeds across the row until he reaches the column for the appropriate housing type and size, in this case garden apartnents, one bedroom. The multiplier is 1.686. The product of this figure and the anticipated number of housing untis (one hundred) provides a projection of the population increase that will require future municipal services (1.686 × 100 or 169 people).

The analyst repeats this process to tabulate future school district service demand. He enters Exhibit 13-2 at the extreme left hand column first under the appropriate region and moves across the row of the applicable subregion (South Atlantic) to the column of the desired type and size of housing—garden apartments, one bedroom. Under this column he would find for the South Atlantic region a school-age children multiplier of .009. The product of this figure and the number of housing units, one hundred, produces an estimate of incremental school load—for this development, one school-age child (.009 × 100 or 1 school-age child). The new service population generated by one hundred, one-bedroom garden apartments proposed for a Virginia municipality is thus 170—169 people for whom municipal service departments must provide and one school-age child for whom the school district must provide. Once service demand is known, any one of several fiscal impact techniques may be employed to obtain cost estimates.

Field Surveys and Demographic Multipliers: Specialized Housing Types

Sample

Multipliers for total household size and school-age children have been developed for four special housing types. They supplement the multipliers presented in Exhibits 13-1 and 13-2 for standard housing types. Specialized housing types are those forms of shelter for which Census information as of 1970 was not readily available or regularly maintained by locality or census tract in published summaries. In this handbook they include vacation homes, condominiums, elderly and singles residences. The absence of Census-maintained information is due primarily to a lack of clarity in definition—housing type is specified not by number of units, stories or the presence of an elevator but rather by who will occupy the unit, for what purpose and/or in what relationship.

EXHIBIT 13-3

REGION AND SUBREGION INTO WHICH VARIOUS STATES FALL FOR THE PURPOSE OF DEMOGRAPHIC MULTIPLIERS

STATE	REGION	SUBREGION	(ABBREVIATIONS)
Alabama	South	East South Central	ESC
Alaska	West	Pacific	P
Arizona	West	Mountain	M
Arkansas	South	West South Central	WSC
California	West	Pacific	P
Colorado	West	Mountain	M
Connecticut	Northeast	New England	NE
Delaware	South	South Atlantic	SA
Florida	South	South Atlantic	SA
Georgia	South	South Atlantic	SA
Hawaii	West	Pacific	P
Idaho	West	Mountain	M
Illinois	North Central	East North Central	ENC
Indiana	North Central	East North Central	ENC
Iowa	North Central	West North Central	WNC
Kansas	North Central	West North Central	WNC
Kentucky	South	East South Central	ESC
Louisiana	South	West South Central	WSC
Maine	Northeast	New England	NE
Maryland	South	South Atlantic	SA
Massachusetts	Northeast	New England	NE
Michigan	North Central	East North Central	ENC
Minnesota	North Central	West North Central	WNC
Mississippi	South	East South Central	ESC
Missouri	North Central	West North Central	WNC
Montana	West	Mountain	M
Nebraska	North Central	West North Central	WNC
Nevada	West	Mountain	M
New Hampshire	Northeast	New England	NE
New Jersey	Northeast	Middle Atlantic	MA
New Mexico	West	Mountain	M
New York	Northeast	Middle Atlantic	MA
North Carolina	South	South Atlantic	SA
North Dakota	North Central	West North Central	WNC
Ohio	North Central	East North Central	ENC
Oklahoma	South	West South Central	WSC
Oregon	West	Pacific	P
Pennsylvania	Northeast	Middle Atlantic	MA
Rhode Island	Northeast	New England	NE
South Carolina	South	South Atlantic	SA
South Dakota	North Central	West North Central	WNC
Tennessee	South	East South Central	ESC
Texas	South	West South Central	WSC
Utah	West	Mountain	M
Vermont	Northeast	New England	NE
Virginia	South	South Atlantic	SA
Washington	West	Pacific	P
West Virginia	South	South Atlantic	SA
Wisconsin	North Central	East North Central	ENC
Wyoming	West	Mountain	M

The information which is provided here has been obtained by survey sampling. Using the most current national distributions for the specified housing types, both primary and secondary resources were used to derive demographic multipliers from samples in the geographic regions where these housing types are concentrated.

Just as similar information for standard housing types appeared sporadically a decade ago, the information presented here for specialized housing is just a prelude to an increasing variety and amount of information which will be available later. As more research is undertaken, the local fiscal impact of these types of housing can be more accurately gauged. The multipliers in Exhibits 13-4 and 13-5 are based on the samples described in the next few pages.

Definitions

Vacation Homes

The principal definitional characteristic of a vacation home is that it is a temporary residence used by a family or individual maintaining a permanent residence elsewhere. Leisure, recreation, and second homes are synonymous. Vacation homes encompass the range of structural types and amenities from small cabins without plumbing or heating to ultra modern high-rise condominiums. They are generally, however, single-family, detached units. Trailers, campers, houseboats, and commercially operated guest homes are not included in the definition of vacation homes.

Condominiums

The principal feature that distinguishes condominiums from other multifamily housing types is their legal form of ownership. Those who reside in single family attached or multifamily condominium units individually own, rather than rent, their units. This ownership agreement is not fee simple, however, for besides *individual* ownership of units there is also *joint* ownership of the common elements of real property. Typically this ownership is referred to as cooperative. The sample considers condominiums to be those units where individual ownership is limited to a finite space within a structure and joint control is exercised over the remaining real property. The structural form of condominiums do, however, run the gamut in structural type including low-rise/garden, townhouse and high-rise units.

Housing for the Elderly

This specialized housing type is developed for major or total occupancy by elderly people. Two distinctions are commonly found: (1) standard structures or subdivisions which, for reasons of accommodation, location, or climate, become "elderly enclaves," without specific household-head age or children occupancy restrictions; (2) planned retirement communities serving the elderly, which deliberately define minimum age/occupancy restrictions. The range of structural types and forms often are included. Specifically excluded, however, are public housing complexes, age-restricted trailer parks, nursing homes, and institutional environments. In essence, the first category defined here is typically rental housing sought by the elderly; the second is typically condominiums built for the elderly.

284 THE FISCAL IMPACT HANDBOOK

EXHIBIT 13-4

REGIONAL DEMOGRAPHIC MULTIPLIERS FOR COMMON CONFIGURATIONS OF SPECIALIZED[1] HOUSING TYPES FOR TOTAL HOUSEHOLD SIZE, BY HOUSING TYPE AND NUMBER OF BEDROOMS (FIELD SURVEYS, 1970–1975)

REGIONS	VACATION HOMES[3] (Single Family)				HOUSING TYPES CONDOMINIUMS (Low Rise/Garden)[C] (Single Family Attached)[D] (High Rise)[E]				ELDERLY RESIDENCES (High Rise)[F] (Low Rise)[G]			SINGLES RESIDENCES (Low Rise/Garden)		
	Rooms[A] Lot Size[B]	1 Room 5000 Ft^2	2 Room 5000–9999	3 Room 10000–19999	4 Room 20000–29999	One Bedroom	Two Bedroom	Three Bedroom	Four Bedroom	Studio	One Bedroom	Two Bedroom	Studio	One Bedroom	Two Bedroom
NORTHEAST New England[4] Middle Atlantic		3.085^A	3.039^A[2]	3.198^A	3.244^A					—	1.699^G	1.898^G			
NORTH CENTRAL East North Central		3.637^B	3.626^B	3.699^B	3.514^B								—	1.163	1.947
SOUTH South Atlantic										1.380^F	1.650^F	1.850^F			
WEST Pacific													1.089	1.282	—
NATIONAL						2.714^C — 2.368^E	2.614^C 3.133^D 2.966^E	3.735^D	4.731^D						

EXHIBIT 13-5

REGIONAL DEMOGRAPHIC MULTIPLIERS FOR COMMON CONFIGURATIONS OF SPECIALIZED HOUSING TYPES FOR SCHOOL AGE CHILDREN, BY HOUSING TYPE AND NUMBER OF BEDROOMS (FIELD SURVEYS, 1970–1975)

REGIONS	1 Room	2 Room	3 Room	4 Room	One Bedroom	Two Bedroom	Three Bedroom	Four Bedroom	Studio	One Bedroom	Two Bedroom	Studio	One Bedroom	Two Bedroom
NORTHEAST New England Middle Atlantic	0.780^A	0.703^A	0.794^A	0.915^A					—	0.000^G	0.000^G			
NORTH CENTRAL East North Central	1.510^B	1.354^B	1.454^B	1.378^B								—	0.000	0.000
SOUTH South Atlantic									0.000^F	0.000^F	0.000^F			
WEST Pacific												0.000	0.000	—
NATIONAL					1.190^C — 1.000^E	0.982^C 1.308^D 1.225^E	1.804^D	2.615^D						

Notes: [1] New units.
[2] No surveys at this location.
[3] See text for definitions.
[4] See Exhibit 3 for inclusive states.

Source: Survey samples at various locations, see footnote 8.

Singles Residences

There is generally no definite way to identify singles' residences. For this handbook they are defined as housing whose major occupancy is intended for unmarried, childless, adults under the age of fifty. In some areas of the country (California and Texas, for example), singles developments are readily acknowledged in the locality as being primarily for the elderly. In other areas (Georgia and Colorado, for example), "adult" communities clearly cater to young singles rather than young marrieds or elderly adults. In these areas both the designation and accompanying restrictive policies are clearly stated. In Massachusetts, however, residences for singles only (regardless of age) cannot be designated as such because the courts have held the designation discriminatory.

A further difficulty in isolating singles developments is that some singles residences, contrary to advertising, do not, in fact, restrict entry to singles. In one complex in Florida, over 40 percent of a total population of 1,500 residents is married. Similarly, an apartment complex in Minnesota originally built specifically for singles, now seeks a more traditional market. Over 50 percent of the residents are married couples.

Furthermore, with the growing population of singles, a singles unit is often a shared rental, i.e., multiple "singles" living together. There seems to be no general policy regarding children—some "singles" complexes restrict, others allow only children under five; a few allow only teenagers. Obviously the presence of married couples, unrelated individuals, and children represents a significant departure from the traditional view of singles developments, which consequently may have a considerable effect on the projection of the fiscal impact of such projects.

Household Size and School-Age Children Multipliers: Specialized Housing Types

Exhibits 13-4 and 13-5 present multipliers for total household size and school-age children obtained from surveys for the four specialized housing types. They too are presented by type and size of configuration as well as by the region of the country where the data were obtained. As much of this information has been drawn from secondary data sources, the format of the original study must be relied upon for multiplier presentation. For instance, for vacation homes, demographic multipliers for size and configuration are presented by lot size and numbers of rooms rather than by bedroom. In most instances, however, the more common size indication, number of bedrooms, is used.

To illustrate assume that a developer has asked a California city for a zoning variance to permit the construction of 300 low-rise housing units for the elderly. The board of adjustment has asked the municipal staff planner to prepare a fiscal impact analysis projecting both demand for municipal services and future service costs.

Demographic multipliers are employed by the planner for the demand estimate. To obtain total household size the planner first enters Exhibit 13-4 at the extreme left and finds that two major samples of elderly demographic characteristics are reported here. Only one of them involves low rise structures. As this is one of the few sources of information for such demographic multipliers, the planner selects first the total household size figure (Exhibit 13-4) from the appropriate column, elderly residences–low rise, one bedroom (1.699) and further obtains the school-age children multipliers from the same column in Exhibit 13-5 (0.000). (Note: the type of unit is specified by a letter designation, in this case G, which appears both in the column heading and in the data portion of the exhibit.)

The demographic multipliers applied to the number of units anticipated locally provides a projection of future service demand. In this case local development of elderly housing would produce 510 new residents (1.699 × 300) and no additional school-age children (0.000 × 300).

Regional and Temporal Variation of Demographic Multipliers

One of the questions field practitioners ask most frequently is whether or not demographic multipliers for comparable housing types differ by geographic area. They also question the durability of the multipliers over time. Will multipliers for new housing continue to be reliable as this housing ages?

Regional Variation

A preliminary question to be answered when analyzing regional variation in demographic multipliers is what the region under consideration is. Are there obvious urban-suburban or *intraregional* differences in demographic patterns so that demographic multipliers obtained for these areas would be noticeably different? If there are, then the "regions" which should be delineated for comparison might well be central and noncentral cities of metropolitan areas. Or is the important difference an *interregional* one, i.e., a large variation in demographic patterns between those who live in the Northeast versus the West, Southeast, etc.? If this is the case, then the regional variation to be isolated would center on an analysis of differences in demographic multipliers reflecting the characteristics of those who live in one or another sector of the country.

Employing the county group Public Use Sample, Rutgers University Center for Urban Policy Research developed demographic multipliers for both urban and rural areas within regions of the country, and averages for the regions themselves to compare intra- and interregional variations in these multipliers. The housing types for which multipliers were derived consisted of a full range of sizes for the five standard housing types [single family homes, garden apartments, high-rise apartments, townhouses and mobile homes] as well as for some less common housing types [duplex; mid-rise, walk-ups; mid-rise elevators]. Intraregional variation was calculated by comparing the demographic multipliers by housing type from counties both in and outside Standard Metropolitan Statistical Areas (SMSAs) to average values for the entire SMSA. Interregional variation was determined by comparing the same demographic multipliers by housing type for the entire SMSA to demographic multipliers developed for the nation as a whole. For the nine regions, interregional variation exceeded intraregional variations in all situations examined. The difference in demographic multipliers was larger between an average for a region and a national average than between the average for a region and its components. For most regions, the level of both intra-and interregional variation was largest for the least common housing types in the housing stock distribution and smallest for the most frequently represented housing types.

After the geographic area most affecting differences in demographic multipliers was determined, the demographic multipliers for these regions were checked to ascertain the magnitude of the variation. Multipliers representing a region were compared to each other and to a national average.

For common configurations of standard housing types results for the majority of the regions were within 5 percent of one another. There was an even closer spread between the demographic multipliers of a particular region and those derived for the nation as a whole.

Essentially, for *common figurations of standard housing types,* multipliers used in New Jersey are equally applicable in Illinois or California. In fact, a single set of national multipliers can be used for the more common housing types and configurations with nearly as much accuracy as a set derived from the region where the development is located. For less common configurations of standard housing types (one-bedroom single-family homes or four bedroom garden apartments, for example) and nonstandard housing types (duplexes, mid-rise walk-ups, etc.), significant regional variation appears to exist. Thus, significantly different numbers of residents and school-age children occupy a one-bedroom single-family home in the various regions of the country. For fiscal impact analyses, negligible differences will be introduced if a national demographic multiplier or demographic multipliers of another region are used for common configurations of standard housing types. For odd configurations of standard housing types or for odd housing types, however, the more specific regional multiplier should be employed.

Temporal Variation

The temporal variation of demographic multipliers focuses on two basic issues: (1) the accuracy over time of projections made on the basis of a given set of multipliers, and (2) the validity of multipliers calculated for the current period for longer periods of time. The first question involves a mobile population—whether the number of people who initially occupy a dwelling unit will be the same as the number who occupy it as it ages. The second question involves the durability of multipliers over time given changing nationwide trends in family size and rates of family formation—whether demographic multipliers in 1970 be valid in 1980.

To answer these two questions, the Center for Urban Policy Research analyzed several data sets from the county group Public Use Sample. To answer the first question, demographic multipliers for housing units built from 1950 to 1960 were calculated in both 1960 and 1970 to see if they had changed. For both total household size and school-age children multipliers, no significant difference was found to exist in numbers of people occupying the same housing the different time periods.

In pursuit of the second question, demographic multipliers were calculated by housing type and size in 1960 for new housing built from 1950 to 1960 and in 1970 for new housing built from 1960 to 1970. Again no significant difference was found to exist between the two sets of multipliers.

At least in the recent past, dwelling units have contained similar numbers of people after a period of time as they did initially, and a demographic multiplier which initially described the number, was as good ten years later as it was when it was derived. As with regional variation, the results of the analysis hold much more for common configurations of standard housing types than they do for uncommon configurations, or for specialized housing types.

Temporal variation in demographic multipliers is a thorny problem. Trends, while fairly constant from 1960 to 1970, may not remain so in the future. The most current Census reports reveal a decline in current average household size (for all dwelling types) from 3.14 members in 1970 to 2.89 in 1976. During this same period, total elementary school enrollment dropped from 34.0 million to 29.8 million. In addition, the fertility rate has decreased from 2.480 in 1970 to 1.760 in 1976, suggesting that household size and numbers of school-age children will decline even more. The analyst must be sensitive to these trends for they indicate that the demographic multipliers presented here are likely to be revised downward after 1980. The exact magnitude of change cannot be pinpointed until the 1980 Public Use Samples are available.

Conclusion: Which Multipliers Are Used; Where?

The multipliers for standard and specialized housing types presented here represent the most accurate information the authors have been able to compile. The Census sample for standard housing types is large, statistically reliable and quite representative of various housing types and size configurations. The same may be said, although somewhat less emphatically, for the private survey research on specialized housing types. For most purposes, both sets of multipliers will meet the needs of fiscal impact practitioners. The multipliers presented in Exhibits 13-1 through 13-4 should be viewed as replacing most previously published sources except: (1) where other published multipliers exist for the *exact* location, housing type and configuration as the one being considered and (2) there are definite indications that these multipliers are reliable, (sample size, procedures employed, etc.)

If there are indications, however, that the population to be studied differs *significantly* from that for which demographic multipliers were derived, additional demographic multipliers may need to be calculated. The procedural guides on the following pages show how to calculate these multipliers.

One additional item must be stressed when using school-age children multipliers. The multipliers presented here for both standard and specialized housing represent *potential* school district demand. They are exactly what their name implies—school-age children *not* public school attendees. In the interest of simplicity, in the examples presented here the potential or gross estimate of school load has *not* been refined by the proportion of local school-age children attending private primary and secondary schools to derive public school attendees or actual school district demand.

In an actual fiscal impact analysis the gross school-age children demand figure is reduced by the percent of the local school population attending private schools.

It is important that the practitioner understand the difference between a public school attender and a school-age child and further realize that in the past demographic multipliers have been provided for each. Most multipliers produced currently from Public Use Samples or other sources reflect school-age children or gross school district service demand; those which have been produced in the past more often are public school attendees, students or pupils and thus reflect net or actual school district service demand. It is incumbent upon the analyst to know what type of multiplier is being employed to correctly interpret the level of demand which is indicated.

NOTES

1. Dominic Del Guidice, "Cost-Revenue Implications of High Rise Apartments," *Urban Land,* February 1963, pp. 3-5; Fairfax County Planning Division, *Student Contribution from Apartments and Mobile Homes*, Fairfax County Planning Division, Fairfax, Virginia, 1966; Maryland, National Capital Park and Planning Commission, "Dwelling Unit Density, Population and Potential Public School Enrollment Yield by Existing Zoning Classification for Montgomery and Prince Georges Counties," Maryland, National Capital Park and Planning Commission, Silver Spring, Maryland, 1965.

2. George Sternlieb, *The Garden Apartment Development: A Municipal Cost-Revenue Analysis* (New Brunswick, N.J.: (Bureau of Economic Research, Rutgers University, 1964), condensed in *Urban Land,* September 1964; Rolde Company, *Garden Apartments and School-Age Children,* Washington, D.C.: National Association of Homebuilders, 1962).

3. Paul N. Holley, *School Enrollment By Housing Type,* Planning Advisory Service Report No. 210, American Society of Planning Officials, Chicago, Illinois, 1966.

4. Barton-Aschman Associates, *The Barrington, Illinois, Area: A Cost-Revenue Analysis of Land Alternatives* (Chicago, Illinois: Barton-Aschman Associates, 1970), condensed by Darwin G. Stuart and Robert B. Teska in "Who Pays for What: A Cost-Revenue Analysis of Suburban Land Use Alternatives," *Urban Land,* March 1971, pp. 3-16; Robert W. Burchell, *Planned Unit Development: New Communities American Style,* (New Brunswick, N.J.: Rutgers University, Center for Urban Policy Research, 1972).

5. George Sternlieb, et al *Housing Development and Municipal Costs* (New Brunswick, N.J.: Rutgers University, Center for Urban Policy Research, 1972), portions reproduced in George Sternlieb and Robert W. Burchell, "The Numbers Game: Forecasting Household Size," *Urban Land,* January 1974, pp. 3–20.

6. Sternlieb *et al., op cit.,* Chapter 3.

7. Franklin J. James, Jr., and Oliver Duane Windsor, "Fiscal Zoning, Fiscal Reform and Exclusionary Land Use Controls," *Journal of the American Institute of Planners,* Vol. 42-2 (April 1976), pp. 130-141; Wayne R. Archer "Improving Estimates of Local Populations through Public Use Samples," *Journal of the American Institute of Planners,* Volume 43-3 (July 1977), pp. 242-246.

8. Description of Specialized Housing Samples

Vacation Home Samples Vacation home sample data relating to household size and school-age children multipliers, were derived from two independent studies conducted for other analytic purposes. These samples reflect the national distribution of these housing types. The northeast sample includes data for 1,122 vacation home users in five states—Maine, Vermont, New Jersey, Pennsylvania and Delaware—representing 0.2 percent of the universe in the region. Adequate information for the purposes of constructing the multipliers was available for 901 of the respondents. The study from which this data was obtained focused on the environmental impacts of such developments. The principal authors and publication information are as follows: Hays B. Gamble, Gerald L. Cole, Malcolm I. Bevins, Donn Derr and Donald M. Tobey. *Environmental Quality: Effects Associated with Seasonal Home Communities* (University Park, Pa.: Pennsylvania State University, Agricultural Experiment Station, July 1975).

The northcentral sample includes data for 572 vacation home users in the "lakes area" of Northern Michigan, and constitutes 0.12 percent of the northcentral region's total vacation homes. The state of Michigan in 1970 had the largest number of second homes of any state, constituting 8.8 percent of the total national stock. The sample was derived from a study undertaken by the Institute of Social Research of the University of Michigan. The purpose of this study was to analyze changes over time in the residential patterns of northern Michigan recreational counties and is cited as follows: Robert W. Marans *et al., Study of Lake-Oriented Residents in Northern Michigan* (Ann Arbor: University of Michigan, Survey Research Center, forthcoming).

Condominium Samples The National condominium sample employs data on 475 households drawn from five market areas: Boston, Mass., Columbus, Ohio, San Jose, California, Washington, D.C., and Fort Lauderdale, Florida, and includes both new construction and conversions providing data on urban and suburban primary residences. The data were derived from a survey conducted by the A.D. Little Company in 1975 under contract to the U.S. Department of Housing and Urban Development. This nationwide *HUD Condominium/Cooperative Study* was mandated by the Housing and Community Development Act of 1974 as the basis for determining the needs for national legislation regulating the condominium market. An additional sample was derived from a CUPR survey of 100 condominium owners in Washington, D.C., in buildings which had just undergone conversion. This sample was a byproduct of research undertaken by the Rutgers University Center for Urban Policy Research and the Raymond, Parish and Pine Development Economics Group for the Office of Housing and Community Development of the District of Columbia to look into the question of municipal policy concerning condominium conversion. The larger study is cited as follows: *Condominiums In The District of Columbia: The Impact of Conversions on Washington's Citizens, Neighborhoods and Housing Stock, 1975* (New Brunswick, N.J.: Rutgers University, Center for Urban Policy Research, 1974).

Elderly Samples The elderly samples were drawn from two surveys completed by the Rutgers University Center for Urban Policy Research in 1975 on the housing of retirees. One sample in Miami Beach, Florida, concentrates on middle to upper class residents and consists of households in post-1960 high-rise rental units. These 1,003 units, although they contain no specific age limitations, cater almost exclusively to an elderly clientele.

The Miami Beach study involving rent control and the luxury retired housing sector was undertaken for Sibley, Giblin, Levonson, and Ward, Miami Beach, Florida, and is cited as follows: *A Study of Rent Control in the Greater Miami Beach Luxury Housing Market* (New Brunswick, N.J.: Rutgers University, Center for Urban Policy Research, 1975).

The second sample consists of information on 1,033 moderate to middle income households occupying condominium and townhouse units within the confines of age-restricted retirement communities. The sample was derived from surveys of five retirement communities in southern New Jersey. These two samples reflect both elderly enclave and retirement community subsets of the market as well as climate/recreation and metro area housing choice options.

The New Jersey study was undertaken for the Retirement Communities Council, Inc., Lakewood, New Jersey, and is cited as follows: Katherine M. Heintz, *Retirement Communities: For Adults Only* (New Brunswick, N.J.: Rutgers University, Center for Urban Policy Research, 1976).

Singles Residences Singles developments were surveyed by Barton-Aschman Associates, Inc., in San Jose, California, and Schaumberg, Illinois. The California sample includes data for 143 households residing in studio, one and two bedroom garden apartments which are available both furnished and unfurnished. The Illinois sample consists of information on 176 households residing in one to three bedroom garden apartments, typically unfurnished.

The California sample development is designated as an "adult community" while the Illinois sample is identified as a "singles" development. Both, however, cater primarily to single individuals and young couples although a variety of age groups are present. These developments are distinctive in the extensive array of organized social programs which they provide for their residents.

14

USING CENSUS DATA TO CALCULATE DEMOGRAPHIC MULTIPLIERS

The information in the previous chapter drawn from the Census Public Use Samples barely scratches the surface of this rich data source. Public Use Samples from the 1970 Census are available for every state, most major metropolitan areas, and numerous large urban counties. Public Use data offer significant potential for local, regional and state.

The purpose of this chapter is to outline the definitions, assumptions and computer work necessary to determine demographic multipliers and socioeconomic characteristics of residents of housing types within a specific geographic area, using data available in the U.S. Census Public Use Samples.

This outline will give the analyst an idea of how Public Use data may be employed, and what is involved in using the data. The following procedures are simple and straightforward. They are within the reach of both private planning consultants and local public staff planners. Using the data need not be difficult or expensive.

The following pages discuss Public Use data in detail, describe how the data are employed, and show how to obtain and process the data. The analyst must be aware that to calculate demographic multipliers from Census data requires the use of rather extensive computer facilities. However, virtually all major universities have or have access to the required facilities, and many have a staff of programmers already familiar with Public Use data.

Public Use Sample

Public Use data from the decennial national Census offer detailed descriptions, of individual households.* Public Use data are different from standard Census data, because they describe the characteristics of individual households rather than groups of households. The Public Use Samples include detailed descriptions of the housing unit and a complete list of data on every person in the household. The purpose of the samples is to permit researchers to compute statistical tables which regular Census reports do not include. The derivation of demographic multipliers, is one of the most important ways these data may be employed for local fiscal planning. Public Use Samples are available for both 1960 and 1970, which allows planners to determine whether multipliers have changed over time.

The samples do not describe every household contacted in the course of the decennial Census; instead, one in every 100 is included. Even so, the total number of households and persons recorded is very large. In 1970 the national sample comprised more than 700,000 households and 2,000,000 persons.

There are several types of Public Use Samples. They differ in the data they provide on housing units and their occupants, and in the geographic area that they cover. The best overall description of the various public use samples is provided in:

> U.S. Bureau of the Census, "Public Use Samples of Basic Records from the 1970 Census: Description and Documentations," Washington, D.C., 1972 (no charge).

This report will be cited throughout the following discussion. Data items are accompanied by variable identification numbers, which are also found in the document. Potential users should acquire and study this report before making any final decisions regarding the employment of this data base.

Geography in Public Use Data

Public Use Samples have been provided for three different levels of geographic detail: state, county group, and neighborhood.

State Public Use Samples

State Public Use Samples present 1 percent samples of completed census questionnaires for each of the fifty states. Limited geographic information is provided to describe the location of households within most states. In larger states, the samples denote whether each household in the sample is in an urban or rural area,** inside or outside a metropolitan area.*** For households in metropolitan areas, the data further identify whether or not the household lives in the central city.†

---

*A household is a group of people occupying a single housing unit — a family, a single individual living alone, or a group of unrelated roommates. Answers provided by household members, except those which would make it possible to identify individuals, are reported in public use samples.

**According to the Census, urban areas comprise incorporated localities with populations of 2,500 or more; densely settled suburban areas surrounding major cities; towns and townships in New Jersey, Pennsylvania, and New England with populations of 25,000 persons or more, or with population densities over 1,500 persons per square mile; and counties in other areas with population densities of 1,500 persons per square mile or more.

***The Census defines Metropolitan areas as a group of whole counties surrounding a major city or twin cities of 50,000 population or more. They were formally termed standard metropolitan statistical areas.

†Central cities are the major city or cities around which metropolitan areas are grouped.

For state analysis the Public Use Samples permit measurement of demographic multipliers for the state as a whole, and for several types of areas within the state. They are:

1. Major cities (central cities);
2. Urban concentrations of population in the suburbs of major cities (households living in urban areas, outside central cities, within metropolitan areas);
3. Rural areas in suburbs of major cities (households living in rural areas, outside central cities, within metropolitan areas);
4. Nonmetropolitan concentrations of population (households in urban areas outside metropolitan areas); and
5. Rural areas outside metropolitan areas.

County Group Public Use Samples

The second type of Public Use Samples permits the separate identification of specific counties or groups of counties. The United States Census Bureau is enjoined from releasing Public Use Samples for geographic areas containing fewer than 250,000 persons. While this limit sometimes affects the Bureau's ability to identify types of areas within states (for example, the state Public Use Samples for twelve states* do not report metropolitan or nonmetropolitan residences), it has the greatest effect on the delimitation of county groups. Maps of county groups are provided in "Public Use Samples of Basic Records from the 1970 Census." There are over 3,000 counties and 400 county groups in the nation. Because SMSAs are defined as whole groups of counties, county groups often coincide with SMSAs. The county group Public Use Samples can be used to calculate demographic multipliers for SMSAs. Eight major cities are exactly coterminous with counties.** There are over sixty major cities in the United States whose populations exceed 250,000. In most cases the county group Public Use Samples can be used to calculate multipliers for each of the counties containing these cities.

Some county groups are quite large and heterogeneous. Since county group samples contain no information on a household's address or neighborhood type, the usefulness of the samples for some types of analysis is reduced. For instance, all of the state of Nevada is defined as a single county group. Because the state Public Use Sample identifies types of areas (metropolitan, rural, urban) within the state, it may actually offer greater geographic detail than the county group public use sample for Nevada.

Neighborhood Public Use Samples

Neighborhood Public Use Samples are available for only nine major regions of the United States. The samples list characteristics of the household and of the neighborhood in which the household lives. This type of Public Use Sample is of little real use for local or state planning.

Household Descriptions in the Public Use Samples

Public Use Samples report answers by individual households to virtually all the questions asked in the course of the Census. Only information which might allow households to be personally identified is excluded. This means that Public Use data provide a wealth of information on

---

*Arizona, Delaware,
**Baltimore, San Francisco, New Orleans, Philadelphia, New York, St. Louis, Denver, and Washington, D.C.

physical and economic aspects of housing accommodations as well as demography and socioeconomic characteristics of housholds throughout the nation.

Public Use Samples differ in the types of the data they provide, however. In the 1970 Census, the Census Bureau used three types of questionnaires. Every household in the nation was asked a basic list of questions (the 100 percent questionnaire). Two different questionnaires which required more detailed answers were sent to some households. One of these longer questionnaires was sent to 15 percent of the national households (the 15 percent questionnaire). The second was sent to 5 percent of national households (the 5 percent questionnaire).

The 1970 Public Use Samples are based on these two longer questionnaires. One set of public use data provides copies of one of every 15 responses to the 15 percent questionnaire. A second set is based on one of every five responses to the 5 percent questionnaire. There are thus two groups of Public Use Samples available: one of the state, county, and neighborhood samples based on the 15 percent questionnaire, and one of state, county and neighborhood samples based on the 5 percent questionnaire.

With only a few exceptions, data reported in the two groups of Public Use Samples are virtually identical. Both are useful for fiscal impact analyses. The 5 percent sample is more useful, however, because it reports the number of stories in a building and the presence or absence of a passenger elevator — crucial pieces of information in the definition of housing types. The bulk of the description which follows assumes the use of data from the 5 percent questionnaire, although data from the 15 percent questionnaire may be useful in some cases, as noted.

Sample Size in the Public Use Samples

Limited sample size is one potential drawback of the Public Use data for fiscal impact analysis. This fact may be surprising, given the enormous size of the sample. Demographic multipliers are best calculated for recently constructed housing, however, and this restriction directly affects the sample size available for Public Use data. The sample size is reduced by a factor of at least three, and, for some housing types, by as much as 10. The effect of this restriction on sample size can be illustrated by the following example.

There are likely to be only about 1,000 households in the Public Use Samples for a state or county group containing 250,0900 persons. Moreover, calculations of demographic multipliers are typically based on only recently constructed housing units — housing units built within ten years of the Census.* A state or region with a population of 250,000 might expect to have only 100 to 300 such constructed housing units in the Public Use Samples. Effective sample size can be increased by combining them into larger files. It is thus possible to obtain as much as a four percent sample of newly constructed housing in a state or region.

There are two situations where two or more Public Use Samples can be combined to increase the size of the available sample of households. First, for state level analysis of demographic multipliers, the county group and state public use samples based on the five percent questionnaire can be combined and analyzed as a single sample of two-out-of-one hundred households in the state. Second, the Public Use Samples based on the fifteen percent questionnaire can be used where measures of the number of stories or the presence of passenger elevators in a structure is required. This type of combination can be made for either county groups or for states.

For state level analysis, Public Use Samples can effectively provide between a 1 and 4 percent sample of state households. For county group analysis, the Public Use Samples can provide a 1 or 2 percent sample, depending on the study's objectives.

---

*For most well populated states, sample size is not a problem, except for special types of housing units which comprised a small portion of new housing during the 1960s. Unfortunately, townhouses and condominiums fall into this category.

Housing Type Specifications Using Public Use Samples

The Census does not record whether a family lives in a garden apartment, a walk-up flat, a luxury high rise apartment, or a row house. Rather, the analyst must infer these various housing configurations from several individual descriptions of housing structures.

The 1970 Census collected information on a number of separate characteristics; they can be assembled to identify several important types of housing units. For the purposes of calculating demographic multipliers, the most important housing characteristics include the following:

1. Number of rooms in housing unit
    (5 percent data, H21)*;
2. Year structure built
    (5 percent data, H52);
3. Number of housing units in structure
    (5 percent data, H53);
4. Number of stories in structure
    (5 percent data, H56);
5. Availability of a passenger elevator
    (5 percent data, H57);
6. Number of bedrooms in housing unit
    (5 percent data, H61).

Together, these six variables permit the identification of several types of housing structures. They also enable analysts to measure roughly the interior space provided in housing units of each structure type. Both of these characteristics are of key importance in calculating demographic multipliers.

Defining Housing Structure Types

Single family detached homes, townhouses, duplexes and mobile homes can be identified by using the Census codes for the number of housing units in each structure. Multifamily housing, generally apartments, can be divided into several categories, defined by the number of stories in the structure and whether an elevator is present. Garden apartments can be identified as single structures with (a) more than three housing units and (b) three or fewer stories. Mid-rise walk-up apartments are housing units in four- to six-story structures not equipped with a passenger elevator. Mid-rise elevator apartments are housing units in multifamily four- to six-story structures with an elevator. High-rise apartments are housing units in structures with seven or more stories serviced by an elevator.

Together, these eight housing types are fully adequate for most planning purposes; they comprise over 99 percent of the recently constructed housing units in the nation. Moreover, additional refinements in identifying housing types are possible. The analyst can use Census codes identifying whether the housing unit is owned fee simple, owned as a condominium or cooperative, etc. In addition, the Census reports homeowners' estimates of the market values of their properties (5 percent data, H29-H30), tenants' contract rents (the monthly amounts actually paid to landlords — 5 percent data, H31-H33), or tenants' gross rents (contract rents adjusted to

---

*Figures in parentheses denote the type of questionnaire providing the corresponding variable and the identification number the Census Bureau assigns this variable. Both pieces of information are reported in "Public Use Samples of Basic Records from the 1970 Census."

include the costs of utilities — 5 percent data, H34-H36). These data permit the separate identification of higher value from lower value homes or apartments.*

Housing Unit Space: Rooms and Bedrooms

Conventionally, household size and number of school-age children are assumed to depend on housing structure type and on the number of bedrooms in the housing unit. This linkage is so strong that demographic multipliers are frequently termed "bedroom multipliers." Bedrooms need not be the key space variable, because the number of bedrooms is difficult to measure exactly. Typically, housing units contain one or more rooms that may be used as a bedroom or for some other purpose. For instance, some developers advertise a room as a den, although it may be physically indistinguishable from adjoining rooms advertised as bedrooms. Such advertising may cause a miscalculation in the expected number of school-age children who will reside in the unit.

Multipliers based on a simple count of the number of rooms in a housing unit are often a useful alternative to bedroom multipliers. As noted above, the Public Use Samples based on the 1970 Census present both the number of bedrooms and other rooms in individual housing units, making it possible to calculate both room and bedroom multipliers.

Calculation of Demographic Multipliers/Profiles

Multipliers

The Public Use Samples include two groups of records for each household. The first group is a single record describing the characteristics of the housing unit, such as its residence, location and the total number of persons living in the unit (5 percent data, H12-H13). The second group includes a separate record describing each individual in the family. There are varying numbers of records in this second group, depending on the number of persons in the household.

The Public Use Samples provide detailed descriptions of up to thirty members of the household. Three crucial pieces of information are listed for each person:

1. Age (5 percent data, P9-P11)
2. The highest school grade attended
   (5 percent data, P11-P18)
3. A code indicating whether or not the person
   was currently attending school at the time
   of the census (5 percent data, P19)

Because the Census is taken during the regular school year (in April) the above items identify school attendance.

1. identify all persons in each household whose
   ages fall into the normal bounds of public
   school attendance, i.e., persons between the
   ages of 5 and 20 years;**

---

*The Census Bureau makes it possible to identify owner-occupied homes whose values fall into several categories. High value single family homes might be defined as those valued at $35,000 or more. The Public Use Sample also makes it possible to measure multipliers in homes valued at $50,000 or more.

**These age limits are flexible. Virually no children under the age of five will be attending public kindergarten in April. Very few high school seniors, except those who are enrolled in adult education classes, will be over the age of 20.

2. Identify persons of school-age who are actually attending school;
3. Determine the school grade being attended, using Census information on the highest grade attended.

For most purposes, three groups of school grades are necessary for planning purposes: kindergarten, elementary and intermediate school (grades one to eight); and high school (grades nine to twelve). However, the Census identifies each of the twelve regular grades of elementary and high school, so local users have a good deal of discretion.

Multipliers calculated using this method have one major deficiency. They do not distinguish between children attending public school and private school. The importance of this deficiency differs a great deal among areas. If individual analysts feel that private or parochial schools account for a large part of the school attendance in their areas, they can adjust school-age children multipliers on the basis of local estimates of the proportion of pupils not attending private schools. This distinction cannot be made using Census data.

Socioeconomic Profiles

One of the questions most often asked about new housing is what kinds of people will live in it — rich or poor, professional or blue collar, old or young. The Public Use Samples describe these characteristics of residents of new housing. The household record presents four variables which can be used to determine socioeconomic profiles:

1. Household type (5 percent data, H70);
2. Race of the head of the household (5 percent data, H71);
3. Age of the head of the household (5 percent data, (H72-73);
4. Total annual income of family or primary individual (5 percent data, H85-87).

The Census defines five types of households: husband-wife families; other types of families with a male head (such as a father living with his children, or an adult son living with his mother); families with a female head; male individuals living alone or with other people to whom they are not related by blood or marriage; and females in the same situation. Information on the age and race of the head of household is also quite detailed.

Income actually received by the family in 1969 is presented in hundreds of dollars, up to $50,000. Income data are most useful for defining the relative economic status of residents of new housing of various types. To be useful for any other planning purpose, 1969 income would have to be adjusted to general inflation and to the particularly rapid increase in housing costs in recent years.

If other socioeconomic data are required, the analyst must examine the descriptions of individual members of the family. Socioeconomic data on the head of the household may be particularly useful. The head of the household is identified in the person records (5 percent data, P1). The person record can be used to determine the education of the head of the household (5 percent data, P17-P18) and his or her occupation (5 percent data, P27-P29). Other information is also available. Using these data, the analyst can easily describe a number of socioeconomic characteristics of residents of whatever type of housing units he wishes to define.

Data Processing and the Public Use Samples

The Public Use Samples do not require sophisticated programming, but they do require the use of a reasonably sophisticated computer — one capable of reading magnetic tape and processing large quantities of data. They also require access to special programs designed to read and process the data, or to programmers who have and know how to use such programs.

Where to Get the Data

The 1970 Census was the first one the Census Bureau used to prepare extensive reports coded on magnetic tape for easy computer use. To maximize the accessibility of these data, the Census Bureau and other government agencies contracted with the Data Use and Access Laboratories (DUALABS) to design tape specifications and computer programs to process the data. For most users interested in acquiring and using the Public Use Samples, DUAL ABS is the place to begin.* DUAL ABS can provide all the data and programming necessary to use the Public Use Samples.

Many universities acquired major parts of the computer files for the 1970 Census to use in research. Such universities will already possess the programming necessary to use the Public Use Samples or will know who does have the programming. They will also often know where actual copies of Public Use Samples can be obtained, and they may be able to provide access to Public Use data more inexpensively than DUAL ABS.

Programming and Using the Public Use Samples

Typically, using the Public Use Samples requires a three-stage procedure.

The first state consists of reading the Census tapes and translating them into records which can be easily manipulated by most computer programmers using a standard computer language, such as FORTRAN IV. DUALABS has prepared computer programs to accomplish this task.

DUALABS programs enable the user to edit in the Public Use Samples by eliminating everything but the data about the household and its members for the analysis being undertaken. Exhibit 14-1 lists the basic variables required for calculating demographic multipliers. The list includes all items likely to be required for the calculation and analysis of demographic multipliers. As indicated in the exhibit, a number of items are optional, but they may be useful for special types of analysis.

One crucial usefulness of the PUSH program (Exhibit 14-2) is that it can be applied to eliminate households living in older housing. Multipliers most useful for fiscal analyses are those describing newer housing, built between 1960 and 1970. Housing unit age is reported in data item H52 of the 5 percent sample.

The Census Bureau collects information on up to thirty members in each household. Records in the following form will be created for all households living in new housing:

I	II		
	Person Data Items		
Household Data Items	Person 1	Person 2	Person 30

---

*The address is
  Suite 900,
  1601 N. Kent Street,
  Arlington, Virginia 22209;
  telephone (703) 525-1480

Using Census Data 299

EXHIBIT 14-1

HOUSEHOLD AND PERSON DATA FROM
THE PUBLIC USE SAMPLE REQUIRED
TO CALCULATE DEMOGRAPHIC MULTIPLIERS[1]

I. Household Information

   A. Geographic Identifiers
      1. State Samples Only[2]
         a. State of Residence (H7-H8)
         b. Urban/Rural Residence (H9)
         c. Metropolitan/Nonmetropolitan Residence (H10)
         d. Central City/Non Central City Residence (H11)
      2. County Group Samples Only[3]

   B. County Group Identification Code (H7-H11)
   C. Number of Persons (H12-H13)
   D. Number of Rooms (H21)
   E. Tenure (H27)[4]
   F. Value of Property[4] (H29-H30)
   G. Contract Monthly Rent[4] (H31-H33)
   H. Gross Monthly Rent[4] (H34-H36)
   I. Year Structure Built (H52)
   J. Units in Structure (H53)
   K. Number of Stories (H56)
   L. Passenger Elevator (H57)
   M. Number of Bedrooms (H61)
   N. Household Type (H70)[4]
   O. Race of Head (H71)[4]
   P. Age of Head (H72-H73)[4]
   Q. Total Income of Family or Primary Individual[4] (H85-H87)

II. Person Information

   A. Basic Relationship (P1)[4]
   B. Age (P9-P11)
   C. Highest Grade Attended (P17-P18)
   D. Finished Grade (P19)
   E. Current Occupation[4] (P27-P29)

Notes: [1] The table describes data available from the 5 percent questionnaire. Data names and identifier numbers are those reported in "Public Use Samples of Basic Records from the 1970 Census."

[2] These geographic identifiers are available only from the state Public Use Samples. They are relevant only to users undertaking state level analyses.

[3] The county group Public Use Samples enable users to identify individual areas. No other geographic data are provided.

[4] These data items are optional and are required for various types of special analyses described in the text. Strictly speaking, they are not required for calculating demographic multipliers.

Source: Rutgers University, Center for Urban Policy Research, Summer 1976.

EXHIBIT 14-2

SAMPLE FORTRAN PROGRAM FOR EDITING THE OUTPUT OF THE PUSH PROGRAM

```
      INTEGER P,Ø.
      DIMENSION ID(   J), IA(   K, 3Ø)
C     NOTE J IS THE NUMBER OF DATA ITEMS DESCRIBING THE HOUSEHOLD
C          K IS THE NUMBER OF DATA ITEMS DESCRIBING EACH PERSON
C          THESE PARAMETERS MUST BE FILLED IN
    1 READ (   ,2, END=5)  ID, IA
C          NOTE THAT THE LOGICAL INPUT FILE MUST BE SPECIFIED
C          THE FORMAT WILL DEPEND ON ITEMS SELECTED USING PUSH
    2 FORMAT (
      IS = Ø
C          IS COUNTS TOTAL NUMBERS OF SCHOOL AGE CHILDREN
      IK = Ø
C          ID COUNTS KINDERGARTEN PUPILS
      IE = Ø
C          IE COUNTS ELEMENTARY SCHOOL PUPILS BETWEEN THE GRADE OF
C          1 and 8
      IH = Ø
C          IH COUNTS HIGH SCHOOL PUPILS IN GRADES 9 TO 12
      IHD = Ø
C          IHD IDENTIFIES THE SEQUENCE NUMBER OF THE HEAD OF HOUSEHOLD
C          IN THE LIST OF PERSON RECORDS (IF EDUCATION OF HEAD IS
C          DESIRED)
      NPERS = ID(L)
C              L IS THE SEQUENCE WITHIN THE HOUSEHOLD DATA ITEM H12-13
C          WHICH MEASURES NUMBER OF PERSONS IN THE FAMILY
      IF(NPERS. EQ.Ø) GO TO 1
C     THIS STATEMENT ELIMINATES VACANT UNITS
      DO 3 1 = 1, NPERS
      IF (IA(M, I).  EQ.Ø. AND   IA(N,I). NE. Ø) IHD =1
C          M IS THE SEQUENCE IN THE PERSON RECORD OF THE DATA DESCRIBING
C          A PERSON'S RELATIONSHIP TO THE HEAD OF HOUSEHOLD.  THIS IS DATA
C          ITEM (P1).  M MUST BE SPECIFIED BY USER 9
C          N IS THE SEQUENCE IN THE PERSON RECORD OF THE DATA ITEM MEASURING
C          PERSONS AGE(P9-11) ZERO VALUE DENOTES INFANTS.
      IF (IA(N, 1). GT. 2Ø) GO TO 3
      IF (IA(N, 1). LT. 5) GO TO 5
      IF (IA(P,1). NE.Ø) GO TO 3
C          P IS THE SEQUENCE WITHIN THE PERSON RECORD OF DATA ITEM P19, WHICH
C             TAKES THE VALUE OF ZERO FOR PERSONS ATTENDING SCHOOL.
C          P MUST BE SPECIFIED
      IF (IA(Q, 1). LT. 2) GO TO 3
C          Q IS THE SEQUENCE NUMBER WITHIN THE PERSON RECORD OF DATA ITEM
C          P17-18.  NUMBER OF YEARS OF SCHOOL ATTENDED (VALUES LESS THAN 2
C          DENOTE)
C          NURSERY SCHOOL PUPILS
C          VALUES GREATER THAN 14 DENOTE COLLEGE STUDENTS.
      IF (IA(Q,1). GT. 14) GO TO 3
      IS = IS + 1
      IF (IA(Q, 1). EQ. 2) ID = IK + 1
      IF (IA(Q,1). GT. 1Ø) IH = IH + 1
      IF (IA(Q,1). GT. 2. AND. IA(Q,1). LT.11) IE = IE + 1
    3 CONTINUE
      WRITE (   ,4) ID, IS, IK, IE, IH, (IA(KV, IHD), KV = 1, K)
C          NOTE THAT THE LOGICAL OUTPUT UNIT MUST BE SPECIFIED AS WELL AS K
C          THE PORTION ',(IA(KV, IHD), KV = 1, K)' IS NEEDED ONLY IF INFORMATION
C          ON THE HEAD OF HOUSEHOLD IS DESIRED
    4 FORMAT (
C          FORMAT MUST BE SPECIFIED
      GO TO 1
    5 ENDFILE --
      STOP
      END
```

Source: Rutgers University, Center for Urban Policy Research, Summer 1976

Identical data items will be included for each person in the family, up to thirty individuals. Only a miniscule number of households will actually contain thirty persons. For smaller households, most of the person records will be empty. (Technically, all data items in excess person records will take the value of zero.)

The second stage of estimating demographic multipliers is to summarize these unwieldly records so that the multipliers can be calculated. The data file created will define housing types, and calculate average number of persons, school-age children at various grade levels, and other socioeconomic data required. For most users this will require a special program designed to calculate the number of school-age children living in each household, by grade level.

The logic and mechanics of such a program are straightforward, and any competent programmer can accomplish this task easily. A sample program is included here for guidance (Exhibit 14-2).

The third stage is to read the data file created by the second step. This last step can be accomplished quite easily with standard computation programs used in social science research. One of the simplest tools to use for reading the file is the breakdown procedure in the *Statistical Package for the Social Sciences* (SPSS). SPSS programs are widely available and are described in: Norman Nie, C. Hadlay Hall, Jean C. Jenkins, Karin Steinbrenner, Dale H. Bent, *Statistical Package for the Social Sciences* (New York: McGraw-Hill, 1975).

The breakdown procedure defines a number of subgroups within a basic data sample, and the program calculates the mean value of selected variables for each subgroup as well as for the sample as a whole. This method is perfect for calculating demographic multipliers. Subgroups defined in the breakdown program could be made on the basis of housing type, and other characteristics of the household.

For analysis of other characteristics of residents of housing units, SPSS also permits the cross-tabulation of variables. Cross-tabulation of housing types could be made with respect to the occupation of the head of household, his or her age, household type, and so forth.

15

USING FIELD SURVEYS TO CALCULATE DEMOGRAPHIC MULTIPLIERS

Neither available studies of demographic multipliers[1] nor public use data can meet the information needs of local planners in all cases. Regional multipliers do not always apply to local conditions. For instance, regional multipliers may be misleading for specific localities where private or parochial schools play important roles in educating children. More importantly, physically similar housing units may serve quite different housing functions in different locations. A high-rise condominium in Florida will attract a much different clientele than one located in suburban Washington or San Francisco.[2] Special household surveys[3] provide one way to make sure that a local cost-revenue analysis is as accurate and useful as possible. If correctly conducted, special surveys can result in demographic multipliers that better reflect local conditions. They can also be targeted to newly popular types of housing being built today, such as condominiums or townhouses.

Surveys can further be used to increase the sophistication of fiscal impact analyses by ascertaining shopping patterns, incomes, and workplaces of residents of new housing in the community. These types of data are invaluable for measuring additional sales tax or income tax revenues likely to be generated by a housing development. Surveys permit communities to determine how their residents view priorities for additional public spending or cut-backs, and how satisfied they are with the existing quality of public services.

Surveys have a number of drawbacks. First, they are quite expensive. Second, if they are conducted improperly, they may prove unreliable. Third, they are time-consuming, especially since they must be completed before the remainder of the fiscal impact analysis is undertaken.

This chapter describes many of the important considerations and decisions the analyst must make during the course of a survey to ensure a useful product. First, the chapter addresses two basic questions about survey sampling: (1) whether or not to undertake a survey, and (2) if so, what kind. Second, the processes of sample and questionnaire design are described. Both guidelines for sample selection and a model questionnaire are provided. The reader is then shown the benefits of survey efficiency, how to calculate survey costs, and a simple method of determining sample size. Examples of required sample size for various levels of survey accuracy are also provided. Finally, the necessary coding, keypunching, and programming requirements, and the more basic data presentation formats are included. The chapter concludes with a list of additional resources that can be used to augment the information in this chapter.

Deciding to Undertake a Survey

The first step in survey research is to decide whether or not a survey is necessary. The answer to this question depends on the balance between the potential benefits of the survey and its cost.

Potential Benefits of Surveys

The benefits of a survey will depend on three prime considerations, which vary considerably among localities:

1. What type of information is required for intelligent local planning?
2. How much of this information is known already or can be inferred from other studies?
3. What can a survey add to this knowledge?

It is very important to remember that numerous special studies have been already undertaken. They provide most of the data required for fiscal impact analysis. The maximum contribution a survey can make is to fill in whatever gaps exist in this basic information. In some instances, upon reflection, the gaps will prove to be quite small. Special surveys ought not to be undertaken before data needs are aired, measured, and balanced very carefully.

Potential Costs of Surveys

The costs of special surveys differ enormously depending, in part, on such a relatively simple factor as the price of available labor. Usually, however, cost is a direct reflection of the survey's design. A survey has three basic components:

1. The choice of questions to be asked (questionnaire design) and the design of the sample to be contacted during the survey;
2. The actual field work; and
3. The processing, verification, and analysis of survey results.

The design of questionnaires for fiscal impact analyses is generally relatively inexpensive because so many earlier surveys have been done that questions can follow standard formats. Sample design is crucially important in determining the costs of field work. It should be done very carefully; if not, the sample can be very costly.

The costs of field work depend on the size of the survey, and exactly how the sample is organized. This aspect of survey work will be described below in detail, but the most basic and obvious determinant of the costs of field work is the number of persons to whom the questionnaire will be administered, i.e., sample size.

Another important determinant of the costs of special surveys is the way in which households are contacted after they are selected for interview. There are a number of ways to undertake a sample survey. People may be mailed the questionnaire, asked to complete it, and then return it by mail, or they may be visited by interviewers and have the questionnaire completed in person.

Mail and phone surveys pose problems since they involve inherent biases. Mail surveys reach only people willing to read and act upon what is generally termed "junk mail." Telephone surveys are biased because a significant number of households either do not have a telephone or have unlisted numbers.[4] Successful surveys require a combination of methods. The method most likely to be successful by itself, however, is the personal interview. It also is the most expensive method, but it has many advantages which justify its costs. Most importantly, interviewers can apply gentle but effective pressure on people to answer questions. In addition, they are able to clarify questions for people and they generally get more accurate data.

There is no real upper limit to the cost per interview. However, there is a minimum: the cost of selecting people to be interviewed, making contact with them, obtaining answers to the array of questions, and preparing the answers for processing. A general minimum cost for work will entail the expenditure of at least several hours of the analyst's labor per interview.

Processing and using the data are always surprisingly expensive to the novice. This element will cost at least as much as the rest of the survey combined, and frequently more. Great care must be made to allow for sufficient time to perform this last stage of the work. The beginner often spends all his resources in the field and leaves no time to check or analyze data.

Sample Design and Survey Methods

The objective of a survey is to find out something about a large group of households or persons. The group to which the survey is directed is termed the target population (or, technically, the "universe" of the survey). The basic idea of a survey is to contact a group of households or people (the sample) selected from the target population in such a way as to guarantee that they will represent the target population.

Thus, sample design requires two basic decisions:

1. Choosing the target population; and
2. Specifying the methods for selecting the sample.

Choosing the Target Population

Household surveys for fiscal impact analysis generally aim at examining the characteristics and attitudes of *residents of recently constructed housing* in the community so that planners can confidently predict who will live in similar units constructed in the community in the future.[5]

Thus, the choice of target population is relatively straightforward. In general, local surveys will want to examine the type of housing that is being built in and around the community. A truly meaningful survey requires that a substantial number of housing units in a number of different developments be surveyed. Otherwise, survey results will be too unreliable to be worth the effort. Many communities will not contain enough housing units in the target population to satisfy this requirement. In this case, it will be necessary to include housing developments in surrounding communities similar to your own. It is unlikely that this factor will bias survey results with respect to the socioeconomic or demographic characteristics of housing residents, although it would render questions regarding residents' perceptions and priorities regarding local public services or amenities less meaningful.

Once the target population is chosen, a complete inventory of all housing units of the selected structure types in the area must be made so that a sample can be determined.

Sample Design

The next step in undertaking a survey is to determine which housing units in the target population are to be selected for the sample. Formal statistical texts generally emphasize the definition and merits of the random sample.[6] Random sampling procedures for a fiscal impact analysis would choose sample housing units in such a way so as to guarantee that each individual housing unit in the target population had an equal probability of being selected. One way of making this would be to assemble the addresses of all the individual housing units in a box, mix them, and then select single addresses, one at a time. For a fiscal impact analysis, however, such a sampling procedure can lead to a prohibitively expensive field survey.

One sampling method which has proven successful permits cost-efficient surveys without sacrificing data quality. The essence of the method is to select a random sample of all recent housing *developments* that are potential survey targets because of their location and constituent housing type. Every household in each of the sample developments is a potential interview. If this sampling method is selected, groups of interviewers may be sent door to door in each of the developments without making prior appointments and administer the questionnaire in person. This method enables interviewers to accomplish a large number of interviews in a relatively short period of time.

There are two important points to remember if this method is selected. First, at least two or three developments must be included for each basic housing type to have any probability of success.* Developments of the same housing type may differ in their characteristics and the kinds of residents they attract. These differences can be neutralized only by examining a reasonable number of them.

Second, and perhaps more importantly, this method must be supplemented by techniques designed to guarantee that *all* residents of the development are equally represented in the survey. There is an inevitable bias in surveys that interview only households where people are usually found at home. If the interviews are conducted during the day, the survey is quite likely to be biased in favor of families with young children rather than families with dual incomes.

There are a number of methods which will minimize such a bias. For instance, interviews can be conducted on weekends or early evenings. Second, the interviewers can note addresses and names on post boxes or doors of housing units where no one was at home, and then attempt to reach these people later — either by personal visits or by telephoning (reverse telephone directories can be used for this purpose).

The analyst must also remember to allow for vacant units. It would be incorrect to include vacant units indetermining the weight to be applied to follow-up interviews. During initial contacts with housing managers or owners, the analyst should ascertain exactly which (or at least how many) housing units in the development are vacant. Interviewers must also be directed to note units which appear to be vacant.

Questionnaire Design

The basic element of survey design is to determine what questions must be asked. The choice of specific questions depends upon the survey's objectives. This section describes one group of questions that should meet the needs of most users. A sample questionnaire used in a recent national survey is used as the basis for the discussion. (The entire questionnaire is included at the

---

*Prior arrangements must be made with owners or managers of apartment developments, as well as with the local police department. Otherwise, interviewers may be guilty of trespassing or other crimes.

Using Field Surveys 307

end of this chapter.) It is designed for personal interviews. It could be used largely unchanged for a phone survey and would have to be altered slightly for a mail survey.

The questionnaire is designed to ascertain general demographic information for residents of standard housing types (single-family homes, garden apartments, high rise, etc.). It was planned as a multipurpose survey instrument, however. This means that questions have been included to handle situations and housing types (i.e., vacation homes and mobile homes) which may not be part of the survey as planned. Thus, the questionnaire may be shortened, depending on the analyst's particular objectives.

Estimating Demographic Multipliers

For the purpose of fiscal impact analysis, the two most important data items are the number of people living in the housing unit and the number of pupils attending public schools at various grade levels. For some types of analyses it is useful to know the age and sex of household residents as well.

Household demographic characteristics have been shown to be very strongly related to housing costs, to the number of rooms or bedrooms in the housing unit, and to structure type.[7] Multipliers also differ considerably among developments, each of which has a character of its own.[8] As a result of these relationships, typical data required to describe a housing unit usefully include the following:

1. The number of bedrooms in the particular unit;
2. The number of rooms in the unit;
3. Housing unit structure type (e.g., single-family detached home, garden apartment, etc.);
4. For owner-occupants, their estimate of housing unit market value; and
5. For renters, their monthly rent.

Other Potential Questions

The main difficulty in designing a questionnaire is its length. There is never a shortage of questions which might be asked, but as each question is added, the cost of the survey escalates. Two important areas not included in this sample questionnaire are household satisfaction with the quality of public services[9] and priorities for improving these services. Questions about these areas might be phrased as follows:

There are many services a municipality provides.
How would you rate the following?

| | | | Rating | | | |
Service	Very Good	Good	Neutral	Poor	Very Poor	No Answer/ Don't Know
Public Education						
Government Administration						
Public Safety						
Public Works						
Health and Welfare						
Recreation and Culture (Libraries)						
Other (Specify)						

(A more specific categorization for local services could be used.)
In which of the previous list of services are improvements most pressingly needed?

Public Education	_____
Government Administration	_____
Public Safety	_____
Public Works	_____
Health and Welfare	_____
Recreation and Culture (Libraries)	_____
Other (Specify)	_____
No Answer/Don't Know	_____

If the revenue portion of fiscal impact analysis is to be reasonably detailed, several other questions can be asked. For instance, if a sales tax is a primary revenue source, it might be important to ascertain shopping patterns. Similarly, if the community obtains significant revenues from beach user fees, it might be important to ask about the frequency of use of this and other revenue-producing recreational facilities.

The best advice, however, is to keep the questionnaire as short as possible. Adding more questions without very careful planning is likely to affect the survey's reliability.

Questionnaire Layout and Survey Efficiency

A good questionnaire is more than a series of good questions. The first key to successful surveys is careful organization.

Interviewer Notes and Pre-Interview Data

As shown on the sample questionnaire at the end of this chapter, the first page is designed to be filled out before the interview. The basic data required on this page are:

1. The type of housing unit to which the questionnaire is to be administered
2. The particular unit of this type to be examined
3. The interviewer and
4. The type of interview to be administered.

The first two data items assist in organizing field work during the effort and allow the completed interviews to be stored easily before they are analyzed. Identifying the particular interviewer provides a record of the productivity of individual interviewers and a basis for checking on data accuracy and job performance. Questions will inevitably arise during an analysis, and the interviewer is often able to answer them.

The final area on the first page denotes the type of interview. A number of attempts are sometimes required to complete an interview. It is crucial to keep track of how many attempts of various kinds were actually necessary. The exact types of entries under "type of interview" will depend on study design. However, the function of this information slot is to record both the procedure used and the relative difficulty in obtaining the information.

Preamble for Interviewers

The second page of the questionnaire is a sample preamble for interviewers to use when they contact residents. It is very important to give interviewers some idea of how to begin a conversation. They may elaborate on the recommended introduction, but this basic format provides a useful starting place.

Computer Coding and Question Design

One of the most important ways in which a questionnaire helps to organize a survey is by making the recording of data as simple and clear as possible. This clarity has the side advantage of helping to ensure the accuracy of the data. Almost inevitably, computers play an important role in analyzing survey results. This means that the information collected during the survey will have to be keypunched on computer cards. Answers to questions should therefore be recorded so as to make this task a relatively easy one. To the degree possible, keypunching should be done directly from the questionnaire itself. While this effort helps to eliminate coding errors, it also means that every question that will be subjected to computer analysis must be structured so that some kind of numeric code can be used. Answers to some types of questions, e.g. the amount of monthly rent, are inherently easy to encode. For others, numeric codes have to be imposed on the answers: "Yes" might be coded "one" and "no" as "zero." The sample questionnaire is designed with this in mind. Users should follow its lead whenever possible.

One point must be reemphasized at this time. *It would be a serious mistake to assume that survey reliability can be increased by focusing field work on getting as many interviews as possible. Larger samples are more useful than smaller samples only when both are equally unbiased, i.e., only when equal care is taken in both samples to collect information from people who are uncooperative or difficult to locate.* A considerable amount of effort must be diverted to undertaking follow-up interviews. These reinterviews can be difficult. Doing them conscientiously means that sample size must be sacrificed. The sacrifice is more than worth it, however.

Another point to be emphasized with regard to sample size is that *overall sample size* is of less importance than the *size of the sample used in analyses*. Although it sounds confusing, the basic idea is simple. Calculating demographic multipliers is usually focused on a particular type and size of housing unit. The sample sizes used in the analysis are the numbers of units in each separate type of housing divided by number of bedrooms, for instance. Unless the sample is carefully designed so that each separate type of housing unit and size dimension is sufficiently represented, samples quickly get too thin for effective analysis.

The Determination of Sample Size

Statistical rules governing sample size have two main objectives (for the purposes of this section). First, they give some guidance regarding sample size required for reliable estimates of demographic multipliers. Second, once the survey is taken and the data are analyzed, these rules can be used to ascertain the likely reliability of estimates of demographic multipliers resulting from the survey. There are a number of fine statistical texts which describe these rules.[10] Special data, from the 1970 Census, have been used to estimate demographic multipliers in the nation, by region, for several types of housing. The results of this analysis provide guidelines for selecting sample size and the sample's likely effect on the accuracy of the findings of the surveys.

Exhibit 15-1 presents estimates, based on national Census data, about average numbers of residents, of school-age children and household size multipliers for four structure types and a variety of sizes. These figures are tabulated in columns 1 and 2. For example, Census data show that the mean number of school-age children residing in one-bedroom garden apartments across the nation was 0.04 in 1970.

The more important portion of this exhibit is columns 3 to 10. They present estimates of likely errors from random factors in sample sizes ranging from 25 to 500 housing units. The size of the random error which will occur is best measured by a statistical term called the standard error. It measures the range of differences in survey estimates of average data which might arise entirely because of chance. A useful rule of thumb is that random factors can cause survey estimates of average values of demographic multipliers or other data to vary from true values by as much as two standard errors. As shown in the exhibit, the standard error of estimates of school-age children multipliers in one-bedroom garden apartments is 0.06 when demographic multipliers are estimated from a survey of twenty-five such apartments. The average multiplier to be expected in such units is 0.04 (column 1). Thus, chance elements may cause this multiplier to vary from 0.00 to 0.16. A survey based on twenty-five units might be off by a factor of four, simply because of chance.

Taking another example, the mean number of school-age children living in four-bedroom, single-family detached homes was 1.9 in the nation as a whole in 1970. If a sample of 100 of these units were taken, the standard error of estimates of this demographic multiplier would be approximately 0.15. Thus, purely by chance, survey results might range from 1.6 to 2.2, or vary by almost 40 percent.

The data in the table may also be used to obtain a rough idea of required sample size for fiscal impact surveys. The approach is to set some minimum acceptable standard for survey reliability, ascertain the sample size required to get this level of reliability, and then make sure that this level is attained in the course of the work. For this method, the most reasonable measure of the reliability of results is some standard which the user is willing to accept for the likely percent error (plus or minus) in demographic multipliers.

For instance, a user may wish to calculate school-age children (SAC) multipliers for three-bedroom, single-family homes. After reflection, he decides to accept results that may be in error by plus or minus 10 percent. This means that

$$\frac{(2) \times (\text{Standard Error})}{\text{SAC}} \leq .10$$

where SAC is the mean number of school-age children likely to reside in this type of unit. The average number of school-age children residing in a three-bedroom detached home is typically 1.1 in the nation. This means that the chosen reliability level implies that the standard error must be 0.06 or less. Exhibit 15-1 shows that to achieve this level of accuracy would require a sample of 500 three-bedroom houses. Other standards for survey accuracy would yield different estimates of the requisite sample size. The reader is urged to undertake these calculations for all types of units and for all other accuracy standards when designing the sample.

National data provide useful but rough guides to the demographic multipliers that will be encountered in the course of the survey. The first step after local fiscal surveys are completed should be the calculation of "confidence intervals" for survey estimates of the multipliers. A confidence

EXHIBIT 15-1
SAMPLE SIZE AND THE RELIABILITY OF SURVEY ESTIMATES OF DEMOGRAPHIC MULTIPLIERS

Housing Unit Type	Mean Number in Nation as a Whole		Standard Error of Estimates of Number of School-Age Children Based on Sample Sizes Of:				Standard Error of Estimates of Number of Resident Persons Based on Sample Sizes Of:			
	(1) School-Age Children	(2) Household Size	(3) 25 Units	(4) 50 Units	(5) 100 Units	(6) 500 Units	(7) 25 Units	(8) 50 Units	(9) 100 Units	(10) 500 Units
Garden apartment										
1 bedroom	0.04	1.70	0.06	0.04	0.03	0.01	0.16	0.11	0.08	0.04
2 bedroom	0.27	2.60	0.16	0.11	0.08	0.04	0.24	0.17	0.12	0.06
Single-family House										
2 bedroom	0.40	2.70	0.18	0.13	0.29	0.04	0.28	0.20	0.14	0.06
3 bedroom	1.10	3.80	0.26	0.18	0.13	0.06	0.30	0.21	0.15	0.07
4 bedroom	1.92	4.70	0.30	0.21	0.15	0.07	0.32	0.23	0.16	0.07
Townhouse										
1 bedroom	0.10	1.90	0.06	0.04	0.03	0.01	0.16	0.11	0.08	0.04
2 bedroom	0.35	2.70	0.16	0.11	0.08	0.04	0.26	0.18	0.13	0.06
3 bedroom	1.33	4.10	0.26	0.18	0.13	0.06	0.34	0.24	0.17	0.08
High-Rise Apartment										
0 bedroom (Studio)	0.01	1.10	0.02	0.014	0.01	0.004	0.14	0.10	0.07	0.03
1 bedroom	0.17	1.40	0.02	0.014	0.01	0.004	0.14	0.10	0.07	0.03
2 bedroom	0.18	2.30	0.12	0.08	0.06	0.030	0.24	0.17	0.12	0.06

Source: Rutgers University Center for Urban Policy Research analyses of 1970 Census Public Use Samples from 11 states.

interval is the range within which each of the multipliers can be expected to vary, simply as a result of chance, i.e., (two standard errors). Virtually all computer programs likely to be used for analyzing survey results will calculate the standard error of estimated demographic multipliers for the user.

The Mechanics of Sample Surveys: After the Field Work

During survey planning, it is easy to underestimate the effort and cost of processing the results. When interviewers return from the field, large parts of the job remain. Typically, they involve:

1. Editing questionnaires and verifying data;
2. Coding questionnaires for keypunching on computer cards;
3. Keypunching and verification;
4. Computer programming and statistical manipulations; and
5. Analyzing results

Few useful surveys will contain so small a number of observations that hand tabulations are feasible. Generally computers will be an inevitable accompaniment to data analysis.

The logic and mechanics of most of this final stage of survey work are clear. For instance, data verification involves filling in gaps in completed questionnaires or clearing up ambiguous answers. Some verification may be accomplished simply by talking to interviewers. Some questions require more extensive effort, occasionally a re-interview.

Preparing interview data for computer analysis involves coding answers so that they can be keypunched and analyzed by computers. Computers understand only "yes's" and "no's." Good coding must be logically clear, permit discrete classification and exact counts of data, and be as simple as possible. The attached questionnaire is largely self-coding, which greatly simplifies its use.

It is vitally necessary to assemble coding instructions into a clear and concise manual, which must be preserved. Otherwise, survey data will quickly become meaningless to future users.

Keypunching data on computer cards is itself a source of a number of errors. The cards should always be verified, and the initial computer analyses of the data must focus on making sure that each data item on each card falls within permissible limits defined by the coding manual. Blank columns on computer cards must be checked to make sure that they really *should* be blank. If they are not supposed to be blank, the entire card should be reviewed for the possible error. The data in multiple columns may be wrong because of this error.

With regard to the mechanics of computer analyses, a number of standard packages of computer programs are widely available. They permit the variety of statistical computations which will be required in the course of the analysis. The most popular of them is *Statistical Package for the Social Sciences* (SPSS).[11] A "breakdown" procedure in SPSS permits users to define a number of subgroups within a basic data sample. This program calculates average values of data items for each subgroup as well as for the sample as a whole. This is perfect for calculating demographic multipliers. The breakdown program can be refined on the basis of housing type and other household characteristics. For analysis of other characteristics of residents, SPSS also permits the cross-tabulation of multiple variables. Cross-tabulation of housing types may be made with respect to the occupation of the head of household, his or her age, household type, and so forth.

Conclusion

It is impossible within the confines of this chapter to explore in depth the intricacies of survey research. The information should be augmented when the analyst wants to begin significant field research. The following is a list of survey research resources for further reference.

Background

Backstrom, Charles H., and Hursh, D. *Survey Research.* Evanston, Illinois, Northwestern University Press, 1963.
Hyman, Herbert H., *et al. Interviewing in Social Research.* Chicago: University of Chicago Press, 1954.
_____. *Survey Design and Analysis.* New York: The Free Press, 1955.
Lansing, John B., and Morgan, James N. *Economic Survey Methods.* Ann Arbor, Michigan: Survey Research Center, 1971.

Statistical Texts

Blalock, Hubert M. *Social Statistics.* New York: McGraw-Hill Book Company, 1972.
Kish, Leslie L. *Survey Sampling.* New York: John Wiley and Sons, Inc., 1965.
Slonim, Morris. *Sampling in a Nutshell.* New York: Simon and Schuster, 1970.

Procedural Guides

Community Planning and Evaluation Institute. *A Manual on Conducting Interview Studies.* Washington, D.C.: Community Planning and Evaluation Institute, 1972.
National Opinion Research Center (NORC). *Manual of Procedures for Hiring and Training Interviewers.* Chicago: NORC, 1972.
National Opinion Research Center (NORC). *A Brush Up on Interviewing Technique.* Chicago: NORC, 1962.
Saroff, Jerome R., and Alberta Z. Levitan. *Survey Manual for Comprehensive Urban Planning.* Fairbanks, Alaska: Institute of Social, Economic and Government Research.
Survey Research Center. *Interviewers' Manual.* Ann Arbor, Michigan: Survey Research Center, 1976.
Webb, Kenneth, and Hatry, Harry P. *Obtaining Citizen Feedback: The Application of Citizen Surveys to Local Governments.* Washington, D.C.: The Urban Institute, 1973.
Weiss, Carol H., and Hatry, Harry P. *An Introduction to Sample Surveys for Government Managers.* Washington, D.C.: The Urban Institute, 1971.

NOTES

1. Appendix 2 of this Handbook.
2. *Ibid.*
3. John B. Lansing, and James N. Morgan, *Economic Survey Methods* (Ann Arbor, Michigan: Survey Research Center, 1971), Chapter VII.
4. Leslie Kish, *Survey Sampling* (New York: John Wiley and Sons, Inc., 1967), Chapter 13.
5. George Sternlieb, *Garden Apartment Development: Municipal Cost-Revenue Analysis* (New Brunswick, N.J.: Rutgers University, Bureau of Economic Research, 1964), p.20.
6. Kish, *op. cit.,* Chapter 9.
7. George Sternlieb, et al., *Housing Development and Municipal Costs* (New Brunswick, N.J.: Rutgers University, Center for Urban Policy Research, 1973).
8. George Sternlieb, and Robert W. Burchell, "The Numbers Game: Forecasting Household Size," *Urban Land,* January 1974, pp. 8-9.
9. U.S. Department of Commerce, *Classification Manual, Government Finances* (Washington, D.C.: Government Printing Office, 1972).
10. See page 313, "Statistical Texts."
11. Norman Nie, *et al., Statistical Package for the Social Sciences* (New York: McGraw-Hill Book Publishing Company, 1975).

Sample Questionnaire for Local Surveys

Cover Sheet

COMPLETE PRIOR TO INTERVIEW:

Type of Interview: _____

Name of Interviewer: _____

Date of Interview: _____

Location: _____

    Street Address _____

    Development Name _____

    Housing Type _____

    Community _____

    County _____

    State _____

Introduction

I'm _____ from the _____. We're conducting a survey of people who live in various types of housing for the _____.

The purpose of our survey is to see what types of families live in different types of housing units and their need for public services. The information that is collected here will be employed in a report that we think will be useful for you and other community residents.

Your participation in this survey is completely voluntary, and of course there's no penalty for refusal. We'd appreciate a few minutes of your time to answer this short questionnaire.

0.   *TYPE OF STRUCTURE*
   [Complete Prior to Interview]

       (1) Single family detached
       (2) Single family attached
       (3) Garden apartment (1–3 stories)
       (4) Mid-rise apartment (4–6 stories)
       (5) High-rise apartment (7 + stories)
       (6) Mobile home
       (7) Other (Specify: _____)
       (9) NA/DK

1. *HOW LONG HAVE YOU BEEN LIVING HERE IN THIS UNIT?*

    (1) Less than 1 year
    (2) 1 to less than 2 years
    (3) 2 to less than 3 years
    (4) 3 to less than 4 years
    (5) 4 to less than 5 years
    (6) 5 to less than 7 years
    (7) 7 to less than 10 years
    (8) 10 years or more
    (9) NA/DK

2a. *DO YOU OWN OR RENT THIS UNIT?*
[For mobile home, code Q.2b instead.]

    (1) Own conventionally
    (2) Cash rent
    (3) Occupying without cash rent
    (4) Condominium
    (5) Cooperative
    (6) Other (Specify: _____)
    (9) NA/DK

2b. *[IF MOBILE HOME:]*

    (1) Owns home and site
    (2) Owns home, rents site
    (3) Rents home and site
    (9) NA/DK

3. *IS THIS YOUR PRIMARY RESIDENCE OR IS YOUR USUAL RESIDENCE ELSEWHERE?*

    (1) Primary [Go to Q.5]
    (2) Usual residence elsewhere [Go to Q.4a]
    (9) NA/DK

[IF USUAL RESIDENCE ELSEWHERE, ASK Q.4a and 4b]

4a. *WHEN DO YOU USUALLY OCCUPY THIS UNIT?*
[Check all that apply:]

    (1) Spring
    (2) Summer
    (3) Fall
    (4) Winter
    (5) Occasionally throughout the year
    (6) Other (Specify: _____)
    (9) NA/DK

4b. *DO YOU INTEND TO MAKE THIS STRUCTURE YOUR PRIMARY RESIDENCE SOMETIME IN THE FUTURE?*

    (1) Yes, definitely
    (2) Yes, possibly
    (3) No
    (9) NA/DK

[SKIP TO Q.8]

[IF PRIMARY RESIDENCE, ASK Q.5, 6 and 7:]

5. *WHAT WAS THE COMMUNITY, COUNTY, AND STATE THAT YOU LIVED IN JUST BEFORE YOU MOVED HERE?*

    Community _____
    County _____
    State _____

6. *WHAT TYPE OF HOUSING UNIT DID YOU MOVE FROM?*

    (1) Single family detached
    (2) Single family attached
    (3) Garden apartment (1–3 stories)
    (4) Mid-rise apartment (4–6 stories)
    (5) High-rise apartment (7 + stories)
    (6) Mobile home
    (7) Other (Specify: _____)
    (9) NA/DK

7. *DID YOU OWN OR RENT YOUR PREVIOUS UNIT?*

    (1) Owned conventionally
    (2) Cash rent
    (3) Occupied without cash rent
    (4) Condominium
    (5) Cooperative
    (6) Other (Specify: _____)
    (9) NA/DK

[ASK EVERYONE:]

8. *HOW LONG DO YOU EXPECT TO BE LIVING HERE?*

    (1) Less than 1 year
    (2) 1–2 years
    (3) 3–5 years
    (4) 6–10 years
    (5) More than 10 years
    (6) Indefinitely
    (9) NA/DK

9a.   HOW MANY ROOMS DO YOU HAVE HERE?   _____

9b.   AND HOW MANY BEDROOMS?   _____

10.   RENT/VALUE
        If Rental Unit:

10a. HOW MUCH IS YOUR MONTHLY RENT?   _____

10b. WHAT UTILITIES, IF ANY, ARE INCLUDED IN YOUR RENT?

         _____ heating
         _____ air conditioning
         _____ electricity for purposes other than
         heating or air conditioning
         _____ gas for purposes other than heating
         or air conditioning
         _____ water

10c. IS YOUR UNIT AIR CONDITIONED?

        Yes ____ No ____ NA/DK ____

        [If Mobile Home:]

10d. HOW MUCH IS YOUR MONTHLY RENT FOR THIS UNIT AND
        FOR THE SITE?

            Unit: $ _____
            Owns unit
            NA/DK

            Site: $ _____
            Owns site
            NA/DK

        [If Owned Unit (Conventional, Mobile home, Cooperative, Condominium)]

10e. WHAT WOULD YOU SAY IS THE ESTIMATED VALUE OF THIS UNIT
        IF YOU WERE TO PUT IT ON THE MARKET TODAY?

            (1) Less than $5,000
            (2) $ 5,000 to $ 9,999
            (3) $10,000 to $14,999
            (4) $15,000 to $19,999
            (5) $20,000 to $24,999
            (6) $25,000 to $34,999
            (7) $35,000 to $49,999
            (8) $50,000 to $74,999
            (9) $75,000 or more
            (99) NA/DK

Using Field Surveys

[ASK EVERYONE:]

Now I'd like to ask you just a few questions about the people who live here.

11. *WHAT IS THE MARITAL STATUS OF THE HEAD OF THE HOUSEHOLD?*

    (1) Single or unrelated individuals
    (2) Married
    (3) Separated/divorced
    (4) Widowed
    (5) Other (Specify: _____)
    (9) NA/DK

12. *WHAT IS THE TOTAL NUMBER OF PEOPLE LIVING IN THE HOUSEHOLD?*

    _____

13. *NOW, I'D LIKE TO LIST ALL THE PEOPLE IN THE HOUSEHOLD IN TERMS OF THEIR RELATIONSHIP TO THE HEAD OF THE HOUSEHOLD, AND THEN GET THEIR AGE. LET'S START WITH THE HEAD OF THE HOUSEHOLD.*

| Relation to Head | Age | Sex | | In School | | 20 Years Old or Under | | | |
| | | | | | | Grade | Type of School | | |
		M	F	Yes	No		Public	Private	Parochial
1. Head		1	2	1	2		1	2	3
2.		1	2	1	2		1	2	3
3.		1	2	1	2		1	2	3
4.		1	2	1	2		1	2	3
5.		1	2	1	2		1	2	3
6.		1	2	1	2		1	2	3
7.		1	2	1	2		1	2	3
8.		1	2	1	2		1	2	3
9.		1	2	1	2		1	2	3
10.		1	2	1	2		1	2	3

14. *WHAT IS THE PRESENT OCCUPATION OF THE HEAD OF THE HOUSEHOLD?*

    (01) Professional or technical
    (02) Manager, administrator, proprietor
    (03) Sales
    (04) Clerical

(05) Craftsman, foreman
(06) Operative
(07) Laborer
(08) Service worker
(09) Retired
(10) Student
(11) Armed Forces
(12) Other (Specify: _____)
(99) NA/DK

15. *HOW FAR DOES THE HEAD OF HOUSEHOLD TRAVEL (ONE WAY) FROM HOME TO PLACE OF WORK?*

(1) Less than 5 miles
(2) 5 to 9 miles
(3) 10 to 24 miles
(4) 25 to 49 miles
(5) 50 miles or more
(9) NA/DK

16. *HOW MANY YEARS OF SCHOOL HAS THE HEAD OF HOUSEHOLD COMPLETED?*

(1) Eight or less
(2) Some High School
(3) High School grad
(4) Some College
(5) College grad
(6) Vocational training
(7) Graduate school
(8) Other (Specify: _____)
(9) NA/DK

17. *NOW, WOULD YOU PLEASE LOOK AT THIS CARD AND TELL ME WHAT WAS YOUR TOTAL FAMILY INCOME LAST YEAR FROM ALL SOURCES. JUST TELL ME THE LETTER NEXT TO THE RIGHT AMOUNT ON THE CARD.*

(a) Less than $5,000   (01)
(b) $5,000 to $9,999   (02)
(c) $10,000 to $11,999   (03)
(d) $12,000 to $13,999   (04)
(e) $14,000 to $15,999   (05)
(f) $16,000 to $17,999   (06)
(g) $18,000 to $19,999   (07)
(h) $20,000 to $21,999   (08)
(i) $22,000 to $24,999   (09)
(j) $25,000 to $34,999   (10)
(k) $35,000 to $49,999   (11)

(l) $50,000 or more (12)
(m) Refused (13)
(n) NA/DK (99)

[Interviewer complete without asking:]

18. ETHNICITY

   (1) Black
   (2) White
   (3) Spanish
   (4) Other (Specify: _____)
   (9) NA/DK

ADDITIONAL QUESTIONS FOR MOBILE HOMES

[Insert after Q.9b]

9c. HOW MANY BEDS IN THE UNIT ARE ACTUALLY USED FOR SLEEPING PURPOSES BY MEMBERS OF THE HOUSEHOLD?

   _____

9d. IS THIS A SINGLE WIDE, DOUBLE WIDE, OR EXPANDABLE UNIT?

   (1) Single wide
   (2) Double wide
   (3) Expandable
   (4) Other (Specify: _____)
   (9) NA/DK

9e. AND HOW WIDE IS THE UNIT?

   (1) 8 feet
   (2) 10 feet
   (3) 12 feet
   (4) 14 feet
   (5) 16 feet
   (6) Other (Specify: _____)
   (9) NA/DK

16

SECTION I:

GROSS INCOME MULTIPLIERS FOR RESIDENTIAL AND COMMERCIAL PROPERTIES

Increasingly, local property assessors are using the *income* of multifamily residential and commercial real properties as the basis upon which to estimate their value.* Although information which would gauge the value of these properties based on replacement costs or comparative sales** is available, the income approach is often preferred by the local assessors. Preference for the income approach typically occurs when elected officials are apprehensive of subsequent reduced local assessments based on decreasing income flows to property owners.

The estimate of value obviously affects future real property tax revenues. This revenue source, although diminishing in importance somewhat, continues to dominate local revenues. Thus, if the fiscal impact practitioner is to adequately project the revenue half of the fiscal impact equation, he

---

*There are three accepted approaches for estimating the value of a real property. These are the *income approach,* a property's worth based on the income it generates; the *market approach,* a property's worth based on the sales-evaluated worth of other comparable properties; and the *cost approach,* a property's worth based on what it would cost to reproduce it. More explicit definitions are found in the glossary.

**An additional procedure to calculate gross income multipliers is to compare sales to income ratios at time of sale of a structure. While there is an increasing trend towards monitoring and computerizing real property transactions, the income of the structure is very rarely reported or required as an inclusive element of these data assemblages. Thus, only one-half of the necessary data to calculate gross income multipliers is available to practitioners. One of the few sources of both segments of information is unofficial tabulations by multiple listing agencies of reported income and actual sales prices of income-producing properties.

must be familiar with the income or capitalization approach of estimating the market value of real property. Further, not only is it necessary to understand the process, it is also desirable to have, as a basic frame of reference, the magnitude of the ratio of a property's market value to its annual income as well as the types of financial parameters which affect this relationship.

This chapter thus presents *multipliers* of annual income which reflect a property's market value as well as *procedural guides* to derive the value if this is the approach preferred by local officials. The former are useful for quick approximations of real property value; the latter are used in instances where more detailed analysis is desired.

In the past, income multipliers have been used in fiscal impact analyses with little, if any, indication of origin or authenticity. Information, such as the real property value of high-rise apartments established at six to eight times their annual income, is used recurrently without practitioners realizing what went into this statement of capitalized value, and whether it varies over time or from place to place. The multipliers and procedures presented here are a first step away from this approach. The multipliers are based on the precedural guides and Exhibits 16-5 through 16-10. The guides have been derived from basic appraisal texts; the information in them for residential and commercial operating patterns has been obtained from surveys and augmented where necessary by standard reporting sources for these classifications of properties.

The Organization of the Information and How it was Obtained

The following information is presented in three sections. First, Exhibit 16 presents income to value multipliers for garden apartments, mid- to high-rise structures, regional/community/neighborhood shopping centers and office space. Second, procedural guides outline necessary steps to *tabulate* the market value of these two classes of residential and four classes of commercial property. Finally, Section II of this chapter contains the component information required by the procedural guides to compile the multipliers found in Exhibit 16-1. The multipliers have been derived using financial parameters which vary over time and by geographic area. Although presented by region, they may vary slightly within regions and indeed reflect 1977 financial conditions i.e., interest rates, time etc. Essentially, however, the multipliers will provide excellent first appropriations to estimate real property value based on annual gross income for these classes of property.

The information contained here was obtained from a national survey of fifty-four appraisers — six from each of nine census-defined regions. Appraisers were chosen within regions to reflect both geographic spread and significant experience in the appraisal of residential and commercial income properties. These individuals were asked to provide basic information on rent per square foot, vacancies and expense ratios for real property within their jurisdiction. In addition, they were asked for financial information consisting of typical mortgage interest rates and terms, mortgage-equity ratios, and expected equity dividend by class of property.

With this information, net operating income and capitalization rates could be determined. With these pieces of information, real property value was tabulated and divided by gross income to obtain multipliers of income for newly constructed buildings by region of the country. These multipliers appear in Exhibit 16-1. In each case, gross income multipliers derived from field data are augmented with similar multipliers for existing buildings as determined from published data.

Gross Income Multiplier Procedural Guide: Need and Basic Strategy

The fiscal impact practitioner at times may find it necessary to estimate real property value using financial parameters which pertain to a more current time period or a more specific location than

Sect. I: Gross Income Multipliers

EXHIBIT 16-1
GROSS INCOME MULTIPLIERS FOR NEWLY CONSTRUCTED RESIDENTIAL AND COMMERCIAL PROPERTIES BY REGION OF THE UNITED STATES

Region	RESIDENTIAL		COMMERCIAL			
	Garden Apartment (IREM)	Mid to High-Rise (IREM)	Regional Center (ULI)	Community Center (ULI)	Neighborhood Center (ULI)	Office Space (BOMA)
New England (I)	5.35	4.86	5.91	5.85	6.43	4.70
	(4.33)	(3.77)	(6.20)	(6.73)	(7.17)	(2.29)
Middle Atlantic (II)	4.84	4.55	5.81	5.88	6.39	4.71
	(4.06)	(3.60)	(6.10)	(6.76)	(7.12)	(2.13)
South Atlantic (III)*	5.76	5.34	6.84	6.81	6.71	5.17
	(4.95/4.38)	(4.37/4.98)	(7.40)	(7.08)	(7.70)	(3.46)
E. South Central (IV)	5.18	4.95	6.28	6.53	6.44	5.02
	(3.94)	(4.62)	(6.79)	(6.80)	(7.16)	(3.23)
E. North Central (V)	4.92	4.57	5.87	6.30	6.26	4.59
	(4.76)	(4.28)	(5.77)	(6.68)	(7.08)	(2.78)
W. North Central (VI)	5.24	4.77	5.70	5.73	6.04	4.80
	(4.36)	(4.99)	(6.44)	(6.87)	(6.44)	(2.64)
W. South Central (VII)	4.89	5.06	6.37	5.92	6.34	5.10
	(4.00)	(4.69)	(6.45)	(6.14)	(7.17)	(3.87)
Mountain (VIII)**	5.02	4.84	5.90	5.89	6.41	4.99
	(4.34)	(5.05)	(6.54/6.62)	(6.55/7.07)	(6.92/6.62)	(3.70/4.09)
Pacific (IX)***	5.41	5.02	6.41	5.73	6.24	5.31
	(4.77/4.43)	(3.68/5.06)	(6.56)	(6.37)	(6.73)	(3.81)

*In the following states the gross income multipliers for older garden apartments and mid to high-rise structures were found to be 4.95 and 4.37: Delaware, Maryland and District of Columbia, Virginia and West Virginia. For the remainder of the states in Region III the multipliers were: 4.38 and 4.98 for older mid to high-rise structures.

**In the following states the gross income multipliers for older regional, community and neighborhood shopping centers were found to be 6.62, 7.07 and 6.62: Montana, Wyoming, Colorado and New Mexico. For the remainder of Region VIII the following multipliers were in evidence: 6.54 for regional shopping centers; 6.55 and 6.92 respectively for similar community and neighborhood centers. The gross income multipliers for old office space were found to be 4.09 in Colorado and New Mexico. For the rest of Region VII the multiplier was 3.70.

***In the following states the gross income multipliers for older garden apartments and mid-high rise structures were found to be 4.43 and 5.06: Washington, Oregon and Alaska. For the remainder of Region IX the following multipliers were found to be in evidence: 4.77 and 3.68 respectively for older garden and mid to high-rise structures.

Note: The reason for two different multipliers in the same geographic region is the variation in the definitions of regions. Industrial reporting standards (IREM, ULI, and BOMA) typically vary from the regions that have been established in this Handbook for the Southeast and West.

Source: Rutgers University Center for Urban Policy Research — *National Appraisal Survey: 1976*. (Figures in parentheses are multipliers for older structures which have been calculated from information on building operations reported by industry standards — See "Method" (pages 326–339) for procedures, "Notes" (page 340) for industry standards and Section II for raw data.)

that from which the multipliers in Exhibit 16-1 of the previous section were derived. The procedural guides in this section illustrate the series of calculations necessary to determine current real property value at a particular site.

Guides are provided for both residential income properties (garden apartments, mid and high-rise apartments) and commercial income properties (neighborhood/community/regional shopping centers, office space). All guides are essentially similar except for different terminology specific to their operating patterns. These terminology differences are reflected in operating pattern reporting standards for each class of property, i.e. Institute of Real Estate Management, *Income/Expense Analysis* for garden apartment and mid and high-rise residential income properties, Urban Land Institute's *Dollars and Cents of Shopping Centers,* and Building Owners and Managers Association's *Office Building Experience Exchange Report* for commercial income properties.*

Each guide consists of six steps to determine real property value and a seventh step to demonstrate the procedure used to tabulate the multipliers found in Exhibit 16-1. The steps are shown below.

Step 1 —	*Determine annual gross income.*
Step 2 —	*Calculate effective annual gross income by applying an occupancy factor to annual gross income.*
Step 3 —	*Calculate total annual expenses by applying an expense ratio to annual gross income.*
Step 4 —	*Determine annual net operating income by subtracting total annual expenses from annual gross income.*
Step 5 —	*Calculate the capitalization rate using empirical information on mortgage-equity ratio, interest rate/term, and the equity dividend.*
Step 6 —	*Determine real property value by dividing annual net operating income by the capitalization rate.*
Step 7 —	*Derive income multipliers by dividing real property value by annual gross income.*

Calculating Residential Real Property Value: Garden and High Rise Apartments

Gross income of a property is used to estimate real property value for two distinct types of multifamily housing, garden apartments and high-rise apartments.** (In the example used in this section, the garden apartment complex has 100 units and the mid/high-rise apartment contains 200 units.) The computation procedure employs data which has been assembled by the Rutgers University Center for Urban Policy Research and the Institute of Real Estate Management. The intent of the procedure is not only to illustrate the actual step-by-step computations to derive real property value but also to demonstrate how regional variations in data alter the final estimate of value. Exhibit 16-2 contains the pertinent data for the residential examples in two selected regions — Region I (New England) and Region III (South Atlantic).

Determining Net Operating Income

Step 1 Determine Annual Gross Income.

The first major step in the computation of real property value for these two housing types is to determine potential annual gross income. Annual gross income for this example is the annual gross

---

*Notes at the end of this chapter explain in detail each of these sources, the information they contain and where they may be obtained.

**Garden apartments are structures with three or more units and three or fewer stories which offer rental tenure. Mid- to high-rise apartments are structures with three or more units and four or more stories with elevator service, which offers rental tenure.

Sect. I: Gross Income Multipliers

rent that is generated by a specific unit or development plus income from common appliances or vending machines and on-site parking, garage space, etc. The magnitude of income other than rent is usually very slight and is frequently ignored. Both the garden and mid- to high-rise apartments are assumed to be one-bedroom units with approximately 800 square feet of gross rentable space.

The calculation of annual gross income for each residential type is as follows:

Annual Rental per Square Foot
(from Exhibit 16-2)
X
Total Square Feet of Rentable Floor Area Space per Unit =
Potential Annual Gross Income per Unit

This results in the following income profiles:

Region I		Region III	
Garden Apartments	– $3,120	Garden Apartments	– $3,080
Mid-to High-Rise Apartments	– $4,400	Mid-to High-Rise Apartments	– $4,720

EXHIBIT 16-2

INPUT DATA TO DERIVE REAL PROPERTY VALUE
FOR NEW RESIDENTIAL USES

REGION I (NEW ENGLAND)		REGION III (SOUTH ATLANTIC)	
Garden Apartment	Mean	*Garden Apartment*	Mean
Annual rental per square foot of rentable floor area*	$3.90	Annual rental per square foot of rentable floor area	$3.80
Vacancy factor	3.0% (97.0%)	Vacancy factor	5.0% (95.0%)
Expense ratio	44.9%	Expense ratio	41.0%
Mortgage terms: 30 years @	9.75%	Mortgage Terms: 27 years @	9.75%
Mortgage/equity ratio	75:25	Mortgage/equity ratio	75:25
Annual constant	0.1031	Annual constant	0.1051
Equity dividend	0.080	Equity dividend	0.060
Mid to High-Rise Apartment		*Mid to High-Rise Apartment*	
Annual rental dollar per square foot of rentable floor area	$5.50	Annual rental dollar per square foot of rentable floor area	$5.90
Vacancy factor	4.0% (96.0%)	Vacancy factor	5.0% (95.0%)
Expense ratio	47.9%	Expense ratio	44.0%
Mortgage terms: 30 years @	10%	Mortgage terms: 27 years @	10%
Mortgage/equity ratio	75:25	Mortgage/equity ratio	75:25
Annual constant	0.1053	Annual constant	0.1073
Equity dividend	0.080	Equity dividend	0.060

*Rentable Floor Area is computed by measuring the inside finish of permanent outer building walls or from the glass line in cases where at least 50 percent of the outer building wall is of glass construction. Rentable area *shall not include* area within air conditioning rooms, janitor closets, electrical closets, balconies, and other rooms not actually available to the tenant for his furnishings and personal use.

Source: Rutgers University, Center for Urban Policy Research, "National Appraisal Survey 1976" (unpublished survey, 1976); Institute of Real Estate Management of the National Association of Realtors, *Income/Expense Analysis*, 1975.

Step 2 Calculate Effective Annual Gross Income.

This step involves the determination of the *actual* gross income for each unit. To do so, an occupancy factor must be applied to the potential annual gross income derived in step 1. The occupancy factor is the reciprocal of the vacancy factor, or 1.00 minus the vacancy factor.*

1. 1.00 - Vacancy Factor = Occupancy Factor
2. Potential Gross Income × Occupancy Factor = Effective Gross Income

Employing the above relationships, the following effective gross incomes were computed:

Region I		Region III	
Garden Apartments	- $3,026	Garden Apartments	- $2,888
Mid to High-Rise Apartments	- $4,224	Mid to High-Rise Apartments	- $4,484

Step 3 Calculate Total Annual Expenses.

Once the effective annual gross income has been calculated, total expenses for each unit must be estimated. Total expenses are made up of three general categories:** operating expenses and repairs, fixed expenses, and reserves for replacement. To estimate total expenses for a given unit, the best method is to apply an expense ratio to the potential gross income. Expense ratios*** may be obtained either from the Institute of Real Estate Management for various categories of multifamily buildings by region and year constructed or from local surveys of similar building types. The calculation is as follow:

Potential Annual Gross Income per Unit (from step 1)
×
Expense Ratio =
Total Annual Expenses per Unit

The following are the total expenses for each example:

Region I		Region III	
Garden Apartments	- $1,401	Garden Apartments	- $1,246
Mid to High-Rise Apartments	- $2,108	Mid to High-Rise Apartments	- $2,077

---

*The vacancy factor is made up of actual vacancies and other losses resulting from rent non-payment expressed as a decimal.

***Operating Expenses* include all out-of-pocket costs involved in providing services to tenants and maintaining the income stream — for example, administration, utilities, payrolls, supplies, contracted services such as cleaning, etc.; *Fixed Expenses,* real estate taxes and building insurance may be shown on an actual or accrual basis. *Reserves for Replacement* funds to provide for the replacement of short-lived equipment items, such as stoves, refrigerators, washers, driers, and air conditioning, and for portions of the building that require periodical replacement during the life of the building. *Source:* American Institute of Real Estate Appraisers, *The Appraisal of Real Estate,* 6th edition, pp. 331-332.

***Expense ratio.* The relationship of total expenses to gross income expressed as a decimal.

Sect. I: Gross Income Multipliers

Step 4 Determine Annual Net Operating Income.

The final step in deriving net operating income* is its actual computation. Net operating income is determined through the following simple procedure:

Effective Annual Gross Income per Unit (step 2) −
Total Annual Expenses per Unit (step 3) =
Annual Net Operating Income per Unit

Listed below are the resultant net operating incomes for each prototype:

Region I		Region III	
Garden Apartments	− $1,625	Garden Apartments	− $1,642
Mid to High-Rise Apartments	− $2,116	Mid to High-Rise Apartments	− $2,407

Determining the Capitalization Rate

The second half of this approach involves the construction of a capitalization rate and the projection of an estimated value for each unit. The construction of the capitalization rate** is accomplished using three of the financial parameters listed in Exhibit 16-2: the mortgage-equity ratio, mortgage interest rate and term and equity dividend.

The mortgage equity ratio is the relationship to total value of the proportion of value that is mortgaged and the proportion which represents developer equity. For example, in a typical residential multifamily development, 75 percent may represent the segment of overall value which is financed by the mortgage loan; 25 percent, the equity funds (down payment) which an investor commits to the specific project.

The mortgage interest rate is the interest the investor has to pay on the mortgage; the term is simply the period of time over which the mortgage is repaid. The mortgage interest rate and term are translated into an annual constant, which is the annual debt service (principal plus interest) per dollar borrowed. (Annual constants at intervals of one quarter percent interest for a period of up to sixty years may be found in the appendices of most real estate texts.

The equity dividend is the rate of return on invested capital which is satisfactory to an investor in a current market. A typical rate of return for residential multifamily structure in 1976 was 9 percent. The equity dividend or rate of return is expressed as a decimal.

Step 5 Calculate the Capitalization Rate

The development of the capitalization rate for a garden apartment in Region I is illustrated below. The rate is the sum of the portion of the loan which is mortgaged times the annual constant, plus

---

Net Operating Income. The annual net income remaining after deducting all operating expenses and reserves for replacement but before deducting financial charges such as recapture or debt service. Net operating income may also be referred to as net income before recapture. *Source:* American Institute of Real Estate Appraisers, *Capitalization Theory and Techniques,* p. 77.

**See step 5.

the portion of the loan which is equity times the expected equity dividend.*Equity dividend is used here rather than equity yield**

Source of Capital	Portion		Rate		Weighted Rate
Mortgage Loan	.75[1]	×	.1031[2]	=	.0773
Down Payment	.25	×	.080[3]		.0200
			Overall Rate	=	.0973

1. Mortgage/equity Ratio
2. Mortgage interest rate and loan maturity (expressed as an annual constant — 30 years @ 9.7% for Region I).
3. Equity Dividend

Using the above procedure the following capitalization rates for each prototype may be determined:

Region I		Region III	
Garden Apartments —	.0973	Garden Apartments —	.0938
Mid to High-Rise Apartments	.0990	Mid to High-Rise Apartments	.0955

Step 6 *Determine Real Property Value*

The next step is to convert net operating income (obtained in step 4) into an estimated value for each unit the capitalization rates obtained in step 5.*** This procedure is a very simple one, involving only the quotient of net operating income and the capitalization rate:

$$\frac{\text{Net Operating Income}}{\text{Capitalization Rate}} \times \text{Number of Units} = \text{Real Property Value}$$

---

*Equity Dividend = $\frac{\text{Net Operating Income} - \text{Mortgage Debt Service}}{\text{Equity}}$

**A classic problem confronting those who prepare guides for the practitioner is reflected in procedures recommended to calculate a capitalization rate: theoretical purity versus practical reality. In this case, does one recommend a strict definition of capitalization rate which uses a weighted average of the mortgage constant and the *equity yield rate* (which makes allowances for capital gains and losses) or does one recommend a more pragmatic approach which ignores predicted capital gains and losses and instead uses a weighted average of the mortgage constant and the *equity dividend rate*.

Since the investor does not know what the future holds in terms of appreciation or depreciation of his property and typically confines his interest to estimated return rather than actual yield on investment, the more practical or equity dividend as a component of the capitalization rate will be employed here. This procedure opts for inclusive information which is familiar to the practitioner i.e., his desired return on investment. It does not ask him to employ a data element which requires a simultaneous prediction of future capital gains or losses related to this investment.

In an inflationary economy the use of *equity dividend* rather than *equity yield* slightly underestimates the true capitalization rate. Thus resulting gross income multipliers are somewhat higher than if equity yield was the financial parameter used.

For those who desire to pursue the *equity yield* approach see: Robert H. Zerbst and Daniel P. Kohlne, "An Examination of Equity Rates in Real Estate Valuation" (Norman, Oklahoma, Center for Economic and Management Research, College of Business Administration, University of Oklahoma, 1975).

***There are 100 units in the garden apartment prototypes and 200 units in the mid- to high-rise prototype — unit value × number of units = structure value.

Sect. I: Gross Income Multipliers

Region I
Garden Apartments — $1,670,092
($1,625 X 100)
.0973

Mid/High-Rise Aparts. — $4,274,747
($2,116 X 200)
.0990

Region III
Garden Apartments — $1,750,533
($1,642 X 100)
.0938

Mid/High-Rise Aparts. — $5,040,838
($2,407 X 200)
.0955

Step 7 Derive Income Multiplier

The gross income multiplier is obtained by dividing the real property value (obtained in step 6) by the gross income per structure (step 1). The resultant multipliers are those shown in Exhibit 16-1.

$$\frac{\text{Estimated Structure Value}}{\text{Potential Annual Gross Income Per Structure}} = \text{Gross Income Multiplier}$$

Region I
Garden Apartments — 5.35 ($1,670,092)
($ 312,000)

Mid- to High-Rise — 4.86 ($4,274,747)
($ 880,000)

Region III
Garden Apartments — 5.76 ($1,750,553)
($ 304,000)

Mid- to High-Rise — 5.34 ($5,040,838)
($ 944,000)

Summary

The use of gross income multipliers in fiscal impact analysis is a reasonably standard procedure. For example, a planner in Region I may be called upon to calculate the property tax revenue that will be generated by a proposed garden apartment complex. He is provided with a rent schedule that indicates the estimated potential gross income (rent) from the complex will be $500,000 per year. Applying the gross income multiplier for garden apartments in Region I and then the equalized real property tax rate, the planner can project the tax revenue likely to result from the complex.

Real property value is projected as follows:

Potential Gross Income (step 1)
X
Gross Income Multiplier (step 7) =
Estimated Value
($500,000 X 5.35 = $2,675,000)

Real property tax revenue is determined as follows:

Estimated Real Property Value
X
Total Equalized Property Tax =
Potential Property Tax Revenue
($2,675,000 X .0300 = $80,250)

These computations may be used to project revenues from proposed residential and nonresidential developments in which data on income rather than value of a structure are known. The next two sections examine the use of data on income to attain real property value for nonresidential uses — shopping centers and office space.

Calculating Nonresidential Real Property Value: Shopping Centers

The procedures to determine real property value for commercial uses are essentially similar to those employed for residential uses. Slight differences do exist, however, in the terminology of various data inputs. They vary according to the reporting standard used. Shopping center operations are summarized in the Urban Land Institute's *Dollars and Cents of Shopping Centers*. This triennial publication has a broad industry following.

The per square foot measure of space for commercial uses is termed gross leasable area* (compared to rentable floor area for residential properties). Essentially they are identical measures of the space for which tenants pay rent.

Total operating receipts** *is* the commercial equivalent to the gross income measure for residential properties. Again, the two definitions are very close; total operating receipts is money received from tenant rentals plus miscellaneous income. One note of caution, however. For residential rental properties, miscellaneous income is seldom more than 1 percent of total gross income; for commercial properties, it may be as much as 15 percent (rentals from intermittent tenants who occupy concessions in common areas or from levied common area shares on permanent tenants). For residential uses, if specific information is not available, the category can generally be ignored; for commercial uses, it typically cannot.

Total operating expenses,*** the equivalent of total expenses for residential properties, has the same constituent elements as its residential equivalent — fixed expenses and reserves for replacement in addition to operating expenses.

Finally, the net income figure is called the operating balance but it is handled in exactly the same way as the net operating income for residential uses.

Besides the differences in terminology, there is one procedural change of significant note. Vacancy figures are not reported in *Dollars and Cents of Shopping Centers* and the information is not easily obtained from the field. Retailers do not divulge this information to the same extent that operators of residential income properties or office space do. Total operating receipts are thus somewhat of an overstatement of effective income. This will have a tendency to inflate the multipliers slightly.

---

*Gross leasable area (GLA) is the total floor area designed for tenant occupancy and exclusive use including basements, mezzanines, and upper floors, if any. It is expressed in square feet and measured from the center-line of joint partitions and the outside wall face. GLA is the area within a structure for which tenants pay rent. GLA lends itself readily to measurement and comparison. As such, it has been adopted by the shopping center industry as the standard for statistical comparison.

**Total Operating Receipts – total income received by the owner of the shopping center (all money accruing from rentals, common area charges, and other income). *Source:* Urban Land Institute, *Dollar and Cents of Shopping Centers: 1975,* p.314.

***Total Operating Expenses – building maintenance; parking lot, mall and other common areas; central utility systems; office area services; advertising and promotion; real estate taxes; insurance; and general administration. *Source:* Urban Land Institute, *Dollars and Cents of Shopping Centers: 1975,* p. 315.

Sect. I: Gross Income Multipliers

Regional gross income multipliers for three types of commercial shopping centers* — regional (400,000 ft² GLA), community (150,000 ft² GLA), and neighborhood (50,000 ft² GLA) for the nine regions are shown in Exhibit 16-1. This section demonstrates their derivation as well as a method of estimating shopping center real property value, given only information on income. Exhibit 16-3 contains the pertinent data for each category of shopping center.

EXHIBIT 16-3

INPUT DATA TO DERIVE REAL PROPERTY VALUE FOR
NEW COMMERCIAL USES (SHOPPING CENTERS)

REGION I (NEW ENGLAND)		REGION IX (PACIFIC)	
Regional Center	Mean	*Regional Center*	Mean
Annual operating receipts per square foot of gross leasable area	$8.84	Annual operating receipts per square foot of gross leasable area	$8.60
Operating expense ratio	42.0%	Operating expense ratio	36.0%
Mortgage terms: 30 years @	9.5%	Mortgage terms: 27 years @	9.5%
Mortgage/equity ratio	75:25	Mortgage/equity ratio	75:25
Annual constant	0.1009	Annual constant	0.1030
Equity dividend	0.090	Equity dividend	0.090
Size: 400,000 square feet of GLA			
Community Center		*Community Center*	
Annual operating receipts per square foot of gross leasable area	$4.87	Annual operating receipts per square foot of gross leasable area	$4.70
Operating expense ratio	39.7%	Operating expense ratio	41.0%
Mortgage terms: 27 years @	10%	Mortgage terms: 27 years @	10%
Mortgage/equity ratio	75:25	Mortgage/equity ratio	75:25
Annual constant	0.1073	Annual constant	0.1073
Equity dividend	0.090	Equity dividend	0.090
Size: 150,000 square feet of GLA			
REGION I (NEW ENGLAND)		REGION IX (PACIFIC)	
Neighborhood Center		*Neighborhood Center*	
Total operating receipts per square foot of gross leasable area	$4.43	Total operating receipts per square foot of gross leasable area	$4.66
Operating expense ratio	33.8%	Operating expense ratio	35.7%
Mortgage terms: 27 years @	10%	Mortgage terms: 27 years @	10%
Mortgage/equity ratio	75:25	Mortgage/equity ratio	75:25
Annual constant	0.1073	Annual constant	0.1073
Equity dividend	0.090	Equity dividend	0.090
Size: 50,000 square feet of GLA			

Source: Rutgers University, Center for Urban Policy Research, "National Appraisal Survey 1976" (unpublished survey, 1976); Institute of Real Estate Management of the National Association of Realtors, *Income/Expense Analysis*, 1975.

*Regional shopping center – A shopping center built around at least one and more typically two to four full-line department stores. The typical size, for definition purposes, is considered to be 400,000 square feet of GLA.
 Community shopping center – A shopping center built around a junior department store or a variety store, as the major tenant, plus a supermarket. It does not have a full-line department store and has an average size of 150,000 square feet of GLA.
 Neighborhood shopping center – A shopping center built around a supermarket as the principal tenant with a typical GLA of 50,000 square feet.
Source: Urban Land Institute, *Dollars and Cents of Shopping Centers: 1975,* p. 314.

Determining the Operating Balance

Step 1 *Determine Actual Annual Operating Receipts*

Annual Operating Receipts per Square Foot of GLA
(From Exhibit 16-3)
X
Total Square Feet of Gross Leasable Area =
Actual Annual Operating Receipts per Structure.

Results:

Region I		Region IX	
Regional Center	$3,536,000	Regional Center	$3,440,000
Community Center	730,500	Community Center	705,000
Neighborhood Center	221,500	Neighborhood Center	233,000

Step 2 *Effective Annual Operating Receipts (Not Computed)*

Step 3 *Total Annual Operating Expenses*

Actual Annual Operating Receipts (step 1)
X
Operating Expense Ratio (Exhibit 16-3) =
Total Annual Expenses per Structure.

Region I		Region IX	
Regional Center	$1,485,120	Regional Center	$1,238,400
Community Center	290,009	Community Center	289,050
Neighborhood Center	74,867	Neighborhood Center	83,181

Step 4 *Determine Operating Balance*

Annual Operating Receipts (step 1)
−
Total Annual Operating Expenses (step 3) =
Operating Balance

Results:

Region I		Region IX	
Regional Center	$2,050,880	Regional Center	$2,201,600
Community Center	440,491	Community Center	415,950
Neighborhood Center	146,633	Neighborhood Center	149,819

Determining the Capitalization Rate

Step 5 *Calculate the Capitalization Rate*

The capitalization rate for the regional center in Region I is calculated as follows:

Sect. I: Gross Income Multipliers

Source of Capital	Portion[1]		Rate		Weighted Rate
Mortgage Loan	.75	×	.1009[2]	=	.0757
Down Payment	.25	×	.090[3]	=	.0225
			Overall Rate	=	.0982

1. Mortgage/equity ratio
2. Mortgage interest rate and loan maturity as an annual constant (30 years @ 9.5%)
3. Equity dividend

Results:

Region I		Region IX	
Regional Center	.0982	Regional Center	.0998
Community Center	.1030	Community Center	.1030
Neighborhood Center	.1030	Neighborhood Center	.1030

Step 6 Determine Real Property Value

$$\frac{\text{Balance After Operating Expenses (step 4)}}{\text{Capitalization Rate (step 5)}} = \text{Real Property Value}$$

Results:

Region I		Region IX	
Regional Center	$20,884,725	Regional Center	$22,060,120
Community Center	4,276,612	Community Center	4,038,350
Neighborhood Center	1,423,621	Neighborhood Center	1,454,553

Step 7 Derive Operating Receipts Multiplier

$$\frac{\text{Real Property Value}}{\text{Actual Annual Operating Receipts (step 1)}} = \text{Operating Receipt Multiplier}$$

Results:

Region I		Region IX	
Regional Center	5.91	Regional Center	6.41
Community Center	5.85	Community Center	5.73
Neighborhood Center	6.43	Neighborhood Center	6.24

Summary

The application of gross income multipliers to commercial uses is identical to the procedure illustrated for residential uses. For example, assume that, again, in Region I, a local planning consultant finds it necessary to determine the property tax revenue that would be generated by a proposed regional shopping center. The planner has information indicating that the estimated operating receipts for the proposed center are $1,500,000 per year after the project is fully rented and income is stabilized. By performing the following computations, the planner can quickly obtain a projection of forthcoming revenue.

Real property value is projected as follows:

$$\begin{array}{c} \text{Estimated Annual Operating Receipts per Structure} \\ \times \\ \text{Gross Income Multiplier (step 7)} = \\ \text{Estimated Real Property Value} \\ (\$1,500,000 \times 5.91 = \$8,865,000) \end{array}$$

Real property tax revenue is determined as follows:

$$\begin{array}{c} \text{Estimated Real Property Value} \\ \times \\ \text{Equalized Property Tax Rate} = \\ \text{Property Tax Revenue} \\ (\$8,865,000 \times .0300 = \$265,950) \end{array}$$

Calculating Nonresidential Real Property Value: Office Space

Information on the annual operations of office space was obtained from field appraisers and augmented, where necessary, by the *Office Building Experience Exchange Report,* distributed by the Building Owners and Managers Association. The terms which appear in this section follow closely those found in this industry-wide annual reporting source. Again slight differences from previous procedures are those associated with terminology.

The square foot measure of rentable space for office structures is termed net rentable area.* Net rentable area is the space a tenant occupies, excluding common corridors, entranceways, etc.

The income measure is total operating income**; it consists of income from offices, stores, storage areas, etc. It is basically the same index used for residential investment properties and shopping centers. Income other than from offices is frequently significant — 10–20 percent of total operating income — and should not be ignored. Total operating income multiplied by an occupancy factor yields the total effective income.

Total operating expenses*** is the same measure of expenditures used for shopping centers. Again it consists of three constituent elements: operating expenses, fixed expenses, and reserves for replacement.

Net rentable area – The net rentable area of a multiple tenancy floor, whether above or below grade, is the sum of all rentable areas on that floor. The rentable area of an office on a multiple tenancy floor is computed by measuring to the inside finish of permanent outer building walls, or the glass line if at least 50 percent of the outer building wall is glass, to the office side of corridors and/or other permanent partitions, and to the center of partitions that separate the premises from adjoining rentable areas. No deductions are allowed for colums and projections necessary to the building.

**Total operating income* – gross annual dollars per square foot received for occupied space. Includes income from offices, stores, storage areas and special areas.
Source: Building Owners and Managers Association International, *Office Building Experience Exchange Report: 1975,* p. 88.

***Total operating expenses* – Consists of three main accounts — for various utility and maintenance costs (e.g., heating and cleaning), for alterations and improvements in the tenant area (space occupied by tenants), for taxes and insurance. Also expressed in annual dollars per square foot.

Sect. I: Gross Income Multipliers

The net income* measure represents the difference between total effective income and total operating expenses. It is exactly the same index used in the value determinations for multifamily residential properties and shopping centers.

With these definitions and the procedures outlined previously, gross income multipliers have been developed for new office space in the nine regions of the country. Similar multipliers have been calculated for existing older buildings using BOMA data. Both sets of multipliers appear in Exhibit 16-1. Listed in Exhibit 16-4 is the pertinent data for office space in two of the nine regions.

Determining Net Income

Step 1 Determine Total Annual Operating Income

Annual Operating Income per Square Foot
(Exhibit 16-4)
×
Total Net Rentable Area =
Total Annual Operating Income

Results:

	Region I		Region IX	
Office Space	$825,000	Office Space	$800,000

EXHIBIT 16-4

INPUT DATA TO DERIVE REAL PROPERTY VALUE FOR NEW COMMERCIAL USES (OFFICE SPACE)

REGION I (NEW ENGLAND)	Mean	REGION IX (PACIFIC)	Mean
Annual operating income per square foot	$8.25	Annual operating income per square foot	$8.00
Vacancy factor	6.0% (94.0%)	Vacancy factor	7.5% (92.5%)
Expense ratio	49.0%	Expense ratio	40.0%
Mortgage terms: 30 years @	9.5%	Mortgage terms: 27 years @	9.75%
Mortgage/equity ratio	75:25	Mortgage/equity ratio	75:25
Annual constant	0.1009	Annual constant	0.1051
Equity dividend	0.080	Equity dividend	0.080
Size: 100,000 square feet of net rentable area			

Source: Rutgers University Center for Urban Policy Research, "National Appraisal Survey" (unpublished survey, 1976), BOMA — *Office Building Experience Exchange Report: 1975.*

---

*Net income – the difference between total effective income and total operating expenses, in annual dollars per square foot.
Source: Building Owners and Managers Association International, *op. cit.*

Step 2 *Calculate Total Annual Effective Income*

1. 1.00 − Vacancy Factor = Occupancy Factor
2. Total Annual Operating Income × Occupancy Factor = Total Annual Effective Income

Results:

	Region I		Region IX
Office Space	$775,500	Office Space	$740,000

Step 3 *Calculate Total Annual Operating Expenses*

Total Annual Operating Income (step 1)
×
Expense Ratio (Exhibit 16-4) =
Total Annual Operating Expenses

Results:

	Region I		Region IX
Office Space	$404,250	Office Space	$320,000

Step 4 *Determine Annual Net Income*

Total Annual Effective Income (step 2)
−
Total Annual Expenses (step 3) =
Annual Net Income

Results:

	Region I		Region IX
Office Space	$371,250	Office Space	$480,000

Determination of the Capitalization Rate

Step 5 *Calculate the Capitalization Rate*

The capitalization rate for office space in Region I is calculated as follows:

Source of Capital	Portion[1]		Rate		Weighted Rate
Mortgage Loan	.75	×	.1009[2]	=	.0757
Down Payment	.25	×	.080[3]	=	.0200
			Overall Rate	=	.0957

1. Mortgage/equity ratio
2. Mortgage interest rate and loan maturity expressed as an annual constant (30 years at 9.5%)
3. Equity dividend

Sect. I: Gross Income Multipliers

Results:

	Region I			*Region IX*	
Office Space		.0957	Office Space		.0988

Step 6 Determine the Real Property Value

$$\frac{\text{Net Income (step 4)}}{\text{Capitalization Rate}} = \text{Real Property Value}$$

Results:

	Region I			*Region IX*	
Office Space		$3,879,310	Office Space		$4,858,300

Step 7 Derive Operating Income Multiplier

$$\frac{\text{Estimated Real Property Value (step 6)}}{\text{Total Annual Operating Income (step 1)}} = \text{Operating Income Multiplier}$$

Results:

	Region I			*Region IX*	
Office Space		4.70	Office Space		6.07

Summary

The use of the gross income multiplier, for office space, is identical to the procedures discussed for residential multifamily and commercial shopping centers. Assume that a developer in Region I desires to demonstrate the magnitude of property tax revenue that a structure will generate. The developer expects an annual total operating income of $500,000. Applying the region's gross income multiplier (Region I – 4.70), he can estimate potential revenues.

Real property value is projected as follows:

$$\begin{array}{c}\text{Total Annual Operating Income (step 1)}\\ \times\\ \text{Gross Income Multiplier (step 7)} =\\ \text{Estimated Real Property Value}\\ (\$500{,}000 \times 4.70 = \$2{,}350{,}000)\end{array}$$

Real property tax revenue is determined as follows:

$$\begin{array}{c}\text{Estimated Real Property Value}\\ \times\\ \text{Equalized Property Rate} =\\ \text{Potential Property Tax Revenue}\\ (\$2{,}350{,}000 \times .0300 = \$70{,}500)\end{array}$$

NOTES

(A DESCRIPTION OF INDUSTRY-WIDE REPORTING SOURCES USED IN THE PREVIOUS CALCULATIONS)

1. *Income/Expense Analysis: 1975, Institute of Real Estate Management, 155 East Superior Street, Chicago, Illinois 60611, 168 pp., price $30.00.*

The Income/Expense Analysis is an annual publication. It examines income and expenses for multifamily residential structures — low-rise, garden and condominiums. The assembled data, presented on the basis of dollars per room per annum and dollars per square foot per annum, represent the average income and expense patterns that may be attributed to a particular residential apartment configuration. Under income such factors as rental incomes, miscellaneous income and occupancy rates are tabulated. The expense summary lists multiple categories of operating, fixed and replacement expenses.

The survey, conducted in the United States and Canada, annually monitors the following number of residential units:

High-Rise – 75,398
Garden – 197,108
Low-Rise – 48,384
Condominiums – Not Available

2. *Dollars and Cents of Shopping Centers: 1975, Urban Land Institute, 1200 18th Street N.W., Washington, D.C. 20036, 325 pp., price $35.00.*

Dollars and Cents of Shopping Centers is a triennial report on the incomes and expenses of shopping centers published by ULI. The report examines the operating profiles of four major types of shopping centers: superregional, regional, community, and neighborhood. The composite operating statement, presented on a basis of dollars per square foot of gross leasable area, is categorized into operating receipts, operating expenses, and operating balance.

Tenant characteristics include average sales volume and rent per square foot of gross leasable area by category of retailer. Information in this report is assembled on a national and regional level, as well as by age groups and type of shopping center.

The number of operations currently monitored is as follows:
Superregional Shopping Centers – 33
Regional Shopping Centers – 109
Community Shopping Centers – 170
Neighborhood Shopping Centers – 163

3. *Office Building Experience Exchange Report: 1975, Building Owners and Managers Association International, Washington, D.C. 20036, 92 pp., price $95.00.*

BOMA publishes the *Office Building Experience Exchange Report* annually. The report covers the average expenses and income in cents per square foot per annum for a building's rentable area, office rentable area, and actual rented office area. Income information includes that from offices, lobby concessions or stores, and storage areas. The expenses that are reported are the characteristic operating, fixed and replacement expenses that may be attributed to office space.

The data are aggregated on a number of bases: by region, age of building, city size, height of building, etc. The survey monitors 721 buildings across the United States.

16

SECTION II:
INPUT DATA USED TO DETERMINE REAL PROPERTY VALUE OF RESIDENTIAL AND COMMERCIAL PROPERTIES

EXHIBIT 16-5

INPUT DATA USED TO DERIVE GROSS INCOME MULTIPLIERS FOR NEW GARDEN APARTMENTS

Region	Mean Rental per Square Foot of Rentable Floor Area		Vacancy Factor	Expense Ratio	Mortgage Term and Interest Rate	Capitalization Rate
New England	$3.90	3.0	(97.0)	44.9%	30 yrs. @	.0973[1]
	(2.82)	(3.8)		(54.1)	9.75 (.080)[2]	
Middle Atlantic	3.90	5.0	(95.0)	44.9	26 yrs. @	.1036
	(2.82)	(3.8)		(54.1)	10% (.090)	
South Atlantic	3.80	5.0	(95.0)	41.0	27 yrs. @	.0938
	(2.46/2.37)	(3.9/12.5)		(49.7/46.4)	9.75 (.060)	
East So. Central	2.64	5.0	(95.0)	41.0	27 yrs. @	.1043
	(2.37)	(12.5)		(46.4)	10% (.095)	
East No. Central	3.84	5.0	(95.0)	44.3	27 yrs. @	.1030
	(2.60)	(5.8)		(45.3)	10% (.090)	
West No. Central	3.60	3.0	(97.0)	43.9	27 yrs. @	.1013
	(3.39)	(9.7)		(46.1)	9.75 (.090)	
West So. Central	3.20	8.0	(92.0)	41.7	30 yrs. @	.1028
	(2.37)	(12.5)		(46.4)	10% (.095)	
Mountain	3.60	6.0	(94.0)	42.9	27 yrs. @	.1018
	(2.39)	(9.7)		(46.1)	10% (.085)	
Pacific	3.60	5.0	(95.0)	41.0	30 yrs. @	.0998
	(2.70/2.39)	(8.1/9.7)		(44.3/46.1)	9.75 (.090)	

Notes: Multiple values per column indicate partitioning of a region by industrial reporting source. Specific definitions of regions may be found in IREM.

[1]The capitalization rate is constructed by the band of investment approach using a mortgage/equity ratio of 75%:25%.
[2]Equity dividend.

Source: Rutgers University Center for Urban Policy Research, "National Appraisal Survey 1976" (unpublished survey, 1976); Institute of Real Estate Management, *Income/Expense Analysis: 1975* (IREM results are shown in parentheses.)

EXHIBIT 16-6
INPUT DATA USED TO DERIVE GROSS INCOME MULTIPLIERS FOR NEW MID-TO HIGH-RISE ELEVATOR APARTMENTS

Region	Mean Rental per Square Foot of Rentable Floor Area	Vacancy Factor	Expense Ratio	Mortgage Term and Interest Rate	Capitalization Rate
New England	$5.50 (3.76)	4.0 (3.9)	(96.0)	47.9 (58.8)	30 yrs. @ 10% (.080)[2]	.0990[1]
Middle Atlantic	5.50 (3.76)	5.0 (3.9)	(95.0)	47.9 (58.8)	26 yrs. @ 10% (.090)	.1036
South Atlantic	5.90 (3.27/2.96)	5.0 (3.7/4.3)	(95.0)	44.0 (54.6/48.1)	27 yrs. @ 10% (.060)	.0955
East So. Central	4.04 (2.96)	5.0 (4.3)	(95.0)	44.0 (48.1)	27 yrs. @ 10% (.090)	.1030
East No. Central	5.52 (3.40)	5.0 (3.6)	(95.0)	47.3 (51.8)	25 yrs. @ 10% (.090)	.1043
West No. Central	5.52 (3.03)	3.0 (5.0)	(97.0)	47.9 (43.6)	27 yrs. @ 10% (.090)	.1030
West So. Central	4.95 (2.96)	6.0 (4.3)	(94.0)	44.7 (48.1)	30 yrs. @ 10% (.090)	.1015
Mountain	5.08 (3.03)	5.0 (5.0)	(95.0)	45.7 (43.6)	27 yrs. @ 10% (.085)	.1018
Pacific	4.30 (3.36/3.03)	5.0 (9.3/5.0)	(95.0)	44.0 (53.4/43.6)	30 yrs. @ 10% (.090)	.1015

Notes: Multiple values per column indicate partitioning of a region by industrial reporting source. Specific definitions of regions may be found in IREM.
[1] The capitalization rate is constructed by the band of investment approach using a mortgage/equity ratio of 75%:25%.
[2] Equity dividend.

Source: Rutgers University Center for Urban Policy Research, "National Appraisal Survey 1976" (unpublished survey, 1976); Institute of Real Estate Management, *Income/Expense Analysis: 1975* (IREM results are shown in parentheses.)

EXHIBIT 16-7
INPUT DATA USED TO DERIVE GROSS INCOME MULTIPLIERS FOR NEW REGIONAL SHOPPING CENTERS

Region	Mean Rental per Square Foot of Gross Leasable Area	Vacancy Factor	Expense Ratio	Mortgage Term and Interest Rate	Capitalization Rate
New England	$8.84 (4.32)	—	42.0 (39.1)	30 yrs. @ 9.5 (.090)[2]	.0982[1]
Middle Atlantic	8.97 (4.32)	—	42.0 (39.1)	30 yrs. @ 9.75 (.090)	.0998
South Atlantic	8.92 (3.43)	—	34.5 (29.2)	30 yrs. @ 9.5 (.080)	.0957
East So. Central	7.84 (3.43)	—	34.5 (29.2)	25 yrs. @ 10% (.090)	.1043
East No. Central	9.00 (5.12)	—	39.5 (40.6)	27 yrs. @ 10% (.090)	.1030
West No. Central	8.15 (3.71)	—	41.3 (33.7)	27 yrs. @ 10% (.090)	.1030
West So. Central	7.53 (3.16)	—	34.4 (33.6)	27 yrs. @ 10% (.090)	.1030
Mountain	7.91 (4.10/3.71)	—	40.9 (34.5/33.7)	27 yrs. @ 9.75% (.085)	.1001
Pacific	8.60 (4.10)	—	36.0 (34.5)	27 yrs. @ 9.5 (.090)	.0998

Notes: Multiple values per column indicate partitioning of a region by industrial reporting source. Specific definitions of region may be found in ULI.
[1] The capitalization rate is constructed by the band of investment approach using a mortgage/equity ratio of 75%:25%.
[2] Equity dividend.

Source: Rutgers University Center for Urban Policy Research, "National Appraisal Survey 1976" (unpublished survey, 1976); The Urban Land Institute, *Dollars and Cents of Shopping Centers: 1975* (ULI results are shown in parentheses).

Sect. II: Input Data Used

EXHIBIT 16-8

INPUT DATA USED TO DERIVE GROSS INCOME MULTIPLIERS FOR NEW COMMUNITY SHOPPING CENTERS

Region	Mean Rental per Square Foot of Gross Leasable Area	Vacancy Factor	Expense Ratio	Mortgage Term and Interest Rate	Capitalization Rate
New England	$4.87 (2.43)	—	39.7 (30.6)	27 yrs. @ 10% (.090)[2]	.1030[1]
Middle Atlantic	4.87 (2.43)	—	39.7 (30.6)	28 yrs. @ 10% (.090)	.1025
South Atlantic	4.50 (2.40)	—	32.7 (30.0)	27 yrs. @ 9.75% (.080)	.0988
East So. Central	4.50 (2.40)	—	32.7 (30.0)	27 yrs. @ 10% (.090)	.1030
East No. Central	4.94 (2.20)	—	35.1 (31.2)	27 yrs. @ 10% (.090)	.1030
West No. Central	4.80 (2.56)	—	41.0 (29.2)	27 yrs. @ 10% (.090)	.1030
West So. Central	4.54 (2.00)	—	39.0 (36.8)	27 yrs. @ 10% (.090)	.1030
Mountain	5.54 (2.66/2.56)	—	41.0 (34.4/29.2)	27 yrs. @ 9.75% (.085)	.1001
Pacific	4.70 (2.66)	—	41.0 (34.4)	27 yrs. @ 10% (.090)	.1030

Notes: Multiple values per column indicate partitioning of a region by industrial reporting source. Specific definitions of regions may be found in IREM.
[1] The capitalization rate is constructed by the band of investment approach using a mortgage/equity ratio of 75%:25%.
[2] Equity dividend.

Source: Rutgers University Center for Urban Policy Research, "National Appraisal Survey 1976" (unpublished survey, 1976); The Urban Land Institute, *Dollars and Cents of Shopping Centers: 1975* (ULI results are shown in parentheses).

EXHIBIT 16-9

INPUT DATA USED TO DERIVE GROSS INCOME MULTIPLIERS FOR NEW NEIGHBORHOOD SHOPPING CENTERS

Region	Mean Rental per Square Foot of Gross Leasable Area	Vacancy Factor	Expense Ratio	Mortgage Term and Interest Rate	Capitalization Rate
New England	$4.43 (2.87)	—	33.8 (26.2)	27 yrs. @ 10% (.090)[2]	.1030[1]
Middle Atlantic	4.43 (2.87)	—	33.8 (26.2)	27 yrs. @ 10% (.090)	.1036
South Atlantic	4.31 (2.31)	—	33.7 (26.3)	27 yrs. @ 9.75% (.080)	.0988
East So. Central	4.31 (2.31)	—	33.7 (26.3)	27 yrs. @ 10% (.090)	.1030
East No. Central	4.57 (2.51)	—	35.5 (27.1)	27 yrs. @ 10% (.090)	.1030
West No. Central	4.56 (2.80)	—	37.8 (33.7)	27 yrs. @ 10% (.090)	.1030
West So. Central	4.44 (2.09)	—	34.7 (26.1)	27 yrs. @ 10% (.090)	.1030
Mountain	5.07 (2.66/2.80)	—	36.8 (30.7/33.7)	27 yrs. @ 10% (.085)	.0986
Pacific	4.66 (2.66)	—	35.7 (30.7)	27 yrs. @ 10% (.090)	.1030

Notes: Multiple values per column indicate partitioning of a region by industrial reporting source. Specific definitions of regions may be found in IREM.
[1] The capitalization rate is constructed by the band of investment approach using a mortgage/equity ratio of 75%:25%.
[2] Equity dividend.

Source: Rutgers University Center for Urban Policy Research, "National Appraisal Survey 1976" (unpublished survey, 1976); The Urban Land Institute, *Dollars and Cents of Shopping Centers: 1975* (ULI results are shown in parentheses).

EXHIBIT 16-10
INPUT DATA USED TO DERIVE GROSS INCOME MULTIPLIERS FOR NEW OFFICE SPACE

Region	Mean Rental per Square Foot of Rentable Floor Area		Vacancy Factor	Expenses Ratio	Mortgage Term and Interest Rate	Capitalization Rate
New England	$8.25 (7.26)	6.0 (3.8)	(94.0)	49% (74.4)	30 yrs. @ 9.5 (.080)[2]	.0957[1]
Middle Atlantic	8.75 (7.26)	7.7 (3.8)	(92.3)	44 (74.4)	27 yrs. @ 9.75 (.095)	.1026
South Atlantic	7.25 (5.26)	8.0 (6.6)	(92.0)	41 (59.3)	30 yrs. @ 9.75 (.085)	.0986
East So. Central	7.25 (5.26)	8.0 (6.6)	(92.0)	39 (59.3)	25 yrs. @ 10% (.095)	.1056
East No. Central	7.75 (6.64)	7.8 (4.5)	(92.2)	45 (67.2)	30 yrs. @ 10% (.095)	.1028
West No. Central	7.37 (5.47)	8.4 (6.6)	(91.6)	45 (67.8)	30 yrs. @ 9.75 (.085)	.0970
West So. Central	7.00 (5.71)	9.3 (6.5)	(90.7)	36 (52.0)	25 yrs. @ 10.25% (.095)	.1072
Mountain	7.00 (5.49/5.71)	8.4 (6.0/6.5)	(91.6)	41 (56.4/52.0)	25 yrs. @ 9.75 (.085)	.1015
Pacific	8.00 (6.99/5.49)	7.5 (5.8/6.0)	(92.5)	40 (56.6/56.4)	27 yrs. @ 9.75 (.080)	.0988

Notes: Multiple values per column indicate partitioning of a region by industrial reporting source. Specific definitions of regions may be found in IREM.
[1] The capitalization rate is constructed by the band of investment approach using a mortgage/equity ratio of 75%:25%.
[2] Equity dividend.

Source: Rutgers University Center for Urban Policy Research, "National Appraisal Survey 1976" (unpublished survey, 1976); Building Owners and Managers Association International, *Office Building Experience Exchange Report: 1975* (BOMA results are shown in parentheses).

17

COMPUTER MODELS FOR FISCAL IMPACT ANALYSIS

Fiscal impact analyses are often time consuming. After completing an initial analysis the planner typically is faced with repeating the entire process should he desire to calculate either variations of a specific proposal or alternative growth strategies. The necessity to increase speed of computations and the desire for a more rigorous approach to fiscal impact analysis have led to the rise of cost-revenue models for computers. Since most calculations are routine and repetitive they lend themselves to computer use.

In addition to simplifying the task of performing sensitivity analysis, computer models usually have the capacity to store information such that the cumulative effect of historical development decisions become a part of each current fiscal impact analysis. For example, assume that a community has recently adopted a planned unit development (PUD) ordinance. Several development proposals are received each containing multiple housing types and each having a specific fiscal impact on the community. Most computerized fiscal impact approaches are able to assess the impact of each development on the local fisc serially — taking into account the fiscal effects of previous developments. Further, it is possible through computerized approaches to view the impact of multiple proposals simultaneously at a selected point in the future. Thus the fiscal impact of a development 70 percent completed may be viewed simultaneously with one 25 percent completed and with one just being initiated.

Despite all this, with some exceptions, models developed to date have not met with much success. Their problems have been twofold. One has been the amount of front-end effort needed to initiate a computerized approach. This front-end effort normally includes gathering necessary data, computer programming and educating the local planning agency in the use of the model. It has not been uncommon to spend six months and many times the cost of a single analysis just to get the model operating. This time-consuming and costly process has proved disastrous to both the model developers who cannot move on to new locations and to the users who, as often as not, find they have complicated rather than simplified their task.

Another problem has been the "black box" or concealed nature of some models. This "black box" effect may be due to either the inability of the planner to understand the complex or sophisticated methodology of a particular model, or the desire of a model developer to avoid revealing the model's workings to potential competitors. In both cases the model is of little or no use to the planner who must not only obtain fiscal impact solutions but also justify and explain those solutions to the local electorate and to the public at large.

Yet models remain an important part of fiscal impact analysis. They simplify the tasks of county, regional and state agencies that must review locally submitted fiscal impact statements. They can provide small municipalities with quick and sophisticated analysis of a specific development. If used judiciously, models may become an intricate part of the every day planning analysis performed in larger cities or counties where rapid growth is occurring or areas where there is a desire for more intensive econometric analyses than is currently available.

This chapter describes various computer models for fiscal impact analysis and briefly explains how they work, the data they require, how they deal with issues such as inflation, interim projections, intergovernmental revenues, etc. and finally, where the user may turn to find out more about them.

Model Description

This study reviews twelve models. They give an overview of the state of the art of computerized cost-revenue analyses. They span a wide range of concepts and applications and vary from simple to quite sophisticated.

Alachua County Econometric Model (ACEM)

The Alachua County Econometric Model (ACEM) was developed by Professors Henry Fishkind, Jerome Milliman and Richard Ellson of the University of Florida's Bureau of Economic and Business Research and Department of Economics, under contract to the Gainesville-Alachua County Regional Utilities Board. The model attempts to evaluate the need for economic development in the region and to determine the fiscal impacts of alternative growth strategies. Although currently being marketed, ACEM has been applied only in Alachua County.

Community Development Model (CDM)

CDM was developed by the Urban Studies Center at the University of Louisville in 1974 for the Louisville and Jefferson County (Kentucky) Planning Commission. The model predicts future demand and costs of supplying municipal and county public services caused by demographic changes in the population and corresponding changes in distribution of the housing stock. The model has not been applied anywhere else and is currently not being marketed.

Community Impact Model (CIM)

CIM was developed in 1971-'72 for the Michigan State Housing Development Authority (MSHDA) by Applied Decision Systems, Inc., (now a part of Temple, Barker, and Sloan) located in Wellesley Hills, Massachusetts. The model's purpose was to assess the impact of MSHDA-financed, low and moderate income housing on the state and local economies of Michigan. The model was designed to compare the impacts of different development scenarios, including public housing, on local communities. CIM was to be used in towns and cities with a population range of 10,000-200,000. The model is no longer in use.

The Community Development Impact Model (CODIM)

CODIM was developed by S. Awerbuch formerly of the New York State Economic Development Board and W.A. Wallace of Rensselaer Polytechnic Institute in 1974-75. The model is designed to assess the impact of residential and light industrial development on small cities. CODIM has been applied in Cohoes, New York, and Dunbar, Pennsylvania. While the model is still available, it is not presently being applied or marketed.

Cost-Revenue Analysis Model (CRAM)

The Cost-Revenue Analysis Model was developed by Metcalf and Eddy, Inc. of Boston, Massachusetts for the Strafford (New Hampshire) Regional Planning Commission. It was to be used for fiscal impact analysis by Strafford County and its various jurisdictions. Its original application was to a site in Dover, New Hampshire in 1974 to evaluate alternative land development schemes there. While CRAM in its original application was not computerized, it is designed to be used as such. Versions of the model have been applied in Medford and Ipswich, Massachusetts. The model is not currently being marketed.

Fiscal Impact Model for Rural Industrialization (FIMRI)

This model was developed under the sponsorship of the North Dakota Environmental Assessment Program for the evaluation of the impact of major electric generating facilities and related mining activity.

FIMRI is presently available and applicable to municipalities within North Dakota. To date the model has been applied approximately 50 times in the state. Its developers, however, have expressed a willingness to increase its geographic applicability. The model is available and currently being marketed.

Fiscal Impact Research Project (FIRP)

FIRP was developed in 1974–'75 by James E. Frank of Florida State University for the Florida Department of Community Affairs. The primary purpose of the model is to analyze the fiscal impact of new development on both local and county jurisdictions. The model was applied, as part of the project in Tallahassee/Leon County and Bradenton/Manatee County. It is currently available for use elsewhere.

Municipal Impact Evaluation System (MUNIES)

MUNIES was developed by Westinghouse and Marcou, O'Leary and Associates of Washington, D.C., in 1973 as a tool to aid in local planning agencies in evaluating the fiscal impact of both alternative growth strategies and specific developments. MUNIES attempts to examine the effects of proposed developments through Needs Analyses (demand for municipal services) and Fiscal Analyses (resulting budget structure to accomodate services). The most widely publicized of the models, it is in various stages of operation at multiple sites, including three counties in Maryland, Baltimore Regional COG, Southeast Idaho COG, Atlanta, Georgia; and San Diego, California. The model is currently being marketed nationally by Tischler, Marcou Associates, Washington, D.C.

New Haven Model (NHM)

The New Haven expenditure model was developed by Claudia DeVita Scott, a member of the Urban Public Finance Group of the Urban Institute, in 1969 for the City of New Haven, Connecticut. The model projects current and capital expenditures for all departments in the city's budget annually over a five year period. A revenue submodel was developed by several members of the Planning Research Corporation of Los Angeles, California, and McLean, Virginia. Its purpose is to measure future changes in municipal revenues and expenditures resulting from development, redevelopment or alternative financing mechanisms. The model has not been applied at sites other than New Haven.

Public Finance Model (PFM)

PFM was developed by Parsons, Brinckerhoff, Quade and Douglas, Inc., for the City of Lakewood, Colorado. The model is driven by and essentially a part of a larger land use allocation model called DYLAM. At present PFM is used to determine only a limited number of costs (streets, sewer, water and elementary schools) associated with alternative development scenarios generated by DYLAM. The model is in the process of refinement so that it may be employed to evaluate a broader range of impacts.

Although DYLAM has been used in a number of locations, the PFM submodel has been applied only in Lakewood. It is not currently being marketed.

Provincial Municipal Simulator (PROMUS)

PROMUS was developed in 1971–'73 for the City of Toronto by Decision Sciences Corporation of Jenkintown, Pennsylvania. It is based on two subsystems: (1) the community model subsystem (CMS), which describes an existing or new community in terms of size, location, internal diversity, etc., and (2) the financial policy planning subsystem (FPPS), which provides the basis for analyzing the costs, cash flow, and revenues of given community programs or development decisions. PROMUS has been applied in varying degrees in Detroit and Philadelphia, and its developers claim it is equally applicable to smaller cities and towns.

Selle Model (SELLE)

The Selle Model was devised by Henry F. Selle, a private consultant in Hanover, New Hampshire. The model was initially applied in Walpole and Charlestown, New Hampshire in 1975 to evaluate the fiscal impact of industrial development. It has also been used in York, Maine to evaluate alternative growth strategies. It is currently being marketed as generally applicable to smaller cities and towns for both development and growth strategy analysis.

Methods and Techniques

Overview

As indicated in Exhibit 17-1, the twelve models examined in this chapter use a variety of procedural approaches discussed elsewhere in this handbook. These are:

1. Per Capita Multiplier
2. Case Study
3. Service Standard
4. Comparable City
5. Proportional Valuation
6. Employment Anticipation

In addition to these essentially arithmetic methods, other estimation approaches are employed by some of the models. Two of the most frequent are *regression analysis* and *systems dynamics*. Regression analysis is used in fiscal impact analysis to establish a relationship between current municipal costs and current community socioeconomic characteristics. The equation which is produced links, at a particular time, local costs (dependent variable) and local conditions (independent variables). Coefficients are developed to refine this relationship. Future changes in local conditions occasion changes in expected costs; they are projected using the more current information as independent variables and the derived regression coefficients of the previous period. An example of how this technique is used follows: a regression equation based on

EXHIBIT 17-1
BASIC TECHNIQUE USED TO PROJECT COSTS IN THE
FISCAL IMPACT SECTION OF THE COST-REVENUE MODEL

Technique	ACEM	CDM	CIM	CODIM	CRAM	FIMRI	FIRP	MUNIES	NHM	PFM	PROMUS	SELLE
Per Capita Multiplier			√	√	√		√	√		√	√	
Case Study				√				√				
Service Standard					√	√	√	√	√		√	
Comparable City						√		√				
Proportional Valuation						√						
Employment Anticipation							√					
Regression Analysis	√	√	√						√		√	√
Systems Dynamics	√										√	√

Source: Field Survey, Rutgers University Center for Urban Policy Research, Spring 1977.

historical data is developed. It defines a community's total expenditures in terms of, for instance, total real property value, total population, percent of population over 65, percent of population under the poverty level, etc. When a new development is anticipated, planners may use a variety of predictive methods to determine future values for local conditions. These new estimates appear in the regression equation as independent variables; they impact on the dependent variable to determine future total local costs.

Systems dynamics is a time-dependent technique which describes the long-range development of an area through a simulation of the interaction between the area's many variables, i.e., population, employment, housing and municipal services. The model which projects the future based upon these relationships is constantly refined through feedback responses. One example of a feedback response is the linkage between urban migration, the availability of housing and the level of required public services. When a significant number of new apartments is built in a city, occupancy levels in existing rental structures fall to a point where landlords must respond by lowering rents. Potential renters' interest in the area is renewed by lower rents, and occupancy levels increase. As renewed demand increases occupancy, supply is diminished and the cost of housing rises, forcing people to stop migrating to the area. Residents attracted to an area demand municipal services. Both the quantity and quality of services required are related to the number and income of consumers. The number of residents, their income, and ultimately their demand on services are reflected in the rents new residents are willing to pay. Feedback loops consider the relationship between these variables as well as the time required for the system to perceive the changes which are occurring. Feedback loops are designed using observed relationships between one or more variables. In the aggregate, when used in fiscal impact analyses, they form a "systems dynamics" approach to estimating future municipal costs.

Use of Techniques by Models

CRAM uses primarily the Service Standard method to determine future municipal service costs. As originally developed, it was used to compare three alternatives for land development for a single tract of 500 acres in Dover, New Hampshire. Each development scenario was specifically defined (e.g., two-bedroom apartment, retail store, etc.) and employed both locally derived and published demographic and employment characteristics, such as population per unit and employees per acre, to generate an estimate of the future service population. Service population was converted to service demand using a combination of locally derived and published standards on pupils per classroom, policemen per 1,000 population, etc. Existing local costs per classroom, per policeman, etc., were used to project incremental annual operating costs.

MUNIES also relies heavily on local demographic data and service standards to generate future service demand and the cost of meeting these demands. School district and Census-generated information on school age children and total household size are used to project demand. Existing local service standards per capita or per pupil are employed to indicate future levels of supply. Cost per unit of service is also based on existing conditions. New capital facilities are projected using current local service standards. Future capital facility projections are related to anticipated revenues through bonding capacity.

FIRP uses a framework similar to that of MUNIES. The major difference is that FIRP emphasizes short-term costs and, as a result, uses the Case Study Method to sum existing service excess and deficient capacities. This sum of service capacity is used to refine aggregate demand estimates. In addition to multipliers and service standards, FIRP uses a simple systems dynamics technique to determine existing capacities of special services (specifically water) in which there is a high degree of interdependence between demand variables.

PFM uses the Case Study Method to project three types of location-specific costs (streets, water and sewers, and elementary schools) associated with new development. The type and location of the new development is determined by DYLAM, which divides the city into numerous grid squares and specifies a land use type within each grid. Each land use type describes the number and mix of units to be constructed. City officials are then interviewed to determine the amount of services needed and cost of providing the services to a particular land use type. The model also uses demographic (school-age children) multipliers to determine the cost of providing elementary school services.

CODIM also uses the Case Study Method. The model combines this method with regression analysis to determine anticipated public service demands of proposed development. In the initial stage of the public sector submodel, local government officials are shown maps of vacant land in the community and are asked to quantify the effects which alternative development configurations would have on local expenditures. Service levels are assumed to remain constant.

Population estimates are derived for each development scenario. The results of the interviews and estimates of current population and expenditures are used to develop a simple regression equation defining the relationship between population and municipal service costs. The actual value of the projected population is then entered into the equation to determine future servicing costs associated with residential development. Interviews are conducted to determine costs per acre of industrial development. This figure is multiplied by the number of acres to be developed. Educational costs are projected by multiplying cost per student times projected number of students. The total cost to the community is the sum of the three individual estimates.

FIMRI uses a variation of the Employment Anticipation Method to determine both primary and secondary impacts of a new industry. Initially, a study is made to determine specific characteristics (work force, distribution of expenditures and amount of land taken out of agricultural production). Input/output coefficients are applied to the expenditure information to calculate net changes in other industries by sector. Numerous multipliers obtained from surveys of other facilities defining the relationship between business volume and employment population are used to calculate net changes in population caused by the new facility. A gravity model is used to distribute the new population; regression equations are used to relate future service costs to population increases.

Both *PROMUS* and *SELLE* use systems dynamics as the main mode of analysis. These two models also use other arithmetic and regression approaches within a systems dynamics framework. *PROMUS* uses the most complex methodology of the models surveyed. The function of the community model subsystem is to simulate the community's attributes. This is done through three submodels.

The small area submodel serves to determine the way in which population and employment are distributed throughout the community. The neighborhood submodel deals with each neighborhood individually to produce estimates of future socioeconomic characteristics. The population and income submodel computes age and income distribution for each small area.

The community model subsystem is used as a basis for the financial policy planning subsystem. The major function of FPPS is to forecast budgets and detailed expenditure patterns related to community growth. Examining the refuse collection program within the streets department, for example, allows this subsystem to be clearly understood. The budgeting requirements for the refuse collection program are set up as an algorithm. The quantity of garbage generated by commercial and residential units, the relationship between the kinds of equipment used, the service levels concerning the location and frequency of pickup, new ratios, and budgetary requirements are some of the equations entered into the computer to simulate this particular program. The equations are simultaneously solved to produce an operating budget. This method is used within the budgeting expense and performance planning submodels of the FPPS.

SELLE is a regional simulation model. In the model's application to a new pulp mill to be located in either Walpole or Charlestown, N.H., systems dynamics was used to determine the fiscal impact on communities within the normal commuting range. Impact was projected to three units of government — county, school district and municipality — each of which derives a large portion of its operating revenue from real property tax revenues. A change in population, school enrollment, or taxable valuation will affect component elements of the systems. Variation in one or more component elements was tested simultaneously.

A derivative of the Comparable City Method was used to determine secondary impact as a result of the location of the pulp mill. A 1973 U.S. Chamber of Commerce research project in Rutland, Vermont, found that for every 100 new factory workers entering an area, a total of 351 new residents move in. The residents would include ninety-seven new families and seventy-nine school children. In addition, sixty-eight nonfactory jobs would be created and one retail store would open. These figures were made part of the simulations model.

CDM, CIM, NHM, and *ACEM* are based on regression analysis. *CDM* uses regression to extrapolate current trends in public expenditures. Data relating to government expenditures are examined on a departmental basis for the preceding ten years. These figures are divided by user populations to establish per capita service costs. *CDM* then applies a number of different regression equations (e.g., linear, multiplicative, exponential, etc.) to the data. The equation with the highest r^2 value in predicting current service costs is chosen to project per capita costs twenty years into the future. This process is repeated for each service category to be considered. The results are then multiplied by the appropriate user populations to determine total costs.

CIM uses regression analysis as a research method to set up a typology of cities. In one application, twenty-seven towns and cities were surveyed. Data describing the demographic, physical, economic, and fiscal characteristics from 1960 and 1970 were entered into the data file. Approximately one thousand regression analyses were solved to determine general coefficients for forecasting purposes.

The regression analysis followed a procedure in which independent variables (e.g., population, total housing stock) were regressed against the dependent variable of annual municipal operating costs (total general fund expenditures) on a cross-sectional basis for 1960 and 1970.

CIM produced cost-revenue forecasts for three cases:

1. Construction of housing units in the city continues to operate under "normal" supply-demand mechanisms; or
2. MSHDA-financed housing is constructed incrementally to the "normal" estimates of new construction; or
3. Privately-financed housing is constructed incrementally to the "normal" estimates of new construction.

CIM has two submodels — house and impact. The house submodel produces future five-year population forecasts based on historical trends. Data on the three alternative development scenarios are then entered into the model. The house submodel with the addition of housing development data is used in the impact submodel to develop fiscal impact forecasts on both the city and local school district(s).

NHM projects a city's expenditures based on the interaction of a number of variables. Three kinds of variables are used: (1) population variables, which are projections of the size, age, and racial composition of the city; (2) wage increases, which are projections of the rates of increase for employees in various wage categories; and (3) service variables, which are projections of the degree to which the level or manner of service provided will change, given an assumed change in the demand for services. Municipal department heads supply raw data to the model.

NHM treats each service category independently. Regression equations based on the value of the variable and historical data are used to determine personnel and nonpersonnel expenditures for each service category. Demand for services is projected by equations also based on the value of the variables and historical data. For instance, the number of teachers required is determined by the number of pupils divided by the average class size, which is then multiplied by a refinement coefficient developed from historical data.

ACEM used a system of thirty-eight simultaneously solved regression equations to project base line costs, revenues and a variety of other economic and demographic information for Alachua County and the City of Gainesville. The regression coefficients were based on least square analyses of historical data. Those equations most accurately predicting current conditions were selected to predict the future.

Data Base and Data Base Sources

The information stored in the program is referred to as the data base (Exhibit 17-2). This information may be either programmed into the model or developed internally by other subsystems of the model. Socio-economic characteristics which form the data base are delivered from published data for an area or from local survey. Both data base and data base sources are often the most flexible components of a model.

CODIM, MUNIES, FIRP, CRAM and *PFM* use demographic multipliers to project the specific population change caused by development. *ACEM, CDM, PROMUS, SELLE,* and *FIMRI* all use cohort-survival techniques to forecast the future population of the entire community. (Exhibit 17-2). *CIM* projects population based on a linear model using change from 1960 to 1970 as an index of future growth. *NHM* projects population primarily as a function of migration based on employment and demographic information obtained from samples of thirty-two metropolitan areas using data for 1950 to 60. For all of the models, the nature of the population projection can range from very general to very specific depending on the type of data available and the level of analysis desired.

Revenues Considered

Three sources of general revenue are considered in most models: real property tax revenues, intergovernmental transfers, and other revenues (Exhibit 17-2). Real property tax revenues are generated by multiplying assessed valuation by the local real property tax rate. Intergovernmental transfers are projected using formulas determined by local, state, and federal enabling legislation and allocation guides. Other revenues are most frequently projected on a per capita basis.

The general approach of the models with regard to property tax revenues is to assume that the difference between intergovernmental/other categories of revenues and costs is what must be made up by the property tax. Based on this assumption, changes in real property tax rates are projected for the future.

Troublesome Issues

Impact Over Time

With the exception of *CODIM* and *FIRP*, all of the models surveyed project fiscal impact data over a number of years. *CODIM* and *FIRP* project impact as if the development were completed under current fiscal conditions.

Several advantages are associated with projecting fiscal impact analysis over time. One advantage is that the user is able to determine the fiscal effects of development at interim stages of project completion. For instance, a development may generate a long-term positive fiscal impact but during the intervening years impose a significant deficit on the locality. Knowledge of project

EXHIBIT 17-2
DATA RESOURCES DRAWN UPON: COST-REVENUE MODELS/COSTS AND REVENUES CONSIDERED

Source	ACEM	CDM	CIM	CODIM	CRAM	FIMRI	FIRP	MUNIES	NHM	PFM	PROMUS	SELLE
U.S. Census socioeconomic data	✓	✓	✓	✓						✓	✓	✓
U.S. Census total household size information				✓		✓					✓	✓
Published multipliers for total household size and school-age children					✓		✓			✓		
School District information school-age children				✓	✓			✓				
Revenue Tabulation (includes inter-governmental transfers)	✓	✓	✓	✓	✓	✓	✓	✓	✓	✓	✓	
Cost calculations (includes capital costs)	✓	✓		✓	✓	✓	✓	✓	✓	✓	✓	✓

Source: Field Survey, Rutgers University Center for Urban Policy Research, Spring 1977.

fiscal impact at interim stages as well as at completion may indeed influence local decisions with regard to the approval or disapproval of other development proposals. A further advantage of this detailing is that it provides vital information to the planner who must determine optimal size and timing of service expansions, such as the capacity of a new high school and when it should be available.

Inflation

The ten models that project impact into the future use a variety of techniques to cope with inflation. *CDM* and *FIMRI* convert all amounts into constant dollars based on the Consumer Price Index. By doing so, these models avoid the problem of predicting future inflation rates. Yet the basis of their inflation estimates is private rather than public sector costs. The Consumer Price Index provides constant dollars using monitored price changes in a number of privately produced goods and services. These price changes may or may not reflect the annual expenditure increases occurring within the publicly provided services of municipalities and school districts. *ACEM, CIM, MUNIES, PFM, PROMUS* and *SELLE* provide for the aplication of annual percentage increases to costs and revenues. This method is based on past trends noted in the particular cost or revenue concerned or on a number of user assumptions regarding future inflation rates within each service category. *NHM* only applies inflation rates to personnel expenditures based on an analysis of contract negotiations between a city and its employees over a ten-year period. *CODIM* and *CRAM* ignore inflation because of the difficulties involved in applying differential inflation rates to costs and revenues. They assume that over time inflation rates will have a negligible effect on current estimates of the net cost-revenue surplus or deficit.

User Sophistication

Two levels of user sophistication are considered. The first is based on the difficulty of theoretical underpinnings of the model. In general, those models which are a straightforward automation of arithmetic techniques are rated low, while those using more sophisticated econometric techniques are rated high (*ACEM, CIM, NHM, PROMUS* and *SELLE*).

The second level of user sophistication is based on the amount of front-end effort required of the user to operate the model. In situations where a municipality purchases a model, must stock it with local data and learn to operate it themselves, user sophistication is considered high (*ACEM, CDM, CIM, NHM, PFM* and *PROMUS*). At the other extreme are those models which are operated by the developer as a consultant to the municipality. In cases where different packages may be purchased, user sophistication is said to vary.

Cost of Implementation

The cost of a model depends on a number of items — what is supplied in response to the client's demand, the level of consulting services provided, first run versus successive implementation cost, where and when the model was instituted, etc. Exhibit 17-3 details the cost of models; they were obtained from interviews at sites of implementation. Models able to handle routine tasks for medium size population jurisdictions cost from $10,000 to $20,000 without consulting services (except for orientation). For more complex models, implementation costs are typically over $30,000, with an equivalent amount for consulting services, usually extending over several years.

Conclusion

As for the demand for fiscal impact analysis increases, so too will the necessity for cost-revenue models. If continuing models are to serve practitioner's needs, improvements must be based on the experience of their predecessors. Fiscal impact analyses are often used in land use policy to either

EXHIBIT 17-3
TROUBLESOME ISSUES IN FISCAL IMPACT ANALYSIS AND THEIR
HANDLING BY COST-REVENUE MODELS

Issue	ACEM	CDM	CIM	CODIM	CRAM	FIMRI	FIRP	MUNIES	NHM	PFM	PROMUS	SELLE
Schedule of development	✓	✓	✓						✓	✓		
Inflation considered	✓	✓	✓	✓	✓	✓		✓	✓	✓	✓	✓
Difficult theoretical underpinnings	✓		✓						✓		✓	
Significant front-end effort required	✓	✓	✓						✓	✓	✓	✓
Cost of implementation	$10,500	Not Available	Not Available	$5,000 or under	$15,000 or under	$1,000 (Free to North Dakota jurisdictions)	Not Available	$10,000 and up	$35,000	Not Available	$25,000 and up	$2,000

Source: Field Survey, Rutgers University Center for Urban Policy Research, Spring 1977.

deny or grant development rights. As such, they are highly visible and usually stir a great deal of controversy. To be effective those who present the conclusions of such analyses must be intimately familiar with both the nature of the process which produced results as well as variations in results given certain changes in the computational process.

To date, field practitioners have insufficient knowledge and confidence in the results produced by models to air these conclusions in defense of local development policy. At public hearings for example, practitioners have been critized for blindly using models to project excessively far into the future with unreasonable results. More complex econometric models lack a simple, believable explanation and thus also evoke voter skepticism.

The message from current practitioners is clear — models should be conceptually straightforward, clearly detailed and easy to implement and interpret. Furthermore, users must devote sufficient care to avoid misuse.

Bibliography for Fiscal Impact Models

ACEM

Fishkind, Henry; Milliman, Jerome; and Ellson, Richard. *Alachua County Econometric Study*. Gainesville, Florida: Bureau of Economic and Business Research and Department of Economics, University of Florida, 1977.

Fishkind, Henry; Milliman, Jerome; and Ellson, Richard. "Alachua County Econometrics Study; A Methodology for Assessing the Impacts of Growth and Development on Local Economies." *Land Economics* (forthcoming, Winter 1978).

CDM

Urban Studies Center, University of Louisville. *Louisville and Jefferson County Community Development Model: CDM User Manual*. Louisville: Urban Studies Center, 1974.

CIM

Applied Decision Systems, Inc. *The Fiscal Consequences of MSHDA – Financed Housing: Overview of the Project*. Wellesley Hills, Massachusetts: Applied Decision Systems, Inc., 1973.

CODIM

Awerbuch, Shimon, and Wallace, William A. *A Goal-Setting and Evaluation Model for Community Development*. Troy, N.Y.: Rensselaer Polytechnic Institute, 1976.

Awerbuch, Shimon and Wallace, W.A. *Policy Evaluation for Community Development: Decision Tools for Local Government*. New York: Praeger Publishers, Inc., 1976.

Cohen, R.; Awerbuch, S.; and Wallace, W.A. "A Test of an Interactive Community Development Impacts Model in a Rural Environment." *Interfaces,* Vol. 7 #1 (1976), pp. 51–62.

CRAM

Strafford Regional Planning Commission. *The Cost-Revenue Analysis Model and Its Application to a Site in Dover, New Hampshire*. Dover, N.H.: Strafford Regional Planning Commission, 1974.

FIMRI

Leistritz, F. Larry, and Murdock, Steven H. *Economic, Demographic, and Social Factors Affecting Energy-Impacted Communities: An Assessment Model and Implications for Nuclear Energy Centers.* Fargo, N.D.: North Dakota State University, 1977.

Tomar, Norman E., et al. "A Fiscal Impact Model for Rural Industrialization." (Prepared for the Western Agricultural Economics Association Annual Meeting. Fort Collins, Colorado, July 18-20, 1976.)

Tomar, Norman E., et al. *Economic Impacts of Construction and Operation of the Coal Creek Electrical Generation Complex and Related Mine.* Fargo, N.D.: Department of Agricultural Economics, North Dakota State University, 1976.

FIRP

de Corla-Souze, Patrick. *A Report on the Results Obtained from an Empirical Analysis of Fiscal Impact of New Development, Using Computerized Fiscal Impact Models.* Tallahassee, Florida: Florida State University, 1976.

The Fiscal Impact Study Group. *The Fiscal Consequences of Alternative Growth Patterns: A Simulation.* Tallahassee, Florida: Department of Urban and Regional Planning, Florida State University, 1976.

Frank, James E. *Final Report on the Fiscal Impact Research Project.* Tallahassee, Florida: Department of Urban and Regional Planning, Florida State University, 1975.

Frank, James E. *Fiscal Impact Research Project. Volume 1: Report on First Generation Model Development.* Tallahassee, Florida: Department of Urban and Regional Planning, Florida State University, 1976.

MUNIES

Gale, Dennis E. "The Municipal Impact Evaluation System." *ASPO Planning Advisory Service Report, No. 297 (September 1973).*

Marcou, O'Leary and Associates. *MUNIES — Municipal Impact Evaluation System: A Computerized System for Evaluating Fiscal Impact.* Washington, D.C.: Marcou, O'Leary and Associates, 1974.

NHM

Scott, Claudia DeVita. *Forecasting Local Government Spending.* Washington, D.C.: Urban Institute, 1972.

PFM

Department of Community Development, Lakewood, Colorado. *Planning Report 10.G DYLAM/Lakewood: Development of a Land Use Allocation Model.* Lakewood, Colorado: Department of Community Development, 1973.

Department of Community Development, Lakewood, Colorado. *Public Finance Model Final Report.* New York: Parsons, Brinckerhoff, Quade and Douglas, Inc., 1974.

PROMUS

Decision Sciences Corporation. *PROMUS: The Provincial Municipal Simulator.* Jenkintown, Pennsylvania, 1973.

SELLE

Selle, Henry, et al. *Feasibility Study for a Proposed Pulp Mill toBe Built by Parsons Wittemore in Walpole, N.H.* (Chapter 4). The Environmental Study Department Sayer Engineering School, Dartmouth, N.H.

APPENDIX 1

NATIONAL SUMMARY OF CASE LAW RELATING TO COST-REVENUE

Alabama

Aldridge v. *Grund,* 293 Ala. 333, 302 So.2d 847 (1974)

Board of Commissioners rezoned land from single-family to multi-family; lower court invalidated the rezoning. The Supreme Court upheld the Board's decision to rezone. "There was evidence that the population in metropolitan Birmingham and its environs was rapidly increasing and that in the area of the rezoning and nearby there were *school facilities,* that the subject property was served by *water and sewer lines,* that there was *adequate drainage,* that widening the road was under consideration, that police and fire protection was good, and that the subject property had good highway access to Birmingham's business district. These are only *some of the factors that the commissioners might have considered** from the evidence in concluding that it would promote the general welfare of the county to rezone the property." [p.855]

Arkansas

City of Little Rock v. *Hocott,* 220 Ark.421, 247 S.W. 2d 1012 (1952).

Applicant wanted rezoning from single-family residential to multi-family. City denied request but lower court directed change in zoning and Supreme Court affirmed. Court mentioned that evidence had been presented that "schools in the area were already overcrowded but most witnesses conceded this to be a statewide condition." [p.1014] Thus the court's decision did not turn on that consideration and there was no indication that *the availability of schools* was a crucial consideration in this situation.

---

*Emphasis in this and all following citations added.

California

Robinson v. City of Los Angeles, 146 A.2d 810, 304 P.2d 814 (1956).

Challenge to zoning change from agricultural use to light industrial use was allowed. Speaking to the issue of traffic congestion and inadequate sewerage facilities to support such a use, the Court stated that this difficulty "presupposes that roads and sewers will remain in their present limited capacity rather than growing in proportion to increasing public demand. This is a faulty notion of the basis for testing validity of zoning, which *necessarily looks to the future and proceeds upon the assumption that development of properties and facilities within and without the zoned area will proceed harmoniously with its requirements."*

Construction Industry Association of Sonoma County v. City of Petaluma, 375 F. Supp. 574 (N.D. Cal. 1974).

Court invalidated zoning ordinance limiting the number of new entrants into city, based on unconstitutional violation of right to travel. In its decision, the Court stated that a municipality capable of supporting a natural population growth *may not limit its growth simply because it does not prefer to grow at the rate which would be dictated by prevailing market demands."* Decision was reversed on appeal.

Colorado

Sundance Hill Homeowners Association v. Board of Commissioners, 188 Col. 321, 534 P.2d 1212 (1975).

Planning Board recommended rezoning for a PUD at 10.6 units per acre. Board of Commissioners rezoned. Lower court overturned rezoning. Supreme Court upheld Board of Commissioners. "The lower court erred in making a finding that, because adequate sewage facilities were unavailable at that time, such deficiency was fatally defective to the proposed rezoning grant." [p. 1215] The Board has regulations that will serve as multilevel checks to assure that development will be in the best interest of the public. It is during those processes (presumably subdivision control, site plan review etc.) that *"the availability of adequate sewage facilities must finally be resolved, not at the rezoning stage."* [p.1215]

Also note that in this case the representative of the Board of Education was allowed to present testimony verifying the developer's school impact statement. [p. 1215]

Rondo Land, Inc. v. Board of Commissioners of Boulder, Colorado

Court upheld Board's decision to deny rezoning to multifamily use. Board had listed as one of its reasons for denial that it must see to it *"that police, fire protection should not be jeopardized. . ."* [p.874]

Connecticut

Jablon v. Town Plan and Zoning Com'n. of Town of Newton 157 Ct. 434, 254 A.2d 914 (1969).

Court upheld rezoning from farming and residential to industrial. In discussing the issue of growth, it stated, "Balancing the preservation of the status quo with the reasonable *pressures for change due to growth* in population and the onslaught of business needs and community requirements is a function of zoning which *must best be resolved by the duly authorized legislative municipal body through a logical development of its comprehensive plan."*

Florida

Watson v. Mayflower Property Inc., 223 So.2d 368(District Court of Appeals, Fourth District 1969).

Applicant sought to rezone to increase the density of land use which was already multi-family. The lower court ordered the rezoning and stated that the increase in traffic congestion was a matter to be resolved by the City. The Court of Appeals held that the ordinance "was reasonably calculated to prevent excessive traffic. . .and prevent aggravation of an already serious traffic problem. . ." [p.374] Some of the *factors deemed appropriate for consideration as objectives of zoning are* "*adequacy of drainage and storm sewers, public streets, pedestrian walkways. . ."* [p. 373]

Florida Palm-Aire Corporation v. *Deluin,* So.2d 26 (District Court of Appeals, Fourth District, 1969).

Neighbors sought to overturn rezoning which allowed four-story apartment buildings on the adjoining property. Lower court granted the invalidation. Court of Appeals reversed and allowed rezoning. "The proofs establish that plantiffs' injuries, i.e., obstruction of view, increased use of utilities, increased traffic, etc., to be not special but those which follow as a natural consequence of increased population and thereby sustained by the public as a whole in that particular area." [pp.27–28]

City of Naples v. *Central Plaza of Naples, Inc.,* 303 So.2d 423(District Court of Appeals Second District, 1974).

Applicant petitioned for a special exception to construct apartments, which City of Naples denied. Lower court overturned the City's determination. Court of Appeals held that the City did *not have the right to consider evidence* that erection of apartments would substantially increase traffic on the main commercial street, and *that construction could result in overpopulation of the area, creating excessive demands on utilities and other services* where zoning ordinance did not refer to such considerations.

City of Miami Beach v. *Lachman,* 71 So.2d 148 (Supreme Court, 1953).

City sought to keep beachfront property in single-family residences. Owners wished to rezone to hotels and apartments. Lower court held for owners. Supreme Court said issues were fairly debatable and upheld City's restrictions. City argued that the *rezoning "will result in overcrowding, the increase of fire and other hazards and would overtax the sewer, water, and fire fighting facilities, thus endangering the public health and safety."* p.152.

Georgia

Pendley v. *Lake Harbin Civic Association,* 230 Ga. 631, 198 S.F.2d 503 (1973)

This case was decided on procedural grounds. In the opinion the court mentioned approvingly that the objectors "had introduced unrebutted lay and expert evidence that such construction would be harmful to the area, causing dangerous traffic conditions, inadequate water and sewage, overcrowded schools and other land use problems" which had caused the Planning Commission to deny the rezoning. [p.507]

Barton v. *Atkinsokn,* 228 Ga. 733, 187 S.E.2d 835 (1972).

Counties with a population of over 500,000 had to have their Directors of the Board of Health, Board of Education, and Planning Board submit reports concerning each rezoning application as to how it would affect their departments. The Court did not question that procedure. The case dealt with the statutory construction as to whether those reports had to be read aloud at public hearings and decided that they did not.

Pruitt v. *Meeks,* 177 S.E.2d 41 (Supreme Court, 1970).

Applicant wished to erect a mobile home park and shopping center. Board denied and lower court reversed Board's decision. Supreme Court upheld Board's denial. Two of the five reasons for the Board's denial were that there were *"no provisions for sewerage for the 200 trailer sites and that schools could not adjust to resulting increase in enrollment."* [p.43]

Illinois

Mistretta v. *Village River Forest,* 223 N.E.2d 282 (1966).

Court upheld the denial of a request for a zoning change from single-family dwellings to permit multiple-family apartments. *Based on testimony as to the added burden such a development would place on existing sewer, utilities, and water, the Court ruled that the denial of this request was not "capricious or arbitrary."*

Central National Bank of Chicago v. *Village of Hoffman Estates,* 293 N.E. 2d 481 (1973).

Zoning change permitting a planned residential development was held invalid. The Court stated, however, that *mere incidence of higher municipal costs is not a justifiable basis for rejecting an appropriate use of property.*

Chicago City Bank and Trust Co. v. *City of Highland Park* 137 N.E. 2d 835 (1956).

Court upheld a prohibition against expanding an existing apartment complex based on the existence of an already overburdened sewerage facility.

First National Bank of Skokie v. *Village of Skokie,* 229 N.E.2d 378,(1967).

Court upheld challenge to a zoning ordinance preventing construction of apartment complex despite argument that such use would burden existing services. Court held that *a use cannot be denied simply because it requires more services.*

Brent Glassey v. *County of Taxewell,* 297 N.E.2d 235, (1973).

In granting request for a rezoning from agricultural use to use as a mobile home park, the court held that *a zoning change cannot be denied simply because it may increase government costs.*

Duggan v. *The County of Cook,* 60 Ill. 107, 324 N.E.2d 406 (1975).

The Court declared invalid the County's denial of a zoning change from single-family dwellings to allow for a mobile home development. In response to the County's argument that such development would overburden its ability to provide educational facilities, it stated, *"While these problems may be considered in weighing the comparative benefits and burdens upon the public and the private landholder, they are by no means conclusive."*

Kansas

Hukle v. *City of Kansas City,* 212 Kan. 627, 512 P.2d 457, (1973).

Superior Court overruled lower court's refusal to allow neighboring landowners to challenge a rezoning which would permit the building of a townhouse complex. In discussing the question of whether such a zoning change was proper, the Court stated, "The record here is clear, that the city in denying rezoning was concerned that the proposed development would overtax certain essential facilities, namely sewers, streets, and already overcrowded neighborhood schools... *We know of no reason why at any given point in time the city fathers may not call a halt to substantial increase in density in a particular area. In any event the matter is primarily one for municipal or legislative policy as distinguished from judicial."*

Kentucky

Pierson Trapp Company v. *Peak,* 340 S.W. 2d 456 (1960).

Action brought to enjoin property owner from using tract of land rezoned from residential to commercial. In denying plaintiff's argument based on inadequacy of sewerage facilities, the Court stated, *"What sewerage facilities will be provided for the particular structure* that eventually may be erected on the land in question *is not a proper factor of consideration on the question of whether there shall be a change of zoning classification."*

J.E.Johnson III v. *La Grew,* 447 S.W. 2d 98 (1969).

Court upheld planning commission's approval of zoning change. The commission's decision was ruled to be not arbitrary or unreasonable, in part, based on its *proper consideration of the availability of "all urban services."*

Louisiana

Gandet v. *Economical Super Market,* 163 La. 785, 112 So.2d 720 (1959).

Court refused to deny permit which allowed store owner to use nearby vacant lot for parking. City ordinance pertaining thereto required that the Council grant a permit where "such land use will not have an unduly detrimental effect upon the character of the neighborhood, traffic conditions, public utility facilities or other matters pertaining to the public health, public safety or general welfare."

Maryland

Redden v. Montgomery County, 270 Md. 688, 313 A.2d 481 (1974).

Board allowed a rezoning to permit construction of a 428 unit senior citizen building for the elderly in an area zoned for single-family dwellings. Lower court affirmed. Court of Appeals held that *applicants had not established "by a preponderance of the evidence that the proposed use would not overburden existing public sanitary sewer services."* It remanded the case for further examination.

Storch v. Zoning Board of Howard County, 267 Md. 476, 398 A.2d 8 (1972).

Board rezoned to eliminate two-family dwellings except as a special exception. Owners appealed. Courts upheld the Board. There was evidence presented relating to two-family dwellings as to "consequent dangers from increased traffic, overburdening of public facilities and the like. Their testimony was admissible; its weight was for the Zoning Board, and not the courts." [p.15]

Marcus v. Montgomery County Council, 253 Md. 535, 201 A.2d 777 (1964).

Council rezoned land from single family residential to commercial and apartment uses. Lower court and Court of Appeals affirmed the County actions. Nearby land owners had protested that the rezoning would bring in more people and *increase traffic and school population.* Court held that *such effects are "inconveniences likely to be suffered by any member of the public, far or near, and do not require a denial of the application.* [p.781]

Renz v. Bonfield Holding Company, 223 Md. 34, 158 A.2d 611 (1960).

County Zoning Board denied request to rezone for town houses. Lower court reversed. Court of Appeals upheld Board refusal in that there was insufficient evidence to show error in the original zoning. In upholding the Board denial of rezoning the Court stated that "the objections as to *increased pressure on highways and schools* (which currently seem to be greater than that as to sewer or water facilities), still remain as to each, and they *are proper subjects for considerations by the Board in a proceeding such as this."* [p.614]

Shapiro v. Montgomery County Council, 269 Md. 380, 306 A.2d 253 (1973).

Board and lower court refused to rezone property from single-family residential to multifamily use, citing the resulting overcrowding of schools. The Court of Appeals, stating that the question of overcrowded schools was fairly debatable, affirmed the Board's decision.

Gorin v. Board of County Commissioners of Anne Arundel Co., 260 Md. 223 A.2d 237 (1966).

Court upheld Board denial for rezoning from agricultural to commercial and garden apartments. *It accepted the argument that inadequate traffic and sewerage facilities*

Appendix 1: National Summary

existed to permit such use on land, particularly since "how and when such financing (for public facilities) could be secured was not made clear."

Malasky v. Montgomery County Council, 294 Md. 91, 267 A.2d 182 (1970).

Court affirmed Council's denial of a request for rezoning from single-family to multifamily residential. In part the Court *based its acceptance* of the Council's decision on an adverse report submitted by the Planning Board's technical staff which stated *that the roads and schools were inadequate to meet the increased demand if the rezoning were granted.*

Furnace Branch Land Co. v. Board of County Commissioners of Anne Arundel County, 232 Md. 536, 194 A.2d 640 (1963).

Court upheld Board's decision to deny rezoning request which would have permitted construction of garden apartments *based on the existence of a "continued, dangerous and increasing problem" of inadquate sewage disposal facilities.*

Norbeck Village Joint Venture v. Montgomery County Council, 254 Md. 59, 254 A.2d 700 (1969).

County sought to control growth through plan that preserved open space and protected watershed area. Lower court and Court of Appeals affirmed County plan. "The Olney area roads, sewers, schools and fire and police protection will not according to the record presently support urban or intense development, and to install the additional facilities that would be necessary to support a *changed pattern would place a burden on the taxpayers that the County legislative body thinks is unwarranted and beyond its present reasonable capabilities."* [p.706]

Massachusetts

122 Main Street Corporation v. City of Brockton,

Challenge to validity of minimum height requirement for buildings in central business district was upheld. The Court held in part that, *"It is not within the scope of the act to enact zoning regulations for the purpose of assisting a municipality. .to inflate its taxable revenue."*

Michigan

Johnson v. Township of Lyon, 45 Mch. 491, 206 N.W.2d 761 (1973).

Applicant petitioned for a rezoning to permit mobile homes. Lower court upheld township's refusal to rezone. Court of Appeals reversed and remanded to lower court for new findings of fact. During the course of the opinion, the Court of Appeals cited *Cohen* with approval and stated that *"the use of surrounding area, traffic patterns, and available water supply and sewage disposal systems certainly are relevant considerations in the reasonableness of a particular exclusion."* [p.764]

Cohen v. Township of Canton, 38 Mch. 680, 197 N.W.2d 101 (1972).

Applicant sought to rezone land from agricultural to mobile home use. Township refused. Lower court upheld Township. Court of Appeals upheld the lower court's findings of fact that were *used to uphold the ordinance*. "The area is *presently poorly served by roads and highways*. . . . The area is *not served by any public water supply* and it will be years before public water can be brought into the area. . . . The area is *not served by any public sewage disposal system*. . . ." [p.103]

South Central Improvement Association v. *City of St. Clair Shores,* 348 Mch. 153, 82 N.W.2d 453 (1957).

City rezoned residential area to commercial to accommodate non-conforming businesses in the area. Nearby homeowners complained and lower court and Supreme Court declared the rezoning invalid. City attempted to defend by saying that "St. Clair Shores has only very small areas for industrial use from which tax revenues may be obtained and that *rapid growth creates serious financial problems in the furnishing of adequate school facilities and municipal services*." [p.456] The court held that *this factor would not justify in this case the rezoning of the area in issue*." [p.456]

Snookler v. *Township of Wheatfield,* Mch. 162, 207 N.W. 646 (1973).

Township wished to have land rezoned from agricultural and residential to mobile home use. Town denied; lower court upheld town and found that the township had *no police protection*. .no fire protection and the park would double the population of the township. The Court of Appeals overruled the lower court and held that *"all of the foregoing facts relate to an increase in burdens, economic and otherwise, on the township for future services. This type of economic justification for exclusionary zoning was rejected in Green.*" [p. 465]

Wilkins v. *Village of Birch Run,* 48 Mch. 57, 209 N.W.2d 863 (1973).

Applicant wished to have its land rezoned for mobile homes, the Township denied the application and the lower court granted rezoning. Court of Appeals reversed and upheld Township. One of the reasons the Court gave for its decision was *"that the water supply. . .was just adequate to serve existing population, and with population increases new wells would have to be obtained."*

Green v. *Township of Lima,* 40 Mch. 655, 199 N.W.2d 243 (1972).

Township zoned land from mobile homes to agriculture. Owner sought to rezone to mobile homes. Lower court upheld Township. Court of Appeals reversed. The evidence presented merely established that the building of a mobile home park would increase the burdens, economic and otherwise, on the township for future services." [p.246] This court has adopted the unequivocal statement in *National Land* (Pennsylvania case) which *rejects "Any type of economic justification for exclusionary zoning."* [p.246]

Minnesota

State of Minnesota v. *Larson,* 195 N.W.2d 180 (1972).

Court upheld zoning ordinance limiting trailer homes to designated mobile home parks as a valid exercise of the police power. It stated that, "By limiting trailer

Appendix 1: National Summary 369

homes to designated parks, cities have found it easier to provide police and fire protection and to regulate health conditions, as well as provide necessary services such as water, sewerage and lighting."

Mississippi

Adam v. Reed, 239 Mis. 437, 123 So.2d 606 (1960).

City rezoned area along highway from residential to commercial. Nearby property owners objected. Lower court and Supreme Court affirmed rezoning to commercial. City argued that "the rezoning of the property. . .would enable the municipality to obtain more tax revenue. . .and the cost of schools and the performance of other governmental functions has greatly increased." [p.607] The Supreme Court stated that such factors are not in themselves sufficient but that *"the need for more revenue for these purposes may be entitled to consideration in determining whether or not the amendment would tend to promote the general welfare. . . ."* [p.608]

Fowler v. City of Hattiesburg, 296 So.2d 358 (1967).

Applicant wished to change zoning from residential to commercial for the construction of a shopping center. He presented evidence that the shopping center would provide $250,000 in additional tax revenues to the City each year. Supreme Court affirmed the City's rezoning to allow the shopping center but on grounds of the presumption of validity of a municipality's actions. It did not find the City's action to be clearly unreasonable and did not specifically speak to the monetary considerations.

Missouri

Desloge v. County of St. Louis, 431 S.W.2d 126 (1968).

Nearby homeowners sought to overturn the County's zoning designation of a 350-acre tract from nonurban (3 acres) to R-4 (7,500 square feet). The Supreme Court upheld the rezoning. "The tract was ripe for development and *problems of roads, schools, fire and police services do not have to be solved prior to zoning a tract for development."* [p.134]

Flora Realty & Investment Co. v. City of Ladue, 246 S.W. 2d 771 (1972).

Applicant sought to overturn the 3 acre minimum lot size for his property. Town refused. Lower court and Supreme Court upheld Town. Although the case was not decided on the following grounds, the Court did say that "the record clearly shows conflicting evidence on issues of fact. . .as to roads and traffic conditions and the results to be anticipated from subdivision and development in smaller tracts on traffic, city services, fire and police protection and schools. . . ." [p.777]

Miller v. Kanas City, 141 Kan. 459, 358 S.W.2d 100 (1962).

City rezoned area from residential to commercial. Lower court overturned the City, and the Court of Appeals reversed the City's rezoning. In discussing *the purposes of zoning the court said that among other purposes they were to be designed to "provide adequate transportation, water, sewerage, schools and parks. . ."* [p.104]

Nebraska

Stahla v. Board of Zoning Adjustment in and for Hall County, 186 Neb. 219, 182 N.W.2d 209 (1970).

A challenge to the requirement of a conditional use permit for mobile home parks within a medium density residential use district was disallowed. The school board filed an objection, *claiming that facilities were already overextended.* The Court stated, *"These factors while not alone controlling, are circumstances the zoning board of adjustment could consider."*

Nevada

Cocnet Homes, Inc. v. McKenzie, 84 Nev. 250 (1968).

Ct. upheld validity of a special use granted for a proposed cluster zone. The Court stated, "Zoning is a means by which a government body and its citizens can plan and build for the future—it *may not, however be used as a means to deny the future."*

New Hampshire

Steel Hill Development, Inc. v. Town of Sanbortown et al., 335 F. Supp. 947 (1971).

Court upheld town's upgrading minimum lot size of property owned by developer was not arbitrary or unreasonable. It held that "We recognize, as *within the general welfare, concerns relating to the construction and integration of hundreds of new homes which would. . .pose substantial financial burdens on the town for police, fire, sewer and road service."* Court went on to state, however, that this should not be interpreted as a general approval of six-acre zoning.

New Jersey

Rockaway Estates v. Rockaway Twp., 119 A.2d 461 (1955).

Attack on township's zoning ordinance claiming it was not adopted pursuant to a reasonable comprehensive plan was disallowed; The Court deemed it a proper exercise of police power: "So long as grounds exist for zoning as are demanded by the statute, *there is no sound objection to the consideration of cost of municipal services in the establishment of the zones."*

Newark Milk and Cream Corporation v. Township of Parsippany-Troy Hills, 47 Su 306, 135 A2d 682 (1957).

Amendment to zoning ordinance to create a specialized economic development district was upheld: *"a zoning scheme seeking. .to obtain a sound municipal economy by encouraging industry. . .is a proper exercise of the zoning power,* subject always to the reasonableness of the classification and regulations enacted to achieve the end both generally and with respect to particular property."

Ward v. Township of Montgomery, 28 N.J.52, 9, 147A.2d 248 (1959).

Zoning amendment to enlarge a manufacturing zone was upheld: "Manifestly its fiscal picture was such that *a new source of income would serve the general economic welfare. Pursuit of that objective is entirely worthy of the attention of the municipal fathers."*

Gruber v. Mayor and Township Commission of Raritan, 39 N.J. 1, 186 A.2d 489 (1962).

Court approved rezoning from residential to light industry: *The attempt to achieve a better economic balance falls within the concept of "general welfare,"* but can only be done "as part of and in furtherance of a legitimate comprehensive plan for. . .the entire municipality."

Vickers v. Township of Gloucester, 37 N.J. 232, 181 A.2d 129 (1962).

Court upheld an ordinance precluding trailer parks from an industrial zone; Justice Hall's dissent proposes an increase in judicial review of zoning power and discusses economic segregation caused by zoning.

Kunzler v. Hoffman, 48 N.J.277, 255 A.2d 321 (1966).

Court upheld rezoning for construction of a hospital. The court stated, *"Effect of zoning on municipal tax revenues. . .may be considered by zoning authorities along with other valid reasons when they act legislatively to enact the zoning ordinance."*

Oakwood at Madison Inc. v. Twp. of Madison, 117 Su, 283 A.2d 353 (1971).

Zoning ordinance invalidated: The Court stated that *"fiscal zoning per se is irrelevant to the statutory purposes of zoning."* The test is whether it promotes a reasonably balanced and well ordered plan for the municipality.

Molina v. Mayor of Glassboro, 116 Su 195, 287 A.2d 401 (1971).

Court struck down ordinance limiting number of bedrooms. It stated, *"The governmental cost must be an official concern, but not to an extent that it limits who shall live in the municipality."*

South Burlington County NAACP v. Mount Laurel Township 67 N.J. 151, 336 A.2d 713 (1975)

Court invalidated exclusionary sections of zoning ordinance. Township must allow for its "fair share" of the regional low- and moderate-income housing in the region.

New York

Wachsberger v. Michalis, 191 N.Y.S.2d 62 (1969).

Application for a variance to permit construction of a two-family residence in an area zoned for single-family was remanded by the Court for further investigation. It stated, *"In its determination the Board should consider. . .the effect,* if the variance is allowed, *of the increased population density thus produced on available government facilities."*

Josephs v. Town Board of Clarkstown, 24 N.Y. Misc. Rpts 366, 198 N.Y.S. 2d 695 (1960).

Challenge to denial of a special exception based on inadequacy of public services was denied. Addressing this issue the Court stated, "It is all very well to speak generally of an absolute duty on the part of a municipality to supply necessary school, highway and other facilities as it grows and expands in population and as the need for increased facilities arises, *but it is clear that the duty of a municipality in this regard will not bar it from the right to reasonably regulate and control the density of population in specified districts in the interest of public welfare and to avoid unnecessary hardship to individuals and taxpayers.* The question should be and is whether or not the action of the municipal authorities is reasonable in a particular case."

Raynor v. Village of Rockville Center, 62 N.Y. Misc. Rpts. 870, 310 N.Y.S. 2d 210 (1969).

Challenge to validity of zoning amendment permitting only single-family dwellings was rejected. *Court cited inadequate sewerage and school facilities as a valid reason for the Board's refusal to permit construction of apartments.*

Nattin Reality, Inc. v. Ludewig, 67 N.Y. Misc. Rpts. 828, 324 N.Y.S. 2d 668 (1971).

Unsuccessful challenge to rezoning of plaintiff's property from permitting multifamily dwellings to single-family residences. *Court held that inadequate water supply and sewerage disposal facilities were a proper justification for using zoning to restrict density.*

Westwood Forrest Estates Inc., v. *Village of South Nyack,* 23 N.Y.2d 424, 297 N.Y.S. 2d 129 (1969).

Zoning ordinance prohibiting the construction of multiple dwellings anywhere in the Village *was invalid, where it was based on inadequate sewage disposal facilities.*

Golden v. *Planning Board of the Town of Ramapo,* 30 N.Y.2d 359, 285 N.E. 2d (1972).

Court upheld development plan which tied future development to the availability of adequate public facilities, the purpose being *"to phase residential development to the Town's ability to provide* the *facilities or services."*

North Carolina

Jackson v. *Guilford County Board of Adjustment,* 275 N.C. 155, 166 S.E.2d 78 (1969).

Court upheld grant of a special exception to permit construction of a mobile home park in an agriculture zone, *despite language in the statute* establishing such a zone which stated as one of its purposes, "to discourage any use, which because of its character or size, *would create unusual requirements and costs for providing public services,* such as law enforcement, fire protection, water supply and sewerage disposal before such services are generally needed."

Ohio

Willott v. Village of Beachwood, 175 Oh. 557, 197 N.E.2d 201 (1964).

Challenge to the validity of an amendment to the zoning ordinance permitting the building of a shopping center was disallowed. The Court asked "Where the council of a municipality makes a determination of land use policy which involves the control of traffic, the burden of traffic. ., the *municipal revenue* which will be produced for the city, and the land use consistent with the best interests of the general welfare and prosperity and development of the community as a whole, does the court have the authority to invalidate such an ordinance in the absence of a showing that such power has been exercised in such an arbitrary, confiscatory and unreasonable manner as to be in violation of constitutional guarantees?" Its answer is that *"the courts are without authority to interfere."*

Pennsylvania

Appeal of Santa F. Cisco et al. from Aston Twp. Zoning Board, 60 Dela Co.199 (1972).

Application for rezoning from industrial to residential use was denied. Court relied upon same argument as in *Pumo—that an increase in tax revenue as a coincidence to a previous zoning change is not reason for invalidation of that change.*

Pumo Applicant v. Norristown Borough, 404 Pa. 475, 172 A.2d 828 (1961).

Challenge to zoning amendment which changed an area zoned for residential use to commercial use was disallowed with regard to the applicant's argument that the zoning power may not be used for the purpose of producing tax revenue. The Court stated that "The facts coincidentally and incidentally, show valid exercise of the Borough's authority in zoning to bring about an increase in tax revenue."

Appeal of Girsh, 437 Pa. 237, 263 A.2d 395 (1970).

Court held that failure of township's zoning scheme to provide for apartments, although not explicity prohibited, was unconstitutional. Quoting *National Land, the Court rejected the argument that such an exclusionary ordinance can be justified on the basis of inadequate municipal services.* Pointing to the recent growth of residential suburbs, it stated "Municipal services must be provided somewhere, and if Nether Providence is a logical place for development to take place, it should not be heard to say that it will not bear its rightful part of the burden."

In re: Application of Calvary Methodist Church, 81 Dauphin County Reports 397 (1963).

Court upheld refusal of a rezoning application to allow residential construction on land previously zoned for commercial use. Quoting with approval from *Pumo v. Norristown Borough,* it stated, "The fact that coincidentally, and incidentally, a valid exercise of the Borough's authority in zoning may bring about an increase in tax revenue cannot invalidate the Borough's action, otherwise proper and legal."

Township of Williston v. *Chesterdale Farms, Inc.,* 7 Pa. C453, 300A.2d 107 (1973).

Zoning ordinance permitting apartments only by special exception was declared unconstitutional. Citing both *National Land* and *Girsh,* the Court ruled that *the future economic burden of providing municipal services was not a proper justification for utilizing the zoning ordinance as an exclusionary device.*

Surrick v. *Zoning Hear. Bd. of Upper Providence,* 11 Pa. C607, 314 A.2d 565 (1974).

Court upheld constitutionality of zoning ordinance requiring a one-acre minimum lot size. Although recognizing the holding in *National Land*, the Court suggested that "it is impossible for a court to say that any minimum acreage requirement is unconstitutional per se." In this instance it found such a restriction to be reasonable.

Appeal of Manns, 3 Pa. C242, 281 A.2d 355 (1971).

Court overruled denial of a special exception to allow use of land for a stone quarry. In addressing a finding of fact by the Board of Adjustment "that the proposed use would be economically disadvantageous to the township and community as a whole, since it would require more services in terms of roadwork and police protection, while returning less revenue to the community than non-quarry uses," it stated that "we do not believe that this consideration is a justification for a denial to a property owner of the lawful use of his land. It is now clear that *zoning may not be used to avoid the increased responsibilities and economic burdens which time and natural growth invariably bring.*"

Appeal of Kit-Mar Builders, Inc., 439 Pa. 466, 268 A.2d 765 (1970).

Court held as unconstitutional a zoning ordinance which required lots of no less than 2 acres along roads and no less than 3 acres in the interior. Citing with approval *National Land,* the Court stated that communities *"may not refuse to confront the future by adopting zoning regulations that effectively restrict population to near present levels."*

National Land and Investment Company v. *Kohn,* 419 Pa. 504, 215, A.2d 597 (1965).
Pennsylvania Supreme Court held unconstitutional a zoning ordinance requiring four acre minimum lot size in residential districts. It stated *"A zoning ordinance whose primary purpose is to prevent the entrance of newcomers in order to avoid future burdens, economic and otherwise, upon the administration of public services and facilities cannot be held valid.* Of course, we do not mean to imply that a governmental body may not utilize its zoning power in order to insure that the municipal services which the community requires are provided in an orderly and rational manner."

Rhode Island

Town of Gloucester v. *Divio's Mobile Home Court, Inc.,* 111 RI. 120, 300 A.2d 465 (1973).

Town brought action to enjoin operator of mobile home park from violating provision of licensing and zoning ordinances limiting number of mobile homes that could be parked in such a facility to 30. Operator filed an answer challenging the constitutionality of the 30 unit limitation.

Court invalidated ordinance restricting the number of units in a mobile home development. "The municipality's contention that its limitation of 30 units constitutes an effort to lesser congestion seems to be a diplomatic way of expressing its real concern, that of finding some way *to maintain the population of its schools at a point where a stable tax rate can be preserved. We do not believe that a zoning ordinance was ever intended to fulfill such a function."*

Merlino Enterprises, Inc. v. Fenlon, 112 RI. 653, 314 A.2d 155 (1974).

Court held that applicant could not attack validity of ordinance on which he relied in filing application and that town council's denial of license was not arbitrary and capricious and did not deny applicant due process. [p.160]

[Kelleher (J) concurring] "No one could dispute the principle that owners of mobile homes should pay their fair share of cost of the municipal services which they enjoy. The problem is in deciding how such share can be determined and its payment enforced."

Tennessee

Connor v. City of Tennessee, 142 S.W.2d 706 (1940).

Ordinance forbidding offices in residential areas was upheld as a valid exercise of the police power; *Court cited both increased traffic and costs of operating municipality as basis for restriction.*

Virginia

Board of County Supervisors of Fairfax, County v. Carper 200 Va. 653, 107 S.E.2d 390 (1959).

County sought to restrict development in western two-thirds of County to 2 acre lots. From 1947–1957 Fairfax County was fastest growing county in the nation. The sewers located in the eastern one-third of the County were financed by revenue bonds. That indebtedness grew from $800,000 in 1947 to a projected $67,000,000 in 1958. Bond ratings dropped. The county justified its restrictions by saying that they did away with a health problem and that schools could be built more cheaply in the eastern part of the county. The County argued that "the general economic effect or the county's having to furnish police and fire protection, the construction and maintenance of public schools, and other public conditions should be considered in determining the reasonableness of the ordinance. [p.396]. In overturning the Board, the Court said that the "real purpose. . .was to. . .channel the county's population into the eastern ⅓ where the cost of government would be more economical. *The purpose of preventing development that could reasonable reasonably be expected, in order to channel the population to a more congested area in the interest of economy, was unreasonable and arbitrary."* [p.395] The Court considered the County's economic argument at best to "be considered as more or less incidentital." [p.396]

The Court also found that a service company could supply water if asked, that septic tanks could be used on lots smaller than 2 acres, and that the county's financial conditions could be improved by imposing higher taxes.

Wilhelm v. Morgan, 208 Va. 298, 157 S.E.2d 920 (1967).

The local board allowed a rezoning of an 8 acre parcel to permit a quarry. The Court upheld the rezoning and stated that *"the advisability of encouraging industry in Botetourt County. . .is not an improper motive."* [p.923] Although the Court said this the above was not the only reason for allowing the rezoning, it did not specifically mention others except for the broad category of "the general good of the county."

Board of County Supervisors of Fairfax County v. DeGroff Enterprises, Inc., 214 Va. 235, 198 S.E.2d 600 (1963).

The zoning ordinance required 15 percent of the units built to be low or moderate incomes. The Court struck down the ordinance. "We conclude that the legislative intent was to permit localities to enact only traditional zoning ordinances directed to physical characteristics and having the purpose neither to include nor exclude any particular socio-economic group." [p.602]

Board of Supervisors of Fairfax County v. Allman, 215 Va. 434, 211 S.E. 48 (1975).

In 1971, Roy G. Allman filed an application for rezoning approximately 300 acres of land on the northwestern border of Fairfax County near the new town of Reston. The rezoning request was for a change from the RE-1 category (one-acre zoning, which would yield 273 conventionally situated single-family units) to the PDH-3 category (approximately three units per acre, which would yield 988 units in a planned development community).

At the first hearing, the Planning Commission denied approval of the Allman application, *citing an inadequacy of facilities, in particular roads and sewers, to serve development on the land.* Next, the Board of Supervisors voted five to three to deny the application, also claiming that public facilities were already overburdened around the Allman tract and that such a large population increase would worsen conditions. Allman promptly filed suit against the county, claiming the board's action to be "arbitrary and capricious."

The lower court found Fairfax County's action "arbitrary and capricious" and ordered the Board of Supervisors to reconsider its decision to deny rezoning. The board then reconsidered the *Allman* decision and again refused to rezone. However, in November 1973, the court ordered the property in question to be rezoned to the PDH-3 category. The board appealed, claiming that the court had exceeded its authority. A stay was granted and the case was then appealed to the State Supreme Court.

The Virginia Supreme Court handed down its decision on the Allman case late in January 1975, putting what the county's lawyers interpreted as the *"last nail in the coffin" for prospects of using adequacy of facilities as a development timing test.* The state court remanded the case to the lower court, affirming the lower court's original decision.

Washington

Anderson v. City of Seattle, 64 W.2d 198, 390 P.2d 994 (1964).

Rezoning land to high-density residential held valid as spot zoning. *Court referred to the inadequacy of school facilities, roads and fire protection as a valid basis to deny increased density.*

Daslowsview Preservation v. City of Tacoma, 84 W.2d 416, 526 P.2d 897 (1974).

Court upheld rezoning from single family residential to planned residential development, citing comments from the departments of health, fire, school and public works that *the impact from either land use would be similar.*

District of Columbia

Shenk v. Zoning Commission of District of Columbia, 440 F.2d 295 (District Court of Appeals, D.C. Cir., 1971).

Denial of zoning from single-family dwellings to garden apartments was overturned. Court refused to give weight to argument that overburdened public facilities was valid justification for denying request. Citing the lower court's opinion, it stated, "Progress and growth cannot be stopped for the lack of facilities. *It is putting the cart before the horse to say that because there are not enough governmental facilities in a particular area we will not commence to grow.*"

APPENDIX 2

EXPERIENCE OF THE FIELD ANNOTATED LITERATURE SEARCH

The information in this appendix is an overview in chart form of current field experience with fiscal impact analysis in the United States. The 136 studies summarized in Chapter 12 are presented individually in this annotated matrix. For each study is shown the focus of the analysis, its application and context, the technical procedures employed, and the local practitioner's evaluation of the effort.

The fiscal impact analyses received and selected as a result of the request for information discussed in chapter 12 include a wide range of studies: large and small, costly and modest, sophisticated and simple. They were conducted by several categories of practitioners in all areas of the country, for many different purposes and sponsors. The reports thus provide an excellent cross section of why, where, and for whom fiscal impact analyses have been undertaken.

The annotation matrix presented here is particularly useful to planning practitioners. It arrays field examples of fiscal impact analysis. These have been initiated by typical sponsors — developers and public officials, and undertaken by line practitioners — private planning consultants and public staff planners.

The annotation matrix may be employed several ways. In embarking on a study of a particular fiscal impact problem, the analyst can locate from the matrix a number of studies dealing with the same issue with which he is concerned. These studies may be obtained from the indicated sources (usually at reproduction cost) by writing to the addresses provided. From these studies of similar substantive concern, the practitioner is able to ascertain which fiscal impact method was employed; the range of costs and revenues considered; and the fiscal, legal and demographic context of the area where the study was completed. The latter may provide insight as to why certain costs and revenues were considered or why a particular method was chosen for analysis.

Appendix 2: Annotated Literature Search 379

Another typical problem facing the fiscal impact analyst is to obtain a firm grasp of the local fiscal system of the area in which he plans to work. By obtaining studies which have been completed in the region, state or county of the intended analyses, excellent insight into local revenue emphases, the extent of dependency on inter-governmental revenues, etc., may be obtained by the analyst.

Annotation Organization

Each study listed in the matrix has been reviewed by a number of professionals familiar with fiscal impact procedures and compared over a set of standard parameters; i.e., why was the study done, for what purpose, what was analyzed, where and under what revenue contexts was it undertaken, what types of methods and data sources were utilized and finally, what type of results were observed?

The studies are summarized via information displayed along axes of the matrix. The vertical axis along the left side of the page identifies the analyses via alphabetical listings (by author) of the titles of the studies and where they were undertaken. The horizontal axis, across the page, provides coded information about each study under four main categories which comprise 114 descriptive variables.

The Vertical Axis - Study Identification

The following information is found within the title block of each alphabetical listing: author, title, locality and state where the analysis was conducted, date of study, number of pages, and an assigned study identification number. To illustrate, an individual listing would be interpreted as follows:

Abt Associates, *Effect of High Density Development on Municipal Finances in the City of Boston*. Boston, Mass. April 1974, 115 pp. 001

AUTHOR:	Abt Associates
TITLE:	Effect of High Density Development on Municipal Finances in the City of Boston
CONDUCTED IN:	Boston, Massachusetts
PUBLICATION DATE:	April 1974
PAGE TOTAL:	115 pages
IDENTIFICATION NO.	001

The identification number is keyed to a list of publication information (see page 423) where the reader may obtain the analyses shown in the matrix. Using the Abt study as an example, the following information on availability, price, source, etc., is provided:

001   Abt Associates, 55 Wheeler Street, Cambridge, Massachusetts 02138. $4.00

IDENTIFICATION NUMBER:	001
AUTHOR:	Abt Associates
ADDRESS:	55 Wheeler Street, Cambridge, Massachusetts 02138

PRICE: $4.00

The Horizontal Axis - Study Characteristics
The listing of studies is repeated four times to individually display for each study:
1. Subject, Jurisdictional Focus, Method, and Land Use Analyzed
2. Geographical, Fiscal, and Legal Context of the Study
3. Scope of Study and Data Resources
4. Author, Audience, and Significance of Study

The matrix is thus divided into four sections. The first explores such traits as the specific nature of the cost-revenue inquiry, the fiscal impact strategy employed and the type and form of development that was examined. The second indicates the regional population base and growth rate, revenue and legal context of the report. The third reviews how costs and revenues were reported and detailed, what data were utilized, the procedures employed in the analysis, and, what results were shown. The last section evaluates the analysis in terms of quality, accuracy, sophistication and coherence. It heavily relies on field level feedback, specifically the reaction of those at the site who commissioned the reports.

The study characteristics are shown in a coded numeric form. The codes are shown in the matrix and are explained before each matrix section (see pages 384, 394, 404 and 414). To illustrate there are seven codes cited for the subject of fiscal impact analysis. Code "1" refers to a residential/mixed use proposal, code "2" a land use alternative study, code "3" a zone variance, etc. (see page 384). There are four possibilities for the jurisdictional focus of a study: Code "8" indicates a local focus while codes 9 through 11 refer to county, regional and state impacts. The ABT study cited above has a code 2 and 8 under the Subject Jurisdictional Focus section of the matrix for it considered the local fiscal consequences of land use alternatives.

Using the Matrix

The matrix is easy to use. A reader interested in identifying the individual characteristics of a single study should read across the row for that report. A coded number in the row indicates that the study displays at least one of the characteristic features there grouped. Thus, a reader wishing to see what method Booz, Allen and Hamilton used in their Reston, fiscal impact study can easily tell from Section One that a combined Per Capita Multiplier and Case Study approach (code 14 under method) was followed. An analyst wishing to identify several studies sharing certain tracts, rather than the individual characteristics of a single investigation, should read down the columns of the study characteristics, and search for identical codes. To illustrate, a user requiring information from studies analyzing planned communities (code 26) would note under the Subject Jurisdictional Focus section that the Barton-Aschman Associates, and Rutgers University analyses, among others, all examined the fiscal impact of PUDs or new towns.

Definitions

Following is a brief definition of each of the twenty-seven characteristics (as used in Appendix 2) grouped under the four sections.

Subject, Jurisdictional Focus, Method, and Land Use Analyzed
    SUBJECT   The general type of planning issue analyzed in the study, includes procedural guides.

Appendix 2: Annotated Literature Search

JURISDICTIONAL FOCUS	The level of government on which the analysis specified impact.
METHOD	The principal technique or group of fiscal impact techniques used to undertake the analysis.
LAND USE TYPE	The main category of land use analyzed.
LAND USE FORM	The development configuration of land use analyzed.

Geographical, Fiscal, and Legal Context

REGION	U.S. Census region in which the analysis was undertaken.
POPULATION BASE	1970 U.S. Census population of the jurisdiction.
ANNUAL 1960–1970 GROWTH RATE	The jurisdiction's annual percentage population change from 1960 to 1970.
SCHOOL DISTRICT REVENUE SOURCES	Significant sources of public school district revenues.
MUNICIPAL REVENUE SOURCES	Significant sources of municipal revenues for noneducational purposes.
C/R (COST-REVENUE) STATE CASE LAW	State lower court reaction to the cost-revenue argument as the sole criterion upon which to base zoning decisions. (See General Applicability Part).

Scope of Study and Data Resources

NUMBER OF PROJECTION POINTS	A single fiscal impact projection or interim projections staged over time.
IMPACT BREADTH	The direct fiscal impact of what is studied, or the fiscal impact of both what is examined plus its catalytic effect on local growth (sometimes called accumulative effects or secondary effects).
IMPACT SCOPE	Impact confined to the jurisdiction under study or extending beyond its borders.
DATA RESOURCES	The sources of data employed in the analysis.
REVENUES CONSIDERED	The range of revenues examined.
COSTS CONSIDERED	The range of municipal and school district, aggregated versus and nonaggregated, costs examined.
ANALYSIS PROCEDURE	The procedure — computer or manual — used for calculations.
C/R (COST-REVENUE) IMPACT	The results of the cost-revenue analysis, i.e., a positive, negative or mixed fiscal result.

Author, Audience and Significance of Study

AUTHOR	The person, municipality, etc., that performed the analysis.

QUALITY	Extensiveness and thoroughness of the analysis — a reviewer evaluation, taking into account such criteria as the soundness of the basic data (demographic multipliers), a balanced treatment of costs and revenues, the range of costs and revenues considered and whether the implications of the determined fiscal impact were discussed.
LOGICAL SEQUENCE	The presentation of the major steps of the analysis and their explication — a user evaluation of whether the assumptions of the procedural steps were clearly presented and seemed to follow logically.
ACCURACY	The study's ability to predict actual fiscal impact — a user evaluation comparing the actual versus predicted fiscal impact.
DURATION	Time required to complete the analysis.
COMPLEXITY	Difficulty in understanding methods and procedures employed — a reviewer evaluation taking into account the analytical tools used, e.g. arithmetic calculations versus regression.
USER SOPHISTICATION	The level of planning knowledge required to interpret the analysis.
FOLLOW-UP STUDY	The presence of a second or follow-up study.

*SUBJECT,
JURISDICTIONAL
FOCUS, METHOD
AND
LAND USE
ANALYZED*

CODES
SUBJECT, JURISDICTIONAL
FOCUS, METHOD, AND
LAND USE ANALYZED

Subject

1. Residential/Mixed Use Proposal
2. Land Use Alternatives
3. Zone Variance or Rezoning
4. Annexation or Boundary Change
5. Fiscal Planning/Budgeting
6. Redevelopment/Public Facility
7. Method/Procedural Guide

Jurisdictional Focus

8. Local (city or town)
9. County
10. Regional
11. State

Method

12. Per Capita Multiplier
13. Case Study
14. Per Capita Multiplier/Case Study
15. Service Standard
16. Proportional Valuation
17. Model Regression
18. Multiple Methods

Land Use Type

19. Single Family Residential
20. Multifamily Residential
21. Single-Family and Multifamily Residential
22. Industrial/Commercial
23. Residential and Nonresidential
24. Multiple Alternatives

Land Use Form

25. Standard Subdivision/Site Plan
26. PUD/New Community
27. Retirement/Vacation Homes
28. Mobile Homes
29. Multiple Alternatives

Appendix 2: Annotated Literature Search 385

SUBJECT, JURISDICTIONAL FOCUS, METHOD, AND LAND USE ANALYZED		
STUDY	ID NO.	CHARACTERISTICS
Abt Associates, *Effect of High Density Development on Municipal Finances in the City of Boston.* Boston, Massachusetts, April, 1974, 115 pp.	001	2, 8, 18, 24, 25
Ada Council of Governments, *The Urban Forum: Urban Expansion in the Boise Area.* Boise, Idaho, August 1973, 106 pp.	002	2, 8, 18, 21, 23, 25
Akron Department of Planning and Urban Renewal, *Ellet Hills Mall: A Report on the Third Request for Conditional Zoning.* Akron, Ohio, November 1974, 16 pp.	003	1, 8, 13, 22, 26
Albuquerque Planning Department, *Costs and Revenues from a Typical New Subdivision.* Albuquerque, New Mexico, May 1972, 17 pp.	004	1, 8, 18, 19, 25
Alexandria, Virginia, Committee on Potential Growth Areas, *Report.* City of Alexandria, Virginia, August 1975, 230 pp.	005	2, 8, 12, 24, 25
Anaheim Development Services, *Cost Revenue Analysis of Single Family Homes, Mobile Home Parks and Multi-family Residential Developments.* Anaheim, California, August 1970, 70 pp.	006	2, 8, 12, 19, 28
Ann Arbor Planning Department, *The Ann Arbor Growth Study.* Ann Arbor, Michigan, February 1973, 250 pp.	007	5, 8, 18, 21, 25
Applied Decision Systems, Inc., *Fiscal Consequences of MSHDA — Financed Housing Community Impact Model.* Lansing, Michigan, June 1973, 120 pp.	008	6, 8, 18, 20, 25
Ashley Economic Services, *The Fiscal Impact of Urban Growth: The California Experience.* San Diego, California, July 1973, 500 pp.	009	2, 8, 13, 23, 25
Ashley Economic Services, *Fountain Valley Cost-Revenue Study.* Fountain Valley, California, August 1974, 54 pp.	010	3, 8, 18, 24, 25
Atlanta Regional Commission, *Fiscal Impact Model for Evaluation of Public Service Costs and Revenues.* Atlanta, Georgia, March 1975, 27 pp.	011	7, 9, 18, 24, 25
Baldwin and Gregg Ltd., *Planned Unit Development: Justification Study of Stonehenge, York County, Virginia.* York County, Virginia, January 15, 1974, 26 pp.	012	1, 8, 12, 23, 26
Barton-Aschman Associates, *The Barrington Area: A Cost-Revenue Analysis of Land Use Alternatives.* Barrington, Illinois, February 1970, 74 pp.	013	2, 11, 12, 24, 25
Barton-Aschman Associates, *Comparative Evaluation of New Community Growth versus Trend Development Growth,* Charles County, Maryland, August 1975, 200 pp.	014	1, 11, 18, 23, 26
Barton-Aschman Associates, *Cost-Revenue Impact Analysis for Proposed Regional Development.* Dundee Township, Illinois, February 1974, 30 pp.	015	1, 8, 12, 23, 25
Barton-Aschman Associates, *Cost-Revenue Impact Analysis of Cedar Square West.* Minneapolis, Minnesota, July 1974, 50 pp.	016	1, 8, 18, 23, 26
Barton-Aschman Associates, *Fiscal Impact Analysis of Alternative Development on Sheffner Property.* Hoffman Estates, Illinois, March 1975, 12 pp.	017	3, 8, 15, 22, 25
Barton-Aschman Associates, *Impact of a New Community on Charles County, Maryland.* Charles County, Maryland, August 1975, 103 pp.	018	1, 11, 12, 23, 26

SUBJECT, JURISDICTIONAL FOCUS, METHOD, AND LAND USE ANALYZED

STUDY	ID NO.	CHARACTERISTICS
Barton-Aschman Associates, *Tax Impact Study for Lombard Office Center*. Lombard, Illinois, September 1975, 11 pp.	019	4, 8, 15, 22, 25
Barton-Aschman Associates, *Tax Impact Study for Dupage County Regional Planning Commission*. Dupage County, Illinois, February 1975, 148 pp.	020	5, 9, 16, 24, 25
Bill Elliot and Associates, Inc., *Cost-Revenue Analysis of Development for a Tract Located on Connor Road, Mount Lebanon Township, Pennsylvania*, Mount Lebanon Township, Pennsylvania, March 1974, 51 pp.	021	3, 8, 12, 21, 26
Booz, Allen and Hamilton, Inc., *Cost-Revenue Analysis: Four Alternative Plans for Growth*. Tucson, Arizona, July 1974, 84 pp.	022	2, 8, 14, 24, 25
Booz, Allen and Hamilton, Inc., *Economic Impact of Reston, Fairfax County, Virginia*. Reston, Virginia, April 1973, 70 pp.	023	1, 9, 14, 23, 26
Boulder, Colorado, Planning Department, *Annexation: Cost-Revenue, Boulder, Colorado*. Boulder, Colorado, October 1965, 21 pp.	024	4, 8, 15, 19, 25
Brookline, Massachusetts, Planning Department, *Residential Cost-Revenue Analysis*. Brookline, Massachusetts, July 1973, 45 pp.	025	2, 8, 14, 21, 25
CKR Investments, Inc., *Fiscal Impact Study: Chapel Spring, Illinois*. Monroe County, Illinois, March 1974, 27 pp.	026	1, 9, 18, 24, 26
Clark Associates, *Alternative Forms of Future Residential Development*. New Castle, New York, July 1975, 88 pp.	027	2, 8, 12, 20, 25
Clearwater, Florida, Planning Department, *Cost-Revenue of Housing in Clearwater, Florida*. Clearwater, Florida, June 1975, 20 pp.	028	2, 8, 13, 21, 27
Connecticut Development Group, Inc., *Cost-Revenue Impact Analysis for Residential Developments*. Hartford, Connecticut, 1972, 323 pp.	029	7, 8, 13, 23, 25
Contra Costa, California, Planning Department, *East County/Delta Cost Effectiveness Study, Parts I and II*. Contra Costa, California, June 1975, 450 pp.	030	7, 8, 15, 23, 25
Delaware County Planning Commission, *Housing: Cost-Revenues Public Costs and Revenues*. Delaware County, Pennsylvania, June 1975, 64 pp.	031	7, 8, 14, 21, 25
Doxiadis Urban Systems, Inc., *Fiscal and Land Use Analysis of Prince Georges County, Vols. I and II*. Prince Georges County, Maryland, June 1970, 200 pp.	032	5, 9, 12, 23, 25
East Providence, Rhode Island, Planning Department, *Multi-family Housing Study*. East Providence, Rhode Island, December 1972, 54 pp.	033	2, 8, 18, 20, 25
Envico, *Effect of Second Home Development on Ludlow, Vermont*. Ludlow, Vermont, June 1973, 68 pp.	034	2, 8, 18, 21, 27
Envirland Associates, *Estimate of Tax Cost and Revenue: Tobacco Farms PUD*. Agawam, Massachusetts, April 1974, 17 pp.	035	1, 8, 12, 21, 26
Environmental Analysis Foundation, *Cost-Benefit Analysis of Alternative Land Uses for Coyote Hills*. Fullerton, California, May 1975, 180 pp.	036	2, 8, 14, 21, 26

Appendix 2: Annotated Literature Search   387

SUBJECT, JURISDICTIONAL FOCUS, METHOD, AND LAND USE ANALYZED		
STUDY	ID NO.	CHARACTERISTICS
Fairfax County Planning Commission, *Fiscal Impact of the Larwin-Atlantic Rezoning.* Fairfax County, Virginia, April 1973, 100 pp.	037	3, 9, 12, 23, 26
Fleck/Sterling, *An Analysis of the Costs and Benefits of the Hampton Coliseum and the Proposed Convention Center.* Hampton, Virginia, September 1975, 167 pp.	038	6, 8, 13, 22, 25
Fort Collins, Colorado, Planning Department, *Assessment of Residential Impact on the Public School and Municipal Services in Fort Collins.* Fort Collins, Colorado, November 1975, 55 pp.	039	2, 8, 18, 24, 25
Fresno, California, Planning Department, *Urban Growth Management Process and Cost-Revenue Analysis.* Fresno, California, January 1975, 49 pp.	040	7, 8, 15, 23, 25
Frontera del Norte Fund, *Growth Impact Study Effects on New Construction.* Santa Fe, New Mexico, June 1973, 12 pp.	041	2, 8, 15, 24, 25
Genesee County Metropolitan Planning Commission, *Density Study of Genesee County.* Genesee County, Michigan, April 1974, 126 pp.	042	2, 9, 18, 21, 25
Georgia Institute of Technology, *Study of Housing and Its Effects on County Fiscal Capacity.* Bibb County, Georgia, September 1970, 101 pp.	043	2, 9, 12, 21, 29
Gladstone Associates, *Beaumont, Texas Central Business District Development Plan.* Beaumont, Texas, December 1973, 46 pp.	044	6, 8, 13, 23, 25
Goochland County Office of County Administrators, *Costs and Revenues of Growth in Goochland County, Virginia.* Goochland County, Virginia, September 1975, 19 pp.	045	2, 9, 12, 24, 25
Griffinhalgen-Kroeger, Inc., *Cost and Revenue Analysis of Public Services.* Prince Georges County, Virginia, September 1975, 69 pp.	046	5, 9, 13, 24, 29
Hammer, Siler and George, *Fiscal Impact Analysis, Cherokee Village, Arkansas.* Cherokee Village, Arkansas, October 1974, 34 pp.	047	1, 9, 12, 23, 25, 27
Hampton Planning Commission, *Cost of City Services vs. Revenues—Apartments and Single Family Homes.* Hampton, Virginia, April 1972, 10 pp.	048	2, 8, 12, 21, 25
Harmon, O'Donnell, and Henninger Associates, Inc., *Community Impact Study for Buchanan Mill.* Elgin, Illinois, November 1974, 17 pp.	049	1, 9, 14, 23, 26
Honolulu Planning Department, *Planning for Oahu: An Evaluation of Alternative Residential Policies.* Oahu, Hawaii, March 1974, 198 pp.	050	2, 9, 18, 23, 25
HOK Associates, *Main Street Mall Feasibility Study.* Midland, Michigan, June 3, 1975, 58 pp.	051	6, 8, 13, 23, 25
Howard P. Hoffman Associates, *BATA Plans for the Future in Harford County, Maryland.* Harford County, Maryland, May 1975, 200 pp.	052	3, 9, 18, 23, 26
New Community Interim Non-Profit Corporation, *Fiscal Impact Statement-Brookwood New Community.* Dayton, Ohio, March 1973, 100 pp.	053	1, 9, 13, 23, 26

SUBJECT, JURISDICTIONAL FOCUS, METHOD, AND LAND USE ANALYZED

STUDY	ID NO.	CHARACTERISTICS
Inglewood, California, City Planning Department, *Cost-Benefit Study: Inglewood, California.* Inglewood, California, August 1973, 26 pp.	054	5, 8, 14, 23, 25
Institute for Government and Business Research, Inc., *Cost-Revenue Analysis of Public Services in De Kalb County, Georgia.* De Kalb County, Georgia, June 1972, 105 pp.	055	5, 9, 12, 23, 25
Institute of Regional and Urban Studies, *Fiscal Impacts of Proposed Pleasanton General Plan.* Pleasanton, California, March 1975, 18 pp.	056	5, 8, 13, 23, 25
John Donaho Associates, Inc., *Howard County, Columbia Fiscal Impact Study.* Howard County, Maryland, June 1970, 110 pp.	057	1, 9, 14, 22, 26
Joliet, Illinois, Planning Department, *Ridgewood Annexation: Cost-Revenue Impact Analysis.* Joliet, Illinois, November 1975, 17 pp.	058	4, 8, 18, 21, 25
Kings County Regional Planning Agency, *Revenue/Cost Analysis in Environmental Resources Management Element-Phase 2.* Kings County, California, July 1974, 26 pp.	059	2, 9, 18, 24, 25
Lake County, Illinois, Regional Planning Commission, *Lake Bluff Annexation: Alternatives in School District 65.* Lake Bluff, Illinois, May 1974, 37 pp.	060	4, 8, 12, 24, 25
Lehigh Valley Joint Planning Commission, *Comparative Costs of Residential Development.* Lehigh City, Pennsylvania, September 1974, 139 pp.	061	2, 8, 12, 24, 25
Lima, Ohio, Planning Department, *Quality Growth and the Annexation Issue.* Lima, Ohio, October 1974, 16 pp.	062	4, 8, 14, 24, 25
Livingston and Blayney, *Santa Rosa Optimal Growth Study.* Santa Rosa, California, January 1973, 125 pp.	063	2, 8, 18, 24, 29
Longmont, Colorado, Planning Department, *Cost-Revenue Analysis—Longmont, Colorado.* Longmont, Colorado, March 1973, 58 pp.	064	5, 8, 16, 21, 25
Lorain County, Ohio, Regional Planning Commission. *Mobile Homes in Lorain County, Ohio.* Lorain County, Ohio, December 1970, 35 pp.	065	2, 8, 12, 19, 28
Lower Merion, Pennsylvania, Planning Office, *Study of Property Tax Revenue and Expenditures According to Land Use.* Lower Merion, Pennsylvania, April 1964, 20 pp.	066	5, 8, 13, 23, 25
McDonald & Smart, Inc., *Fiscal Impact Study for the County of Sacramento, Vols. I & II.* Sacramento County, California, June 1975, 200 pp.	067	7, 9, 13, 21, 25
Manuel S. Emanuel Associates, *Impact Study: Town of Minisink, Orange County, New York.* Minisink, New York, May 1973, 27 pp.	068	1, 8, 12, 23, 26
Marlett and Associates, *Economic Implication of Fringe Development Adjacent to Major Cities: A Case Study: Eugene, Oregon.* Eugene, Oregon, July 1973, 75 pp.	069	4, 8, 14, 23, 25
Maryland National Capital Planning Commission, *Fiscal Impact Analysis: Germantown Master Plan.* Germantown, Maryland, January 1974, 61 pp.	070	5, 9, 12, 23, 25
Metcalf and Eddy, Inc., *The Cost-Revenue Analysis Model and Its Application to a Site in Dover, New Hampshire.* Dover, New Hampshire, March 1974, 62 pp.	071	2, 8, 18, 23, 25

Appendix 2: Annotated Literature Search 389

SUBJECT, JURISDICTIONAL FOCUS, METHOD, AND LAND USE ANALYZED

STUDY	ID NO.	CHARACTERISTICS
Metro Metrics, Inc., *Economics of Urban Growth: Cost-Benefits of Residential Construction*. Fairfax, Virginia, October 1971, 144 pp.	072	5, 9, 13, 21, 25
Miami Valley, Ohio, Regional Planning Commission, *Salem Mall-Cost-Revenue and Economic Policy Analysis*. Trotwood, Ohio, May 1975, 17 pp.	073	3, 8, 16, 22, 25
Mid-American Appraisal and Research, *Budgetary Allocation Model for Residential Properties*. Chicago, Illinois, September 1973, 50 pp.	074	2, 8, 12, 20, 25
Monroe County, New York, Planning Department, *Henrietta Management/Riverton Impact Study*. Henrietta, New York, October 1973, 50 pp.	075	1, 8, 13, 23, 26
Montgomery County, Maryland, Planning Board, *Cost-Revenue Study of the Bethesda CBD Sector Plan-Final Draft*. Silver Spring, Maryland, September 1975, 57 pp.	076	6, 9, 14, 23
Montgomery County, Maryland, Planning Board, *Fiscal Impact Analysis*. Montgomery County, Maryland, September 1975, 187 pp.	077	5, 9, 12, 21, 25
Murphy/Williams, *Eastport Study: Benefit/Cost Analysis*. Annapolis, Maryland, January 1973, 34 pp.	078	2, 8, 14, 23, 25
N.J. County and Municipal Government Study Commission, *A Model for the Evaluation of the Cost/Revenue Effect of Multifamily Housing*. Trenton, New Jersey, 1973, 33 pp.	079	7, 8, 12, 23, 25
New Jersey Department of Community Affairs, *Cost-Revenue Analysis of Flemington Commons*. Raritan Township, New Jersey, February 1974, 19 pp.	080	1, 8, 12, 21, 26
New Jersey Planning Association, *Cost-Revenue Analysis of Bear's Nest Land Use Proposals*. Park Ridge, New Jersey, January 1974, 24 pp.	081	1, 8, 12, 23, 25
Newark, Delaware, Planning Department, *Demographic, Capacity Cost Analysis for Blair Village*. Newark, Delaware, March 1974, 14 pp.	082	1, 8, 13, 20, 25
Nicholas, James C., and Charles W. Blowers, *Socioeconomic Impact of the Marco Island Development*. Collier County, Florida, October 1974, 230 pp.	083	1, 9, 12, 23, 26
Northeast Illinois Planning Commission, *Fiscal Impact Analysis of Regional Shopping Center Proposals*. Carpentersville Illinois, January 1974, 8 pp.	084	1, 8, 18, 22, 25
Northern Virginia Planning District Commission, *Handbook for Cost/Revenue Analysis of Land Development*. Fairfax County, Virginia, October 1973, 50 pp.	085	7, 8, 18, 23, 25
Oak Creek, Wisconsin, Planning Department, *Cost-Revenue Analysis of a Proposed Rezoning at S. Howell Ave. and W. Puetz Rd*. Oak Creek, Wisconsin, March 1975, 23 pp.	086	3, 8, 14, 23, 26
Oakland County, Michigan, Planning Commission, *Cost-Revenue Analysis for Milford Village*. Milford, Michigan, September 1972, 22 pp.	087	5, 8, 14, 23, 25
Oliver T. Carr Company, *Cost-Revenue Study for the West End Plan*. Washington, D.C., October 1973, 30 pp.	088	6, 8, 14, 23, 26
Orange County, New York, Planning Department, *Residential Uses: Students and School Taxes in Orange County: A Cost Benefit Analysis*. Orange County, New York, April 1975, 38 pp.	089	2, 8, 12, 20, 25

390　THE FISCAL IMPACT HANDBOOK

SUBJECT, JURISDICTIONAL FOCUS, METHOD, AND LAND USE ANALYZED

STUDY	ID NO.	CHARACTERISTICS
Oregon State University, *Impacts of Urban Growth on Local Government Costs and Revenues*. Salem, Oregon, November 1974, 37 pp.	090	2, 8, 18, 21, 25
Oshawa, Ontario, Planning Department. *Oshawa: Preliminary Analysis of Ontario Housing Action Program*. Oshawa, Canada, April 1974, 100 pp.	091	2, 8, 18, 21, 25
Ottowa, Canada, Ministry of State. *Impact of Alternative Residential Land Uses on Municipal Government Finances: A Cost-Revenue Model and Case Study*. North York, Canada, December 1973, 53 pp.	092	6, 8, 18, 21, 25
Pasadena Research Institute, *Economic Impact of Watson Industrial Center*. Carson, California, December 1973, 64 pp.	093	1, 9, 13, 22, 25
Patton, Harris, Rust and Guy, *Impact Study, Town of Culpeper, Virginia*. Culpeper, Virginia, June 1974, 84 pp.	094	2, 8, 18, 24, 25
Peat, Marwick, Mitchell & Company. *Users Manual-Impact Estimation Relationships*. Arlington, Virginia, January 1975, 129 pp.	095	7, 9, 18, 24, 29
Phoenix, Arizona, Office of Budget and Research, *Cost-Benefit Analysis of the 1972 Deer Valley Annexation*. Phoenix, Arizona, October 1974, 15 pp.	096	4, 8, 14, 23, 25
Portsmouth, Virginia, Office of Economic Analysis, *Planned Unit Development: Impact and Cost Revenue Analysis*. Portsmouth, Virginia, November 1972, 60 pp.	097	1, 8, 18, 21, 26
Prince William County, Virginia, Planning Department, *Mobile Home Study - Planning Bulletin #2*. Prince William County, Virginia, April 1971, 31 pp.	098	5, 8, 12, 19, 28

SUBJECT, JURISDICTIONAL FOCUS, METHOD, AND LAND USE ANALYZED

STUDY	ID NO.	CHARACTERISTICS
Prudential Insurance Company, *Fiscal Impact Report: North Ranch Tract 2343*. Thousand Oaks, California, September 1975, 32 pp.	099	1, 9, 12, 23, 26
Pueblo, Colorado, Council of Governments, *Fiscal Impact of Urban Development: A Cost-Revenue Analysis*. Pueblo, Colorado, September 1974, 60 pp.	100	2, 8, 18, 23, 25
Quincy, Massachusetts, Planning Department, *Residential Development in the City of Quincy, A Cost-Revenue Analysis*. Quincy, Massachusetts, May 1975, 38 pp.	101	2, 8, 13, 20, 25
Raymond, Parish, Pine and Plavnick, *The Piedmont Development Center: Feasibility Study and Master Plan*. Crewe, Nottoway County, Virginia, June 1975, 129 pp.	102	1, 8, 12, 21, 25
Real Estate Research Corporation, *The Costs of Sprawl*. Hypothetical, April 1974, 278 pp.	103	1, 8, 17, 23, 29
Real Estate Research Corporation. *Public Service Costs and Development*. Madison, Wisconsin, October 1975, 84 pp.	104	2, 10, 15, 24, 25
Real Estate Research Corporation, *Shenandoah: Fiscal Impact of New Community on Local Government*. Coweta County, Georgia, October 1972, 70 pp.	105	1, 9, 12, 23, 26
Rivkin Associates, *Cost-Revenue Analysis for the Seton-Briefing Paper*. Baltimore, Maryland, February 1975, 50 pp.	106	2, 9, 14, 24, 25
Rutgers University Bureau of Economic Research, *Garden Apartment Development: Municipal Cost-Revenue Analysis*. Highland Park, New Jersey, November 1964, 26 pp.	107	5, 8, 12, 20, 25

Appendix 2: Annotated Literature Search 391

SUBJECT, JURISDICTIONAL FOCUS, METHOD, AND LAND USE ANALYZED

STUDY	ID NO.	CHARACTERISTICS
Rutgers University Center for Urban Policy Research, *Fiscal Implications of Municipal Growth.* Dover Township, New Jersey, June 1972, 100 pp.	108	2, 8, 12, 21, 25
Rutgers University Center for Urban Policy Research, *Planned Unit Development: New Communities American Style.* East Windsor, New Jersey, January 1972, 254 pp.	109	1, 8, 14, 23, 26
St. Louis County Planning Department, *Apartments in St. Louis County: Cost-Revenue Impact.* St. Louis, Missouri, February 1972, 40 pp.	110	2, 9, 12, 20, 25
San Antonio, Texas, Planning and Community Development Department, *Alternative Growth Study: San Antonio Master Plan.* San Antonio, Texas, June 11, 1975, 75 pp.	111	1, 8, 12, 24, 25
San Buenaventura, California, Planning Department, *Fiscal Effects of Residential Growth: An Analytical Model with Comparative Case Studies.* San Buenaventura, California, June 1974, 33 pp.	112	7, 8, 17, 24, 25
San Diego, California, Environmental Development Agency, *Basic Fiscal Impact Model.* San Diego, California, February 1975, 119 pp.	113	7, 9, 18, 24, 26
San Diego, California, Planning Department, *Cost-Revenue Analysis: Acadia Village.* San Diego, California, July 1974, 52 pp.	114	1, 8, 18, 20, 26
San Francisco, California, Planning and Urban Renewal Association, *Impact of Intensive High Rise Development on San Francisco.* San Francisco, California, March 1975, 59 pp.	115	2, 8, 13, 22, 27
San Jose, California, Planning Department, *IBM West Coast Programming Development Center: Cost-Revenue Analysis.* San Jose, California, October 1974, 18 pp.	116	1, 8, 13, 22, 25
San Luis Obispo, California, Planning Department, *Residential Land Use Economic Study: Revenue-Expenditure Comparison.* San Luis Obispo, California, June 1972, 23 pp.	117	1, 8, 18, 21, 28
Santa Clara County, California, Planning Department, *Cost and Revenues of Residential Growth in the City of Cupertino: A Case Study.* Cupertino, California, October 1974, 62 pp.	118	6, 8, 18, 24, 25
Santa Clara, California, Planning Department, *Municipal Cost-Revenue Analysis - South Santa Clara Planning Program.* Morgan Hill, California, May 1973, 10 pp.	119	2, 8, 14, 24, 25
Saunders-Thalden and Associates, *Review of Proposed Annexation-Royal Acres Tract.* Des Peres, Missouri, February 1974, 25 pp.	120	4, 8, 14, 19, 25
Southeastern Connecticut Regional Planning Agency, *Cost-Revenue Analysis of Alternative Land Uses on Two Sites in the Town of Groton.* Groton, Connecticut, February 1971, 29 pp.	121	2, 8, 18, 24, 25
Southeastern Michigan Council of Governments, *Fiscal Impact Analysis: A Technical Report.* Detroit, Michigan, December 1969, 70 pp.	122	5, 8, 14, 24, 27
Smith, Bruce W., and John Hittner, *Cost-Revenue Analysis of Calderon Annexation.* Bowling Green, Ohio, December 1974, 20 pp.	123	4, 8, 12, 23, 25

SUBJECT, JURISDICTIONAL FOCUS, METHOD, AND LAND USE ANALYZED

STUDY	ID NO.	CHARACTERISTICS
Spindletop Research, *Analysis of Growth Alternatives for Lexington.* Fayette County, Kentucky, June 1973, 116 pp.	124	2, 9, 18, 23, 25
Taylor, Wiseman and Taylor, *Comparative Cost-Revenue Study: Cherry Hill Townhouse Single Family Home.* Cherry Hill, New Jersey, June 1973, 6 pp.	125	1, 8, 12, 19, 25
University of California Center for Real Estate and Urban Economics, *Municipal Cost-Revenue Analysis for PUD.* Fremont, California, June 1973, 44 pp.	126	1, 8, 18, 23, 26
U.S. Department of Housing and Urban Development, *New Communities Administration Fiscal Impact Study Guide.* Hypothetical, April 1975, 24 pp.	127	1, 9, 18, 23, 26
University of Delaware, Division of Urban Affairs, *Hidden Valley: Impact Analysis.* Newark, Delaware, December 1974, 31 pp.	128	1, 8, 18, 23, 26
Urban Institute, Washington, D.C., *Fiscal Impact of Residential and Commercial Development: A Case Study.* Albemarle County, Virginia, December 1972, 140 pp.	129	1, 9, 18, 23, 25
Urban Institute, Washington, D.C., *Forecasting Local Government Spending.* New Haven, Connecticut, 1973, 142 pp.	130	5, 8, 14, 17, 23, 25
Urban Institute, Washington, D.C., *Impact of Annexation on City Finances: Case Study: Richmond, Virginia.* Richmond, Virginia, May 1973, 74 pp.	131	4, 8, 14, 23, 25
Waltham, Massachusetts, Office of Planning, *Tax Revenues and Service Costs Associated with Community and Single Family Development Along Route 128 in Waltham, Massachusetts.* Waltham, Massachusetts, January 1974, 117 pp.	132	2, 8, 13, 22, 25
Westchester County, New York, Planning Department, *School Taxes and Residential Development.* Westchester County, New York, November 1971, 87 pp.	133	2, 8, 12, 24, 25
Western Interstate Commission for Higher Education, *The City of Antioch General Plan: A Reevaluation of the Land Use Element.* Antioch, California, July 1974, 313 pp.	134	2, 8, 18, 23, 25
Wilbur Smith and Associates, Inc., *Planning and Traffic Evaluation Proposed Clustered, Residential Development.* East Hills, New York, August 1974, 14 pp.	135	1, 8, 14, 20, 26
Zech, F., *Multiple Family Housing for Oak Bay: A Cost Benefit Analysis.* Oak Bay, British Columbia, July 1972, 250 pp.	136	7, 8, 18, 20, 25

GEOGRAPHICAL, FISCAL, AND LEGAL CONTEXT

CODES
GEOGRAPHICAL, FISCAL AND LEGAL CONTEXT

Region

1. Northeast
2. North Central
3. South
4. West
5. Canada

1970 Population Base

6. Less than 10,000
7. 10,000–24,999
8. 25,000–49,999
9. 50,000–99,999
10. 100,000–499,999
11. 500,000+

Annual 1960–1970 Growth Rate

12. Decline
13. 0–2 Percent
14. 3–4 Percent
15. 5–6 Percent
16. Over 6 percent

School District Revenue Sources

17. Over 50% from Local Taxes
18. Over 40% from State Aid
19. Over 10% from Federal Aid

Municipal Revenue Sources

20. Over 40% from Property Tax
21. Over 20% from Sales and Gross Receipt Taxes
22. Over 10% from Other Taxes
23. Over 15% from Other Revenue
24. Over 15% from Intergovernmental Transfers

C/R State Case Law

25. Limited Case Law Permits Fiscal Impact
26. Limited Case Law Prohibits Fiscal Impact
27. Significant Case Law Permits Fiscal Impact
28. Significant Case Law Prohibits Fiscal Impact
29. No Case Law

Appendix 2: Annotated Literature Search 395

GEOGRAPHICAL, FISCAL, AND LEGAL CONTEXT		
STUDY	ID NO.	CHARACTERISTICS
Abt Associates, *Effect of High Density Development on Municipal Finances in the City of Boston.* Boston, Massachusetts, April 1974, 115 pp.	001	1, 11, 12, 17, 20, 24, 26
Ada Council of Governments, *The Urban Form: Urban Expansion in the Boise Area.* Boise, Idaho, August 1973, 106 pp.	002	4, 9, 13, 20, 29
Akron Department of Planning and Urban Renewal, *Ellet Hills Mall: A Report on the Third Request for Conditional Zoning.* Akron, Ohio, November 1974, 16 pp.	003	2, 10, 12, 17, 22, 23, 25
Albuquerque Planning Department, *Costs and Revenues from a Typical New Subdivision.* Albuquerque, New Mexico, May 1972, 17 pp.	004	4, 10, 13, 18, 21, 23, 29
Alexandria, Virginia, Committee on Potential Growth Areas Report. City of Alexandria, Virginia, August 1975, 230 pp.	005	3, 10, 13, 18, 19, 23, 24, 28
Anaheim Development Services, *Cost Revenue Analysis of Single Family Homes, Mobile Home Parks and Multi-family Residential Developments.* Anaheim, California, August 1970, 70 pp.	006	4, 10, 15, 17, 21, 23, 25
Ann Arbor Planning Department, *The Ann Arbor Growth Study.* Ann Arbor, Michigan, February 1973, 250 pp.	007	2, 10, 14, 18, 22, 23, 28
Applied Decision Systems, Inc., *Fiscal Consequences of MSHDA-Financed Housing Community Impact Model.* Lansing, Michigan, June 1973, 120 pp.	008	2, 6, 14, 18, 24, 27
Ashley Economic Services, *The Fiscal Impact of Urban Growth: The California Experience.* San Diego, California, July 1973, 500 pp.	009	4, 11, 14, 17, 21, 23, 26
Ashley Economic Services, *Fountain Valley Cost-Revenue Study.* Fountain Valley, California, August 1974, 54 pp.	010	4, 8, 16, 17, 21, 23, 26

GEOGRAPHICAL, FISCAL, AND LEGAL CONTEXT		
STUDY	ID NO.	CHARACTERISTICS
Atlanta Regional Commission, *Fiscal Impact Model for Evaluation of Public Service Costs and Revenues.* Atlanta, Georgia, March 1975, 27 pp.	011	3, 11, 14, 18, 19, 23, 27
Baldwin and Gregg Ltd., *Planned Unit Development: Justification Study of Stonehenge, York County, Virginia.* York County, January 15, 1974, 26 pp.	012	3, 6, 14, 17, 20, 24, 28
Barton-Aschman Associates, *The Barrington Area: A Cost-Revenue Analysis of Land Use Alternatives.* Barrington, Illinois, February 1970, 74 pp.	013	2, 8, 13, 17, 21, 23, 28
Barton-Aschman Associates, *Comparative Evaluation of New Community Growth versus Trend Development Growth.* Charles County, Maryland, August 1975, 200 pp.	014	3, 9, 14, 18, 20, 27
Barton-Aschman Associates, *Cost-Revenue Impact Analysis for Proposed Regional Development.* Dundee Township, Illinois, February 1974, 30 pp.	015	2, 7, 13, 17, 21, 23, 28
Barton-Aschman Associates, *Cost-Revenue Impact Analysis of Cedar Square West.* Minneapolis, Minnesota, July 1974, 50 pp.	016	2, 10, 13, 18, 23, 24, 25
Barton-Aschman Associates, *Fiscal Impact Analysis of Alternative Development on Sheffner Property.* Hoffman Estates, Illinois, March 1975, 12 pp.	017	2, 7, 16, 18, 22, 23, 27
Barton-Aschman Associates, *Impact of a New Community on Charles County, Maryland.* Charles County, Maryland, August 1975, 103 pp.	018	3, 8, 15, 18, 20, 27
Barton-Aschman Associates, *Tax Impact Study for Lombard Office Center.* Lombard, Illinois, September 1975, 11 pp.	019	2, 8, 15, 17, 21, 28

396   THE FISCAL IMPACT HANDBOOK

GEOGRAPHICAL, FISCAL, AND LEGAL CONTEXT		
STUDY	ID NO.	CHARACTERISTICS
Barton-Aschman Associates, *Tax Impact Study for Dupage County Regional Planning Commission*. Dupage County, Illinois, February 1975, 148 pp.	020	2, 11, 15, 18, 24, 28
Bill Elliot and Associates, Inc., *Cost-Revenue Analysis of Development for a Tract Located on Connor Road, Mount Lebanon, Pennsylvania*. Mount Lebanon, Pennsylvania, March 1974, 51 pp.	021	1, 9, 14, 17, 19, 20, 22, 28
Booz, Allen and Hamilton, Inc., *Cost-Revenue Analysis: Four Alternative Plans for Growth*. Tucson, Arizona, July 1974, 84 pp.	022	4, 10, 13, 17, 22, 29
Booz, Allen and Hamilton, Inc., *Economic Impact of Reston, Fairfax County, Virginia*. Reston, Virginia, April 1973, 70 pp.	023	3, 10, 16, 18, 19, 24, 28
Boulder, Colorado, Planning Department, *Annexation: Cost-Revenue, Boulder, Colorado*. Boulder, Colorado, October 1965, 21 pp.	024	4, 9, 16, 17, 21, 23, 26
Brookline, Massachusetts, Planning Department, *Residential Cost-Revenue Analysis*. Brookline, Massachusetts, July 1973, 45 pp.	025	1, 9, 13, 17, 20, 26
CKR Investments, Inc., *Fiscal Impact Study: Chapel Spring, Illinois*. Monroe County, Illinois, March 1974, 27 pp.	026	2, 7, 13, 17, 19, 21, 23, 28
Clark Associates, *Alternative Forms of Future Residential Development*. New Castle, New York, July 1975, 88 pp.	027	1, 6, 13, 17, 18, 20, 23, 26
Clearwater, Florida, Planning Department, *Cost-Revenue of Housing in Clearwater, Florida*. Clearwater, Florida, June 1975, 20 pp.	028	3, 9, 15, 18, 19, 21, 23, 28
Connecticut Development Group, Inc., *Cost-Revenue Impact Analysis for Residential Developments*. Connecticut, 1972, 323 pp.	029	

GEOGRAPHICAL, FISCAL, AND LEGAL CONTEXT		
STUDY	ID NO.	CHARACTERISTICS
Contra Costa, California, Planning Department, *East County/Delta Cost Effectiveness Study Parts I and II*. Contra Costa, California, June 1975, 450 pp.	030	4, 11, 14, 17, 21, 22, 24, 25
Delaware County Planning Commission, *Housing: Cost-Revenues, Public Costs and Revenues*. Delaware County, Pennsylvania, June 1975, 64 pp.	031	1, 8, 13, 18, 22, 27
Doxiadis Urban Systems, Inc., *Fiscal and Land Use Analysis of Prince Georges County, Vols. I and II*. Prince Georges County, Maryland, June 1970, 200 pp.	032	3, 11, 16, 18, 20, 26
East Providence, Rhode Island, Planning Department, *Multi-family Housing Study*. East Providence, Rhode Island, December 1972, 54 pp.	033	1, 8, 13, 17, 20, 28
Envico, *Effect of Second Home Development on Ludlow, Vermont*. Ludlow, Vermont, June 1973, 68 pp.	034	1, 6, 13, 17, 23, 24, 29
Envirland Associates, *Estimate of Tax Cost and Revenue: Tobacco Farms PUD*. Agawam, Massachusetts, April 1974, 17 pp.	035	1, 8, 16, 17, 20, 23, 24, 26
Environmental Analysis Foundation, *Cost-Benefit Analysis of Alternative Land Uses for Coyote Hills*. Fullerton, California, May 1975, 180 pp.	036	4, 9, 15, 17, 21, 22, 24, 26
Fairfax County Planning Board, *Fiscal Impact of the Larwin-Atlantic Rezoning*. Fairfax County, Virginia, April 1973, 100 pp.	037	3, 11, 15, 17, 19, 20, 28
Fleck/Sterling, *An Analysis of the Costs and Benefits of the Hampton Coliseum and the Proposed Convention Center*. Hampton, Virginia, September 1975, 167 pp.	038	3, 10, 13, 17, 19, 24, 28

Appendix 2: Annotated Literature Search 397

GEOGRAPHICAL, FISCAL, AND LEGAL CONTEXT

STUDY	ID NO.	CHARACTERISTICS
Fort Collins, Colorado, Planning Department, *Assessment of Residential Impact on the Public School and Municipal Services in Fort Collins*. Fort Collins, Colorado, November 1975, 55 pp.	039	4, 9, 16, 17, 21, 22, 24, 26
Fresno, California, Planning Department, *Urban Growth Management Process and Cost-Revenue Analysis*. Fresno, California, January 1975, 49 pp.	040	4, 10, 13, 17, 22, 24, 26
Frontera del Norte Fund, *Growth Impact Study Effects on New Construction*. Sante Fe, New Mexico, June 1973, 12 pp.	041	4, 8, 13, 18, 21, 29
Genesee County Planning Commission, *Density Study of Genesee County*. Genesee County, Michigan, April 1974, 126 pp.	042	2, 10, 13, 18, 20, 28
Georgia Institute of Technology, *Study of Housing and Its Effects on County Fiscal Capacity*. Bibb County, Georgia, September 1970, 101 pp. (Atlanta, Georgia 30332)	043	3, 9, 13, 18, 19, 20, 22, 24, 27
Gladstone Associates, *Beaumont, Texas, Central Business District Development Plan*. Beaumont, Texas, December 1973, 46 pp.	044	3, 10, 12, 18, 19, 20, 21, 29
Goochland County Office of County Administrators, *Costs and Revenues of Growth in Goochland County, Virginia*. Goochland County, Virginia, September 1975, 19 pp.	045	3, 6, 13, 17, 19, 22, 23, 28
Griffinhalgen-Kroeger, Inc., *Cost and Revenue Analysis of Public Services*. Prince Georges County, Virginia, September 1975, 69 pp.	046	3, 10, 15, 18, 19, 20, 24, 28
Hammer, Siler and George, *Fiscal Impact Analysis, Cherokee Village, Arkansas*. Cherokee Village, Arkansas, October 1974, 34 pp.	047	3, 6, 13, 18, 19, 22, 23, 24, 25
Hampton Planning Commission, *Cost of City Services vs. Revenues—Apartments and Single Family Homes*. Hampton, Virginia, April 1972, 10 pp.	048	3, 10, 13, 17, 19, 24, 28
Harmon, O'Donnell, and Henninger Associates, Inc., *Community Impact Study for Buchanan Mill*. Elgin, Illinois, November 1974, 17 pp.	049	2, 9, 13, 17, 22, 28
Honolulu Planning Department, *Planning for Oahu: An Evaluation of Alternative Residential Policies*. Oahu, Hawaii, March 1974, 198 pp.	050	4, 10, 13, 18, 20, 23, 29
HOK Associates, *Main Street Mall Feasibility Study*. Midland, Michigan, June 3, 1975, 58 pp.	051	2, 8, 13, 17, 21, 22, 24, 28
Howard Hoffman Associates, *BATA Plans for the Future in Harford County, Maryland*. Harford County, Maryland, May 1975, 200 pp.	052	3, 10, 15, 18, 20, 23, 27
New Community Interim Non-Profit Corporation, *Fiscal Impact Statement-Brookwood New Community*. Dayton, Ohio, March 1973, 100 pp.	053	2, 11, 14, 18, 22, 24, 25
Inglewood, California, City Planning Department, *Cost-Benefit Study: Inglewood, California*. Inglewood, California, August 1973, 26 pp.	054	4, 9, 14, 18, 19, 23, 24, 26
Institute for Government and Business Research, Inc., *Cost-Revenue Analysis of Public Services in De Kalb County, Georgia*. De Kalb County, Georgia, June 1972, 105 pp.	055	3, 10, 15, 18, 23, 27
Institute of Regional and Urban Studies, *Fiscal Impacts of Proposed Pleasanton General Plan*. Pleasanton, California, March 1975, 18 pp.	056	4, 7, 16, 17, 21, 23, 24, 26

GEOGRAPHICAL, FISCAL, AND LEGAL CONTEXT		
STUDY	ID NO.	CHARACTERISTICS
John Donaho Associates, Inc., *Howard County Columbia Fiscal Impact Study*. Howard County, Maryland, June 1970, 110 pp.	057	3, 9, 13, 18, 23, 24, 27
Joliet, Illinois, Planning Department, *Ridgewood Annexation: Cost-Revenue Impact Analysis*. Joliet, Illinois, November 1975, 17 pp.	058	2, 9, 13, 17, 21, 23, 24, 28
Kings County Regional Planning Agency, *Revenue/Cost Analysis in Environmental Resources Management Element-Phase 2*. Kings County, California, July 1974, 26 pp.	059	4, 9, 14, 17, 21, 23, 26
Lake County, Illinois, Regional Planning Commission, *Lake Bluff Annexation: Alternatives in School District 65*. Lake Bluff, Illinois, May 1974, 37 pp.	060	2, 6, 14, 17, 21, 23, 28
Lehigh Valley Joint Planning Commission, *Comparative Costs of Residential Development*. Lehigh City, Pennsylvania, September 1974, 139 pp.	061	1, 10, 13, 17, 18, 22, 23, 28
Lima, Ohio, Planning Department, *Quality Growth and the Annexation Issue*. Lima, Ohio, October 1974, 16 pp.	062	2, 9, 13, 17, 22, 23, 25
Livingston and Blayney, *Santa Rosa Optimal Growth Study*. Santa Rosa, California, January 1973, 125 pp.	063	4, 9, 15, 17, 21, 26
Longmont, Colorado, Planning Department, *Cost-Revenue Analysis—Longmont, Colorado*. Longmont, Colorado, March 1973, 58 pp.	064	4, 7, 16, 17, 21, 23, 26
Lorain County, Ohio, Regional Planning Commission, *Mobile Homes in Lorain County, Ohio*. Lorain County, Ohio, December 1970, 35 pp.	065	2, 9, 13, 17, 23, 25

GEOGRAPHICAL, FISCAL, AND LEGAL CONTEXT		
STUDY	ID NO.	CHARACTERISTICS
Lower Merion, Pennsylvania, Planning Office, *Study of Property Tax Revenue and Expenditures According to Land Use*. Lower Merion, Pennsylvania, April 1964, 20 pp.	066	1, 9, 16, 18, 22, 23, 28
McDonald & Smart, Inc., *Fiscal Impact Study for the County of Sacramento, Vols. I & II*. Sacramento County, California, June 1975, 200 pp.	067	4, 11, 13, 17, 21, 23, 26
Manuel S. Emanuel Associates, *Impact Study: Town of Minisink, Orange County, New York*. Minisink, New York, May 1973, 27 pp.	068	1, 6, 13, 17, 18, 20, 23, 27
Marlett and Associates, *Economic Implication of Fringe Development Adjacent to Major Cities: A Case Study: Eugene, Oregon*. Eugene, Oregon, July 1973, 75 pp.	069	4, 9, 14, 17, 23, 25
Maryland National Capital Planning Commission, *Fiscal Impact Analysis: Germantown Master Plan*. Germantown, Maryland, January 1974, 61 pp.	070	3, 11, 15, 18, 20, 27
Metcalf and Eddy, Inc., *The Cost-Revenue Analysis Model and Its Application to a Site in Dover, New Hampshire*. Dover, New Hampshire, March 1974, 62 pp.	071	1, 7, 13, 17, 22, 25
Metro Metrics, Inc., *Economics of Urban Growth: Cost-Benefits of Residential Construction*. Fairfax, Virginia, October 1971, 144 pp.	072	3, 10, 15, 19, 22, 23, 28
Miami Valley, Ohio, Regional Planning Commission, *Salem Mall—Cost-Revenue and Economic Policy Analysis*. Trotwood, Ohio, May 1975, 17 pp.	073	2, 6, 13, 17, 22, 23, 25
Mid-American Appraisal and Research, *Budgetary Allocation Model for Residential Properties*. Chicago, Illinois, September 1973, 50 pp.	074	2, 11, 13, 17, 28

Appendix 2: Annotated Literature Search

GEOGRAPHICAL, FISCAL, AND LEGAL CONTEXT		
STUDY	ID NO.	CHARACTERISTICS
Monroe County, New York Planning Department, *Henrietta Management/Riverton Impact Study*. Henrietta, New York, October 1973, 50 pp.	075	1, 8, 16, 17, 18, 20, 24, 26
Montgomery County, Maryland, Planning Board, *Cost-Revenue Study of the Bethesda CBD Sector Plan–Final Draft*. Silver Spring, Maryland, September 1975, 57 pp.	076	3, 11, 15, 18, 24, 26
Montgomery County, Maryland, Planning Board, *Fiscal Impact Analysis*. Montgomery County, Maryland, September 1975, 187 pp.	077	3, 11, 13, 18, 20, 23, 24, 26
Murphy/Williams, *Eastport Study: Benefit/Cost Analysis*. Annapolis, Maryland, January 1973, 34 pp.	078	3, 7, 13, 17, 27
New Jersey County and Municipal Government Study Commission, *A Model for the Evaluation of the Cost/Revenue Effect of Multi-family Housing*. Trenton, New Jersey, 1973, 33 pp.	079	1
New Jersey Department of Community Affairs, *Cost-Revenue Analysis of Flemington Commons*. Raritan Township, New Jersey, February 1974, 19 pp.	080	1, 6, 15, 17, 23, 24, 28
New Jersey Planning Association, *Cost-Revenue Analysis of Bear's Nest Land Use Proposals*. Park Ridge, New Jersey January 1974, 24 pp.	081	1, 6, 14, 17, 20, 28
Newark, Delaware, Planning Department, *Demographic, Capacity, Cost Analysis for Blair Village*. Newark, Delaware, March 1974, 14 pp.	082	3, 7, 13, 17, 24, 29
Nicholas, James C., and Charles W. Blowers, *Socioeconomic Impact of the Marco Island Development*. Collier County, Florida, October 1974, 230 pp.	083	3, 9, 16, 18, 19, 21, 22, 23, 28
Northeast Illinois Planning Commission, *Fiscal Impact Analysis of Regional Shopping Center Proposals*. Carpentersville, Illinois, January 1974, 8 pp.	084	2, 7, 14, 17, 21, 23, 28
Northern Virginia Planning District Commission, *Handbook for Cost/Revenue Analysis of Land Development*. Fairfax County, Virginia, October 1973, 50 pp.	085	3, 11, 15, 17, 19, 24, 28
Oak Creek, Wisconsin, Planning Department, *Cost-Revenue Analysis of a Proposed Rezoning at S. Howell Ave. and W. Puetz Rd*. Oak Creek, Wisconsin, March 1975, 23 pp.	086	2, 7, 15, 17, 24, 29
Oakland County, Michigan, Planning Commission, *Cost-Revenue Analysis for Milford Village*. Milford, Michigan, September 1972, 22 pp.	087	2, 6, 13, 17, 19, 20, 24, 28
Oliver T. Carr Company, *Cost-Revenue Study for the West End Plan*. Washington, D.C., October 1973, 30 pp.	088	3, 11, 12, 17, 19, 22, 24, 26
Orange County, New York, Planning Department, *Residential Uses: Students and School Taxes in Orange County: A Cost Benefit Analysis*. Orange County, New York, April 1975, 38 pp.	089	1, 10, 13, 17, 18, 20, 23, 27
Oregon State University, *Impacts of Urban Growth on Local Government Costs and Revenues*. Salem, Oregon, November 1974, 37 pp.	090	4, 6, 13, 17, 23, 24, 26
Oshawa, Ontario, Planning Department, *Oshawa: Preliminary Analysis of Ontario Housing Action Program*. Oshawa, Canada, April 1974.	091	5, 9, 13, 18, 20, 25
Ottawa, Canada, Ministry of State, *Impact of Alternative Residential Land Uses on Municipal Government Finances: A Cost-Revenue Model and Case Study*. North York, Canada, December 1973, 53 pp.	092	5, 11, 14, 18, 20, 25

GEOGRAPHICAL, FISCAL, AND LEGAL CONTEXT

STUDY	ID NO.	CHARACTERISTICS
Pasadena Research Institute, *Economic Impact of Watson Industrial Center.* Carson, California, December 1973, 64 pp.	093	4, 9, 13, 17, 21, 23, 26
Patton, Harris, Rust and Guy, *Impact Study, Town of Culpeper, Virginia.* Culpeper, Virginia, June 1974, 84 pp.	094	3, 6, 13, 17, 19, 22, 28
Peat, Marwick, Mitchell & Company, *Users Manual—Impact Estimation Relationships.* Arlington, Virginia, January 1975, 129 pp.	095	3, 10, 13, 17, 19, 22, 29
Phoenix, Arizona, Office of Budget and Research, *Cost-Benefit Analysis of the 1972 Deer Valley Annexation.* Phoenix, Arizona, October 1974, 15 pp.	096	4, 11, 14, 17, 18, 21, 23, 24, 29
Portsmouth, Virginia, Office of Economic Analysis, *Planned Unit Development: Impact and Cost Revenue Analysis.* Portsmouth, Virginia, November 1972, 60 pp.	097	3, 10, 12, 17, 19, 24, 29
Prince William County, Virginia, Planning Department, *Mobile Home Study—Planning Bulletin #2.* Prince William County, Virginia, April 1971, 31 pp.	098	3, 10, 16, 17, 19, 20, 28
Prudential Insurance Company, *Fiscal Impact Report: North Ranch Tract 2343.* Thousand Oaks, California, September 1975, 32 pp.	099	4, 6, 16, 17, 22, 24, 26
Pueblo, Colorado, Council of Governments, *Fiscal Impact of Urban Development: A Cost-Revenue Analysis.* Pueblo, Colorado, September 1974, 60 pp.	100	4, 9, 13, 17, 21, 23, 26
Quincy, Massachusetts, Planning Department, *Residential Development in the City of Quincy, A Cost-Revenue Analysis.* Quincy, Massachusetts, May 1975, 38 pp.	101	1, 9, 13, 18, 20, 26
Raymond, Parish, Pine and Plavnick, *The Piedmont Development Center: Feasibility Study and Master Plan.* Crewe, Nottoway County, Virginia, June 1975, 129 pp.	102	3, 7, 12, 17, 19, 20, 22, 28
Real Estate Research Corporation, *The Costs of Sprawl.* Hypothetical, April 1974, 278 pp.	103	1, 8, 16, 18, 26
Real Estate Research Corporation, *Public Service Costs and Development.* Madison, Wisconsin, October 1975, 84 pp.	104	2, 11, 13, 17, 20, 24, 29
Real Estate Research Corporation, *Shenandoah: Fiscal Impact of New Community on Local Government.* Coweta County, Georgia, October 1972, 70 pp.	105	3, 8, 16, 18, 19, 22, 23, 27
Rivkin Associates, *Cost-Revenue Analysis for the Seton-Briefing Paper.* Baltimore, Maryland, February 1975, 50 pp.	106	3, 11, 12, 18, 24, 27
Rutgers University Bureau of Economic Research, *Garden Apartment Development: Municipal Cost-Revenue Analysis.* Highland Park, New Jersey, November 1964, 26 pp.	107	1, 7, 14, 17, 20, 23, 28
Rutgers University Center for Urban Policy Research, *Fiscal Implications of Municipal Growth.* Dover Township, New Jersey, June 1972, 100 pp.	108	1, 7, 16, 17, 20, 23, 28
Rutgers University Center for Urban Policy Research, *Planned Unit Development: New Communities American Style.* East Windsor, New Jersey, January 1972, 254 pp.	109	1, 7, 16, 17, 20, 23, 28
St. Louis County Planning Department, *Apartments in St. Louis County: Cost-Revenue Impact.* St. Louis, Missouri, February 1972, 40 pp.	110	2, 11, 14, 17, 21, 23, 28
San Antonio, Texas, Planning and Community Development Department, *Alternative Growth Study: San Antonio Master Plan.* San Antonio, Texas, June 11, 1975, 75 pp.	111	3, 11, 13, 18, 20, 23, 24, 27

Appendix 2: Annotated Literature Search 401

GEOGRAPHICAL, FISCAL, AND LEGAL CONTEXT

STUDY	ID NO.	CHARACTERISTICS
San Buenaventura, California, Planning Department, *Fiscal Effects of Residential Growth: An Analytical Model with Comparative Case Studies.* San Buenaventura, California, June 1974, 33 pp.	112	4, 9, 13, 17, 21, 22, 24, 26
San Diego, California, Environmental Development Agency, *Basic Fiscal Impact Model.* San Diego, California, February 1975, 119 pp.	113	4, 11, 14, 17, 23, 26
San Diego, California, Planning Department, *Cost-Revenue Analysis: Acadia Village.* San Diego, California, July 1974, 52 pp.	114	4, 11, 13, 17, 23, 26
San Francisco, California, Planning and Urban Renewal Association, *Impact of Intensive High Rise Development on San Francisco.* San Francisco, California, March 1975, 59 pp.	115	4, 11, 12, 17, 20, 23, 26
San Jose, California, Planning Department, *IBM West Coast Programming Development Center: Cost-Revenue Analysis.* San Jose, California, October 1974, 18 pp.	116	4, 10, 16, 17, 21, 23, 26
San Luis Obispo, California, Planning Department, *Residential Land Use Economic Study: Revenue-Expenditure Comparison.* San Luis Obispo, California, June 1972, 23 pp.	117	4, 8, 14, 17, 21, 23, 26
Santa Clara County, California, Planning Department, *Cost and Revenues of Residential Growth in the City of Cupertino: A Case Study.* Cupertino, California, October 1974, 62 pp.	118	4, 7, 16, 17, 21, 23, 24, 26
Santa Clara, California, Planning Department, *Municipal Cost-Revenue Analysis—South Santa Clara Planning Program.* Morgan Hill, California, May 1973, 10 pp.	119	4, 6, 15, 17, 24, 26

GEOGRAPHICAL, FISCAL, AND LEGAL CONTEXT

STUDY	ID NO.	CHARACTERISTICS
Saunders-Thalden and Associates, Inc., *Review of Proposed Annexation—Royal Acres Tract.* Des Peres, Missouri, February 1974, 25 pp.	120	2, 6, 13, 17, 23, 28
Southeastern Connecticut Regional Planning Agency, *Cost-Revenue Analysis of Alternative Land Uses on Two Sites in the Town of Groton.* Groton, Connecticut, February 1971, 29 pp.	121	1, 8, 13, 19, 20, 25
Southeastern Michigan Council of Governments, *Fiscal Impact Analysis: A Technical Report.* Detroit, Michigan, December 1969, 70 pp.	122	2, 11, 13, 18, 20, 28
Smith, Bruce, W., and John Hittner, *Cost-Revenue Analysis of Calderon Annexation.* Bowling Green, Ohio, December 1974, 20 pp.	123	2, 7, 14, 17, 22, 23, 25
Spindletop Research, *Analysis of Growth Alternatives for Lexington.* Fayette County, Kentucky, June 1973, 116 pp.	124	3, 10, 14, 18, 22, 23, 27
Taylor, Wiseman and Taylor, *Comparative Cost-Revenue Study: Cherry Hill Townhouse Single Family Home.* Cherry Hill, New Jersey, June 1973, 6 pp.	125	1, 8, 14, 17, 20, 28
University of California Center for Real Estate and Urban Economics, *Municipal Cost-Revenue Analysis for PUD.* Fremont, California, June 1973, 44 pp.	126	4, 10, 16, 17, 26
U.S. Department of Housing and Urban Development, *New Communities Administration Fiscal Impact Study Guide.* Hypothetical, April 1975, 24 pp.	127	
University of Delaware, Division of Urban Affairs, *Hidden Valley: Impact Analysis.* Newark, Delaware, December 1974, 31 pp.	128	3, 8, 14, 18, 22, 23, 24, 29

GEOGRAPHICAL, FISCAL, AND LEGAL CONTEXT		
STUDY	ID NO.	CHARACTERISTICS
Urban Institute, Washington, D.C., *Fiscal Impact of Residential and Commercial Development: A Case Study*. Albamarle County, Virginia, December 1972, 140 pp.	129	3, 8, 13, 17, 18, 19, 20, 23, 24, 28
Urban Institute, Washington, D.C., *Forecasting Local Government Spending*. New Haven, Connecticut, 142 pp.	130	2, 10, 12, 19, 23, 24, 25
Urban Institute, Washington, D.C., *Impact of Annexation on City Finances: Case Study: Richmond, Virginia*. May 1973, 74 pp.	131	3, 10, 13, 17, 19, 24, 28
Waltham, Massachusetts, Office of Planning, *Tax Revenues and Service Costs Associated with Community and Single Family Development Along Route 128 in Waltham, Massachusetts*. Waltham, Massachusetts, January 1974, 117 pp.	132	1, 9, 13, 17, 20, 26
Westchester County, New York, Planning Department, *School Taxes and Residential Development*. Westchester County, New York, November 1971, 87 pp.	133	1, 9, 12, 17, 18, 20, 24, 28
Western Interstate Commission for Higher Education, *The City of Antioch General Plan: A Reevaluation of the Land Use Element*. Antioch, California, July 1974, 313 pp.	134	4, 8, 14, 17, 21, 23, 26
Wilbur Smith Associates, Inc., *Planning and Traffic Evaluation, Proposed Clusters, Residential Development*. East Hills, New York, August 1974, 14 pp.	135	1, 6, 13, 17, 18, 20, 24, 27
Zech, F., *Multiple Family Housing for Oak Bay: A Cost Benefit Analysis*. Oak Bay, British Columbia, July 1972, 250 pp.	136	5, 7, 13, 17, 18, 20, 24, 25

SCOPE OF STUDY AND DATA RESOURCES

CODES
SCOPE OF STUDY AND DATA RESOURCES

Number of Projection Points

1. At Full Development
2. At Full Development plus Interim Projection
3. (Code Not Used)

Impact Breadth

4. Direct Costs
5. Direct plus Induced Costs

Impact Scope

6. Jurisdictional
7. Jurisdictional plus Extrajurisdictional

Data Resources

8. Published HHS & SAC Multipliers
9. School District SAC Multipliers
10. U.S. Census, HHS Multipliers
11. SAC/HHS Multipliers–Resident Survey
12. Per Capita Expenditure Data (Local)
13. Gross Expenditure Data from Public Officials

Revenues Considered

14. Property Tax
15. Sales and Gross Receipts Tax
16. Other Taxes
17. Other Revenues
18. Intergovernmental Transfers

Costs Considered

19. Education Aggregated
20. Noneducation Aggregated
21. Noneducation Detailed
22. Education Detailed
23. Education Aggregated/Noneducation Detailed
24. Education Aggregated/Noneducation Aggregated

Analysis Procedure

25. Computer
26. Manual

C/R Impact

27. Positive Cost Revenue
28. Negative Cost Revenue
29. Mixed Cost Revenue
30. No Conclusion

Appendix 2: Annotated Literature Search 405

SCOPE OF STUDY AND DATA RESOURCES

STUDY	ID NO.	CHARACTERISTICS
Abt Associates, *Effect of High Density Development on Municipal Finances in the City of Boston*. Boston, Massachusetts, April 1974, 115 pp.	001	1, 4, 6, 10, 12, 13, 14, 22, 23, 26, 27
Ada Council of Governments, *The Urban Form: Urban Expansion in the Boise Area*. Boise, Idaho, August 1973, 106 pp.	002	2, 4, 7, 9, 10, 12, 13, 14, 23, 26, 30
Akron Department of Planning and Urban Renewal, *Ellet Hills Mall: A Report on the Third Request for Conditional Zoning*. Akron, Ohio, November 1974, 16 pp.	003	2, 5, 6, 9, 12, 13, 14, 21, 26, 28
Albuquerque Planning Department, *Costs and Revenues from a Typical New Subdivision*. Albuquerque, New Mexico, May 1972, 17 pp.	004	1, 4, 6, 10, 12, 13, 14, 15, 16, 17, 18, 22, 26, 28
Alexandria, Virginia, Committee on Potential Growth Areas Report. City of Alexandria, Virginia, August 1975, 230 pp.	005	1, 4, 6, 8, 9, 12, 13, 14, 15, 16, 17, 18, 23, 26, 28
Anaheim Development Services, *Cost Revenue Analysis of Single Family Homes, Mobile Home Parks and Multi-family Residential Developments*. Anaheim, California, August 1970, 70 pp.	006	1, 4, 6, 14, 15, 16, 17, 21, 25, 30
Ann Arbor Planning Department, *The Ann Arbor Growth Study*. Ann Arbor, Michigan, February 1973, 250 pp.	007	1, 4, 6, 8, 9, 10, 11, 12, 13, 14, 17, 18, 22, 26, 27
Applied Decision Systems, Inc., *Fiscal Consequences of MSHDA-Financed Housing Community Impact Model*. Lansing, Michigan, June 1973, 120 pp.	008	2, 4, 6, 8, 9, 10, 12, 14, 15, 16, 17, 18, 25, 28
Ashley Economic Services, *The Fiscal Impact of Urban Growth: The California Experience*. San Diego, California, July 1973, 500 pp.	009	2, 5, 6, 8, 9, 11, 12, 13, 14, 15, 16, 17, 18, 23, 25, 27
Ashley Economic Services, *Fountain Valley Cost-Revenue Study*. Fountain Valley, California, August 1974, 54 pp.	010	2, 4, 6, 10, 12, 13, 14, 15, 16, 17, 18, 23, 25, 28

SCOPE OF STUDY AND DATA RESOURCES

STUDY	ID NO.	CHARACTERISTICS
Atlanta Regional Commission, *Fiscal Impact Model for Evaluation of Public Service Costs and Revenues*. Atlanta, Georgia, March 1975, 27 pp.	011	1, 4, 6, 10, 12, 14, 15, 16, 17, 18, 23, 26
Baldwin and Gregg Ltd., *Planned Unit Development: Justification Study of Stonehenge, York County, Virginia*. York County, January 15, 1974, 26 pp.	012	1, 4, 6, 8, 9, 12, 14, 15, 16, 17, 18, 23, 26, 29
Barton-Aschman Associates, *The Barrington Area: A Cost-Revenue Analysis of Land Use Alternatives*. Barrington, Illinois, February 1970, 74 pp.	013	1, 5, 7, 8, 9, 11, 12, 13, 14, 23, 26, 28, 29
Barton-Aschman Associates, *Comparative Evaluation of New Community Growth versus Trend Development Growth*. Charles County, Maryland, August 1975, 200 pp.	014	2, 4, 7, 8, 9, 10, 12, 13, 14, 15, 16, 17, 18, 23, 26, 27
Barton-Aschman Associates, *Cost-Revenue Impact Analysis for Proposed Regional Development*. Dundee Township, Illinois, February 1974, 30 pp.	015	2, 4, 7, 8, 12, 13, 14, 15, 16, 17, 18, 24, 26, 27
Barton-Aschman Associates, *Cost-Revenue Impact Analysis of Cedar Square West*. Minneapolis, Minnesota, July 1974, 50 pp.	016	2, 4, 6, 8, 9, 11, 12, 13, 14, 16, 17, 18, 23, 26, 27
Barton-Aschman Associates, *Fiscal Impact Analysis of Alternative Development on Sheffner Property*. Hoffman Estates, Illinois, March 1975, 12 pp.	017	2, 4, 6, 12, 13, 14, 15, 17, 18, 21, 26, 27
Barton-Aschman Associates, *Impact of a New Community on Charles County, Maryland*. Charles County, Maryland, August 1975, 103 pp.	018	3, 4, 7, 9, 12, 13, 14, 15, 16, 17, 18, 23, 26, 27
Barton-Aschman Associates, *Tax Impact Study for Lombard Office Center*. Lombard, Illinois, September 1975, 11 pp. (Available at Reproduction Costs, Evanston, Illinois 60204)	019	2, 5, 6, 12, 13, 14, 15, 21, 26, 27

SCOPE OF STUDY AND DATA RESOURCES

STUDY	ID NO.	CHARACTERISTICS
Barton-Aschman Associates, *Tax Impact Study for Dupage County Regional Planning Commission*. Dupage County, Illinois, February 1975, 148 pp.	020	2, 4, 6, 8, 9, 12, 15, 16, 17, 18, 23, 25, 29
Bill Elliot and Associates, Inc., *Cost-Revenue Analysis of Development for a Tract Located on Connor Road, Mount Lebanon Township, Pennsylvania*. Mount Lebanon, Pennsylvania, March 1974, 51 pp.	021	2, 4, 6, 8, 9, 11, 12, 14, 16, 17, 18, 24, 26, 29
Booz, Allen and Hamilton, Inc., *Cost-Revenue Analysis: Four Alternative Plans for Growth*. Tucson, Arizona, July 1974, 84 pp.	022	3, 4, 6, 11, 12, 13, 14, 15, 16, 17, 18, 23, 26, 29
Booz, Allen and Hamilton, Inc., *Economic Impact of Reston, Fairfax County, Virginia*. Reston, Virginia, April 1973, 70 pp.	023	3, 4, 6, 8, 9, 12, 13, 14, 15, 16, 17, 23, 26, 27
Boulder, Colorado, Planning Department, *Annexation: Cost-Revenue, Boulder, Colorado*. Boulder, Colorado, October 1965, 21 pp.	024	2, 4, 6, 12, 13, 14, 15, 22, 26, 29
Brookline, Massachusetts, Planning Department, *Residential Cost-Revenue Analysis*. Brookline, Massachusetts, July 1973, 45 pp.	025	1, 4, 6, 8, 9, 12, 13, 14, 17, 18, 23, 26, 29
CKR Investments, Inc., *Fiscal Impact Study: Chapel Spring, Illinois*. Monroe County, Illinois, March 1974, 27 pp.	026	2, 4, 7, 8, 12, 13, 14, 15, 17, 18, 23, 26, 27
Clark Associates, *Alternative Forms of Future Residential Development*. New Castle, New York, July 1975, 88 pp.	027	1, 4, 7, 8, 9, 11, 12, 13, 14, 23, 26, 29
Clearwater, Florida, Planning Department, *Cost-Revenue of Housing in Clearwater, Florida*. Clearwater, Florida, June 1975, 20 pp.	028	1, 4, 6, 10, 12, 13, 14, 16, 17, 21, 26, 29
Connecticut Development Group, Inc., *Cost-Revenue Impact Analysis for Residential Developments*. Connecticut, 1972, 323 pp.	029	2, 5, 6, 10, 12, 13, 14, 15, 16, 17, 18, 23, 26, 30

SCOPE OF STUDY AND DATA RESOURCES

STUDY	ID NO.	CHARACTERISTICS
Contra Costa, California, Planning Department, *East County/Delta Cost Effectiveness Study Parts I and II*. Contra Costa, California, June 1975, 450 pp.	030	1, 4, 6, 8, 9, 10, 12, 13, 14, 15, 16, 17, 18, 23, 26, 27
Delaware County Planning Commission, *Housing: Cost-Revenues, Public Costs and Revenues*. Delaware County, Pennsylvania, June 1975, 64 pp.	031	1, 4, 6, 8, 9, 11, 12, 13, 14, 17, 18, 23, 26, 28
Doxiadis Urban Systems, Inc., *Fiscal and Land Use Analysis of Prince Georges County, Vols. I and II*. Prince Georges County, Maryland, June 1970, 200 pp.	032	2, 5, 6, 8, 9, 10, 14, 16, 17, 18, 23, 26, 28
East Providence, Rhode Island, Planning Department, *Multi-family Housing Study*. East Providence, Rhode Island, December 1972, 54 pp.	033	1, 4, 6, 8, 9, 11, 12, 13, 14, 24, 26, 29
Envico, *Effect of Second Home Development on Ludlow, Vermont*. Ludlow, Vermont, June 1973, 68 pp.	034	2, 4, 6, 12, 13, 14, 15, 18, 21, 26, 29
Envirland Associates, *Estimate of Tax Cost and Revenue: Tobacco Farms PUD*. Agawam, Massachusetts, April 1974, 17 pp.	035	2, 4, 6, 8, 9, 11, 12, 14, 24, 26, 27
Environmental Analysis Foundation, *Cost-Benefit Analysis of Alternative Land Uses for Coyote Hills*. Fullerton, California, May 1975, 180 pp.	036	1, 5, 6, 8, 9, 10, 12, 13, 14, 15, 16, 17, 18, 23, 26, 29
Fairfax County Planning Board, *Fiscal Impact of the Larwin-Atlantic Rezoning*. Fairfax County, Virginia, April 1973, 100 pp.	037	2, 4, 6, 8, 9, 12, 13, 14, 24, 26, 27
Fleck/Sterling, *An Analysis of the Costs and Benefits of the Hampton Coliseum and the Proposed Convention Center*. Hampton, Virginia, September 1975, 167 pp.	038	2, 5, 6, 12, 13, 14, 15, 17, 20, 26, 28

Appendix 2: Annotated Literature Search 407

SCOPE OF STUDY AND DATA RESOURCES		
STUDY	ID NO.	CHARACTERISTICS
Fort Collins, Colorado, Planning Department, *Assessment of Residential Impact on the Public School and Municipal Services in Fort Collins*. Fort Collins, Colorado, November 1975, 55 pp.	039	1, 4, 6, 8, 9, 10, 12, 13, 14, 15, 16, 17, 23, 26, 29
Fresno, California, Planning Department, *Urban Growth Management Process and Cost-Revenue Analysis*. Fresno, California, January 1975, 49 pp.	040	2, 5, 6, 12, 13, 14, 15, 16, 17, 18, 21, 26, 30
Frontera del Norte Fund, *Growth Impact Study Effects on New Construction*. Sante Fe, New Mexico, June 1973, 12 pp.	041	2, 4, 6, 12, 13, 14, 15, 16, 17, 21, 26, 28
Genesee County Planning Commission, *Density Study of Genesee County*. Genesee County, Michigan, April 1974, 126 pp.	042	1, 4, 6, 8, 9, 12, 13, 14, 17, 21, 26, 30
Georgia Institute of Technology, *Study of Housing and Its Effects on County Fiscal Capacity*. Bibb County, Georgia, September 1970, 101 pp.	043	1, 4, 6, 9, 12, 13, 14, 16, 17, 21, 26, 29
Gladstone Associates, Beaumont, Texas, *Central Business District Development Plan*. Beaumont, Texas, December 1973, 46 pp.	044	2, 5, 6, 12, 13, 14, 15, 17, 20, 26, 28
Goochland County Office of County Administrators, *Costs and Revenues of Growth in Goochland County, Virginia*. Goochland County, Virginia, September 1975, 19 pp.	045	1, 4, 6, 8, 9, 12, 14, 15, 16, 17, 23, 26, 29
Griffinhalgen-Kroeger, Inc., *Cost and Revenue Analysis of Public Services*. Prince Georges County, Virginia, September 1975, 69 pp.	046	2, 4, 6, 12, 13, 14, 15, 16, 17, 18, 23, 26, 27
Hammer, Siler and George, *Fiscal Impact Analysis, Cherokee Village, Arkansas*. Cherokee Village, Arkansas, October 1974, 34 pp.	047	1, 4, 6, 9, 10, 12, 13, 14, 15, 17, 18, 23, 26, 27

SCOPE OF STUDY AND DATA RESOURCES		
STUDY	ID NO.	CHARACTERISTICS
Hampton Planning Commission, *Cost of City Services vs. Revenues—Apartments and Single Family Homes*. Hampton, Virginia, April 1972, 10 pp.	048	1, 4, 6, 8, 9, 12, 13, 14, 17, 23, 26, 29
Harmon, O'Donnell, and Henninger Associates, Inc., *Community Impact Study for Buchanan Mill*. Elgin, Illinois, November 1974, 17 pp.	049	2, 4, 6, 8, 9, 12, 13, 14, 15, 16, 17, 23, 26, 27
Honolulu Planning Department, *Planning for Oahu: An Evaluation of Alternative Residential Policies*. Oahu, Hawaii, March 1974, 198 pp.	050	1, 4, 6, 13, 23, 26, 30
HOK Associates, *Main Street Mall Feasibility Study*. Midland, Michigan, June 3, 1975, 58 pp.	051	2, 4, 6, 12, 13, 14, 15, 21, 26, 27
Howard Hoffman Associates, *BATA Plans for the Future in Harford County, Maryland*. Harford County, Maryland, May 1975, 200 pp.	052	2, 4, 6, 8, 9, 13, 14, 16, 17, 18, 24, 26, 27
New Community Interim Non-Profit Corporation, *Fiscal Impact Statement-Brookwood New Community*. Dayton, Ohio, March 1973, 100 pp.	053	2, 4, 7, 9, 12, 13, 14, 15, 16, 17, 21, 26, 30
Inglewood, California, City Planning Department, *Cost-Benefit Study: Inglewood, California*. Inglewood, California, August 1973, 26 pp.	054	2, 4, 6, 8, 9, 10, 12, 13, 14, 15, 16, 17, 18, 23, 26, 30
Institute for Government and Business Research, Inc., *Cost-Revenue Analysis of Public Services in De Kalb County, Georgia*. De Kalb County, Georgia, June 1972, 105 pp.	055	1, 5, 6, 8, 9, 11, 12, 13, 14, 16, 17, 18, 23, 26, 30
Institute of Regional and Urban Studies, *Fiscal Impacts of Proposed Pleasanton General Plan*. Pleasanton, California, March 1975, 18 pp.	056	2, 4, 6, 12, 13, 14, 15, 16, 17, 18, 21, 26, 28

SCOPE OF STUDY AND DATA RESOURCES			SCOPE OF STUDY AND DATA RESOURCES		
STUDY	ID NO.	CHARACTERISTICS	STUDY	ID NO.	CHARACTERISTICS
John Donaho Associates, Inc., *Howard County Columbia Fiscal Impact Study*. Howard County, Maryland, June 1970, 110 pp.	057	2, 4, 7, 8, 9, 10, 12, 13, 14, 15, 16, 17, 18, 23, 26, 28	Lower Merion, Pennsylvania, Planning Office, *Study of Property Tax Revenue and Expenditures According to Land Use*. Lower Merion, Pennsylvania, April 1964, 20 pp.	066	1, 4, 6, 8, 9, 12, 13, 14, 23, 26, 29
Joliet, Illinois, Planning Department, *Ridgewood Annexation: Cost-Revenue Impact Analysis*. Joliet, Illinois, November 1975, 17 pp.	058	2, 4, 6, 12, 13, 14, 15, 16, 17, 18, 21, 26, 28	McDonald & Smart, Inc., *Fiscal Impact Study for the County of Sacramento, Vols. I & II*. Sacramento County, California, June 1975, 200 pp.	067	2, 4, 6, 8, 9, 10, 12, 13, 14, 15, 16, 17, 18, 23, 26, 30
Kings County Regional Planning Agency, *Revenue/Cost Analysis in Environmental Resources Management Element-Phase 2*. Kings County, California, July 1974, 26 pp.	059	1, 4, 6, 9, 10, 12, 14, 15, 16, 17, 18, 23, 26, 29	Manuel S. Emanuel Associates, *Impact Study: Town of Minisink, Orange County, New York*. Minisink, New York, May 1973, 27 pp.	068	2, 4, 6, 8, 9, 10, 12, 13, 14, 19, 26, 27
Lake County, Illinois, Regional Planning Commission, *Lake Bluff Annexation: Alternatives in School District 65*. Lake Bluff, Illinois, May 1974, 37 pp.	060	1, 4, 6, 12, 13, 14, 15, 16, 17, 18, 23, 26, 29	Marlett and Associates, *Economic Implication of Fringe Development Adjacent to Major Cities: A Case Study: Eugene, Oregon*. Eugene, Oregon, July 1973, 75 pp.	069	1, 4, 6, 8, 12, 13, 14, 17, 21, 26, 28
Lehigh Valley Joint Planning Commission, *Comparative Costs of Residential Development*. Lehigh City, Pennsylvania, September 1974, 139 pp.	061	1, 4, 7, 12, 13, 14, 16, 17, 18, 23, 26, 29	Maryland National Capital Planning Commission, *Fiscal Impact Analysis: Germantown Master Plan*. Germantown, Maryland, January 1974, 61 pp.	070	2, 4, 7, 9, 12, 13, 14, 16, 17, 18, 23, 26, 29
Lima, Ohio, Planning Department, *Quality Growth and the Annexation Issue*. Lima, Ohio, October 1974, 16 pp.	062	1, 4, 6, 12, 13, 14, 16, 21, 26, 29	Metcalf and Eddy, Inc., *The Cost-Revenue Analysis Model and Its Application to a Site in Dover, New Hampshire*. Dover, New Hampshire, March 1974, 62 pp.	071	2, 4, 6, 8, 10, 14, 15, 16, 23, 26, 28
Livingston and Blayney, *Santa Rosa Optimal Growth Study*. Santa Rosa, California, January 1973, 125 pp.	063	2, 5, 6, 10, 12, 13, 14, 15, 16, 17, 21, 26, 28	Metro Metrics, Inc., *Economics of Urban Growth: Cost-Benefits of Residential Construction*. Fairfax, Virginia, October 1971, 144 pp.	072	2, 5, 6, 8, 9, 12, 13, 14, 15, 16, 17, 18, 23, 26, 27
Longmont, Colorado, Planning Department, *Cost-Revenue Analysis–Longmont, Colorado*. Longmont, Colorado, March 1973, 58 pp.	064	2, 4, 6, 12, 13, 14, 15, 16, 17, 21, 26, 29	Miami Valley, Ohio, Regional Planning Commission, *Salem Mall–Cost-Revenue and Economic Policy Analysis*. Trotwood, Ohio, May 1975, 17 pp.	073	1, 4, 6, 9, 12, 14, 16, 21, 26, 27
Lorain County, Ohio, Regional Planning Commission, *Mobile Homes in Lorain County, Ohio*. Lorain County, Ohio, December 1970, 35 pp.	065	1, 4, 6, 8, 9, 10, 11, 12, 13, 14, 19, 26, 27	Mid-American Appraisal and Research, *Budgetary Allocation Model for Residential Properties*. Chicago, Illinois, September 1973, 50 pp.	074	1, 4, 6, 8, 9, 12, 13, 14, 15, 16, 17, 18, 23, 26, 29

Appendix 2: Annotated Literature Search

SCOPE OF STUDY AND DATA RESOURCES		
STUDY	ID NO.	CHARACTERISTICS
Monroe County, New York Planning Department, *Henrietta Management/Riverton Impact Study*. Henrietta, New York, October 1973, 50 pp.	075	2, 4, 6, 12, 13, 14, 21, 26, 28
Montgomery County, Maryland, Planning Board, *Cost-Revenue Study of the Bethesda CBD Sector Plan—Final Draft*. Silver Spring, Maryland, September 1975, 57 pp.	076	1, 4, 7, 8, 9, 10, 11, 12, 13, 14, 15, 16, 17, 18, 23, 26, 27
Montgomery County, Maryland, Planning Board, *Fiscal Impact Analysis*. Montgomery County, Maryland, September 1975, 187 pp.	077	2, 4, 6, 8, 9, 12, 14, 15, 16, 17, 18, 23, 25, 29
Murphy/Williams, *Eastport Study: Benefit/Cost Analysis*. Annapolis, Maryland, January 1973, 34 pp.	078	1, 4, 7, 8, 9, 10, 12, 13, 14, 17, 18, 23, 26, 27
New Jersey County and Municipal Government Study Commission, *A Model for the Evaluation of the Cost/Revenue Effect of Multi-family Housing*. Trenton, New Jersey, 1973, 33 pp.	079	1, 4, 6, 8, 14, 23, 26, 30
New Jersey Department of Community Affairs, *Cost-Revenue Analysis of Flemington Commons*. Raritan Township, New Jersey, February 1974, 19 pp.	080	1, 4, 6, 8, 9, 12, 13, 14, 18, 24, 26, 27
New Jersey Planning Association, *Cost-Revenue Analysis of Bear's Nest Land Use Proposals*. Park Ridge, New Jersey, January 1974, 24 pp.	081	2, 4, 6, 8, 9, 12, 13, 14, 23, 26, 29
Newark, Delaware, Planning Department, *Demographic, Capacity, Cost Analysis for Blair Village*. Newark, Delaware, March 1974, 14 pp.	082	1, 4, 6, 8, 12, 13, 16, 17, 21, 26, 27
Nicholas, James C., and Charles W. Blowers, *Socioeconomic Impact of the Marco Island Development*. Collier County, Florida, October 1974, 230 pp.	083	2, 5, 6, 8, 9, 12, 13, 14, 15, 16, 17, 18, 23, 26, 27
Northeast Illinois Planning Commission, *Fiscal Impact Analysis of Regional Shopping Center Proposals*. Carpentersville, Illinois, January 1974, 8 pp.	084	1, 4, 7, 12, 13, 14, 15, 18, 21, 26, 27
Northern Virginia Planning District Commission, *Handbook for Cost/Revenue Analysis of Land Development*. Fairfax County, Virginia, October 1973, 50 pp.	085	2, 4, 6, 9, 12, 13, 14, 15, 16, 17, 18, 23, 26, 30
Oak Creek, Wisconsin, Planning Department, *Cost-Revenue Analysis of a Proposed Rezoning at S. Howell Ave. and W. Puetz Rd.* Oak Creek, Wisconsin, March 1975, 23 pp.	086	1, 4, 6, 8, 9, 10, 12, 13, 14, 18, 24, 26, 27
Oakland County, Michigan, Planning Commission, *Cost-Revenue Analysis for Milford Village*. Mildord, Michigan, September 1972, 22 pp.	087	1, 4, 6, 8, 9, 12, 13, 14, 15, 17, 18, 23, 26, 29
Oliver T. Carr Company, *Cost-Revenue Study for the West End Plan*. Washington, D.C., October 1973, 30 pp.	088	1, 4, 6, 8, 12, 13, 14, 15, 16, 23, 26, 27
Orange County, New York, Planning Department, *Residential Uses: Students and School Taxes in Orange County: A Cost Benefit Analysis*. Orange County, New York, April 1975, 38 pp.	089	1, 4, 6, 11, 12, 14, 18, 19, 26, 29
Oregon State University, *Impacts of Urban Growth on Local Government Costs and Revenues*. Salem, Oregon, November 1974, 37 pp.	090	1, 4, 6, 12, 13, 14, 15, 16, 17, 18, 23, 26, 29
Oshawa, Ontario, Planning Department, *Oshawa: Preliminary Analysis of Ontario Housing Action Program*. Oshawa, Canada, April 1974.	091	1, 4, 6, 8, 9, 12, 13, 14, 23, 26, 28
Ottawa, Canada, Ministry of State, *Impact of Alternative Residential Land Uses on Municipal Government Finances: A Cost-Revenue Model and Case Study*. North York, Canada, December 1973, 53 pp.	092	1, 4, 6, 8, 9, 12, 13, 14, 17, 18, 23, 26, 28

410　THE FISCAL IMPACT HANDBOOK

SCOPE OF STUDY AND DATA RESOURCES

STUDY	ID NO.	CHARACTERISTICS
Pasadena Research Institute, *Economic Impact of Watson Industrial Center*. Carson, California, December 1973, 64 pp.	093	2, 5, 7, 13, 14, 15, 16, 17, 26, 29
Patton, Harris, Rust and Guy, *Impact Study, Town of Culpeper, Virginia*. Culpeper, Virginia, June 1974, 84 pp.	094	2, 4, 6, 8, 12, 14, 15, 16, 17, 18, 21, 26, 27
Peat, Marwick, Mitchell & Company, *Users Manual—Impact Estimation Relationships*. Arlington, Virginia, January 1975, 129 pp.	095	2, 4, 7, 8, 9, 10, 11, 12, 13, 14, 15, 16, 17, 18, 23, 25, 30
Phoenix, Arizona, Office of Budget and Research, *Cost-Benefit Analysis of the 1972 Deer Valley Annexation*. Phoenix, Arizona, October 1974, 15 pp.	096	2, 4, 6, 12, 13, 14, 15, 16, 17, 18, 21, 26, 29
Portsmouth, Virginia, Office of Economic Analysis, *Planned Unit Development: Impact and Cost Revenue Analysis*. Portsmouth, Virginia, November 1972, 60 pp.	097	2, 4, 6, 10, 12, 14, 15, 16, 17, 18, 24, 26, 27
Prince William County, Virginia, Planning Department, *Mobile Home Study—Planning Bulletin #2*. Prince William County, Virginia, April 1971, 31 pp.	098	1, 4, 6, 8, 9, 11, 12, 14, 19, 26, 28
Prudential Insurance Company, *Fiscal Impact Report: North Ranch Tract 2343*. Thousand Oaks, California, September 1975, 32 pp.	099	1, 4, 6, 8, 9, 10, 12, 13, 14, 15, 17, 18, 23, 26, 27
Pueblo, Colorado, Council of Governments, *Fiscal Impact of Urban Development: A Cost-Revenue Analysis*. Pueblo, Colorado, September 1974, 60 pp.	100	2, 4, 6, 8, 9, 12, 13, 14, 15, 16, 17, 18, 24, 26, 29
Quincy, Massachusetts, Planning Department, *Residential Development in the City of Quincy, A Cost-Revenue Analysis*. Quincy, Massachusetts, May 1975, 38 pp.	101	1, 4, 6, 8, 9, 12, 13, 14, 17, 18, 23, 25, 29
Raymond, Parish, Pine and Plavnick, *The Piedmont Development Center: Feasibility Study and Master Plan*. Crewe, Nottoway County, Virginia, June 1975, 129 pp.	102	1, 4, 6, 8, 9, 10, 12, 14, 16, 17, 24, 26, 27
Real Estate Research Corporation, *The Costs of Sprawl*. Hypothetical, April 1974, 278 pp.	103	2, 4, 6, 8, 9, 11, 12, 14, 24, 26, 27
Real Estate Research Corporation, *Public Service Costs and Development*. Madison, Wisconsin, October 1975, 84 pp.	104	2, 4, 7, 9, 12, 23, 26, 30
Real Estate Research Corporation, *Shenandoah: Fiscal Impact of New Community on Local Government*. Coweta County, Georgia, October 1972, 70 pp.	105	2, 4, 7, 8, 12, 14, 16, 17, 18, 23, 25, 27
Rivkin Associates, *Cost-Revenue Analysis for the Seton-Briefing Paper*. Baltimore, Maryland, February 1975, 50 pp.	106	2, 4, 6, 8, 9, 10, 12, 13, 14, 16, 17, 18, 23, 26, 27
Rutgers University Bureau of Economic Research, *Garden Apartment Development: Municipal Cost-Revenue Analysis*. Highland Park, New Jersey, November 1964, 26 pp.	107	1, 4, 6, 11, 12, 14, 19, 26, 27
Rutgers University Center for Urban Policy Research, *Fiscal Implications of Municipal Growth*. Dover Township, New Jersey, June 1972, 100 pp.	108	1, 4, 6, 8, 12, 13, 14, 23, 26, 29
Rutgers University Center for Urban Policy Research, *Planned Unit Development: New Communities American Style*. East Windsor, New Jersey, January 1972, 254 pp.	109	2, 4, 6, 8, 9, 10, 12, 13, 14, 15, 16, 17, 18, 23, 26, 27
St. Louis County Planning Department, *Apartments in St. Louis County: Cost-Revenue Impact*. St. Louis, Missouri, February 1972, 40 pp.	110	1, 4, 6, 8, 9, 11, 12, 13, 14, 23, 26, 29
San Antonio, Texas, Planning and Community Development Department, *Alternative Growth Study: San Antonio, Master Plan*. San Antonio, Texas, June 11, 1975, 75 pp.	111	2, 4, 6, 8, 9, 12, 14, 15, 16, 17, 18, 23, 25, 28

Appendix 2: Annotated Literature Search

SCOPE OF STUDY AND DATA RESOURCES

STUDY	ID NO.	CHARACTERISTICS
San Buenaventura, California, Planning Department, *Fiscal Effects of Residential Growth: An Analytical Model with Comparative Case Studies.* San Buenaventura, California, June 1974, 33 pp.	112	2, 4, 6, 8, 12, 13, 14, 15, 16, 17, 18, 21, 26
San Diego, California, Environmental Development Agency, *Basic Fiscal Impact Model.* San Diego, California, February 1975, 119 pp.	113	2, 4, 6, 8, 9, 12, 13, 14, 15, 16, 17, 18, 23, 25, 30
San Diego, California, Planning Department, *Cost-Revenue Analysis: Acadia Village.* San Diego, California, July 1974, 52 pp.	114	1, 4, 6, 9, 12, 13, 14, 15, 16, 17, 18, 23, 26, 27
San Francisco, California, Planning and Urban Renewal Association, *Impact of Intensive High Rise Development on San Francisco.* San Francisco, California, March 1975, 59 pp.	115	2, 5, 6, 9, 12, 13, 14, 15, 16, 17, 18, 23, 26, 27
San Jose, California, Planning Department, *IBM West Coast Programming Development Center: Cost-Revenue Analysis.* San Jose, California, October 1974, 18 pp.	116	2, 4, 6, 12, 13, 14, 16, 17, 21, 26, 27
San Luis Obispo, California, Planning Department, *Residential Land Use Economic Study: Revenue-Expenditure Comparison.* San Luis Obispo, California, June 1972, 23 pp.	117	1, 4, 6, 8, 13, 14, 16, 17, 18, 23, 26, 29
Santa Clara County, California, Planning Department, *Cost and Revenues of Residential Growth in the City of Cupertino: A Case Study.* Cupertino, California, October 1974, 62 pp.	118	2, 4, 7, 12, 13, 14, 15, 16, 17, 21, 26, 29
Santa Clara, California, Planning Department, *Municipal Cost-Revenue Analysis—South Santa Clara Planning Program.* Morgan Hill, California, May 1973, 10 pp.	119	1, 4, 6, 8, 9, 10, 12, 13, 14, 15, 16, 17, 18, 21, 26, 30
Saunders-Thalden and Associates, Inc., *Review of Proposed Annexation—Royal Acres Tract.* Des Peres, Missouri, February 1974, 25 pp.	120	2, 4, 6, 12, 13, 14, 16, 17, 18, 21, 26, 29
Southeastern Connecticut Regional Planning Agency, *Cost-Revenue Analysis of Alternative Land Uses on Two Sites in the Town of Groton.* Groton, Connecticut, February 1971, 29 pp.	121	1, 4, 6, 8, 9, 11, 12, 13, 14, 23, 26, 27
Southeastern Michigan Council of Governments, *Fiscal Impact Analysis: A Technical Report.* Detroit, Michigan, December 1969, 70 pp.	122	2, 5, 6, 8, 9, 10, 12, 13, 14, 15, 16, 17, 18, 23, 25, 30
Smith, Bruce, W., and John Hittner, *Cost-Revenue Analysis of Calderon Annexation.* Bowling Green, Ohio, December 1974, 20 pp.	123	1, 5, 6, 8, 9, 12, 13, 14, 16, 18, 24, 26, 29
Spindletop Research, *Analysis of Growth Alternatives for Lexington.* Fayette County, Kentucky, June 1973, 116 pp.	124	1, 4, 7, 8, 9, 10, 12, 13, 14, 15, 16, 17, 23, 25, 27
Taylor, Wiseman and Taylor, *Comparative Cost-Revenue Study: Cherry Hill Townhouse Single Family Home.* Cherry Hill, New Jersey, June 1973, 6 pp.	125	1, 4, 6, 8, 9, 12, 13, 14, 23, 26, 27
University of California Center for Real Estate and Urban Economics, *Municipal Cost-Revenue Analysis for PUD.* Fremont, California, June 1973, 44 pp.	126	1, 4, 6, 11, 12, 13, 14, 15, 16, 17, 18, 23, 26, 28
U.S. Department of Housing and Urban Development, *New Communities Administration Fiscal Impact Study Guide.* Hypothetical, April 1975, 24 pp.	127	2, 4, 6, 8, 9, 10, 12, 14, 15, 16, 17, 18, 24, 26, 27
University of Delaware, Division of Urban Affairs, *Hidden Valley: Impact Analysis.* Newark, Delaware, December 1974, 31 pp.	128	2, 5, 6, 9, 12, 14, 16, 24, 26, 27

SCOPE OF STUDY AND DATA RESOURCES

STUDY	ID NO.	CHARACTERISTICS
Urban Institute, Washington, D.C., *Fiscal Impact of Residential and Commercial Development: A Case Study*. Albamarle County, Virginia, December 1972, 140 pp.	129	2, 4, 6, 8, 9, 10, 12, 13, 14, 15, 16, 17, 18, 23, 26, 28
Urban Institute, Washington, D.C., *Forecasting Local Government Spending*. New Haven, Connecticut, 142 pp.	130	2, 4, 6, 12, 13, 14, 15, 16, 17, 18, 23, 25, 30
Urban Institute, Washington, D.C., *Impact of Annexation on City Finances: Case Study: Richmond, Virginia*. May 1973, 74 pp.	131	2, 4, 6, 12, 13, 14, 15, 16, 17, 23, 26, 27
Waltham, Massachusetts, Office of Planning, *Tax Revenues and Service Costs Associated with Community and Single Family Development Along Route 128 in Waltham, Massachusetts*. Waltham, Massachusetts, January 1974, 117 pp.	132	2, 4, 6, 9, 10, 12, 13, 14, 26, 27

SCOPE OF STUDY AND DATA RESOURCES

STUDY	ID NO.	CHARACTERISTICS
Westchester County, New York, Planning Department, *School Taxes and Residential Development*. Westchester County, New York, November 1971, 87 pp.	133	1, 4, 6, 8, 9, 11, 12, 13, 14, 18, 19, 26, 29
Western Interstate Commission for Higher Education, *The City of Antioch General Plan: A Reevaluation of the Land Use Element*. Antioch, California, July 1974, 313 pp.	134	1, 4, 6, 9, 12, 13, 14, 15, 17, 23, 26, 29
Wilbur Smith Associates, Inc., *Planning and Traffic Evaluation, Proposed Clusters, Residential Development*. East Hills, New York, August 1974, 14 pp.	135	1, 4, 6, 8, 9, 12, 13, 14, 23, 26, 27
Zech, F., *Multiple Family Housing for Oak Bay: A Cost Benefit Analysis*. Oak Bay, British Columbia, July 1972, 250 pp.	136	2, 4, 6, 12, 13, 14, 16, 17, 18, 24, 26, 27

AUTHOR, AUDIENCE, AND SIGNIFICANCE OF STUDY

CODES
AUTHOR, AUDIENCE, AND SIGNIFICANCE OF STUDY

Author

1. Planning Consultant
2. Municipality
3. County
4. State/Regional
5. Institute/University/Corporation

Quality

6. Significant
7. Average
8. Modest

Logical Sequence

9. Yes, Complete
10. Yes, Incomplete
11. No

Accuracy

12. Substantially Accurate
13. Reasonably Accurate
14. Rough Gauge
15. Not Able to Determine

Duration

16. 1 Month or Less
17. 2-5 Months
18. 6 Months-1 Year
19. 1 Year +

Complexity

20. Simple
21. Moderate
22. Difficult

User Sophistication

23. Low
24. Medium
25. High

Follow-up Study

26. Yes
27. No

Appendix 2: Annotated Literature Search 415

AUTHOR, AUDIENCE, AND SIGNIFICANCE OF STUDY

STUDY	ID NO.	CHARACTERISTICS
Abt Associates, *Effect of High Density Development on Municipal Finances in the City of Boston*. Boston, Massachusetts, April 1974, 115 pp.	001	1, 7, 9, 12, 19, 21, 24, 27
Ada Council of Governments, *The Urban Form: Urban Expansion in the Boise Area*. Boise, Idaho, August 1973, 106 pp.	002	4, 7, 9, 13, 19, 20, 24, 27
Akron Department of Planning and Urban Renewal, *Ellet Hills Mall: A Report on the Third Request for Conditional Zoning*. Akron, Ohio, November 1974, 16 pp.	003	2, 8, 11, 15, 17, 20, 23, 27
Albuquerque Planning Department, *Costs and Revenues from a Typical New Subdivision*. Albuquerque, New Mexico, May 1972, 17 pp.	004	2, 7, 9, 12, 17, 20, 23, 27
Alexandria, Virginia, Committee on Potential Growth Areas Report. City of Alexandria, Virginia, August 1975, 230 pp.	005	2, 6, 9, 13, 19, 21, 24, 27
Anaheim Development Services, *Cost Revenue Analysis of Single Family Homes, Mobile Home Parks and Multi-family Residential Developments*. Anaheim, California, August 1970, 70 pp.	006	2, 8, 10, 13, 19, 20, 23, 27
Ann Arbor Planning Department, *The Ann Arbor Growth Study*. Ann Arbor, Michigan, February 1973, 250 pp.	007	2, 7, 10, 15, 17, 21, 24, 27
Applied Decision Systems, Inc., *Fiscal Consequences of MSHDA-Financed Housing Community Impact Model*. Lansing, Michigan, June 1973, 120 pp.	008	1, 6, 9, 13, 19, 22, 25, 27
Ashley Economic Services, *The Fiscal Impact of Urban Growth: The California Experience*. San Diego, California, July 1973, 500 pp.	009	1, 6, 9, 13, 19, 21, 24, 26
Ashley Economic Services, *Fountain Valley Cost-Revenue Study*. Fountain Valley, California, August 1974, 54 pp.	010	1, 6, 10, 13, 17, 22, 25, 27
Atlanta Regional Commission, *Fiscal Impact Model for Evaluation of Public Service Costs and Revenues*. Atlanta, Georgia, March 1975, 27 pp.	011	4, 7, 9, 14, 17, 21, 24, 27
Baldwin and Gregg Ltd., *Planned Unit Development: Justification Study of Stonehenge, York County, Virginia*. York County, January 15, 1974, 26 pp.	012	1, 7, 9, 13, 17, 20, 24, 27
Barton-Aschman Associates, *The Barrington Area: A Cost-Revenue Analysis of Land Use Alternatives*. Barrington, Illinois, February 1970, 74 pp.	013	1, 7, 9, 12, 18, 21, 24, 27
Barton-Aschman Associates, *Comparative Evaluation of New Community Growth versus Trend Development Growth*. Charles County, Maryland, August 1975, 200 pp.	014	1, 6, 10, 12, 19, 21, 24, 27
Barton-Aschman Associates, *Cost-Revenue Impact Analysis for Proposed Regional Development*. Dundee Township, Illinois, February 1974, 30 pp.	015	1, 8, 9, 14, 16, 20, 23, 26
Barton-Aschman Associates, *Cost-Revenue Impact Analysis of Cedar Square West*. Minneapolis, Minnesota, July 1974, 50 pp.	016	1, 7, 9, 14, 16, 21, 24, 26
Barton-Aschman Associates, *Fiscal Impact Analysis of Alternative Development on Sheffner Property*. Hoffman Estates, Illinois, March 1975, 12 pp.	017	1, 7, 9, 15, 16, 21, 24, 27
Barton-Aschman Associates, *Impact of a New Community on Charles County, Maryland*. Charles County, Maryland, August 1975, 103 pp.	018	1, 7, 9, 15, 19, 21, 24, 27
Barton-Aschman Associates, *Tax Impact Study for Lombard Office Center*. Lombard, Illinois, September 1975, 11 pp.	019	1, 7, 9, 15, 17, 20, 24, 27

AUTHOR, AUDIENCE, AND SIGNIFICANCE OF STUDY

STUDY	ID NO.	CHARACTERISTICS
Barton-Aschman Associates, *Tax Impact Study for Dupage County Regional Planning Commission*. Dupage County, Illinois, February 1975, 148 pp.	020	1, 7, 9, 14, 18, 21, 24, 27
Bill Elliot and Associates, Inc., *Cost-Revenue Analysis of Development for a Tract Located on Connor Road, Mount Lebanon, Pennsylvania*. Mount Lebanon, Pennsylvania, March 1974, 51 pp.	021	1, 7, 10, 13, 17, 21, 24, 27
Booz, Allen and Hamilton, Inc., *Cost-Revenue Analysis: Four Alternative Plans for Growth*. Tucson, Arizona, July 1974, 84 pp.	022	1, 6, 9, 13, 17, 21, 24, 27
Booz, Allen and Hamilton, Inc., *Economic Impact of Reston, Fairfax County, Virginia*. Reston, Virginia, April 1973, 70 pp.	023	1, 6, 9, 12, 18, 21, 24, 27
Boulder, Colorado, Planning Department, *Annexation: Cost-Revenue, Boulder, Colorado*. Boulder, Colorado, October 1965, 21 pp.	024	2, 7, 11, 15, 17, 21, 24, 26
Brookline, Massachusetts, Planning Department, *Residential Cost-Revenue Analysis*. Brookline, Massachusetts, July 1973, 45 pp.	025	2, 7, 9, 13, 17, 20, 23, 26
CKR Investments, Inc., *Fiscal Impact Study: Chapel Spring, Illinois*. Monroe County, Illinois, March 1974, 27 pp.	026	5, 8, 9, 15, 17, 20, 23, 27
Clark Associates, *Alternative Forms of Future Residential Development*. New Castle, New York, July 1975, 88 pp.	027	1, 7, 10, 15, 18, 21, 24, 26
Clearwater, Florida, Planning Department, *Cost-Revenue of Housing in Clearwater, Florida*. Clearwater, Florida, June 1975, 20 pp.	028	2, 8, 11, 15, 16, 20, 23, 26
Connecticut Development Group, Inc., *Cost-Revenue Impact Analysis for Residential Developments*. Connecticut, 1972, 323 pp.	029	1, 6, 9, 15, 19, 21, 24, 27
Contra Costa, California, Planning Department, *East County/Delta Cost Effectiveness Study Parts I and II*. Contra Costa, California, June 1975, 450 pp.	030	3, 6, 9, 14, 19, 21, 24, 26
Delaware County Planning Commission, *Housing: Cost-Revenues, Public Costs and Revenues*. Delaware County, Pennsylvania, June 1975, 64 pp.	031	3, 7, 10, 12, 18, 20, 23, 26
Doxiadis Urban Systems, Inc., *Fiscal and Land Use Analysis of Prince Georges County, Vols. I and II*. Prince Georges County, Maryland, June 1970, 200 pp.	032	1, 6, 9, 14, 19, 21, 24, 26
East Providence, Rhode Island, Planning Department, *Multi-family Housing Study*. East Providence, Rhode Island, December 1972, 54 pp.	033	2, 7, 9, 15, 18, 20, 23, 27
Envico, *Effect of Second Home Development on Ludlow, Vermont*. Ludlow, Vermont, June 1973, 68 pp.	034	1, 7, 9, 14, 18, 21, 23, 27
Envirland Associates, *Estimate of Tax Cost and Revenue: Tobacco Farms PUD*. Agawam, Massachusetts, April 1974, 17 pp.	035	1, 8, 9, 15, 17, 20, 23, 27
Environmental Analysis Foundation, *Cost-Benefit Analysis of Alternative Land Uses for Coyote Hills*. Fullerton, California, May 1975, 180 pp.	036	1, 8, 9, 13, 17, 21, 24, 26
Fairfax County Planning Board, *Fiscal Impact of the Larwin-Atlantic Rezoning*. Fairfax County, Virginia, April 1973, 100 pp.	037	3, 8, 9, 13, 16, 20, 23, 27
Fleck/Sterling, *An Analysis of the Costs and Benefits of the Hampton Coliseum and the Proposed Convention Center*. Hampton, Virginia, September 1975, 167 pp.	038	1, 7, 9, 13, 18, 21, 24, 27

Appendix 2: Annotated Literature Search 417

AUTHOR, AUDIENCE, AND SIGNIFICANCE OF STUDY

STUDY	ID NO.	CHARACTERISTICS
Fort Collins, Colorado, Planning Department, *Assessment of Residential Impact on the Public School and Municipal Services in Fort Collins*. Fort Collins, Colorado, November 1975, 55 pp.	039	2, 7, 9, 15, 17, 21, 24, 27
Fresno, California, Planning Department, *Urban Growth Management Process and Cost-Revenue Analysis*. Fresno, California, January 1975, 49 pp.	040	2, 6, 9, 12, 18, 22, 25, 26
Frontera del Norte Fund, *Growth Impact Study Effects on New Construction*. Sante Fe, New Mexico, June 1973, 12 pp.	041	2, 8, 11, 12, 18, 20, 23, 27
Genesee County Planning Commission, *Density Study of Genesee County*. Genesee County, Michigan, April 1974, 126 pp.	042	3, 7, 10, 13, 17, 21, 24, 27
Georgia Institute of Technology, *Study of Housing and Its Effects on County Fiscal Capacity*. Bibb County, Georgia, September 1970, 101 pp.	043	5, 7, 9, 15, 17, 21, 24, 27
Gladstone Associates, *Beaumont, Texas, Central Business District Development Plan*. Beaumont, Texas, December 1973, 46 pp.	044	1, 7, 10, 13, 18, 21, 24, 27
Goochland County Office of County Administrators, *Costs and Revenues of Growth in Goochland County, Virginia*. Goochland County, Virginia, September 1975, 19 pp.	045	3, 7, 10, 15, 17, 21, 24, 26
Griffinhalgen-Kroeger, Inc., *Cost and Revenue Analysis of Public Services*. Prince Georges County, Virginia, September 1975, 69 pp.	046	1, 7, 10, 12, 18, 21, 24, 27
Hammer, Siler and George, *Fiscal Impact Analysis, Cherokee Village, Arkansas*. Cherokee Village, Arkansas, October 1974, 34 pp.	047	1, 7, 9, 12, 17, 21, 24, 27

AUTHOR, AUDIENCE, AND SIGNIFICANCE OF STUDY

STUDY	ID NO.	CHARACTERISTICS
Hampton Planning Commission, *Cost of City Services vs. Revenues—Apartments and Single Family Homes*. Hampton, Virginia, April 1972, 10 pp.	048	2, 8, 11, 13, 16, 20, 23, 27
Harmon, O'Donnell, and Henninger Associates, Inc., *Community Impact Study for Buchanan Mill*. Elgin, Illinois, November 1974, 17 pp.	049	1, 7, 11, 15, 16, 21, 24, 27
Honolulu Planning Department, *Planning for Oahu: An Evaluation of Alternative Residential Policies*. Oahu, Hawaii, March 1974, 198 pp.	050	3, 8, 11, 15, 19, 21, 25, 27
HOK Associates, *Main Street Mall Feasibility Study*. Midland, Michigan, June 3, 1975, 58 pp.	051	2, 7, 9, 15, 17, 21, 24, 27
Howard Hoffman Associates, *BATA Plans for the Future in Harford County, Maryland*. Harford County, Maryland, May 1975, 200 pp.	052	1, 7, 11, 15, 19, 21, 24, 27
New Community Interim Non-Profit Corporation, *Fiscal Impact Statement-Brookwood New Community*. Dayton, Ohio, March 1973, 100 pp.	053	1, 7, 9, 14, 18, 21, 24, 26
Inglewood, California, City Planning Department, *Cost-Benefit Study: Inglewood, California*. Inglewood, California, August 1973, 26 pp.	054	2, 6, 9, 14, 17, 21, 24, 27
Institute for Government and Business Research, Inc., *Cost-Revenue Analysis of Public Services in De Kalb County, Georgia*. De Kalb County, Georgia, June 1972, 105 pp.	055	5, 7, 9, 15, 18, 21, 24, 27
Institute of Regional and Urban Studies, *Fiscal Impacts of Proposed Pleasanton General Plan*. Pleasanton, California, March 1975, 18 pp.	056	5, 8, 11, 15, 17, 20, 23, 27

AUTHOR, AUDIENCE, AND SIGNIFICANCE OF STUDY

STUDY	ID NO.	CHARACTERISTICS
John Donaho Associates, Inc., *Howard County Columbia Fiscal Impact Study*. Howard County, Maryland, June 1970, 110 pp.	057	1, 7, 10, 15, 17, 21, 24, 26
Joliet, Illinois, Planning Department, *Ridgewood Annexation: Cost-Revenue Impact Analysis*. Joliet, Illinois, November 1975, 17 pp.	058	2, 8, 9, 12, 17, 20, 23, 27
Kings County Regional Planning Agency, *Revenue/Cost Analysis in Environmental Resources Management Element-Phase 2*. Kings County, California, July 1974, 26 pp.	059	3, 7, 9, 13, 17, 21, 24, 27
Lake County, Illinois, Regional Planning Commission, *Lake Bluff Annexation: Alternatives in School District 65*. Lake Bluff, Illinois, May 1974, 37 pp.	060	4, 7, 11, 13, 17, 21, 24, 26
Lehigh Valley Joint Planning Commission, *Comparative Costs of Residential Development*. Lehigh City, Pennsylvania, September 1974, 139 pp.	061	5, 6, 9, 15, 18, 21, 24, 27
Lima, Ohio, Planning Department, *Quality Growth and the Annexation Issue*. Lima, Ohio, October 1974, 16 pp.	062	2, 8, 11, 13, 17, 20, 23, 27
Livingston and Blayney, *Santa Rosa Optimal Growth Study*. Santa Rosa, California, January 1973, 125 pp.	063	1, 7, 10, 13, 18, 21, 24, 27
Longmont, Colorado, Planning Department, *Cost-Revenue Analysis—Longmont, Colorado*. Longmont, Colorado, March 1973, 58 pp.	064	2, 7, 9, 12, 18, 20, 23, 27
Lorain County, Ohio, Regional Planning Commission, *Mobile Homes in Lorain County, Ohio*. Lorain County, Ohio, December 1970, 35 pp.	065	3, 8, 10, 15, 16, 20, 23, 26
Lower Merion, Pennsylvania, Planning Office, *Study of Property Tax Revenue and Expenditures According to Land Use*. Lower Merion, Pennsylvania, April 1964, 20 pp.	066	2, 8, 9, 12, 18, 21, 24, 27
McDonald & Smart, Inc., *Fiscal Impact Study for the County of Sacramento, Vols. I & II*. Sacramento County, California, June 1975, 200 pp.	067	1, 6, 9, 13, 18, 21, 24, 27
Manuel S. Emanuel Associates, *Impact Study: Town of Minisink, Orange County, New York*. Minisink, New York, May 1973, 27 pp.	068	1, 8, 11, 15, 16, 20, 23, 27
Marlett and Associates, *Economic Implication of Fringe Development Adjacent to Major Cities: A Case Study: Eugene, Oregon*. Eugene, Oregon, July 1973, 75 pp.	069	1, 7, 9, 13, 18, 22, 25, 27
Maryland National Capital Planning Commission, *Fiscal Impact Analysis: Germantown Master Plan*. Germantown, Maryland, January 1974, 61 pp.	070	3, 7, 9, 13, 19, 21, 24, 27
Metcalf and Eddy, Inc., *The Cost-Revenue Analysis Model and Its Application to a Site in Dover, New Hampshire*. Dover, New Hampshire, March 1974, 62 pp.	071	1, 7, 9, 15, 18, 22, 24, 27
Metro Metrics, Inc., *Economics of Urban Growth: Cost-Benefits of Residential Construction*. Fairfax, Virginia, October 1971, 144 pp.	072	1, 7, 9, 15, 18, 20, 23, 26
Miami Valley, Ohio, Regional Planning Commission, *Salem Mall—Cost-Revenue and Economic Policy Analysis*. Trotwood, Ohio, May 1975, 17 pp.	073	4, 8, 10, 13, 17, 20, 23, 27
Mid-American Appraisal and Research, *Budgetary Allocation Model for Residential Properties*. Chicago, Illinois, September 1973, 50 pp.	074	1, 7, 10, 15, 17, 21, 24, 27

Appendix 2: *Annotated Literature Search* 419

AUTHOR, AUDIENCE, AND SIGNIFICANCE OF STUDY			AUTHOR, AUDIENCE, AND SIGNIFICANCE OF STUDY		
STUDY	ID NO.	CHARACTERISTICS	STUDY	ID NO.	CHARACTERISTICS
Monroe County, New York Planning Department, *Henrietta Management/Riverton Impact Study*. Henrietta, New York, October 1973, 50 pp.	075	3, 8, 9, 12, 17, 20, 23, 26	Northeast Illinois Planning Commission, *Fiscal Impact Analysis of Regional Shopping Center Proposals*. Carpentersville, Illinois, January 1974, 8 pp.	084	5, 7, 9, 15, 16, 21, 24, 27
Montgomery County, Maryland, Planning Board, *Cost-Revenue Study of the Bethesda CBD Sector Plan—Final Draft*. Silver Spring, Maryland, September 1975, 57 pp.	076	3, 7, 10, 15, 17, 21, 24, 27	Northern Virginia Planning District Commission, *Handbook for Cost/Revenue Analysis of Land Development*. Fairfax County, Virginia, October 1973, 50 pp.	085	5, 6, 9, 15, 19, 20, 23, 27
Montgomery County, Maryland, Planning Board, *Fiscal Impact Analysis*. Montgomery County, Maryland, September 1975, 187 pp.	077	3, 6, 9, 15, 17, 22, 25, 26	Oak Creek, Wisconsin, Planning Department, *Cost-Revenue Analysis of a Proposed Rezoning at S. Howell Ave. and W. Puetz Rd*. Oak Creek, Wisconsin, March 1975, 23 pp.	086	2, 8, 10, 15, 16, 20, 23, 27
Murphy/Williams, *Eastport Study: Benefit/Cost Analysis*. Annapolis, Maryland, January 1973, 34 pp.	078	1, 7, 10, 12, 17, 21, 24, 27	Oakland County, Michigan, Planning Commission, *Cost-Revenue Analysis for Milford Village*. Milford, Michigan, September 1972, 22 pp.	087	3, 8, 9, 15, 16, 20, 23, 27
New Jersey County and Municipal Government Study Commission, *A Model for the Evaluation of the Cost/Revenue Effect of Multi-family Housing*. Trenton, New Jersey, 1973, 33 pp.	079	5, 7, 9, 13, 18, 21, 24, 27	Oliver T. Carr Company, *Cost-Revenue Study for the West End Plan*. Washington, D.C., October 1973, 30 pp.	088	1, 7, 9, 12, 17, 21, 24, 27
New Jersey Department of Community Affairs, *Cost-Revenue Analysis of Flemington Commons*. Raritan Township, New Jersey, February 1974, 19 pp.	080	4, 7, 9, 15, 16, 21, 24, 27	Orange County, New York, Planning Department, *Residential Uses: Students and School Taxes in Orange County: A Cost Benefit Analysis*. Orange County, New York, April 1975, 38 pp.	089	3, 7, 9, 12, 17, 20, 23, 26
New Jersey Planning Association, *Cost-Revenue Analysis of Bear's Nest Land Use Proposals*. Park Ridge, New Jersey, January 1974, 24 pp.	081	5, 8, 9, 15, 18, 20, 23, 27	Oregon State University, *Impacts of Urban Growth on Local Government Costs and Revenues*. Salem, Oregon, November 1974, 37 pp.	090	5, 8, 11, 13, 19, 20, 24, 27
Newark, Delaware, Planning Department, *Demographic, Capacity, Cost Analysis for Blair Village*. Newark, Delaware, March 1974, 14 pp.	082	2, 8, 11, 15, 16, 20, 23, 27	Oshawa, Ontario, Planning Department, *Oshawa: Preliminary Analysis of Ontario Housing Action Program*. Oshawa, Canada, April 1974.	091	2, 7, 10, 12, 19, 21, 24, 27
Nicholas, James C., and Charles W. Blowers, *Socioeconomic Impact of the Marco Island Development*. Collier County, Florida, October 1974, 230 pp.	083	1, 7, 11, 12, 18, 22, 25, 27	Ottawa, Canada, Ministry of State, *Impact of Alternative Residential Land Uses on Municipal Government Finances: A Cost-Revenue Model and Case Study*. North York, Canada, December 1973, 53 pp.	092	4, 8, 11, 15, 17, 20, 23, 26

420 THE FISCAL IMPACT HANDBOOK

AUTHOR, AUDIENCE, AND SIGNIFICANCE OF STUDY		
STUDY	ID NO.	CHARACTERISTICS
Pasadena Research Institute, *Economic Impact of Watson Industrial Center.* Carson, California, December 1973, 64 pp.	093	1, 7, 10, 12, 18, 21, 24, 27
Patton, Harris, Rust and Guy, *Impact Study, Town of Culpeper, Virginia.* Culpeper, Virginia, June 1974, 84 pp.	094	1, 7, 9, 12, 17, 21, 24, 27
Peat, Marwick, Mitchell & Company, *Users Manual—Impact Estimation Relationships.* Arlington, Virginia, January 1975, 129 pp.	095	1, 6, 9, 15, 19, 22, 25, 27
Phoenix, Arizona, Office of Budget and Research, *Cost-Benefit Analysis of the 1972 Deer Valley Annexation.* Phoenix, Arizona, October 1974, 15 pp.	096	2, 7, 10, 15, 18, 21, 24, 26
Portsmouth, Virginia, Office of Economic Analysis, *Planned Unit Development: Impact and Cost Revenue Analysis.* Portsmouth, Virginia, November 1972, 60 pp.	097	2, 8, 10, 14, 17, 20, 23, 27
Prince William County, Virginia, Planning Department, *Mobile Home Study—Planning Bulletin #2.* Prince William County, Virginia, April 1971, 31 pp.	098	3, 8, 10, 15, 17, 20, 23, 26
Prudential Insurance Company, *Fiscal Impact Report: North Ranch Tract 2343.* Thousand Oaks, California, September 1975, 32 pp.	099	5, 8, 10, 14, 17, 20, 23, 26
Pueblo, Colorado, Council of Governments, *Fiscal Impact of Urban Development: A Cost-Revenue Analysis.* Pueblo, Colorado, September 1974, 60 pp.	100	4, 7, 9, 15, 17, 21, 24, 27
Quincy, Massachusetts, Planning Department, *Residential Development in the City of Quincy, A Cost-Revenue Analysis.* Quincy, Massachusetts, May 1975, 38 pp.	101	2, 8, 10, 15, 17, 20, 23, 27
Raymond, Parish, Pine and Plavnick, *The Piedmont Development Center: Feasibility Study and Master Plan.* Crewe, Nottoway County, Virginia, June 1975, 129 pp.	102	1, 7, 10, 15, 18, 21, 24, 27

AUTHOR, AUDIENCE, AND SIGNIFICANCE OF STUDY		
STUDY	ID NO.	CHARACTERISTICS
Real Estate Research Corporation, *The Costs of Sprawl.* Hypothetical, April 1974, 278 pp.	103	1, 6, 9, 15, 19, 21, 24, 27
Real Estate Research Corporation, *Public Service Costs and Development.* Madison, Wisconsin, October 1975, 84 pp.	104	1, 7, 9, 15, 19, 21, 24, 27
Real Estate Research Corporation, *Shenandoah: Fiscal Impact of New Community on Local Government.* Coweta County, Georgia, October 1972, 70 pp.	105	1, 6, 9, 14, 18, 21, 23, 26
Rivkin Associates, *Cost-Revenue Analysis for the Seton-Briefing Paper.* Baltimore, Maryland, February 1975, 50 pp.	106	1, 7, 9, 13, 17, 21, 24, 27
Rutgers University Bureau of Economic Research, *Garden Apartment Development: Municipal Cost-Revenue Analysis.* Highland Park, New Jersey, November 1964, 26 pp.	107	5, 7, 9, 12, 18, 20, 23, 27
Rutgers University Center for Urban Policy Research, *Fiscal Implications of Municipal Growth.* Dover Township, New Jersey, June 1972, 100 pp.	108	5, 7, 9, 14, 16, 21, 24, 27
Rutgers University Center for Urban Policy Research, *Planned Unit Development: New Communities American Style.* East Windsor, New Jersey, January 1972, 254 pp.	109	5, 6, 9, 12, 19, 21, 24, 26
St. Louis County Planning Department, *Apartments in St. Louis County: Cost-Revenue Impact.* St. Louis, Missouri, February 1972, 40 pp.	110	2, 7, 9, 12, 19, 21, 24, 26
San Antonio, Texas, Planning and Community Development Department, *Alternative Growth Study: San Antonio, Master Plan.* San Antonio, Texas, June 11, 1975, 75 pp.	111	2, 7, 9, 13, 19, 21, 24, 26

Appendix 2: Annotated Literature Search 421

AUTHOR, AUDIENCE, AND SIGNIFICANCE OF STUDY		
STUDY	ID NO.	CHARACTERISTICS
San Buenaventura, California, Planning Department, *Fiscal Effects of Residential Growth: An Analytical Model with Comparative Case Studies*. San Buenaventura, California, June 1974, 33 pp.	112	2, 7, 9, 12, 17, 22, 25, 26
San Diego, California, Environmental Development Agency, *Basic Fiscal Impact Model*. San Diego, California, February 1975, 119 pp.	113	3, 6, 9, 15, 19, 21, 25, 27
San Diego, California, Planning Department, *Cost-Revenue Analysis: Acadia Village*. San Diego, California, July 1974, 52 pp.	114	2, 7, 9, 15, 16, 21, 24, 27
San Francisco, California, Planning and Urban Renewal Association, *Impact of Intensive High Rise Development on San Francisco*. San Francisco, California, March 1975, 59 pp.	115	5, 7, 9, 12, 19, 21, 24, 27
San Jose, California, Planning Department, *IBM West Coast Programming Development Center: Cost-Revenue Analysis*. San Jose, California, October 1974, 18 pp.	116	2, 8, 10, 12, 17, 20, 23, 27
San Luis Obispo, California, Planning Department, *Residential Land Use Economic Study: Revenue-Expenditure Comparison*. San Luis Obispo, California, June 1972, 23 pp.	117	2, 8, 9, 13, 16, 20, 23, 27
Santa Clara County, California, Planning Department, *Cost and Revenues of Residential Growth in the City of Cupertino: A Case Study*. Cupertino, California, October 1974, 62 pp.	118	3, 7, 9, 13, 19, 21, 24, 27
Santa Clara, California, Planning Department, *Municipal Cost-Revenue Analysis—South Santa Clara Planning Program*. Morgan Hill, California, May 1973, 10 pp.	119	3, 6, 9, 15, 18, 21, 24, 27

AUTHOR, AUDIENCE, AND SIGNIFICANCE OF STUDY		
STUDY	ID NO.	CHARACTERISTICS
Saunders-Thalden and Associates, Inc., *Review of Proposed Annexation—Royal Acres Tract*. Des Peres, Missouri, February 1974, 25 pp.	120	1, 7, 10, 15, 17, 21, 24, 27
Southeastern Connecticut Regional Planning Agency, *Cost-Revenue Analysis of Alternative Land Uses on Two Sites in the Town of Groton*. Groton, Connecticut, February 1971, 29 pp.	121	4, 8, 10, 15, 18, 20, 24, 26
Southeastern Michigan Council of Governments, *Fiscal Impact Analysis: A Technical Report*. Detroit, Michigan, December 1969, 70 pp.	122	4, 6, 10, 15, 19, 22, 25, 27
Smith, Bruce, W., and John Hittner, *Cost-Revenue Analysis of Calderon Annexation*. Bowling Green, Ohio, December 1974, 20 pp.	123	5, 7, 9, 14, 17, 21, 24, 27
Spindletop Research, *Analysis of Growth Alternatives for Lexington*. Fayette County, Kentucky, June 1973, 116 pp.	124	1, 7, 10, 15, 17, 21, 24, 27
Taylor, Wiseman and Taylor, *Comparative Cost-Revenue Study: Cherry Hill Townhouse Single Family Home*. Cherry Hill, New Jersey, June 1973, 6 pp.	125	1, 8, 10, 12, 16, 21, 24, 26
University of California Center for Real Estate and Urban Economics, *Municipal Cost-Revenue Analysis for PUD*. Fremont, California, June 1973, 44 pp.	126	5, 7, 9, 15, 17, 21, 24, 27
U.S. Department of Housing and Urban Development, *New Communities Administration Fiscal Impact Study Guide*. Hypothetical, April 1975, 24 pp.	127	5, 7, 10, 12, 18, 21, 24, 27
University of Delaware, Division of Urban Affairs, *Hidden Valley: Impact Analysis*. Newark, Delaware, December 1974, 31 pp.	128	5, 7, 10, 13, 19, 21, 24, 27

AUTHOR, AUDIENCE, AND SIGNIFICANCE OF STUDY

STUDY	ID NO.	CHARACTERISTICS
Urban Institute, Washington, D.C., *Fiscal Impact of Residential and Commercial Development: A Case Study*. Albamarle County, Virginia, December 1972, 140 pp.	129	5, 6, 9, 14, 18, 21, 24, 27
Urban Institute, Washington, D.C., *Forecasting Local Government Spending*. New Haven, Connecticut, 142 pp.	130	5, 6, 9, 15, 19, 22, 25, 27
Urban Institute, Washington, D.C., *Impact of Annexation on City Finances: Case Study*. Richmond, Virginia. May 1973, 74 pp.	131	5, 7, 9, 14, 19, 21, 24, 26
Waltham, Massachusetts, Office of Planning, *Tax Revenues and Service Costs Associated with Community and Single Family Development Along Route 128 in Waltham, Massachusetts*. Waltham, Massachusetts, January 1974, 117 pp.	132	2, 7, 9, 12, 18, 21, 25, 27
Westchester County, New York, Planning Department, *School Taxes and Residential Development*. Westchester County, New York, November 1971, 87 pp.	133	3, 7, 9, 15, 19, 21, 25, 26
Western Interstate Commission for Higher Education, *The City of Antioch General Plan: A Reevaluation of the Land Use Element*. Antioch, California, July 1974, 313 pp.	134	2, 7, 9, 12, 17, 21, 24, 27
Wilbur Smith Associates, Inc., *Planning and Traffic Evaluation, Proposed Clusters, Residential Development*. East Hills, New York, August 1974, 14 pp.	135	1, 8, 11, 15, 19, 20, 23, 27
Zech, F., *Multiple Family Housing for Oak Bay: A Cost Benefit Analysis*. Oak Bay, British Columbia, July 1972, 250 pp.	136	4, 7, 9, 12, 19, 21, 24, 27

SOURCES AND PRICES OF ANNOTATED FISCAL IMPACT STUDIES

SOURCES AND PRICES OF ANNOTATED FISCAL IMPACT STUDIES

ID NUMBER	SOURCE/PRICE		ID NUMBER	SOURCE/PRICE	
001	Abt Associates, 55 Wheeler Street, Cambridge, MA 02138	$4.00	014	Barton-Aschman Associates 820 Davis St., Evanston, IL 60201 Reproduction Cost	
002	Ada Council of Governments 525 W. Jefferson Street, Boise ID 83700	$2.00	015	Barton-Aschman Associates 820 Davis St., Evanston, IL 60201 Reproduction Cost	
003	Department of Planning and Urban Renewal 401 Municipal Building, Akron, OH 44308 Reproduction Cost		016	Barton-Aschman Associates 820 Davis St., Evanston, IL 60201 Reproduction Cost	
004	Albuquerque Planning Department P.O. Box 1293, Albuquerque, NM 87111 Reproduction Cost		017	Barton-Aschman Associates 820 Davis St., Evanston, IL 60201 Reproduction Cost	
005	Alexandria Planning Department 320 King Street, Alexandria, VA 22300	$5.00	018	Barton-Aschman Associates 820 Davis St., Evanston, IL 60201 Reproduction Cost	
006	Anaheim Development Services Department P.O. Box 3222, Anaheim, CA 92803 Reproduction Cost		019	Barton-Aschman Associates 820 Davis St., Evanston, IL 60201 Reproduction Cost	
007	Ann Arbor Planning Department 100 N. 5th Ave., P.O. Box 647 Ann Arbor, MI 48107 Reproduction Cost		020	National Technical Information Service 5285 Port Royal Road, Springfield, VA 22161	$7.50
008	National Technical Information Service 5285 Port Royal Road, Springfield, VA 22161	$8.00	021	Planning Department 710 Washington Rd., Pittsburgh, PA 15228 Reproduction Cost	
009	Ashley Economic Services, Inc. 500 Newport Center Drive, Suite 915 Newport Beach, CA 92660 Reproduction Cost		022	Booz, Allen and Hamilton, Inc. 555 California Street, San Francisco, CA 94104 Reproduction Cost	
010	Presley of Southern California P.O. Box 2200, Newport Beach, CA 92663	$5.50	023	Booz, Allen and Hamilton, Inc. 1025 Connecticut Avenue, N.W., Washington, DC 20036 Reproduction Cost	
011	Atlanta Regional Commission Suite 910, 100 Peachtree Street, Atlanta, GA 30303 Reproduction Cost		024	Municipal Government Reference Center Boulder Public Library 1000 Canyon Boulevard, P.O. Drawer 4 Boulder, CO 80302 Reproduction Cost	
012	Baldwin and Gregg, Ltd. 620 May Avenue, Norfolk, VA 23504 Reproduction Cost		025	Brookline Planning Department 333 Washington Street, Brookline, MA 02146 Reproduction Cost	
013	Barton-Aschman Associates 820 Davis St., Evanston, IL 60201 Reproduction Cost				

Appendix 2: Annotated Literature Search 425

SOURCES AND PRICES OF ANNOTATED FISCAL IMPACT STUDIES (continued)

ID NUMBER	SOURCE/PRICE	ID NUMBER	SOURCE/PRICE
026	Southwestern Illinois Planning Commission 203 W. Main Street, Collinsville, IL 62234 Reproduction Cost	038	Hampton Planning Department, City Hall 22 Lincoln Street, Hampton, VA 23369 Reproduction Cost
027	Frederick P. Clark Associates 29 Locust Avenue, Rye NY 10580 Reproduction Cost	039	Fort Collins Planning Department P.O. Box 580, Fort Collins, CO 80521 Reproduction Cost
028	Clearwater Planning Department P.O. Box 4748, Clearwater, FL 33500 Reproduction Cost	040	Fresno City Manager's Office P.O. Box 12706, Fresno, CA 93779 Reproduction Cost
029	Connecticut Development Group, Inc. Hartford, CT 06101 Reproduction Cost	041	Frontera del Norte Fund 338 E. DeVargas, Santa Fe, NM 87501 $2.00
030	Contra Costa County Planning Department County Administration Building P.O. Box 951, Martinez, CA 94553 Reproduction Cost	042	Genesee County Metropolitan Planning Commission 1101 Beach Street, Flint, MI 48502 $2.50
031	Delaware County Planning Commission 3rd and Orange Sts., Media, PA 19063 Reproduction Cost	043	Graduate City Planning Program Georgia Institute of Technology Atlanta, GA 30332 Reproduction Cost
032	Doxiadis Urban Systems, Inc. 2435 Virginia Ave., N.W., Washington, DC 20037 Reproduction Cost	044	Gladstone Associates 2030 M Street, N.W., Suite 500, Washington, DC 20036 Reproduction Cost
033	Department of Planning and Urban Development East Providence, RI 02914 Reproduction Cost	045	Richmond Regional Planning District Commission 6 North Sixth Street, Suite 500 Richmond, VA 23219 Reproduction Cost
034	Envico, Star Route #4, Windsor, VT 05089 Reproduction Cost	046	Prince George County Planning Department Prince George Court House P.O. Box 68, Prince George, VA 23875 Reproduction Cost
035	Envirland Associates P.O. Box 74, Hadlyne, CT 06439 Reproduction Cost	047	Cooper Communities, Inc. Bella Vista, AR 72712 Reproduction Cost
036	Development Services Department, City Hall 300 West Commonwealth Avenue Fullerton, CA 92632 $4.00	048	Office of the City Planning Commission, City Hall 22 Lincoln Street, Hampton, VA 23369 Reproduction Cost
037	Fairfax County Planning Commission Massey Building, Fairfax, VA 22030 Reproduction Cost	049	Harmon, O'Donnell, and Henninger Associates 2727 East Second Ave., Denver, CO 80206 Reproduction Cost

SOURCES AND PRICES OF ANNOTATED FISCAL IMPACT STUDIES (continued)

ID NUMBER	SOURCE/PRICE	ID NUMBER	SOURCE/PRICE
050	Department of General Planning City and County of Honolulu Suite 2100, Pacific Trade Center 190 South King Street, Honolulu, HI 96813 Reproduction Cost	061	Joint Planning Commission Lehigh-Northampton Counties ABE Airport, Lehigh Valley, PA 18103 $3.00
051	HOK Associates, 200 East Main St. P.O. Box 2185, Midland, MI 48640 Reproduction Cost	062	Planning Department Municipal Building, Lima, OH 45801 Reproduction Cost
052	Howard P. Hoffman Associates 122 East 42nd Street, New York, NY 10017 Reproduction Cost	063	Santa Rosa Planning Department, City Hall P.O. Box 1678, Santa Rosa, CA 95403 Reproduction Cost
053	New Community Interim Non-Profit Corporation Brookwood Community Authority, Dayton, OH 45400 Reproduction Cost	064	Longmont Planning Department, City Hall Longmont, CO 80501 Reproduction Cost
054	Department of Planning and Development Civic Center, Inglewood, CA 90301 Reproduction Cost	065	Lorain County Regional Planning Commission 21 Turner Block Court St., Elyria, OH 44035 Reproduction Cost
055	De Kalb County Planning Department Court House Square, Decatur, GA 30030 Reproduction Cost	066	Office of Planning 75 E. Lancaster Avenue, Ardmore, PA 19003 Reproduction Cost
056	Institute of Regional and Urban Studies 610 University Avenue, Palo Alto, CA 94301 Reproduction Cost	067	Community Development Agency 827 Seventh Street, Sacramento, CA 95814 $10.00
057	John Donaho and Associates Room 320 – 10 Light Street, Baltimore, MD 21202 Reproduction Cost	068	Manuel S. Emanuel Associates P.O. Box 629, 50 Piermont Ave., Nyack, NY 10960 Reproduction Cost
058	Department of Community Development Joliet, IL 60431 Reproduction Cost	069	Lane County Local Government Boundary Commission 541 Willamette St., Room 402, Eugene, OR 97401 Reproduction Cost
059	Kings County Regional Planning Agency Courthouse Box C, Hanford, CA 93230 Reproduction Cost	070	Montgomery County Planning Board 8787 Georgia Avenue, Silver Spring, MD 20907 Reproduction Cost
060	Lake County Regional Planning Commission Waukegan, IL 60085 Reproduction Cost	071	Strafford Regional Planning Commission 90 Washington Street, Dover, NH 03820 Reproduction Cost
		072	Metro Metrics, Inc. P.O. Box 34451, Washington, DC 20034 Reproduction Cost

Appendix 2: Annotated Literature Search 427

SOURCES AND PRICES OF ANNOTATED FISCAL IMPACT STUDIES (continued)

ID NUMBER	SOURCE/PRICE	ID NUMBER	SOURCE/PRICE
073	Miami Valley Regional Planning Commission 333 W. First Street, Dayton, OH 45402 Reproduction Cost	085	Northern Virginia Planning District Commission 7309 Arlington Boulevard, Falls Church, VA 22030 Reproduction Cost
074	Department of Development and Planning City Hall, Chicago, IL 60602 Reproduction Cost	086	Oak Creek Planning Department 8640 S. Howell Avenue, Oak Creek, WI 53154 Reproduction Cost
075	Monroe County Department of Planning 301 County Office Building, Rochester, NY 14614 Reproduction Cost	087	County Planning Commission 1200 North Telegraph Road, Pontiac, MI 48053 Reproduction Cost
076	Montgomery County Planning Board 8787 Georgia Avenue, Silver Spring, MD 20907 Reproduction Cost	088	Oliver T. Carr Company 1700 Pennsylvania Avenue, N.W., Suite 900 Washington, DC 20006 Reproduction Cost
077	Montgomery County Planning Board 8787 Georgia Avenue, Silver Spring, MD 20907 Reproduction Cost	089	Orange County Department of Planning County Government Center Main Street, Goshen, NY 10924 $1.50
078	Murphy/Williams 3426 Sansom Street, Philadelphia, PA 19104 Reproduction Cost	090	Oregon State University Extension Service Corvallis, OR 97331 Reproduction Cost
079	County and Municipal Government Study Commission 115 West State Street, Trenton, NJ 08625 Reproduction Cost	091	Oshawa Planning Department Municipal Building, Oshawa, Ontario, Canada Reproduction Cost
080	Division of State and Regional Planning Department of Community Affairs 329 W. State Street, Trenton, NJ 08625 Reproduction Cost	092	Ministry of State for Urban Affairs Ottawa, Canada Reproduction Cost
081	The Planning Association of New Jersey 400 Clifton Ave., Clifton, NJ 07011 Reproduction Cost	093	Pasadena Research Institute 607 Laguna Road, Pasadena, CA 91105 Reproduction Cost
082	Newark Planning Department P.O. Box 390, Newark, DE 19711 Reproduction Cost	094	Planning Department 118 West Davis Street, Culpeper, VA 22701 Reproduction Cost
083	The Deltona Corporation 3250 Southwest 3rd Ave., Miami, FL 33129 Reproduction Cost	095	Peat, Marwick, Mitchell and Co. 1025 Connecticut Avenue, N.W., Washington, DC 20036 Reproduction Cost
084	Northeast Illinois Planning Commission 10 S. Riverside Plaza, Chicago, IL 60602 Reproduction Cost	096	Office of Budget and Research 251 West Washington, Phoenix, AZ 85003 Reproduction Cost

SOURCES AND PRICES OF ANNOTATED FISCAL IMPACT STUDIES (continued)

ID NUMBER	SOURCE/PRICE		ID NUMBER	SOURCE/PRICE	
097	Office of Economic Analysis Planning Department Portsmouth, VA 23700 Reproduction Cost		108	Center for Urban Policy Research Building 4051, Kilmer Campus Rutgers University, New Brunswick, NJ 08903 Reproduction Cost	
098	Prince William County Planning Department 15920 Jefferson Davis Highway, Woodbridge, VA 22191 Reproduction Cost		109	Center for Urban Policy Research Building 4051, Kilmer Campus Rutgers University, New Brunswick, NJ 08903	$12.95
099	Prudential Insurance Company Westlake Project Office P.O. Box 3969, Westlake Village, CA 91359 Reproduction Cost		110	St. Louis County Planning Department Municipal Building, St. Louis, MO 63155	$2.00
100	Pueblo Council of Governments Pueblo, CO 81003	$6.00	111	Planning and Community Development P.O. Box 9066, San Antonio, TX 78285	$1.50
101	Department of Planning City Hall, Quincy, MA 03169 Reproduction Cost		112	Research and Budget Division City of San Buenaventura P.O. Box 99, Ventura, CA 93001	$5.00
102	Piedmont Planning District Commission 205 North Virginia St., Farmville, VA 23901 Reproduction Cost		113	County Planning Office, County Administration Center 1600 Pacific Highway, San Diego, CA 92101 Reproduction Cost	
103	U.S. Government Printing Office Washington, DC 20402	$3.45	114	San Diego Planning Department City Administration Building 202 C Street, San Diego, CA 92101 Reproduction Cost	
104	Wisconsin Department of Administration Madison, WI 53702 Reproduction Cost		115	San Francisco Planning and Urban Renewal Association 126 Post St., San Francisco, CA 94108 Reproduction Cost	
105	Real Estate Research Corporation 72 West Adams Street, Chicago, IL 60603 Reproduction Cost		116	San Jose Planning Department City Hall, San Jose, CA 95100 Reproduction Cost	
106	Division of Planning, Department of Housing and Community Development 222 East Saratoga Street, Baltimore, MD 21202 Reproduction Cost		117	American Mobile Home Appraisal Co. P.O. Box 1422, San Luis Obispo, CA 93401 Reproduction Cost	
107	Center for Urban Policy Research Building 4051, Kilmer Campus Rutgers University, New Brunswick, NJ 08903 Reproduction Cost		118	Santa Clara County Planning Department 70 W. Hedding Street, San Jose, CA 95110 Reproduction Cost	

Appendix 2: Annotated Literature Search 429

SOURCES AND PRICES OF ANNOTATED FISCAL IMPACT STUDIES (continued)

ID NUMBER	SOURCE/PRICE	ID NUMBER	SOURCE/PRICE
119	Santa Clara County Planning Department 70 W. Hedding Street, San Jose, CA 95110 Reproduction Cost	127	U.S. Department of Housing and Urban Development Washington, DC 20410 Reproduction Cost
120	Saunders-Thalden and Associates 3740 Undell Boulevard, St. Louis, MO 63108 Reproduction Cost	128	Division of Urban Affairs University of Delaware, Newark, DE 19711 $5.00
121	Southeastern Connecticut Regional Planning Agency 139 Boswell Ave., Norwich, CT 06360 Reproduction Cost	129	Publication Office, Urban Institute 2100 M St., N.W., Washington, DC 20037 $3.00
122	Southeastern Michigan Council of Governments 8th Floor, Book Building, 1249 Washington Blvd. Detroit, MI 48226 Reproduction Cost	130	Publications Office, Urban Institute 2100 M St., N.W., Washington, DC 20037 $7.50
		131	The Urban Institute 2100 M St., N.W., Washington, DC 20037 $3.00
123	Department of Geography Bowling Green State University Bowling Green, OH 43403 Reproduction Cost	132	Urban Planning, Design, and Decision 37 Fanwood Ave., Chicopee, MI 01020 Reproduction Cost
124	Lexington-Fayette County Planning Commission 227 North Upper Street, Lexington, KY 40507 Reproduction Cost	133	Westchester County Planning Department 910 County Office Building, White Plains, NY 10601 Reproduction Cost
125	Taylor, Wiseman and Taylor 306 Fellowship Road, Mt. Laurel, NJ 08057 Reproduction Cost	134	Antioch Planning Department, City Hall P.O. Box 369, Antioch, CA 94509 Reproduction Cost
		135	Wilbur Smith and Associates 1212 Avenue of the Americas, New York, NY 10036 Reproduction Cost
126	Center for Real Estate and Urban Economics University of California, Berkeley, CA 94720 $1.50	136	Corporation of the District of Oak Bay, Municipal Hall 2167 Oak Bay Avenue, Oak Bay, B.C., Canada $6.00

GLOSSARY

Reference numbers indicate sources of definitions which follow glossary.

AD VALOREM: a tax or duty levied in the form of percentage of value of property.³

AMORTIZATION: the systematic reduction of debt through use of serial bonds or term bonds with actuarial basis sinking fund.⁵

ANNEXATION: the addition of territory to a unit of government. Annexation usually denotes the addition by a city of land adjacent to it to meet the problems of metropolitan expansion. Procedures for annexation are established by state law and generally require an affirmative vote of both the annexing city and the area concerned.⁷

ASSESSED VALUATION: the value at which property is appraised for tax purposes.¹

ASSESSOR: a public official who determines the value of real and personal property for purposes of taxation. Assessors are commonly elected in towns, townships, or counties.⁷

AUTHORITY: a governmental unit or public agency created to perform a single function or a restricted group of related activities. Usually such units are financed from service charges, fees, and tolls, but in some instances they also have taxing powers.⁵

AVERAGE COSTING: costs assigned to a future growth increment according to the existing average cost of present government services. Cost assignment does not consider existing excess or deficient capacity that might exist for particular services or the possibility that a new development might fall at the threshold level, calling for major new capital construction to accommodate increased growth.

BEDROOMS: the count of rooms used mainly for sleeping, even if also used for other purposes. Rooms reserved for sleeping such as guest rooms, even though used infrequently, are counted as bedrooms. Rooms used mainly for other purposes, even though used also for sleeping, such as a living room with a hideaway bed, are not considered bedrooms. A housing unit consisting of only one room, such as a one-room efficiency apartment, is classified, by definition, as having no bedroom.²

BOND (MUNICIPAL OR PUBLIC): certificates of indebtedness issued by a state or local government authority as a promise to repay money over a period of time. They are used to finance the costs of public capital facilities, i.e., roads, schools, hospitals, and other projects that cannot be financed out of current revenues.

BUDGET: an estimate of receipts and expenditures needed by the government to carry out its program in some future period, usually a fiscal year.[7]

CAPITAL BUDGET: a plan for capital expenditures, including commitments, to be incurred during the budget year from funds subject to appropriation by the governing body of the concerned government for projects scheduled in a given year of the capital program.[5]

CAPITALIZATION: the process of estimating the present investment value of a property by reducing anticipated future income to present worth.[4]

CAPITAL OUTLAY: expenditures by ordinance or budget appropriation for the construction, purchase, or improvement of fixed assets such as buildings and equipment, parks and playgrounds, vehicular equipment, streets, roads, sidewalks, storm sewers, etc.[1]

CAPITAL PROGRAM: a plan for capital expenditures, including commitments, to be incurred each year over a fixed period of years to meet capital needs arising from the long-term work program. It thus sets forth each project or other contemplated expenditure in which the local government is to have a part, and it specifies the full resources estimated to be available to finance the projected expenditures.[5]

CASE STUDY METHOD: a method to project the fiscal impact of a proposed development, annexation, land use alternative, etc., it assigns impact costs to a growth increment according to the sum of all specific immediate local expenditures, taking into account existing service deficiencies and excesses.

CENTRAL CITIES: the major city or cities around which Standard Metropolitan Statistical Areas (SMSAs) are defined.[14]

CHARGES AND MISCELLANEOUS REVENUE: all general revenue other than taxes and intergovernmental transfers.[2]

CHIEF FINANCIAL OFFICER: the director of revenue and finance, comptroller, treasurer, collector, or other financial officer of a municipality, or the treasurer of a county.[1]

COMMON MUNICIPAL FUNCTIONS: frequently provided municipal services. Includes financial administration, general control, police, fire, highways, sewerage, sanitation, water supply, parks and recreation, and libraries.

COMMUNITY SHOPPING CENTER: a shopping complex built around a junior department store or variety store, in addition to a supermarket. It usually does not contain a full-line department store; the average size is 150,000 square feet of gross leasable area."

COMPARABLE CITY METHOD: a method to project the fiscal impact of a proposed development, annexation, land use alternative, etc. It recognizes a relationship between expenditure levels of cities of similar size and growth rate and assigns an impact cost to a growth increment based on the service profiles of the population size to which the city will grow at a specified rate.

CONDOMINUM: residential attached structures of single or multifamily construction in which occupants hold legal title to an apartment and a communal interest in the land and all improvements.

CONTRACT RENT: the monthly rent agreed to, or contracted for, regardless of any furnishings, utilities, or services that may be included.[2]

CONVENIENCE GOODS: goods from grocery, drug, liquor, and hardware stores; services from beauty, barber, and bake shops; and services from laundry and dry cleaning establishments.[11]

Glossary

Cost: a municipal or school district actual cash disbursement (plus amounts reserved to meet bills incurred during the year but unpaid at the close of the calendar year) incurred as a result of providing a local public service. As used in this handbook it is synonymous with the term expenditure.

County: the major unit of local government in the United States, except in Connecticut, Rhode Island, and Alaska.[7]

Credit: an outstanding asset.

Debit: an outstanding charge.

Debt Limit: the maximum amount of debt that a governmental unit may incur under constitutional, statutory, or charter requirements. The limitation is usually a percentage of assessed valuation.[5]

Deficient Capacity: capacity below that needed to accommodate the existing service or target population.

Demographic Multiplier: estimate of average household size and school-age children for various sizes and configurations of housing.

Duplex: residential structure containing two attached dwelling units.

East North Central Region: Illinois, Indiana, Michigan, Ohio, Wisconsin.

East South Central Region: Alabama, Kentucky, Mississippi, Tennessee.

Education: public schools, institutions of higher education, and other educational institutions and services; support of private educational activities; supervision of education; and any other activities and facilities related to education that are administered by school boards, systems, or commissions.[2]

Elderly Housing: housing developed for major or exclusive occupancy by adult households with or without specific age or occupancy restrictions.

Employment Anticipation Method: a method to project the fiscal impact of proposed commercial or industrial development. It utilizes coefficients developed for industrial and commercial uses which show the percentage increase in public costs attributable to commercial or industrial employment changes.

Equalization Ratio: ratio of assessed value to true (market) value of real property.[1]

Equalized Tax Rate: the local tax rate multiplied by a county- or state-recognized ratio of assessed value by the equalization ratio.[1]

Excess Capacity: capacity beyond that needed to accommodate the existing service or target population at current public service levels.

Expenditures: see cost.

Expense Ratio: the relationship of total expenses to gross income, expressed as a decimal.[9]

Financial Administration: office of the finance director, auditor, comptroller, treasurer, and other central accounting, budgeting, and purchasing activities; tax administration; and other finance services not included under other functional headings. Includes tax assessment and collection, custody and disbursements of funds, state supervision of local government finance, debt management, and administration of investment, employee retirement, and other trust funds.[2]

Fire Protection: includes fire fighting organization and auxiliary services, fire charges, support of volunteer fire forces, rescue squads, and related fire protection activities. Includes any identifiable amounts for services rendered by other agencies of the government for the fire protection function, including water and other utility services.[2]

Fiscal Impact Analysis: an evaluation of the net public costs or revenues resulting from actual or planned growth.

Fixed Expenses: may be shown on an actual or accrual basis. Real estate taxes and building insurance.

GARDEN APARTMENT: single structures of more than three housing units of few stories.

GENERAL CONTROL: judicial, legislative, executive, and staff agencies of the government. Includes office of the chief executive, legal activities, recording and general public reporting, overall planning or zoning, central personnel and other staff and executive or administrative services.

JUDICIAL: courts and activities associated with courts (e.g., law libraries, medical and social service activities, juries, etc.). For cities, includes registrar of wills and similar probate functions.

LEGISLATIVE: legislative bodies, research and investigation agencies, and committees responsible to the legislature.

EXECUTIVE: office of the chief executive and central staff services other than financial administration. Includes office of the chief executive, legal activities, recording and general public reporting, overall planning and zoning, central personnel, and other staff executive and administrative services.[2]

GENERAL GOVERNMENT: a collective term for municipal, administrative, executive and tax functions. As used here, it includes financial administration and general control.

GENERAL REVENUE: all revenue of a government except utility revenue, liquor store revenue, and insurance trust revenue. The basis for this distinction is not the fund or administrative unit established to account for and control a particular activity, but rather the nature of the revenue sources involved. Three primary categories of general revenue are recognized in Census reporting—taxes, charges and miscellaneous general revenue, and intergovernmental transfers.[2]

GENERAL TAX RATE: the rate applied to net taxable assessed valuation of a municipality to yield the required tax levy.[1]

GROSS INCOME MULTIPLIER: a figure that, when applied to the annual rent and miscellaneous income of a building, projects its true or market value.

GROSS RENT: the contract rent plus the estimated average monthly cost of utilities (electricity, gas, water) and fuels (oil, coal, kerosene, wood, etc.), if these items are paid for by the renter or by someone else.

HEALTH AND WELFARE: establishment and operation of hospital facilities, provision of hospital care, support of other public or private hospitals, and conservation and improvement of public health.[2]

HIGH-RISE APARTMENT: housing units in structures with seven or more stories, and serviced by an elevator.

HIGHWAYS: expenditure for streets and highways and related structures (including highway garages and highway agency administration buildings), snow and ice removal, and street or highway lighting. Includes street and highway planning and engineering, and related traffic engineering administered by highway or public works agencies. For cities, includes snow and ice removal performed by the city's sanitation or street cleaning agency, when identifiable; and cost of street lighting services furnished by an electric utility operated by the city, when identifiable. (An identical amount is excluded from utility current operation expenditure.)[2]

HOUSEHOLD SIZE: the total number of persons, both related and unrelated, residing in a housing unit.

HOUSING AND URBAN RENEWAL: construction and operation of housing and redevelopment projects and other activities to promote or aid housing and urban renewal. Housing projects include constructing, furnishing, and operating housing projects administered by the city government concerned. Urban renewal projects include land clearance and urban renewal projects administered by the city government concerned.[2]

Housing Units: a house, an apartment, a group of rooms, or a single room occupied or intended for occupancy as separate living quarters.[2]

Housing For The Elderly: see elderly housing.

Income Approach To Value Estimation: estimate of the market value of a property by capitalizing the net income produced from the application of market rates of interest and a rate reflecting the return on investment.

Income Taxes, Corporation Net: on incorporated and unincorporated businesses (when taxed distinctively from individual income), measured by net income. May be called "license" or "franchise" taxes. Includes net income taxes on special kinds of corporations, such as financial institutions.[2]

Income Taxes, Individual: taxes on individuals measured by net income and taxes distinctively imposed on special types of income (e.g., interest, dividends, income from intangibles, etc.).[2]

Insurance Trust Revenue: revenue derived from contributions required of employers and employees for financing of compulsory or voluntary social insurance programs operated by the government, and earnings on assets held for such funds or accounts.[2]

Intergovernmental Transfers: includes grants, shared taxes, and contingent loans and advances for support of particular functions or for general financial support; any significant and identifiable amounts received from other governments as reimbursement for performance of governmental functions; and any other form of revenue representing the sharing by other governments in the financing of activities administered by the receiving government. Intergovernmental transfers exclude amounts received from the sale of property, commodities, and utility services to other governments.[2]

Land-use Regulations: zoning official maps, and sub-division regulations to guide or control land development.[6]

Libraries: includes libraries operated by the government concerned, support of privately operated libraries, and any intergovernmental expenditure for library purposes.[2]

License Taxes: taxes exacted either for revenue raising or for regulation, for a business or nonbusiness privilege, at a flat rate or measured by such bases as capital stock or surplus, number of business units, or capacity.[2]

Line Agency: categorization of a public agency according to its work. Carries out operating programs and deals directly with the public[7] See also Staff Agency.

Liquor Store Revenue: revenue from sale of liquor and related operations of publicly operated liquor stores. Excludes sales and license taxes on alcoholic beverages collected through liquor stores.[2]

Marginal Costing: costs assigned to a growth increment. They represent the sum of all immediate expenditures undertaken by the jurisdiction that otherwise would not have occurred.

Market Analysis: process of determining the characteristics of the market and the measurement of its capacity to buy a commodity.[4]

Market Approach To Value Estimation: estimate of the market value of a property based on a comparative analysis of sales of similar properties.

Mean: the average value.

Median: the value of the middle case.

Metropolitan Areas: a group of whole counties surrounding a major city or twin cities of 50,000 population or more. They were formally termed standard metropolitan statistical areas.[14]

Mid-rise Apartment: residential structure with three or more units, four to six stories, with or without an elevator, offering rental tenure.

MIDDLE ATLANTIC REGION: New Jersey, New York, Pennsylvania.

MILL: a unit of monetary value equal to one-thousand U.S. dollar or one-tenth cent. A fifty mill local tax rate is equivalent to a five dollar tax levy per one-hundred dollars of property valuation.

MOBILE HOMES: mobile homes other than those used only for business or vacation.

MODE: the value of the most frequent case.

MODEL: a theoretical construction designed to represent a situation in the real world.

MORTGAGE: an agreement under which property or land is given as security for repayment of a loan.[3]

MOUNTAIN REGION: Arizona, Colorado, Idaho, Montana, Nevada, New Mexico, Utah, Wyoming.

MUNICIPAL: any governmental unit below or subordinate to the state.[5]

MUNICIPAL FUNCTIONS: expenditures (except for education) necessary to operate the municipality and provide the required public services.[1]

NEIGHBORHOOD SHOPPING CENTER: a shopping complex built around a supermarket as the principal tenant and having a typical gross leasable area of 50,000 square feet.[11]

NET INCOME: the difference between total effective income and total operating expenses, in annual dollars per square foot.[10]

NET INCOME BEFORE RECAPTURE: see net operating income.

NET OPERATING INCOME: the annual net income remaining after deducting all operating expenses, fixed expenses, and reserves for replacement but before deducting financial charges such as recapture or debt service. Net operating income may also be referred to as net income before recapture.[12]

NET RENTABLE AREA: the net rentable area of a multiple tenancy floor, whether above or below grade, is the sum of all rentable areas on that floor. The rentable area of an office on a multiple tenancy floor is computed by measuring to the inside finish of permanent outer building walls, or the glass line if at least fifty percent of the outer building wall is glass, to the office side of corridors and/or other permanent partitions, and to the center of partitions that separate the premises from adjoining rentable areas. No deductions are allowed for columns and projections necessary to the building.[10]

NEW ENGLAND REGION: Connecticut, Maine, Massachusetts, New Hampshire, Rhode Island, Vermont.

NONRESIDENTIAL USE: local use of land for the primary purpose of commercial or industrial facilities.

NORTH CENTRAL REGION: Illinois, Indiana, Iowa, Kansas, Michigan, Minnesota, Missouri, Nebraska, North Dakota, Ohio, South Dakota, Wisconsin.

NORTHEAST REGION: Connecticut, Maine, Massachusetts, New Hampshire, New Jersey, New York, Pennsylvania, Rhode Island, Vermont.

OCCUPATION AND BUSINESS PRIVILEGE TAX: taxes commonly regarded as licenses levied on individuals engaged in particular occupations, on owners of businesses, and on corporations either at a flat amount or at a variable amount such as a percentage of gross receipts.[13]

OPERATING EXPENSES: all out-of-pocket costs involved in providing services to tenants and maintaining the income stream—for example, administration, utilities, payrolls, supplies, and contracted services such as cleaning, etc.[9]

OPERATIONS: direct expenditure for compensation of officers and employees and for supplies, materials, and contractual services, except any amounts for capital outlay.[2]

ORDINANCE: a legislative enactment by a local governing body. Ordinances are issued under authority granted by the state and must comply with state constitutions, charters, and general laws.[7]

OVERAGE CAPACITY: see deficient capacity.

OWN-SOURCE REVENUE: revenue raised either through a municipality's or school district's taxing powers or through locally imposed user charges.

PACIFIC REGION: Alaska, California, Hawaii, Oregon, Washington.

PARCEL: a piece of property entered on the tax map as one unit and carried on the tax rolls for assessment and tax collection purposes as one unit.[1]

PER CAPITA: a means of expressing total municipal expenditures by dividing them by the total user or resident population.

PER CAPITA MULTIPLIER METHOD: a method to project the fiscal impact of a proposed development, annexation, land use alternative, etc. It expresses current average educational and noneducational costs per pupil and per resident, respectively, and subsequently assigns them as impact costs to a growth increment based upon detailed demographic profiles of constituent housing types.

PER CAPITA TAX: small lump sum tax levied on resident adults ages 18 to 65 with exemptions for disabilities (i.e., deafness, blindness, or insanity.)[13]

PER PUPIL: a means of expressing total school district expenditures by dividing them by the total user or student population.

PERSONAL PROPERTY TAX: a tax levied on personal possessions such as automobiles, jewels, silverware, fur coats, pianos, etc.[4]

POLICE PROTECTION: preservation of law and order and traffic safety, whether administered as part of a police department or by a separate agency. Includes regular police services; detention and custody of persons awaiting trial; traffic control and traffic safety activities, including related traffic engineering activities (but not highway planning and engineering); vehicular inspection; and buildings used exclusively for police purposes.[2]

PROPERTY TAXES: taxes conditioned on ownership of property and measured by its value. General property taxes relate to property as a whole, real and personal, tangible or intangible, whether taxed at a single rate or at classified rates.[2]

PROPORTIONAL VALUATION METHOD: a method to project the fiscal impact of proposed commercial or industrial development. It assigns a share of local municipal costs to a nonresidential growth increment according to the increment's percentage share of total local property valuation.

PROTECTIVE INSPECTION AND REGULATION: regulation of private enterprise for the protection of the public and inspection of hazardous activities (except where done incidentally to major functions) such as fire prevention, health, natural resources, etc. Includes building, plumbing, electrical, gas, boiler, elevator, and weights and measures inspection; regulation of financial institutions, public service corporations, insurance companies, and other corporations; regulation of professional occupations (including professional examinations and licensing for health-related occupations); regulation of working conditions; and regulation of sales of alcoholic beverages.[2]

PUBLIC SAFETY: a collective term for municipally-provided, protective services. As used here, it includes police and fire.

PUBLIC SECTOR: the part of the economy that comes within the scope of the government.[3]

PUBLIC USE SAMPLE: one percent sample of housing and demographic characteristics, counties and regions, as reported by the U.S. Census.

PUBLIC UTILITY: an agency created to perform specific functions within a municipal, county, or regional area. Operations are separate and distinct from the local unit, but not autonomous with respect to it.[1]

PUBLIC WELFARE: support of and assistance to needy persons contingent upon their need, including provision and operation of welfare institutions.[2]

PUBLIC WORKS: a collective term for municipal maintenance and repair services. As used here, it includes highway, sewerage, sanitation and water supply.

QUASI-MUNICIPAL: agencies invested by the state with limited corporate character to perform a particular function in a particular locality. Examples are schools, sanitation, irrigation, roads, sewer districts, etc.[5]

RATABLE: a taxable parcel of real property.[1]

REAL ESTATE TRANSFER TAX: a tax on the turnover of real property, usually based on market value and taxed at the rate of one percent of the sales price.[13]

REAL PROPERTY: land and appurtenances and man-made improvements attached to it.[4]

RECREATION AND CULTURE: provision by the city of recreational and cultural-scientific facilities and activities except those operated as part of a school system.[2]

REGIONAL SHOPPING CENTER: a shopping complex built around at least one, and more typically two to four, full-line department stores. The average size is considered to be at least 400,000 square feet of gross leasable area."

RENT: regular periodic payments by a tenant to a landlord for the use of real property.[4]

REPLACEMENT COST APPROACH TO VALUE ESTIMATION: estimate of the market value of a property obtained through an analysis of the cost to replace the structure at the time of assessment.

RESERVES FOR REPLACEMENT: funds to provide for the replacement of short-lived equipment items, such as stoves, refrigerators, washers, driers, air conditioning, and for portions of the building that require periodical replacement funds during the life of the building.[9]

RESIDENTIAL USE: local use of land for the primary purpose of housing accommodations.

REVENUE: all amounts of money received by a government from external sources—excluding refunds and other correcting transactions—other than from issuance of debt, liquidation of investments, and agency and private trust transactions. Excludes any amounts transferred between funds or agencies of the same government.[2]

REVENUE SHARING: see State and Local Fiscal Assistance Act of 1972.

ROOMS: whole rooms used for living purposes, such as living rooms, dining rooms, bedrooms, kitchens, finished attics or basements, recreation rooms, permanently enclosed porches that are suitable for year-round use, and lodger's rooms. Also includes rooms used for offices by a person living in the unit.[2]

SALES AND GROSS RECEIPTS TAXES: taxes (and licenses levied at more than nominal rates) based upon the volume or value of transfers of goods or services, upon gross receipts therefrom, or upon gross income; and related taxes based upon use, storage, production, importation, or consumption of goods.[2]

SANITATION: includes sewerage, street cleaning, and waste collection and disposal activities. Excludes smoke regulation, sanitary engineering, and other sanitary regulation and health purposes. Sewerage includes the provision and maintenance of municipal sewers and sewage disposal facilities, and any intergovernmental payments by local governments for such services. For combined water supply and sewage disposal systems, includes segregable expenditures relating to sewage disposal.[2]

SCHOOL-AGE CHILDREN: all persons aged 5 to 18 residing in the housing unit.

SCHOOL DISTRICT: a governmental unit for the maintenance of schools.[7]

SCHOOL DISTRICT FUNCTIONS: see Education.

SERVICE STANDARD: a given or determined level of manpower expenditure or capital commitment per unit of user demand, typically expressed either areally or demographically.

SERVICE STANDARD METHOD: a method to project the fiscal impact of a proposed development, annexation, land use alternative, etc. It develops average service

Glossary

ratios per 1,000 people for cities of various sizes and locations and assigns these costs to a growth increment according to the number of thousands of people it will introduce locally.

SEWERAGE: *see* Sanitation.

SHOPPING GOODS: goods from variety, department, and general merchandise stores—toys, hobbies, sporting goods, small appliances, household, textile, garden and lawn supplies, luggage and leather, music, books, housewares, children's apparel, candy, radios and televisions, and gasoline.[11]

SINGLE-FAMILY HOUSES: single, detached structures of one unit.

SINGLES DEVELOPMENT: single and multifamily residences of various configurations built for primary occupancy by unmarried, single-person households.

SLACK CAPACITY: *see* excess capacity.

SOCIAL INSURANCE: a form of protection designed primarily to protect against loss of earning power. Old age, unemployment, and disability insurance are forms of social insurance. Benefits are financed by taxation or other form of compulsory contribution based on payrolls.[4]

SOUTH ATLANTIC REGION: Delaware, Florida, Georgia, Maryland, North Carolina, South Carolina, Virginia, West Virginia.

SOUTHERN REGION: Alabama, Arkansas, Delaware, Florida, Georgia, Kentucky, Louisiana, Maryland, Mississippi, North Carolina, Oklahoma, South Carolina, Tennessee, Texas, Virginia, West Virginia.

SPECIAL ASSESSMENT: a charge made by a government against a property owner for that part of the cost and public improvements made adjacent to his property that is especially useful or beneficial to his property.[7]

SPECIAL DISTRICTS: independent governmental corporations created within a local municipal unit to provide definite functions, and having power to tax, impose service charges, and incur debt. About half of the special districts in the United States are for fire protection, soil conservation, and drainage.

SPECIALIZED HOUSING TYPE: shelter configuration that, because of numerical representation in the overall housing stock of occupancy characteristics, the U.S. Census does not report on regularly. This handbook includes vacation homes, condominiums, and housing for singles or the elderly.

STAFF AGENCY: categorization of a public agency according to its work. Serves in an advisory capacity, assisting the chief executive and line officials through such activities as planning, coordinating, and budgeting.[7] *See also* Line Agency.

STANDARD HOUSING TYPE: shelter configuration of sufficent number and national distribution to be reported on regularly by the U.S. Census. This handbook includes single-family houses, garden apartments, high-rise apartments, town houses, and mobile homes.

STATE AID: revenues received from the state under various programs authorized by the state legislature. Includes state road aid, highway lighting, building allowances for schools, etc.[1]

STATE AND LOCAL FISCAL ASSISTANCE ACT OF 1972 (Revenue Sharing): funds received by units of local government from the federal government that may be used only for priority expenditures, maintenance, and operating expenses for (1) public safety, environmental protection, public transportation, health, recreation, libraries, social services for the poor and aged, and financial administration; or (2) ordinary and necessary capital expenditures authorized by law.[1]

STATUTORY: rules that have been formulated into law by legislative action.

TAXES: compulsory contributions exacted by a government for public purposes.[2]

TAX EXEMPTION: the privilege granted by a government that legally frees certain types of properties, sales, or incomes from general obligations to pay taxes.

TAX RATE: a percentage applied to all taxable property to raise general revenues. It is derived by dividing the total tax levy by the taxable net property valuation.

TENURE: the classification of occupants of a housing unit. A housing unit is owner occupied if the owner or co-owner lives in the unit, even if it is mortgaged or not fully paid for. A cooperative or condominium is owner occupied only if the owner or co-owner lives in it. All other occupied units are classified as renter occupied, including units rented for cash rent and those occupied without payment of cash rent.[2]

TOTAL OPERATING EXPENSES: expenses for shopping centers, including maintenance of the building, parking lot, mall, and other common areas; central utility systems; office area services; advertising and promotion; real estate taxes; insurance; and general administration.[11]

TOTAL OPERATING INCOME: gross annual dollars per square foot received for occupied space. Includes income from offices, stores, storage areas, and special areas.[10]

TOTAL OPERATING RECEIPTS: the total income received by the owner of the shopping center (all the money received from rentals, common area charges, and other income).[11]

TOWN HOUSE: attached residential structure of one unit.

URBAN AREAS: comprise incorporated localities with populations of 2,500 or more; residents of densely settled suburban areas surrounding major cities; towns and townships in New Jersey, Pennsylvania and New England with populations of 25,000 persons or more, or with population densities in excess of 1,500 persons per square mile; and counties in other areas with population densities of 1,500 persons per square mile or more.[14]

UTILITY REVENUE: amount received from the sale of utility commodities or services to the public or to other governments. Includes receipts from sales of commodities and services, rentals from operating property, customers' forfeitures and penalties, and charges received for installing and servicing connections and meters.[2]

WESTERN REGION: Alaska, Arizona, California, Colorado, Hawaii, Idaho, Montana, Nevada, New Mexico, Oregon, Utah, Washington, Wyoming.

WEST SOUTH CENTRAL REGION: Arkansas, Louisiana, Oklahoma, Texas.

ZONING: the partitioning of land parcels in a community by ordinance into zones and the establishment of regulations in the ordinance to govern the land use and the location, height, use, and land coverages of buildings within each zone. The zoning ordinance usually consists of text and a zoning map. The districts or zones shown on the zoning map are usually identified as to the permitted type of land use.[6]

SOURCE OF DEFINITIONS

1. State of New Jersey, Department of Community Affairs, *Thirty-Eighth Annual Report of the Division of Local Government Services* (Trenton, New Jersey: Division of Local Government Services, 1975).
2. U.S. Department of Commerce, *Classification Manual, Governmental Finances* (Washington, D.C.: Government Printing Office, 1972).
3. Davis, William, *The Language of Money* (Boston: Houghton-Mifflin Company, 1973).
4. *The Prentice Hall Encyclopedic Dictionary of Business Finance* (Englewood Cliffs, New Jersey; Prentice Hall, 1960).
5. Moak, Lennox L., *Administration of Local Government Debt* (Chicago; Municipal Finance Officers Association, 1970).
6. J. Robert Dumouchel, *Dictionary of Development Terminology* (New York: McGraw Hill, 1975).
7. Plano, Jack, C., and Milton Greenberg, *The American Political Dictionary* (New York: Holt, Rinehart and Winston, 1973).
8. Aronson, J. Richard, and Eli Schwartz, *Management Policies in Local Government Finance* (Chicago; International City Managers Association, 1975).
9. American Institute of Real Estate Appraisers, *The Appraisal of Real Estate* (Cambridge, MA.; Ballinger Publishing Co., 1973).
10. Building Owners and Managers Association International, *1975 Office Building Experience Exchange Report,* (Chicago, Ill: B.O.M.A.I., 1975).
11. Urban Land Institute, *Dollars and Cents of Shopping Centers* (Washington, D.C.: ULI, 1975).
12. American Institute of Real Estate Appraisers, *Capitalization Theory and Techniques* (Cambridge, MA.: Ballinger Publishing Co., 1973).
13. International City Managers Association, *Management Policies in Local Government Finance* (Washington, D.C.: ICMA, 1975).
14. U.S. Department of Commerce, Office of Economic Affairs, U.S. Census Bureau, *Dictionary of Social and Economic Terms* (Washington, D.C.: Government Printing Office, 1972)

Bibliography

BOOKS

Appelbaum, Richard P. et al. *The Effects of Urban Growth: A Population Impact Analysis.* New York, Praeger, 1976.

Awerbuch, Shimon, and Wallace, William A. *Policy Evaluation for Community Development: Decision Tools for Local Government.* New York, Praeger Publishers, Inc., 1976.

Bahl, Roy W. *Metropolitan City Expenditures: A Comparative Analysis.* Lexington, University of Kentucky Press, 1969.

Bahl, Roy W.; Campbell, Alan; and Greytak, David. *Taxes, Expenditure and the Economic Base: A Case Study of New York City.* New York, Praeger, 1974.

Baumol, William, J. *Public Expenditure Decisions in the Urban Community.* Baltimore, Johns Hopkins Press, 1962.

Beaton, W. Patrick, ed. *Municipal Needs, Services and Financing: Readings on Municipal Expenditures.* New Brunswick, Center for Urban Policy Research, 1974.

Beeman, William Joseph. *The Property Tax and the Spatial Pattern of Growth Within Urban Areas.* Washington, D.C., Urban Land Institute, 1969.

Benson, S. Charles and Long, Peter B. *Neighborhood Distribution of Local Public Services.* Berkeley, California, Institute of Governmental Studies, University of California, 1969.

Breese, Gerald, et al. *The Impact of Large Installations on Nearby Areas – Accelerated Urban Growth.* Beverly Hills, Sage Publications, 1965.

Brownrigg, Mark, *A Study of Economic Impact: The University of Stirling.* New York, Halsted Press, 1974.

Buchanan, James, ed. *Public Finance: Needs, Sources and Utilization.* Princeton, N.J. Princeton University Press, 1961.

Burchell, Robert W. and Hughes, James W. *Planned Unit Development – New Communities American Style.* New Brunswick, New Jersey, Rutgers University, 1972.

Burkhead, James & Mines, J. *Public Expenditure.* New York, Aldine—Atherton, 1971.

Campbell, Alan K. and Sachs, Seymour. *Metropolitan America: Fiscal Patterns and Governmental Systems.* New York, The Free Press' 1967.

Catanese, Anthony, J. *Scientific Methods of Urban Analysis.* Chicago, Illinois, University of Illinois Press, 1972.

The Center for Auto Safety. *Mobile Homes; the Low-Cost Housing Hoax.* New York, Grossman Publishers, 1975.

Cerf, Allen. *Real Estate and Federal Tax.* Englewood Cliffs, NJ, Prentice Hall, 1965.

Chapin, F. Stuart, Jr. *Cost-Revenue Studies in Urban Land Use Planning.* 2nd edition Urbana, Illinois, University of Illinois Press, 1972.

Chapin, F. Stuart and Weiss, Shirley. ed. *Urban Growth Dynamics in a Regional Cluster of Cities.* New York, John Wiley and Sons, Inc., 1962.

Chase, Samuel B, Jr. *Problems in Public Expenditure Analysis.* Washington, The Brookings Institution, 1968.

Chinitz, Benjamin. *City and Suburb: The Economics of Metropolitan Growth.* Englewood Cliffs, NJ, Prentice-Hall, 1964.

Clawson, Marion. *Suburban Land Conversion in the United States.* Baltimore, Md., Johns Hopkins Press, 1972.

Cohn, Elchanan. *Public Expenditure Analysis with Special Reference to Human Resources.* Lexington, Massachusetts, Lexington Books, 1972.

Coughlin, Robert E. and Isard, Walter. *Municipal Costs and Revenues from Community Growth.* Wellesley, Chandler-Davis Publishing Co., 1957.

Council of State Governments. *Land: State Alternatives for Planning and Management.* Lexington, Ky., Council of State Governments, 1975.

Crecine, John P. *Governmental Problem-Solving: A Computer Simulation of Municipal Budgeting.* Skokie, Illinois, Rand McNally, 1969.

Dearden, John. *Cost and Benefit Analysis.* Englewood Cliffs, NJ, Prentice-Hall, 1962.

DeChiara, Joseph, and Koppelman, Lee. *Manual of Housing, Planning and Design Criteria.* Englewood Cliffs, N.J., Prentice-Hall, 1975.

Dorfman, Robert *Measuring Benefits of Government Investments.* Washington, D. C., Brookings Institution, 1965.

Downing, Paul B. *The Economics of Urban Sewage Disposal.* New York, Praeger, 1969.

Ecker-Racz, L. Laszlo. *The Politics and Economics of State-Local Finance.* Englewood Cliffs, N.J., Prentice-Hall, 1970.

Fabricant, Solomon. *The Trend of Government Activity in the United States since 1900.* New York, National Bureau of Economic Research, 1952.

Fisher, Benjamin H. *Evaluation of Alternative Plans for New Communities: Toward Application of the Competition for Benefits Model.* Chapel Hill, N.C., Center for Urban and Regional Studies, University of North Carolina, 1971.

Fowler, Floyd J. *Citizens Attitudes Toward Local Government Services and Taxes.* Cambridge, Massachusetts, Ballinger Publishing Co., 1974.

Gibson, N.L., Jr., Hildreth, R.J. and Wunderlich, Gene. *Methods for Land Economics Research.* Lincoln, Nebraska, University of Nebraska Press, 1966.

Goldman, George. *Explanations and Application of County Input-Output Models.* Berkeley, California, Cooperative Extension, University of California, March 1974.

Goldman, Thomas A. *Cost-Effectiveness Analysis: New Approaches in Decision-Making.* New York, Praeger, 1967.

Green, Kenneth V., Neenan, William B., and Scott, Claudia D. *Fiscal Interaction in a Metropolitan Area.* Washington, D.C., The Urban Institute, 1974.

Hardenbergh, W.A. and Rodie, Edward B. *Water Supply and Waste Disposal.* Scranton, Pennsylvania, International Textbook Company, 1960.

Harris, Curtis C., Jr. *Regional Economic Effects of Alternative Highway Systems.* Cambridge, Massachusetts, Ballinger Publishing Co., 1974.

Haveman, Robert H. et al. *Benefit-Cost and Policy Analysis: 1973.* Chicago, Aldine, 1974.

Haveman, Robert H. *The Economic Performance of Public Investments: An Expost Evaluation of Water Resources Investments.* Baltimore, Md., John Hopkins Press, 1972.

Haveman, Robert H. and Margolis, Julius, eds. *Public Expenditures and Policy Analysis.* Chicago, Markham, 1970.

Helliwell, John F. *Public Policies and Private Investment.* Oxford, Clarendon Press, 1968.

Hicks, Ursula K. *Development Finance; Planning and Control.* New York, Oxford University Press, 1965.

Hirsch, Werner Zvi. *The Economics of State and Local Government.* New York, McGraw-Hill, 1970.

Hirsch, Werner Z., *Urban Economic Analysis.* New York, McGraw-Hill, 1973.

Isaacs, Herbert H. & Tyre, Robert D. *A Municipal Services Cost Model.* Los Angeles, Calif. March, 1973.

Isard, Walter, et al. *Ecologic-Economic Analysis for Regional Development.* New York, The Free Press, 1972.

Isard, Walter, et al. *Methods of Regional Analysis.* Baltimore, Johns Hopkins Press, 1965.

Isard, Walter & Coughlin, Robert. *Municipal Costs and Revenues Resulting From Community Growth.* Wellesley, Massachusetts, Chandler-Davis, 1957.

Jump, Bernard. *The Cost of Providing Retirement and Social Security Benefits to New York City Employees: Trends, Causes, and Prospects, 1961–1972.* Syracuse, N.Y., Syracuse University Research Corp., 1973.

Lindholm, Richard W. *Property Taxation and the Finance of Education.* Madison, Wisc., University of Wisconsin Press, 1974.

Mace, Ruth L. *Costing Urban Development and Redevelopment: Selected Readings on Costs, Revenues, Cost-Benefit and Cost-Revenue Analysis in Relation to Land Use.* Chapel Hill, North Carolina, University of North Carolina, Institute of Government, 1964.

Mace, Ruth L. *Municipal Cost-Revenue Research in the United States.* Chapel Hill, University of North Carolina, 1961.

Marglin, Stephen A. *Public Investment Criteria: Benefit-Cost Analysis for Planned Economic Growth.* Cambridge, MIT Press, 1967.

Margolis, Julius. *Land Use Related to Selected Fiscal Issues.* Berkeley, California, University of California, Bureau of Business and Economic Research, 1957.

Miner, Jerry. *Social and Economic Factors in Spending for Public Education.* Syracuse, New York, Syracuse University Press, 1963.

Mishan, Exra J. *Cost-Revenue Analysis: An Introduction.* New York, Praeger, 1971.

Mishan, Ezra J. *The Costs of Economic Growth.* New York, Praeger, 1967.

Mitchell, William E. and Ingo, Walter. *State and Local Finance.* New York, The Ronald Press Company, 1970.

Musgrave, Richard A., and Musgrave, Peggy B. *Public Finance in Theory and Practice,* San Francisco McGraw-Hill Book, 1973.

Mushkin, Selma. *Public Prices for Public Products.* Washington, D.C., Urban Institute, 1972.

Netzer, Dick. *Economics and Urban Problems-Diagnoses and Prescriptions.* New York, Basic Books, Inc., 1970.

Neutze, Graeme Max. *The Suburban Apartment Boom: Case Study of a Land Use Problem.* Baltimore, Md., John Hopkins Press, For Resources of the Future, Washington, D.C., 1968.

Oberman, Joseph. *Planning and Managing the Economy of the City.* New York, Praeger Publishers, 1972.

Rubinowitz, Leonard S. *Low Income Housing: Suburban Strategies.* Cambridge, Mass., Ballinger Publishing Co., 1974.

Scott, Stanley & Feder, Edward L. *Factors Associated with Variation in Municipal Expenditure Levels: A Statistical Study of California Cities.* Berkeley, University of California Press, 1957.

Seiler, Karl. *Introduction to Systems Cost-Effectiveness.* New York, Wiley-Interscience, 1969.

Sewell, W.R.D. et al. *Guide to Benefit-Cost Analysis.* Ottawa, Roger Duhamel F.R.G.C. (RFF), 1962.

Sharkansky, Ira. *Policy Analysis in Political Science.* Chicago, Illinois, Markham, 1970.

Sharkansky, Ira. *The Politics of Taxing and Spending.* Indianapolis, Indiana, Bobbs-Merrill, 1969.

Sternlieb, George. et al. *Housing Development and Municipal Costs.* New Brunswick, N.J., Rutgers University, Center for Urban Policy Research, 1972.

Stone, P.A. *The Structure, Size and Costs of Urban Settlements,* New York, Cambridge University Press, 1973.

Wendt, Paul, and Cerf, Alan. *Real Estate Investment Analysis and Taxation.* New York, McGraw-Hill, 1969.

Wheaton, William L., and Schussheim, Morton J. *The Cost of Municipal Services in Residential Areas.* Washington, D.C., Government Printing Office, 1955.

ARTICLES

Acharya, S. N. "Public Enterprise Pricing and Social Benefit-Cost Analysis". *Oxford Economic Papers* 24, 1972, 36-53.

Ahlbrandt, Roger S., Jr. "Implications of Contracting for a Public Service". *Urban Affairs Quarterly* 9, 1974, 337-358.

Akin, John S. and Aufch, Gerald E. "City School and Suburban Schools: A Fiscal Comparison". *Land Economics* 52, 1976, 452-66.

Albin, S. Peter "Distributional Effects of State and Local Finance - A Skeptical View". *Land Economics* 48, 1972, 86-87.

American Society of Planning Officials. "School Enrollment by Housing Type". *Planning Advisory Services Information Report* 210, 1966.

American Society of Planning Officials and the International City Managers Association. "Apartments in the Suburbs". *Planning Advisory Report* 187, 1964.

Anderson, A. C. "The Effect of Rapid Transit on Property Values". *Appraisal Journal* 38, 1970, 59-68.

Anderson, Marshall L. "Community Improvements and Services Costs". *Journal of the Urban Planning and Development Division of the American Society of Civil Engineers* 99, 1973, 77-92.

Andrews, Richard B. and Dasso, Jerome J. "The Influence of Annexation on Property Tax Burdens" *National Tax Journal* 14, 1961, 88-97.

Bibliography

Aronson, J. Richard and Schwartz, Eli. "Forecasting Future Expenditures". *Management Information Service* 2, No. S-7, July 1970.

Ashley, Thomas J. "Cost Revenue Analysis of New Housing Development in the City of San Diego". In *Growth Cost-Revenue Studies,* William T. Leonard, Berkeley, California, Associated Home-Builders of the Greater Eastbay, Inc., 1972.

Bahl, Roy W. and Jump, Bernard. "The Budgetary Implications of Rising Employee Retirements System Costs". *National Tax Journal* 27, 1974, 479-90.

Bahl, Roy W., Jr. and Saunders, Robert J. "Determinants of Changes in State and Local Government Expenditures". *National Tax Journal* 18, 1965, 50-57.

Bahl, Roy W. "Studies on Determinants of Public Expenditures: A Review". In Selma J. Mushkin and John Cotton, *Functional Federalism: Grants-in-Aid and PPB Systems,* Washington, D.C., George Washington University, 1968.

Banks, F. E. "A Note on Fiscal Policy Models and Economic Development". *Public Finance* 29, 1974, 225-30.

Barnes, Ralph M., and Raymond, George M. "The Fiscal Approach to Land Use Planning". *Journal of the American Institute of Planners* 21, 1955, 71-75.

Barr, James L., and Davis, Otto A. "An Elementary Political and Economic Theory of the Expenditures of Local Government". *Southern Economic Journal* 33, 1966, 149-165.

Batchelor, Thomas R., Jr. "Albemarle County/Measuring the Cost of Growth". *Public Management* 56, 1974, 30-31.

Baumol, William J. "Macroeconomies of Unbalanced Growth: The Anatomy of Urban Crisis". *American Economic Review* 57, pt. 2, 1967, 415-26.

Baumol, William J. "Urban Services: Interactions of Public and Private Decisions". *Public Expenditure Decisions in the Urban Community,* Howard G. Schaller, ed. Baltimore, Md, Johns Hopkins Press, 1963.

Beaton, W. Patrick. "The Determinants of Police Protection Expenditures". *National Tax Journal* 27, 1974, 335-49.

Beaton, W. Patrick "The Municipal Cost Revenue Implications of Proposed New Business Activity: Method and Analysis". *Land Economics* (pending).

Bergson, A. "Optimal Pricing for Public Enterprise". *Quarterly Journal of Economics* 86, 1972, 519-44.

Bergstrom, T.O., and Goodman, R.P. "Private Demands for Public Goods". *The American Economic Review* 63, 1973, 280-296.

Berolzheimer, Joseph. "Influences Shaping Expenditures for Operation of State and Local Government". *Bulletin of the National Tax Association* 32, 1947.

Berry, Brian J. L. and Bednarz, Robert S. "A Hedonic Model of Prices and Assessments for Single-Family Homes: Does the Assessor Follow the Market or the Market Follow the Assessor?". *Land Economics* 51, 1975, 21-40.

Birdsall, William C. "A Study of the Demand for Public Goods". In *Essays in Fiscal Federalism,* Richard A. Musgrove, ed. Washington, The Brookings Institution, 1965.

Bishop, George A. "Stimulative Versus Substitutive Effects of State School Aid in New England". *National Tax Journal* 17, 1964, 133-43.

Blomquist, G. "The Effect of Electric Utility Power Plant Location on Area Property Value". *Land Economics* 50, 1974, 97-100.

Bloom, Max Robert. "Fiscal Productivity and the Theory of Urban Renewal". *Papers and Proceedings of the American Economic Association,* 1967.

Bloom, Max Robert. "Fiscal Productivity and the Pure Theory of Urban Renewal". *Land Economics* 38, 1962, 134-144.

Booms, Bernard H. "City Governmental Form and Public Expenditure Levels". *National Tax Journal* 19, 1966, 187-99.

Booms, Bernard H. and Hu, T. "Toward a Positive Theory of State and Local Public Expenditures: An Empirical Example". *Public Finance* 26, 1971, 419-36.

Borcherding, Thomas E. and Deacon, Robert T. "The Demand for the Services of Non-Federal Governments". *The American Economic Review* 62, 1972, 891-901.

Bottum, J. S. "Non-Local Funding of Rural Public Services". *American Journal Agricultural Economics* 56, 1974, 953-58.

Bowman, John H. "Tax Exportability, Intergovernmental Aid and School Finance Reform". *National Tax Journal* 27, 1974, 163-173.

Bradford, D. F.; Malt, R. A; and Oates, W. E. "The Rising Costs of Local Public Services". *National Tax Journal* 22, 1969, 185-202.

Brazell, E. C. "Comparative Costs for Open Space Communities: Rancho Bernardo Case Study". *Land-Use Controls* 1, 1967, 35-40.

Brazer, Harvey E. "The Role of Major Metropolitan Centers in State and Local Finance". *American Economic Review* 48, 1958, 305-316.

Breck, G. "The Incidence and Economic Effects of Taxation". In Washington, D.C., [A.S. Binder, et al.,] *The Economics of Public Finance,* The Brookings Institution, 1974.

Brigham, Eugene F. "The Determinants of Residential Land Values". *Land Economics* 41, 1965, 325-334.

Buchanan, James M. "Principles of Urban Fiscal Strategy". *Public Choice* 11, 1971, 1-16.

Buchanan, James and Stubblebine, W. Craig. "Externality". *Economica* n.s. 29, 1962, 371-384.

Buchanan, James M. and Tullock, G. "Polluters' Profits and Political Response: Direct Control Versus Taxes". *American Economic Review* 65, 1975, 139-47.

Burchell, Robert W. and Hughes, James W. "Financial Aspects of PUDs". *The Appraisal Journal* 42, 1974, 372-390.

Burkhead, Jessie. "Metropolitan Area Budget Structures and Their Significance for Expenditures". *Proceedings of the National Tax Association: 1959.* Harrisburg, 1960.

Campbell, Alan K. and Meranto, Philip J. "The Metropolitan Education Dilemma: Matching Resources to Needs". *Urban Affairs Quarterly* 2, 1966, 42-63.

Cardwell, Rosson L. "How to Measure Metropolitan Bed Needs". *Modern Hospital* 103, 1964, 107-112.

"The Case for Mobile Homes". *Housing Ontario* April/May 1975, 8-9.

Carroll, S.J. "School District Expenditure Behaviors". *Journal of Human Resources* 11, 1976, 317-27.

Chamberlain, Gary M. "Local Revenues vs. Land Uses". *American City* May 1974.

Chambers, John W. "Do Single Family Homes Pay Their Way?: Summary and Comment" In *Growth Cost-Revenue Studies,* William T. Leonard, Berkeley, California, Associated Home Builders of the Greater Eastbay, Inc., 1972.

Chapin, F. Stuart, Jr. "A Model for Simulating Residential Development". *Journal of the American Institute of Planners* 31, 1965, 120-125.

Chinitz, Benjamin. "The Effect of Transporation Forms on Regional Economic Growth". *Traffic Quarterly* 14, 1960.

Cho, Yong Hyo. "Fiscal Implications of Annexation: The Case of Metropolitan Central Cities in Texas". *Land Economics* 45, 1969, 368-72.

Clark, Douglas. "Urban Renewal & Municipal Taxation". *Canadian Tax Journal* 10, November-December 1962.

Clark, T. N. "Community Structure, Decision-Making, Budget Expenditures, and Urban Renewal in 51 American Communities". *American Sociological Review* 33, August 1968, 576-593.

Clark, William H. "Apartments and Local Taxes: Are Apartment Projects Really Good Ratables?". *New Jersey Municipalities*, October and November, 1963.

Clark, William H. "An Area of Need for Cost-Revenue Studies". *Municipal Finance* 36, 1964, 130-135.

Cochrane, Robert A. & Womble, Joseph E. "Technical Report: Discounted Cash Flow Analysis and Plan Evaluation – (Cost Effectiveness Analysis)". *Journal of the American Institute of Planners* 37, 1971, 338-343.

Cohen, R.; Awerbuch, S.; and Wallace, W. A. "A Test of an Interactive Community Development Impacts Model in a Rural Environment". *Interfaces* 7, 1976, 51-62.

Crecine, John P. "A Computer Simulation Model of Municipal Budgeting". *Management Science* 12, 1967, 786-815.

Crecine, J. P. "Empirical Evidence of Political Influences Upon the Expenditure Policies of Public Schools". In *The Public Economy of Urban Communities* Julius Margolis, ed. Washington, D.C., Resources for the Future, 1964.

Crouch, R. L. and Weintraub, R. E. "Cost-Benefit Analysis of a PUD". *Urban Land* 32, June 19 3-13.

Czamanski, S. "Effects of Public Investment on Urban Land Values". *Journal of the American Institute of Planners* 32, 1966, 204-217.

Darting, A. H. "Measuring Benefits Generated by Urban Water Parks". *Land Economics* 49, 1973, 22-34.

David, Elizabeth Likert. "Public Preferences and State-Local Taxes". In *Essays in State and Local Finance,* Ann Arbor, Michigan, University of Michigan Institute of Public Administration, 1967.

David, Irwin T. "Slow to Evaluate Revenue Sources". *Municipal South* 23, March/April 1976, 10-13.

Davis, Otto A. "Empirical Evidence of Political Influence Upon the Expenditure Policies of Public Schools". In *The Public Economy of Urban Communities,* Julius Margolis, ed. Washington D.C., Johns Hopkins Press; 1965, 92-111.

Davis, Otto A. and Haines, George H., Jr. "A Political Approach to a Theory of Public Expenditure: The Case of Municipalities". In *Readings in State and Local Finance,* William E. Mitchell and Ingo Walter, eds. New York, Ronald Press, 1970.

Del Guidice, Dominic. "Cost-Revenue Implications of High Rise Apartments". *Urban Land* 22, 1963, 1, 3-5.

Dickinson, Thomas E. & Blackmarr, James R. "Evaluation of Private and Public Economic Impacts Caused by Developments". In *Evaluation of Social Impacts,* James McEvoy, ed. New York, Wiley, 1975.

Dienstfrey, T. "A Note on the Economics of Community Building". *Journal of the American Institute of Planners* 32, 1967, 120-123.

Downing, Donald. "Sewer, Water and Urban Growth Policies". *Ekistics* 43(254), 1977, 27-30.

Downing, Paul B. "Extension of Sewer Service at the Urban-Rural Fringe". *Land Economics* 45, 1969, 103-111.

Ducker, Richard D. "Louden County's Pay-as-you-Grow Plan". *Land Use Law and Zoning Digest* 26(1), 1974.

Eckstein, Otto. "A Survey of the Theory of Public Expenditure Criteria". IN *Public Finances: Needs, Sources, Utilization,* Princeton, Princeton University Press, 1961.

Eddleman, B. R. "Financing Public Services in Rural Areas: A Synthesis" *American Journal of Agricultural Economics* 56, 1974, 959-63.

Einham, David. "Trends in Local Governmental Revenues: the Impact of General Revenue Sharing". *HUD Challenge* November 1974, 20.

Einsweiler, Robert C. and Smith, Julius C. "New Town Locates in a Municipality: Jonathan Saves Money and Chaska Increases Tax Base". *Planners Notebook* 1, June-July 1971, 3-4.

Eisen, Albert. "Condo Conversion – From Feasibility to Completion". *Journal of Property Management* 39, 1974, 217-222.

Elias, C. E., Jr. "Land Development and Local Public Finance". IN *Essays in Urban Land Economics,* Los Angeles, University of California, Real Estate Research Program, 1966.

Ellickson, Robert C. "Suburban Growth Controls: An Economic and Legal Analysis". *The Yale Law Journal* 86, 1977, 385-511.

Esser, George H., Jr. "Urban Growth and Municipal Services. I: Municipal Service Patterns; II: Cost and Revenues". *Popular Government* 23, October 1956, 3-8; 23, November 1956, 5-12.

Etzold, David J. "Benefit-Cost Analysis: An Integral Part of Environmental Decisioning". *Journal of Environmental Systems* Fall 1973, 253-256.

Feinberg, Mordecai S. "The Implications of Core-City Decline for the Fiscal Structure of the Core-City". *National Tax Journal* 17, 1964, 213-31.

"Figures Show How Apartments Benefit City". *Homebuilding Magazine* April 1970.

Finney, G. S. "The Intergovernmental Context of Local Planning". IN *Principles and Practice of Urban Planning,* W.I. Goodman and E.C. Freud, ed., Washington, D.C., International City Manager's Association, 1968.

Fisher, Glenn. "Determinants of Public Education Expenditures". *National Tax Journal* 13, 1960, 29-40.

Fisher, Glenn. "Determinants of State and Local Government Expenditures: A Preliminary Analysis". *National Tax Journal* 14, 1961, 349-355.

Fisher, Glenn. "Expenditure Implications of Metropolitan Growth and Consolidation". *Review of Economics and Statistics* 41, 1959, 232-241.

Fisher, Glenn. "Fiscal Impact of Industrialization on Schools". *Review of Economics and Statistics* 46, 1964, 198-208.

Fisher, Glenn. "Interstate Variation in State and Local Government Expenditures". *National Tax Journal* 17, 1964, 57-74.

Fishkind, Henry; Milliman, Jerome; and Ellson, Richard. "'Alachua County Econometric Study: A Methodology for Assessing the Impacts of Growth and Development on Local Economies". *Land Economics,* in press.

Fitch, Lyle C. "Planning and Property Tax". *Jersey Plans.* January and February, 1960.

Fuerst, J. S. and Ditton, Andrew. "Reducing Property Taxes: An Evaluation of a Collective Action". *Land Economics* 51, 1975, 94-97.

Gabler, L. R. "Economies and Diseconomies of Scale in Urban Public Sectors". *Land Economics* 45, 1969, 425-434.

Gabler, L. R. "Population Size as a Determinant of City Expenditures and Employment – Some Further Evidence". *Land Economics* 47, 1971, 130-138.

Gale, Dennis E. "The Municipal Impact Evaluation System". *Planning Advisory Service Report* 297, September 1973, (entire issue).

Gappert, Gary. "The Future of Economic Inequality and the Planning of Urban Services". *Journal of the American Institute of Planners* 39, 1973, 188-202.

Garrison, Charles B. "New Industry in Small Towns: The Impact on Local Government". *National Tax Journal* 24, 1971, 493-500.

Glendening Parris N. "Municipal Finances: Charge and Continuity". *Urban Data Service Reports* 6, December 1974. (entire issue).

Goldman, George H. "Are Mobile Home Parks a Good Investment?" *Journal of Property Management* 38, 1973, 262-266.

Granfield, Michael. "Residential Location: A Comparative Econometric Analysis". *Applied Economics* 6, 1974, 95-108.

Grasberger, Freidrich H. "UDC Housing: Effects on School Taxes". *Overview* (Monroe County Planning Council) September 1972.

Graybeal, Ronald S. "Condominium Computerized Feasibility Analysis". *Appraisal Journal* 41, 1973, 526-533.

Greene, Kenneth V. "Collective Decision Making Models and the Measurement of Benefits in Fiscal Incidence Studies". *National Tax Journal* 26, 1973, 177-88.

Greytak, David; Gustely, Richard and Dinlekmeyer, Robert J. "The Effects of Inflation on Local Government Expenditures". *National Tax Journal* 27, 1974, 583-98.

Grossman, Howard J. "Cost-Revenue Statistics Can Help Get Apartment Approval". *Apartment Construction News* 1967.

Groves, Harold M. and Riew, John. "The Impact of Industry on Local Taxes - A Simple Model". *National Tax Journal* 16, 1963, 137-146.

Grubb, W. N. "The Distribution of Costs and Benefits in an Urban Public School System". *National Tax Journal* 24, 1971, 1-12.

Guldburg, Peter H. "Secondary Impacts of Major Land Use Projects". *Journal of the American Institute of Planners* 43, 1977, 260-70.

Gustely, R.D. "Local Taxes, Expenditures and Urban Housing: A Reassessment of the Evidence". *Southern Economic Journal* 42, 1976, 659-65.

Hambor, John C., et al. "A Tax Revenue Forecasting Model for the State of Hawaii". *Public Finance Quarterly* 2, 1974, 432-450.

Hanke, Steve H. "Pricing Urban Water". IN *Public Prices for Public Products,* Mushkin, Selma, ed., Washington, The Urban Institute, 1972.

Harvey, Robert O. and Clark, W.A.V. "The Nature and Economics of Urban Sprawl". *Land Economics* 41, 1965, 1-9.

Haskell, Mark A. and Leshinski, Stephen. "Fiscal Influences on Residential Choice: A Study of the New York Region". *Quarterly Review of Economics and Business* 9, 1969, 47-56.

Hawley, Amos H. "Metropolitan Population and Municipal Government Expenditures in Central Cities". *Journal of Social Issues* 7, 1951, 100-108.

Hawley, Amos H. "Metropolitan Population and Municipal Government Expenditures in Central Cities". In *Cities and Society,* Paul K. Hatt and Albert J. Reiss, eds. New York, The Free Press, 1957.

Hellman, Daryl. "External Impacts of Housing Developments". *Urban Land* 33, 1974, 25-28.

Hepworth, N.P. "Local Government and the Economic Situation". *National Westminster Bank Quarterly Review,* February 1976, 7-18.

Hirsch, Werner Zvi. "Cost Functions of an Urban Government Service: Refuse Collection". *Review of Economics and Statistics* 47, 1965, 87-92.

Hirsch, Werner Zvi. "Determinants of Public Education Expenditures." *National Tax Journal* 13, 1960, 29-40.

Hirsch, Werner Zvi. "Expenditure Implication of Metropolitan Growth and Consolidation." *Review of Economics and Statistics* 41, 1959, 232-41.

Hirsch, Werner Zvi. "Fiscal Impact of Industrialization on Local Schools". *Review of Economics and Statistics* 46, 1964, 191-199.

Hirsch, Werner Zvi. "The Supply of Urban Public Services". IN *Issues in Urban Economics,* Perloff and Wingo, eds. Baltimore, Maryland, Johns Hopkins Press, 1968, 477-525.

Holtmann, A.G. Taba S2, T. and Kruse, W. "The Demand for Local Public Services, Spillovers, and Urban Decay; the Case of Public Libraries". *Public Finance Quarterly* 4, 1976, 97-113.

Horowitz, Julian. "Municipal Fiscal Structure in a Metropolitan Region". *Southern Economics Journal,* June 1972.

Hu, Teh-wei and Booms, Bernard H. "A Simultaneous Equation Model of Public Expenditure Decisions in Large Cities". *The Annals of Regional Science* 5, 1971, 73-85.

Hudson, Barclay M.; Wachs, Martin, and Schofer, J.L. "Local Impact Evaluation in the Design of Large Scale Urban Systems". *Journal of the American Institute of Planners* 40, 1974, 255–265.

Hudson, James F., and David H. Marks "Screening the Impacts of Municipal Service Policy Changes". *Socio-Economics Planning Science* 11, 1977, 49–59.

Hyman, D.N. and Pasour, E.C., Jr. "Real Property Taxes, Local Public Services and Residential Property Values". *Southern Economic Journal* 39, 1973, 601–11.

James, Franklin J. Jr. and Windsor, Oliver Duane "Fiscal Zoning, Fiscal Reform, and Exclusionary Land Use Controls". *Journal of the American Institute of Planners* 42, 1976, 130–141.

Kaserda, John D. "The Impact of Surburban Service Functions". *The American Journal of Sociology* 77, 1972, 1111–1124.

Kee, Woo Sik. "Central City Expenditures and Metropolitan Areas". *National Tax Journal* 18, 1965, 337–353.

Kee, Woo Sik. "City-Suburban Differentials in Local Government Fiscal Effort". *National Tax Journal* 21, 1968, 183–89.

Kee, Woo Sik. "Industrial Development and its Impact on Local Finance". *Quarterly Review of Economics and Business* 8, 1968, 19–24.

Kent, Calvin A. "User charges for Municipalities". *Governmental Finance* 1(1), 2–7.

King, Thomas. "Property Taxes, Amenities and Residential Land Values". *Journal of the American Institute of Planners* 40, 1974, 377–378.

Kirlin, J.J. "The Impact of Contract Services arrangements on the Los Angeles Sheriff's Department and Law-Enforcement Services in Los Angeles County". *Public Policy* 21, 1973, 553–84.

Kitchen, Harry M. "A Statistical Estimation of An Operating Cost Function for Municipal Water Provision". *Urban Analysis* 4, 1977, 119–133.

Krauss, B. Melvin and Johnson, G. 'Learry. "The Theory of Tax and Expenditure Incidence – A Diagramatic Analysis". *Public Finance* 31, 1976, 340–62.

Kurnow, Ernest. "Determinants of State and Local Expenditures Re-Examined". *National Tax Journal* 16, 1963, 252–55.

Ladd, Helen F. "Local Education Expenditures, Fiscal Capacity, and the Composition of the Property Tax Base". *National Tax Journal* 28, 1975, 145–58.

Lauthold, Jane H. "The Impact of Industrial Development on Local Finance: A Comment". *Quarterly Review of Economics and Business* 8, 1968, 76–80.

Lauthold, Jane H. and Due, J.F. "A Fiscal Policy Model for Economic Development: A Reply". *Public Finance* 29, 1974, 231–35.

Levin, Michael S. "Cost-Revenue Impact Analysis: State of the Art". *Urban Land* 34, 1975, 8–15.

Lichfield, Nathaniel. "Cost-Benefit Analysis in City Planning". *Journal of the American Institute of Planners* 26, 1960, 273–279.

Lichfield, Nathaniel. "Cost-Benefit Analysis in Plan Evaluation". *Town Planning Review* 35, 1964, 159–169.

Lichfield, Nathaniel and Chapman, H. "Cost-Benefit Analysis in Urban Expansion: A Case Study, Ipswich". *Urban Studies* 7, 1970, 153–188.

Lichfield, Nathaniel. "Cost-Benefit Analysis in Urban Expansion: A Case Study – Petersborough". *Regional Studies* 3, 1969, 123–155.

Lichfield, Nathaniel. "Cost-Benefit Analysis in Urban Redevelopment: A Case Study, Swanly". *Regional Science Association Papers,* European Congress, Cracow, 1965. University of Pennsylvania, 1966.

Liebert, Roland J. "Municipal Functions, Structure and Expenditures: a Re-analysis of Recent Research". *Social Science Quarterly* 54, 1974, 765–783.

Liebert, Roland J. "Theory Construction and Measurement Error in City Expenditure Analysis: Response to Clark". *Social Science Quarterly* 55, 1974, 791–94.

Lima Neito, Roberto P. "Choosing Among Proposals: The Making Of Investment Decisions". *Finance and Development,* June 1971, 42-45.

Loewenstein, Louis K. "The Impact of New Industry on Revenues and Expenditures of Suburban Communities". *National Tax Journal* 16, June 1963, 113-37.

Ludlow, William H. "Urban Densities and Their Costs". IN *Urban Redevelopment: Problems and Practices,* Coleman Woodbury, ed. Chicago, The University of Chicago Press, 1953, 101-220.

Luft, Harold S. "Benefit Cost Analysis and Public Policy Implementation: From Normative to Positive Analysis". *Public Policy* 24, 1976, 437-62.

Maass, Arthur. "Benefit Cost Analysis: Its Relevance to Public Investment Decisions". *Quarterly Journal of Economics* 80, 1966, 208-226.

McBride, Howard J. "Benefit Cost Analysis and Local Government Decision-making: Utilizing Benefit-Cost Analysis Can Mean the Difference Between an Unnecessary Extravagance and a Beneficial Expenditure". *Governmental Finance* 4, 1975, 31-34.

Mace, Ruth Lowens. "Cost-Revenue Research and the Finance Officer". *Municipal Finance* 36, 1964, 122-29.

McGuire, M. and Aaron, H. "Efficiency and Equity in Optimal Supply of a Public Good". *Review of Economics and Statistics* 51, 1969, 31-39.

McHugh, F. Dodd. "Cost of Public Services in Residential Areas". *Transactions, American Society of Civil Engineers* 107, 1942, 1401-1446.

McKee, John. "Coastal Development: Cost-Benefit Models". *Maine Townsman* July 1969.

McMahon, Walter W. "An Economic Analysis of Major Determinants of Expenditures on Public Education". *Review of Economics and Statistics* 52, 1970, 242-52.

Mao, James T. "Efficiency in Public Urban Renewal Expenditures Through Benefit-Cost Analysis". *Journal of the American Institute of Planners* 33, 1966, 95-107.

Margolis, Julius. "Metropolitan Finance Problems, Territories, Functions, and Growth". IN *Public Finances: Needs, Resources and Utilization,* Princeton, New Jersey, National Bureau of Economic Research, 1961.

Margolis, Julius. "Municipal Fiscal Structure in a Metropolitan Region". *Journal of Political Economy* 65, 1957, 225-36.

Margolis, Julius. "On Municipal Land Policy for Fiscal Gains". *National Tax Journal* 8, 1957, 247-257.

Masotti, Louis H. and Bowen, Don R. "Communities and Budgets: The Sociology of Municipal Expenditures". *Urban Affairs Quarterly* 1, 1965, 39-58.

Mass, A. "Benefit-Cost Analysis: Its Relevance to Public Investment Decisions". *Quarterly Journal of Economics* 80, 1966, 208-226

Masten, John T., Jr., and Quindry, Kenneth E. "A Note on City Expenditure Determinants". *Land Economics* 46, 1970, 79-81.

"Method Used to Assess and Tax Condominiums in Cook County". *Real Estate News,* October 14, 1974, 5.

Meyer, P.A. and Singer, N.M. "Local Fiscal Effects of Subsidized Housing". *Public Finance Quarterly* 4, 1976, 409-30.

Miller, S.M. and Tabb, W.K. "A New Look at a Pure Theory of Local Expenditures". *National Tax Journal* 26, 1973' 161-76.

Miiliman, J.W. "Policy Horizons for Future Water Supply". *Land Economics* 39, 1963, 109-132.

Mitchell, George W. "The Financial and Fiscal Implications of Urban Growth". *Urban Land,* July and August 1959.

Mohring, Herbert. "Land Values and Measurement of Highway Benefits". *Journal of Political Economy* 69, 1961, 236-249.

Muller, Thomas. "Fiscal Issues of Local Growth". *Public Management* 56, 1974, 5-7.

Muller, Thomas and Dawson, Grace. "Implicit Grants to Property Owners at the Local Level". IN *Redistribution to the Rich and Poor,* Boulding, Kenneth E., and Pfatt, Martin, eds., Belmont, Wadsworth Publishing Company, 1972.

Murphy, J.F. "Quiet Revolution in Government Planning". *Management Review* 57, 1968, 4-11. (Bandel, J.E. "Reply" Nov. 1968)

Musgrave, Richard A. et al. "The Distribution of Fiscal Burdens and Benefit". *Public Finance Quarterly* 2, 1974, 259-311.

Mushkin, Selma J. "Intergovernmental Aspects of Local Expenditure Decisions". IN *Public Expenditure Decisions in the Urban Community,* . Howard G. Schaller, ed. Baltimore, Johns Hopkins Press, 1963.

Netzer, Dick. "Federal, State, and Local Finance in a Metropolitan Context". IN *Issues in Urban Economics,* Harvey S. Perloff and Lowdon Swingo, Jr., ed. Baltimore, Johns Hopkins Press, 1968, 435-76.

Netzer, Dick. "Financing Suburban Development: Economic Aspects of Suburban Growth," IN *Studies of the Nassau-Suffolk Planning Region,* Deiter K. Zschock, ed. Stony Brook, New York, Economic Research Bureau of the State University of New York, 1969.

Netzer, Dick. "The Incidence of the Property Tax Revisited". *National Tax Journal* 26, 1973, 515-36.

Oates, Wallace E. "The Effects of Property Taxes and Local Public Spending on Property Values: An Empirical Study of Tax Capitalization and the Tiebout Hypothesis". *Journal of Political Economy* 77, 1969, 957-71.

Odell, Robert M. "Use of Recreational Service Charges." *Governmental Finance* 1, 1972, 15-20.

Ohls, J.C. & Wales, T.J. "Supply and Demand for State and Local Services". *Review of Economics and Statistics* 54, 1972, 424-30.

Okner, B.A. "Taxes and Income: A Microunit Analysis". *Review of Income and Wealth* 21, 1975, 276-99.

Ordway, Nicholas and Weave, William, Weaver C. "Preparing for a Zoning Ambush". *Real Estate Review* 7, 1977, 40-43.

Osban, Jack. "The Dual Impact of Federal Aid on State and Local Government Expenditures". *National Tax Journal* 19, 1966, 362-72.

Osburn, Donald D. "Economics of Size Associated with Public High Schools". *The Review of Economics and Statistics* 52, 1970, 113-15.

Ostrom, Elinor and Parks, Roger B. "Suburban Police Departments: Too Small and Too Many?" *The Urbanization of Suburbs,* Louis H. Masotti and Jeffrey Hadde, eds. Vol. 7, Beverly Hills, Sage Publications, 1973.

Pacey, Elizabeth and Philip. "The Costs of Development". *City Magazine* (Toronto, Ontario) no. 4, May-June, 1974.

Patterson, George M. "Allocating Expenditures to Land Use Categories". *Municipal Finance* 36, May 1964, 136-9.

Peterson, Thomas. "Cost-Benefit Analysis for Evaluating Transportation Proposals: Los Angeles, Case Study". *Land Economics* 50, 1975, 72-79.

Pidot, George B. Jr. "A Principal Components Analysis of the Determinants of Local Government Fiscal Patterns". *The Review of Economics and Statistics* 51, 1969, 176-88.

Pigeon, Carol A. "Personnel Compensation, and Expenditures in Police, Fire, and Refuse Collection and Disposal Departments". *Urban Data Service Reports* 7, April 1975, (entire issue).

Pogue, Thomas F. and Sgontz, L.G. "The Effect of Grants-in-Aid on State-Local Spending". *National Tax Journal* 21, 1968, 190-97.

Pollak, William. "Pricing Fire Protection Services". IN *Public Prices for Public Products,* Selma Mushkin, ed. Washington, D.C., The Urban Institute, 1972.

Bibliography

Prest, A.R. and Turvey, R. "Cost Benefit Analysis: A Survey". *Economic Journal* 75, 1965, 683-735.

Renshaw, Edward F. "A Note on the Expenditure Effect of State Aid to Education". *Journal of Political Economy* 68, 1960, 170-74.

Riew, John. "Economies of Scale in High School Operation". *The Review of Economics and Statistics* 48, 1966, 280-87.

Riew, John. "Scale Economies in Public School". *The Review of Economics and Statistics* 54, 1972. 100.

Robin, Robert. "A Taxpayer's Choice Incentive System: An Empirical Approach to Community Economic Development Tax Incentives". *Law and Contemporary Problems* 36, 1971, 98-118.

Robinson, J.Y. "New Data for Cost Estimating at the Conceptual Stage". *AIA Journal,* November 1974, 33.

Ross, William B. "A Proposed Methodology for Comparing Federally Assisted Housing Programs". *American Economic Review* 57, 1967, 91-100.

Runyan, Dean "Tools for Community Managed Impact Assessment". *Journal of the American Institute of Planners* 43, 1977, 125-35.

Sacks, Seymour and Campbell, Alan K. "The Fiscal Zoning Game". *Municipal Finance* 36, 1964, 141-49.

Sacks, Seymour, and Harris, Robert. "The Determinants of State and Local Government Expenditures and Inter-Governmental Flow of Funds". *National Tax Journal* 17, 1964, 75-85.

Sacks, Seymour and Ranney, David C. "Suburban Education: A Fiscal Analysis". *Urban Affairs Quarterly* 2, 1966, 103-119.

Schmandt, Henry J., and Stephens, G. Ross. "Local Government Expenditures". *Land Economics* 39, 1963, 397-406.

Schmandt, Henry J. and Stephens, G. Ross. "Measuring Municipal Output". *National Tax Journal* 13, 1960, 369-75.

Shaffer, Ron and Tweeten, Luther. "Measuring Net Economic Changes from Rural Industrial Development, Oklahoma". *Land Economics* 50, 1974, 261-270.

Shapiro, Harvey. "Economies of Scale and Local Government Finance". *Land Economics* 39, 1963, 175-186.

Shapiro, Sherman. "Some Socio-Economic Determinants of Expenditures for Education; Southern and Other States Compared". *Comparative Education Review,* 6, 1962, 160-167.

Sharkansky, Ira. "Environment, Policy, Output and Impact: Problems of Theory and Method in the Analysis of Public Policy". IN *Policy Analysis in Political Science,* Ira Sharkansky, ed. Chicago, Markham, 1970.

Sharkansky, Ira. "Government Expenditures and Public Services in the American States". *American Political Science Review* 61, 1967, 1066-1077.

Sharkansky, Ira. "Some More Thoughts About the Determinants of Government Expenditure". *National Tax Journal* 20, 1967, 171-179.

Stuart, Darwin G. and Teska, Robert B. "Who Pays for What: A Cost-Revenue Analysis of Suburban Land-Use Alternatives". *Urban Land* 30, 1971, 3-16.

Sunley, Emile M. Jr. "Some Determinants of Government Expenditures Within Metropolitan Areas". *The American Journal of Economics and Sociology* 30, 1971, 345-64.

Tiebout, Charles M. "A Pure Theory of Local Expenditures". *Journal of Political Economy* 64, 1956, 416-24.

Turvey, Ralph. "On Divergences Between Social Cost and Private Cost". *Economica* 30, 1963, 309-313.

Walzer, Norman. "Economies of Scale and Municipal Police Services: The Illinois Experience". *The Review of Economics and Statistics* 54, 1972, 431-38.

Warren, Robert. "A Municipal Services Market Model of Metropolitan Organization". *Journal of the American Institute of Planners* 30, 1964, 193-204.

Weicher, John C. "Aid, Expenditures, and Local Governmental Structures". *National Tax Journal* 25, 1972, 573-83.

Weicher, John C. "The Allocation of Police Protection by Income Class". *Urban Studies* 8, 1971, 207-20.

Weicher, John C. "Determinants of Central City Expenditures: Some Overlooked Factors and Problems". *National Tax Journal* 23, 1970, 379-96.

Weicher, John C. "The Effect of Urban Renewal on Municipal Service Expenditures". *Journal of Political Economy* 80, 1972, 86-101.

Shaw, David. "New Towns vs. Trends: Comparative Costs". *AIP Newsletter,* August 1968, 11.

Shaw, E.A. "Rail Transportation's Effect Upon Real Estate Values". *Appraisal Journal* 37, 1969, 532-537.

Shoup, D.C. "Effects of Suboptimization on Urban Government Decision Making". *Journal of Finance* 26, 1971, 547-64.

Singell, Larry D. "Optimum City Size: Some Thoughts on Theory and Policy". *Land Economics* 5, 1974, 202-212.

Smith, William C. "Municipal Economy and Land Use Restrictions". *Law and Contemporary Problems* 20, 1955, 481-492.

Solow, R.M. "Congestion Cost and Use of Land for Streets". *Bell Journal of Economics and Management Science* 4, 1973, 602-18.

Spangler, Richard. "The Effect of Population Growth Upon State and Local Government Expenditures". *National Tax Journal* 16, 1963, 193-96.

Stein, Erwin. "Cost-Revenue Allocation Model: A Tool for Financial City Planning". *Urban Land* 35, 1976, 13-22.

Stephens, George M. "Fiscal Impact Model for Land Development" *Urban Land* 34, 1975, 16-23.

Sternlieb, George and Burchell, Robert W. "The Numbers Game: Forecasting Household Size". *Urban Land* 33, 1974, 3-16.

Stocker, F. D. "Some Effects of Suburban Residential Development on Local Finance". *Agricultural Economics Research*, April, 1957.

Weisbrod, Burton A. "Geographical Spillover Effects and the Allocation of Resources to Education". IN *The Public Economy of Urban Communities,* Julius Margolis, ed. Washington, D.C., Resources for the Future, Inc., 1965.

Well, Robert E. "Scalor Economies and Urban Service Requirements". *Yale Economic Essays* 5, 1965, 3-61.

Wertz, Kenneth L. "Financing the Collection and Disposal of Households Refuse". *Urban Affairs Quarterly* 9, 1973, 37-56.

Wheaton, William C. "Application of Cost-Revenue Studies to Fringe Areas". *Journal of the American Institute of Planners* 25, 1959, 170-174.

Wildavsky, A. "Political Economy of Efficiency: Cost-Benefit Analysis". *Public Administration Review* 26, 1966, 292-310.

Williams, David and Finkler, Earl. "Containing Growth Does Save Money". *A.S.P.O. Planning* 41, 1975, 9-12.

Wilenski, Gail. "Determinants of Local Government Expenditures". In *Financing the Metropolis: Public Policy in Urban Economics,* John P. Crecine, ed., Beverly Hills, Sage Publications 1970, 197-218.

PAPERS, REPORTS, THESES

Adams, Robert F. *Determinants of Local Government Expenditures.* Ph.D.. Dissertation, Ann Arbor, University of Michigan, 1963.

Adams, S. Charles. *Land Use and Municipal Finance.* West Hartford, Connecticut, Town Plan and Zoning Commission, 1960.

Alabama Regional Council of Governments. *The Revenue Potential of the Government of DeKalb County, Alabama.* Huntsville, Alabama, June 1971.

Alesch, Daniel J., and Dougharty, L. A. *Economies-of-Scale Analysis in State and Local Government.* Santa Monica, California, RAND Institute, May 1971.

American Institute of Planners. "Improving State and Metropolitan Planning." *Proceedings of Technical Seminars on Planning Program Management and Urban Development Costs.* Washington, D.C., January 6-7, 1969.

Arlington County, Virginia. Office of Planning. *Fiscal Aspects of Land Use, Arlington County, Va. Part II, Report No. 3, Master Plan Study.* Arlington, Office of Planning. May 1957.

Aronson, J. Richard and Schwartz, Eli. "Forecasting Future Expenditures," Washington, D.C., Management Information Service, International City Management Association, II, No. S-7, July 1970.

Aurora, Colorado. Department of Planning and Community Development. *Annexation Study of the Areas Generally Located to the Northeast and Southeast of the City of Aurora.* Aurora, Department of Planning, April 1973.

Aurora, Colorado. Department of Planning and Community Development. *Cooper Annexation: Cost-Revenue Study.* Aurora, Department of Planning, March 1972. 12 p.

Aurora, Colorado. Department of Planning and Community Development. "*Revenues and Costs of Hutchinson Annexation.*" Aurora, Department of Planning, 1973.

Awerbuch, Shimon and Wallace, William A. *A Goal-Setting and Evaluation Model for Community Development.* Troy, N.Y., Rensselaer Polytechnic Institute, 1976.

Bahl, Roy W. "*Quantitative Public Expenditure Analysis and Public Policy.*" Paper presented at the Sixty-Second Annual Conference on Taxation of the National Tax Association, Boston, Mass., September 29, 1969.

Banovetz, James M. *Government Cost Burdens and Service Benefits on the Twin Cities Metropolitan Area.* Minneapolis, Public Administration Commission, University of Minnesota, 1965.

Barnett, Larry D. *Population Growth and the Expenditures and Debt of State and Local Governments: 1957-1968.* Los Angeles, California State College, 1970.

Barr, James L.; Gibson, Lay James; and O'Keefe, Terrence B. *Local Economic Analysis – A Case Study in Casa Grande, Arizona, Including A Methodology Handbook.* Division of Economic and Business Research, College of Business and Public Administration, University of Arizona, 1974.

Barton-Aschman Associates, Inc. *Urban Development Cost-Revenue Model. Work Paper #1: Typology of Existing Cost-Revenue Models and Discussion of Major Issues.* For the Tri-County Regional Planning Commission, Lansing, Michigan. Evanston, Ill., nd.

Beaton, C. Russell. *Costs of Urban Growth for the Salem, Oregon Area.* Salem, Oregon, Mid Willamette Valley Council of Government, July 1972.

Beaton, W. Patrick. *"Analyzing Municipal Expenditures: A Cross City Approach."* Institute for Urban Studies and Community Service, University of North Carolina at Charlotte, 1974. (unpublished).

Beaton, W. Patrick *"The Impact of Commercial and Industrial Development upon the Municipal Budget."* Institute for Urban Studies and Community Service, University of North Carolina at Charlotte, 1976. (unpublished)

Beaton, W. Patrick, *"Multivariate Nonresidential Cost-Revenue Analysis."* Institute for Urban Studies and Community Service, University of North Carolina at Charlotte, 1976. (unpublished)

Beck, Morris. *Property Taxation and Urban Land Use in Northeastern New Jersey. Interaction of Local Taxes and Urban Development in the Northeastern New Jersey Metropolitan Region.* Research Monograph 7, Washington, D.C., Urban Land Institute. 1963.

Becker, Arthur, P. *Local Government Finance in the Milwaukee SMSA Vol.: Past Trends and Projections of Expenditures and Revenues,* Springfield, Virginia, National Technical Information Service, 1974.

Bowman, John H.; Hovey, Harold, A.; and Stocker, F. D. *Final Report on Fiscal Equity: A Study of Comparative Revenue Payments, Fiscal Capacity, and Public Expenditure Benefits and Needs in Seven Areas in Missouri.* Columbus, Ohio, 1970.

Boyce, David E. et al. *Impact of Rapid Transit on Suburban Residential Property Values and Land Development.* Philadelphia, University of Pennsylvania, November 1972.

Boykin, James H. *Industrial Potential of the Central City.* Washington, D.C., Urban Land Institute, Research report no. 21, 1973.

Boyle, Gerald J. *Use of Service Charges in Local Government.* Washington, D.C., National Industrial Conference Board, 1967.

Bradley, Richard C. *The Costs of Urban Growth: Observations and Judgements.* Colorado Springs, Pikes Peak Area Council of Governments, July 1973.

Brazer, Harvey E. *City Expenditures in the United States.* Occasional Paper no. 66, New York, National Bureau of Economic Research, 1959.

Brown, William H. *Redevelopment Decisions, Alternative Land Uses and Their Influence on Operating Costs.* Philadelphia, Office of the Redevelopment Coordinator, 1961.

Burchell, R. W.; Hughes, J. W.; Listokin, D. C.; and James, F. *PUD Evaluation Methodology.* Center for Urban Policy Research, Rutgers University, New Brunswick, New Jersey.

Bureau of Municipal Research. *Nottingham – Tecumseh Area Annexation: Financial Considerations to the City of Syracuse.* Syracuse, New York, 1957.

Bureau of Municipal Research and Statistics: Department of Audit and Control. *Analysis of the Use of Federal Revenue Sharing Funds by Local Governments in New York State.* April 1975. (unpublished)

Cantrell, Jay. *An Analysis of the Impact of Price Increases on Governmental Operations in the North Texas Planning Region.* Wichita Falls, Tx. Nortex Regional Planning Commission, December 1974.

Capitol Region Planning Agency. *Municipal Taxation and Regional Development.* Hartford, Capitol Region Planning Agency, March 1963.

Carroll, John J., and Sacks, Seymour. "Local Sources of Local Revenues". *1961 Proceedings of the National Tax Association,* Seattle, 294-311.

Carroll, John J. and Sacks, Seymour. "The Property Tax Base and the Pattern of Local Government Expenditures: The Influence of Industry." *Regional Science*

Bibliography

Association Papers and Proceedings IX. Philadelphia, Regional Science Association, 1962.

Chaiken, Jan M. and Larson, Richard C. *Methods for Allocating Urban Emergency Units,* New York. The New York City Rand Institute, May 1971.

Chapin, F. Stuart, Jr. and Weiss, Shirley. *Factors Influencing Land Developments Evaluation of Inputs for a Forecasting Model.* Chapel Hill, N.C., Institute for Research in Social Science, 1962.

Clark, Frederick P. & Associates. *Land Use and Community Taxes. A Planning Program for the Northeast Section of Yorktown, NY.* Rye, New York, 1958.

Clark, Sally D. *Plain Facts: An Arlington County Fiscal Profile 1960-1974.* Arlington, Virginia, July 1975.

Clayton, Reva, *Municipal Expenditures and Revenues under Contracting.* Los Angeles Institute of Government and Pulbic Affairs, University of California, 1974.

Comprehensive Planning Organization. *Emerging Governmental Responsibilities.* San Diego County, California, Comprehensive Planning Organization, January 1972.

Congressional Research Service. *Property Taxation: Effects on Land Use and Local Government Revenues.* Washington, D.C. Government Printing Office, 1971.

Connecticut Development Group, Inc. *Cost-Revenue Impact Analysis for Residential Devlopments.* New Haven, Connecticut, Connecticut Development Group, 1973.

Consad Research Corporation. *A Study of the Effects of Public Investment.* Washington, D.C., Economic Development Administration, 1969.

Council of Planning Librarians. *Benefit – Cost Analysis: A Select Bibliography.* Exchange Bibliography #267. Monticello, Illinois, Council of Planning Librarians, 1972.

Cuthbertson, Ida D. *The Fiscal Impact of New Town and Suburban Development: An assessment of the Effects of Reston and West Springfield on Fairfax County, Virginia.* Unpublished M.U.A. Thesis for Virginia Polytechnic Institute, November 1973.

Darley/Gobar Associates, Inc. *Cost Benefit Manual for Los Angeles City Planning Department.* Los Angeles Civil Systems, Inc., November 1969.

Dasgupta, Ajit K. and Pearce, D. W. *Cost-Benefit Analysis: Theory and Practice.* New York, Barnes and Noble, 1972.

Dean, Gillian et al. *Local Economic Impacts of Tennessee State Parks.* Nashville, Tennessee, Institute for Public Policy Studies, Vanderbilt University, November 1975.

Decision Sciences Corporation. *PROMUS: The Provincial Municipal Simulator.* Jenkintown, Pa., Decision Science Corporation, 1973.

deCorla-Souze, Patrick. *A Report on the Results Obtained from an Empirical Analysis of Fiscal Impact of New Development, Using Computerized Fiscal Impact Models.* Tallahassee, Fla., Florida State University, 1976.

Delware County (PA). Planning Commission. *Housing: Cost Revenue; Public Costs and Revenues.* Media. Pa., Delaware County Planning Commission. June 1975.

Detroit City Plan Commission. *An Evaluation of the Urban Renewal Program in Detroit. Renewal and Revenues: A Demonstration Grant Study.* Detroit, Michigan, City Plan Commission, 1962.

Development Research Associates. *Economic Impact of A Regional Open Space Program for the San Francisco Bay Area.* Los Angeles, California, People for Open Space, 1969.

Dickey, John W. et al. *A Guide for Analyzing Local Government Service Pricing Policies.* 5 Vols. Blacksburg, Virginia, June 1975.

Downing, Paul B. *The Distributional Impact of User Charges.* Presented to the Southern Economic Association, Atlanta, 1974.

Economic Consultants Organization, Inc. *Housing Subsidies and Municipal Finances. Rochester, New York.* Syracuse, New York, November 1973.

"Economic Impact of Reston on Fairfax County Government," Memorandum to County Executive from Fairfax County Office of Research and Statistics, Fairfax County, Virginia, June 1973.

Eckberg, Myron Gustav, Jr. *Cost of Public Facilities and Services for an Urban Residential Development in Midwest City, Oklahoma.* Master's Thesis. Norman, University of Oklahoma, 1965.

Eckmann, Michael and Steed, Philip. *Basic Fiscal Impact Model.* San Diego County, Environmental Development Agency, February 1975.

English, John Christopher. *The Impact of Land Use Patterns on Public Service Expenditures in the Twin Cities Metropolitan Area.* Ph.D Dissertation. St. Paul, Minnesota, University of Minnesota, 1967.

Esser, George H., Jr. "Land Use and Local Finances," IN *Proceedings of the 41st Annual Meeting of the American Institute of Planners, October 26-30, 1958, New York City.* Washington, D.C., American Institute of Planners, 1959.

Esser, George H., Jr. *Urban Growth and Municipal Services: Uses and Methods of Cost-Revenue Analysis.* Chapel Hill, N.C., Institute of Government, University of North Carolina., 1957.

Fels Institute of State and Local Government. *Special Education and Fiscal Requirements of Urban School Districts in Pennsylvania. A Research Inquiry: The Impact of Social and Economic Conditions on Urban Education and State Fiscal Policy.* Philadelphia, University of Pennsylvania, 1964.

Finkler, M.D. *Summary, Joint City/County Economic Analysis Project.* San Diego County, California, 1974.

The Fiscal Impact Study Group. *The Fiscal Consequences of Alternative Growth Patterns: A Simulation.* Tallahassee, Fla. Department of Urban and Regional Planning, Florida State University, 1976.

Fiscam: Impact Assessment Technique. Philadelphia, Rahenkanp Sachs and Wells Associates, 1977.

Fisher, Glenn. *Measuring Factors Affecting Expenditure Levels for Local Government Services.* St. Louis, Metropolitan St. Louis Survey, 1957. (Mimeographed.)

Fisher, Glenn. "Spillover of Public Education Costs and Benefits," Cooperative Research Project No. 1045. 1965 (Mimeographed.)

Fisher, Glenn W. and Simonson, Lloyd L. "Recent Developments in Illinois Municipal Financial Management," Commission Papers, Institute of Government and Public Affairs, 1970.

Fisher, Robert Moore. *The Boom in Office Buildings: An Economic Study of the Past Two Decades.* Washington, D.C., Urban Land Institute, Technical bulletin no. 58, 1967.

Fisher, Robert. *Public Costs of Urban Renewal.* Paper presented at the American Finance Association. New York, New York. December 29, 1966.

Fishkind, Henry; Milliman, Jerome; and Ellson, Richard. *Alachua County Econometric Study.* Gainesville, Fla., Bureau of Economic and Business Research and Department.

Fisk, Donald M. and Lancer, Cynthia A. *Equality of Distribution of Recent Services: A Case Study of Washington, D.C.,* Washington, D.C., Urban Institute, July 1974.

Frank, James E. *Final Report on the Fiscal Impact Research Project.* Tallahassee, Fla., Department of Urban and Regional Planning, Florida State University, 1975.

Frank, James E. *Fiscal Impact Research Project. Volume I: Report on First Generation Model Development.* Tallahassee, Fla., Department of Urban and Regional Planning, Florida State University, 1976.

Bibliography

Frey, J.C., et al. *Planned versus Unregulated Development in a Suburban Community: A Case Study.* University Park, Pennsylvania, The Pennsylvania State University, Department of Agricultural Economics and Rural Sociology, March 1960.

Friedman, Stephen B. *Public Service Costs and Development: A Study of Wisconsin's Future Development. Summary Report.* Madison Wisconsin State Planning Office, September 1975.

General Electric Company – Tempo. *Developing a Methodology for the Evaluation of Proposed New Communities.* Santa Barbara, California, General Electric Company, October 1971.

Gordon, B.B., Drozda, W., and Stacey, G.S. *Cost-Effectiveness in Fire Protection.* Columbus, Battelle Memorial Institute, December 1969.

Grove, William R. *Economies of Scale in the Provision of Urban Public Services.* (Masters thesis) Massachusetts Institute of Technology, September 1967.

Gruen, Gruen and Associates. *The Impacts of Growth: An Analytical Framework and Fiscal Example.* Berkeley, California, The California Better Housing Foundation, Inc., 1972.

Hanford, Lloyd D., Sr. *Feasibility Study Guidelines.* Chicago, Ill., Institute of Real Estate Management of the National Association of Real Estate Boards, 1942.

Harman, O'Connell & Henninger Associates, Inc. *Community Impact Study for Burnham Mill in Elgin, Illinois.* Denver, November 1974.

Hinrichs, Harley H. and Taylor, Graeme M. *Systematic Analysis: A Primer on Benefit-Cost Analysis and Program Evaluation.* Pacific Palisades, California, Goodyear, 1972.

Hirsch, Werner, Zvi., Segelhorst, Albert W. and Marcus, Morton J. *Spillover of Public Education Costs and Benefits.* Los Angeles, Institute of Public Affairs, University of California, 1964.

Hitzhusen, Frederick J., *Public-Private Fire Protection Cost Trade-Offs in Texas and New York: A Benefit-Cost Analysis.* Ph.D. dissertation, Cornell University, 1972.

Hitman Associates, Incorporated. *Price, Demand, Cost, and Revenue in Urban Water Utilities.* Washington, D.C., U.S. Department of Commerce, September 1970.

Holley, Paul *School Enrollment by Housing Type.* Chicago, Illinois, American Society of Planning Officials, 1966.

Institute of Real Estate Management. Experience Exchange Committee *A Statistical Compilation and Analysis of Actual Income and Expenses Experience in Apartment, Condominium, and Cooperative Building Operation.* Chicago, National Association of Realtors. (Annual).

Kain, John F. "Urban Form and the Costs of Urban Services." Cambridge, Mass., Program on Regional and Urban Economics, Harvard University, 1967. (unpublished)

Knapp, John W. & Rawls, Walter J. *Prediction Model for Investment in Urban Drainage Systems.* Blacksburg, Virginia, Virginia Polytechnic Institute, 1969.

Leach, Richard H. *Cost-Benefit Analysis in Urban Redevelopment.* Berkeley, Real Estate Research Program, Institute of Business and Economic Research, University of California, 1962.

Leistritz, F. Larry, and Murdock, Steven H. *Economic, Demographic, and Social Factors Affecting Energy-Impacted Communities: An Assessment Model and Implications for Nuclear Energy Centers.* Fargo, N.D., North Dakota State University, 1977.

Leiter, Robert A. *Fiscal Effects of Residential Growth: An Analytical Model with Comparative Case Studies.* Prepared for the City of San Buenaventura, Calif. Ventura, Calif., June, 1975.

Leonard, William N. and Clarke, William F. *Does Industry Pay Its Way?* Long Island Industrial Survey #2. Hempstead, N.Y., Hofstra College, Bureau of Business and Community Research. 1956.

Libera, Charles J. *An Investigation of the Determinants of Municipal Expenditures in the United States.* Ph.D. dissertation, University of Minnesota, 1969.

Lichfield, Nathaniel. *Cost-Benefit Analysis in Urban Development.* Berkeley, University of California, Real Estate Research Program, Institute of Business & Economic Research, 1962.

Lind, Roger William. *Determinants of Local Public Expenditures: A Study of Rhode Island's Thirty Nine Cities and Towns.* Ph.D. dissertation. University of Maryland, 1971.

Los Angeles. City Planning Department. *Cost Benefit Manual.* Los Angeles, Planning Department, 1969.

Lucas, Therese C. *The Direct Costs of Growth; A Comparison of Changes in Local Government Expenditure in Growth and Non-Growth Counties in Colorado.* Colorado Land Use Commission, April 1974.

McCallum, David Livingston. *A Case Study of the Cost of Governmental Activity in Single Family Residential Areas of Different Density.* Masters Thesis. Chapel Hill, North Carolina, Department of City and Regional Planning, University of North Carolina, 1956.

Mace, Ruth L. and Wicker, Warren J. *Do Single Family Homes Pay Their Way?: A Comparative Analysis of Costs and Revenues for Public Services:* Research Monograph No. 15, Washington, D.C., Urban Land Institute, 1968.

McKeever, J. Ross. *Business Parks, Office Parks, Plazas and Centers.* Technical Bulletin no. 65. Washington, D.C., Urban Land Institute, 1970.

Marcou, O'Leary and Associates. *MUNIES—Municipal Impact Evaluation System: A Computerized System for Evaluating Fiscal Impact.* Washington, D.C., Marcou, O'Leary and Associates, 1974.

Margolis, H. *Nonresidential Fiscal Analysis.* Los Angeles, Planning Department, 1953. (unpublished report).

Marshall, Peter J. *Impact of Alternative Residential Land Uses on Municipal Government Finances: A Cost-Revenue Model and Case Study.* Ottawa, December 1973.

Maryland National Capitol Park and Planning Commission. *Dwelling Unit Density, Population, and Potential Public School Enrollment Yield by Existing Zoning Classification for Montgomery and Prince George's Counties.* Silver Springs, Maryland, Park & Planning Commission, 1965.

Massey, M.G., Novick, David and Peterson, R.E. *Cost Measurement: Tools and Methodology for Cost Effectiveness Analysis.* Santa Monica, California, Rand Institute, February 1973.

Memphis State University. *Fiscal Capacity Analysis of Counties and Municipalities.* Memphis, Tennessee, Memphis State University, June 1974.

Michigan Municipal League. *Fiscal Crisis for Michigan's Cities and Villages. A Report to Michigan Legislators.* Ann Arbor, Michigan, Michigan Municipal League, July 1971.

Miller, William. *Revenue-Cost Ratios of Rural Townships With Changing Land Uses: A Report of Study for The Rural Advisory Council of New Jersey.* Trenton, New Jersey, New Jersey Department of Agriculture, 1965.

Muller, Thomas. *Fiscal Differences Related to Urban Size and Changes in Population* Western Regional Science Association, February 1975.

Muller, Thomas and Dawson, Grace. *The Fiscal Impact of Residential and Commercial Development: A Case Study.* Washington, D.C., The Urban Institute, December 1972.

Muller, Thomas and Dawson, Grace. *The Impact of Annexation on City Finances: A Case Study in Richmond, Virginia.* Washington, D.C., Urban Institute, May 1973.

Netzer, Dick. "The Property Tax and Alternatives in Urban Development." *Presented at a meeting of the Regional Science Association.* New York, December 27, 1961.

Pattie, Preston S. *Impacts of Urban Growth on Local Government Costs and Revenues.* Oregon State University Extension Service Special Report 423. Corvallis, Oregon, Oregon State University, November 1974.

Peters, Richard M. *Techniques for Fiscal Analysis, including Analyses of Revenues and Expenditures.* Blacksburg, Virginia, Virginia Polytechnic Institute and State University, 1973. (unpublished Research Paper)

Pikielek, Frederick et al. *Boston's Southwest Corridor Development Potential: Analysis and Projection of Social and Economic Impact.* Boston, 1974.

Polinsky, A. Mitchell. *Essays in Public Sector Economics: Central and Local.* Washington, Urban Institute, 1975.

Polk, Lon. *Fiscal Impact Analysis: A Technical Report of TALUS, the Detroit Regional Transportation and Land Use Study.* Detroit, Michigan, December 1969.

Quade, E.S. *A History of Cost-Effectiveness.* Report No. P-4557, Santa Monica, California, RAND Institute, April 1971.

Real Estate Research Corporation. *Economic and Financial Feasibility Models for New Community Development.* Washington, D.C., Department of Housing and Urban Development, 1971.

Regional Plan Association. *Public Services in Older Cities.* New York, Regional Plan Association, 1968.

Regional Science Research Institute, *Cost-Benefit and Cost Effectiveness Analysis: Their Application to Urban Public Services and Facilities.* Philadelphia, Regional Science Research Institute, 1971.

"Residential Growth – Who Pays and Who Benefits?" *Wide Scope of Planning Newsletter.* Corvallis, Oregon, Cooperative Extension Service, Oregon State University, 1972.

Rothenburg, Jerome. *Economic Evaluation of Urban Renewal.* Washington, The Brookings Institution, 1967.

Sacks, Seymour. *Spatial and Locational Aspects of Local Government Expenditures in Urban Areas.* Prepared for the Conference on Public Expenditures Decisions in the Urban Community. Sponsored by the Committee on Urban Economics of Resources for the Future Inc., Washington, D.C., May 14–15, 1962.

Santa Clara County California Planning Department. *Cost-Revenue Aspects of Urban Growth and Development: A Preliminary Bibliography.* 1971.

Schaeffer, Beldon H. *Small Homes and Community Growth: A Study of the Small Low-Cost Home—Community Asset or Liability.* Storrs, Conn., Institute of Public Service, University of Connecticut, 1954.

Schaenman, Philip S. and Muller, Thomas. *Measuring Impacts of Land Development: An Initial Approach.* Washington, D.C., Urban Institute, 1974.

Scott M. and Douglas Scott. *Citizens Evaluation of Local Government Services: Some Measurement Questions.* Los Angeles, Institute of Government and Public Affairs, University of California, 1974.

Scott, Stanley, and Feder, Edward L. *Factors Associated with Variations in Municipal Expenditure Levels.* Berkeley, Calif., Bureau of Public Administration, University of California at Berkeley, 1957.

Seitz, John C. and Taremae, Olev. *Comparative Costs of Residential Devleopment.* Lehigh Valley, Pa., Joint Planning Commission, Leigh-Northampton Counties, 1974.

Selle, Henry, et al. *Feasibility Study for a Proposed Pulp Mill to Be Built by Parsons Wittemore in Walpole, N.H.* Dartmouth, N.H., Environmental Study Department, Sayer Engineering School.

Simon, Herbert A. *Fiscal Aspects of Metropolitan Consolidation.* Berkeley, Bureau of Public Administration, University of California, 1943.

Stauber, Richard L. *A Technical Guide for Measuring the Impact of Tax Base Changes on the Property Tax Burden in Wisconsin.* Revised, Madison, Wis., November 1974.

Sternlieb, George. *The Garden Apartment Development: A Municipal Cost Revenue Analysis.* New Brunswick, Bureau of Economic Research. Rutgers University, 1964.

Stull, William J. *An Essay on Externalities, Property Values and Urban Zoning.* Doctoral dissertation. Cambridge, Massachusetts Institute of Technology, October, 1971.

Syracuse, Lee. *Arguments for Apartment Zoning.* Washington, D.C., National Association of Home Builders, 1968.

Syrek, Daniel B. *The Fiscal Impact of California Residential Growth — Analysis and Supporting Tabulations.* University of California, Davis, 1974.

Taylor, Milton C. and Bourdon, Richard E. *Financing Michigan Local Governments.* East Lansing' Michigan. Institute for Community Development and Services, Michigan State University, 1969. 454.

Tomar, Norman E., et al. *Economic Impacts of Construction and Operation of the Coal Creek Electrical Generation Complex and Related Mine.* Fargo, N.D., Department of Agricultural Economics, North Dakota State University 1976.

Tomar, Norman E. *A Fiscal Impact Model for Rural Industrialization.* Prepared for the Western Agricultural Economics Association Annual Meeting, Fort Collins, Colo., July 18–20, 1976.

University of California. Institute for Governmental Studies. *General Municipal Cost-Revenue Studies.* 1972.

University of Maryland. Bureau of Business and Economic Research. *Industry as a Local Tax Base.* College Park, Maryland, 1960.

University of Oregon. Bureau of Governmental Research and Service. "Analysis of Factors Affecting Expenditures of State and Local Governments in Oregon." (Mimeographed.) Eugene, Oregon, University of Oregon, 1971.

U.S. Department of Agriculture, Economic Research Service. *The Impact of New Industry on Local Government Finances in Five Small Towns in Kentucky.* By Charles B. Garrison. Agricultural Economic Report No. 191. Washington, D.C., Government Printing Office, September 1970.

U.S. Environmental Protection Agency. *Estimating Costs and Manpower Requirements for Conventional Wastewater Treatment Facilities.* Washington, D.C., U.S. Government Printing Office, October 1971.

Urban Institute. *Measuring the Effectiveness of Basic Municipal Services: Initial Report.* Washington, D.C., Urban Institute, February 1974.

Urban Land Institute. *The Relationship of Land Use to Municipal Operating Expenditures.* Washington, D.C., Urban Land Institute, 1972.

Urban Studies Center, University of Louisville. *Louisville and Jefferson County Community Development Model: CDM User Manual.* Louisville, Ky., Urban Studies Center, 1974.

RELATED MATERIAL

American Institue of Real Estate Appraisers. *The Appraisal of Real Estate. 6th ed.* Chicago, American Institute of Real Estate Appraisers, 1973.

American Institute of Real Estate Appraisers. *Capitalization Theory and Techniques.* Chicago, American Institute of Real Estate Appraisers, 1973.

Blalock, Hubert M. *Social Statistics.* New York, McGraw-Hill Book Co., 1972.

Building Owners and Managers Association International. *Office Building Experience Exchange Report: 1975.* Washington, D.C., Building Owners and Managers Association, 1975.

Commuity Planning and Evaluation Institute. A Manual on Conducting Interview *Studies.* Washington, D.C., Community Planning and Evaluation Institute, 1972.

Hyman, Herbert H., et al. *Interviewing in Social Research.* Chicago, University of Chicago Press, 1954.

Hyman, Herbert H. *Survey Design and Analysis.* New York, The Free Press, 1955.

International City Management Association. *The Municipal Year Book.* Washington, D.C., International City Management Association: (Annual).

Kish, Leslie L. *Survey Sampling.* New York, John Wiley and Sons, Inc., 1965.

Lansing, John B., and Morgan, James N. *Economic Survey Methods.* Ann Arbor, Mich., Survey Research Center, 1971.

Moskowitz, Harvey S. *Useful Planning Standards.* New Brunswick N.J., Rutgers University, Bureau of Government Research, 1976.

National Opinion Research Center. *A Brush Up on Interviewing Technique.* Chicago, National Opinion Research Center, 1962.

National Opinion Research Center. *Manual of Procedures for Hiring and Training Interviewers.* Chicago, National Opinion Research Center, 1972.

National Research Bureau. *Shopping Center Directory.* Chicago, National Research Bureau, 1976.

Nie, Norman H., et al. *Statistical Package for the Social Sciences.* New York, McGraw-Hill, 1975.

Saroff, Jerome R., and Levitan, Alberta Z. *Survey Manual for Comprehensive Urban Planning.* Seattle, University of Washington Press, 1969.

Simon, Julian. *Basic Research Methods in Social Science: The Art of Empirical Investigations.* New York, Random House, 1969.

Slonim, Morris, *Sampling in a Nutshell.* New York, Simon and Schuster, 1970.

Suchman, Edward A. *Evaluative Research, Principles and Practice in Public Service and Social Action Programs.* New York, Russell Sage Foundation, 1967.

Survey Research Center. *Interviewers' Manual.* Ann Arbor, Mich., Survey Research Center, 1976.

U.S. Advisory Commission on Intergovernmental Relations. *Federal-State-Local Finances: Significant Features of Fiscal Federalism 1974-1975.* Washington, D.C., Advisory Commission on Intergovernmental Relations, 1977.

U.S. Advisory Commission on Intergovernmental Relations. *Local Revenue Diversification: Income, Sales Taxes, and User Chargers-Commission Report A-47.* Washington, D.C., Government Printing Office, 1974.

U.S. Advisory Commission on Intergovernmental Relations. *The Property Tax in a Changing Environment: Selected State Studies.* U.S. Government Printing Office, Wash., D.C., March 1974.

U.S. Bureau of the Census. *Census of Business and Manufacturing.* Washington, D.C., Government Printing Office, 1972.

U.S. Bureau of the Census. *Census of Governments – Public Employment.* Washington, D.C., Government Printing Office, 1974.

U.S. Bureau of the Census. *Census of Retail Trade.* Washington, D.C., Government Printing Office, 1972.

U.S. Bureau of the Census. *Composite Finances in Selected City Areas.* Washington, D.C., Government Printing Office, 1974.

U.S. Bureau of the Census. *Government Finances: Finances of Municipalities and Township Governments,* vol. 4-4. Washington, D.C., Government Printing Office, 1974.

U.S. Bureau of the Census. *Government Finances: Finances of School Districts,* vol. 4-3. Washington, D.C., Government Printing Office, 1974.

U.S. Bureau of the Census. *Local Government Finances in Selected Metropolitan Areas and Large Counties:* 1969-70. Washington, D.C., Government Printing Office, 1971.

U.S. Bureau of the Census. *Public Use Samples of Basic Records from the 1970 Census: Description and Documentations.* Washington, D.C., Government Printinq Office, 1972.

U.S. Bureau of the Census. *State and Local Ratio Studies and Property Assessment. Washington, D.C., Government Printing Office, 1975.*

U.S. Department of Commerce. *Classification Manual, Government Finances.* Washington, D.C., Government Printing Office, 1972.

U.S. Department of Health, Education and Welfare. *Public School Finance Programs.* Washington, D.C., Government Printing Office, 1975.

U.S. Department of Labor, Bureau of Labor Statistics. *Consumer Expenditure Survey Series Diary Data.* Report no. 448-1. Washington, D.C., Government Printing Office, 1976.

Urban Land Institute. *The Dollars and Cents of Shopping Centers.* Washington, D.C., Urban Land Institute, 1974.

Urban Land Institute. *Industrial Development Handbook.* Community Builders Handbook Series. Washington, D.C., Urban Land Institute, 1972.

Webb, Kenneth, and Hatry, Harry P. *An Introduction to Sample Surveys for Government Managers.* Washington, D.C., The Urban Institute, 1971.

Webb, Kenneth, and Hatry, Harry P. *Obtaining Citizen Feedback: The Application of Citizen Surveys to Local Governments.* Washington, D.C., The Urban Instiue, 1973.

Williams, Norman. *American Land Planning Law.* Chicago: Callaghan and Co., 1974.

Index

ACEM (Alachua County Econometric Model), 346, 353, 354, 356, 357
ABT Associates, 258
"Adult" communities. *See* Singles complexes
Adult resident population, 189, 190
Adults per unit (of residential development), 189, 190
Ad valorem, defined, 431
Advanced Land Acquisition programs, federal. *See* Community Development Block Grants (CDBGs)
Advisory Commission on Intergovernmental Relations, 179, 197
Aggregate family income (of new development), 187, 197
Alabama, 157, 162, 174, 247, 250
Alachua County (Florida), 346, 353
Albemarle (Virginia), 261
Alaska, 173, 245
Alcoholic beverage tax, state-levied, 161, 201-202
Alternative development scenarios. *See* Land use alternatives
American Society of Planning Officials, 276
Amortization, 26, 431
Amusement park, 121
Anderson, Robert, M., 249
Animal, insect, and rodent control, 30
Animal licenses, 192

Ann Arbor (Michigan) Growth Study, 260
Annexation(s), costs associated with, 1, 42, 57, 153, 257, 258
Annexations(s), defined, 431   fiscal impact of, 8, 21, 27, 67, 99, 240   insufficient data associated with, 18-19, 71, 101   intergovernmental transfers associated with, 213, 217, 218   large-scale, 215, 261   of mid-size suburban areas, 16   of second-order cities, 16   of unincorporated area, 22   revenues associated with, 91, 151, 181, 257, 258   servicing levels associated with, 70   state enabling legislation regarding, 242, 246-248
Annual amortized amount, of capital outlays, 57
Annual earned income, family, 185
Annual gross income (from real property), 323-344
Annual sales income (of nonresidential development), 187
Anti-recession aid, federal, 216-218
Applied Decision Systems, Inc., 346, 357
Archer, Wayne R., 277
Arizona, 173, 242
Arkansas, 162, 242, 251
Assessed value (or valuation), 181, 184, 192, 431
Assessment, 122

467

Assessments, special, 156, 173, 439
Athletic facility income, 90
Average costing, approach to municipal cost allocation, 4, 22, 25, 67, 70, 94   defined, 431   in moderate growth suburbs or cities, 18   in small, rapidly growing areas, 18   for nonresidential impact, 119   for residential impact, 20
Average versus marginal cost projections, 21
Average daily attendance (ADA), 29, 220
Average daily enrollment (or pupil membership), 102, 206
Average expenditures (of cities), 97–98
Average sales per square foot (of nonresidential development), 187–188
Average valuation (for guaranteed state aid to education), 209
Awerbuch, Shimon, 346, 357

Bagby, Scott, 133
Bahl, Roy W., 100
Barrington (Illinois), 21, 258
Barton-Aschman Associates, 258, 261, 276
Basic support of education, state, 206–211
Baumol, William J., 100
Beach user fees, 308
Beaton, W. Patrick, 100, 135, 139
Bedroom configuration (of housing units), 71, 285
"Bedroom multipliers," 296
Bedrooms, defined, 431
Bedrooms, expected number of pupils by, 207
Bedrooms, number of (in apartments), 213, 236, 275–278, 295, 307, 309
Bibliography for Fiscal Impact Models, 357–359
Bilingual education, state aid to, 212
Birth or death certificates, 192
"Blended" multipliers, 101, 281
Board of adjustment, local, 239, 250, 251, 285
Bonds, 57, 160, 245, 431
Booms, Bernard, 70
Booz, Allen and Hamilton study, 261
Boston (Massachusetts), 258
Boulder (Colorado), 261
Boundary, municipal or school district, 99, 213, 246–247, 258, 264
Bowman, John H., 135
Bradenton/Manatee County (Florida), 346
Brazer, Harvey E., 70, 100, 135
Budget crunch, municipal, 1, 56
Budget officer, local, 261
Budget projections, 46
Budgeting (or budget planning), 99, 213, 258, 261
Budgets, defined, 432   line-item, 82   published (official), 28, 110, 137 266   operating (municipal), 4, 137, 1j1, 179, 246,   school district, 4, 57, 82, 110, 151, 179, 213   working (unpublished), 28, 57, 82
Building codes, 2, 192
Building inspector, local, 192
Building lot size, minimum, 236
Building moratoria, 236
Building Owners and Managers Association International (BOMA), 138, 190, 326, 336–337
Building permits, 29, 192
Burchell, Robert W., 276
Business administrator, local, 193, 194, 222
Business administrator, school district, 207, 213
Business personal property tax, 183–185
Business privelege tax, 171, 188–190, 202

CDM (Community Development Model), 346, 352, 353, 355, 357
CETA (Comprehensive Employment Training Act of 1972), 58, 68, 90, 149, 155–157, 214–218
CETA municipalities, 216–217
CIM (Community Impact Model), 346, 352, 353, 355, 357
CMS (Community Model Subsystem). See PROMUS (Provincial Municipal Simulator)
CODIM (Community Development Impact Model), 346–347, 351, 353, 355, 357
CRAM (Cost-Revenue Analysis Model), 347, 350, 353, 355, 357
Cable TV franchise tax, 188
California, case law regarding, 245, 251   demographic multipliers for, 285, 286   field experience in, 261, 263   moderate-size community in, 101–117(passim)   revenue trends in, 160, 161, 162, 171, 173, 206
Capital budget, defined, 432
Capital cost(s), 2, 9, 98, 100, 110–112, 116–117   amortization of, 26, 57   See also Debt service
Capital expenditure multiplier(s), 106–110, 114
Capitalization, defined, 432
Capitalization rate, 323–340
Capital outlay, defined, 432
Capital program, defined, 432
Capital-to-operating cost ratios, 52–54, 67–70, 84, 92, 94
Carr study, 263
Carroll, John J., 135
Carson (California), 261
Case law on fiscal impact, state, 235, 238, 249–254, 361–377
Case studies, retrospective, 126–130
Case Study Method, as marginal costing strategy, 4, 21   defined, 432   for areas with excess or deficient service capacity, 16–18, 20, 22, 350   relationship to Comparable City Method, 98–100, 110, 114,

Index

116 relationship to Employment Anticipation Method, 136, 137, 146 relationship to Per Capita Multiplier Method, 24, 27, 43 relationship to Proportional Valuation Method, 119-121, 130, 132 relationship to Service Standard Method, 67-70, 92, 95 use of, 5, 8, 45-65, 257, 260-261, 267 use with regression analysis, 348
Categorial aid to education, state, 206, 211
Census data. *See* U.S. Census data
Center for Urban Policy Research, Rutgers University, 97, 100, 135, 197, 278, 286, 287, 326. *See also* Rutgers University
Central city (or cities), 22, 258, 286 defined, 291-292, 432 large, declining, 21, 46, 99
Certificates of occupancy (or occupancy permits), 29, 192
Charges (local), 58, 68, 112, 127, 152, 173. *See also* Fees and permits; Fines; User charges
Charlestown (New Hampshire), 348, 351
Cherokee Village (Arizona), 263
Cigarette taxes, state-levied, 201-202
City manager, 193, 202, 261
Classrooms, 20, 50, 206
Cluster development(s), 236, 260
Cohoes, (New York), 347
Colorado, 162, 173, 247, 251, 261, 285
Commercial development. *See* Nonresidential development
Commissioner of education, state. *See* Department of education, state
"Common group" cities, 104
Community Development Block Grants (CDBGs), 58, 143, 150, 157, 196, 218-219
Community development office, local, 219
Comparable City Method, as marginal costing strategy, 4, 21 defined, 432 for areas with excess or deficient service capacity, 19-20, 22 relationship to Case Study Method, 47, 63 relationship to Employment Anticipation Method, 136, 264 relationship to Per Capita Multiplier Method, 42, 260, 264 relationship to Service Standard Method, 69, 70, 95 use of, 6, 8, 97-117, 257, 352
Comprehensive planning (or plans), local, 236-237, 247, 248, 252
Computer models (for fiscal impact analysis), 10, 25, 345-359, 436
Condominium(s), 72, 101, 260, 281-283, 295, 303 defined 432
Connecticut, 158, 250
Connecticut Development Group Inc., 48
Consortia of local governments, 214
Constitutional rights, infringement upon, 234
Consumer durables, 186
Consumer expenditure patterns, 197

Contingent loans, 154
Contract rent, defined 432
Convenience goods, 196-197, 432
Convenience shopping center, 18
Cost benefit analysis, defined, 3
Cost effectiveness analysis, defined, 3
Cost-revenue analysis. *See* Fiscal Impact analysis
Cost-Revenue Impact Analysis for Residential Developments, 48
Costs, defined, 2, 433 *See also* Local costs, School costs per pupil; Capital costs; Operating costs
Countercyclical Aid, federal. *See* Public Works Employment Act of 1976
County, defined 433
County governments, 181, 263
County Group Public Use Samples, 293
County long-range (or "horizon") plans, 19
County planners, 267, 346
County registry of deeds, 188
Court fees, municipal, 173
Courts, federal, 250
Courts (or court action), state, 240, 241, 243, 248, 249-254, 264
Crowther, Inc. v. Johnson, 251
Current costs, 2, 27, 100, 110, 112
"Current multipliers," 104
DUALABS (Data Use and Access Laboratories), 298
DYLAM, in PFM (Public Finance Model), 348, 351
Daily occupancy rates (for hotels or motels), 191
Dawson, Grace, 119
Dayton (Ohio), 347
Debt limit, defined, 433
Debt service, 185, 246, 329 use of Comparable City Method for, 98, 110 use of Employment Anticipation Method for, 135-137, 139, 146 use of Per Capita Multiplier Method for, 30, 31, 37 use of Proportional Valuation Method for, 120 use of Service Standard Method for, 68, 84, 89
Decision Sciences Corporation, 348
Deficient service capacity, defined, 433 in small, rapidly growing areas, 18 insufficient data about, 22 use of Case Study Method for, 45-48, 50-52, 56, 60, 63-65, 260 use of Comparable City Method for, 19, 99 use of Per Capita Multiplier Method for, 16, 26, 43 use of Proportional Valuation Method for, 120 use of Service Standard Method for, 68, 94
Delaware, 157, 162, 171, 173, 206, 247
Del Guidice, Dominic, 276
Demand, for local (or school district) services, 12, 281, 289

Demographic multipliers, calculating, 266, 291–301, 303–321 defined, 433 for different housing types, 10, 269, 275–289 for different regions, 5 for household size and school-age children, 189, 264 use of in Case Study Method, 52, 60, 71–72 use of in Comparable City Method, 101 use of in Per Capita Multiplier Method, 26–27, 32–33, 39, 42–43
Department of education, state, 207, 211, 212, 213, 219, 220
Department of transportation, state, 203
Depressed areas, 204
Detroit (Michigan), 348
Developed properties, 192
Development proposals, 16
Direct costs, 151, 264
Direct impact, 2
Diseconomies of scale, 6, 19, 110
District of Columbia, 171, 251, 263
Dollars and Cents of Shopping Centers, 138, 188, 190, 326, 332–333
Dover (New Hampshire), 347, 350
Downtown mall, 261
Drainage, 241, 245
Dunbar (Pennsylvania), 347
Dupage County (Illinois), 261
Duplex, defined, 433

Earned income tax, 161, 185–186
East North Central (region), 160, 175, 433
East South Central (region), 157, 173, 175, 433
East Windsor (New Jersey), 21, 258
Economically disadvantaged persons, 214, 240
Economies of scale, 6, 19, 20, 21, 110
Education, 6, 25, 49, 110, 157, 433
Educational services, charges for, 173–174
Educationally disadvantaged, aid to, 212
"Efficiency and economy," as a planning purpose, 242
Efficiency studies, 67
Elderly housing. *See* Housing for the elderly
Elementary and Secondary Education Act (ESEA), 212
Elevators, passenger (in apartments), 294, 295
Eligibility for assistance (from government), 195
Ellson, Richard, 346, 357
Employees per square foot, 138
Employment Anticipation Method, as marginal casting strategy, 4 defined, 433 relationship to Proportional Valuation Method, 120–121, 130, 132 use of, 8, 63, 135–147, 257, 264 use of for nonresidential facilities, 7, 20, 27, 348
Employment-based taxes, 89
Employment change, defined, 2
Employment levels, 135–136, 138, 147

Enabling legislation on fiscal impact, state, 239–254
Environmental impact statement(s), 16, 27, 240, 241
Equalization ratio, defined, 433
Equalized tax rate, defined, 181, 433
Equalized valuation, defined, 433
Equalized valuation per pupil, local, 207, 208
Equally weighted share (of population and road mileage), 199–201
Equity dividend, 323
Excess service capacity, defined, 433 in large, declining cities, 16–18 insufficient data about, 22 use of Case Study Method for, 45–48, 50–52, 56, 60, 63–65, 260 use of Comparable City Method for, 19, 21, 99 use of Per Capita Multiplier Method for, 16, 26, 43 use of Proportional Valuation Method for, 120 use of Service Standard Method for, 68, 94
Excess unemployment rate, 217
"Exclusionary zoning," 241, 244, 249, 251, 252, 253
Existing costs, 20, 125
Expenditure multipliers, 103–107, 114, 116, 117
Expense ratio, defined, 433
Exurban (development), 258, 263

FICA (Social Security), 30, 57
FIMRI (Fiscal Impact Model for Rural Industrialization), 347, 351, 353, 355, 358
FIRP (Fiscal Impact Research Project), 347, 350, 353, 358
FPPS (Financial Policy Planning Subsystem). *See* PROMUS (Provincial Municipal Simulator)
Fabricant, Solomon, 70
Fairfax County (Virginia), 276
Fair share (of housing for employees), 252
Family earned income, 185, 196, 198
Farm land, 122
Feder, Edward L., 135
Federal aid (to municipalities and school districts), 196, 212–221
Federal grants, direct, 155–163
Federal impact school assistance,(l.c.) 90, 150, 157, 219–220
Federal-local funding, 155
Federal school aid, 179, 213–220
Federal-State Cooperation for Population Estimates, 200
Federal transfers. *See* Intergovernmental transfers; Revenue Sharing; Community Development Block Grants; CETA; Public Works Eloyment Act of 1976
Feedback responses (in systems dynamics), 350
Feeder roads, 49
Fees and permits, 37, 58, 89, 112, 127, 150, 192

Index

Fee simple ownership, 283, 295
Feinberg, Mordecai S., 100
Field experience (or surveys), 257–270, 303–321, 378–429
Financial administration, 77, 82–84
Financial officer, local, 222
Fines, forfeitures and penalties, 68, 150, 173, 192–193
Fire codes, 2, 192
Fire department, 63, 245
Firemen, 46, 55, 68, 77
Fire outlays (or costs), 84, 89
Fire protection, 3, 84, 250, 433. *See also* Public safety
Fiscal impact analysis, defined, 1–3, 433
Fiscal impact methods, 4–9, 15–24, 222–234   advantages and disadvantages of, 42–43, 53–64, 92–94, 114–116, 130–132, 144–146   mix and match of, 22   user sophistication needed for, 42, 60–61, 92, 114, 130, 143, 357
Fiscal responsibility (or stability), local, 239–240, 254, 257, 264
Fiscal zoning, 249, 251, 252, 253
Fishkind, Henry, 346, 357
Fixed expenses, defined, 433
Flat fees, 188, 193
Flat grants to education, state, 206–207, 210, 211
Fleck/Sterling study, 119, 260
Floor space requirements, minimum, 241
Florida, 174, 246, 247, 251, 261, 285, 303   case law regarding, 246, 247, 251   field experience in, 261, 303   revenue trends in, 174
Florida Department of Community Affairs, 347
Florida State University, 347
Foundation aid to education, state, 206, 207–210, 211
Franchise taxes, business or utility, 37, 68, 89, 152, 188–190, 202–204
Frank, James E., 347, 358
Free-standing discount store, 187
Fremont (California), 258
Frequency of unit transfer (of real property), 188
Fresno (California), 21
Fringe benefits, employee, 21, 30, 110
Future annual growth rate, 105
Future assessed valuation, 192
Future costs, calculating, 27, 110–112, 266, 285
Future costs (of nonresidential development), 20, 144
Future costs (of residential development), 94, 98–100
Future growth (or development), 242, 261, 263
"Future multipliers," 104

Future (or potential) Service demands, 19, 285, 288
Future size (of community), 105
Future-to-current expenditure ratio, 107
Future-to-current service multipliers, 21

Gabler, L.R., 70
Gainesville (Florida), 353
Gainesville-Alachua County (Florida) Regional Utilities Board, 346
Garbage collection. *See* Sanitation services
Garden apartments, calculating revenues from, 181, 186   defined, 295, 434   demographic multipliers for, 32, 275–286, 310   field experience concerning, 260   gross income multipliers for, 324–332, 341   use of Comparable City Method for, 101–102   use of Per Capita Multiplier Method for, 16, 26, 32–33   use of Service Standard Method for, 71–72, 94
Gasoline tax, state. *See* Motor fuels tax, state
General government, as municipal service category, 30, 49, 110   costs of, 110–111, 126–127, 139   defined, 434   expenditure multipliers for, 106, 118
General revenue(s), 154, 159, 173, 434
General sales tax, defined, 161
Georgia, case law regarding, 243, 247, 250   moderate-size community in, 72–95 (passim)   revenue trends in, 157, 174, 204
Gladstone Associates, 119
Golden v. Planning Board of the Town of Ramapo, 251
Governmental revenues. *See* Public revenues; Local revenues
Greenwich (Connecticut), 347
Gross annual sales income (of nonresidential development), 198
Gross annual sales per square foot (of nonresidential development), 198
Gross income multiplier(s), 323–340, 434
Gross leaseable area (GLA), 138, 332–334
Gross receipts, 188–200, 202–204
Gross receipts per square foot (of nonresidential development), 190
Gross receipts tax, defined, 203   revenues from, 58, 112, 127, 266
Gross rent (or income), 181, 434
Growth, direction of, 19, 136, 146
Growth–no growth alternatives, 45
Growth nuclei (within regions), 261
Growth, orderly, 8, 240
Growth, rapid, 99
Growth rate, 19, 97, 100, 103–108, 110, 114, 116–117
Gruber v. Mayor and Township Commission of Raritan Township, 252
Guaranteed state yield (for aid to education), 211

Guaranteed valuation (for state aid to education), 211

HEW (Health, Education, and Welfare, Department of), 212
HOK Associates, 261
HUD (Housing and Urban Development, Department of), 45, 218, 219, 257
Hammer, Siler and George study, 263
Hampton (Virginia), 260-261
Hawaii, 245, 247, 263
Health and Welfare, as municipal service category, 30 defined, 127, 434 expenditure multipliers for, 95, 108, 110 police power regarding, 243-245, 250-251
Health codes, 2, 192, 241
Health department, local, 77, 251
Health inspection services, 127
"Health, safety and general welfare," 243-244
High-rise apartments, defined, 295, 434 demographic multipliers for, 276-283 field experience concerning, 258, 276-281, 303 gross income multipliers for, 324-332, 342
Highway department, 92
Highways, defined, 434. *See also* Roads
Hold harmless clauses, 205, 208-209, 215, 218, 219
"Holding capacity" (of a site), 241
Holley, Paul N., 276
Homeowners, 188
Homestead rebate (or relief reimbursement), state, 205-206
"Horizon plans," 19, 99
Horowitz, Julian, 70
Hospital services, 173
Hotels, 18, 190-191
Household, defined, 292
Household personal property tax, 183-185
Household size (HHS), as demographic multiplier, 189-190, 264-266, 275-289, 291-301, 307, 310 defined, 434 use in Case Study Method, 52, 60 use in Comparable City Method, 101, 114 use in Per Capita Multiplier Method, 26, 29 use in Service Standard Method, 71, 93
House Submodel (in CIM), 352
Housing. *See also* New housing
Housing and Community Development Act of 1974, Title I. *See* Community Development Block Grants (CDBGs)
Housing costs, monthly, 185, 187, 297
Housing, court decisions regarding, 8, 240, 252-253
Housing Development and Municipal Costs, 195, 276
Housing for the elderly, 205, 281-285, 435
Housing multipliers, 33, 275-289, 291-301

Housing overcrowding, 218
Housing type(s), in Comparable City Method, 101, 114 in Per Capita Multiplier Method, 26, 32-33, 39 in Service Standard Method, 71-72, 92, 261
Housing type(s), specialized, 269, 281-289 defined, 260, 439
Housing type(s), standard, 275-281, 286-288, 295-301, 305-307, 309-310, 312 defined, 439
Housing (or dwelling) units, 188-190, 192 defined, 435
Housing (or dwelling) unit size, 27, 32. *See also* Bedrooms
Hukle v. City of Kansas City, 250

Idaho, 243, 246
Illinois, 54, 158, 245, 251, 261, 263, 286
Impact aid (to schools), federal, 219-220
Impact submodel (in CIM), 352
Impacted school districts, defined, 219
Income approach (to property valuation), 323-340, 435
Income/Expense Analysis, 326
Income multipliers, 10
Income tax, corporate, 435 defined, 162 federal, 198 individual, 435 local (or locally levied), 153-154, 157, 162-171, 175, 185-186, 303 state-levied, 112, 127, 149, 157, 198-199, 204
Incoming dwelling units, estimated, 19
Incorporated/unincorporated business tax, state-levied, 202
Indiana, 162, 246
Indianapolis (Indiana), 347
Indirect impacts, 2
Industrial complex, large, 18
Industrial development. *See* Nonresidential development
Industrial Development Handbook, 138
Industrial plants, 138
Institute for Survey Research, University of Michigan, 197
Institute for Urban Studies, University of North Carolina at Charlotte, 97, 135
Institute of Real Estate Management, 326, 328
Insurance, monthly cost of, 185
Insurance trust revenue, 154, 435
Intangible personal property, defined, 159-160
Interest earnings, 112, 127, 149, 154, 173, 192-192
Intergovernmental subsidies to education, state-administered, 206, 212-213
Intergovernmental transfers, calculating revenue from, 195-221, 230-235, 353 defined, 154-157, 435 growing importance of, 7, 9, 153, 171, 175, 266 in

Index

Case Study Method, 46, 60 in Comparable City Method, 112-114 in Employment Anticipation Method, 143 in Per Capita Multiplier Method, 21, 26, 37 in Proportional Valuation Method, 120, 127 in Service Standard Method, 68, 90, 92
International City Managers Association, 179
Interregional differences, 286
Interview(s), in Case Study Method, 47, 49, 52, 60, 63, 120 Interview(s) in field surveys, 304, 309
Intraregional differences, 286
Inventory (per square foot), 184
Investments (of unused revenues), 191
Iowa, 208, 247
Ipswich (Massachusetts), 347

James, Franklin J., Jr., 277
Job holders per unit (of residential development), 189
Journal of the American Institute of Planners, 277

Kansas, 250
Kentucky, 157, 162, 173, 174, 245, 250
Kettering (Ohio), 347

Labor force participation rates, 189
Ladd, Helen F., 135
Lakewood (Colorado), 348
Land dedication (for parks or schools), 245, 246
Land parcels, nonresidential, 29, 122, 125
Land use alternatives, use of field experience for, 257-258, 260-261, 263, 267 use of Per Capita Multiplier Method for, 16, 27, 99, 102, 112, 114, 117
Land use controls (or regulations), 240-241, 243, 246, 248, 251, 254, 435
Land use decisions, 1, 239-241, 249, 250, 254
Land-use development patterns, 4
Land use, intensity of, 121, 247, 250
Land use laws (or plans), state, 8, 239, 242, 247-248
Land use(s), nonresidential, 5, 121-122, 126, 132, 136, 252
Land use planning (or policy), local, 43, 240-241, 243, 245-250, 254, 264
Landfill permits, 192
Large-lot zoning, 241
Large cities, declining, 16-18, 19, 21 stable or slow-growing, 16-18, 19
Large, rapidly growing communities, 19, 99, 100, 139, 263
Large-scale development, effect on federal aid, 213, 217 effect on state aid, 204, 207 fiscal impact of, 98-99, 240, 246, 257, 260-261, 267

Libera, Charles J., 70
Libraries, municipal, 22, 77, 127, 435
Library fines, 192
License fees (or taxes), 171, 188-190, 192, 435
Line-item expenditures, 82, 92
Liquor store revenue, state, 154, 435
Local Contribution Rate (LCR) (for school impact aid), 220
Local costs (public), associated with private development, 1-3, 281 by service category, 8-9, 266, 275 use of Case Study Method for, 45, 49, 57-58 use of Comparable City Method for, 97-98, 100, 110-112 use of Employment Anticipation Method for, 135-147 use of Per Capita Multiplier Method for, 25, 31, 33-37 use of Proportional Valuation Method for, 119-127 use of Service Standard Method for, 67, 90. *See also* Operating costs (local)
Local ordinances, 179, 192
Local revenues (own source), defined, 7
Local revenues (public), associated with private development, 2-3, 21 calculating, 179-194 220-234 forms of, 153-178, 266 use of Case Study Method for, 46, 60 use of Comparable City Method for, 97-101, 112-114 use of Employment Anticipation Method for, 135-136, 143, 147 use of Per Capita Multiplier Method for, 26, 37 use of Proportional Valuation Method for, 119-120, 127, 130 use of Service Standard Method for, 67-68, 89-90. *See also* Intergovernmental transfers
Local service demand, 281, 285
Local wealth or affluence, 195
Louisiana, 173, 186, 245, 250
Louisville and Jefferson County (Kentucky) Planning Commission, 346
Lowenstein, Louis K., 119
Low-income (or poverty) families, 214, 216, 241, 254
Low-income housing, 241, 252
Low-rise apartments. *See* Garden apartments

MSHDA (Michigan State Housing Development Authority), 346
MUNIES (Municipal Impact Evaluation System), 25, 347, 350, 353, 355, 358
Mace, Ruth, 257
Machinery (per square foot), 184
Maine, 157, 159
Manpower assistance grants, 157
Manpower levels, 18-19, 20
Manpower ratios, 6, 77, 84, 92
Marco Island Development (Florida), 263
Marcou and Tischler, 347
Marcou, O'Leary and Associates, 347, 358

Marginal costing, approach to municipal cost allocation, 4, 19, 22, 45, 97-100, 112, 135   defined, 435
Marginal versus average costing, 21
Margolis, H., 119
Market analysis, defined, 435
Market approach to value estimation, 435
Market (or true) value, 181, 188, 192, 295, 307, 323-324
Marriage licenses, 192
Maryland, case law regarding, 246, 250, 251   field experience in, 261, 263   revenue trends in, 157, 162, 171
Maslin, John T., 100
Massachusetts, 160, 251, 285
Master plan(s), 45, 242, 257
Material costs, 82, 90, 103, 110
Mechanized storage facility, 121
Medford (Massachusetts), 347
Metcalf and Eddy, Inc., 347
Metropolitan areas, defined, 292, 435
Miami Valley (Ohio) Regional Planning Commission, 119
Michigan, 162, 247, 251, 254, 261, 346
Michigan State Housing Development Authority (MSHDA), 346
Middle Atlantic (region), 33, 173, 175, 436
Midland (Michigan), 261
Mid-rise apartments, 295, 324-329, 342, 435.
Mid-sized communities, 16, 100, 103, 263
Miller, William, 100
Milliman, Jerome, 346, 357
Minimum lot requirement,**251**
Minnesota, 162, 173, 247, 250, 285
Miscellaneous revenues (local), 58, 68, 112, 127, 154, 173-175. *See also* Interest earnings; Fees and permits; Fines; Property transfer tax; Special assessments
Mississippi (state), 157, 174, 245, 246, 250
Missouri (state), 162, 243, 246, 251
Mixed-use (or mixed) development, 72, 94, 101, 258, 260
Mobile homes, 241, 251, 260, 278-281, 436
Moderate-growth suburbs or cities, 21
Moderate income families (or persons), 241, 254
Moderate-income housing, 252
Model Cities program federal. *See* Community Development Block Grants (CDBGs)
Montana, 173, 245, 246
Montgomery County (Maryland), 276, 347
Mortgage, defined, 436
Mortgage applications, 185
Mortgage equity ratio, 329
Mortgage interest rate, 329
Motels, 190-191
Motor fuels tax, state, 157, 161, 199-200, 201, 203
Mountain (region), 171, 175, 436

Mount Laurel Township (New Jersey), 253
Muller, Thomas, 63, 119
Multi-family dwellings, 16, 241, 260, 283, 295
Multivariate analysis, 119, 135, 136, 143, 276
Municipal, defined, 436
Municipal costs. *See* Local costs
Municipal functions. *See* Service categories
Municipal revenues. *See* Local revenues

NHM (New Haven Model), 347, 352, 353, 355, 358
National Association of Homebuilders, 276
National demographic multipliers, 286-287
National Land and Investment v. Easttown Twp., 251
National Research Bureau, 138
Nebraska, 206, 246, 250, 251
Neighborhood facilities programs, federal. *See* Community Development Block Grants (CDBGs)
Neighborhood Public Use samples, 293
Net income (of office space), 337-339, 436
Net leaseable area (NLA), 138, 139
Net operating income, defined, 436
Net rentable area (of office space), 336-337, 436
Net variable guarantee aid (to education), 211
Net worth (of a business), 202
Netzer, Dick, 100
Nevada, 246, 247, 251, 293
Newark Milk & Cream Corp. v. Parsippany-Troy Hills Twp., 252
New England (region), 160, 171, 175, 275-276, 326-327, 436
New Hampshire, 160, 245, 246, 250
New Haven (Connecticut), 347
New housing (or dwelling units), costs of, 16, 143   field surveys concerning, 303, 305   population increase from, 275, 277, 287, 294 298,   revenues from, 143, 189-190, 220, 324
New industry, 252
New Jersey, case law regarding, 241, 243, 245, 251-254, 261, 263-264   field experience in, 97, 126, 146   moderate-size community in, 29-37 (passim)   revenue trends in, 162, 181, 204
New Mexico, 173, 242, 246-247
New population (or residents), 193, 196, 275, 285
New school(s), 18
New town(s), 2, 19, 260
New York (state), 157, 162, 171, 206, 245, 250-251
New York State Economic Development Board, 346
Nicholas and Blowers study, 263
Nie, Norman H., 143, 301
No-growth alternative, 45

Index

Non-CETA municipalities, 216–217
Nonimpacted school districts, 220
Nonresidential development,
  defined, 436 field surveys, 258, 269 revenues from, 187–191, 198, 240, 324–339 use of Case Study Method for, 18, 47 use of Employment Anticipation Method for, 7, 135–147 use of Proportional Valuation Method for, 6, 8, 20, 119–125, 260, 261
North Carolina, 206, 207, 245, 247, 250, 263
North Central (region), 24, 54, 72, 261, 436
North Dakota, 173, 247, 347
North Dakota Environmental Assessment Program, 347
Northeast (region), 24, 68, 72, 261, 286, 436
"The Numbers Game: Forecasting Household Size," 276

Oakwood at Madison, Inc. v. Township of Madison, 252, 253
Occupational privilege tax, 171, 188–190, 436
Occupied dwelling units, anticipated, 190
Office Building Experience Exchange Report, 138, 323, 336
Office complex, large, 18, 138
Office space, 324–325, 331, 336–339
Office Space Guide, 190
Ohio (state), 160, 162, 171, 186, 243, 246, 250
Oklahoma, 173
One-of-a-kind public facilities, 18, 261, 267
Open space, 72, 101
Open Space programs, federal. *See* Community Development Block Grants (CDBGs)
Operating costs (local), associated with private development, 2, 9 defined, 50 use of Case Study Method for, 57–57 use of Comparable City Method for, 100, 103, 108–112, 114, 116–117 use of Employment Anticipation Method for, 135–136 use of Proportional Value Method for, 120, 125–126 use of Per Capita Multiplier Method for, 26–28, 30, 37, 39 use of Service Standard Method for, 68, 77, 82–84, 89, 93
Operating expenditure ratio, 97–98
Operating expenses (of nonresidential development), defined, 436
Oregon, 247
Outmigration (of population), 99
Overage capacity. *See* Excess service capacity
Overzoning (for industry), 251
Owner-occupied housing, 188
Own source revenue, defined, 436. *See also* Local revenue(s)

PFM (Public Finance Model), 348, 350, 353, 355, 358
PROMUS (Provincial Municipal Simulator), 25, 348, 351, 353, 355
PUSH program 298–300
Pacific (region), 171, 175, 437
Parcel (of land), defined, 437
Pari-mutuel tax, state, 157
Parking fees, 173, 193
Parks, 243, 245
Parsons, Brinckerhoff, Quade and Douglas, Inc., 348
Pasadena Research Institute, 261
Pennsylvania, case law regarding, 247, 251, 254 revenue trends in, 162, 171, 173, 188, 190
Pensions, 30
Per capita costs (or expenditures), 20, 264. *See also* Per Capita Multiplier Method
Per capita, defined, 437
Per Capita Multiplier Method, as average costing strategy, 4, 5, 18 defined, 437 for mid-size, moderate growth communities, 6, 21 relationship to Case Study Method, 46, 47, 52, 63 relationship to Comparable City Method, 100, 116, 117 relationship for Proportional Valuation Method, 20 relationship to Service Standard Method, 67, 69, 70, 92, 94 use of, 12–14, 22, 25–44, 257, 260, 267
Per capita tax, 171, 190, 437
Per pupil, defined, 437
Per pupil costs. *See* School costs per pupil
Per pupil multipliers, 25
Personal property, defined, 159
Personal property tax, 182–185, 437
Personnel costs, 90
Petaluma (California) 251, 261
Philadelphia (Pennsylvania) 202, 348
Physical aspects of development plan, 242, 243
Planned unit development (PUD), approval process for, 8, 240, 344 case law regarding, 241, 242, 246, 248, 253 field surveys regarding, 258, 260 use of Case Study Method for, 46–65 use of Per Capita Multiplier Method for, 33–43
Planning consultant, private, 43, 187, 203, 260, 267, 291
Planning office (or department), local, 187, 192–193, 199, 200, 203, 260
Planning powers, 241
Planning process, local, 251
Planning, rational, 253
Planning Research Corporation, 347
Plant closings or openings, 18
Police cars, 63
Police commissioner, 52
Police manpower, 22
Policemen (or patrolmen), 47, 54, 57, 69, 77, 92

Police operating expenditure, 57
Police power, state legislation regarding, 239, 240-241, 243, 244, 248, 249-254
Police protection, defined, 437
Police protection. *See also* Public safety
Pollution control, 155
"Pool" of revenues (state-levied), 198
Population change, defined, 2
Population, current, 202
Population decline or loss, 99, 104
Population densities (or concentrations), 243
Population estimates, use in Case Study Method, 52-55 use in Comparable City Method, 19-20, 28-29, 101, 105, 114 use in Employment Anticipation Method, 137, 143 use in Per Capita Multiplier Method, 28-29 use in Service Standard Method, 71-72, 92. *See also* New housing
Population expansion, 252
Population-induced demand, 52-54, 64
Population movement, 261
Population, share of state, 198-200, 201, 203
Population size (of communities or school districts), 97-100, 103-108, 114, 116-117, 136, 146
Poverty-impacted areas, 211
Poverty level, 216
Power station, 121
Primary impacts, 2
Priorities (for public spending or cut-backs), 313, 315
"Prioritizing" (of revenue flows), 179-180
Private costs, 2
Private development(s), 1, 239
Private revenues, 2
Private (or individual's) rights 248, 264
Private schools, 33, 288, 297, 303
"Profitable" development (or land use), 240, 263
Projected incomes (of residents), 185
Property, defined, 159
Property tax (local), 153-162, 175, 178-184, 202, 266 defined, 437. *See also* Local revenue
Property tax base (local), 29, 149, 160, 244, 252
Property tax rate (local), 181, 241, 251, 252-253, 353
Property tax relief reimbursement (state), 205-206
Property transfer tax, 154, 171, 173, 188-190, 437
Property values, 160
Proportional Valuation Method, as average costing strategy, 4, 119-133 defined, 437 relationship to Case Study Method, 46-47, 63 relationship to Employment Anticipation Method, 136, 146 relationship to Per Capita Multiplier Method, 31-32, 36 use of for nonresidential development, 6, 8, 20, 26, 257, 261
Public costs. *See* Local costs
Public facilities (or services) component, in enabling legislation, 242, 243-245, 247, 250-251, 253, 260
Public (or publicly assisted) housing, 3, 45-46, 212-213, 215, 218, 257
Public (staff) planners, local, 267, 285, 291, 303
Public revenues, 2, 3, 68
Public safety, as municipal service category, 30, 49, 110 defined, 437 effect of nonresidential development on, 18, 126, 139
Public school attenders, 288
Public School Finance Programs, 207, 211
Public sector, defined 437
Public Use Samples. *See* U.S. Census Public Use Samples; State Public Use Samples; County Group Public Use Samples; Neighborhood Public Use Samples
Public utilities, 245, 246, 251, 252, 253, 437
Public utilities commission, state, 204
Public utilities tax. *See* Utility tax
Public works, as municipal service category, 30, 49, 110 capital improvements in, 22 defined, 437 effect of nonresidential development on, 20, 126 grants for, 155, 157, 216
Public Works Employment Act of 1976, 216-218
Puerto Rico, 245
Pulp mill, 353-354
Pupil-teacher ratios, 45-46

Questionnaire design (in survey research), 277, 303, 304, 306-309
Quincy (Massachusetts), 260
Quindry, Kenneth E., 100
Ramapo (New York), 251
Random Sample (in survey research), 306
Ratable, defined, 438
Rate-of-change ratios, 110
Real estate transfer tax. *See* Property transfer tax
Real property, defined, 159, 438
Real property, equalized valuation of, 207
Real property tax. *See* Property tax
Real property value (local), approaches for estimating, 323-324, 326, 332-336 in Per Capita Multiplier Method, 37, 43 in Proportional Valuation Method, 6, 119-121, 125-126, 130. *See also* Property tax (local)
Reapportionment rate (of state taxes), 196-199
Recreation and culture, as municipal service

Index

category, 30, 49, 110 defined, 438 effect of nonresidential development on, 127
Recreation charges (or fees), 89, 173, 183, 308
Redevelopment, 27, 153, 157, 258, 260-261, 263
Redevelopment area, 18
Redistribution rate (of state taxes), 196-199
Refinement coefficients, 20, 120, 123-126, 130
Regional government, 257
Regional multipliers, 278-281, 303
Regional needs, 8, 240
Regional patterns of revenue, 171-175, 197
Regional/state planners, 267, 346
Regional variation, 19, 26, 67, 72, 286, 324
Regression analysis, 135, 147, 348-350, 351, 352
Regression coefficients, 20
Regression equation(s), 348-350, 351, 352, 353
Rehabilitation Loans, federal. *See* Community Development Block Grants (CDBGs)
Rensselaer Polytechnic Institute, 346
Rental costs, monthly, 185, 295, 307, 309
Rental housing, 283
Rental income, gross, 327, 331
Rents, estimated, 197
Replacement cost approach to value estimation, 438
Required local tax effort (RLTE) (for foundation aid to education), 207, 208
Research Corporation of Connecticut, 48
Reserves for replacement, defined, 438
Resident family earned income, 185
Residential development (or growth), 186-187, 240, 258, 264. *See also* New housing
Residential fiscal impact, 8
Residential use, defined, 438
Restaurants, 121
Retirement communities, planned, 260, 283. *See also* Housing for the elderly
Revenues, defined, 2, 438
Revenue projections (or calculations), for alternative fiscal impact methods, 222-234
Revenue Sharing (federal), 155, 196, 213, 216
Revenues, governmental (local). *See* Local revenues
Revenues, miscellaneous (local). *See* Miscellaneous revenues
Revenues, public. *See* Public revenues
Revenues, school district. *See* School district revenues
Rezoning(s), field experience with, 261, 263 fiscal impact of, 1, 8, 27, 99, 240 revenues associated with, 89, 213
Rhode Island, 160, 251
Richmond (Virginia), 21
Road construction, 202
Road maintenance and repair, 30, 126, 202
Road miles (or mileage), share of state, 198, 199-200, 203

Roads, 110, 132, 202-203, 250, 253, 266
Robinson v. Boulder, 251
Rolde Company, 276
Rooms (in housing units). *See* Bedrooms
Rural areas, 18, 204-205, 263, 293-294
Rural developing communities, 192
Rural-fringe areas, rapidly growing, 16
Rural, undeveloped area(s), 19, 20
Rutgers University, 258, 276, 277. *See also* Center for Urban Policy, Rutgers University
Rutland (Vermont), 354

SELLE (Selle Model), 348, 351, 353, 355
Sacks, Seymour, 135
Safety ordinances (or constraints), 192, 241, 245
Salaries and wages, 57, 77, 82, 92, 103, 110
Sales/assessment ratio (of real property)' 181
Sales Management Magazine, 188, 190
Sales price (of real property), 188, 197
Sales tax (local), 157, 161-166, 171, 175, 186-188 defined, 161, 438 field experience with, 266, 303, 308. *See also* Local revenues
Sales tax redistribution, 196-198
Sales tax, state-levied, 157, 161-162, 175, 186, 196-199, 201. *See also* Intergovernmental transfers
Sample design (in survey research), 277, 303, 304-306
Sample size (in survey research), 277, 294, 304, 309-312
Sample Questionnaire for Local Surveys, 315-321
Sample surveys, 303-321
San Diego (California), 347
San Francisco (California), 303
Sanitation, 69, 110, 143, 193-194, 438
Sanitation charges, 46
School-age children (SAC), as demographic multiplier, 189, 190, 264-266, 275-289, 291-301, 307 by Comparable City Method, 101, 114 by Service Standard Method, 69, 71, 77, 92 by Case Study Method, 54, 60 by Per Capita Multiplier Method, 26, 29, 33 defined, 438. *See also* Demographic multipliers
School Assistance to Local Educational Agencies in Federally Affected Areas. *See* Federal impact school assistance
School budgets. *See* Budgets, school
School congestion, 252
School construction, 252
School costs per pupil, by Comparable City Method, 20, 99, 110 by Per Capital Multiplier Method, 5, 25, 26, 32, 33, 39, 43
School district, defined, 438
School district costs, by Comparable City Method, 97, 98, 112 by Per Capita

Multiplier Method, 32, 33–37 impact of development on, 19, 258, 266, 281
School district revenues, calculating, 179–194, 195–220 forms of, 153–178 use of Case Study Method for, 46, 58 use of Comparable City Method for, 97, 98, 112–114 use of Per Capita Multiplier Method for, 26, 37 use of Proportional Valuation Method for, 120, 127 use of Service Standard Method for, 67, 68, 89–90
School district service demand, 281, 285, 288
School enrollment (student body size), 107, 110, 112, 207–208
School libraries, aid to, 212
School lunch income, 90, 173, 193
Scott, Claudia DeVita, 347, 358
Scott, Stanley, 135
Secondary impacts, 2
Secondary (or induced) costs, 264
Secondary revenues, 143
Second-order cities, 16, 68
Selective sales tax, defined, 161
Selle, Henry F., 348
Service categories (municipal), defined, 30, 43, 49, 276 in Comparable City Method, 98, 103–104, 108 in Employment Anticipation Method, 135, 137
Service infrastructure, 16
Service standard, defined, 438
Service Standard Method, as average costing strategy, 4, 21 defined, 438 relationship to Case Study Method, 18, 49, 52, 63 relationship to Comparable City Method, 99, 100, 116, 117 relationship to Per Capita Multiplier Method, 6, 26, 30, 42, 43 relationship to Proportional Valuation Method, 20 use of, 8, 22, 67–95, 257, 260–261, 352 use of for moderate growth suburbs or cities, 18–19
Services (local), by Comparable City Method, 107, 108, 110, 114 by Service Standard Method, 69, 77, 89 case law regarding, 246, 251, 252 field surveys regarding, 303, 307 See also Deficient service capacity; Excess service capacity; Service categories (municipal)
Services (school district), by Comparable City Method, 98, 107, 108, 110–112, 114 by Service Standard Method, 69, 77, 89 demographic multipliers for, 275–276
Sewage (or sewerage) facilities, 202, 241, 243, 245, 250, 253
Sewerage charges, 89, 173, 193
Sewers (or sewer lines), 49, 110
Share of local property value (of nonresidential developments), 20
Shared taxes or revenues (state-levied), 154, 157
Shopping Center Directory, 138

Shopping center(s), case law regarding, 250 community, 333–335, 343, 432 field experience regarding, 260, 261 neighborhood, 333–335, 343, 436 regional, 333–336, 342, 438 revenues from, 187–188, 190, 324–326, 332–336 use of Case Study Method for, 18, 46, 47, 52, 56 use of Employment Anticipation Method for, 138 use of Per Capita Multiplier Method for, 25, 29, 32–33, 36–37 use of Proportional Valuation Method for, 120–132
Shopping goods, 196–197, 439
Shopping patterns (of residents), 303, 308
Shopping trips, 196, 197
Short-term marketable securities, 191
Single-family home(s), case law regarding, 251 defined, 439 demographic multipliers for, 275–281, 283, 286–287, 310 field experience regarding, 257, 258, 260 revenues from, 181, 186, 188–194, 208–210 use of Comparable City Method for, 101, 112 use of Per Capita Multiplier Method for, 16, 32, 33 use of Service Standard Method for, 71, 72, 77, 94
Singles complexes, 260, 2S1, 285, 439
Site plan review, 241, 267
Site-specific, 27, 43, 261
Size (of communities or school districts). *See* Population size
Slack capacity. *See* Excess service capacity
Small, declining cities, 24
Small, declining communities, 99, 100
Small, rapidly growing areas (or cities), 16–18, 19
Snow Removal, 202
Socioeconomic profiles (from Public Use Samples), 297
South (region), 77, 84, 90, 157, 175, 261 defined, 439
South Atlantic (region), 157, 175, 281, 326–327, 439
So. Burlington Co. N.A.A.C.P. v. Mt. Laurel Tp., 253
South Carolina, 157, 171, 245
South Dakota, 242
Southeast (region), 286
Southern cities, 21
Special exceptions, 261
Specialized housing types. *See* Housing types, specialized
Specialty stores, 181
Spillover effects (of development), 264
Standard error (in (in surveys), 310–312
Standard housing types. *See* Housing types, standard
Standard Industrial Classification (SIC), 136

Index

Standard Metropolitan Statistical Areas (SMSAs), 218, 286, 293
Standard Zoning Enabling Act. *See* Enabling legislation, state
State and Local Fiscal Assistance Act of 1972 (Revenue Sharing), 155, 439
State and regional planning, Division of, 203
State governments, 181
State grants, 157, 204-205
State income tax. *See* Income tax, state
State land use laws. *See* Land use laws, state
State licensing fees, 189
State long-range (or (or "horizon") plans, 23
State planning agencies, 346
State Public Use Samples, 292-293
State sales tax. *See* Sales tax, state
State school aid, 179, 195-213
State statutes, 179
State transfers. *See* Intergovernmental transfers
State treasurer, 186, 198, 199-200, 202, 204-205, 213
Statewide planning, 247-248
Statistical Package for the Social Sciences (SPSS), 143, 301, 312
Statutory, defined, 439
Statutory costs, by Comparable City Method, 103, 110 by Employment Anticipation Method, 135-136, 137, 139, 146 by Service Standard Method, 77, 82, 90 calculating, 57, 120 defined, 30
Steel Hill Development Inc. v. Town of Sanbornton, 250
Sternlieb, George, 97, 100, 197, 276
Strafford (New Hampshire)Regional Planning Commission, 347, 357
Street lighting, 126, 202-203
Street maintenance or improvements, 47, 245
Stuart, Darwin G., 276
Student-teacher ratio, 56, 207, 210
Subdivision regulations (or controls), 241, 242, 245-246, 248, 267
Subregions, 281-282
Subsidized housing, 18
Suburban areas, 68
Suburban development, 258
Suburbanization movement, 257
Sunley, Emil McKee, Jr., 135
Superintendent of schools, local district, 45, 211, 212, 213, 220
Survey research resources, 313
Surveys, benefits of, 304 costs of, 277, 304-305, 312 drawbacks of, 303 efficiency of, 277, 304
Systems dynamics, 348-350, 351

Tallahassee/Leon County (Florida), 347
Tangible personal property tax, 159, 182, 186, 196

Target population (of surveys), 305
Taxable goods, 196
Taxable retail sales, local, 196
Taxable share (of gross annual sales income), 196
Tax anticiaption notes, 191
Tax assessor, local, 181, 186-187, 190-192, 431
Tax burden, 243, 252
Tax collector, local, 187, 202
Tax delinquency penalties, 192
Taxes. *See* Property tax; Income tax; Sales tax; Property transfer tax
Tax ratables, 252
Tax rate, defined, 440
Teacher-pupil ratio. *See* Student-teacher ratio
Teachers, 50, 55, 56, 63, 69, 206
Temple, Barker, and Sloan, 346
Temporal variation (of demographic multipliers), 288
Tennessee, 157, 173, 174, 243, 250
Teska, Robert B., 276
Texas, 120, 127, 137, 139, 143, 285
Threshold eligibility (for foundation aid to education), 207-208
Time-motion studies, 67, 257
Title I, ESEA (assistance to the educationally disadvantaged), 212, 213
Title II, ESEA (general support and school libraries), 212
Titles III and IV, ESEA (supplementary services and bilingual education), 212
Title V, ESEA (grants and special projects), 212
Tobacco tax, state, 157, 161
Toronto (Ontario), 348
Total operating expenses (of office space), 336-338
Total operating expenses (of shopping centers), 332-336, 440
Total operating income (of office space), 336-339, 440
Total operating receipts (of shopping centers), 332-336, 440
Town clerk, 193
Townhouse(s), defined, 440 demographic multipliers for, 101, 276-281, 283, 303 use of Per Capita Multiplier Method for, 16, 32-33 use of Service Standard Method for, 71-72
Traffic ordinances (or controls), 126, 192, 250
Transfer of development rights, 241
Transfer tax rate, 188
Transient occupancy tax 190-191
Transportion, 243, 245, 247
Tucson (Arizona), 261
Turnover (of real property, 188

U.S. Bureau of Labor Statistics, 196, 197, 216

U.S. Census Bureau, 67, 154
U.S. Census data, calculating demographic multipliers from, 281, 287, 292-298, 310 calculating revenues from, 188, 189, 190, 193, 200 in Comparable City Method, 105 in Per Capita Multiplier Method, 5, 29, 33 in Service Standard Method, 69
U.S. Census of Governments, in Case Study Method, 49-50, 53 in Comparable City Method, 98, 103-108 in Service Standard Method, 6, 18, 67-72, 77, 82, 84, 92
U.S. Census of Housing, 138
U.S. Census Public Use Sample(s), 33, 266, 276-281, 286-288, 291-301, 303
U.S. Department of Commerce, 216
U.S. Department of Commerce, Bureau of the Census. U.S. Census Bureau
U.S. Department of Labor, 214, 216
U.S. Supreme Court, 240
U.S. Treasury Department, 213, 217
Underemployed persons, 214
Unemployed persons, 214
Unemployment, 195, 216, 217
Unemployment compensation, 57
Unincorporated business tax, state-levied, 202
University of California, 258
University of Florida, 277, 346
University of Louisville, Urban Studies Center, 346, 357
University of Michigan, Institute for Survey Research, 197
University of North Carolina, Institute for Urban Studies, 97, 135
Unused revenues, 191
Urban areas, defined, 292-293, 440 state aid to, 204-205
"Urban counties," 218
Urban Institute, 261, 348
Urban Land Institute (ULI), 138, 188, 190, 326, 332-333
Urban League of New Brunswick v. Borough of Carteret, 252
Urban Public Finance Group, Urban Land Institute, 347
Urban renewal, 257, 434
Urban renewal programs, federal.*See* Community Development Block Grants (CDBGs)
User charges, 90, 143, 173, 175, 179, 193-194
Utah, 243
Utility gross receipts (or revenue), 37, 90, 154, 203-204, 440
Utility system(s) or facilities, 18, 22
Utility tax (local), 143, 203-204, 161

Vacant land (or undeveloped property), 122, 191, 192
Vacation homes, 281-283, 285

Variable guarantee aid to education, state, 206, 208, 211
Variance(s), 8, 240, 242, 244-245, 248-249, 285
Vermont, 160, 171, 242, 245, 247
Virginia, case law regarding, 243, 245, 251 field experience in, 261, 263 revenue trends in, 157, 160, 162, 171
Wage scales, 21
Wallace, William A., 346, 357
Walpole (New Hampshire), 348, 351
Ward v. Township of Montgomery, 251
Warehouses, 138
Washington (D.C.), 171, 251, 303
Washington (D.C.) West End Plan, 263
Washington (state), 171, 245, 247, 250
Waste treatment facilities, 155
Water, case law regarding, 243, 245, 250, 253 consumption rates for, 204 user charges for, 90, 193-194.*See also* Public works
Water and Sewer Facilities programs, federal.*See* Community Development Block Grants (CDBGs)
Wealth.*See* Property
Weicher, John C., 70, 100
Weighting (of pupils), 207, 210
Welfare costs, 266
Welfare-public assistance.*See* Health and welfare
West (region), 72, 173, 175, 261, 286, 440
West South Central (region), 173, 175, 440
West Virginia, 157, 171
Williams, Norman, 249
Willot v. Village of Beachwood, 250
Windsor, Oliver Duane, 288
Wisconsin, 160, 245
Work places (of residents), 303
Wyoming, 173
York (Maine), 348
Zone change(s), fiscal impact of, 217, 264 use of Case Study Method for, 52, 57 use of Per Capita Multiplier Method for, 16, 42
Zoning, defined, 440 existing, 12, 72, 240, 246, 264 fiscal impact of, 136, 260, 263 state enabling legislation regarding, 241-246, 248, 249-254. *See also* Fiscal zoning; Variances
Zoning board, local, 244, 250, 251, 285
Zoning for industry, 252